Proceedings

IDEAS 2007

11th International Database Engineering
and Applications Symposium

6-8 September 2007
Banff, Alberta, Canada

Proceedings

IDEAS 2007

11th International Database Engineering and Applications Symposium

6-8 September 2007
Banff, Alberta, Canada

Edited by
Bipin C. Desai and Ken Barker

Los Alamitos, California

Washington • Tokyo

IEEE Computer Society Order Number P2947
ISBN-10: 0-7695-2947-X
ISBN-13: 978-0-7695-2947-9
ISSN Number 1098-8068

Additional copies may be ordered from:

IEEE Computer Society	IEEE Service Center	IEEE Computer Society
Customer Service Center	445 Hoes Lane	Asia/Pacific Office
10662 Los Vaqueros Circle	P.O. Box 1331	Watanabe Bldg., 1-4-2
P.O. Box 3014	Piscataway, NJ 08855-1331	Minami-Aoyama
Los Alamitos, CA 90720-1314	Tel: + 1 732 981 0060	Minato-ku, Tokyo 107-0062
Tel: + 1 800 272 6657	Fax: + 1 732 981 9667	JAPAN
Fax: + 1 714 821 4641	http://shop.ieee.org/store/	Tel: + 81 3 3408 3118
http://computer.org/cspress	customer-service@ieee.org	Fax: + 81 3 3408 3553
csbooks@computer.org		tokyo.ofc@computer.org

Individual paper REPRINTS may be ordered at: <reprints@computer.org>

Editorial production by Patrick Kellenberger
Cover art production by Joe Daigle/Studio Productions
Printed in the United States of America by The Printing House

IEEE Computer Society
Conference Publishing Services (CPS)
http://www.computer.org/cps

IDEAS 2007

11th International Database Engineering and Applications Symposium

Table of Contents

Full Papers

Short Papers

IDEAS 2007

Foreword

The aim of the IDEAS series of symposia and workshops is to address issues on the engineering and application of databases. The series was inaugurated in 1997 and has been held annually ever since, in North America, Europe, and Asia. It has attracted researchers, practitioners, and attendees from academic, industry and government agencies, to exchange ideas and share experience. Following the IDEAS tradition, these proceedings include quality papers presenting original ideas and new findings on applied technological and theoretical aspects of information technology. The Program Committee and the referees have ensured this quality for the papers through careful refereeing of the submitted papers. Each paper was reviewed by at least three external referees who acquired consensus through extensive discussions whenever necessary.

Both IDEAS and the field of databases in general have made quite some progress since the inception of IDEAS, part of which is reflected in the present proceedings volume. The conference has matured substantially over the years in that it is now able to attract top-level papers at the forefront of research. The field itself has brought along a number of new developments unheard of only a few of years ago and IDEAS has grown with these changes. The topics discussed this year center around novel issues such as data exploration, service orientation and its applications,, data streams, and P2P, issues that are now in the mainstream of database research such as XML data, queries on trees, OLAP and data mining, enterprise and Web data, and traditional issues such as concurrency control, data integration, query processing, storing and indexing, DBMS operation, security and privacy. The program reflects a high quality as indicated by the less than 35 % acceptance rate and consists of full and short papers. All submissions have gone through a full review process and the average review per paper was over 3.7.

We are grateful to a number of people without whom we would not have been able to put the program together. These include our international program committee, which has done an excellent job; whose commitment to IDEAS is reflected by a nearly perfect return rate that provided an excellent foundation upon which to make acceptance decisions. We would also like to thank the many external reviewers who have helped ``in the background," and who made sure that we met our schedule despite a very short turnaround between the last IDEAS and this one. We are grateful to the large number of authors who have considered IDEAS as the target for their work, and although we could not accommodate every submission, we hope that the reviews can be of help to many people.

We wish to express my gratitude to many people for their help in organizing this event. We wish to also express my thanks to the sponsors: BytePress, Concordia University, and University of Calgary. The local organizing committee has worked hard to arrange the meeting in Banff, undoubtedly, one of the most beautiful places in the world.

We would like to thank IEEE, for their continued support of IDEAS and our editor for the care in ensuring the quality of these proceedings. Thanks are due to our editor Patrick Kellenberger who made the timely production of the proceedings possible.

Ken Barker (Local Chair)   **Bipin C. Desai (General Chair)**
                        Program co-chairs

IDEAS 2007

Program Committee

Foto Afrati	National Technical University of Athens
Gilbert Babin	HEC Montréal
James Bailey	University of Malbourne
Punam Bedi	University of Delhi
Zohra Bellahsene	Universite de Montpellier
Jorge Bernardino	Instituto Politecnico de Coimbra
Vasudha Bhatnagar	University of Delhi
Peter Bodorik	Dalhousie University
Reynold Cheng	Hong Kong Polytechnic University
Nihan Cicekli	Middle East Technical University
Andre Clouatre	University of Montreal
Christine Collet	INP Grenoble
Stefan Conrad	Universitat Duesseldorf
Bin Cui	Peking University
Alfredo Cuzzocrea	University of Calabria
Bipin C. Desai	Concordia University
Anne Doucet	Universite Pierre et Marie Curie(Paris VI)
Todd Eavis	Concordia University
Christie Ezeife	University of Windsor
Sara Foresti	University of Milan
Lukasz Golab	AT&T
Matteo Golfarelli	University of Bologna
Theo Haerder	Universitat Kaiserlautern
Moustafa Hammad	University of Calgary
Candan K. Selcuk	Arizona State University
Shri Kant	DRDO
Bettina Kemme	McGill University
Brigitte Kerhervé	University of Quebec at Montreal
W. Knight	BytePress
A. Kumaran	Microsoft Research, India
Krishna Kummamuru	IBM
Christian Lang	IBM T.J. Watson Research Center
Dominique Laurent	Universite de Cergy-Pontoise
Carson K. Leung	University of Manitoba
Mark Levene	University of London
Arturas Mazeika	Free University of Bozen
Mohamed Mokbel	University of Minnesota
Yiu-Kai Dennis Ng	Brigham Young University
Wendy Osborn	University of Lethbridge

IDEAS 2007

External Reviewers

Alfredo Garro	DEIS Dept - University of Calabria
Anne Laurent	LIRMM, Universite Montpellier 2
Arnaud Giacometti	University of Tours, France
Bolin Ding	Chinese University of Hong Kong
Chi-Yin Chow	University of Minnesota
Christophe Bobineau	Grenoble Institute of Technology
Claudia Roncancio	Grenoble Institute of Technology
Debapriyo Majumdar	BM India Research Lab
Dora Souliou	National Technical University of Athens
Neelam Verma	Defence Research and Development Organisation
Ediz Saykol	Bilkent University
Elias Frentzos	University of Piraeus
Fatima M. Farrag	University of Calgary
Francesco Buccafurri	University of Reggio Calabria
Genoveva Vargas-Solar	CNRS
Ilyas Cicekli	Middle East Technical University
Islam Hegazy	University of Calgary
Ismail Sengor Altingovde	Bilkent University
Jean-Marc Petit	INSA, Lyon, France
Tao-Yuan Jen	University of Cergy-Pontoise
Jens Lechtenboerger	University of Muenster, Germany
Johanna Vompras	University of Duesseldorf, Germany
K Hima Prasad	IBM India Research Lab
Lina Peng	Arizona State University
Maxwell Ejelike	School of Computer Science, University of Windsor
Mohand-Said Hacid	University of Lyon-1, France
Rifat Ozcan	Bilkent University
Sharanjit Kaur	AND College, University of Delhi, Delhi, India.
Stephan Hagemann	University of Muenster, Germany
Sylvie Calabretto	INSA, Lyon, France
Thierry Delot	Université de Valenciennes et du Hainaut Cambrésis
Yan Qi	Arizona State University

IDEAS 2007

Full Papers

A Two Layered Approach for Querying Integrated XML Sources

Felipe Victolla Silveira and Carlos A. Heuser
UFRGS – Porto Alegre, Brazil
victolla,heuser@inf.ufrgs.br

Abstract

The problem of data integration (query decomposition, data fragmentation) has been widely studied in literature, but the inherent hierarchical nature of XML data presents problems that are specific to this data model. Each many-to-many conceptual relationship must be mapped to a specific hierarchical structure in XML. Different XML sources may implement the same many-to-many conceptual relationship in different ways. In our approach the problem of integration of XML data sources is decomposed in two problems: (1) that of fragmentation of a global graph-like model (e.g., an ER model) into several local graph-like models conceptually representing data sources and (2) that of mapping the local graph-like model into an XML tree-like schema. This paper presents a set of fragmentation operators specifically designed for our approach, as well as a query decomposition mechanism that allows a query stated at the conceptual level to be decomposed into an XQuery statement at the XML level. As the query language at the conceptual level, we adopt CXPath (conceptual XPath) a query language we have defined in previous work.

Keywords: *XML, data integration, data fragmentation, query decomposition*

1 Introduction

In this paper we handle the problem of querying several XML data sources that possibly have different schemata and relate to a common domain. We apply the mediator approach [24], in which queries are submitted against a mediated or global schema. In this context an important decision is to choose the abstraction level of the data model used at the global level. One approach taken by some authors is to use the same abstraction level at the global and local levels [19, 5, 11, 12]. In the integration of XML sources this means that the global schema is an XML model. This approach has the potential advantage of simplifying the translation of queries from the global schema to the local schemata, but presents also a major problem: due to the inherent hierarchical structure of XML documents, non-hierarchical conceptual constructs like many-to-many relationships must be hierarchically represented in the XML schemata.

In previous work we have followed another approach, namely that of using a more abstract data model at the global level. In [15, 16, 6] we propose the use of an entity-relationship like conceptual model for the global and local levels, and show how each local XML schemata is abstracted to a local conceptual schema, and how these local conceptual schemas are integrated in the global conceptual schema. Queries against the conceptual model are stated in CXPath (conceptual XPath), an XPath based language, and translated into regular XPath by a query rewriting approach [3].

However, the mechanism proposed in [3] is limited to the translation of one source at a time. The local queries generated by this mechanism are stated against one single source, limiting this approach to queries that don't need to interact with several sources to build the answer. In this work we address the problem of decomposing a global query stated against the conceptual model into local queries stated against several sources. Given this context, there are two major problems which need to be handled. One is to define how a global conceptual schema is fragmented into several local schemas. The other problem is to define an algorithm that decomposes a global query into several local queries and then constructs the answer.

In this paper, we propose a solution for both problems. First, fragmentation operators for XML data are introduced, considering the existence of a global conceptual schema. We define three fragmentation operators against the conceptual model and the conceptual base: *split* fragmentation, *vertical* fragmentation and *horizontal* fragmentation. Additionally, we propose a query decomposition algorithm, based on the use of mapping information between the conceptual model and the XML documents. This algorithm generates XPath expressions to access the individual sources, and then integrates this queries into a single XQuery [23] expression, handling the fragmentation and constructing the answer for the query. The behavior of this algorithm is based on how the sources are fragmented. It means that it implements fragmentation reduction algorithms, similarly to what is done in distributed databases [18].

This paper is organized as follows. Section 2 presents the related work and better motivates our approach. Section 3 presents the data model and the query language used in our approach. Section 4 describes the fragmentation operators. Section 5 describes the mapping information and Section 6 describes the decomposition algorithm and its application to an example. Section 7 is dedicated to the conclusions and future work.

2 Related Work

The problem of fragmentation of XML documents has been investigated by several authors [11, 12, 2, 1]. Most of these work follow the approach of generalizing relational fragmentation operators to the XML data model [11, 12, 2]. Schewe et.al. [11, 12] present three fragmentation operators: vertical fragmentation, horizontal fragmentation and the split operator. The vertical and horizontal fragmentation operators are generalizations of the relational operators, while the split operator is based on a previous work of the same group dealing with fragmentation in the object-oriented model [21].

However, the hierarchical and navigational nature of XML introduces additional issues into the problem of fragmentation. As XML documents are trees, non-hierarchical conceptual constructs like many-to-many relationships may be represented in XML in several different ways (corresponding to different traversal directions of a relationship). Further, a relationship at the conceptual level may be represented in two different ways in XML. One solution is to employ an explicit parent-child relation (the *navigational* solution) and the other is to implement the relationship by associations between key values, as in the relational model (the *associative* solution).

Thus, defining fragmentation operators directly over the XML data model means that one has to deal in a single step with what actually are two different problems: that of abstracting from representation details in XML and that of dealing with fragmentation of data in several sources itself. In our approach we clearly separate both problems. Although aiming at XML fragmentation, our fragmentation operators are defined at the conceptual level, i.e., they define how a global mediated conceptual schema is fragmented to local conceptual schemata. The problem of abstracting from XML representation details is handled by the mapping from each local XML schema to the corresponding local conceptual model. Given the context of fragmentation in XML documents, we are unaware of any work in literature which follows this approach.

There is vast literature dealing with the problem of query processing over several and heterogeneous sources . Most of these work adopt the mediator approach [20, 14, 13, 10]. In the Agora Integration System [14], the global model is XML, and the integrated sources can be relational or XML. Agora adopts the LAV (local-as-view) approach, in which local sources are defined as views against the global schema. The Yacob mediator [20] adopts a different approach. It uses a graph-like global model, based on RDF, that defines concepts and relationship between concepts, being similar to the work presented here in many aspects. However in [20] the author focus on the construction of a query execution engine defining its architecture and functionalities, whereas in our approach we focus on the fragmentation operators and on the query decomposition algorithm. In this sense, our work complements the work done on the Yacob system [20]. To the best of our knowledge, there is no work in literature concerning query processing in XML that is based on the fragmentation of the sources, despite the existence of several work that addresses fragmentation in XML.

3 Data Model and Query Language

This section presents the data model used at the conceptual level, as well as the query language CXPath, used to state queries at the conceptual level.

3.1 Conceptual Model

The conceptual model is a high level abstraction of the XML data source models. It is build by a bottom-up approach described in [15, 16]. First, each local XML schema is abstracted into a local conceptual schema and after that local conceptual schemas are integrated resulting in a global conceptual schema.

The conceptual model is a simplified version of the ORM model [8]. It defines *concepts* and *relationships* between concepts. There are two kinds of concepts: *lexical* and *non-lexical*. Lexical concepts represent objects that have a textual content. Lexical concepts abstract atomic XML elements, like #PCDATA elements or attribute values. Non-lexical concepts do not have a direct textual representation and are abstractions of XML elements that contain other elements. Relationships at the conceptual model level are abstractions of two kinds of constructs at the XML levels. A relationship may have a *navigational* implementation, i.e. it may represent an access path relationship at the XML level. A relationship may further have an *associative* implementation, i.e, it may represent an identifier reference between data in two different XML data sources. For details on the process of abstraction of an XML schemata into a conceptual schema, please refer to [16]. A non-lexical concept may

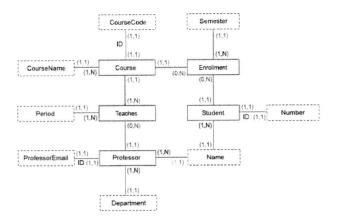

Figure 1. A conceptual schema

have an *identifier*. An identifier is a set of relationships that uniquely identifies an instance of the concept.

Figure 1 shows a conceptual schema for student enrollment in a university. There are five non-lexical concepts: *Course*, *Enrollment*, *Student*, *Teaches* and *Professor*, which are represented by solid rectangles. Each of these concepts is related to at least one lexical concept (dotted rectangle). For example, *Student* is related to *Name* and *Number*. The diagram represents also the cardinality of the relationships between concepts. For example, in this model, *Course* and *Enrollment* have a one-to-many relationship. The identifier relationships are labeled with 'ID' (for example *Student* is identified by the relationship with *Number*).

A formal definition of the conceptual model is given in [22].

3.2 CXPath

CXPath [3] is a query language, based on XPath [23], which is used to state queries at the conceptual level. Queries written in CXPath are *path expressions* over the concepts of a global schema. Path expressions may be enriched with *selection predicates*. Some examples of CXPath queries over the conceptual schema of figure 1 are presented below (for details please refer to [3].

Example 3.1. Retrieve the name of the students registered in the course with code "INF001" in the semester "2006/1".

```
/Course[CourseCode="INF001"]
/Enrollment[Semester="2006/1"]
/Student/Name
```

Example 3.2 Retrieve the name of the professors who will be teaching the course which code is "CSE 241".

```
/Course[CourseCode="CSE
241"]/Teaches/Professor/Name
```

4 Fragmentation Operators

In this work a set of fragmentation operations over a graph-like conceptual model is proposed. These operations have been originally developed for different data models. Horizontal and vertical fragmentations were defined over the relational data model [17, 4]. The split fragmentation was originally developed for the object-oriented data model [21] and afterward was adopted to the XML data model [11, 12]. The result of the fragmentation process is a set of local conceptual schemas and local conceptual bases, which are then directly mapped to XML documents by the process described in [16].

Notice that in our approach we clearly separate two different problems, the problem of fragmentation (decomposition of the global model into several local models) and the problem of abstraction of implementation details in an XML source into a local conceptual schema. If we apply fragmentation directly at the XML model level, we will have to deal with the problem that the same conceptual information may have several different representations at the XML level. In our approach, XML sources that have different schema but have conceptually the same content will be described by a single local conceptual model.

Below, we define first the local models that are obtained by the fragmentation operators and after that we discuss the fragmentation operators themselves.

4.1 Local Conceptual Model

A local conceptual model is a subset of a given global conceptual model. A global conceptual schema can be fragmented into several local schemas through fragmentation operators. The operators that produce local conceptual schemas are the vertical fragmentation and the split fragmentation, which will be detailed below.

When two non-lexical concepts that are associated by a relationship in the global conceptual model are fragmented into different local schemas, *identifier references* need to be included in these local schemas. An identifier reference is an information that implements a relationship between two local conceptual schemas in the same way a foreign-key implements a relationship between two relations in a relational database. The local schema in which an identifier reference is included will depend on the cardinality of the relationships. Each identifier reference is mapped to the identifier of the related non-lexical concept.

Figure 2 shows local schemas that may obtained by fragmentation of the conceptual schema on Figure 1. The non-lexical concepts *Enrollment*, *Course*, *Professor* and

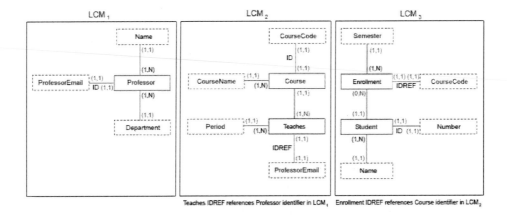

Figure 2. Local conceptual schemas produced through split fragmentation operations

Teaches, which are related in the global conceptual schema shown in Figure 1, were fragmented into the local conceptual schemas in Figure 2. Some relationships in the global schema are implemented in the local schemas through identifier references. For example, take the relationship between *Enrollment* and *Course* that appears at the global level. As the concepts *Enrollment* and *Course* are distributed in two different local schemas (LCM_3 and LCM_2 respectively) the relationship at the global conceptual level must be implemented through an identifier reference at the local level. In this example, the concept *CourseCode* was added to the local schema LCM_3. The instances of this concept are references the *Course* identifier in local schema LCM_2. The same idea is valid for the concept *ProfessorEmail* in LCM_2.

A formal definition of the local conceptual model is given in [22].

4.2 Operators

The *split fragmentation* operator is based on the operator presented in [11], where a given element of an XML document is replaced by a reference to a new element. This operator originates from previous work on object-oriented databases [21]. There, a complex operation in a class is replaced by a reference to a new class. In this work, the split operator has a different behavior. It takes a conceptual schema and divides it into two distinct local conceptual schemas. The relationships in the global schema that are splitted into different local schemas are implemented through identifier references. Figure 2 presents an example of the result of split operations applied to the conceptual schema in figure 1.

Vertical fragmentation is based on the corresponding relational operator [17], which produces fragments projecting subsets of attributes. In the context of this work, each fragment contains subsets of lexical concepts of the conceptual

schema. This operator was also presented in [11, 12], but there it is defined over the XML data model, instead of the conceptual model. However, the behavior of both operators are very similar.

Horizontal fragmentation is also based on the corresponding relational operator [4], which produces fragments that correspond to subsets of the tuples. In the context of this work, this operator produces fragments that correspond to a subset of the instances of a given conceptual base. Each fragment is defined through a selection predicate. If the instance obeys the predicate, it is included in the fragment.

For more details and the formal definitions of this operators, please refer to [22].

5 Mapping Between Local Model and XML Source

This section describes the mapping between a local schema and the corresponding local XML schemata. This mapping is used by the decomposition algorithm during the translation of a global query into a local query. We apply the global-as-view (GAV) approach [7]. The mapping approach presented here is an extension of the mapping approach we have previously defined for translating queries over a single data source [3].

Two types of mappings are applied: *absolute* and *relative* mappings. Absolute mappings are used to describe how a concept at the conceptual level is found at the XML level. Absolute mappings are given by absolute XPath expressions, one for each concept and each source. Relative mappings are used to describe how a relationship traversal at the conceptual level is mapped to a navigation between elements at the XML level. Relative mappings are given by relative XPath expressions that navigate from an element to another at the XML level.

Below we present examples of mapping information for

Figure 3. Schemata for LCM_2 XML source

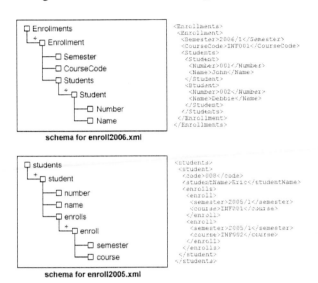

Figure 4. Schematas for LCM_3 XML sources

the local conceptual schemas shown at figure 2, considering the structure of the XML files shown at figures 3 and 4.

Table 1 shows examples of absolute mappings. For each non-lexical concept in a given local conceptual schema and for each XML source, there will be one XPath expression that retrieves the XML elements which represent that concept. For example, consider LCM_2 (Figure 2) and the single XML source (*courses.xml*) that is associated to it (Figure 3). LCM_2 contains two non-lexical concepts: *Course* and *Teaches*. The concept *Course* at the conceptual level is mapped to the XPath expression `/Courses/Course` at the XML source. In the same way the mapping of the concept *Teaches* to this source is given by the XPath expression `/Courses/Course/Professor/Period`.

Table 2 shows examples of relative mappings. For each relationship traversal in a local conceptual schema and for each XML source, there is one relative XPath expression that defines how the relationship traversal at the conceptual level is mapped at the XML level. For example, consider the relationship between the concepts *Course* and *CourseCode* in the local conceptual schema LCM_2 (Figure 2). The traversal of this relationship from *Course* to *CourseCode* is mapped to the relative XPath expression `CourseCode`. This expression specifies that, in order to navigate in this

Table 1. Absolute Mapping Information

concept	LCM	url	expression
Course	LCM_2	courses.xml	/Courses/Course
Teaches	LCM_2	courses.xml	/Courses/Course /Professor/Period
Enrollment	LCM_3	enroll2005.xml	/students/students /enrolls/enroll
Enrollment	LCM_3	enroll2006.xml	/Enrollments /Enrollment
Student	LCM_3	enroll2005.xml	/students/student
Student	LCM_3	enroll2006.xml	/Enrollments /Enrollment/Students /Student

XML source from the element that corresponds to the concept *Course* to the element that corresponds to the concept *CourseCode*, the relative XPath expression `CourseCode` must be applied. The relative XPath expression that maps the traversal of the same relationship in the reverse direction (from *CourseCode* to *Course*) is `..` (the XPath ancestor axis operator).

For a formal definition of the mapping information, please refer to [22].

6 Decomposition Algorithm

In this section, we describe how a query expressed at the conceptual level through a CXPath expression (Section 3.2) is rewritten into an XQuery expression at the XML level. More specifically, the decomposition algorithm first translates the CXPath expression into several XPath expressions, one for each XML source, and then groups these XPath subqueries into a single XQuery expression.

The main steps of the decomposition algorithm are the following:

1. **Parse the CXPath query**

2. **Handle horizontal fragments**

3. **Navigate inside fragments**

4. **Join split fragments**

5. **Implement the selection predicates**

The decomposition algorithm is explained here by discussing the results of each step of the algorithm on an example CXPath query. For details please refer to [22]. Further, due to lack of space the version of the algorithm explained here does not handle vertical fragmentation. At [22] the necessary changes in the algorithm to include this type of fragmentation are discussed.

In the following subsections we will show how the CXPath expression below (Example 3.1 of Section 3) is translated when it is executed against the global conceptual schema described in Figure 1 and the local conceptual

Table 2. Relative Mapping Information

source	destination	LCM	url	expression
Course	CourseCode	LCM_2	courses.xml	CourseCode
Course	CourseName	LCM_2	courses.xml	Name
CourseCode	Course	LCM_2	courses.xml	..
CourseName	Course	LCM_2	courses.xml	..
Enrollment	Semester	LCM_3	enroll2005.xml	semester
Enrollment	CourseCode	LCM_3	enroll2005.xml	course
Enrollment	Student	LCM_3	enroll2005.xml	../..
Semester	Enrollment	LCM_3	enroll2005.xml	..
CourseCode	Enrollment	LCM_3	enroll2005.xml	..
Student	Enrollment	LCM_3	enroll2005.xml	enroll/enrolls
Student	Number	LCM_3	enroll2005.xml	number
Student	Name	LCM_3	enroll2005.xml	name
Number	Student	LCM_3	enroll2005.xml	..
Name	Student	LCM_3	enroll2005.xml	..
Enrollment	Semester	LCM_3	enroll2006.xml	Semester
Enrollment	CourseCode	LCM_3	enroll2006.xml	CourseCode
Enrollment	Student	LCM_3	enroll2006.xml	Students/Student
Semester	Enrollment	LCM_3	enroll2006.xml	..
CourseCode	Enrollment	LCM_3	enroll2006.xml	..
Student	Enrollment	LCM_3	enroll2006.xml	../..
Student	Number	LCM_3	enroll2006.xml	Number
Student	Name	LCM_3	enroll2006.xml	Name
Number	Student	LCM_3	enroll2006.xml	..
Name	Student	LCM_3	enroll2006.xml	..

Table 3. Result of *parseQuery*

oid	concept	LCM	sources	predicate
1	Course	LCM_2	courses.xml	CourseCode= "INF001"
2	Enrollment	LCM_3	enroll2005.xml enroll2006.xml	Semester= "2006/1"
3	Student	LCM_3	enroll2005.xml enroll2006.xml	
4	Name	LCM_3	enroll2005.xml enroll2006.xml	

Table 4. Result of *handleHorizontalFragments* - **FOR clauses**

var	expression
$v1	doc("courses.xml")/Courses/Course
$v2	doc("enroll2005.xml")/students/student /enrolls/enroll | doc("enroll2006.xml") /Enrollments/Enrollment

schemas described in Figure 2, with the mapping information declared in tables 1 and 2 being considered.

```
/Course[CourseCode="INF001"]
/Enrollment[Semester="2006/1"]
/Student/Name
```

6.1 Parse Query

The first decomposition step is to parse the query and generate a tuple for each concept in the CXPath query. CX-Path subqueries that appear in the selection predicates are handled by recursive calls of this algorithm as explained below. Each tuple contains a tuple identifier (*object id*), the *concept*, the local conceptual model which the concept belongs to, its sources, and the selection predicates associated to the concept in the XPath expression.

The tuple identifier is used during the generation of the FOR clause of the resulting XQuery expression to name each variable with a $v followed by the object id. Table 3 contains the result of this step for the example query.

6.2 Handle Horizontal Fragments

In this step, the algorithm begins to build the XQuery expression. For each local conceptual schema that is referenced by the concepts in the CXPath expression, one binding of an XQuery variable will be constructed. These bindings will be used in the FOR clause of the resulting XQuery expression. For the example query, the bindings in Table 4 will be constructed.

These variable bindings are constructed as follows. For each local conceptual schema, the algorithm takes the first concept in the parsed query (Table 3). In the example, these will be the concepts *Course* in LCM_2 and *Enrollment* in LCM_3. For each concept one binding is constructed. This binding contains a reference to each XML source that is associated to the local schema, as well as the absolute mapping expressions (Section 5) for the concept in each source, that specifies how instances of this concept are found in the XML source. For a definition of this algorithm, please refer to [22].

The first concept of LCM_2 found in the example query is *Course*. LCM_2 corresponds to the XML source courses.xml and the absolute mapping expression for

Table 5. Result of *navigateInsideFragments* **- FOR clauses**

var	expression
$v3	$v2[base_uri(.)="enroll2005.xml"]/../.. | $v2[base_uri(.)="enroll2006.xml"]/Students/Student
$v4	$v3[base_uri(.)="enroll2005.xml"]/name | $v3[base_uri(.)="enroll2006.xml"]/Name

Table 6. Result of *joinSplitFragments* **- WHERE clauses**

expression
($v2[base_uri(.)="enroll2005.xml"]/course | $v2[base_uri(.)="enroll2006.xml"]/CourseCode) = $v1/CourseCode

Course in `courses.xml` is `/Courses/Course`. This leads to the first binding shown in Table 4. Local conceptual schema LCM_3 is represented by two different XML data sources, `enroll2005.xml` and `enroll2006.xml`. In this case, the binding will correspond to the union of the elements that represent the concept *Enrollment* in these sources (second line in Table 4).

6.3 Navigate Inside Fragments

In the second step we have defined variables that are bound to absolute XPath expressions that will be used to iterate over each fragment, i.e., over each local conceptual schema. In this step we will implement the navigation inside each fragment through relative XPath expressions. To handle this problem, we adopted the same approach as in [3].

The algorithm compares each pair of adjacent concepts in the parsed query. If the pair belongs to the same local conceptual schema, it means that a relationship between two concepts is being traversed. To implement this relationship traversal at the XML source level, the relative path expression defined by the relative mapping for this traversal (Section 5) is bound to a variable. The complete algorithm for this step is defined in [22]. For example, consider the relationship traversal from *Enrollment* to *Student* in LCM_3. This traversal is implemented in source `enroll2005.xml` by the relative XPath expression `../..`, and in source `enroll2006.xml` by the relative XPath expression `Students/Student` (see Table 2). This leads to the first line in Table 5.

These lines defines a binding for a new variable $v3 that is bound to an expression that is relative to the $v2 variable. Recall that $v2 is bound to an absolute XPath expression that retrieves the XML elements that represent the *Enrollment* concept, source of the relationship traversal being handled. The $v3 binding constructed in this step specifies the traversal of the relationship from *Enrollment* to *Student* at the conceptual level. As this relationship is implemented in two different XML sources, the terms in form `base_uri(.)` are used to ensure that the relative path is being applied over the correct source.

Analogously a variable $v4 is bound to the relative XPath expression that specifies the traversal from concept

Student to concept *Name*.

6.4 Join Split Fragments

A CXPath query may access concepts from different local schemas, which means that several split fragments (local schemas) need to be accessed and joined to answer the query. For each local schema, a variable bound to an absolute XPath expression that retrieves elements in the fragment was constructed in the second step. In this step, the criteria to join the elements from different sources is constructed. This criteria will take part of the WHERE clause in the resulting XQuery expression. The join criteria will be constructed using the *identifiers* and *identifier references* that have been defined during the the split operation, which generated the local schemas from the global schema (Section 3.1)

In the parsed query table (Table 3), for each adjacent pair of concepts that belong to different local schemas, a join must be defined. For each such pair of concepts, the algorithm finds the identifiers and the identifier references that are used to navigate from one fragment to the other. In the example (Table 3), there is a single pair of concepts that corresponds to the navigation from one fragment to the other, namely the traversal from concept *Course* to concept *Enrollment*. This relationship is implemented by identifier reference *Enrollment.CourseCode* that references the identifier *Course.CourseCode*.

Next, for each XML source, the algorithm takes the relative path expressions that implement the traversal from *Course* to the identifier *CourseCode* and from *Enrollment* to the identifier reference *CourseCode*. Finally, an equality predicate among this two relative XPath expressions is included in the WHERE clause, as shown in Table 6.

The algorithm for this step is defined in [22].

6.5 Handle Selection Predicates

This step of the algorithm is in charge of handling the selection predicates that may appear in the CXPath query. This selection predicates will be rewritten into terms in the WHERE clause of the resulting XQuery expression. The algorithm supports a simplified form of the selection predicate, which has the following structure:

9

```
for
    $v1 in doc("courses.xml")/Courses/Course,
    $v2 in doc("enroll2005.xml")/students/student/enrolls/enroll
        | doc("enroll2006.xml")/Enrollments/Enrollment,
    $v3 in $v2[base-uri(.)="enroll2005.xml"]/../.. |
        $v2[base-uri(.)="enroll2005.xml"]/Students/Student,
    $v4 in $v3[base-uri(.)="enroll2005.xml"]/studentName |
        $v3[base-uri(.)="enroll2006.xml"]/Name
where
    ($v2[base-uri(.)="enroll2005.xml"]/course |
    $v2[base-uri(.)="enroll2006.xml"]/CourseCode) =
    $v1/CourseCode and
    (for $v1-1 in $v1/CourseCode return $v1-1) = "INF001" and
    (for $v2-1 in $v2[base-uri(.)="enroll2005.xml"]/semester |
        $v2[base-uri(.)="enroll2006.xml"]/Semester
        return $v2-1) = "2006/1"
return
    $v4
```

Figure 5. XQuery generated by the decomposition algorithm to example 3.1

```
CXPathLeft comp [CXPathRight OR
constant]
```

where *CXPathLeft* and *CXPathRight* are CXPath subqueries, which may be relative or absolute expressions, $comp \in \{=, \neq, <, >, \leq, \geq\}$ is a comparison operator, and *constant* is a string.

The CXPath subqueries that may appear in the selection predicate are translated by a recursive execution of the decomposition algorithm.

For example, the selection predicate CourseCode="INF001" that contains an expression that is relative to the *Course* concept is translated into the predicate:

```
(for $v1-1 in $v1/CourseCode
return $v1-1)
= "INF001"
```

The XQuery expression for $v1-1 ... is obtained by the recursive execution of the decomposition algorithm on the relative CXPath expression CourseCode that appear in the CXPath selection predicate. When the CXPath expressions inside a selection predicate are relative, the context, i.e. the tuple identifier and the concept, must be passed as parameter to the decomposition algorithm. In the example, the parameters are the object id 1 and the concept Course. The details regarding to the recursive call are shown in [22].

The final XQuery for the example 2.1 is shown at figure 5.

7 Conclusion and Future Work

This paper presents an approach to handle the problem of querying integrated XML documents. We first present a set of fragmentation operators for XML documents that belong to a specific domain described by a conceptual schema, and

then, on the basis of these fragmentation operators, present a query decomposition mechanism that translates a CXPath query expression at the global level into an XQuery expression at the XML level.

Our contribution is twofold. One contribution is to clearly separate the problem of fragmentation of a global schema into several local schemata from the problem of abstracting from different XML representations of the same conceptual information. This separation is achieved by the introduction of a conceptual layer at the local source level and at the global (mediated) level as well. The fragmentation operators are defined at this conceptual level. This concepts are formally defined in a separate document [22].

Another contribution is the query decomposition algorithm itself, which is based on the fragmentation of sources. The presented version of the algorithm handles split fragmentation and most of the horizontal fragmentation scenarios that can be described through the fragmentation operators. With the changes presented in [22], it can handle also vertical fragmentation. A scenario that is not handled by this version of the decomposition algorithm is when the horizontal fragmentation operations are not disjoint - i.e. when the same instance appears in more then one XML source. We leave this issue for future work.

A further problem that is not handled by this version of the decomposition algorithm is query optimization. The queries generated by this algorithm are not the most efficient ones, and the performance of the query execution can be improved by rewriting the generated query. Future work should decide among alternatives like improving the generated XQuery or using a XML algebra (e.g., TAX [9]) after the decomposition is concluded.

Acknowledgments

This work is partially supported by FAPERGS (project PRONEX 0408993) and CNPq (projects 473310/2004-0, 550.845/2005-4 and Gerindo).

References

[1] S. Bose, L. Fegaras, D. Levine, and V. Chaluvadi. A query algebra for fragmented xml stream data. In *DBPL*, pages 195–215, 2003.

[2] J.-M. Bremer and M. Gertz. On distributing xml repositories. In *WebDB*, pages 73–78, 2003.

[3] S. Camillo, R. Mello, and C. Heuser. Querying heterogeneous xml sources through a conceptual schema. *ER International Conference on Conceptual Modeling*, 2003.

[4] S. Ceri, M. Negri, and G. Pelagatti. Horizontal data partitioning in database design. In *SIGMOD '82: Proceedings of the 1982 ACM SIGMOD international conference on Management of data*, pages 128–136, New York, NY, USA, 1982. ACM Press.

[5] A. Doan, P. Domingos, and A. Y. Halevy. Reconciling schemas of disparate data sources: A machine-learning approach. In *SIGMOD Conference*, 2001.

[6] R. dos Santos Mello and C. A. Heuser. Binxs: A process for integration of xml schemata. In *CAiSE*, pages 151–166, 2005.

[7] A. Elmagarmid, M. Rusinkiewicz, and A. Sheth, editors. *Management of heterogeneous and autonomous database systems*. Morgan Kaufmann Publishers Inc., San Francisco, CA, USA, 1999.

[8] T. Halphin. *Object-Role Modeling (ORM/NIAM). Handbook on Architectures of Information Systems*. Springer-Verlag, 1998.

[9] H. V. Jagadish, L. V. S. Lakshmanan, D. Srivastava, and K. Thompson. Tax: A tree algebra for xml. In *Revised Papers from the 8th International Workshop on Database Programming Languages*, pages 149–164. Springer, 2002.

[10] V. Josifovski and T. Risch. Query decomposition for a distributed object-oriented mediator system. *Distributed and Parallel Databases*, 11(3):307–336, 2002.

[11] H. Ma and K.-D. Schewe. Fragmentation of xml documents. In *SBBD*, pages 200–214, 2003.

[12] H. Ma, K.-D. Schewe, S. Hartmann, and M. Kirchberg. Distribution design for xml documents. In *ICeCE*, 2003.

[13] L. M. Mackinnon, D. H. Marwick, and M. H. Williams. A model for query decomposition and answer construction in heterogeneous distributed database systems. *J. Intell. Inf. Syst.*, 11(1):69–87, 1998.

[14] I. Manolescu, D. Florescu, and D. Kossmann. Answering xml queries on heterogeneous data sources. In *Proceedings of the 27th International Conference on Very Large Data Bases*, pages 241–250. Morgan Kaufmann Publishers Inc., 2001.

[15] R. Mello, S. Castano, and C. Heuser. A method for the unification of xml schemata. *Information and Software Technology*, 44:241–249, 2002.

[16] R. Mello and C. Heuser. A rule-based convertion of a dtd to a conceptual schema. *ER International Conference on Conceptual Modeling*, pages 133–148, 2001.

[17] S. Navathe, S. Ceri, G. Wiederhold, and J. Dou. Vertical partitioning algorithms for database design. *ACM Trans. Database Syst.*, 9(4):680–710, 1984.

[18] M. T. Ozsu and P. Valduriez. *Principles of distributed database systems*. Prentice-Hall, Inc., Upper Saddle River, NJ, USA, 1991.

[19] C. Reynaud, J.-P. Sirot, and D. Vodislav. Semantic integration of xml heterogeneous data sources. In M. E. Adiba, C. Collet, and B. C. Desai, editors, *IDEAS*, pages 199–208. IEEE Computer Society, 2001.

[20] K.-U. Sattler, I. Geist, and E. Schallehn. Concept-based querying in mediator systems. *The VLDB Journal*, 14(1):97–111, 2005.

[21] K.-D. Schewe. Fragmentation of object oriented and semistructured data. In *BalticDB&IS*, pages 253–266, 2002.

[22] F. V. Silveira and C. A. Heuser. Fragmentation and query decomposition in xml. Technical report, UFRGS, Brazil, April 2006. Available from http://www.inf.ufrgs.br/~heuser/papers/repfv.pdf.

[23] W3C. Available at: $http://www.w3.org/$.

[24] G. Wiederhold. Mediators in the architecture of future information systems. *Computer*, 25(3):38–49, 1992.

Adaptive Execution of Stream Window Joins in a Limited Memory Environment

Fatima Farag   Moustafa A. Hammad*

Department of Computer Science, University of Calgary
2500 University Drive NW, Calgary, AB, CANADA
ffarag,hammad@cpsc.ucalgary.ca←

Abstract

A sliding window join (SWJoin) is becoming an integral operation in every stream data management system. In some streaming applications the increasing volume of streamed data as well as the multiplicity of concurrent queries requires an adaptive SWJoin algorithm for the limited memory resources. Previous algorithms of SWJoin address the memory limitation by exploiting external-memory resources while imposing timely ordered arrival of input data streams. In this paper we propose an external-memory sliding-window join algorithm (EM-SWJoin) that addresses general arrival patterns of input streams and exploits disk-based data structures. The algorithm runs in two phases. The first phase partially joins the arriving data of one stream with the memory-resident data of the other streams. The second phase completes the processing of the partially joined data by considering the disk-resident data from the corresponding streams. Swapping from one phase to the other improves the response time of the input data. A comparative study between EM-SWJoin and other related algorithms illustrates the superiority of the proposed algorithm.

1. Introduction

The widespread use of applications that capture streams of data has led to an increasing focus on how to improve their data management techniques. For example, applications that access data from GPS systems, sensors, and Internet traffic are dealing with hundreds and even thousands of streamed data items (tuples) per second. Stream data sources are usually remote and are connected to the streaming application using wired or wireless networks. As networks are subject to failures and congestions, unpredictable delays or bursty arrivals of input data streams are likely to occur. Delays over a network can slow down the processing of the arriving data and increase the overall system response time. Moreover, the high-rate and bursty arrival of data streams can overflow the limited memory buffers. Therefore, network delays and bursty data arrivals challenge the execution of an important class of data management operations that require buffering of the arriving streamed data (*e.g.*, aggregate and join operations).

One approach to address the memory limitation is to develop stream data management algorithms that exploit external memory storage devices such as disks. However, streaming applications have two unique requirements that continuously challenge the development of such algorithms. The first requirement is the notion of the sliding-window execution, which is a practical way of limiting the processing over the infinite data streams. Using a sliding window, a stream data management operation processes only recently arriving data. As the window slides, processing new data as well as expiring previously processed data, which might be disk residents, increase the disk overhead. The second requirement is the stream-in/stream-out processing phenomenon, which requires releasing output tuples in the same time-order as their corresponding input tuples [6]. Releasing the output tuples in an increasing order of timestamp is crucial for a class of applications that predicts trends of variations. One such application is the Wall Street stock market which intends to accurately and rapidly analyze the continuously arriving data streams in an increasing order of timestamp. For example, a query requesting to monitor the traded volume of stocks of value less than $300 and that experienced a drop in the last 10 minutes is an example for a SWJoin operation. Because such a

*Moustafa A. Hammad's research is supported in part by the Natural Sciences and Engineering Research Council (NSERC) of Canada under DG 73-2276, NSERCCRD, and GEOIDE under SII#43.

query can be used in predicting changes in stock prices, releasing answers in an increasing order of timestamp is required. However, in-order stream processing contradicts with the basic principle of developing external-memory algorithms that relies on input re-ordering to hide disk latency (e.g., the sort-merge operations).

In this paper we focus on developing an external memory algorithm for the join operation over data streams. A stream join is a typical operation in virtually all data stream management systems and tuning its execution affects the overall system performance.

Conventional external memory join operations such as hybrid-hash and sort-merge techniques [9] target static (non streaming) data sources and, hence, are not applicable to data streams. On the other hand, recent stream join algorithms such as XJoin[13, 14], HMJoin[8], and RPJoin[11] depend on the out-of-order processing to hide network delays. Therefore, the stream-in/stream-out key requirement is intentionally violated to overlap network latency with disk access.

In this paper we propose an external-memory stream join algorithm that satisfies the above key requirements of stream processing. The algorithm runs in two phases. The first phase partially processes the arriving tuples against the memory-resident tuples of the other joined streams. The second phase completes the processing of a tuple by processing it against the corresponding disk-resident tuples of the other streams. The algorithm satisfies the two key requirements of stream processing in such a way that hides the network and the disk latencies. Specifically, in this paper we contribute as follows:

1. We study the problem of in-order release of output tuples in a limited memory sliding-window join environment and provide an algorithm, termed EM-SWJoin, that adapts input tuple execution in such a way that hides disk latency as well as network delays.

2. We provide a comparative study between EM-SWJoin and two other related classes of algorithms. The first class of algorithms is concerned with releasing output tuples in an increasing time-order while overlooking the problem of external memory latency and network delays, whereas the second class is concerned with hiding the disk latency as well as the network delays while neglecting the stream-in/stream-out notion in a sliding window environment.

3. We experimentally study the performance of EM-SWJoin as well as selective algorithms found in literature. The experimental study shows the

outperformance of our algorithm over the other approaches when evaluated in a limited memory environment. EM-SWJoin achieves a significant performance in terms of the tuple response time as well as in hiding the disk access latency.

The rest of the paper is organized as follows. Section 2 states the addressed problem and presents a review of some preliminary concepts found in literature regarding in-order execution. Section 3 presents our proposed algorithm. Our experimental study is discussed in Section 4. Section 5 presents the related work found in the literature, while a conclusion to the paper is provided in Section 6.

2. Background

2.1. Context and Environment

Let S_1, S_2, . . . , S_n be n input data streams with arrival rates in tuples/second. Each tuple has a set of attributes that include a timestamp attribute and a join attribute. Our goal is to join the tuples of the input streams using the join attribute under the following assumptions. (1) The streaming tuples are continuously arriving in an unbounded manner. (2) Tuples belonging to a single stream arrive in an increasing order of timestamp. (3) The input streams are generated by independent sources, i.e., there is no implicit order between a timestamp of a tuple from one stream and a timestamp of a tuple from another stream. Data streams that satisfy assumptions (2) and (3) are termed *asynchronous* data streams [6]. (4) The application's requirement is to receive an ordered release of output tuples. By ordered output, we mean that if two input tuples, say s and t, are processed by the join operation and the timestamp of s is less than the timestamp of t, then the output from s (if any) must be released before the output from t (if any). (5) A sliding-window execution is considered, i.e., if n tuples are input to a SWJoin, each from a different stream then the tuples join if the join condition is satisfied and the difference between any two timestamps of the joined tuples is less than or equal to the sliding-window size. (6) The join operator has a local clock (i.e., join clock). The join clock equals $Minimum_{\forall 1 \le i \le n}$ (timestamp (s_i)), where s_i is the newest tuple in stream S_i. (7) The memory space is not enough to store tuples of (at least) one of the input streams.

Table 1 gives an example of a SWJoin over stream S and stream T. Tuples with the same alphabetical letters join together and each tuple is indexed by its timestamp. Assume that the last seen tuple arriving at the system and updating the clock was tuple a_3. Notice that tuples arrive over input streams in an asynchronous manner (*e.g.*, tuple c_9 in *S* arrives after tuple a_{11} in *T*). Table 1 shows how SWJoin updates the join clock as time passes (i.e., as the wall clock advances). According to Table 1, after the join clock is set to 7 at time 8, no update to the join clock occurs until c_9 arrives at time 12. Tuple a_8 is processed upon the arrival of tuple c_9, while a_{10} and a_{11} are processed upon arrival of f_{13}.

Table 1. A description of how the join operator clock updates

Wall Clock	5	6	7	8	9	10	11	12	13
Stream(S)			f_7					c_9	f_{13}
Stream(T)	f_5	a_6		a_8		a_{10}	a_{11}		
Join Clock	3	3	6	7	7	7	7	9	11

2.2. Related Algorithms

The authors in [6] discuss two approaches; namely, the *Sync-Filter* and the *Filter-Order* approaches, that are motivated by the importance of releasing ordered output tuples using SWJoin. In *Sync-Filter* the in-order release of outputs is strictly enforced by the in-order processing of inputs such that the timestamp of an input tuple being processed, say t_1, is smaller than the timestamp of the next arriving input tuple, say t_2. Moreover, an input tuple arriving at one stream triggers for processing the earlier arriving tuple(s) of a smaller timestamp from the other stream. For example, in Table 1 tuple f_{13} is the triggering tuple to process tuples a_{10} and a_{11}. Although *Sync-Filter* releases output tuples in an increasing timestamp order, an input tuple may block prior to its processing due to the in-order execution requirement for inputs.

To overcome the blocking delay problem of the previous approach, the authors in [6] propose the *Filter-Order* approach. Filter-Order resolves the problem by background processing the arriving input tuples while waiting for the triggering tuple (*i.e.*, *Filter-Order* overlaps the processing time and the waiting time of an arriving input tuple). Thus, input tuples are processed upon arrival, while output tuples (if any) are buffered. Output tuples are sorted based on timestamp before release. Although *Filter-Order* overcomes the blocking problem found in *Sync-Filter*, it introduces a memory overhead by buffering the outputs. In both approaches a tuple response time (i.e., the time elapsed between the arrival of a tuple and completing the tuple processing using SWJoin) increases significantly when the tuple probes disk-resident tuples. This is due to the fact that the tuple response time is affected by the incurred system delays

as well as the processing cost, which now includes the disk overhead.

Apart from *Sync-Filter* and *Filter-Order* that assume an unlimited memory resource, another class of algorithms addresses the stream join in a limited memory space, e.g., the algorithms in [8, 11, 13]. These algorithms assume a bounded memory environment where an external memory resource is required in order to keep up with the large input size. However, these algorithms overlook the importance of in-order release of output results. Their main concern is to provide an efficient method of releasing a *complete* set of output results as soon as possible, while reducing the disk overhead incurred when probing disk resident tuples. A tuple arriving at one stream probes the corresponding memory-resident tuples of other streams. No disk access occurs as long as data is continuously arriving along (at least) one of the input streams. Probing disk-resident tuples is postponed until no input tuples arrives over all input streams. Notice that enforcing in-order release of output tuples in these algorithms is problematic for the following two reasons. (1) The continuous arrival of data over the input streams will prevent completing the processing of tuples (a tuple is said to *complete* its processing when it probes the corresponding memory as well as disk resident tuples of the other stream, otherwise, the tuple is said to be *partially* processed). Thus, a tuple response time will increase indefinitely. (2) The in-order release requirement of the output enforces buffering the output of the partially processed tuples as long as these tuples have not completed their processing. This will in turn increase the memory overhead.

Because we are concerned with releasing output results in-order under a memory limited assumption, our algorithm combines between a flexible and an aggressive behavior. The flexible behavior comes from the fact that an input tuple probes the corresponding memory resident tuples upon its arrival. Thus, a tuple efficiently utilizes any delay times prior to releasing its outputs. The aggressive behavior of the algorithm occurs when an input tuple is enforced to complete its processing against the corresponding disk-resident tuples of the other stream as soon as it is triggered to do so. Notice that the aggressive property of our algorithm can cause some memory-resident tuples to postpone completing their processing because some earlier arriving tuples are given the priority to complete their processing first. This reduces the tuple response time, as well as the memory overhead incurred from buffering the output. Such an aggressive property is not available in the related algorithms. With these two complementary behaviors, the tuple response time as well as the disk overhead cost are reduced in our proposed algorithm.

3. The Proposed EM-SWJoin Algorithm

Without loss of generality, we describe EM-SWJoin using a hash-based implementation and using two input data streams. The algorithm has two memory hash tables, one for each input stream. A hash table consists of multiple partitions, which are identified by the hash value. Both hash tables apply the same hash function in partitioning the input tuples among the hash partitions. In addition, two disk hash tables are generated, one for each input stream. Similar to the memory hash table, the disk hash table consists of multiple partitions. The

Algorithm 3.1. The EM-SWJoin Algorithm

1) While there exists an input tuple s in one of the input streams S
2)   If Mem(S) is Full
3)   For every partially processed tuple i in the largest hash partition of S
4)   **DP phase** (i, S) /* Run the DP phase */
5)   Flush the largest hash partition of S
6)   Update the join clock /* See Table 1 */
7)   Release output from the output buffer that has timestamp $\leq$ join clock
8)   **MP phase** (s, S) /* Run the MP phase */
9)   For every partially processed tuple i in Stream I and i's timestamp $\leq$ join clock
10)   **DP phase** (i, I) /* Run the DP phase */
11) For every partially processed tuple i in Stream I
12)   **DP phase** (i, I)

total number of tuples in a given hash partition equals the count of the memory-resident tuples and the disk-resident tuples of this partition. Each data stream has its own input buffer in which arriving tuples are located prior to processing. These input buffers are queue-based data structures.

3.1. EM-SWJoin: How it Works

Figure 1 gives a block diagram of the proposed algorithm. Upon arrival of a tuple at the input buffer, EM-SWJoin calculates the hash value of the joined attribute and moves the tuple to the equivalent memory hash partition. Next, EM-SWJoin probes the memory hash partition of the other stream and expires tuples based on the time-based sliding-window. The output results (if any) are placed in the output buffer. Notice that EM-SWJoin postpones the probing of the input tuple to the disk hash partition of the joined stream. Resuming a tuple processing will be explained in Section 3.2.2. When the memory space of an input stream gets full, EM-SWJoin flushes the tuples of the largest memory hash partition to disk. However, these tuples will have to complete their partial processing

prior to flushing. Expiration decisions against the corresponding disk resident tuples should also be

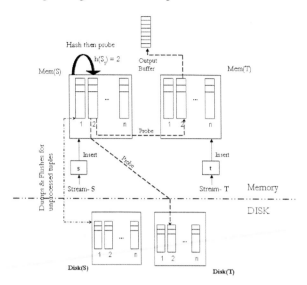

Figure 1. A Block Diagram of EM-SWJoin.

considered. Algorithm 3.1 describes EM-SWJoin. The following symbols are used in the algorithm. Mem(O) represents the memory resident part of object O. Disk(O) is the disk resident part of object O. P(I, n) is hash partition n of stream I, while |W| is the value of the time-based sliding window in seconds. The algorithm runs in two phases; namely the Memory-Probing phase (MP phase) and the Disk-Probing phase (DP phase). The MP phase is responsible for joining memory-resident tuples of both streams, whereas the DP phase is responsible for joining memory-resident tuples of one stream with the corresponding disk-resident tuples of the other stream. Algorithms 3.2 and 3.3 describe the MP phase and the DP phase, respectively.

3.1.1. The *MP* phase. This phase is responsible for matching a newly arriving tuple over one stream against the memory-resident tuples of the other stream that lie within the sliding window. Thus, when a tuple, say t, arrives at one stream, EM-SWJoin calculates t's hash value and moves t to the memory-resident hash partition of the same hash value as that of t. Next, t probes the corresponding memory hash partition of the other stream. Prior to probing, expiring tuples from the corresponding memory hash partition occurs based upon the defined time-based sliding window. Matching results are placed in the output buffer. Note that EM-SWJoin partially processes a tuple in this phase as the tuple completes its processing after probing the corresponding disk hash partition of the other stream. This memory to disk joining process is achieved in the

DP phase (explained in section 3.2.2). The algorithm executes the DP phase when one of the following three conditions is satisfied. (a) The arrival of a new tuple that results in an update to the join clock (e.g., c_9 in Table 1). (b) There is no enough memory to accommodate newly arriving tuple(s). (c) Stalling of tuple arrivals along both input streams. We call these three conditions the *blocking conditions* of the *MP* phase.

Algorithm 3.2. The MP phase of the EM-SWJoin Algorithm

Input: Tuple i, and Stream S.

1) Calculate n as the hash value of i's join attribute.
2) Add i to Mem($P(S,n)$)
3) Compare tuple i with tuples in partition n of other streams that are within window of i and that satisfies the join condition.
4) Add the output of joining i (if any) to the output buffer.

3.1.2. The *DP* phase. This phase is responsible for matching memory-resident tuples of one stream against the corresponding disk-resident tuples of the other stream that lie within the sliding window. Thus, the *DP* phase completes the processing of a tuple. The *DP* phase runs if any of the blocking conditions is satisfied. However, each of these conditions runs the *DP* phase in a different manner which we clarify as follows.

a) *The MP phase blocks when the clock is updated.* Thus, the *DP* phase will run against each of the partially processed memory-resident tuples in a *FIFO* (First In First Out) manner. Using the *FIFO*-ordering to complete the processing of tuples immediately releases from the output buffer an ordered set of output results, thus, no need to buffer the output.

b) *The MP phase blocks if the memory portion of any of the input streams is running short of space.* In such a situation, EM-SWJoin schedules the flushing process, which selects the largest hash partition (victim partition) and appends its resident tuples to the complementary disk partition. To reduce the number of disk accesses, EM-SWJoin schedules the *DP* phase prior to flushing tuples of the largest hash partition. The *DP* phase runs over the partially processed tuples that reside in this victim partition and output results are buffered.

c) *The MP phase blocks if the input tuple arrivals over both streams temporarily stall.* Once delays over both input data streams are detected, EM-SWJoin schedules the *DP* phase to run in a similar fashion to that of the first condition. However, output tuples are buffered.

3.1.3. Discussions. Overhead Costs. EM-SWJoin trades-off between two overhead costs, the memory overhead cost, and the disk I/O cost. As EM-SWJoin tends to avoid the memory overhead incurred in

Algorithm 3.3. The DP phase of the EM-SWJoin Algorithm

Input: Tuple i and Stream S (T).

1) Calculate n as the hash value of i's join attribute
2) Compare tuple i with tuples in disk partition n of other streams that are within window of i and that satisfies the join condition.
3) Add the output of joining i (if any) to the output buffer.

buffering output tuples that are not scheduled for immediate release, excessive disk accesses take place instead. On the other hand, when EM-SWJoin tends to reduce the number of disk accesses (*i.e.*, by packing the processing of input tuples that lie within the same hash partition), buffered output tuples become more than expected. Thus, the partial processing of tuples takes place upon a tuple arrival (*i.e.*, *MP* phase), while complete processing (*i.e.*, *DP* phase) occurs when a compromise between the performance of these two extremes is possible.

Duplicate Avoidance. EM-SWJoin avoids releasing duplicate outputs that are subject to occur in one of the following situations:

(a) *The DP phase executes after the MP phase blocks (i.e., Section 3.2.2 condition (b)).* As the *DP* phase migrates all the residing tuples of the victim partition from memory to disk, a situation where previously processed tuples (*i.e.*, completely processed tuples) that lie in this partition are subject to reprocessing. Thus duplication of output results can occur. EM-SWJoin guarantees that output duplications are avoided by keeping track of the last completely processed tuple in every hash partition. It is worth mentioning that newly arriving tuples are located on top of every hash partition, such that tuples at the head of a hash partition represent newly arriving tuples, while tuples at the tail of the partition represent older arriving ones. In other words, tuples at the head of a hash partition are the partially processed tuples, while tuples at the tail of a hash partition represent the completely processed tuples. EM-SWJoin differentiates between completely processed tuples, and partially processed tuples by recording the last tuple in each hash partition that has completed its processing. Tuples ahead of this tuple are considered as partially processed tuples.

(b) *The DP phase executes after the MP phase blocks (i.e., Section 3.2.2 condition (a)).* This requires the *DP* phase to complete the processing of the partially processed tuples in a *FIFO* scheduled manner. EM-SWJoin avoids duplication of output results by determining the partially processed tuples that need to complete their processing within a hash partition. This is done by running the *DP* phase against tuples that are ahead of the last completely processed tuple in each partition. Thus, tuples at the top of each hash partition participate in the current run of the *DP* phase as long as their timestamp is larger than the timestamp of the last completely processed tuple in every partition.

(c) *The tuples arrive in an asynchronous fashion.* Consider the example found in Table 1. c_9 arrives after tuples a_{10} and a_{11}. Assume that tuples a_8, a_{10}, and a_{11} are partially processed. As c_9 arrives, EM-SWJoin updates the clock, and tuple a_8 completes its processing. Because EM-SWJoin tends to reduce the number of disk accesses, tuples a_{10}, and a_{11} will join a_8 in completing their processing in the same *DP-phase*. Only output tuples of a_8 are released. However, upon arrival of f_{13}, the clock is updated to reflect the existence of tuples a_{10}, and a_{11}. Updating the clock causes the *DP* phase to run. EM-SWJoin avoids duplicating the outputs of a_{10} and a_{11} by checking their processing status which is set to *complete*.

4. Performance Study

4.1. Experimental Setup

We implemented EM-SWJoin, *Sync-Filter*, *Filter-Order*, and *X*Join using Visual C++ 6. All algorithms use the same data structures defined for EM-SWJoin. However, every approach processes in a different manner. Notice that *Sync-Filter* as well as *Filter-Order* process tuples in a complete manner (*i.e.*, a tuple probes both the memory resident tuples followed by the disk resident tuples of the corresponding stream). Moreover, in order to make *X*Join comply with our application requirements, modifications are applied. For example, the original *X*Join algorithm found in [13] assumes a definite arrival of input data streams, which causes a *Disk-to-Disk* probing phase to run. For the indefinite input arrivals in a streaming application, this phase is not considered in our implementation. Moreover, *X*Join does not consider the SW notion, as well as the in-order release of output tuples, which are required for a fair comparison against EM-SWJoin. Thus, we modified the *X*Join algorithm as follows. First, in our implementation, the *MP* phase, which is equivalent to the *Memory-to-Memory* phase in the original *X*Join, runs upon tuple arrivals. Second, running the *DP* phase, which is equivalent to the *Memory-to-Disk* phase in the original *X*Join, occurs

upon clock updates or during silence periods of tuple arrivals over input data streams. Third, tuples are scheduled to run the *DP* phase in a *FIFO* scheduled manner. All approaches are compared in a set of experiments. We give an experimental evidence that the performance of EM-SWJoin outperforms the performance of the other approaches in the conducted experiments. Two input streams are generated such that the inter-arrival time between two consecutive tuples arriving over the same data stream follows an exponential distribution. Our implementation builds two hash tables, one for each stream. Each hash table is divided into two portions, a memory-resident portion, and a disk-resident portion. Tuples arrive at the input buffers of both streams. An input buffer is implemented as a queue-based structure. A tuple is mapped into its corresponding hash partition by applying a hash function to its join attribute. The size of the memory portion of each stream is set to accommodate at most 1000 tuples. In addition, each hash table has a number of partitions (i.e., 100 partitions), which is fixed in all the experiments. Unless mentioned otherwise, the data set involved in the experiments is 1,000,000 tuples over both data streams. Output tuples are placed in a queue-based structure, where the key is the timestamp attribute. The memory resident output buffer can accommodate 1000 tuples at a time. Exceeding this boundary calls for a disk flushing process, which appends newly arriving tuples to a disk resident output buffer. For most experiments, we measure the performance of the implemented approaches in terms of the *average response time per input tuple*. Measuring the response time includes the waiting time, the processing time, as well as the time to produce output results (if any). All experiments are conducted on Intel Pentium IV CPU 3.4GHz with 1GB RAM running Windows XP.

4.2. Experimental Results

4.2.1 Varying the Input Rates

In the following set of experiments we measure the average response time as the performance metric by varying the input arrival rate over one input stream while fixing the arrival rate of the other stream. The following set of experiments measures the response time of 1,000,000 tuples arriving over two data streams, where stream 1 has ≈ 512,000 tuples and stream 2 has ≈ 490,000 tuples. The average response time is calculated for every arriving 200,000 tuples. All the readings are taken at a fixed window size of 10 minutes. We consider a fast arrival rate over one stream of 50 tuples/second and a variable arrival rate over the other stream that ranges between 10 tuples/second and 50 tuples/second. Figure 2 gives the average response time of EM-SWJoin, *XJoin*, *Sync-Filter*, and *Filter-Order* while changing the ratio between the arrival rates of both streams. As seen in figure, the four approaches have a high average response time when the ratio between tuple arrivals over both input streams is $<< 1$. This is due to the fact that when the ratio between the arrival rates of both input streams is high, the tuple response time increases. The average response time of *Sync-Filter* is the highest. The reason is that each tuple has to wait for a clock update in order to be processed. In addition, a tuple response time increases due to disk accessing. Because a tuple in *Filter-Order* does not suffer from any pre-processing delays, the average response time of *Filter-Order* is lower than that of *Sync-Filter*. However, the disk accesses incurred when matching against the corresponding disk resident tuples is still a significant overhead. Note that the performance of *XJoin* is quite similar to that of *Filter-Order* at fast input rates over both input streams. This is due to the fact that clock updates tend to run the *DP* phase more frequently for a small number of partially processed tuples, which is quite similar to the *Filter-Order* behavior. However, *XJoin* performs better when the ratio between the input arrival rates of both data streams is high. The reason is because *XJoin* has the ability to complete the processing of the partially processed tuples at silence periods of input arrivals. In this experiment EM-SWJoin performs the best. This is because the number of disk accesses that EM-SWJoin experiences is lower than that incurred by the other approaches. Note that EM-SWJoin does not move any tuple into disk unless it completes its processing. Not only this, it also completes the processing of all the incompletely processed tuples that lie within same hash partition. This tends to reduce the number of disk accesses to a lower level than that achieved by the other approaches.

4.2.2 Processing Overhead

Studying the processing overhead incurred by the different approaches shows how stable these approaches are when experiencing high input arrival rates over both streams. Figure 3 gives the performance of each of the approaches when the arrival rate of tuples over one stream (λ_1) is 70 tuples/second and the arrival rate over the other stream (λ_2) is 150 tuples/second. For the system to keep up with

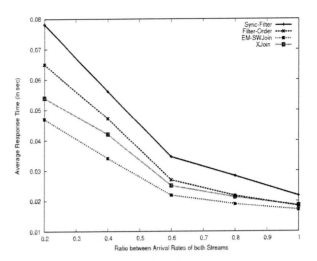

Figure 2. An experiment showing the average response time of *Sync-Filter*, *Filter-Order*, *XJoin*, and EM-SWJoin at variable arrival rates.

processing, 220 tuples should be processed in 1 second or a tuple response time should be less than 5 milliseconds. As shown in figure, *Sync-Filter* is unable to keep up with processing the arriving tuples while *Filter-Order* gets unstable after processing more $\approx 10,000$ input tuples. The performance of *Filter-Order* is better than that of *Sync-Filter* due to its ability to background process input tuples. Although *Filter-Order* outperforms *XJoin*, they are close to each others in performance. However, *XJoin* breaks earlier due to its inability to process disk resident tuples in a background processing way. This increases the number of partially processed tuples with time until it breaks its stability after the arrival of $\approx 650,000$ tuples. EM-SWJoin outperforms the other approaches by keeping up with input processing for a larger number of input tuples ($\approx 830,000$ input tuples).

4.2.3 Varying the Window Sizes

In this experiment we measure the average response time of the implemented approaches when fixing the input arrival rates over both data streams while varying the size of the sliding window. In order to run these experiments we first need to determine the stability point of these approaches. We define the stability point as the point at which every approach can keep up with processing its inputs. We noticed that all the algorithms

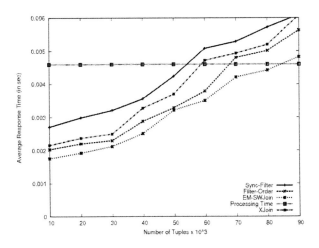

Figure 3. Comparison between *Sync-Filter*, *Filter-Order*, *X*Join, and EM-SWJoin by measuring their stability at high data arrival rates.

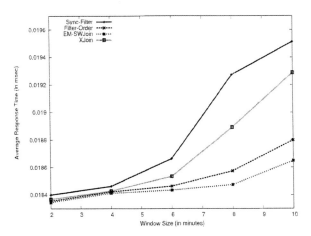

Figure 4. Comparison between *Sync-Filter*, *Filter-Order*, *X*Join, and EM-SWJoin while varying the window size.

reach the stability state when λ_1 is $\approx$ 50 tuples/second over one stream and λ_2 is $\approx$ 80 tuples/second over the other stream. The sliding window size is set to 10 minutes. Based on these findings, we consider this window size as our maximum boundary for a stable system. We varied the window size from 2 minutes to 10 minutes according to which we collected our readings. Figure 4 shows the performance of the approaches at the various sliding-window sizes. Notice that the performance of all the approaches is close at small window sizes. Although the number of disk accesses incurred by *Sync-Filter* and *Filter-Order* is the same, the difference gets significant when the window size increases. Thus, the advantage of having a background processing step in *Filter-Order* makes the average response time significantly better compared to *Sync-Filter*. As for *X*Join, its performance starts with a quite similarity to that of *Filter-Order* at small window sizes. However, as the window size increases, more disk resident tuples get involved in processing, which is scheduled to occur at delay periods over data streams or at clock updates. This causes the performance of *X*Join to move towards *Sync-Filter*. Because EM-SWJoin is capable of performing combined disk probes, the response time of the input tuples is reduced to a level even lower than that of *Filter-Order*.

5. Related Work

Stream query processing has been an active area of research in the past few years [1, 2, 4, 7]. Although

many accomplishments have been achieved, stream processing still introduces new challenges. *Load Shedding* [3] is a technique that an overloaded system adopts when it is unable to keep up with processing all of its arriving inputs. This technique simply discards portions of the input data tuples during processing on the hope of keeping the system up-to-date. This results in an approximate output. Many variations of this approach have been proposed based upon when, where, and how to apply load shedding in a query plan, so that the degree of inaccuracy in the query answers is minimized [10, 12]. Although being an acceptable solution in applications that require fast release of answers, some applications require producing a full answer set of output results.

Another face of the problem is studied in paper [5]. This paper believes in the fact that the continuous arrival of data tuples will eventually call for using disk as a storage alternative. This requires maintaining disk residing tuples to reduce the index update cost as well as preserve fast access when inserting and expiring these data tuples using a SWJoin notion. However, tuples' arrivals are assumed to be synchronous over all input streams. In contrast to all these accomplishments, we consider the unbounded arrival of data streams that runs memory out of space. Eventually, disk is used in order to keep track of processing all the arriving data tuples. Moreover, our work aims to hide the latency incurred from accessing disk residing tuples as well as releasing output tuples in an increasing order of timestamp.

6. Conclusion

In this paper we studied the problem of in-order release of SWJoin outputs, assuming limited memory resources. We proposed an external-memory sliding-window join algorithm (EM-SWJoin) that addresses general arrival patterns of input data streams. EM-SWJoin runs in two phases, the *MP* phase, which is responsible for matching memory resident tuples of one stream with the memory resident tuples of the other streams, and the *DP* phase, which is responsible for matching memory resident tuples of one stream with the disk resident tuples of the other streams. Both phases run in an interleaving fashion such that the memory overhead cost incurred in buffering output tuples is reduced. Moreover, our algorithm aims to decrease the number of disk accesses when probing disk resident tuples. Besides EM-SWJoin, we studied the performance of three different approaches, namely, *Sync-Filter*, *Filter-Order*, and *X*Join in a limited memory environment. A set of conducted experiments compared the performance of these approaches in terms of average response time and processing overhead cost. We showed through real implementation of the approaches the superiority of our proposed algorithm over the other approaches.

References

[1] D. J. Abadi, Y. Ahmad, and et. al., "The Design of the Borealis Stream Processing Engine", *CIDR Conference*, pages 1–16, 2005.

[2] A. Arasu, B. Babcock, and et al., "Stream: The Stanford Data Stream Management System", *Data Stream Management*, pages 1013–1022, 2004.

[3] B. Babcock, M. Datar, and R. Motwani, "Load Shedding for Aggregation Queries over Data Streams", *ICDE*, 2004.

[4] J. Chen, D. J. DeWitt, F. Tian, and Y. Wang. NiagaraCQ: "A scalable Continuous Query System for Internet Databases", *SIGMOD Conference*, pages 379– 390, 2000.

[5] L. Golab, P. Prahladka, and M. T. Ozsu. "Indexing Time-Evolving Data With Varialble Lifetimes", *SSDBM*, pages 265–274, 2006.

[6] M. A. Hammad, W. G. Aref, and A. K. Elmagarmid, "Optimizing In-Order Execution of Continuous Queries over Streamed Sensor Data", *SSDBM Conference*, pages 143–146, 2005.

[7] M. A. Hammad, M. Mokbel, and et. al., "NILE: A query Processing Engine for Data Streams", *ICDE Conference*, pages 851–863, 2004.

[8] M. F. Mokbel, M. Lu, and W. G. Aref, "Hash-Merge Join: A Non-blocking Join Algorithm for Producing Fast and Early Join Results", *ICDE*, pages 251–263, 2004.

[9] A. Silberschatz, H. F. Korth, and S. Sudarshan, *Database System Concepts*. McGrawHill, New York, 2006.

[10] U. Srivastava and J. Widom, "Memory-Limited Execution of Windowed Stream Joins", *VLDB*, 2004.

[11] Y. Tao, M. L. Yiu, D. Papadias, M. Hadjieleftheriou, and N. Mamoulis, "RPJ: Producing Fast Join Results on Streams through Rate-based Optimization", *SIGMOD*, 2005.

[12] N. Tatbul, U. Cetintemel, S. Zdonik, M. Cherniack, and M. Stonebraker, "Load Shedding in a Data Stream Manager", *VLDB*, 2003.

[13] T. Urhan and M. Franklin, "XJoin: Getting Fast Answers from Slow and Bursty Networks", *IEEE Computer Society Technical Committee on Data Engineering*, 1999.

[14] T. Urhan and M. Franklin, "XJoin: A Reactively-Scheduled Pipelined Join Operator", *CS- TR-3994, UMIACS-TR-99-13*, 2000.

An Approach for Text Categorization in Digital Library

Tao Wang   Bipin C. Desai

Department of Computer Science, Concordia University

Montreal, Quebec, Canada   H3G 1M8

{wan_tao, bcdesai}@encs.concordia.ca

Abstract

Text categorization is a very effective way to organize enormous number of documents in Digital Libraries. Accurate classification of documents is able to not only enhance document search precision, but also facilitate browsing-by-topic functionality. It is, nonetheless, difficult to obtain a satisfactory categorization accuracy compared to the corresponding results given by professional catalogers. This is due largely to the complexity of the pre-defined large-scaled category hierarchies that makes it difficult for learning algorithms to distinguish among categories. This paper describes a top-down document classification approach which takes advantage of the hierarchical structure, more specifically, in two ways: identifying the number of independent local classifiers and guiding top-down classification procedure. We finally evaluate it within the CINDI Digital Library applying ACM Classification System as targeted hierarchy. Experimental results show the promise of this approach.

1. Introduction

Text categorization (TC for short) is a task that assigns, depending on the application, any number of categories c in a pre-defined category set C to a given document d based on its content. There are two obvious advantages of using machines instead of humans for text categorization, efficiency and objectivity. Cost is also another factor. Two types of classification problems can be easily identified: flat-structured and hierarchical. In the former case, the categories or classes in C are treated equally. There is no specific relationship defined among classes. Each document can be classified into, depending on the application, exactly one class (single-label classification) or any number of classes (multi-label classification). If set C consists of only two disjoint and complement classes c and $\bar{c}$, the single-label classification becomes binary. Much research work has been conducted on the flat-structured categoriza-

tion, resulting in a number of popular learning methods such as Probabilistic Model, Support Vector Machine (SVM), kNN, Centroid-based, Logic Rule, Neural Networks, etc. that have been experimentally justified [10, 12, 22].

In the context of Digital Library or Web Portal, the text categorization is exposed to a large-scale category hierarchy, typically organized into a structure of tree (e.g., ACM Classification Scheme) or Directed Acyclic Graph (e.g., Google's Web Directory). Solving this hierarchical classification problem, theoretically, could be done by simply flattening the hierarchy into a set C, and then applying aforementioned methods to the downgraded, flat-structured task. However, its feasibility in terms of efficacy and efficiency for real world applications, e.g., in scenario of Digital Libraries, are very doubtful because of the number and fine-grain nature of category defined. As pointed out in [6, 14], the property of hierarchical structure must be considered and employed when building classifier by learning. This suggests a top-down, coarse-to-fine classification. The key here is to preserve the potential categories at each layer for further classification while aggressively cutting unnecessary branches. Unfortunately, most research works reported do not provide detail of their methods. The commercial systems are trade-secrets, and their accuracy cannot be verified. In this paper, we present our approach for hierarchical TC. Specifically, we propose a method to control the number of categories selected, and examine two different methods for re-ranking categories at each level. The proposed method is implemented and experimented within our CINDI Digital Library [15]. The experimental results to date show a satisfactory improvement in comparison with our previous work in [5, 20] that used a keyword match method for document classification.

The rest of this paper is structured as follows: Section 2 formulates the hierarchical text classification task; Section 3 describes our approach for hierarchical TC; we present our corpora and experiment results in Sections 4 and 5; Section 6 gives conclusions.

2 Formulation of Hierarchical TC

2.1 Structure of Classification Scheme

Depending on the application, the category space given in hierarchical TC has one of the following two structures:

A Tree In this case, the well-known "parent-child" relationship represents generality or specificity between two categories. The set of categories are partitioned into *real categories* for holding documents and *virtual categories* for further classification. Usually, all leaf nodes are mapped to real categories, and all internal nodes to virtual ones, as illustrated in ACM Classification Scheme (ACMCS)[17] and Dewey Decimal Classification System [19].

A Graph More strictly, it is a Directed Acyclic Graph (DAG). An edge, as generally understood, represents a generality/specificity relationship between two related categories. The documents can be categorized into any node in the graph. This type of topic hierarchy has been widely used for the Web Directories that are hosted by the most popular websites (e.g., google.com and yahoo.com [18, 16]).

2.2 The Problem

We characterize a hierarchical text classification system, denoted by $\mathcal{HS}$, as a 3-tuple $\mathcal{HS} = (H, \Omega, F)$, where

- H is a DAG $H := (C, E)$, standing for a classification scheme. C denotes a set of categories contained in H, and E defines the structure of these categories. As such, an edge $(c', c'') \in E$ means category c' is more general (broader) than c''. In some cases, only a subset of C, denoted by C_r, are required to hold documents and referred to as real categories. In contrast, those only being used for auxiliary classification are called virtual categories, denoted by C_v collectively, $C_r \cup C_v = C$.

- Ω represents a corpus or dataset, consisting of a set D of pre-labeled documents. Ω has two distinct formats, depending on the type of classification:

$$single\text{-}label:\ \Omega = \{(d_i, c_j) \mid d_i \in D, c_j \in C\}, \quad (1)$$
$$multi\text{-}label:\ \Omega = \{(d_i, C_i) \mid d_i \in D, C_i \subseteq C_r\}. \quad (2)$$

- F is an unknown hierarchical classification function to be learned on Ω by means of some learning method (algorithm) that maps each document to exactly one (for single-label) or any number of categories (for multi-label) in C_r:

$$single\text{-}label:\quad F_{sl} : D' \to C_r, \quad (3)$$
$$multi\text{-}label:\quad F_{ml} : D' \to 2^{C_r}; \quad (4)$$

where, $D' \supset D$ denotes a set of all possible documents. The accuracy of F can be evaluated, by approximation, on a part of Ω.

Example Consider the hierarchical TC task we deal with in the remainder of this paper. Herein, H corresponds to the ACM CS, a tree-structured topic hierarchy. The set C_r consists of all leaf categories (nodes). The corpus Ω are obtained by carefully choosing documents from ACM Digital Library to make sure that each document chosen is properly pre-classified. As it is a multi-label classification problem, the corresponding function F_{ml} needs to be defined.

3 Approaches for Hierarchical TC

3.1 Related Work

Recent research work on flat-structured text categorization indicates that classifier performance can be improved by means of different approaches. For example, in [3], Bekkerman et al. used the word clusters replacing words for document vector representation to increase performance. Antonie and Zaiane in [1], Ruiz-Raio et al. in [8] examined feature selection by using term association and automatic fashion, respectively. Zhang and Lee [23] even utilized substring as features to build classification. Along the different avenue, Schuetze et al. in [11] reported using the optimal thresholding to improve accuracy. Chen et al. [4] and Shen et al. [13] discussed benefits of applying Neural Networks and Multigram model, respectively, for text classification.

With respect to the hierarchical TC, intuitively, the function F_{ml} can be constructed by combining total $|\,C\,|$ (cardinality of C) independent binary classifiers, each of which corresponds to a node in H. This method would work well for a small hierarchy as given in [7]. However, if there are a large number of categories, its applicability to real world application is very questionable because both training and classification processes involve a total of $|\,C\,|$ repetitions. Another possible approach is to flatten the hierarchical structure, resulting in a "flat" multi-label classification with the $|\,C_r\,|$ number of categories. Since the value C_r is usually large, global discerning among these classes relying on only one classifier is extremely difficult.

Many researchers suggests employing the hierarchical structure in hierarchical TC in two ways, by breaking a large classification into a number of smaller ones to improve effectiveness, and more importantly, by selecting potential branches for further classification to increase efficiency. For instances, Susan & Chen [6] utilize a hierarchical model for web page categorization under some web directory. The authors propose the combination of both upper and lower categorization results to determine a web page classification status at lower level. Even though justified by the accompanying experiments, the specifics for this combination remains unknown. Avancini et al [2] suggests a "soft pruning" scheme in branch selection in order to recover some promising branches cut by threshold. Sun [14] compares this "top-down" method with flattened counterpart on the well-known Reuters corpus. The experimental results show favorable when exploiting the structure of hierarchy during hierarchical classification. All of these work justify the advantages of "top-down" approach in hierarchical TC. Unfortunately, the underlying formulation still remains unknown to the public.

3.2 An Approach

Herein, we present our approach for hierarchical TC. Let $Parent(H)$ be a set of external nodes in a given system $\mathcal{HS} = (H, \Omega, F)$. Firstly, we construct the number of $| Parent(H) |$ flat classifiers, or called local classifiers in the context of hierarchical classification. Each such classifier corresponds to a unique external node. Its classification scheme is a set of child categories of that node. Secondly, we develop strategies to rank, with respect to a document to be classified, categories on the same level based on the relevances of that document belonging to categories given by different local classifiers. As a result, only the first ϕ categories in the level are kept for the next level classification unless the leaf nodes are reached. The value ϕ for different levels can be estimated from training documents. An input document at first goes through the root classifier (at level 0). The output results then trigger the connected level 1 classifiers for finer classification, which, in turn, trigger some level 2 classifiers. The document finally reaches the leaf nodes which contain the classification result.

The problem now is how to construct effective flat classifier. Fortunately, we have a number of learning algorithms available to choose from thanks to extensive research work done on it [2, 12, 22]. As for the second issue, the idea is how to aggressively cut off impossible branches while reserving the possible ones. We discuss below two ranking schemes that consider the possibility or relevance of categories on different levels.

3.2.1 Local Classifiers

As mentioned above, the flat local multi-label classifier serves the basic block in our hierarchical classification system. The strength of the underlying learning methods for flat classifier construction, therefore, has a significant impact on the global effectiveness of system. Because this paper explores the top-down hierarchical method, we choose the following two kinds of classifiers. Both have average strength but are very efficient.

Naive Bayes Classifier The multi-label version of Naive Bayes classifier is:

$$P(c_i \mid d_j) = \frac{P(c_i) \times P(d_j \mid c_i)}{P(d_j)}, \qquad (5)$$

where two event spaces are a set of documents D and a set of categories C, respectively. Thus, $P(d_j)$ is the probability that a randomly picked document has the same representation as d_j; $P(c_i)$ as the probability that a randomly picked document belongs to c_i. The value $P(c_i \mid d_j)$ can be used for ranking categories $c \in C$.

Centroid Classifier We modify the classic centroid computation to reflect the multi-label property. Here, the centroid of each category c_i can be simply represented by the sum of the vector for each document in c_i weighted by inverse of number of categories labeled for that document:

$$\odot_{c_i} = \frac{1}{| Cat_i(d_j) | \times | D_{c_i} |} \sum_{i=1}^{|D_{c_i}|} d_j, \qquad (6)$$

where, D_{c_i} is a set of documents in c_i; $| Cat_i(d_j) |$ is the number of labeled categories associated with d_j. If some document has only c_i class label, it is viewed as a perfect positive example for c_i and therefore giving the maximum weight $\frac{1}{|D_{c_i}|}$.

The cosine-similarity [9] between d_j and c_i

$$Sim(d_j, c_i) = \frac{\odot_{c_i} \cdot d_j}{| \odot_{c_i} || d_j |} \qquad (7)$$

measures the strength of d_j belonging to c_i that can be used for ranking categories for d_j.

3.2.2 Methods for Branch Selection

Once the local multi-label classifiers are trained, we need to estimate a set Φ of parameters, $\Phi = \{\phi_0, \phi_1, \ldots, \phi_{K-1}\}$, each of which determines the maximum number of branches at some level selected for the next classification. For example, the value of ϕ_1 represents the maximum number of branches at level 1 that can be preserved for next level classification. Here, we use

$$\phi_i = \arg \max_{d_j \in Tr(D)} \{Cat^i(d_j)\} + (i + 1) \qquad (8)$$

to obtain parameter ϕ_i, which is the maximum number of categories at level i from all training document plus $i + 1$.

To re-rank the categories at the same level, but in different classifiers (except for level 0 where there is only "root" classifier), the following two schemes are applied:

1. Ranking by addition For some document d_j, the degree of d_j belonging to some category c^n at level n is given by $V(d_j, c^n) + V(d_j, c^{n-1})$, where, $V(d_j, c^n)$ is value given by local classifier, $V(d_j, c^{n-1})$ is value returned by another local classifier. Also note that c^{n-1} is the parent of category c^n.

2. Ranking by multiplication Similar setting to the above, but we re-rank the categories at some level based on their values $V(d_j, c^n) \times V(d_j, c^{n-1})$.

4 Document Preparation

4.1 CINDI Digital Library

The CINDI Digital Library(DL) is a research project currently under development at Concordia University. Its objective is to provide a platform for search, browsing, registration, and annotation of academic and scientific documents under various subjects. We apply the hierarchical TC to generate documents' "subject information".

Our classification experiments in this paper is limited to the domain of Computer Science. The classification scheme adopted by the CINDI DL is the latest ACM Classification Scheme (ACMCS-98). More specifically, it is a tree-like hierarchy that consists of around 2,000 categories. According to stipulation by ACM's classification committee, only leaf categories are used for categorization destination and these total around 1,600. Note that this structure is more complicated than the ones appearing in benchmark corpora such as "Reuters", "20 Newsgroups". Also, scientific papers categorization is harder than news story classification [2]. Therefore, the results of classification could compare unfavorably with other classification results reported in the literature.

4.2 Labeled Documents

As almost every document stored in ACM Digital Library has been labeled, it provide us with a very rich set of labeled documents for the sake of classifier training. Specifically, for each leaf category $c_i \in C_r$, we query the ACM DL with code for c_i (for example, codes "F.4.1" for category "Mathematical Logic", and "H.3.2" for category "Information Storage"). We then choose the most N relevant documents to the query code as the positive examples for that category. The positive examples for some higher level category can be easily obtained by simply taking union of documents belonging to its children categories.

4.3 Properties of Scientific Documents

From the corpus generated, the following facts are observed when each document is represented by a bag-of-word format:

1. *High Dimensional Text Feature Space* If every word (excluding stop words) appears in the documents from corpus Ω is qualified for a text feature, the whole Ω would yield a feature space comprised of around 50,000 words.

2. *Sparse Document Vectors* Compared to a highly dimensional feature space, a document in Ω contains, on average, a few thousands of features

3. *Low Document Correlation* The documents in the same category appear to share a low percentage of words with each other. For example, in the category "F.4.1" (Mathematical Logic), we observe the correlation between two documents with a range of 30% to 35%. This observation indicates the necessity and importance that one must carefully examine the methods for document feature selection.

5 Experiments and Results

5.1 Experimental Settings

We narrow the category space in our experiments into part of ACM CS by selecting six out of eleven top subjects. Table 1 gives the names of these subjects and their respective next level categories:

As with the set of labeled documents, we split them into training $Tr(\Omega)$, validating $Va(\Omega)$, and testing portions $Te(\Omega)$ with a ratio of $Tr(\Omega) : Va(\Omega) : Te(\Omega) = 7 : 1 : 2$. Total words (features) extracted from documents in $Tr(\Omega)$ to be classified under this subtree are 45,000 after stop-word removal and simple stemming processing [20], slightly less than the word number generated using whole corpus Ω. For each local classifier k with category scheme $C_k = \{c_1^k, c_2^k, \ldots, c_m^k\}$, we calculate the term t_i's "Information Gain" (IG) and "Odds Ratio" (OR) statistical measures for feature selection of document. Both measures have been shown quite effective, and are defined respectively by [12, 21]

$$IG(t_i, C_k) = \sum_{c \in C_k} \sum_{t \in \{t_i, \bar{t}_i\}} P(t, c) \cdot \log \frac{P(t, c)}{P(t) \cdot P(c)} \quad (9)$$

$$OR(t_i, C_k) = \sum_{c \in C_k} \frac{P(t_i \mid c) \cdot (1 - P(t_i \mid \bar{c}))}{(1 - P(t_i \mid c)) \cdot P(t_i \mid \bar{c})}, \quad (10)$$

where, $\bar{t}_i$ denotes the term t_i missing in the document, $\bar{c}$ represents any category in C_k other than c, $P(t, c)$ is the

```
A. Computer Systems Organization
    GENERAL
    PROCESSOR ARCHITECTURES
    COMPUTER-COMMUNICATION NETWORKS
    SPECIAL-PURPOSE AND APPLICATION-BASED SYSTEMS
    PERFORMANCE OF SYSTEMS
    COMPUTER SYSTEM IMPLEMENTATION
    MISCELLANEOUS

B. Software
    GENERAL
    PROGRAMMING TECHNIQUES
    SOFTWARE ENGINEERING
    PROGRAMMING LANGUAGES
    OPERATING SYSTEMS
    MISCELLANEOUS
C. Data
    GENERAL
    DATA STRUCTURES
    DATA STORAGE REPRESENTATIONS
    DATA ENCRYPTION
    CODING AND INFORMATION THEORY
    FILES
    MISCELLANEOUS

D. Theory of Computation
    ...

E. Mathematics of Computing
    ...

F. Computing Methodologies
    ...
```

Table 1. Fragment of top two levels of category hierarchy used in experiments

joint distribution of t and c, and $P(t \mid c)$ is the conditional distribution of t given c. We finally choose 100 features with the highest values of IG or OR to make up document vector for the classifier k.

5.2 Performance Measures

We evaluate the effectiveness of the proposed hierarchical TC method through the following measures:

- **Precision and Recall** The precision (Pr) for a flat classifier k with classification scheme $C_k = \{c_1^k, c_2^k, \ldots, c_m^k\}$ is given by

$$Pr(k) = \frac{\sum_{i=1}^{|C_m|} \mid S_i \cap T_i \mid}{\sum_{i=1}^{|C_m|} \mid S_i \mid}, \qquad (11)$$

and the corresponding Re measure on is given by

$$Re(k) = \frac{\sum_{i=1}^{|C_m|} \mid S_i \cap T_i \mid}{\sum_{i=1}^{|C_m|} \mid T_i \mid}, \qquad (12)$$

where, $S_i \subset Te(D')$ is a set of documents classified by our classifier into category $c_i \in C_m$, and $T_i \subset Te(D')$ stands for a set of documents with a label $c_i \in C_m$.

Usually, increase of value of Re (or Pr) causes decrease of value of Pr (or Re). In a trivial case, one can easily obtain a perfect recall of 1 by simply assigning a document with all possible categories. In other words, both Pr and Re measures must be considered in judging classifier's effectiveness.

- F_1 **measure** The widely used combined measure, called F_1, on a given classifier k, is defined by

$$F_1(k) = \frac{2 \cdot Pr(k) \cdot Re(k)}{Pr(k) + Re(k)}. \qquad (13)$$

The F_1 measure is used in our evaluation.

- **Precision/Recall Break-even Point (BEP)** It is another popular combined measure but not used in this paper, given by the value when $Pr(k)$ is equal to $Re(k)$

5.3 Results and Discussion

Finally, we evaluate our approach for hierarchical TC locally and globally, using the widely adopted F_1 measure. One of advantages in our approach is that each local classifier can be evaluated separately. As a result, those with a much worse measure can be more carefully examined in order to boost the overall performance. Table 2 gives performance for the top two levels of classifiers when using a combination of different learning algorithms and different feature selection methods. The "Root" represents the top classifier that classifies the document into any number of categories in $\{A, B, C, D, E, F\}$. In addition, Level_1 A to Level_1 F stand for the next level classifiers that classify the documents into their respective child categories (for Level_1 A, which means classifying into the subject of "A. Computer Systems Organization").

We have observed from the experiments the following facts: 1) Naive Bayes based local classifiers outperform Centroid based classifiers; 2) Ranking by Addition (RBA) scheme is better than Ranking by Multiplication (RBM) one; 3) using "Information Gain" for feature selection is better than "Odds Ratio". The Table 2 presents their performance comparison. In Table 3, we give the comparison of the hierarchical classification performance on the global basis by applying different combination of local classifier and ranking strategy.

Comparing to the performance reported [12], our results from the local classifiers show under-performance. The main reason attributable to this under-performance, in our view, is that the domain and textual data we consider are more complicated than the widely used Reuters-21578 standard corpus. It is not quite reasonable to compare each other directly. However, the obtained results justifies suitability of top-down method for the large hierarchical TC.

6 Conclusions

Text categorization is an effective paradigm in managing large number of documents. In this paper, we present

Local Classifier	Naive Bayes with ING	Naive Bayes with OR	Centroid with ING	Centroid with OR
Root	.784	.743	.743	.739
Level_1 A	.697	.687	.654	.602
Level_1 B	.663	.624	.632	.623
Level_1 C	.604	.577	.587	.567
Level_1 D	.635	.633	.623	.612
Level_1 E	.698	.687	.674	.661
Level_1 F	.667	.655	.652	.632

Table 2. F_1 performance comparison among the top two levels of classifiers

	Naive Bayes with RBA	Naive Bayes with RBM	Centroid with RBA	Centroid with RBM
Overall Performance	.625	.587	.581	.524

Table 3. Comparison of the final hierarchical performances measured by F_1

a generic method for large-scale hierarchical text classification in the context of Digital Library. We evaluate the implemented classification system using a self-generated corpus and ACM Classification Scheme within digital library. The preliminary experimental results justify the promise of our method, though producing poorer performance than those reported by others. Since text data and classification scheme are different in many experimental settings, the simple peer-to-peer comparison, in our view, may not be quite objective.

Further improvement of performance in our future research is expected to be obtained by constructing more accurate local classifiers using better learning methods and/or more careful feature selection. On the other hand, the adaptation of this approach to other domain needs to be justified experimentally.

References

[1] M.-L. Antonie and O. R. Zaïane. Text document categorization by term association. In *ICDM '02: Proceedings of the 2002 IEEE International Conference on Data Mining*, pages 19–26, 2002.

[2] H. Avancini, A. Rauber, and F. Sebastiani. Organizing digital libraries by automated text categorization. Technical report, Historical NCSTRL Collection, 2002.

[3] R. Bekkerman, R. El-Yaniv, N. Tishby, and Y. Winter. Distributional word clusters vs. words for text categorization. *Journal of Machine Learning Research*, 3:1183–1208, 2003.

[4] Z. Chen, C. Ni, and Y. L. Murphey. Neural network approaches for text document categorization. In *IJCNN '06: Proceedings of the International Joint Conference on Neural Networks*, pages 1054–1066, 2006.

[5] B. C. Desai, S. S. Haddad, and A. Ali. Automatic semantic header generator. In *ISMIS '00: Proceedings of the 12th International Symposium on Foundations of Intelligent Systems*, pages 444–452, 2000.

[6] S. Dumais and H. Chen. Hierarchical classification of web content. In *SIGIR '00: Proceedings of the 23rd annual international ACM SIGIR conference on Research and development in information retrieval*, pages 256–263, 2000.

[7] M. E. Ruiz and P. Srinivasan. Hierarchical neural networks for text categorization. In *SIGIR '99: Proceedings of the 22nd annual international ACM SIGIR conference on Research and development in information retrieval*, pages 281–282, 1999.

[8] F. Ruiz-Rico, J. L. Vicedo, and M.-C. Rubio-Sánchez. Newpar: an automatic feature selection and weighting schema for category ranking. In *DocEng '06: Proceedings of the 2006 ACM symposium on Document engineering*, pages 128–137, 2006.

[9] G. Salton, A. Shechet, C. Buckley, and A. Singhal. Automatic analysis, theme generation, and summarization of machine-readable texts. *SCIENCE: Science*, 264:1421–1426, 1994.

[10] M. Sasaki and K. Kita. Rule-based text categorization using hierarchical categories. In *SMC '98: Proceedings of the IEEE International Conference on Systems, Man, and Cybernetics*, pages 2827–2830, 1998.

[11] H. Schütze, E. Velipasaoglu, and J. O. Pedersen. Performance thresholding in practical text classification. In *CIKM '06: Proceedings of the 15th ACM international conference on Information and knowledge management*, 2006.

[12] F. Sebastiani. Machine learning in automated text categorization. *ACM Computer Survey*, 34(1):1–47, 2002.

[13] D. Shen, J.-T. Sun, Q. Yang, and Z. Chen. Text classification improved through multigram models. In *CIKM '06: Proceedings of the 15th ACM international conference on Information and knowledge management*, 2006.

[14] A. Sun and E.-P. Lim. Hierarchical text classification and evaluation. In *ICDM '01, Proceedings of 2001 IEEE International Conference on Data Mining*, pages 521–528, 2001.

[15] URL. http://cindi.encs.concordia.ca/about_cindi.html.

[16] URL. http://dir.yahoo.com/.

[17] URL. http://www.acm.org/class/1998/ccs98.txt.

[18] URL. http://www.google.com/dirhp.

[19] URL. http://www.oclc.org/dewey/.

[20] T. Wang and B. C. Desai. Extracting document semantics for semantic header. In *CCECE '06: Proceedings of the IEEE Canadian Conference on Electrical and Computer Engineering*, pages 1878–1883, 2006.

[21] Y. Yang. An evaluation of statistical approaches to text categorization. *Information Retrieval*, 1(1-2):69–90, 1999.

[22] Y. Yang and X. Liu. A re-examination of text categorization methods. In *SIGIR '99: Proceedings of the 22nd annual international ACM SIGIR conference on Research and development in information retrieval*, pages 42–49, 1999.

[23] D. Zhang and W. S. Lee. Extracting key-substring-group features for text classification. In *KDD '06: Proceedings of the 12th ACM SIGKDD international conference on Knowledge discovery and data mining*, pages 474–483, 2006.

An Effective Multi-Layer Model for Controlling the Quality of Data

Carson Kai-Sang Leung*   Mark Anthony F. Mateo
Department of Computer Science
The University of Manitoba, Canada
{kleung, mfmateo}@cs.umanitoba.ca

Andrew J. Nadler
*Manitoba Agriculture, Food and
Rural Initiatives (MAFRI), Canada*
andy.nadler@gov.mb.ca

Abstract

Data mining aims to search for implicit, previously unknown, and potentially useful information that might be embedded in the data. It is well known that "garbage in, garbage out". Hence, to get meaningful mining results, a clean set of data is essential. In this paper, we propose an effective model for controlling the quality of data. Specifically, this three-layer model focuses on data validity and data consistency. To elaborate, the internal layer ensures that the observed data are valid and their values fall within reasonable ranges. The temporal layer ensures that data are consistent with their temporal behaviour. The spatial layer ensures that data are consistent with their spatial neighbours. A case study on applying our proposed model to real-life weather data for an agricultural application shows that our model is effective in controlling and improving data quality, and thus leading to better mining results. It is important to note the application of our proposed model is not confined to the weather data for agricultural applications. We also discuss, in this paper, how the proposed three-layer model can be effectively applicable to control the quality of data in some other real-life situations.

1. Introduction

Data mining aims to search for implicit, previously unknown, and potentially useful information or patterns that might be embedded in the data. Mined information is valuable in numerous real-life applications such as market analysis, corporate analysis, risk management, fraud detection, e-commerce, as well as decision support. Common data mining tasks include frequent-set mining, clustering, classification, and outlier detection. Many of these tasks (e.g., frequent-set mining, clustering, classification) focus mainly on finding information that applies to the *majority* of data in the dataset [3, 4, 5, 8, 13, 15, 16, 17, 19]. While it is useful to know common trends or frequently occurring patterns, it is also helpful to find out uncommon or rarely occurring events because they can be indications of some

unusual, exceptional, suspicious, or criminal activities. To this end, the data mining task of outlier detection focuses on finding information that applies to the *minority* of data in the dataset [1, 11, 18]. Regardless which data mining task is performed, the quality of the mining results (e.g., frequent patterns or exceptional events) in many applications depends heavily on the quality of the input data. Moreover, it is well known that "garbage in, garbage out". Hence, it is crucial to have a clean set of data [2, 6, 23] for successful data mining. Otherwise, the mining results may be useless or misleading, which in turn may affect decisions made for the applications on which the data mining tasks were performed.

With advances in technology, large amounts of data can be generated from various sources and gathered manually or automatically. For example, in some applications, a staff member may manually record an observed reading from a meter and bring the recorded data to his headquarters for data analysis. In some other applications, data from wired or wireless sensors may be transmitted automatically to a centralized database for further analysis. Note that during these processes of data collection and transmission, data may be mistakenly recorded or accidentally corrupted. Incorrect or unclean data may then be fed into the data mining engine, and result in wrong, anomalous, or misleading results. To elaborate, in the example above, the staff may misread the reading from the meter. Alternatively, he may read the correct values, but may inadvertently record wrong values for such data. Moreover, the meter may be malfunctioning such that it produces wrong data (e.g., the same incorrect reading for a prolonged period of time). Furthermore, for cases where data are automatically transmitted to the centralized database (say, through wireless networks), some data may have been lost or corrupted during transmission. All these problems can lead to wrong input data for data mining, and thus useless or misleading outputs.

To improve the situation (e.g., to avoid getting useless or misleading mining results), it is important to have a clean dataset. Some natural questions to ask are: How can we get a clean dataset? How can we identify unclean, incorrect,

---

*Corresponding author: C.K.-S. Leung

28

or suspicious data from the dataset? How can we assure the quality of data to be fed into the data mining engine? We answer these questions in this paper. Specifically, we propose a generic multi-layer model for effective control of the quality of data. We focus on data validity and data consistency. To elaborate further, our proposed model checks the data in the dataset, and identifies any data that appear to be incorrect or inconsistent. Any incorrect data are then ignored or removed from the dataset. Any suspicious data are then returned to users or domain experts for further analysis or verification to see whether or not the data are *truly invalid data* or *truly exceptional data*. The former are ignored or removed from the dataset, whereas the latter are kept. By doing so, our multi-layer model makes sure the following conditions hold:

- data are within their reasonable ranges,
- data are temporally consistent with their temporal behaviours, and
- data are spatially consistent with their spatial neighbours.

In addition, we also develop a *specific* system that follows our proposed *generic* multi-layer model for controlling the quality of weather data used in real-life agricultural applications. Furthermore, we also discuss how one can use the proposed model for other potential applications.

To summarize, our *key contributions of this paper* include (i) the proposal of such a generic model, which is a non-trivial integration of models for data validity as well as for both temporal and spatial consistency and (ii) the development of a specific system to control the quality of data for a real-life application.

This paper is organized as follows. The next section describes our proposed model for controlling the quality of data. In Section 3, we present a case study demonstrating how this proposed model can be developed into a system to control the quality of real-life weather data for an application in the Canadian provincial government department of Manitoba Agriculture, Food and Rural Initiatives (MAFRI). Evaluation results show the effectiveness of our proposed model and our developed system. Section 4 discusses other potential applications of our model. Finally, conclusions are given in Section 5.

2. Our proposed model for controlling the quality of data

In this section, we describe our proposed model for controlling the quality of data. Specifically, we focus on data validity and data consistency. Here, let us give a quick overview about our proposed model. The model consists of three layers: internal, temporal, and spatial layers. The bottom layer (the internal layer) ensures data lie within reasonable ranges, and it guards the user against any strange data. The middle layer (the temporal layer) assumes that

data follow some sequential cycles or patterns (e.g., weekly, monthly, seasonal, yearly, or other regular cycles). This layer ensures data at any time t in the current cycle be consistent with data at t in most (if not all) of previous and subsequent cycles. The top layer (the spatial layer) assumes that data at a certain location are expected to be very similar to their neighbours. This layer ensures data collected at any location L be consistent with those collected at neighbouring locations of L. In the following, we start describing these three layers one-by-one (in a bottom-up fashion starting from the internal layer) in detail.

2.1. The internal layer

The internal layer of our proposed multi-layer model ensures that data lie within a reasonable or valid range. A skeleton of this internal layer is shown in Figure 1. As shown in the figure, key steps of the internal layer of our proposed model include the following four steps.

In Step 1, the model ensures that data fall within their valid ranges. Data falling outside of the ranges are invalid. In many applications, there are lower and upper limits for data. For example, no merchandise in a grocery store is supposed to be of a negative price as the lower limit for the price range is \$0 (i.e., to ensure that $x_{\text{price}}^{\text{lower bound}} = \$0 \leq x_{\text{price},t,L}$). In the remainder of this paper, we use $x_{A,t,L}$ to represent a datum value for attribute A (e.g., price) at time t at location L. Similarly, a measurement on the speed of a vehicle is incorrect if it is negative or is faster than the speed of light in vacuum (i.e., to ensure that $x_{\text{speed}}^{\text{lower bound}} = 0\text{km/h} \leq x_{\text{speed},t,L} \leq 10^9\text{km/h} = x_{\text{speed}}^{\text{upper bound}}$). Of course, a much tighter upper bound (say, 350km/h) can be set for the speed of a vehicle. As a third example, the number of passengers of a tourist bus can be bounded below by 10 (say, it is not profitable to run a bus with fewer than 10 passengers) and above by 47 (which is the maximum capacity of the bus). In other words, the number of passengers in each record is supposed to fall within the range of 10 to 47 inclusive (i.e., to ensure that $x_{\text{\#passengers}}^{\text{lower bound}} = 10 \leq x_{\text{\#passengers},t,L} \leq 47 = x_{\text{\#passengers}}^{\text{upper bound}}$). These lower and upper bounds can be set based on some prior knowledge (e.g., mechanical limits of a vehicle) or user preference (e.g., ideal number of passengers in a profitable tourist bus). Once these bounds are set, our model checks each datum. Any datum that does not fall within its limits is notified to the user so that appropriate action can be taken (e.g., to fix, or ignore, the wrong datum). This ensures that each datum lies within its valid range. Note that, besides the aforementioned applications, this feature for checking data validity is also useful in other applications such as power/water consumption, stock prices, class sizes, and Web clicks.

While it is important to ensure that data fall within their valid ranges, it is also important to check the relationships among the related data attributes. In many applications, ag-

The internal layer

INPUT: DB, and prior knowledge or user preference on lower and upper bounds of the value of each datum.

OUPUT: Invalid or suspicious data $x_{A,t,L}$ for further investigation.

1. For each datum $x_{A,t,L} \in DB$ (where A represents the attribute, t represents the time, and L represents the location), we ensure that the value of each datum falls within its valid upper and lower bounds (i.e., $x_A^{\text{lower bound}} \leq x_{A,t,L} \leq x_A^{\text{upper bound}}$). For example, we ensure that all temperature values in the database fall within the valid range of temperature values.

2. For a collection of data, we ensure that *relationships* among the related attributes make sense. For example, we ensure that the relationship between two related attributes minimum temperature and maximum temperature is as follows: The former is always lower than or equal to the latter.

3. For a collection of data, we ensure that *values* of the related attributes make sense. For example, we ensure that the difference between the maximum and minimum daily temperatures is reasonable.

4. For a collection of data, we ensure that data do not remain unchanged for a period of time. For example, we ensure that the outdoor temperature readings do not remain unchanged for 20 consecutive days.

Figure 1. A Skeleton of the internal layer.

gregate or summary data (e.g., maximum, average, minimum) are available. For example, in addition to the number of passengers for each trip, a tourist bus company may collect information about the maximum, minimum and average numbers of passengers on a weekly basis so as to get an idea for the utility of the bus. For these applications, we not only need to ensure that the aggregate data make sense (i.e., to ensure each of the aggregate data—such as maximum, minimum, average—falls within its valid range) but also need to ensure that relationships among these aggregate data make sense (i.e., to ensure they are consistent among them). Why? With only Step 1 above, it is possible to have (a) the minimum value exceeds the maximum value, (b) the minimum value exceeds the average value, or (c) the maximum value falls below the average value. Therefore, Step 2 of the internal layer of our proposed model controls the quality of data as follows. It ensures that the minimum value does not exceed the average value, which in turn does not exceed the maximum value. These ensure that relationships among aggregate data (e.g., $x_{\text{min temp},t,L} \leq x_{\text{avg temp},t,L} \leq x_{\text{max temp},t,L}$) make sense.

Similar to Step 2 above, Step 3 of the internal layer of our proposed model ensures that the *values* among related attributed data make sense (i.e., to ensure values of some data are consistent with those of their related ones). Unlike Steps 1 and 2 (which identify *incorrect* data), Step 3 detects *suspicious* data. What are suspicious data? They are data with values that are not impossible—but quite unusual—to obtain. Suspicious data may represent (a) truly exceptional data or (b) truly invalid data. For example, it is acceptable to obtain a reading of minimum temperature = $-25°C$ on a certain day; it is also acceptable to obtain a reading of maximum temperature = $+25°C$ on another day. However, it may sound suspicious to obtain both of these two readings

(with a temperature difference of $50°C$) on the same day. One or both of these temperature readings may be incorrect because it is quite unusual to have such a big temperature difference within the same day.

So far, we have described three key steps of the internal layer. The first two identify incorrect data, and the third one detects suspicious data. Now, let us turn our attention to Step 4, which also detects suspicious data. However, unlike the first three steps, Step 4 is related to temporal consistency check. When data are collected for a period of time, Step 4 checks to see if the values of these data remain unchanged. In some applications, it is possible for data to have the same values over a period of time, especially when the values are at their maximum or minimum limits. For example, it is not uncommon for a class to have the same number of students (say, 100) over the past few academic terms. This may be because 100 students were the maximum capacity of such a class. As another example, it is not uncommon to obtain the same room temperature of $+20°C$ per hour over the past few days. This may be because the thermostat was set at $+20°C$. However, although it is not impossible, it sounds suspicious to obtain the same exterior temperature of $+5°C$ per hour over the past few consecutive days. These suspicious data should be flagged, and the model should notify the user about them. Hence, in Step 4, the internal layer examines some application data for serial continuity, flags suspicious data, and notifies the user if consecutive values of data stay at a "flat line" over a period of time.

2.2. The temporal layer

In the previous section, we described the bottom layer of our proposed model and showed how the four key steps of this internal layer ensures data validity. In this section, let us turn our attention to the middle layer of the proposed model. Specifically, let us show how the temporal layer ensures that data follow, or are consistent with, some sequential cycles.

In many applications, data are collected as a time series. Examples of these applications include (i) readings from power and water meters, (ii) data from sensors measuring temperature, rainfall, and wind, (iii) inventory figures for a grocery store, as well as (iv) Web click streams. Data for these applications are assumed to follow some sequential cycles. Data at some time t in the current cycle are supposed to be consistent with data at t in previous and subsequent cycles. Take the reading from power meters as an example. The value on power consumption for this winter would be more or less the same as (i.e., consistent with) the values on power consumption for winter in previous years. Hence, the temporal layer of our model analyzes these time series and detects any significant inconsistency. Some natural questions to ask are: how to do so? Do we need to analyze all data values in the time series? If not, which data values should we consider?

Figure 2 shows a skeleton of the temporal layer of

The temporal layer

INPUT: Time series containing valid data from the internal layer.

OUTPUT: Suspicious data $x_{A,t,L}$ for further investigation.

1. We extract relevant data from the input time series.
2. We compute the bi-weight mean $\overline{x}_{\text{bw}}$ and bi-weight standard deviation σ_{bw} of the extracted time series.
3. We calculate the standardized Z-score for each datum $x_{A,t,L}$. Any data with Z-scores > 3 are considered suspicious. They are flagged and returned to the user for further investigation.

Figure 2. A Skeleton of the temporal layer.

---

our model. As shown in the figure, to identify inconsistent data, the temporal layer first extracts relevant data from the time series. With loss of generality, let us assume that data are collected on a daily basis and follow a yearly cycle. For each data obtained at a certain date d ($date_{d,year_i}$), our model considers (i) data for the day preceding d ($date_{d-1,year_i}$), (ii) data for the day succeeding d ($date_{d+1,year_i}$), and (iii) data for these three dates in all previous and subsequent years ($date_{d-1,year_j}$, $date_{d,year_j}$, and $date_{d+1,year_j}$ for $j \neq i$). See the following example.

Example 1 Let us assume that data are collected on a daily basis, and the data follow a yearly cycle. If d is September 7 2007, our model would consider the daily observations collected on (i) September 6 2007; (ii) September 8 2007; and (iii) September 6, September 7, and September 8 for all years prior to, and after, 2007 (in this example, data for these three days for all years except 2007). ∎

Although we used a yearly cycle in the above example, such a data extraction technique can be applicable for other cycles (e.g., daily, weekly, monthly, quarterly, seasonal, or some other cycles). Similarly, although we analyzed the daily data in the above example, such a data extraction technique can also be applicable for data collected at a different interval (e.g., hourly basis), as illustrated in the following example.

Example 2 Let us assume that data are collected on an hourly basis, and the data follow a weekly cycle. If d is 12:00 noon on Monday, our model would consider the hourly observations collected at (i) 11:00 am on Monday; (ii) 1:00 pm on Monday; and (iii) the 11:00 am, 12:00 noon and 1:00 pm for all days prior to, and after, Monday (in this example, data for these three time moments for all days except Monday). ∎

Once our model extracts relevant data from the time series and analyzes them, it then computes the mean and standard deviation of the time series. On the one hand, our model can use the traditional mean $\overline{x}$ and standard deviation σ:

$$\overline{x} = \frac{\sum_{t=1}^{n} x_{A,t,L}}{n} \quad (1)$$

and

$$\sigma = \sqrt{\frac{\sum_{t=1}^{n} (x_{A,t,L} - \overline{x})^2}{n}}. \quad (2)$$

On the other hand, the model can also use the bi-weight mean $\overline{x}_{\text{bw}}$ and bi-weight standard deviation σ_{bw} [14]:

$$\overline{x}_{\text{bw}} = med + \frac{\sum_{t=1}^{n} (x_{A,t,L} - med)(1 - w_t^2)^2}{\sum_{t=1}^{n} (1 - w_t^2)^2} \quad (3)$$

and

$$\sigma_{\text{bw}} = \frac{\sqrt{n \sum_{t=1}^{n} (x_{A,t,L} - med)^2 (1 - w_t^2)^4}}{\left| \sum_{t=1}^{n} (1 - w_t^2)(1 - 5w_t^2) \right|}, \quad (4)$$

where (i) med is the median of all $x_{A,t,L}$'s and (ii) w_t's are the weights. Let D_t denote the difference between $x_{A,t,L}$ and med; let $midD$ denote the median among all D_t's, that is, $midD = \text{median}(\{D_t \mid D_t = \text{abs}(x_{A,t,L} - med)\})$. Then, w_i can be computed as follows:

$$w_t = \min \left\{ 1, \frac{c(x_{A,t,L} - med)}{midD} \right\} \quad (5)$$

for some constant c.

Although it may look more complicated to compute the bi-weight mean $\overline{x}_{\text{bw}}$ and bi-weight standard deviation σ_{bw} than the traditional mean $\overline{x}$ and standard deviation σ, an advantage of using the former ($\overline{x}_{\text{bw}}$ and σ_{bw}) is that they are more heavily weighted towards the centre of their distribution than outlying regions. Consequently, they are more resistant to outlying values and thus provide a more robust estimation than $\overline{x}$ and σ. This explains why we use $\overline{x}_{\text{bw}}$ and σ_{bw} for the temporal layer of our model.

Afterwards, the model computes a standardized Z-score (Z) for each datum $x_{A,t,L}$, as follows:

$$Z = \left| \frac{x_{A,t,L} - \overline{x}_{\text{bw}}}{\sigma_{\text{bw}}} \right|. \quad (6)$$

Note that *Z-scores* indicate the number of standard deviation a value is away from the mean. So, data with high Z-scores (e.g., data with Z-scores > 3, which implies that the data are more than 3 standard deviations away from the mean) are identified as suspicious data. Users are notified so that they can check and determine whether (a) the data represent exceptions or (b) the data are incorrect.

2.3. The spatial layer

In previous two sections, we described the bottom and the middle layers of our proposed model. It showed how the internal layer checks data validity and how the temporal layer checks temporal consistency of data. How about spatial consistency of data? In this section, we turn our attention to the top layer of our proposed model. Specifically, we show how the spatial layer ensures that data are consistent with their neighbours spatially.

For many applications, data obtained at location L are expected to be consistent with data obtained at L's neighbours. Examples include (i) power and water consumption for single-family houses within the same neighbourhood, as well as (ii) temperature, rainfall, and wind measures for a region. For instance, one would expect the air temperature of Toronto at a certain time t to be very similar to that of its neighbouring city, Hamilton, at the same time t.

The spatial layer

INPUT: Time series (which contain valid data from the temporal layer) for various locations L, and a user-defined radius for neighbourhood.

OUTPUT: Suspicious data $x_{A,t,L}$ for further investigation.

1. We calculate the distances between the location of interest L and other locations. If the distance between L and a location L' is shorter than the user-defined radius (i.e., L' is located within the neighbourhood of L), then L' is a neighbour of L.
2. For each neighbour L' of L, we compute the correlation (e.g., Pearson's correlation) between L' and L. Any neighbour L' with significant correlation coefficients is selected.
3. For each selected L', we generate a least-square regression line for the $\langle L, L' \rangle$ pair and compute the root-mean-squared-error (RMSE).
4. Based on the RMSE, any data that fall outside of the confidence interval are considered suspicious. They are flagged and returned to the user for further investigation.

Figure 3. A Skeleton of the spatial layer.

Here, the challenge is how to ensure consistency among these spatial data? How to detect suspicious *spatial* data? In other words, how to identify data that significantly deviating from their spatial neighbours? The answers are as follows. The spatial layer of our model verifies the quality of an observed datum by comparing it with data collected from surrounding areas. Although discrepancy in values between neighbours is possible, a datum should be flagged and users should be notified for further verification if the difference be statistically significant. The spatial layer of our model uses the *spatial regression test*, which relies on the statistical decision theory and linear regression models to calculate a confidence interval where the data of interest are checked. See Figure 3 for a skeleton of this layer.

To elaborate, our model applies the spatial regression test as follows. It starts with the calculation of the distances between the location of interest and each of its neighbours (say, via their coordinates). This determines if a neighbour lies within a user-specified radius. Then, the model computes the correlation between the location of interest and each of its neighbours, where the correlation coefficient is tested for significance. All neighbours that (i) fall within a valid user-defined radius and (ii) have significant correlation coefficients are then subjected to regression, where a least-square regression line is generated between the location of interest and each qualified neighbour. For each regression line, the model calculates the root-mean-squared-error (RMSE), which is the standard deviation of the difference between the datum and the estimated least-square line value. Based on the RMSE, any observed data with values falling outside of the confidence interval range are then flagged as suspicious data.

3. A case study on weather data: a real-life application

So far, we have presented our generic model for controlling quality of data. We have explained how different layers of the model identify incorrect data and suspicious data. For example, we have described how the internal layer en-

sures the validity of data. We have also described how the temporal and spatial layers ensure that the data are consistent with their temporal behaviour and spatial neighbours, respectively. In this section, we show how our proposed *generic* model can be applicable to a real-life application. Specifically, we illustrate how we develop a *specific* system, which follows the proposed model, for controlling the quality of weather data for a real-life agricultural application.

Note that weather plays an important role in agriculture. For example, excess rain may cause flood, and an extended period of dry weather may cause drought. These are just two examples showing how weather can deeply affect crop production, which in turn affects our food supply and consequently our quality of life. Nonetheless, having accurate weather information is essential. This is especially important for regions, such as the province of Manitoba in the Canadian Prairie, where agriculture is a major industry and a key source of income.

In many existing situations, the accuracy of weather information is mostly dependant on the collected weather data. For instance, agricultural yield and production is highly correlated to the collected weather data observed (e.g., relative humidity, precipitation levels, and air temperature) in a certain geographical area. To collect weather data, the provincial government department of Manitoba Agriculture, Food and Rural Initiatives (MAFRI) has set up a real-time weather monitoring network consisting of *weather stations* to collect weather or meteorological data. Information based on the weather data collected from these weather stations helps farmers make management decisions about their crops. These decisions include the following: When is the best time to administer fungicides to combat late blight disease in potatoes? Which corn varieties are suitable for production in a specific geographic area of Manitoba? Which soybean varieties are suitable for production from the given seeding data? Hence, it is important to gather accurate weather data. This calls for better quality control of weather data [7, 9, 10, 22]. In other words, to support farmers with wise decisions and make them more competitive, one needs to have techniques that ensure the high-quality of collected weather data. By doing so, such high-quality data can then be used to provide useful information for making decisions.

3.1. Related work on the quality control of weather data

Regarding related work, Reek et al. [20] proposed methods to flag conspicuous errors that discredit weather data and archives. However, their methods are confined to single station (say, only the station of interest L) and fail to consider data observed at stations surrounding L. In other words, their methods do not check whether the data observed at L are spatially consistent with those observed at its neighbouring stations.

The Norwegian Meteorological Institute (DNMI) [21], on the other hand, considered spatial consistency among data observed at various stations. Specifically, the method proposed by DNMI considered 12 neighbours of the station of interest. However, in many real-life applications, there are more than 12 neighbouring stations (say, 30 stations). Moreover, there are no guidelines on which 12 (out of 30) stations should be selected. This gives the prerogative to meteorologists based on their "experience" with the climatology of the area of interest. Since different selections of stations may lead to different results, it is not easy to determine the "best" selection without exhaustively examining most—if not all—of $\binom{30}{12} > 8.64 \times 10^7$ possible selections.

Instead of picking the "best" 12 neighbouring stations, Kondragunta and Shrestha [12] selected all the stations that fall within an inclusion box of $1°$ latitude $\times 1°$ longitude of the station of interest. However, they checked spatial consistency by computing an index for each station using the median, the 25th and the 75th percentiles, as well as the mean absolute deviation of the observation. If the index is greater than the user-defined threshold value, the rain gauge data are flagged as outliers. Unfortunately, it is unclear what value should be set as the user-defined threshold value. With this, meteorologists may have difficulties in setting an appropriate threshold value. Moreover, spatial consistency was checked for *only* rain gauge data but *not* other weather parameters (e.g., temperature, relative humidity), which are equally important in many real-life applications.

3.2. Developing a specific system that follows our proposed generic model

Here, we show how we develop a specific system, which follows our proposed generic model, to control the quality of weather data for a real-life agricultural application.

First, we develop our specific system for an agricultural application in such a way that the **internal layer** of the system compares the data observed at each of the weather stations in the network against extreme values based on archival records for the daily high and low measurements of the specific region in Manitoba (Step 1). Any observations are flagged as *incorrect* if any of the following condition occurs:

- Either the observed minimum or maximum temperature values fall outside of the range of $-60°C$ and $+60°C$ (i.e., to ensure that $-60°C \leq x_{\text{temperature},t,L} \leq +60°C$).
- Either the observed minimum or maximum relative humidity (RH) values fall outside of the range of 0% and 100% (i.e., to ensure that $0\% \leq x_{\text{RH},t,L} \leq 100\%$).
- Either the observed minimum or maximum rainfall values fall outside of the range of 0mm and 190mm (i.e., to ensure that $0\text{mm} \leq x_{\text{rainfall},t,L} \leq 190\text{mm}$).

Moreover, the internal layer of our system also ensures consistent relationships among the related attributes (Step 2). For example, it ensures that the following condition holds for temperature: $x_{\text{min temp},t,L} \leq x_{\text{avg temp},t,L} \leq x_{\text{max temp},t,L}$. Similar comments apply to other weather parameters such as minimum, average, and maximum RH as well as rainfall. Any observations violating these consistency relationships are flagged as *incorrect*.

In addition to identifying incorrect data, the internal layer of our system also detects suspicious data (Step 3). For example, it detects data with extraordinarily large daily range between minimum and maximum observed readings while these maximum and minimum measurements are within their reasonable ranges. To be more concrete, it may sound suspicious to have $|x_{\text{max temp},t,L} - x_{\text{min temp},t,L}| \geq 50°C$ (where $-60°C \leq x_{\text{min temp},t,L} \leq x_{\text{max temp},t,L} \leq +60°C$) because it would be a very unusual weather phenomenon in Manitoba. In a similar manner, it is also very unusual to have $|x_{\text{max RH},t,L} - x_{\text{min RH},t,L}| \geq 80\%$ (where $0\% \leq x_{\text{min RH},t,L} \leq x_{\text{max RH},t,L} \leq 100\%$) in Manitoba. Our system returns these suspicious data to users for further investigation. Furthermore, our system also checks whether observed data remain constant for some (say, at least three) consecutive days (Step 4) for some attributes. Note that it is quite unusual, and may sound suspicious, to have several days with the same daily maximum or daily minimum temperature. Of course, there are some exceptions to this check. For example, while the system flags a sequence of three or more consecutive non-zero rainfall measurements, it does not flag sequences of three or more consecutive zero precipitation measurements. Similarly, while it is possible (and not uncommon) to have a long period of dry days, it sounds suspicious (though not impossible) to observe a long period of rainy days with identical daily precipitation measurements (e.g., daily rainfall of 10mm for five consecutive days). These suspicious data are returned by our system to users for further investigation.

Once the data observed at each weather station passed the above data validity check (by the internal layer), the **temporal layer** of our developed system analyzes these daily data and ensures that they follow a yearly cycle. Specifically, for each datum $x_{A,t,L}$, our system first extracts its relevant data from the time series. See Example 1. Our system then calculates the bi-weight mean $\overline{x}_{\text{bw}}$ and bi-weight standard deviation σ_{bw} for each extracted series, and computes its standardized Z-score. Any datum significantly deviating from its temporal behaviour (e.g., any datum with a Z-score > 3) is flagged as suspicious datum subject for further verification by users (i.e., to determine whether the datum is truly exceptional or is just an incorrect datum).

So far, we have developed both the internal and the temporal layers of our system. The internal layer checks data validity, while the temporal layer checks temporal consistency. These two layers focus on data collected at each station. Next, we develop the **spatial layer**, which analyzes and compares daily weather data at different stations (i.e., *not* just at a single station). Given a user-supplied radius for defining neighbourhood, the spatial layer first calculates the distances between stations and finds those stations that are located within the neighbourhood of the station of interest L. Next, this layer computes correlation among L and its neighbouring stations. Those with significant correlation coefficients are then selected for conducting least-square regression and for computing the RMSE. Based on the RMSE, observations that fall outside of the confidence interval are considered suspicious and are returned to users for further verification.

3.3. Evaluation

We conducted various experiments, and results were consistent. For lack of space, we briefly describe the results of the following dataset. The real-time weather monitoring network consists of more than 30 weather stations. Each station collects and stores data—such as temperature, relative humidity, and rainfall—at a 15-minute interval and transmits them to headquarters via a wireless network. We stored these weather data in a database running MS SQL Server and used T-SQL query scripting language to retrieve our data.

In the first experiment, we compared the functionality of our developed system with related work. The following were some of the results:

- The methods proposed by Reek et al. [20] only check data validity, but do not check spatial consistency. In contrast, our developed system checks data validity (by the internal layer), temporal consistency (by the temporal layer), and spatial consistency (by the spatial layer).
- DNMI [21] considered only 12 neighbours of the station of interest when checking for spatial consistency. Note that there can be more than 30 neighbouring stations in our real-life application. Since different selections of stations may lead to different results, it is unclear how to determine the "best" selection without exhaustively examining most—if not all—of the $\binom{30}{12} > 8.64 \times 10^7$ possible selections. In contrast, our developed system was designed to handle any number (whether 12 or 30) of stations.
- Kondragunta and Shrestha [12] checked spatial consistency *only* for *rain gauge data*, but *not* other weather parameters (e.g., temperature, relative humidity) which are equally important in our as well as many other real-life applications. In contrast, our developed system checks various weather parameters including temperature, rainfall, and relative humidity.

In the second experiment, we tested the performance of our developed system. We ran this experiment several times,

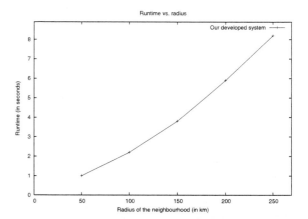

Figure 4. Runtime of our developed system when we varied the radius of the neighbourhood.

and runtime included CPU and I/Os. Results based on the average of multiple runs show that our system is efficient. For example, the temporal layer of our system took only 4 seconds to identify suspicious temporal data on a 40-year dataset. The spatial layer of our system took about 8.2 seconds to detect suspicious spatial data when a radius of 250km was used (i.e., when considering all stations that are located within 250km from the station of interest). Shorter time was required when the radius of neighbourhood was shorter. Figure 4 shows how runtime decreased when the radius decreased.

In the third experiment, we evaluated the accuracy and effectiveness of our model in controlling the quality of data. We randomly seeded several abnormal (e.g., those exceeding limits, those temporally or spatially different from their nearby values) as well as normal observations into our dataset. We tested whether our developed system detects all suspicious observations. Figure 5 shows the precision and recall of our developed system. The x-axis of the figure shows the percentage of observations that were seeded (e.g., 10% of seeded observations means that 90% of observations in the dataset were original and 10% were seeded). The y-axis of Figure 5(a) shows precision, while that of Figure 5(b) shows recall. In both graphs, when the percentage of seeded observations increased (i.e., more seeded observations), the number of abnormal observations (to be detected) also increased. Hence, both precision and recall decreased. Moreover, when the number of standard deviation used for Z-scores (and for confidence interval) increased, abnormal observations lie relatively closer to the normal ones. Hence, both precision and recall decreased. Nonetheless, it is important to note that both precision and recall of our developed system were very high: precision > 88% and recall > 92%. *Almost all of the detected/flagged observations were abnormal*, and *almost all of the abnormal observations were detected*. In other words, the number of false

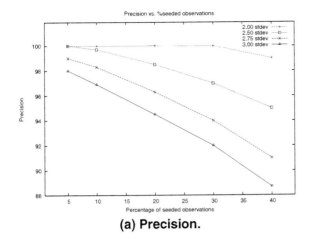

(a) Precision.

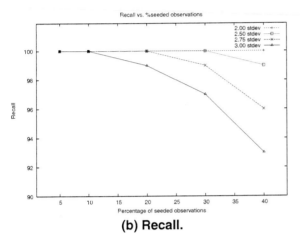

(b) Recall.

Figure 5. Precision and recall.

positives and the number of false negatives were very low.

In the fourth experiment, we applied the two sets of data to a data mining engine for agricultural applications (e.g., weather prediction). The first dataset was the original dataset. We fed this original dataset into our developed system. Some observations were flagged/detected (by any of three layers in our system) and returned to us. After further investigation, we removed those invalid and/or incorrect observations and kept those truly exceptional observations. The resulting dataset were the second dataset for this experiment. Experimental results show that the second dataset led to more useful data mining results (e.g., more accurate weather prediction). This shows the effectiveness of our proposed generic model and of our developed specific system.

To summarize, this case study shows the effectiveness of our developed specific system, in detecting incorrect and suspicious data from weather data for agricultural applications. Although this only shows one application, our proposed generic model can be easily applicable to many other database and data mining applications as discussed in the next section.

4. Discussion: other applications of our generic model

In the previous section, we illustrated the applicability and the effectiveness of using our proposed generic three-layer model for controlling the quality of weather data in a real-life agricultural application. In this section, let us discuss some other potential applications of our model.

First, our model can be applied to the monitoring of utility consumption (e.g., electric power, natural gas, water supply, and telecommunication services). In today's era of modern technology and service delivery, utilities form part of day-to-day consumer consumption. Utilities are considered to be universally needed services or commodities that are provided to homes and businesses. In many parts of the world, people rely on the reliability of their utility services. For example, with sub-zero temperatures during the winter, Canadians rely on the reliability of hydro power or natural gas services to provide heating. With large reliance upon energy sources, it is important that only a suitable amount of energy is consumed so as to prevent wastage and to ensure that these energy resources are utilized efficiently. To this end, one can apply the *internal layer* of our proposed model to ensure that readings from power, gas, or water meters are valid (e.g., within reasonable ranges). One can also apply the *temporal layer* to check the consistency of utility consumption of each household. It is expected that utility consumption mostly follows a yearly cycle (e.g., higher natural gas consumption is expected for heating during the winter). Moreover, one can also apply the *spatial layer* to check the consistency of utility consumption (e.g., applying the spatial regression test to monitor readings on consumer consumption of electricity or natural gas) of households in certain "groups". To elaborate, consumers in a certain locality could be "grouped" together based on their past consumption and compared with each other. This process prevents unfair comparison (e.g., business consumers with residential ones, or consumers occupying large houses with ones owning a starter home). If there is an increase in utility consumption by one consumer, consumption by other consumers in the same "group" is likely to be increased as well (e.g. an increase in natural gas consumption for heating due to record-breaking low temperatures in an area). Any abnormal or outlying data can be detected by the spatial layer of our model. These data could be indications of a malfunction on the meter reading devices or a true heightened utility consumption by the consumer. For the former, the utility company could take appropriate actions (e.g., inspecting the meter of the consumer). For the latter, the utility company could provide the consumer with energy saving tips and/or could recommend house inspection for appropriate preventative actions such as repairs or insulation.

Second, our model can be applied to the monitoring of traffic and law enforcement in highways. To ensure public road safety, various traffic law enforcement agencies have installed cameras for monitoring traffic density and speed limit violation. The *internal layer* of our model could ensure the validity of data captured by these cameras; the *temporal* and *spatial layers* could ensure the temporal and spatial consistency of data, respectively. For example, if the number of over-speeding vehicles captured at a particular camera station is significantly higher than that captured at nearby stations, then either the equipment was malfunctioning or there was a genuine increase of violators in a certain section of a highway. Respective remedies could then be applied (e.g., check the equipment, add traffic enforcers in that section of the highway so as to increase police visibility and public road safety). In addition, the spatial layer could also reveal some abnormal sections of a highway (e.g., more congested sections). Based on this information, appropriate actions (e.g., adjust speed limits, re-route traffic) could then be taken.

5. Conclusions

It is well known that "garbage in, garbage out". A clean set of data is essential to many database as well as data mining applications. However, collected data may be unclean due to various reasons such as human errors, equipment malfunction, and unreliable data transmission. To ensure the quality of data (and to a further extent, the quality of results from database or data mining applications), effective methods for identifying unclean data are in demand. In this paper, we proposed an effective three-layer model for controlling the quality of data. The model focuses on data validity and data consistency. Specifically, the internal layer ensures that the observed data are valid and fall within their ranges. The temporal layer ensures that data are consistent with their temporal behaviour in the time series, and the spatial layer ensures that data collected at location L are consistent with those collected at spatial neighbours of L. In addition to proposing such a *generic* three-layer model to identify unclean data, we also developed a *specific* system that follows our proposed model to control the quality of data for a real-life application. The case study describing this agricultural application showed how our proposed model effectively identifies unclean values from the collected weather data. It also showed that clean data led to more accurate prediction, which subsequently led to better crop management decisions for farmers. Moreover, although the case study only showed an application of our proposed model to weather data, our proposed model can certainly be applicable to control the quality of data for many other practical database and data mining applications.

Acknowledgement

This project is partially supported by (i) Manitoba Agriculture, Food and Rural Initiatives (MAFRI), (ii) Mathematics of Information Technology and Complex Systems (MITACS) in Canadian Networks of Centres of Excellence (NCE), (iii) Manitoba Centres of Excellence Fund (MCEF), (iv) Natural Sciences and Engineering Research Council of Canada (NSERC), and (v) The University of Manitoba.

References

[1] M. Agyemang, K. Barker, and R. Alhajj. A comprehensive survey of numeric and symbolic outlier mining techniques. *Intelligent Data Analysis*, **10**(6), pp. 521–538, 2006.

[2] M. Benedikt, P. Bohannon, and G. Bruns. Data cleaning for decision support. In *Proc. CleanDB 2006*.

[3] P. Bhattacharya, M. Rahman, and B.C. Desai. Image representation and retrieval using support vector machine and fuzzy c-means clustering based semantical spaces. In *Proc. ICPR 2006*, pp. 929–935.

[4] J.-F. Boulicaut and B. Jeudy. Mining free itemsets under constraints. In *Proc. IDEAS 2001*, pp. 322–329.

[5] W. Cheung and O.R. Zaïane. Incremental mining of frequent patterns with candidate generation or support constraint. In *Proc. IDEAS 2003*, pp. 111–116.

[6] B.T. Dai, N. Koudas, et al. Column heterogeneity as a measure of data quality. In *Proc. CleanDB 2006*.

[7] S. Feng, Q. Hu, and W. Qian. Quality control of daily meteorlogical data in China. *Int. J. Climatology*, **24**(7), pp. 853–870, 2004.

[8] M. Halkidi, D. Gunopulos, et al. A framework for semi-supervised learning based on subjective and objective clustering criteria. In *Proc. ICDM 2005*, pp. 637–640.

[9] K. Hubbard, S. Goddard, et al. Performance of quality assurance procedures for an applied climate information system. *J. Atmospheric and Oceanic Technology*, **22**(1), pp. 105–112, 2005.

[10] S. Karatas and L. Yalcin. Data quality management. In *Proc. TECO 2005*.

[11] E.M. Knorr, R.T. Ng, and V. Tucakov. Distance-based outliers: algorithms and applications. *VLDB J.*, **8**(3–4), pp. 237–253, 2000.

[12] C.R. Kondragunta and K. Shrestha. Automated real-time operational rain gauge quality-control tools in NWS hydrologic operations. In *Proc. 20th American Meteorological Society Conf. on Hydrology*, 2006.

[13] L.V.S. Lakshmanan, C.K.-S. Leung, and R.T. Ng. Efficient dynamic mining of constrained frequent sets. *ACM TODS*, **28**(4), pp. 337–389, 2003.

[14] J. Lanzante. Resistant, robust and non-parametric techniques for the analysis of climate data: theory and examples, including applications to historical radiosonde station data. *Int. J. Climatology*, **16**(11), pp. 1197–1226, 1996.

[15] C.K.-S. Leung. Interactive constrained frequent-pattern mining system. In *Proc. IDEAS 2004*, pp. 49–58.

[16] C.K.-S. Leung and Q.I. Khan. Efficient mining of constrained frequent patterns from streams. In *Proc. IDEAS 2006*, pp. 61–68.

[17] C.K.-S. Leung, Q.I. Khan, and T. Hoque. CanTree: a tree structure for efficient incremental mining of frequent patterns. In *Proc. ICDM 2005*, pp. 274–281.

[18] C.K.-S. Leung, R.K. Thulasiram, and D.A. Bondarenko. An efficient system for detecting outliers from financial time series. In *Proc. BNCOD 2006*, pp. 190–198.

[19] R. Rastogi and K. Shim. PUBLIC: a decision tree classifier that integrates building and pruning. *Data Mining and Knowledge Discovery*, **4**(4), pp. 315-344, 2000.

[20] T. Reek, S.R. Doty, and T.W. Owen. A deterministic approach to the validation of historical daily temperature and precipitation data from the cooperative network. *Bulletin of the American Meteorological Society*, **73**(6), pp. 753–762, 1992.

[21] F. Vejen (ed.), C. Jacobsson, et al. Quality control of meteorological observations: automatic methods used in the Nordic countries. Report 8/2002 KLIMA, Norwegian Meteorological Institute, Norway, 2002.

[22] J. You and K.G. Hubbard. Quality control of weather data during extreme events. *J. Atmospheric and Oceanic Technology*, **23**(2), pp. 184–197, 2006.

[23] Y. Zhuang and L. Chen. In-network outlier cleaning for data collection in sensor networks. In *Proc. CleanDB 2006*.

An Extensible and Personalized Approach to QoS-enabled Service Discovery*

Le-Hung Vu, Fabio Porto, Karl Aberer
Swiss Federal Institute of Technology
CH-1015 Lausanne, Switzerland
{lehung.vu, fabio.porto, karl.aberer}@epfl.ch

Manfred Hauswirth
Digital Enterprise Research Institute
National University of Ireland
manfred.hauswirth@deri.org

Abstract

We present an extensible and customizable framework for the autonomous discovery of Semantic Web services based on their QoS properties. Using semantic technologies, users can specify the QoS matching model and customize the ranking of services flexibly according to their preferences. The formal modeling of the discovery process as a query execution plan facilitates the introduction of different discovery algorithms and the automatic generation of parallelized matchmaking evaluations. This enables adapting our approach to unpredictable arrival rates of user queries and scales up to high numbers of published service descriptions.

1 Introduction

In the context of autonomous service usage, users have to be able to discover those services fulfilling their requirements for functional and non-functional properties. QoS is often the decisive criterion for a user to select a specific service among several functionally equivalent ones and in many cases, is the key of a provider's business success. For example, comparing two data-backup services offering similar capabilities in terms of storing data, a user would lean towards the one with higher upload and download speed, employing faster and more reliable recovery mechanisms under better pricing conditions. Many other types of services have QoS features as their main differentiating criteria, for example, Internet TV/radio stations, music stores, or teleconferencing services.

Different from the discovery of services matching functional requirements, the discovery of services based on their QoS is more complicated and the *personalization* of the QoS-based discovery process to adapt to different user's needs is an important requirement impacting on a number of issues: firstly, a Web service description can be used as an electronic advertisement of a real-life service that includes many domain-dependent QoS properties. Such properties are dynamic and depend on many factors, mostly the related user-side contextual or environmental conditions. Secondly, the advertisement of quality in a service description should only be considered as a claim, which the provider offers under certain conditions and to be verified and validated over time. This perception of the reputation information of the services is a subjective process by itself. Thirdly, the suitability of the service to a requirement of the user in terms of a QoS criterion is subject to her own needs. For example, the conclusion whether a certain deviation of quality is still acceptable should only be determined by the user. Finally, users want to obtain the most relevant matched services that are ranked according to their personalized preferences, especially because each of the services can provide many quality properties at different levels and with various reputation scores.

In this paper, we present our solution for the ontology-based discovery of Semantic Web services w.r.t. their QoS properties. Our goal is to automatically find those service descriptions that match the requirements of the users both in terms of functionalities and QoS, assuming that the actual negotiation, selection, and execution of the service can be done later by the user given the result of the service discovery. Extending our previous work in [1, 2], in this paper we introduce a complete discovery solution which combines our previously developed techniques and exploits semantic technologies to enable the personalization of the whole QoS-enabled service discovery process. Specifically, our approach has the following advantages:

- **Expressive and extensible conceptual modeling of service QoS:** Given the above complexity and dynamic of QoS information, we propose an adequate se-

---

*The work presented in this paper was (partly) carried out in the framework of the EPFL Center for Global Computing and was supported by the Swiss National Funding Agency OFES as part of the European project DIP (Data, Information, and Process Integration with Semantic Web Services) No 507483 and by the Swiss National Science Foundation as part of the project: Computational Reputation Mechanisms for Enabling Peer-to-Peer Commerce in Decentralized Networks Contract No. 205121-105287. Manfred Hauswirth was supported by the Líon project funded by the Science Foundation Ireland under Grant No. SFI/02/CE1/I131.

mantic conceptual modeling approach for the flexible specification of user requirements and the QoS offerings of service, which is simple yet expressive. This conceptual model can be seen as compatible with current standards and approaches [3–6].

- **Customizable matchmaking model:** By exploiting semantic technologies, especially rule-based languages and reasoners, users and providers can express their own matching algorithms and preferences flexibly. The QoS-enabled discovery process can be done autonomously by reasoning on the constructed knowledge-bases based on these personalized settings.

- **Personalized ranking algorithm:** We provide useful and informative ranking results supporting a user in the selection of the most appropriate services, taking into account different quality dimensions of the services, their reputation, as well as preferences of the user.

- **Flexible and scalable implementation:** The discovery engine is modeled as an *adaptive query processing* system in which the basic steps of filtering, matchmaking, reputation-based QoS assessment, and ranking of services correspond to logical algebraic operators. This formal modeling enables us to apply cost-based optimization strategies to parallelize the evaluation of the expensive operators, considering that there can be an unpredictable number of queries from many users and that the number of published Web service descriptions may increase substantially in the future. Moreover, it facilitates the *plugging-in, testing, and comparison* of different algorithms on-the-fly.

- **Implemented prototype:** Our prototype validates our approach and confirms the usefulness of semantic technologies in dealing with the above issues. Though we adopt the WSMO ontology framework [8] in our implementation as a proof-of-concept of our work, the proposed approach is generally applicable to other models, e.g., to OWL-S+SWRL [7]. Our prototype as well as the online demonstration, related ontologies, and documentation are freely available[1] and demonstrate how Semantic Web technologies can be exploited in real-world applications.

In the next section we will present our conceptual QoS model. Our personalized matching and ranking algorithms are described in detail in Sections 3 and 4. Section 5 presents the formal discovery process model, followed by a brief description of the discovery prototype and analytical and experimental results in Section 6. We review the related work in Section 7 before ending with our conclusions.

---

[1] http://lsirpeople.epfl.ch/lhvu/download/qosdisc/

2 Semantic Modeling of QoS

Conceptual Modeling

Our conceptual model is developed mostly for the discovery of services based on their QoS properties and serves as a complement to the WSMO conceptual model [8]. To put it more concrete, semantically-annotated Web services are described by conjunctive sets of properties $F \wedge Q$, where F is the functional description and Q defines the QoS offerings. We focus on the modeling of a service's QoS Q and reuse the functionality description F as specified in the WSMO framework. The negotiation between service providers and a user is considered as a later step after the user has already obtained the result from the service discovery and thus is out of the scope of this paper.

We describe a QoS offering Q in the service description as a set $\{\langle C_1'(qi_1), cnd_1, P_1 \rangle, \ldots, \langle C_n'(qi_n), cnd_n, P_n \rangle\}$, where $C_k'(qi_k)$, $1 \leqslant k \leqslant n$ is the concept expression that constrains the instance qi_k of a QoS concept q_k in a QoS domain ontology. cnd_k is an axiom over instances of those concepts describing the environment (context) in which the provider commits to offer C_k', and P_k is the set of preference rules of the provider. We also refer to cnd_k as the *context* to achieve the *QoS level* $C_k'(qi_k)$ henceforth. For example, an online file hosting service specifies $C_k'(qi_k) = \{\text{uploadSpeed} \geqslant 100\text{KBps}\}$ as the average upload speed that it offers, and $cnd_k = \{\text{internetSpeed} \geqslant 1\text{Mbps}, \text{noFilesUploading} = 1, \text{price} = 10\$\}$ is the contextual conditions required by the provider to get the specified average upload speed. Note that in the examples to follow we simply differentiate an ontological concept UploadSpeed from its corresponding instance uploadSpeed by the capitalization of the first letter. The preferences P_k of the provider are a set of rules associating each logical expression in cnd_k with a set of matching results. For instance, the following rules in P_k describe how well a requester satisfies the price demanded by the provider.

userPrice ∈ Price ∧ userPrice ⩾ price → prioritizedClient
userPrice ∈ Price ∧ userPrice < price → acceptedClient

Such preference above is currently used by a provider to specify that a condition to use a service (required contextual condition), e.g., price = 10\$, is optional or mandatory. However, it can also be used by a provider to decide whether to offer its service to a certain user in later negotiation steps.

Similarly, a user query (or a user goal) consists of the description of the functionality and the QoS a Web service should offer to fulfill a user's needs. A QoS requirement in user queries is symmetric to its counterpart in Web service descriptions. Web service consumers indicate by $C_k'(qi_k)$ the condition on QoS parameter instances qi_k they are willing to accept, e.g., $C_k' = \{\text{reqUploadSpeed} \geqslant 20\text{KBps}\}$. This QoS requirement is complemented by the contextual conditions cnd_k the client is able to agree with, e.g., $cnd_k = \{\text{userInternetSpeed} = \text{adsl1Mbps}, \text{ noFilesUploading} = 1,$

userPrice $= 15\$\}$. The set of preferences rules P_k in the goal model comprises various settings for the discovery process: the matching levels for the QoS required by the user, which quality parameters are preferable by the users, how much the user trusts the reputation information on a service, etc. For example, a user can describe her preferences as:

$$qs \in RequploadSpeed \wedge qs \geqslant 100KBps \rightarrow excellent$$
$$qs \in RequploadSpeed \wedge requploadSpeed \leqslant qs < 100KBps$$
$$\rightarrow good$$
$$qs \in RequploadSpeed \wedge qs < requploadSpeed$$
$$\rightarrow acceptable$$
$$\forall qs\neg(qs \in RequploadSpeed) \rightarrow acceptable$$

These above rules enable the discovery component to automatically classify how well a service (with a quality parameter qs) satisfies her requirement on RequploadSpeed. The last rule states that the requirement on RequploadSpeed is only an *optional* one. Other preferences can be described similarly via the use of appropriate rules and will be introduced in detail later on.

QoS Ontological Modeling

We assume that the user and the provider agree on a QoS upper ontology that represents the common knowledge in a specific application domain. This upper ontology can be refined by the user/provider to meet their requirements in terms of more detailed concepts and matching criteria. Because of the high complexity of the QoS information, we propose the use of a rule-based language that supports F-logic [9] to implement the QoS-related ontologies, instead of using DescriptionLogic as in other related work, e.g., [10].

Figure 1 shows the UML diagram representation of the QoS upper ontology. QoSSpecification is the ontological concept corresponding to the QoS offering Q in the conceptual model. QoSParameter is the definition of the foundation quality concepts, such as RangeQuality, DownloadSpeed, ExecutionTime, etc., and their relationships. Users and providers can define their own domain-specific QoS concepts, e.g., AllowableDownloadSpeed, AverageExecutionTime, etc., by specializing the foundation ones. ContextualFactor defines the set of foundation contextual/environmental concepts such as InternetSpeed, Price, etc. that influence the other quality attributes. Other related concepts include the measurement methods (MeasurementModel) of a quality parameter, i.e., which quality attributes can be measured automatically or can only be estimated by human, and their corresponding metrics (MeasurementUnit). ContextualDependency and QualityDependency represent the relations between a quality attribute value with its associated environmental conditions, and the dependencies among the QoS parameters themselves. For instance, in the file hosting scenario, ContextualDependency describes the relation between the offered UploadSpeed parameter with its associated contextual factors, which comprise the InternetSpeed of the user, the number of concurrent uploading files NoFilesUploading to guarantee the specified upload speed, and the Price a user has to pay for the service.

An important aspect of our formalism is the wide use of function symbols and rules to define various constraints, dependencies, matching and ranking preferences in the upper ontology (as well as in the derived ones). To check whether an offered quality value satisfies the user's requirements, we use the function QoSMatchingModel. The matching of contextual specification is similarly defined via the ContextualMatchingModel function. In fact, the rules implementing the ContextualMatchingModel and QoSMatchingModel functions are actually the ontological representation of the conceptual preferences P_k of a provider (or a user) described in Section 2. This ontological modeling enables the customization of both the QoS-based matching and ranking of services according to the preferences of the users and providers without changing the implementation code. Other modeled knowledge includes the personalized comparison between two quality values for the benefit of the ranking (QoSComparisonModel), and the conversion among the different measurement metrics, if possible (UnitChangingModel) and so forth. All of those above functions are implemented in the upper ontology and can be further customized in the derived ontologies.

Our QoS conceptual model is simple yet comprehensive and compatible with most of the current standards and approaches. For example, our conceptual modeling of contextual description cnd can be interpreted as the combination of the Agreement Context, Expiration, and Qualifying Condition in the WS-Agreement specification [4]. Similar, our concept of quality constraint $C'(qi)$ can be implemented to cover the notions of Agreement Creation Constraints, Agreement Offer, and Service level objective. The set of tuples $\langle C'(qi), cnd \rangle$ of each semantic service description is equivalent to the notion of an Agreement Template in WS-Agreement or of a provider's policy in WS-Policy standard [3], etc. The use of F-logic and rule-based languages in our implementation of the conceptual model enables expressive descriptions of service's QoS advertisements for complex application scenarios. Furthermore, our work also includes various user's and provider's preferences into the conceptual model. The result is a powerful QoS modeling that should lead to a refined discovery process as we will show in the paper.

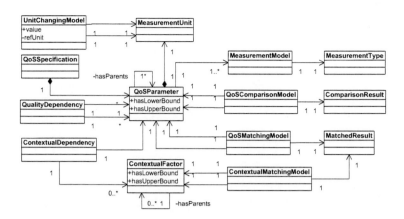

Figure 1: The QoS upper ontology.

3 Personalized QoS Matching Model

We only consider the matchmaking and ranking of services based on the QoS description part of the services, given that a set of services meeting the functional requirements has been obtained by other means already (e.g., via solution in Section 5). Given the presented conceptual model in Section 2, the matching between any complex QoS offering in a service s with a QoS requirement in a query g can be decomposed into a set of basic matches QoSMatching(Q_g, Q_s) between a simplified QoS offering Q_s and a simplified requirement Q_g, where $Q_s = \langle C'_s(qi_s), cnd_s, P_s \rangle$ only refers to one quality concept q_s, and $Q_g = \langle C'_u(qi_u), cnd_u, P_u \rangle$ contains constraints over one concept q_u. Also, to ensure the decidability of the reasoning, we have to reduce some of the expressiveness of our conceptual modeling: (1) a user describes her execution environment cnd_u as a set C_u of instances of related contextual factors; (2) a provider claims its offered QoS level C'_s as a quality instance qi_s. Note that our algorithm does not impose any restriction in the constraint C'_u itself, i.e., depending on the capability of the reasoner, C'_u can be a complex logical expression on the properties of the required QoS instance qi_u. This also applies for the contextual constraints specified in cnd_u.

The personalized matching between a simplified QoS requirement Q_g and a simplified QoS offering Q_s is given in Algorithm 1, with related notations defined as in Table 1. The matching function μ_{ctx} is specified by the provider and needs to conform to the declaration of the ContextualMatchingModel (Figure 1). Symmetrically, a user describes in her goal the personalized QoS matching algorithm μ_{qos} and the match result set M_{qos} that she accepts, in addition to her requirements C'_u. μ_{qos} needs to follow the declaration of the function QoSMatchingModel. The sets M_{qos} and M_{ctx} contain instances of the concept

MatchedResult in the QoS upper ontology. Default implementations of μ_{ctx} and μ_{qos} are available in the QoS upper ontology and thus both the provider and user can customize them flexibly in their own derived ontologies. For example, μ_{qos} can be implemented as in the example at the end of Section 2, where the user needs to define $M_{qos} = \{$excellent, good, acceptable$\}$ as instances of the basic concept MatchedResult in the upper ontology.

More generally, a service s matches a user query g if all *mandatory* requirements of the user on different quality parameter q_u in the query g are satisfied by a certain simple QoS offering of a service, or QoSMatching$(s, g) = m_{qos} \in M_{qos}, \forall q_u \in g$. To conclude whether a service matches with a query or not, the discovery engine formulates the associated queries based on the declarations of the functions μ_{ctx} and μ_{qos}, which it knows about completely, and performs the reasoning on the constructed knowledge-base to find the matching result m_{qos} for each pair (Q_s, Q_g). Thus, the service matchmaking model is highly customizable both by the provider and the user via their own implementations of the functions μ_{ctx} and μ_{qos} in the domain QoS ontologies.

We suppose that the user and the provider may specialize the foundation QoS concept with further properties of their own. However, they would need to provide appropriate mediating rules to translate back and forth between the derived concept and the original one(s) in the upper ontology. With such mediating rules, the reasoner would be able to detect whether the provider offers a quality parameter compatible with what the user expects, i.e., whether q_s and q_u are semantically-equivalent (line 4 of Algorithm 1). For example, a service provider can combine the DownloadSpeed concept in the upper ontology with other domain-dependent concepts and business policies to represent its own quality attributes MinDownloadSpeed, DownloadRate, AllowableDownloadSpeed, etc. This addi-

Provider-side		Client-side	
Q_s	A QoS offering. $Q_s = \langle qi_s, cnd_s, P_s \rangle$	Q_g	A QoS requirement $Q_g = \langle C'_u(qi_u), C_u, P_u \rangle$
qi_s	Provided quality instance. as simplified form of $C'_s(qi_s)$	$C'_u(qi_u)$	Required quality values. $C'_u(qi_u) = f(qi_u, Y) \bigwedge_{i=1}^{m} g_i$. where f, g_i are
cnd_s	Conditions to provide service. $cnd_s = \bigwedge_{i=1}^{n} p_i$. where p_i is any binary		any binary predicates. including the one comparing two quality instances
	predicates. including the one comparing instances of a contextual concept c_i	C_u	user's context described as a set of instances. as simplified form of cnd_u
P_s	Provider's preferences. containing contextual matching rules μ_{ctx}	P_u	User's preferences. containing quality matching rules μ_{qos}
μ_{ctx}	Set of matching rules to check whether user fulfills prerequisites to use the service,	μ_{qos}	Set of matching rules to check if provider's QoS is satisfactory.
	$\mu_{ctx}(m_j) \leftarrow \bigwedge_{p_i \in E_j} p_i : m_j \in M_{ctx}, E_j$ is a subset of $\{p_i\}_{i=1}^{n}$		$\mu_{qos}(m_j) \leftarrow f(qi_u, Y) \bigwedge_{g_i \in F_j} g_i : m_i \in M_{qos}. F_j \in 2^{\{g_i\}_{i=1}^{m}}$
M_{ctx}	Contextual matching levels accepted by provider	M_{qos}	Quality matching levels accepted as satisfactory by client

tional knowledge is integrated into the knowledge-base and can be reasoned about appropriately to detect that a provider also offers a DownloadSpeed at a certain level.

Algorithm 1 QoSMatching(Q_g, Q_s)
___
1: Build the knowledge-base $KB = Q_g \cup Q_s \cup$ related ontologies;
2: Find context matching level $m_j \in M_{ctx}$ so that:
$\quad KB \models \mu_{ctx}(m_j) := \bigwedge_{p_i \in E_j} p_i$;
$\quad$ {*variables in p_i will be bounded by instances in user's context C_u*}
3: If no such m_j found, return $\mu_{qos} = \perp$ (s doesn't match g);
4: Find QoS matching level $m_{qos} \in M_{qos}$ so that:
$\quad KB \models \mu_{qos}(m_{qos}) := C'_u(qi_s)$;
5: Return the QoS matching result m_{qos};

---

4 Personalized Service Ranking

Consider a user query g with QoS requirements $\{\langle C'_1(qi_1), cnd_1, P_1 \rangle, \ldots \langle C'_n(qi_n), cnd_n, P_n \rangle\}$, where all notations have the meanings as introduced in Section 2 and in Table 1. Suppose that the list of services that match the above query is L_g. For each $S_i \in L_g$, we define $\widehat{q_{ik}}$, $1 \leq k \leq n$ as the reputation-based QoS value of the QoS parameter q_{ik} provided by S_i, where q_{ik} is an instance of a QoS concept q_k in the ontology and $\widehat{q_{ik}}$ is estimated as in our previous work [1,2]. Since the evaluation of quality and the perception of the reputation information is subjective, user preferences and own judgements are relevant. Therefore, we include the following user preference information into the ranking procedure:

Firstly, a user may weight different quality parameters q_{ik} of service differently, e.g., she may state that the requirement on UploadSpeed is of lower importance than that of DownloadSpeed. We use $w_k > 0$ (w_k can be a property of a QoSParameter concept) to denote the importance weight of the quality concept q_k to the user. Higher values of w_k mean the user considers q_k as more important and vice versa.

Secondly, the comparison between two quality values q_{ik} and q_{jk} of a QoS concept q_k is also important. We use the relation $q_{ik} \succeq q_{jk}$ (resp. $q_{ik} \prec q_{jk}$) to denote that

the quality value q_{ik} is preferable (resp. less favored) than the value q_{jk} by the user. This relation is specified via the QoSComparisonModel by the user in her preference ontology (derived from the upper QoS ontology). Note that this comparison should include the case where q_{ik} and/or q_{jk} does not exist in the descriptions of S_i and S_j.

Thirdly, each user may want to include the reputation-based estimated value $\widehat{q_{ik}}$ into the rank computation differently, since each individual user have her own confidence on the credibility of the reputation mechanism, as well as on the sensitivity of reputation information to the actual value of different domain-dependent quality parameters. For instance, in the file hosting scenario, the DownloadSpeed offered by the service might be seen as more sensitive to its historical values than the SupportSize quality attribute since the latter is less likely to change. Thus we denote $\alpha_k, 0 \leq \alpha_k \leq 1$ as the (common) subjective probability that the user trusts the advertised QoS of a provider, and $\beta_k = 1 - \alpha_k$ as the probability that she believes in the reputation mechanism and thus in the estimation of $\widehat{q_{ik}}$. The quantity β_k (can be defined as a property of a QoSParameter concept) is used as a measure of confidence the user has on the reputation-based estimate value of that particular QoS parameter. Higher β_k values imply that: (1) the user has higher confidence in the reputation-based estimation $\widehat{q_{ik}}$, and (2) the user prefers the reputable services to the newly published ones. A user who wants to ignore the reputation value of a quality concept q_k simply sets $\beta_k = 0.0$.

The values of those above preferences can be defined by default in the upper QoS ontology or provided by the user in derived ontologies. This strategy enables the user to personalize the ranking as far as she wants, and the discovery solution is reusable for many different application domains without special knowledge about them.

The ranking of services based on their QoS properties is a multi-criteria decision problem, to which there are many possible solutions [11]. Here we employ a preference-based approach to develop our personalized ranking mechanism (Algorithm 2). We use the indicator function 1_P that evaluates to 1 if the predicate P is true and evaluates to 0 otherwise. Algorithm 2 ranks the services in L_g in the decreasing order of the probability that a user favors them (c.f. Proposition 1 of [12]). An advantage of this method is its considerable genericness even for the case we do not know the ideal results for a certain query due to the complexity of the quality requirements $C'_k(qi_k)$. The evaluation $1_{\{q_{ik} \succeq q_{jk}\}}$ and $1_{\{\widehat{q_{ik}} \succeq \widehat{q_{jk}}\}}$ can also be pre-computed to reduce the time cost of the discovery process.

Algorithm 2 QoSRanking(L_g) : RankedList L_r

1: **for** each S_i in L_g **do**
2:    **for** each $S_j \neq S_i$ in L_g **do**
3:      $p_{ij} = \sum_k w_k \alpha_k 1_{\{q_{ik} \succeq q_{jk}\}} + w_k \beta_k 1_{\{\widehat{q_{ik}} \succeq \widehat{q_{jk}}\}}$;
4:    **end for**
5:    $P_i = \prod_{j \neq i} p_{ij}$;
6: **end for**
7: Return L_r as L_g sorted in the descending order of P_i's;

---

5 Formal Model of the Discovery Process

One may envisage a single discovery component managing a large number of Web service descriptions and being targeted by numerous user queries with completely unpredictable arrival rates. In this context, the performance of a discovery process becomes of primordial importance as well as its ability to respond to variations on query arrival rates, while keeping the execution time of each query at an acceptable level. To provide such guarantees, we formally model the discovery process as a cost-based adaptive parallel query processing problem [13]. A query is modeled as an operator execution plan, in which nodes represent discovery operators and edges denote the dataflow between each pair of them. Potentially, a single discovery query may be modeled by a number of different operator execution plans, albeit equivalent in terms of the results they produce. Thus we derive an execution plan producing the smallest estimated cost for a given query.

We have identified a set of discovery operators that together form a discovery algebra (c.f. [14]). Each operator represents a particular function within the discovery process and may be implemented using different algorithms. For example, we have the following main operators: μ_Q to match between a Web service description and a user query in term of QoS, μ_F to assess the functional similarity between service description and a user query, ρ to rank services, and θ to perform the evaluation of various QoS parameter values based on the ratings from the reputable users. In addition to ordering operators into an execution plan, our execution model extends traditional query execution by supporting reasonings and introducing some dynamic optimization techniques. The reasoning task is invoked as part of the execution of the μ_Q and μ_F operators and deserves special attention as it can become a bottleneck for the execution.

Thus an efficient evaluation of a discovery query must target three main issues: (1) reduce the number of reasoning tasks; (2) reduce the elapsed time for each individual Web service description semantic matchmaking evaluation; (3) adapt to variations in execution environment conditions. We cope with these three issues by introducing control operators into the execution plan that manage data transfer, data materialization, reasoning task parallelization and scheduling, etc. For brevity reasons, we refer the interested reader to our previous work [13] which describes the parallelization and adaptive execution strategies in detail.

Figure 2 illustrates a typical query execution plan (generated by the system) for processing general service discovery requests. Once a user query g and preferences a are entered, the scan operator ν will read service descriptions s from the service repository and insert them into the query processing system. The execution process will be performed according to this plan via a parallel-pipelining processing mechanism. In this generated plan, there are a number of operators (μ_F and μ_Q) being parallelized in order to reduce the total number of steps in processing a query. The operators γ and $\circ$ in the query execution plan are automatically inserted by the system to handle the distribution of tasks and the collection of results.

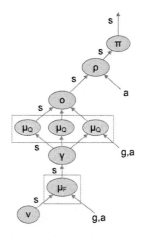

Figure 2: An example query execution plan.

6 Implementation and Experimentation

We implemented the prototype of our QoS-enabled discovery component using KAON2[2] as the reasoning engine and a WSML-Flight reasoner wrapper[3] to translate from WSML ontologies to KAON2's Datalog format. The adaptive discovery query processing system is developed

[2]http://kaon2.semanticweb.org/
[3]http://tools.deri.org/wsml2reasoner/

from the existing implementation of the CoDISM-G framework [13]. Another third party light-weight functionality discovery component [15] is used to performs the matching of services with a user goal by comparing their postconditions. We also implement several ontologies based on real-world use cases using the WSML-Flight language, which covers a subset of F-logic [9]. These ontologies include the general purpose QoS upper ontology, the preferences and related ontologies for three use cases: the online file hosting, the hotel reservation, and the stock market broker application scenarios from one of our EU projects which has just finished [16]. For our online demonstration[4], we develop a dedicated Web-based user interface to analyze the QoS-related ontologies, generate a GUI for user inputs and automatically formulates the ontology-based user preferences and goal descriptions for the discovery process.

Table 2 shows the results of an (illustrative) example service discovery query for a file hosting service offering DownloadSpeed higher than 25KB/s and UploadSpeed higher than 10KB/s. The user is willing to pay at most 10 Euros for her subscription and her Internet connection speed is ADSL 5Mbps. The service providers can specialize the DownloadSpeed concept in the upper ontology by defining various concepts MinDownloadSpeed, DownloadRate, AllowableDownloadSpeed, etc., with additional properties for their own uses. Thus, the use of semantics enables us to evaluate whether a syntactically-different but semantically-equivalent QoS parameter offered by a provider, e.g., DownloadRate, satisfies the user's requirements of DownloadSpeed or not.

The returned services satisfying both functionality and quality requirement of the user are S_1 and S_2, in which S_1 has a higher rank due to its higher reputation-based QoS ($\widehat{q_{11}} \succeq \widehat{q_{21}}$ and $\widehat{q_{12}} \succeq \widehat{q_{22}}$). Other services are rejected and removed from the discovery result since they either offer the quality level under those conditions that the user does not satisfy (S_3, S_4) or since they do not satisfy the required functionality (S_5, S_6). In general our discovery component can be used with more complicated scenarios where the QoS offers and requirements are of high complexity, e.g., a user may specify in her requirements that the statistics on the QoS parameter ExecutionTime of a candidate service (to be integrated in a Web service-based workflow management system) follows a certain distribution over different temporal periods for given input sizes. Similarly, providers can specify whatever prerequisites they want to impose on their potential clients, e.g., different prices according to different quality levels over time.

In our implemented prototype we limit ourselves to consider only exact matches between two QoS concepts during the matchmaking, assuming that we have a set of complete and correct translating rules between the de-

rived concepts, e.g., MinDownloadSpeed, DownloadRate, AllowableDownloadSpeed etc. by a provider (or user) and the original one DownloadSpeed in the upper ontology. As a result, the precision and recall of our ontology-based QoS discovery depends on the capability of the rule-based reasoner being used. The study of correctness of such reasoner is beyond the scope of this paper. The remaining relevant issue we need to analyze is the effectiveness of the ranking algorithm. Regarding this, our ranking approach exhibits the following properties.

- **One-time interaction:** The user provides her preferences only once before the discovery begins. These preferences are comprehensible and can be easily collected via the user interface. The whole matching and ranking processes are then done completely automatically, which is a benefit for users since the number of published services can be considerably high.

- **Informative results:** The services are ranked in decreasing order of the probability that a user favors them, taking into preferences of the users. This means the results are shown to the users in an appropriate way and can effectively support them to select their most favorite services.

- **Dominance detection:** Our ranking mechanism can detect the dominance among the services, i.e., if a service S_a is strictly better than S_b in term of a quality parameter q_k, and S_a is better than or equal to S_b in all other quality criteria, it is assured that S_a gets a higher rank than S_b in the final ranking result (c.f. Proposition 2 in [12]).

The reputation-based QoS estimation approach has been studied under various settings, which yields very accurate and reliable results even in highly vulnerable environments [1].

We also performed experiments running our service discovery engine using a parallel query processing system. The experiment objective was to evaluate the gains obtained by parallelizing operators of the discovery algebra. In particular, we execute in parallel a fragment of the query execution plan comprising the match (μ_Q, μ_F) and the rank (ρ) operators, in this order. We considered a repository containing 1000 web service descriptions synthetically generated. The execution environment comprises 20 homogeneous machines, one for the local operators and 19 parallel nodes. Figure 3 illustrates the obtained results. The values presented correspond to the average of five runs with the same configuration. One can observe that with 10 nodes, the overall response time is 3.6 times faster than the one obtained in the centralized execution. Note that this is the case considering the remote nodes initialization costs. In scenarios with larger number of remote machines (i.e., greater

---

[4]http://lsirpeople.epfl.ch/lhvu/download/qosdisc/

Table 2: Example discovery result

	UploadSpeed(q_1)	DownloadSpeed(q_2)	Price	InternetSpeed	Result
Requirements	$\geqslant$ 10 KB/s	$\geqslant$ 25 KB/s	$\leqslant$ 10 Euros	5Mbps	
Preferences	optional, $w_1 = 1$, $\beta_1 = 0.75$	optional, $w_2 = 2$, $\beta_2 = 0.75$			
FilesRUBasic(S_1)	$\geqslant$ 100 KB/s, $\widehat{q_{11}} = 102.9$ KB/s	$\geqslant$ 500 KB/s, $\widehat{q_{12}} = 514.7$ KB/s	free	5Mbps	**rank=1**
UltraFiles4All(S_2)	$\geqslant$ 10 KB/s, $\widehat{q_{21}} = 10.5$ KB/s	$\geqslant$ 40 KB/s, $\widehat{q_{22}} = 42.5$ KB/s	free	1Mbps	**rank=2**
FilesRUDeluxe(S_3)	$\geqslant$ 100 KB/s	$\geqslant$ 500 KB/s	150CHF	5Mbps	**rejected** *(advertised price too high)*
UltraFilesPro(S_4)	$\geqslant$ 100 KB/s	$\geqslant$ 500 KB/s	100CHF	10Mbps	**rejected** *(advertised price too high, demanded Internet speed unavailable)*
WSGetNewsXignite(S_5)	–	–	100CHF	1Mbps	**rejected** *(functionality unsatisfied)*
ThemesHotel(S_6)	–	–	–	–	**rejected** *(functionality unsatisfied)*

than 10 nodes for 1000 service descriptions), the gains obtained by parallelization start being blurred by initialization costs and remote node interferences. It is, however, interesting to observe that whenever the same query is executed twice, the whole initialization cost is hidden, enlarging the parallelization spectrum. We are currently enhancing our query optimizer to take into account the interference cost caused by remote nodes communicating with the local one. Our intention is to identify a break even point from which the initial input set should be split into multiple local nodes, keeping the interference under reasonable limits and allowing for greater parallelism.

Our modeling of the discovery process as a query execution plan also enables the plugging-in and comparison of the results of different variants of the reputation-based QoS estimation, matching, and ranking approaches. This will be addressed in our future work.

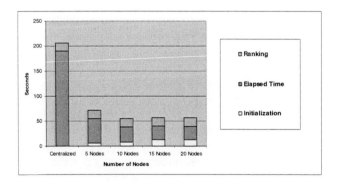

Figure 3: Experimental results

7 Related Work

Amongst the major efforts in using QoS criteria in service discovery are [17, 18] and [10]. The personalization of QoS-based service selection also interests a number of

research work, e.g., Wagner et al. [19,20] and [21]. Reputation information has also been partly used during the selection of services based on their QoS [22–24]. Due to limited space, we refer the readers to the extended version of our paper [12] for a more extensive review. Herein, we summarize the difference between our solution with the most relevant work in Table 3 w.r.t the following dimensions:

- QEXP: the expressiveness of QoS model
- QEXT: the extensibility of the QoS model
- SWSE: whether the approach is semantic-enabled
- CXTE: whether the discovery is also based on checking of prerequisite conditions expressed by providers
- REPE: whether the approach employs reputation mechanisms to evaluate the trustworthiness of the advertised QoS
- PMCH: whether the matching algorithm is customizable (without changing the code)
- PRNK: whether the ranking algorithm can be personalized w.r.t. user preferences
- FLEX: the possibility of integrating different algorithms during the discovery, e.g., using different reputation mechanisms to estimate services' quality
- OPTE: the easy parallelization and optimization of the whole discovery process

A $\checkmark$ in Table 3 denotes that the corresponding feature is supported and a * implies that the issue is (partially) addressed by some work in the mentioned group.

8 Conclusions

We have presented an approach for discovery of services that enables both functional- and quality-based discovery. The proposed discovery framework is highly extensible and customizable, which adequately addresses many relevant issues in the literature: semantic modeling of QoS, personalized matchmaking and ranking of services, and the use of

Table 3: Comparison of our framework with others

	Ours	[17]	[18]	[10]	[19, 20]	[21]	[22]	[23, 24]
QEXP	✓	✓	✓	✓		✓		*
QEXT	✓	✓	✓	✓	✓	✓	✓	*
SWSE	✓	✓	✓	✓	✓	✓		*
CXTE	✓	✓	✓	✓				
REPE	✓						✓	✓
PMCH	✓	✓			✓	✓		
PRNK	✓	✓			✓	✓	✓	*
FLEX	✓							
OPTE	✓							

services' QoS reputation in the discovery process. Additionally, the important steps of the discovery process are implemented as operators in a discovery algebra, making our approach customizable and scalable through implicit parallelization capabilities.

References

[1] L.-H. Vu, M. Hauswirth, and K. Aberer, "QoS-based service selection and ranking with trust and reputation management," in *Proceedings of the Cooperative Information System Conference (CoopIS'05)*, pp. 446–483, 2005.

[2] L.-H. Vu, M. Hauswirth, F. Porto, and K. Aberer, "A search engine for QoS-enabled discovery of Semantic Web services," *International Journal of Business Process Integration and Management*, 1(3): 244–255, 2006.

[3] S. B. et al, *Web Services Policy Framework*. http://www.w3.org/Submission/WS-Policy/, 2006.

[4] A. Andrieux et al, *Web Services Agreement Specification (WS-Agreement) Version 2005/09*. http://www.w3.org/Submission/WS-Policy/, 2005.

[5] H. Ludwig et al, *Web Service Level Agreement (WSLA) Language Specification*. http://www.research.ibm.com/wsla/WSLASpecV1-20030128.pdf, 2003.

[6] V. Tosic, *Service Offerings for XML Web Services and Their Management Applications*. PhD thesis, Department of Systems and Computer Engineering, Carleton University, Canada, 2004.

[7] *SWRL: A Semantic Web Rule Language Combining OWL and RuleML*. http://www.w3.org/Submission/SWRL/.

[8] *D2v1.3. Web Service Modeling Ontology (WSMO)*. http://www.wsmo.org/TR/d2/v1.3/.

[9] M. Kifer, G. Lausen, and J. Wu, "Logical foundations of object-oriented and frame-based languages," *J. ACM*, 42(4): 741–843, 1995.

[10] C. Zhou, L.-T. Chia, and B.-S. Lee, "Web services discovery with daml-qos ontology," *Int. Journal of Web Services Research (JWSR)*, 2(2): 44–67, 2005.

[11] F. Naumann, "Data fusion and data quality," in *Seminar on New Techniques and Technologies for Statistics*, (Sorrento, Italy), 1998.

[12] L.-H. Vu, F. Porto, M. Hauswirth, and K. Aberer, "An Ex-

tensible and Personalized Approach to QoS-enabled Semantic Web Service Discovery," Tech. Rep. LSIR-REPORT-2006-012, EPFL, 2006, available at http://infoscience.epfl.ch/search.py?recid=89160.

[13] F. Porto, V. F. V. da Silva, M. L. Dutra, and B. Schulze, "An adaptive distributed query processing Grid service," in *Proceedings of the Workshop on Data Management in Grids*, VLDB, 2005.

[14] M. Hauswirth, F. Porto, and L.-H. Vu, *P2P and QoS-enabled service discovery specification. DIP Project Deliverable D4.17, available from http://dip.semanticweb.org/documents/D4.17-Revised.pdf*, 2005.

[15] A. Friesen and S. Grimm, *SWS Discovery Module Specification. DIP Project Deliverable D4.8*. http://dip.semanticweb.org/documents/D4.8Final.pdf.

[16] *DIP Integrated project- Data, Information, and Process Integration with Semantic Web Services*. http://dip.semanticWeb.org/.

[17] N. Oldham, K. Verma, A. Sheth, and F. Hakimpour, "Semantic WS-agreement partner selection," in Proceedings of WWW'06, pp. 697–706, 2006.

[18] N. Sriharee, T. Senivongse, K. Verma, and A. P. Sheth, "On using ws-policy, ontology, and rule reasoning to discover web services.," in *Proceedings of INTELLCOMM*, pp. 246–255, 2004.

[19] W.-T. Balke and M. Wagner, "Through different eyes: assessing multiple conceptual views for querying web services," in *Proceedings of WWW'04*, pp. 196–205, ACM Press, 2004.

[20] W.-T. Balke and M. Wagner, "Towards personalized selection of web services.," in *Proceedings of WWW'03*, 2003.

[21] T. D. Noia, E. D. Sciascio, F. M. Donini, and M. Mongiello, "A system for principled matchmaking in an electronic marketplace," in *Proceedings of WWW'03*, pp. 321–330, 2003.

[22] Y. Liu, A. Ngu, and L. Zheng, "QoS computation and policing in dynamic web service selection," in *Proceedings of WWW'04*, pp. 66–73, 2004.

[23] S. Ran, "A model for Web services discovery with QoS," *SIGecom Exch.*, 4(1): 1–10, 2003.

[24] M. Ouzzani and A. Bouguettaya, "Efficient access to Web services," *IEEE Internet Computing*, pp. 34–44, Mar./Apr. 2004.

Applying Hypothetical Queries to E-Commerce Systems to Support Reservation and Personal Preferences

Yu Zhang
Zhejiang University
Hangzhou 310027, Zhejiang, China
yzh@zju.edu.cn

Huajun Chen
Zhejiang University
Hangzhou 310027, Zhejiang, China
huajunsir@zju.edu.cn

Hao Sheng
Zhejiang University
Hangzhou 310027, Zhejiang, China
zjuhsh@gmail.com

Zhaohui Wu
Zhejiang University
Hangzhou 310027, Zhejiang, China
wzh@zju.edu.cn

Abstract

Online travel continues to be one of the most successful e-commerce categories on the Internet. As increasing number of people book online, existing e-ticket systems can not satisfy customers' growing demand. Customers complain about most of the current e-ticket systems for the lack of "reservation" functionality. They also complain that these systems are not "intelligent" enough as a traditional travel agent who can deal with more complicated personal preferences. In this paper, we propose a transaction model for e-commerce system to support reservation functionality while balancing the benefits and risks of both customers and airlines. We introduce the theory of hypothetical query to avoid unnecessary transactions and rollbacks on underlying database. Hypothetical queries can be generated automatically and transformed into relational algebra queries which can be optimized with conventional techniques. We extend the lazy approach for evaluating hypothetical queries with integrity constraints to deal with customers' personal preferences. We also provide the "watch" and "remind" mechanism to help customers to purchase their most desirable tickets. Although we have chosen ticket booking system as our target application, the framework presented in this paper is also applicable to other e-commerce systems.

1. Introduction

Booking travel arrangement online now is a booming business. The most important factor for a successful business web site is to make it customer centered [17]. Since more and more people are booking travel packages online [23], existing e-commerce systems are not capable to satisfy customers' needs in several aspects.

First, most of the online ticket booking systems including some well-known ones such as Expedia.com [13], Travelocity.com [22] and Orbitz.com [20] do not allow customers to *reserve* a ticket. Tickets must be purchased immediately after query and it is impossible to reserve the fare for later ticketing. These systems use an optimistic concurrency model that checks if the ticket is available only when the customer actually purchases it. In this way, the airlines reduce the risks to the minimum to keep revenue high, however it results in a less chance for customers to purchase their most desirable tickets. Studies have indicated that online travel agents offer tickets with substantially different prices and characteristics when given the same customer request [12]. A consumer may want to check whether a better deal could be obtained on the Internet. He will be very unhappy if he finds out the ticket he chose as a candidate is sold out maybe only 5 minutes after his initial query. It becomes more essential for online ticket booking systems to support reservation when customers want to book a travel package consists of several legs of flight or other transportation. Customers would like to compare the prices offered by different e-ticket systems, also they will consider about other factors such as schedule, availability and preferences of successive legs. Supporting reservation function can offer more flexibility to customers and let them to purchase the most satisfying tickets. Some travel web sites such as United [4], American Airline [2], Amadeus.net [1] allow customers to reserve tickets for a certain period of time typically 24 hours, however, the price of the ticket can not be guaranteed and sometimes only tickets of much higher price can be reserved.

46

Second, comparing with traditional travel agents, online ticket booking systems are not "intelligent" enough. Although these systems allow customers to specify their preferences such as a nonstop flight, seat locations and food types, they can not deal with customer's personal requests like "I refuse to take a train as part of my journey" or "I do not want to pass by a place during my travel" etc. Therefore, some customers still rely on traditional travel agents instead of booking online especially when the arrangement seems like a more complicated one. Traditional travel agents take advantage of their expertise and intelligence to help customers to save time on search, meanwhile they can provide support during customers decision making process. Therefore, it is very necessary for the online ticket booking systems to support reasoning functionality and provide more intelligent services.

In this paper, we propose a transaction model for e-commerce system to support reservation functionality while balancing the benefits and risks of both customers and airlines. The model allows the customers to do the following: (a) queries to check availability and airfare of tickets; (b) make reservation of potential ticket after queries are conducted; (c) finally purchase the ticket, perhaps after the reservation. We also provide an approach to deal with customers personal preferences.

Contributions. The main contribution of the paper include the following:

1. Our first contribution is to set up a new model for transaction control, supporting: (a) queries, (b) reservation (after the queries are conducted), (c) purchase (only at this point real transactions take place).

2. Our second contribution is to introduce the theory of hypothetical query into the model to avoid unnecessary transactions and rollbacks on underlying database.

3. Our third contribution is to extend Timothy et al's framework [15] for evaluating hypothetical queries with integrity constraints. The hypothetical rules and inferences can facilitate e-ticket systems to deal with more complicated personal preferences.

Currently, research on online e-ticket systems has focus largely on user interface [17], presentation methods [8], and system usability [3]. To the best of our knowledge, at present, there is no in-depth research about reservation strategy and reasoning functionality to support more customers' personal preferences. This topic is very important yet not studied.

In order to develop the model, we face the following challenges: first, e-ticket systems are at risk of losing customers if it takes lengthy time to load pages or return query results as customers are very concerned about the efficiency of tickets reservation. Therefore, how to automatically generate hypothetical queries and rewrite them into relational

algebra queries become an important issue. Second, after the hypothetical query is generated, we need to provide an approach to answer the query and optimize the evaluation of the query. Third, the real purchase is executed on *fact* tables while the reservation is made on hypothetical data. It is essential to guarantee the consistency of the database especially when there are potentially large number of hypothetical modifications during transactions.

Organization. In Section 2, we introduce our reservation model and implementation technique. In Section 3 we illustrate the extended framework with integrity constraints to provide more "intelligent" services of e-ticket systems. Related work is presented in Section 4, followed by conclusion and future work in Section 5.

2. Supporting Reservation

It is common in practice that customers want to make reservation before they actually make purchase, especially when they need to change flights or other transportation during the trip. The overall booking transaction for the whole trip can be regarded as a long running action and will be divided into several individual activities. When a customer books the whole trip ticket via Internet, he faces a dilemma: purchasing the ticket of each leg one after another or committing to purchase all the tickets together after finding all the candidate tickets. For the former option, maybe the customer can not find appropriate tickets for successive hops after he commits to purchasing a "perfect" first-leg ticket. In this case he has to undo the committed transaction of first-leg ticket and the service charge of the online booking is not refundable. Technically speaking, it would be possible to let also the end-customers to reserve tickets and cancel them later without charge, however, travel web sites do not allow this in order to keep revenue high. Nobody would like to pay extra money without successfully booking the ticket that he wants. For the second option, customers search for ticket of each leg, compare different combinations of transportation and choose the most suitable travel package. That sounds like a good idea, but this approach has some inherent problems. It is entirely possible that after the customer chooses the tickets of the first and second leg, he finds the ticket of the third leg is not acceptable to him. Therefore, he has to start over from the scratch to search for tickets of each leg. It is entirely possible that some other customer manages to purchase the last remaining seat during the time you are still considering about.

From the above analysis, we can see that no matter which approach customers adopt, they are expose to a chance of loss (either the extra service fee or the loss of the most satisfying ticket). In order to best serve customers and let them purchase the tickets that they most want, we introduce the theory of hypothetical queries and propose a transaction control model to support reservation.

2.1. Implementation Technique

To reduce unnecessary rollbacks and transaction management cost, we adapt theory of hypothetical queries to provide reservation functionality. In this paper, reservation of an airplane ticket is regarded as a *hypothetical purchase* while final committing to the transaction is regarded as a *real purchase*. The additions and deletions of reservations are entirely hypothetical, so that the underlying database is in its original state until the customer commits the transaction. By using hypothetical queries, not only the customers can purchase the tickets they most want, but also the e-ticket systems can avoid unnecessary transactions and rollbacks on underlying database.

In order to evaluate hypothetical query for booking tickets online, we adopt a lazy approach of hypothetical evaluation. During the reservation of tickets, the state of underlying database will not be changed until the final confirmation of purchase.

2.2. Data Structure

First of all, we introduce the data structures of the model.

1. Ticket table $T(\text{id}, \sharp, \text{price})$ keeps track of the number $\sharp$ of available seats of a specific flight id.

2. Reservation table $R(\text{id}, \sharp, t_s, \text{price}, \text{info})$ stores reservations made so far. A customer reserves $\sharp$ tickets on flight id with a locked price, where t_s is a timestamp specifying when the reservation expires, and info denotes some basic information about the customer such as name, nationality, number of passengers, etc.

3. Purchase table $P(\text{id}, \sharp, \text{price}, \text{info})$ stores the *real* purchases.

4. Other tables store other information about the flight such as departure time, arrival time and destinations, etc.

Ticket table T and purchase table P of our model are the same as the ones of existing ticket booking systems. They are called *fact* tables. Reservation table R has the same structure as P except for having one more timespan field s.

2.3. Hypothetical Queries

To support reservation functionality, reservations in R should be "taken out" from T during the process. For each query Q on T, we automatically rewrite it into a hypothetical query $Q_T = Q$ when $\{\{U\}\}$ on both T and R, where U

is an update expression generated by the grammar of Hypothetical Query Language (HQL) [15] as follows:

$$U ::= del(T, R) \quad \text{delete the value of } R \text{ from } T$$

In a nutshell, for each occurrence of T in Q, we replace it with $del(T, R)$ by taking out tickets already reserved. Typically only α percent of reservation will lead to real purchases in the end, so we use a parameter α to control it

$$Q_T = Q \text{ when } \{\{del(T, \alpha R)\}\} \tag{1}$$

In order to answer this hypothetical query, we can explore a broad spectrum of implementation strategies from eager to lazy. Traditional way of processing a hypothetical query is eager: copy the data from original fact database to a temporary one. All the views are recomputed according to hypothetical modifications and the query is processed on the temporary database. However, materializing the hypothetical world can cause enormous overhead on replicating data and the materialized representation will become useless if the underlying database state is changed. In fact, there is no need to update the ticket and purchase tables T and P when a reservation is made or canceled. Indeed, only the reservation table R needs to be changed in response to these updates. All three tables T, R and P are updated when a user commits to purchase a reserved ticket. Therefore, in this paper, we adopt lazy approach to evaluate hypothetical queries. The lazy strategy first reformulate Q_T into an equivalent, non-hypothetical query Q'_T by transforming each U into an "explicit substitution", and then applying the substitution in these scopes, to obtain a pure relational algebra query [15]. We illustrate this using query (1), where Q is a normal SQL query about the number of tickets in stock on flight k, namely $Q = \pi_\sharp(\sigma_{\text{id}=k} T)$. We replace the update expression with the explicit substitution as follows:

$$\pi_\sharp(\sigma_{\text{id}=k} T) \text{ when } \{\{(T - \alpha R)/T\}\}$$

Note that R is a bag of records—for each flight there may be several reservations for it by different customers, thus to deduct the total number of reserved tickets in R, we should compute a sum. Now we apply the substitution to the query Q_T and we have

$$Q'_T \equiv \pi_\sharp(\sigma_{\text{id}=k} T) - \alpha \text{ sum}(\pi_\sharp(\sigma_{\text{id}=k} R)) \tag{2}$$

This query is equivalent to Q_T, and more importantly it can be performed without reference to the underlying database state, so we can use conventional techniques to evaluate Q'_T.

2.4. Reservation Queue

Providing reservation functionality of airplane tickets is convenient for customers, however it also brings new problems:

48

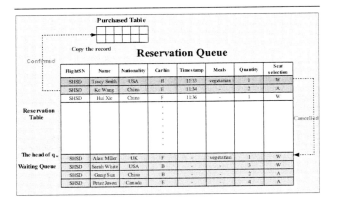

Figure 1. Reservation Queue

1. Suppose that when a customer wants to reserve a ticket, he finds out that there is no ticket available at the moment. However, in most situations, there will be a certain number of customers cancel their previously reserved tickets. Chances are that the customers who come later happen to miss the chance when the locked tickets are released.

2. Some customers may reserve several candidate tickets for the same itinerary while in the end, they confirm only one of the candidates and cancel all the others. Some seats might not get sold which may directly results in loss revenue of the airlines.

In order to benefit both sides of customers and airlines, we introduce a data structure—Reservation queue q_r (See Figure 1). Reservation queue is composed by two parts: the first part corresponds to Reservation table which stores the records of customers who have already reserved the tickets, while the second part corresponds to the Waiting queue (q_w) which stores the customers who try to reserve tickets. Customers in the Waiting queue do not hold any ticket at the moment and they wait to see if someone in the Reservation table may cancel his reservation. Generally speaking, there is a certain percentage $(1 - \alpha)$ of reservations will be canceled before or on deadline. Therefore, the model allows other customers who are interested in the tickets waiting in the queue, meanwhile these customers can still search for other alternatives, so they have more chances to purchase the most desired tickets. When there is some customer cancels his reservation, the e-ticket system will send a reminder to the customer who waits at the front of the queue. The length of q_w is not infinite, it is dynamically adjusted according to the number of unconfirmed reservation records in q_r. For airlines, allowing potential customers waiting in the queue can help lower the risk of unsold tickets.

3. Providing More Intelligent Services

As remarked earlier, customers hope the current e-ticket systems can provide more intelligent services like the traditional travel agents do. For example, the e-ticket system can deal with more complicated personal preferences like "I don't want to take a train as part of my trip" or "I do not want to pass by the Union Station in LA". Meanwhile, the system can "watch" the customer's most wanted ticket and remind him after someone else releases the ticket. In this section, we introduce the reasoning of hypothetical queries and the "remind" mechanism of the e-ticket system.

To illustrate our method, we define the following clauses about e-ticket systems:
$travel(X, Y)$: travel from source X to destination Y;
$travel(X, Y) \leftarrow flight(X, Y)$;
$travel(X, Y) \leftarrow train(X, Y)$;
$travel(X, Y) \leftarrow bus(X, Y)$;
$travel(X, Y) \leftarrow flight(X, Z) \wedge flight(Z, Y)$;
$travel(X, Y) \leftarrow flight(X, W) \wedge train(W, Z) \wedge$
$flight(Z, Y)$;

3.1. Support "Watch" and "Remind"

We use the following notation to denote a hypothetical query combined with customers' preferences:

$$Q_1^{'} \equiv (Q_1 \text{ if } \hbar) \text{ when } \eta$$

where Q_1 is the relational algebra query (which may involve nested when's) of the airplane ticket from source to destination. $\hbar$ specifies customers' personal preferences. We regard customers' personal preferences as integrity constraints which are defined as a finite set of clauses: $\perp \leftarrow A_1 \wedge A_2 \ldots A_n$, where $A_1, A_2, \ldots A_n$ are atoms. η denotes the hypothetical world composed of hypothetical state S and hypothetical update expressions U ($\eta \equiv S \cup U$). When someone cancels a previous reserved ticket, $Q_1^{'}$ will be updated in response to the changes of η. For example, a customer Tom wants to buy a airplane ticket from Beijing (BJ) to Hangzhou (HZ), unfortunately no tickets are available on that specific day (either all the tickets are sold out or some tickets are held by other customers) the moment he is checking tickets availability. If ticket table T still has tickets in stock (note that T is a *fact* table, $\sharp$ will not be 0 until all the tickets are really *purchased*), the system will put Tom's request in the Reservation Queue to queue up for a released ticket. Meanwhile he can reserve an alternative airplane ticket from Beijing(BJ) to Shanghai(SH) and then take a train from Shanghai(SH) to Hangzhou (HZ): $travel(\text{BJ}, \text{HZ}) \leftarrow flight(\text{BJ}, \text{SH}) \wedge train(\text{SH}, \text{HZ})$. Suppose that Tom has an important meeting to attend, so he must arrive in Hangzhou on that specific day. In case of sold out, he can first reserve the ticket package $travel(\text{BJ}, \text{HZ}) \leftarrow flight(\text{BJ}, \text{SH}) \wedge train(\text{SH}, \text{HZ})$ for a timespan s while waiting for the opportunity to get the nonstop flight ticket $travel(\text{BJ}, \text{HZ}) \leftarrow flight(\text{BJ}, \text{HZ})$. During the timespan s, if another customer who has previously reserved the nonstop ticket from Beijing to Hangzhou canceled the ticket, the transaction control model updates the hypothetical query in response to the state changes. A reminder will be sent to the first customer in the queue about the released ticket. When this opportunity comes to Tom, he can first reserve and purchase the nonstop ticket, and then canceled the previous reserved 2-hops tickets. As can be seen from the above analysis, this is what we do with a traditional travel agent: we call them to specify our trip and personal preferences and ask them to come up with a reasonable travel itinerary. If there is no perfectly matched tickets, the travel agent will look for other alternatives that acceptable to us. After finding an acceptable alternative, we ask our travel agent to still keep an eye on our most wanted ticket. If someone else canceled the reservation or purchase, the travel agent will notify us and help us to purchase our most desired one. With the development of the technology, traditional travel agents are gradually replaced by e-ticket systems online, however, current e-ticket systems can not satisfy customers' needs when the trip or personal preferences get complicated. Therefore it is very essential to make our ticket booking system more intelligent such as provide "watch" and "remind" functionality to cater to customers.

3.2. Hypothetical Reasoning with Integrity Constraints

For most customers, usually there is no direct flight from the place of departure to the destination, so the whole trip is composed of 2 or 3 legs, even more legs. There are several transportation can be chosen along the trip according to customers' personal preferences such as airplane, train, bus and taxi, etc. A customer may pose a query to compare the prices of several itineraries under different preferences. Suppose I want to travel from Shanghai (SH) in China to San Diego (SD) in the USA to attend an international conference, there are two major itineraries for me to choose:

1. i_a: Shanghai $\rightarrow$ Tokyo $\rightarrow$ San Diego

2. i_b: Shanghai $\rightarrow$ Los Angeles $\rightarrow$ San Diego

A travel package maybe composed by several transportation such as: flight, train, and bus etc. We extend the denotation T of ticket table in Section 2.2 to T_v, where $v \in (f, t, b)$ denotes flight, train and bus respectively.

For simplicity, on itinerary i_a, we use k_{a1} to denote the id of the first-leg travel: Shanghai $\rightarrow$ Tokyo; k_{a2} to denote the id of Tokyo $\rightarrow$ San Diego of the second-leg travel. By analogy, k_{b1} refers to the first-leg from Shanghai $\rightarrow$ Los Ange-

les on itinerary i_b while k_{b2} illustrates the second-leg travel from Los Angeles $\rightarrow$ San Diego. At present, η refers to the hypothetical state that I have reserved the airplane tickets of each itinerary for the first leg, that is $S \equiv (flight(\text{SH}, \text{TO}), flight(\text{SH}, \text{LA}))$. The e-ticket system allow me to reserve the two tickets for a timespan s_{a1}, s_{b1} respectively, so I have the time to investigate and compare the tickets for successive legs as follows:

$$Q' \equiv ((Q_1 \text{ if } \hbar_1) - (Q_2 \text{ if } \hbar_2)) \text{ when } \eta \qquad (3)$$

where, query Q_1 and Q_2 correspond to itinerary i_a and i_b respectively. Intuitively, Q' is asking for the difference of the value of Q_1 under the constraint $\hbar_1$ vs. the value of Q_2 under the constraint $\hbar_2$. Both of the two queries are within the hypothetical world of η.

As I travel a lot every year, I have my preferences about how to travel for each itinerary. For itinerary i_a, I will not fly from Tokyo to San Diego unless the discount of the ticket is higher than 40%. The reason is that San Diego is not an airline's central hub, so the direct flight to San Diego is more expensive. As known to all, customers are very concerned about the price of ticket as the airlines adjust the discount of the same ticket frequently even within a day. Sometimes customers change other itineraries or transportation if the tickets do not have a reasonable discount. This personal preference can be easily transformed into relational algebra queries by using the operator **selection**, so we have:

$$\hbar_1 \equiv \pi_{\mathsf{d}}(\sigma_{\mathsf{id}=k_{a2}} T_f) > 0.4$$

where, d is the discount of the airplane ticket and T_f denotes the flight ticket table. Referring to the second itinerary i_b, I refuse to pass by Union Station in Los Angeles as I had an unpleasant experience on my last travel there. When a query has a negative hypothesis, it can be treated as an integrity constraint on database [11]. In the evaluation of the query, the negative hypothesis behaves as "filters" which may reduce the search space of the query, so we have

$$\hbar_2 \equiv \forall X (\neg \text{ travel } (X, c)) \wedge \forall Y (\neg \text{ travel } (c, Y))$$
$$c \equiv \text{Union Station}$$

Since Union Station is the only Amtrack station in Los Angeles, therefore excluding Union Station from consideration leads to pruning the search within train tickets database on the second leg of $travel$ (Shanghai, San Diego).

As remarked earlier, η denotes the hypothetical world that composed of hypothetical states (S) and hypothetical update expressions (U). S includes n_k—the number of tickets that can be reserved based on the hypothetical data of taking α percent of tickets in R from T, here k denotes the id of the transportation such as flight, train etc. S also records the reservations been made for the previous legs.

As S illustrates the static characteristics of η while U denotes the dynamic characteristics of η. In this paper, U corresponds to the update of hypothetical world. For example, when another customer makes a reservation of $\sharp$ tickets, it is regarded as a deletion from the pool, $del(n_k, \alpha \times \sharp)$, which means this $\alpha \times \sharp$ tickets are locked and can not be viewed or reserved by other customers. On the contrary, when a customer cancels $\sharp$ number of tickets, the update expression can be regarded as a insertion into the pool: $ins(n_k, \alpha \times \sharp)$ which means $\alpha\,\sharp$ number of tickets are released for other customers to reserve or purchase. Meanwhile the parameter of remaining seats for reservation (n_k) will change dynamically according to reservation and cancelation, and the updates of these figures does not need operations on the underlying databases.

We build the following relational algebra query to evaluate the hypothetical world:

$$Q_1' = (Q_1 \text{ if } \hbar_1) \text{ when } \eta$$
$$Q_2' = (Q_2 \text{ if } \hbar_1) \text{ when } \eta$$

Then we can evaluate Q' by means of evaluating $Q_1' - Q_2'$. We illustrate this by using the normal SQL query

$$Q_1 = Q_2 = \pi_{\text{price}}(\sigma_{\text{id}=k_i} T)$$

to query about the price of different ticket packages $Q_1' - Q_2'$:

$$(\pi_{\text{price}}(\sigma_{\text{id}=k_{a_2}} T_f)) \text{ if } (\pi_{\text{d}}(\sigma_{\text{id}=k_{a_2}} T_f) > 0.4) -$$
$$(\pi_{\text{price}}(\sigma_{\text{id}=k_{b_1}} (T_f \cup T_t))$$
$$\text{if } (\forall X (\neg \text{ travel}(X, c)) \land \forall Y (\neg \text{ travel}(c, Y)))$$
$$\text{when} \{\{ \text{flight(SH,TO), flight(SH,LA)} \}\}$$

Note that η stores the hypothetical states that I have reserved two tickets of first-leg for either of the two itineraries. For Q_1', we could evaluate this query by using algebraic simplification to obtain

$$(\pi_{\text{price}}(\sigma_{\text{id}=k_{a2} \land \text{d}>0.4} T_f)) \text{ when} \{\{ \text{flight(SH,LA)} \}\}$$

For query Q_2', we could obtain the transformation by using "counterfactual reasoning". As remarked earlier, Union Station is the only Amtrack station in LA, therefore excluding Union Station from consideration leads to pruning the search within train ticket table T_t on the second-leg of i_b. Therefore Q_2' is converted to:

$$(\pi_{\text{price}}(\sigma_{\text{id}=k_{b2}} T_f)) \text{ when } \{\{ \text{flight(SH,TO)} \}\}$$

After the queries are conducted on corresponding ticket tables, the price of different itineraries will be returned. Then the system use aggregate function sum to acquire the total expense of the whole trip for each itinerary, then I can make a decision to choose the cheapest itinerary among all

the acceptable candidates. According to the above example, we can see that our model can deal with more complicated personal preferences and help customers to purchase their most desirable tickets.

3.3. Hypothetical Queries in Response to Update

In the above example, we illustrate how to evaluate the hypothetical query with integrity constraints according to hypothetical states. In the following example, we will discuss how to answer the queries with hypothetical state update. We still use Q' as a simple illustration:

$$Q' \equiv ((Q_1 \text{ if } \hbar_1) - (Q_2 \text{ if } \hbar_2)) \text{ when } \eta$$

Suppose there are two update to Q', the first update expression is:

$$del(T_f, (\sigma_{\text{id}=k_{b1} \land \text{d}>0.2} T_f))$$

this expression means the airlines adjust the highest discount to 20%, so query Q_1' is as follows:

$$(\pi_{\text{price}}(\sigma_{\text{id}=k_{a2}} T_f)$$
$$\text{if } (\pi_{\text{d}}(\sigma_{\text{id}=k_{a2}} T_f) > 0.4)) \text{ when } del(T_f, (\sigma_{\text{id}=k_{a2} \land \text{d}>0.2} T_f))$$

We replace the hypothetical-state update expression by using "explicit substitution":

$$(\pi_{\text{price}}(\sigma_{\text{id}=k_{a2} \land \text{d}>0.4} T_f)) \text{ when } (T_f - \sigma_{\text{id}=k_{a2} \land \text{d}>0.2} T_f)/T_f$$

Then we evaluate this query by using algebraic simplification to obtain

$$(\pi_{\text{price}}(\sigma_{\text{id}=k_{a2} \land \text{d}>0.4} T_f)) \text{ when } (\sigma_{\text{id}=k_{a2} \land \text{d}\leq 0.2} T_f)$$

It is obvious that the query would yield an empty result NULL as tickets can not satisfied my needs after the update.

The second update expression is that some customer released three previous reserved flight tickets of the trip from Los Angeles to San Diego. We assumed that at first $n_{b2} = 0$ so there are no tickets available for reservation. After the customer releases three tickets of the same route, we have the update expression $ins(n_k, \alpha \times 3)$. The query Q_2' is updated as follows:

$$(\pi_{\text{price}}(\sigma_{\text{id}=k_{b2}} T_f)) \text{ when } \{\{ins(n_{b2}, \alpha \times 3)\}\}$$

Similarly, we could evaluate this query by converting it into "explicit substitution":

$$(\pi_{\text{price}}(\sigma_{\text{id}=k_{b2}} T_f)) \text{ when } \{\{(n_{b2} + \alpha \times 3)/n_{b2}\}\}$$

As $n_{b2} = 0$ before update (we let $\alpha = 0.8$ unless other specified), so we have:

$$(\pi_{\text{price}}(\sigma_{\text{id}=k_{b2}} T_f)) \text{ when } \{\{(n_{b2} = 2)\}\}$$

As I want to reserve one ticket, $n_{b2} > 1$, so there is enough tickets for me to make the reservation. According to the query results, I can make my final decision.

3.4. Automated Generation of Hypothetical Queries with Integrity Constraints

In this section, we will illustrate how to automatically generate hypothetical queries with integrity constraints. The generation consists of two steps: the first step is to preprocess the customers' input to generate the travel plan with personal preferences. Customers are asked to express their needs by choosing from a fixed set of attributes represented by option sets or dropdown lists. When a customer enters the departure, destination and his personal preference, the *travel plan generator* first work out the travel plan (such as where to change flight, whether need to change transportation etc.) according to the indexed itinerary database. Then the e-ticket system analyzes customers' personal preferences and transforms them into corresponding clauses. Each clause is extended as a "filter" to effectively reduce the search space as the integrity constraint prevents the evaluator from considering the clause which anyhow would not lead to consistent answers. After filtering, the travel itinerary will be divided into corresponding legs if necessary. The second step is to convert the query of each leg into a hypothetical one $Q_T = Q$ when $\{\{U\}\}$ as indicated in Section 2.1. Then we adopt the lazy approach to evaluate the hypothetical query and rewrite it into a relational algebra SQL query by using "explicit substitution". After the transformation, we can use conventional algorithms for optimization.

4. Related Work

The model developed here is inspired partly by Timothy et al's framework for optimizing hypothetical queries [15]. The framework allows exploration of a broad spectrum of implementation strategies from the purely eager to the purely lazy. In our model, we adopt the lazy method in the evaluation of a hypothetical query. We transform each hypothetical query into an equivalent relational algebra query with explicit substitutions to avoid unnecessary rollbacks and transaction control cost.

Hypothetical queries has been studied in logic and datalog community. For example, [10] augments the logic with *negation as failure* and develop the notion of stratified hypothetical rulebases. It was shown that negation does not increase complexity. [9] develops an alternative logic for hypothetical reasoning. By introducing the notion of rulebase independence, these rules can express hypothetical queries which classical logic cannot. Counterfactual reasoning of hypothetical query has been discussed by Henning et al in [6] [11]. Treating negative hypothesis specifically as "counterfactual exception" requires only minor overhead in query evaluation.

In [7], Andrey et al developed system SESAME which models an hypothetical scenario as a list of hypothetical modifications on the warehouse views and fact data. The system provides formal scenario syntax and semantics, which extends view update semantics for accommodating the special requirements of OLAP.

A logic programming language which supports hypothetical updates together with integrity constraints is proposed in [14]. The language makes use of a revision mechanism, which is needed to restore consistency when an update violates some integrity constraints.

In constructing the model, we also refer to some materials in travel research area. [17] reports on a study about examining airlines' Web-based online reservation services. Thirty airlines from three regions (North America, Europe and Middle East, and Asia and Australia) were assessed.

Travel web sites are effectively becoming virtual travel agents, which are replacing traditional travel agents as the most popular way to book a flight or a holiday [5]. Hugo Haas illustrates how travel agent service can interact dynamically with airline services, hotel services and payment services, without a priori knowledge of them or of the way they work [16]. In [21], Marco et al address a process-level composition of an "hotel booking" service and a "flight booking" service to implement a "virtual travel agency". A prototype for Virtual Travel Agency applying Semantic Web service is developed [24], allowing users to use one portal that aggregates multiple tourist services and can be extended with new ones. In [18], the author proposed to add flexibility to B2C booking systems using a virtual intermediate travel agent. [19] addressed the problem of automated Web service composition and execution and proposed an approach to building agent technology based on the notion of generic procedures and customizing user constraints.

5. Conclusion and Future work

In this paper, we present a reservation model for e-ticket systems on the Internet. We adopt the theory of hypothetical queries to avoid unnecessary rollbacks and transaction control cost while providing the reservation functionality. Hypothetical queries can be automatically generated and transformed into relational algebra queries. To balance the benefit and risks of both customers and airlines, we set up a data structure Reservation Queue to queue up potential customers. We also propose the "watch" and "remind" mechanisms of the model to help customers to purchase the most desirable tickets. We extend Timothy et al's framework with integrity constraints to deal with customers personal preferences. Our model and methods improve the existing e-ticket systems and make them more convenient for customers to use. There is much more to be done. First, we should set up a time-framed model to capture the latency between reservation and confirmation. Second, in this paper, we are conducting research on a single ticket booking site. In the future, we will extend the model to multiple web sites. The problem becomes more severe when booking services become more complicated—eg a composed one that consists of several distributed web services. We will take the above aspects into consideration and try to improve them in the future.

References

[1] Amadeus.net. www.Amadeus.net.

[2] American airlines. http://www.aa.com/.

[3] Online travel usability study. http://www.techsmith.com/community/articles/wudreport.asp.

[4] United airlines. http://www.united.com/.

[5] Uk: Travel websites replace agents as most popular way to book a holiday. http://www.hotelmarketing.com/, May 2006.

[6] T. Andreasen and H. Christiansen. Counterfactual exceptions in deductive database queries. In *Proceeding of 12th European Conference on on Artificial Intelligence (ECAI'96)*, pages 340–344, August 1996.

[7] A. Balmin, T. Papadimitriou, and Y. Papakonstantinou. Hypothetical queries in an olap environment. In *Proceedings of 26th International Conference on Very Large Data Bases (VLDB'00)*, pages 220–231, Cairo, Egypt, September 10-14 2000.

[8] A. Bogdanovych, H. Berger, S. Simoff, and C. Sierra. Travel agents vs. online booking: Tackling the shortcomings of nowadays online tourism portals. In *Proceeding of 13th international conference on Information Technologies in Tourism (ENTER'06)*, Lausanne, Switzerland, 2006.

[9] A. J. Bonner. A logic for hypothetical reasoning. In *Proceedings of the Seventh National Conference on Artificial Intelligence (AAAI'88)*, number 480-484, pages 480–484, Saint Paul, August 1988.

[10] A. J. Bonner. Hypothetical datalog complexity and expressibility. *Theoretical Computer Science*, 76:3–51, 1990.

[11] H. Christiansen and T. Andreasen. A practical approach to hypothetical database queries. In *International Seminar on Logic Databases and the Meaning of Change, Transactions and Change in Logic Databases (ILPS'97)*, pages 340–355, 1998.

[12] I.-H. H. Eric K. Clemons and L. M. Hitt. Price dispersion and differentiation in online travel: An empirical investigation. *Management Science*, 48:534–550, 2002.

[13] Expedia.com. http:// www.expedia.com.

[14] D. M. Gabbay, L. Giordano, A. Martelli, and N. Olivetti. A language for handling hypothetical updates and inconsistency. *Journal of IGPL*, 4:385–416, 1996.

[15] T. Griffin and R. Hull. A framework for implementing hypothetical queries. In *Proceedings of the ACM SIGMOD International Conference on Management of Data (SIGMOD'97)*, pages 231–242, Tucson, United States, 1997.

[16] H. Haas. Web service use case: Travel reservation. W3C, may 2002.

[17] R. Law and R. Leung. A study of airlines' online reservation services on the internet. *Journal of Travel Research*, 39:202–211, 2000.

[18] A. Malizia. Adding flexibility to b2c booking systems using a virtual intermediate travel agent. In *Proceedings of the 2005 IEEE Symposium on Visual Languages and Human-Centric Computing (VL/HCC'05)*, pages 337–338, 2005.

[19] S. McIlraith and T. C. Son. Adapting golog for composition of semantic web services. In *Proceedings of the 8th International Conference on Principles of Knowledge Representation and Reasoning (KR'02)*, pages 482–493, Toulouse, France, April, 22-25 2002.

[20] Orbitz. http://www.orbitz.com/.

[21] M. Pistore, P. Roberti, and P. Traverso. Process-level composition of executable web services: "on-the-fly" versus "once-for-all" composition. In *Proceedings of the 2nd European Semantic Web Conference 2005 (ESWC'05)*, Heraklion, Greece, May 29-June 1 2005.

[22] Travelocity.com. http://www.travelocity.com/.

[23] T. N. Tribute. http://www.thenewstribune.com/.

[24] M. Zaremba, M. Moran, and T. Haselwanter. Applying semantic web services to virtual travel agency case study. In *Proceedings of 3rd European Semantic Web Conference (ESWC'06)*, Budva, Montenegro, June 11-14 2006.

Approximate Structural Matching over Ordered XML Documents

Nitin Agarwal
Arizona State University
Nitin.Agarwal.2@asu.edu

Magdiel Galan Oliveras
Arizona State University
Magdiel.Galan@asu.edu

Yi Chen
Arizona State University
yi@asu.edu

Abstract

There is an increasing need for an XML query engine that not only searches for exact matches to a query but also returns "query-like" structures. We have designed and developed XFinder, an efficient top K tree pattern query evaluation system, which reduces the problem of approximate tree structural matching to a simpler problem of subsequence matching. However, since not all subsequences correspond to valid tree structures, it is expensive to enumerate common subsequences between XML data and query and then filter the invalid ones. XFinder addresses this challenge by detecting and pruning structurally irrelevant subsequence matches as early as possible. Experiments show the efficiency of XFinder on various data and query sets.

1 Introduction

Wide acceptance of XML as the standard data exchange format has led to a large amount of XML data that needs to be searched. XML documents are in general viewed as trees, as in Figure 1. The key component in XML query languages (e.g. XPath and XQuery) is tree pattern queries (twig queries).

For document-oriented XML data, such as Shakespeare's plays[1], legislative documents[2], and news in XML format[3], the order of sections, paragraphs, and sentences is important. For instance, we may express a query like "find all the acts before the act that is titled as ACT IV and has a speaker Philo" when searching Shakespeare's plays. This query can be represented as the query tree in Figure 1, if we set the tag A to "Play", B and D to "Act", G to "Title" with a value predicate, and F to "Speaker" with a value predicate.

During a search, a user query may be over-specified. For example, no acts in Shakespeare's plays satisfy the above query. Returning an empty query answer can be frustrating to users. Furthermore, sometimes the user may only have a rough idea of what (s)he is looking for. It is desirable if the top K XML subtrees that *exactly* or *partially* match the query tree are returned, in the order of the degree of matching.

In this paper, we propose XFinder, a system that efficiently searches top K XML subtrees that exactly or partially match input ordered tree pattern query in ranked order. Rank of the match is gauged by the degree of tree structure match, as well as the degree of corresponding node tag and node value match. Existing approaches [9, 3, 6] can be plugged in XFinder to measure similarity of tags and values. In this paper, we focus discussion on approximate structural matching between ordered XML data and queries, the unique challenge in XML data processing.

Although we can compute approximate tree pattern matches directly [13], such an approach involves high complexity. Alternatively, we can relax the input query such that the data subtrees satisfying the relaxed queries are returned [16]. However, in general the size of relaxed queries can be exponential to the input query.

On the other hand, the problem of *exact* ordered tree pattern matching can be reduced to that of subsequence matching [12]. Using Prüfer method that constructs a one-to-one correspondence between trees and sequences, both XML data tree and query tree are transformed into sequences, and the document subsequences that are the same as the query sequence are computed and filtered as the result of evaluating a twig query. There are two advantages of such an approach. First, it allows holistic processing of a twig query to achieve efficiency. Indeed, the approach that decomposes a twig query to subqueries and processes each subquery individually can result in large intermediate results, and therefore can be expensive. Second, sequence matching is inherently simpler than tree pattern

---

[1]http://www.ibiblio.org/xml/examples/shakespeare/
[2]http://xml.house.gov/
[3]http://www.xmlnews.net/

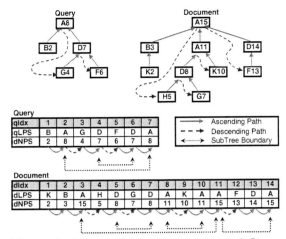

Figure 1. Sample XML Document and Query with their Prüfer Sequences

qidx	1	2	3	4	5	6	7
qLPS	B	A	G	D	F	D	A
dNPS	2	8	4	7	6	7	8

didx	1	2	3	4	5	6	7	8	9	10	11	12	13	14
dLPS	K	B	A	H	D	G	D	A	K	A	A	F	D	A
dNPS	2	3	15	5	8	7	8	11	10	11	15	13	14	15

Ascending Path
Descending Path
SubTree Boundary

matching, which enables various optimizations. The efficiency of a sequence-based tree pattern matching approach has been demonstrated in PRIX [12].

Intuitively, we can extend this technique to retrieve top K document subsequences that have largest length in common to query sequence, such that *partial matches* are returned at same time as exact matches.

However, such an intuitive approach can be inefficient due to a possibly large number of common subsequences that do not correspond to valid tree structures. Recall that after performing sequence matching, PRIX [12] requires a filtering step on each matched document subsequence to ensure that it forms a tree structure and this structure matches query tree. Therefore to retrieve top K valid subtree matches, the matching step needs to return $K'(K' \geq K)$ longest common subsequences, since some subsequences need to be filtered after matching step.

Example 1.1: In Figure 1, top 3 longest document subsequences that match query sequence are $B3\text{-}A15\text{-}G7\text{-}D8\text{-}F13\text{-}D14\text{-}A15$, $B3\text{-}A15\text{-}D8\text{-}F13\text{-}D14\text{-}A15$, and $B3\text{-}A15\text{-}F13\text{-}D14\text{-}A15$. However, the first two matched subsequences do not correspond to valid trees, and therefore are rejected in the filtering step. We only obtain the third subsequence as a valid match. In this example, to find the top $K = 1$ match we have to generate top $K' = 3$ common subsequences. ∎

As we can see, the relationship between K and K' depends on the particular structure of document and query, therefore we are not able to set the value of K' a priori. We need to either set K' to be very large to guarantee that after filtering stage at least K valid sequences are returned; or we need to perform several document passes in matching stage if K' is relatively small and less than K common subsequences are valid. Neither approach is efficient.

To address afore-mentioned challenges, we developed XFinder and make the following technical contributions:

- We propose a novel approximate tree structural matching algorithm by reducing the problem to longest common Prüfer subsequence matching.

- By pruning matching subsequences that do not correspond to valid tree structures as early as possible, and discarding the common subsequences that are not top K matches immediately, we avoid to generate large intermediate query results and achieve efficiency.

- We introduced a ranking function such that similarity measurement between two trees can be obtained by similarity measurement between their Prüfer sequences.

- We developed XFinder system for approximate XML tree pattern query evaluation and demonstrated its effectiveness in experiments.

Next we introduce background knowledge about Prüfer sequence and its application in tree pattern matching in Section 2. Proposed algorithm is presented in Section 3. Section 4 demonstrates a thorough experimental evaluation of XFinder. After discussing related work in Section 5, Section 6 concludes the paper.

2 Background

We introduce PRIX method [12] which retrieves exact tree matches using Prüfer sequences [11].

Prüfer Sequences. Prüfer's method [11] establishes a one-to-one correspondence between trees and sequences. Given a tree T, we first add a dummy node as the child for every leaf in T forming tree T'_N of N nodes, as proposed in [12]. Then nodes in T'_N are numbered during post-order tree traversal. We construct T's Prüfer sequence by deleting nodes in T'_N in the increasing order of their post-order numbers as follows. We start with the deletion of the leaf node with the smallest number in T'_N and record the number of its parent: n_1. The resulting tree is denoted as T'_{N-1}. Then we delete the leaf node with the smallest number in T'_{N-1}, and record its parent's number n_2. We continue the process until only the root node remains. The number sequence obtained $(n_1, n_2, ...)$ is called the *Numbered Prüfer Sequence* (NPS). If each number in NPS is replaced by its corresponding XML label (element tag or attribute name), the new sequence obtained is called as *Labeled Prüfer Sequence* (LPS). We use *qNPS* and *qLPS* to denote the numbered and labeled Prüfer sequences for the XML query, respectively. Similarly, we define *dNPS* and *dLPS* for XML document.

Example 2.1: Consider the sample XML document and twig query in Figure 1, where each node is named as a concatenation of its node label and its post-order number (after adding dummy children to leaf nodes, which are not shown in the Figure). Using the method described above, LPS and NPS can be constructed as shown in Figure 1. *qIdx* and *dIdx*, represent the index of *qLPS/qNPS* and *dLPS/dNPS*, respectively. For instance, for $dIdx = 3$, $dNPS[3]=15$ and $dLPS[3]=A$.

We use dotted lines in the sequences to denote the corresponding subtrees, e.g., an arrow between query sequence at qIdx=4 and qIdx=6 denotes that the nodes between them correspond to a subtree. ∎

Prüfer Sequence Based Tree Structural Matching. Tree pattern queries are evaluated as searching subsequences in dLPS that match qLPS [12]. LPS match ensures content matching between XML tree and query tree. Then filtering step needs to be performed to validate tree structure using their NPS. Three criteria are checked, connectedness, gap consistency and frequency consistency.

Connectedness ensures that nodes in a sequence form a tree. Let i be the index of last occurrence of a post-order number n in NPS. Then $NPS[i+1]$ should record post-order number of n's parent.

Example 2.2: In document sequence *dNPS* in Figure 1, the last occurrence of node D8 is at index 7, then the node at index 8: A11 is its parent. ∎

Gap consistency ensures that node relationships with respect to trees are consistent between document subsequence and query sequence. Gap is defined as difference between two consecutive numbers of an NPS sequence, giving the information about tree structural relationship between corresponding nodes. A negative value indicates a *child-parent* relationship and a positive value indicates an *ancestor-descendant* or *parent-child* relationship. The query sequence Q is gap consistent with respect to a document matching subsequence D if (1) they are of same length; and for every pair of adjacent nodes in Q and the corresponding adjacent nodes in D, their gaps g_Q and g_D (2) have the same sign, and (3) if $|g_Q| > 0$ then $|g_Q| \leq |g_D|$, else $g_Q = g_D = 0$. Intuitively, condition (1) ensures that every node in the query has a match in the data. Condition (2) ensures that the parent-child, ancestor-descendant relationship between adjacent nodes in document sequence and query sequence are consistent. Condition (3) ensures that some document nodes may

be skipped to match the whole query tree.

Example 2.3: In Figure 1, document subsequence B3-A15 with gap −12, is gap consistent with query subsequence B2-A8 with gap −6. ∎

We define *path direction* based on the concept of gaps. Path direction is *ascending* if gap is negative, that is, the post-order number of next node is bigger than that of current node (such as B3-A15); and path direction is *descending*, otherwise (such as A15-H5). We call two paths are *direction matching* if they are both ascending, or both descending, indicating the corresponding tree structure match. The document and query tree in Figure 1 are annotated with arrows. Solid arrows indicate ascending paths, going from a node to its parent; dashed arrows indicate descending paths, going from a node to a child or descendant.

Frequency consistency ensures that number of children of a node in document subsequence matches that of query subsequence. Two sequences are frequency consistent if they are of same length, and nodes at same index in both sequences have the same number of occurrences and always occur at the same index positions. Number of occurrences of a node is determined by number of its children, and position of node occurrence depends on subtree size.

Example 2.4: Query subsequence B2-A8-F6-D7-A8 is frequency consistent with a document subsequence B3-A15-F13-D14-A15. A8 appears twice, at position 2 and 5 in the query subsequence; and A15 appears twice, at position 2 and 5 in the document subsequence. ∎

3 Algorithm

We propose a novel algorithm to compute top K matches between an XML document and a twig query. As discussed in Section 1, it is not efficient to first compute longest common subsequences between the document and query sequences, and then prune invalid ones according to connectedness, gap consistency and frequency consistency, due to large intermediate results. To address this challenge, we explicitly embed gap consistency checking using path direction matching when we perform common subsequence search. Furthermore, our subsequence matching stage also implicitly ensures connectedness and frequency consistency. Therefore generated common subsequences are guaranteed to correspond to valid subtree matches without generating invalid common subsequences as intermediate results.

Algorithm 1

$getTopKCCS(k, qLPS, dLPS, qNPS, dNPS)$

```
 1: dIdx ← 1; qIdx ← 1
 2: (dIdx, qIdx) ← pathInit(dIdx, qIdx)
 3: for i = dIdx + 1 to |dNPS| do
 4:     qLCCS[1] = qLPS[qIdx]; qNCCS[1] = qNPS[qIdx]
 5:     dLCCS[1] = dLPS[dIdx]; dNCCS[1] = dNPS[dIdx]
 6:     for j = qIdx + 1 to |qNPS| do
 7:         if inSubTree then Seq = TEMP
 8:         else Seq = CCS
 9:         end if
10:         if qLPS[j] = dLPS[i] then M
11:         else M̄
12:         end if
13:         if qNCCS[|qNCCS|] > qNPS[j] then q ↓
14:         else q ↑
15:         end if
16:         if dNCCS[|dNCCS|] > dNPS[i] then d ↓
17:         else d ↑
18:         end if
19:         case
20:             M/q ↑ /d ↑: i, j, Seq ← lccsAppendNode(i, j, Seq)
21:             M/q ↑ /d ↓: i ← skipSubTree(i, dNPS)
22:             M/q ↓ /d ↑: j ← skipSubTree(j, qNPS)
23:             M/q ↓ /d ↓: i, j ← pathFinder(i, j, Desc)
24:             M̄/q ↑ /d ↑: i, j ← pathFinder(i, j, Asc)
25:             M̄/q ↑ /d ↓: i ← skipSubTree(i, dNPS)
26:             M̄/q ↓ /d ↑: j ← skipSubTree(j, qNPS)
27:             M̄/q ↓ /d ↓: i, j ← pathFinder(i, j, Desc)
28:         end case
29:     end for
30:     maximalCheck()
31:     scoreNRank(k, CCS)
32:     initializeVars(TEMP, CCS)
33:     (dIdx, qIdx) ← pathInit(dIdx + 1, qIdx + 1)
34:     i ← dIdx
35: end for
```

3.1 Finding Top K Sequences

Our algorithm takes the labeled and numbered Prüfer sequences of query and document (qLPS, dLPS, qNPS, dNPS) as input, and outputs top K matches, as presented in Algorithm 1.

To start the search, we first invoke procedure *pathInit* (Alg 1: line 2) to find a "seed", which is an tree edge, or equivalently, a subsequence of length two in document and query sequences that match labels and have an ascending path direction. We only need to consider ascending paths since they are inherently connected, and every descending path has a corresponding ascending path to reconnect to a root of the subtree.

Procedure *pathInit* (refer to Algorithm 4) starts with finding an initial consecutive node pair in an ascending path ($dNPS[i + 1] > dNPS[i]$) in the document sequence from a given starting index (dIdx). Then it searches the query sequence from a given starting index (qIdx) for an ascending pair ($qNPS[j + 1] > qNPS[j]$) with matching labels ($dLPS[i] = qLPS[j]$ and $dLPS[i + 1] = qLPS[j + 1]$). If no matching query node pair is found for the initial document node pair, *pathInit* advances to the next document ascending node pair and resumes the query search from the initial query start point.

Example 3.1: In Figure 1, *pathInit* finds the first document ascending node pair: $K2\text{-}B3$. Since there is no matching pair in the query sequence, it advances document index and yields next ascending node pair: $B3\text{-}A15$. This time, there is a matching node pair $B2\text{-}A8$ in query sequence that matches label and ascending path direction. So $B3\text{-}A15$ and $B2\text{-}A8$ become the initial "seed" for document and query, respectively. ■

After the initial "seed" is found, the algorithm then proceeds to a pair of nested loops (Alg 1:lines 3 & 6). The outer loop builds the longest common-connected subsequence (CCS) from the seed match. The inner loop matches document and query sequences, and advances them accordingly. We traverse document sequence in outer loop and query sequence in inner loop so that in face of a mismatch only query sequence needs to be "rewound". During the traversal, we compare the labels of the query and document nodes, and compare their numbers with respect to the last node in their corresponding sequences for path direction. We differentiate 8 possible scenarios (Alg 1:lines 20-27) based on the following three conditions of the comparisons: (a) the labels for the next document and query nodes match (M) or not($\overline{M}$); (b) document path direction is ascending ($d \uparrow$) or descending ($d \downarrow$); (c) query path direction is ascending ($q \uparrow$) or descending ($q \downarrow$).

We then take one of three possible actions to handle the above 8 cases: *appending* the nodes to CCS, if labels match and both sequences ascend; *skipping* the subtree for the sequence with a descending path, if only one sequence descends; or *finding* path for reconnecting the root of respective subtrees, if both sequences descend. These actions are illustrated next.

Appending Node. We append the current node to CCS by invoking procedure *lccsAppendNode* (Algorithm 2). This action is taken when current query and document nodes have matching labels and both are on ascending paths ($M/q \uparrow /d \uparrow$ case), representing a matching connected subtree.

Example 3.2: In Figure 2, document's edge $F13\text{-}D14$ matches query's edge $F6\text{-}D7$, and also document's edge $D14\text{-}A15$ matches query's edge $D7\text{-}A8$. ■

Skipping the Subtree. We skip the subsequence that corresponds to a subtree by invoking procedure *skipSubTree* (Algorithm 3). This action is taken if the sequences do not match path direction, indicating a mismatch of their corresponding tree structure. The sequence (document or query) that follows a descending path, leads to a subtree rooted at the prior node. The sequence that follows an ascending path, leads to

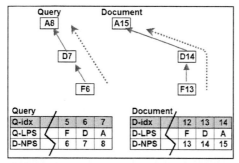

Figure 2. "*lccsAppendNode*" **procedure**

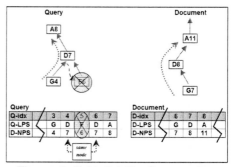

Figure 3. "*skipSubTree*" **procedure**

the parent node. In this case, the algorithm searches for a possible structure match after skipping the subtree of the descending sequence. To identify the subtree, we notice that for every descending path in a Prüfer sequence, there is an ascending path that reconnects to the root of the subtree, forming a closed loop. Therefore the algorithm records the NPS value of the current node in the descending sequence, and advance the sequence until this NPS value is re-encountered.

Example 3.3: In Figure 3, $G4$-$D7$ of query matches with $G7$-$D8$ of document. However, the next node after $G4$-$D7$ in the query sequence, node $F6$, leads to a descending path. While the next node after $G7$-$D8$ in the document sequence, node $A11$, leads to an ascending path. As such, we skip the query subtree rooted at node $D7$. The algorithm records the NPS value 7, and advances the query sequence till the node with the same NPS value is reached, i.e. node $qIdx[6]$. Although the subtree in Figure 3 has only one node, the same principle applies to a subtree of any size. ∎

Finding a Reconnecting Path. We find a matching subsequence within document and query subtrees by invoking procedure *pathFinder* in Algorithm 5. This action is taken when the document and query sequences both follow a descending path direction, indicating that the next node in the sequence is the leftmost node in the subtree rooted at the current node. *pathFinder* searches for common subsequences in these subtrees and ensures that the found common subsequences correspond to a connected tree structure.

This search can be reduced to original problem of finding matching sequences in document and query trees, except that we limit the seed search and appending node to common connected sequence within the boundaries of a subtree and with the constraint that the last node in the common subsequence must contain the root nodes to ensure connectedness. Two stacks are used (qStack and dStack) to record the NPS values of query and document subtree root nodes (named as *pivot nodes*, pNodes), respectively. When the query and document sequences simultaneously descend into subtrees, the algorithm recursively treats the subtrees

and pushes the root nodes onto stacks. The common sequence found in a subtree is recorded in temporary variable TEMP (Alg 5:lines 4-8). If the found common subsequence is connected to the corresponding pNodes at the top of the stacks, then it is appended to the current CCS. We clear off a pivot node that was added to the stacks after its subtree has been traversed.

Example 3.4: Figure 4 illustrates *pathFinder* in two cases. First case, shown in Figure 4(a), after $B3$-$A15$ and $B2$-$A8$ are found, their next corresponding nodes, $H5$ and $G4$ simultaneously follow descending paths into subtrees. *pathFinder* records NPS values of current nodes, 15 and 8, in respective stacks, and proceeds to search for a common subsequence within the subtrees that contain $H5$ and $G4$, rooted at $A15$ and $A8$. *pathInit* is invoked to find a seed in the subtrees, document's $G7$-$D8$ and query's $G4$-$D7$. Then the seed is extended by *lccsAppendNode* to $G7$-$D8$-$A11$ and $G4$-$D7$-$A8$. Looking at document and query stacks, we find that query subsequence connects to root of the subtree:$A8$; while the document subsequence does not connect to root of the subtree:$A15$. This indicates matching document sequence does not correspond to connected subtree; hence this match is discarded.

Then *pathFinder* identifies no valid matches in the current subtrees rooted at $A8$ and $A15$ and advances the document sequence to the next node beyond the subtree, $F13$, resets the query sequence index to the previous match node $G4$, and clears the stacks. This corresponds to the second case, shown in Figure 4(b). The current nodes $F13$ and $G4$ simultaneously follow descending paths into subtrees. *pathFinder* finds matching subsequences $F13$-$D14$-$A15$ and $F6$-$D7$-$A8$ in the subtrees rooted at $A15$ and $A8$, respectively. Since both subsequences simultaneously reach the roots of corresponding subtrees, they are appended to the current CCS, and we have $B3$-$A15$-$F13$-$D14$-$A15$ and $B2$-$A8$-$F6$-$D7$-$A8$ ∎

Exit from inner loop (Alg 1:line 29) indicates a complete traversal of the query sequence. Now we check whether the newly found CCS has already been found using *maximalCheck*. Then *scoreNRank* procedure ranks this CCS and records it if it is among the top K results. All intermediate variables are cleared using *initializeVars*, document sequence is advanced, and the search for a new "seed" starts.

Algorithm 2 $lccsAppendNode(dIdx, qIdx, Seq)$

1: $docPopFlag \leftarrow false; qryPopFlag \leftarrow false$
2: **if** $dNPS[dIdx] = dStack.top()$ **then** $docPopFlag \leftarrow true$
3: **end if**
4: **if** $qNPS[qIdx] = qStack.top()$ **then** $qryPopFlag \leftarrow true$
5: **end if**
6: **if** $docPopFlag \wedge qryPopFlag$ **then** $dStack.pop(); qStack.pop()$
7: **end if**
8: **if** $docPopFlag = qryPopFlag$ **then**
9:   **if** $stacksempty$ **then** $InSubTree \leftarrow false$
10:   **end if**
11:   $dLSeq.append(dLPS[dIdx]); dNSeq.append(dNPS[dIdx])$
12:   $qLSeq.append(qLPS[qIdx]); qNSeq.append(qNPS[qIdx])$
13:   $dIdx \leftarrow dIdx + 1$
14: **else**
15:   $dIdx, qIdx \leftarrow pathFinder(dIdx, qIdx, "Asc")$
16: **end if**
17: **return** dIdx,qIdx,Seq

Algorithm 3 $skipSubTree(dqIndex, dqNPS)$

1: $skipVal \leftarrow dqNPS[dqIndex - 1]$
2: $dqIndex \leftarrow dqIndex + 1$
3: **while** $dqNPS[dqIndex] \leq skipVal \wedge dqIndex < dqNPS.size()$ **do**
4:   $dqIndex \leftarrow dqIndex + 1$
5: **end while**
6: **return** dqIndex

Algorithm 4 $pathInit(dIdx, qIdx)$

1: **if** $stack\ empty$ **then** $doc/qryStopIndex \leftarrow last\ doc/qIdx$
2: **else** $doc/qryStopIndex \leftarrow doc/qryTopOfStack$
3: **end if**
4: $i \leftarrow dIdx; j \leftarrow qIdx$
5: **while** $i < docStopIndex$ **do**
6:   **if** $document\ ascending\ wrt\ next\ node$ **then**
7:     **while** $j < qryStopIndex$ **do**
8:       **if** $query\ label\ =\ document\ label\ \wedge\ next\ query\ label\ =\ next\ document\ label\ \wedge\ query\ ascending\ wrt\ next\ node$ **then return** i, j
9:       **end if**
10:       $j \leftarrow j + 1$
11:     **end while**
12:   **end if**
13:   $i \leftarrow i + 1; j \leftarrow qIdx$
14: **end while**
15: **return** i,j

3.2 Ranking top K Sequences

A top K longest subsequence between query and document can be shorter than the original query sequence. We call each matching query subsequence as *modified query*, and record the number of deletions required to convert the query to a modified query as *edit cost*. We have shown that the matching document subsequence and modified query sequence are *connected*, *gap consistent* and *frequency consistent* in [1]. This

---

Algorithm 5 $pathFinder(dIdx, qIdx, Direction)$

1: $qryPivotNode \leftarrow qNTemp[|qNTemp|]$
2: $docPivotNode \leftarrow dNTemp[|dNTemp|]$
3: **if** $Direction = "Desc"$ **then**
4:   **if** $InSubTree$ **then**
5:     $qLTemp[1] = qLPS[qIdx]$
6:     $qNTemp[1] = qNPS[qIdx]$
7:     $dLTemp[1] = dLPS[dIdx]$
8:     $dNTemp[1] = dNPS[dIdx]$
9:     $qStack.push(qNCCS[|qNCCS|])$
10:     $dStack.push(dNCCS[|dNCCS|])$
11:   **end if**
12:   $InSubTree \leftarrow TRUE$
13:   **if** $qLTemp[|qLTemp|] < qryTopOfStack \wedge dLTemp[|dLTemp|] < docTopOfStack$ **then**
14:     $qStack.push(qLTemp[|qLtemp|])$
15:     $dStack.push(dLTemp[|dLTemp|])$
16:   **end if**
17:   $docReStart, qryReStart \leftarrow pathInit(dIdx, qIdx)$
18:   **return** $docReStart, qryReStart$
19: **else**
20:   **if** $InSubTree$ **then**
21:     $docReStart, qryReStart \leftarrow pathInit(docReStart + 1, qryReStart + 1)$
22:     **return** $docReStart, qryReStart$
23:   **else**
24:     **return** $dIdx, |qNPS|$
25:   **end if**
26: **end if**

---

guarantees that a sequence match corresponds to a valid tree structure match. Therefore, the ranking scheme for partial matches is based on the edit cost (the cost of node deletion) between the original query sequence and the modified one.

Example 3.5: In Figure 1, for the seed match $B2$-$A8$ in the query and $B3$-$A15$ in the document, Algorithm 1 retrieves the CCS $B2$-$A8$-$F6$-$D7$-$A8$ and $B3$-$A15$-$F13$-$D14$-$A15$, which represent valid subtree match. This matching sequence has an edit cost of 2 with the original query sequence. Then the control is returned to the outer loop which invokes *pathInit* (Alg 1:line 33) and finds the next seed, query's $G4$-$D7$ and document's $G7$-$D8$. Then another valid subsequence match, $G4$-$D7$-$A8$ and $G7$-$D8$-$A11$, is found with an edit cost of 4, which has a lower rank than the previous CCS. ∎

4 Experiments

XFinder is implemented in Java. To evaluate XFinder, we compare it with another two approaches[4]: tree matching approach [13], referred as "Tree-Edit Distance approach" henceforth and a Baseline approach for reducing approximate tree pattern matching to subsequence matching. The Baseline approach first computes all the common subsequences (of length greater than or equal to 2) between XML document and query. It then filters out matching subsequences

---

[4]Since the implementations of [10, 2, 16] are not available, we didn't make a comparison with them

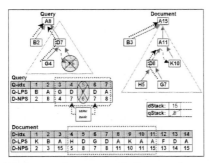

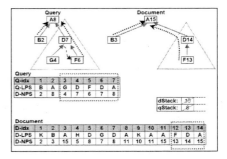

(a) pathFinder - subsequence finds no path to root A15   (b) pathFinder - subsequence finds path to roots A8/A15

Figure 4. *"pathFinder"* **procedure**

that do not correspond to valid tree structures by checking connectedness, gap consistency and frequency consistency. Similar as XFinder, valid subsequences are ranked and the top K ones are output. Notice that XFinder returns the same set of top K matches as the Baseline approach. However, XFinder pushes the tree validity check during the common subsequence search to improve efficiency. We do not include XML tree parsing time while clocking the execution time for a fair comparison with Tree-Edit Distance approach[5] and use an in-memory representation for the XML document/query trees.

Both synthetic and real-world datasets are tested of size from 0.5MB-5.0MB, in 0.5MB increments. Synthetic dataset is generated using XMark[6] XML data generator. DBLP[7] is used as real-world dataset.

Ten queries were designed for each dataset with different sizes as well as different numbers of node matches, as listed in [1]. For first five queries with increasing size, the number of nodes in the query that have data matches remains same, while the number of unmatched query nodes are increased. The remaining fives queries are opposite.

4.1 Experimental Results

Figures 5 through 7 show execution time comparison among XFinder, Tree-Edit Distance and Baseline approach on both DBLP and XMark datasets. Here the execution time is presented in log (to the base 10) scale due to the large difference in execution time of these three approaches. Three sets of experiments are performed, with varying document size, varying query size and varying K for returning top K query results, respectively, to test the effect of each parameter.

Increasing Data Size. Figure 5(a), 5(b) shows query execution time of XFinder, Tree-Edit Distance

and Baseline approach for DBLP dataset when document size increases for queries Q1 and Q5, respectively, (K=1). Performance comparisons for other queries are similar, as shown in [1]. Both Tree-Edit Distance and Baseline approaches run out of memory after 1.0MB and 3.5MB document size, respectively, for Q1 and Q5. The time required by Tree-Edit Distance approach is more than 2 orders of magnitude than that of XFinder, and slope of its curve is also steeper than that of XFinder. Baseline approach is slower than Tree-Edit Distance and much slower than XFinder, with a higher value of the slope of the curve. This is due to the expensive matching step of computing all possible common subsequences between an XML document and a tree pattern query, followed by the filtering step of checking and removing invalid sequences. Similar behavior is observed when we compared XFinder with Tree-Edit Distance and Baseline approaches for XMark dataset as document size increases for queries Q11 and Q15, as presented in Figure 5(c), 5(d).

Increasing Query Size. Figures 6(a), 6(b) and 6(c),6(d) show the execution time of XFinder, Tree-Edit Distance and Baseline approaches for DBLP and XMark dataset, respectively, as the query size increases for fixed document size (100KB), K=1. Particularly, in Figure 6(a) and Figure 6(c) as the query size increases, the number of unmatched query nodes increases, while the number of matched query nodes stays the same. While in Figure 6(b) and Figure 6(d), as the query size increases, only the number of matching query nodes increase. The execution time of XFinder and Tree-Edit Distance only increases a little as the query size increases, while the Baseline approach has a larger increase due to a large number of false positive matches. Again, XFinder is much faster than the other two approaches.

Both Tree-Edit Distance and Baseline approach are more sensitive to the increase in XML document size when compared against XFinder. XFinder may look more sensitive to the increase in query size as compared to Tree-Edit Distance. However, the slope of the curve

---

[5]Tree-Edit Distance approach does not include XML tree parsing time in their execution time.

[6]http://monetdb.cwi.nl/xml/index.html, uses auction DTD

[7]http://www.cs.washington.edu/research/xmldatasets/

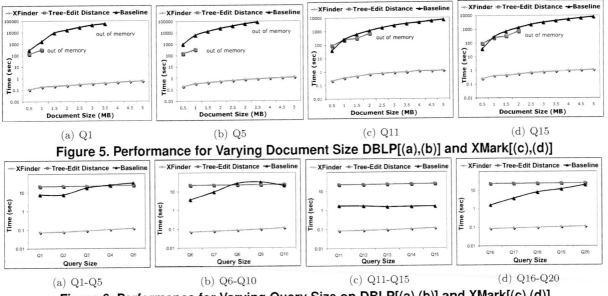

(a) Q1   (b) Q5   (c) Q11   (d) Q15

Figure 5. Performance for Varying Document Size DBLP[(a),(b)] and XMark[(c),(d)]

(a) Q1-Q5   (b) Q6-Q10   (c) Q11-Q15   (d) Q16-Q20

Figure 6. Performance for Varying Query Size on DBLP[(a),(b)] and XMark[(c),(d)]

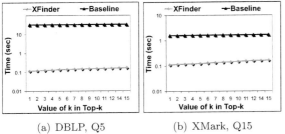

(a) DBLP, Q5   (b) XMark, Q15

Figure 7. Performance with Varying K

is low and in practice the size of a user query is small.

Increasing the Number of Results. Figure 7(a), 7(b) show the running time when K ranges from 1 to 15 for fixed DBLP and XMark document of size $100KB$, and fixed query $Q5$ and $Q15$, respectively. Since Tree-Edit Distance approach only returns the best match between XML document and query (K=1) by computing the minimum number of operations required to transform the document to the query, we only compared the performance between XFinder and Baseline approach. As we can see, Baseline approach stays constant. This is because irrespective of the value of K, all common subsequences are computed, which is the most expensive task, then top K valid sequences are output. While the execution time of XFinder increases slowly and linearly with respect to K. This behavior is very desirable since K is often small, and computing only the top K sequences without generating all the common subsequences is much more efficient.

Verifying Correctness. We record the number of common subsequences found by Baseline approach and the number of valid sequences among them. We also record the number of matches reported by XFinder. For DBLP dataset, Figure 7(a), Baseline approach gen-

erates 623 common subsequences, out of which 15 are valid. XFinder finds all 15 valid subsequences without generating any invalid subsequences if we set $K \geq 15$. For XMark dataset, Figure 7(b), Baseline approach generates 44 common subsequences, out of which 16 are valid. Again, XFinder finds all 16 valid subsequences without generating invalid subsequences if we set $K \geq 16$. This shows that XFinder is very efficient in computing top K query matches by avoiding large intermediate result generation, without compromising search quality.

5 Related Work

Several efforts have been made for supporting approximate XML query processing. [16] proposed FleX-Path to search approximate matches by query relaxation. Later, *Whirlpool* [8] was proposed for adaptive join order evaluation. Ranking schemes inspired by *tf-idf* are used to rank join predicates and to adaptively select the best join order. However, the size of the relaxed query can be exponential to the original query, and decomposing a query to sub-queries followed by joins can generate large intermediate results. TWIX [2] assigns a unique label to each node in the tree and uses string alignment for structural matching. A bottom-up breadth-first search is explored using the matched leaves as initial points and the tree matches are ranked based on tree edit distance. On the other hand, XFinder employs a bottom-up depth-first search looking for similar "path-structures" in the query and document. TreeSketch [10] uses the notion of graph synopsis to estimate the selectivity of XML twigs and compute approximate query answers. It finds all possible match results based on the synopsis of XML document. In contrast XFinder produces top K query results from the document itself. TopX [14] computes approximate matches based on pre-computed index lists for individual tag-term content conditions. XFinder reduces approximate tree matching problem to subsequence matching, where tree validity check is pushed inside subsequence matching.

Another line of research finds similarity between two trees of comparable size. [13] proposed approximate tree matching based on edit distance, i.e., the number of insertion, deletion and relabel operations needed to convert one tree to the other. Due to its high computational complexity, a lot of research approximates the tree edit distance metrics. [5] handles approximate matching in terms of joins, such that two trees that are at most τ tree edit distance apart are considered as matches. [7] proposed algorithms to compute lower bound to tree edit distance using a variety of refinements like maximum leaf path histogram, degree of nodes-histogram and content histogram. Top K documents are picked based on these preliminary scores and tree-edit distance is computed for result ranking. [17] proposed a lower bound to tree-edit distance for ordered XML documents by extending q-grams from string edit distance domain. [4] approximates tree edit distance by emphasizing more on the structure of the tree, e.g. deleting a leaf node is less significant than deleting a non-leaf node. The tree similarity approach assigns a score to a tree depending on its similarity with the other tree. This requires the two trees to be of comparable size. Whereas, XFinder searches for similar query tree patterns in one or more, much larger XML tree(s) and assigns a score depending on the extent of match.

6   Conclusions

In this paper, we present XFinder, a system for approximate tree pattern matching on ordered XML data. It reduces the problem of approximate tree pattern matching to a simpler problem: finding common subsequences in the sequences converted from data and query, which can be more efficiently evaluated. However, not all common subsequences represent valid tree matches. XFinder pushes the tree validity checking into sequence matching stage to achieve performance speedup. Experiments show that XFinder has substantial performance improvement over an existing approach [13] and a baseline approach. As a future initiative, we are extending XFinder by exploiting various indexing schemes which are critical for querying very large XML documents.

References

[1] N. Agarwal, M. Galan, and Y. Chen. Approximate Structural Matching over XML Documents. Technical report, Arizona State University, 2006.

[2] S.A. Aghili, H. Li, D. Agrawal, and A. El Abbadi. TWIX: Twig Structure and Content Matching of Selective Queries using Binary Labeling. In *Proceedings of INFOSCALE*, 2006.

[3] S. Agrawal, S. Chaudhuri, G. Das, and A. Gionis. Automated Ranking of Database Query Results. In *Proceedings of CIDR*, 2003.

[4] N. Augsten, M. Böhlen, and J. Gamper. Approximate matching of hierarchical data using pq-grams. In *Proceedings of VLDB*, 2005.

[5] S. Guha, H. V. Jagadish, N. Koudas, D. Srivastava, and T. Yu. Approximate XML joins. In *Proceedings of SIGMOD*, pages 287–298, 2002.

[6] S. Guha, R. Rastogi, and K. Shim. ROCK: A Robust Clustering Algorithm for Categorical Attributes. *Information Systems*, 25(5):345–366, 2000.

[7] K. Kailing, H. P. Kriegel, S. Schfnauer, and T. Seidl. Efficient Similarity Search for Hierarchical Data in Large Databases. In *Proceedings of EDBT*, 2004.

[8] A. Marian, S. A. Yahia, N. Koudas, and D. Srivastava. Adaptive Processing of Top-k Queries in XML. In *Proceedings of ICDE*, 2005.

[9] U. Nambiar and S. Kambhampati. Answering Imprecise Queries over Autonomous Web Databases. In *ICDE*, 2006.

[10] N. Polyzotis, M. Garofalakis, and Y. Ioannidis. Approximate XML Query Answers. In *SIGMOD*, 2004.

[11] H. Prüfer. Neuer Beweis eines Satzes über Permutationen. *Archiv für Mathematik and Physik*, 27:142–144, 1918.

[12] P. Rao and B. Moon. PRIX: Indexing and querying XML using Prfer sequences. In *Proceedings of ICDE*, 2004.

[13] D. Shasha and K. Zhang. Approximate Tree Pattern Matching. In *Pattern Matching Algorithms*. Oxford University Press, 1997.

[14] M. Theobald, R. Schenkel, and G. Weikum. An efficient and versatile query engine for TopX search. In *Proceedings of VLDB*, 2005.

[15] S. A. Yahia, N. Koudas, A. Marian, D. Srivastava, and D. Toman. Structure and Content Scoring for XML. In *Proceedings of VLDB*, 2005.

[16] S. A. Yahia, Laks V. S. Lakshmanan, and S. Pandit. FleXPath: Flexible Structure and Full-text Querying for XML. In *Proceedings of SIGMOD*, 2004.

[17] R. Yang, P. Kalnis, and A. K. H. Tung. Similarity Evaluation on Tree-Structured Data. In *SIGMOD*, 2005.

Avoiding Infinite Blocking of Mobile Transactions

Sebastian Obermeier
University of Paderborn, Fürstenallee 11
33102 Paderborn, Germany
so @ upb.de

Stefan Böttcher
University of Paderborn, Fürstenallee 11
33102 Paderborn, Germany
stb @ upb.de

Abstract

When a transaction commit decision is lost or delayed in a mobile network, most transaction protocols cannot terminate the transaction and delay conflicting transactions. In contrast to this, we present a concept called Bi-State-Termination (BST) that allows transactions to terminate into two states: one state having the changes applied, and the other state having the transaction aborted. Conflicting transactions that work on these states are not blocked. We prove that BST guarantees atomicity and serializability, and describe a possible implementation using version numbers. Furthermore, our experimental results show that BST is feasibility for mobile networks, and that it enhances the transaction throughput whenever transactions are blocked for a long time.

1. Introduction

Whenever transaction processing is necessary within mobile applications, the fulfillment of the ACID properties is crucial for maintaining data integrity and consistency. Each time a transaction involves more than one site, e.g. if a mobile network serves as a distributed database, the transaction atomicity property guarantees that either all sub-transactions that belong to a global transaction are executed, or no sub-transaction is executed. To ensure this atomicity property, atomic commit protocols, like 2PC [9], 3PC [19], or Paxos Commit [10], and a lot of other protocols and variations (e.g. [2], [14], or [17]) are used. However, these protocols require that either a database checks whether or not the transaction can be processed and then sends a binding commit message, or the protocols require that transactions must be compensated later on if some databases cannot execute the transaction.

We will not focus on protocols based on compensation for the following reason. If a network contains mobile participants, there is no guarantee that a compensating transaction will be received by the destined database. This means that a database may contain inconsistent data, but has no knowledge of this state. Furthermore, the database may participate in other transactions that are based upon this inconsistent data. This means, the state of inconsistency is passed on to other participants. Since this "chain of inconsistency" may be arbitrarily long and compensation is not possible if participants cannot be reached, e.g. if the network is partitioned, protocols relying on compensation cannot guarantee atomicity in each and every situation. For this reason, we focus on protocols where a database is required to vote on a transaction, and wait for the instruction to commit or abort the transaction, e.g. 2PC. However, in 2PC and other protocols, the vote (for commit) message is a proposal to commit the transaction if the coordinator decides so. If this vote message has been sent, the database cannot commit a second transaction that depends on the pending one. If in a such case, the commit decision is delayed or cannot be obtained due to coordinator failure, the database must not process a depending transaction, but block the data as long as a decision on the pending transaction has been made.

1.1. Contributions

The main contributions of this paper are:

- We propose a transaction protocol that does not require compensation but allows a database maintaining control of its resources during the whole transaction execution.

- We present a transaction model, which distinguishes two coordination points in transaction execution time: a lock point, which is the point in time where each sub-transaction that belongs to a global transaction has acquired all necessary locks, and a commit point, which is the point where the transaction is committed. In contrast to other protocols, our protocol takes advantage of the separation of the lock point from the commit point.

- Based on our transaction model, we present a locking-based protocol that guarantees atomicity and serializability, and that allows databases to release locks of non-proceeding transactions at any point in time:

  - When a resource R has been locked for a transaction T that does not proceed, the database can,

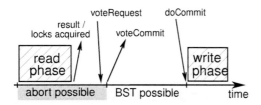

Figure 1. 2PC Transaction Execution

as long as it has not voted for commit, release the lock for R and abort T.

  - After the database has voted for commit of a transaction T, T does not prevent the processing of concurrent depending transactions even if these transactions require conflicting locks. Instead, the database is allowed to release some or all locks of T under certain conditions, which we call *Bi-State-Termination*.

- We explain a concrete implementation of Bi-State-Termination and show how the database processes a transaction T_c that depends on a transaction T_w, while T_w waits for the commit decision.

- We give experimental results that demonstrate the feasibility of Bi-State-Termination in environments where the commit decision may get lost.

2. Transaction Model

Above the time line, Figure 1 shows the standard application of 2PC for a distributed transaction T when a locking mechanism like 2-Phase-Locking [8] is used. Below the time line, Figure 1 illustrates the possible database reactions in case the database does not receive expected messages after a timeout. As long as the database has not voted for commit, it can still abort T and release the locks. Different from traditional 2PC, our protocol allows *Bi-State-Termination* (BST) to terminate a transaction even after the commit vote has been sent. Before we explain BST, we first point out the transaction model.

- T consists of a *read-phase* and a *write phase*.

- During T's read-phase, the database obtains required locks and stores the results of each write operation in its own *private transaction storage*. If any required lock cannot be obtained during the read phase of T since the lock is held by a transaction U, the database has the following possibilities:

  - abort T,
  - wait until U releases the lock,
  - try to abort U, which may not be possible if the database has already voted for the commit of U.

- After the successful execution of T's read-phase, the database sends the result of T to the initiator of the transaction. Then, the initiator collects the results of all transactions belonging to the same global transaction, and starts the commit protocol by notifying the commit coordinator when all results are present.

- The commit coordinator requests the binding commit votes of all participants, and decides for commit when all votes have arrived and are votes for commit. Otherwise, if at least one vote is abort or if a certain time has passed, the coordinator decides for abort.

- When the database receives the doCommit command for T, the write phase is executed. The write phase makes the private transaction storage visible and lets the database release all locks hold for T. If the command was an abort, the database deletes the private transaction storage and releases the locks as well.

The transaction execution involves two messages showing that the locked point was reached: Both the voteRequest message and the doCommit message indicate that all databases obtained all necessary locks. However, for the purpose of ensuring serializability, it is only necessary to reach this locked point once, as protocol optimizations like "unsolicited vote optimization" [21] show.

When we look at Figure 1, we can see that the transaction sequence is already fixed after the voteRequest message has been received by each database, and therefore serializability is guaranteed. However, for ensuring transaction atomicity and validity of the read-phase, each database must hold all locks until the doCommit message is received and the write phase has been finished. Unfortunately, if the doCommit message is lost or cannot reach a database, the database must hold the locks and cannot abort the transaction on its own, which however is possible before the vote for commit message has been sent.

In the remainder of this paper, we develop a solution that not only unblocks and processes concurrent and depending transactions if the commit decision cannot be received by a database for a longer period of time. Our solution, which is called *Bi-State-Termination* (BST) of a transaction T_w, also guarantees atomicity. The main idea of BST is that if the coordinator's decision for a transaction T_w is delayed, a concurrent transaction T_c depending on T_w can be processed by first transferring the required locks from T_w to T_c, and second by executing T_c on two database states: one state having T_w committed, the other state having T_w aborted.

However, it is the database's choice whether or not and after which timeout it applies BST.

3. Definition of Underlying Concepts

Definition 3.1 A *distributed global transaction* consists of a series of read and write operations executed at different sites, each of which returns a result, e.g. a concrete return value or a successful/unsuccessful result. We call the parts of a distributed global transaction that are executed at each site *transactions*. Furthermore, we consider database *triggers* and *consistency checks* that are executed due to the transaction also as belonging to the transaction.

Definition 3.2 Assume, a transaction T is executed on a database in state S_0 that is created by previous transactions. Then, we call $\mathsf{Result}_T(S_0)$ the result value that is returned to the initiator.

Definition 3.3 Two operations O_i and O_j conflict $\iff$ $\exists$ tuple t $\exists$ attribute $a(O_i$ accesses $t.a \land O_j$ accesses $t.a \land ((O_i$ writes $t.a) \lor (O_j$ writes $t.a))$

Definition 3.4 A transaction T_j depends on T_i if and only if on a database D at least one operation O_i of T_i conflicts with an operation O_j of T_j, and O_i precedes O_j.

Definition 3.5 The *serialization graph* of a set of transactions contains the transactions as nodes and a directed edge $T_i \to T_j$ for each pair (T_i, T_j) of transactions for which T_j depends on T_i.

Serializability requires the serialization graph of all committed transactions to be acyclic.

We want to achieve that all transactions belonging to a distributed global transactions are executed in an atomic fashion, and that each concurrent execution of different distributed global transactions is serializable, i.e. the execution produces the same output and has the same effect on the databases as some serial execution of the same distributed global transactions.

Definition 3.6 Assume, a database is in a state S_0 that has been created by some previous transactions, before the write phase of T is executed. Assuming no concurrent transaction has changed the database state while T is executed, we call the database state that is caused by the write phase of T the state S_T. Furthermore, we call the modifications done by T's write phase on the database the *delta of the transaction T based on the state S_0*, i.e. $\Delta_T(S_0)$. When $\Delta_T(S_0)$ based on S_0 becomes visible for other transactions, we get the new database state S_T, for which we write $S_T = S_0 \oplus \Delta_T(S_0)$.

Lemma 3.7 *Assume, a database is in state S_0, a transaction T is executed, and a concurrent transaction U is started, but U does not depend on T, and vice versa. Therefore, the changes of transaction U do not affect the execution of the transaction T. The equations*

$$\Delta_U(S_0) = \Delta_U(S_T) \quad and \quad \Delta_T(S_0) = \Delta_T(S_U)$$

hold, which means that the modifications of a transaction U are independent of any previous modification of a non-dependent transaction T, and vice versa.

Proof Assume the database state before the execution of T and U is S_0.

$$
\begin{aligned}
& U \text{ does not depend on } T \text{ and} \\
& J \text{ does not depend on } T \\
\iff\ & \forall \text{ tuple } t\ \forall \text{ attribute } a\ (\neg O_i \text{ accesses } t.a \\
& \lor \neg O_j \text{ accesses } t.a \\
& \lor (O_i \text{ reads } t.a \land O_j \text{ read } t.a)) \\
\implies\ & S_0 \oplus \Delta_T(S_0) \oplus \Delta_U(S_T) \\
& = S_0 \oplus \Delta_U(S_0) \oplus \Delta_T(S_U) \\
\implies\ & (\Delta_U(S_0) = \Delta_U(S_T)) \land (\Delta_T(S_0) = \Delta_T(s_U))
\end{aligned}
$$

Therefore, whenever a set BT of transactions is blocked, the result of a transaction T may only be influenced by those transactions $DBT \subseteq BT$, which are dependent of T or on which T is dependent.

4. Infinite Blocking Problem Description

We first give *two* definitions for different kinds of blocking and show the effects that these kinds of blocking have on other transactions.

Definition 4.1 *Protocol blocking* occurs, if during an execution of an atomic commit protocol for a transaction T the following situation occurs: an arbitrary sequence of failures leads to a situation where the atomic commit protocol instance cannot terminate with a unique commit or abort decision d.

Example 4.2 *Assume, the coordinator and one database fail in 2PC after all databases voted commit, but before a commit decision was sent out by the coordinator. In this situation, the protocol blocks since it cannot give a decision on the transactions fate, since the remaining databases do not know the vote of the disconnected database.*

If the coordinator is still alive and only databases disconnect, the protocol is not blocked since the coordinator can immediately decide on the transaction (but may first wait a certain time for the failed database to reconnect).

If network partitioning may occur, [20] proved that there is no non-blocking commit protocol (blocking in the sense of definition 4.1). However, the following definition shows, that in consequence of protocol blocking a more serious problem arises, which has an effect on concurrent transactions.

Definition 4.3 We call a *transaction T blocked*, if a database proposed to execute T (e.g. by sending a voteCommit message) and waits for the final decision, but cannot abort or commit T on its own.

Note that transaction blocking means the unilateral impossibility to abort or commit a transaction, but does *not* mean that a transaction U waits until it gets necessary locks from a concurrent transaction, since in this case U can be aborted by the database itself.

Example 4.4 *Assume, 2PC is used and no problems occur. In this situation, transaction blocking occurs at all participating databases for a short period of time, namely within the time interval between the sending of the vote message and the receiving of the commit or abort message.*

While protocol blocking does not necessarily prevent the possibility of an unilateral abort by some of the databases, transaction blocking has an effect on concurrent transactions: they cannot be processed until the final commit decision is received.

One might think that time-out based approaches solve this problem. However, if we add a time-limit for the commit decision, then the scenario fulfills the requirements of the coordinated attack scenario [9], in which the commit decision is that two generals use an unreliable communication channel to agree on a time for a common attack. For this scenario, [9] proves that a commit decision is not possible under the assumption that message loss may occur. The conclusion of this coordinated attack scenario is that the use of time-out votes (e.g. "my commit vote is valid until 3:23:34") does not allow the databases to unilaterally abort the transaction, and therefore does not solve the problem of infinite transaction blocking.

5. Solution

In the following, we focus on the question:

> What can a database D executing a transaction U do, when U is blocked, and a concurrent transaction T requests access to data tuples of T in a conflicting way.

A proposed solution to answer this question can be found in standard literature for databases, and is quite simple: wait. Unfortunately, waiting can be very long, and the number of concurrent transactions that wait may increase if the blocking continues. Another possibility is to abort the concurrent transaction T. Although correct, this behavior is not satisfying.

Our solution called *Bi-State-Termination* is based on the following observation: whenever transaction blocking occurs, the database does not know whether a transaction U waiting for the commit decision will be aborted or committed. However, only if the transaction is committed, the database state changes. Let S_0 denote the database state before U was executed. Although the database does not know the commit decision for U, it knows for sure that either S_0 or $S_0 \oplus \Delta_U(S_0)$ is the correct database state, depending on the commitment of U. Figure 2 shows these two possible states in the tree at Level 1. With this knowledge, the database can try to execute a concurrent conflicting transaction T on both states S_0 and $S_0 \oplus \Delta_U(S_0)$. Whenever the two executions of T on S_0 and on $S_0 \oplus \Delta_U(S_0)$ return the same results to the Initiator, i.e. $\mathsf{Result}_T(S_0) =$

$\mathsf{Result}_T(S_U)$, T can be committed regardless of U, even though they are conflicting. Otherwise it is the application's choice whether it handles two possible transaction results. However, since U and T are depending, we might have $\Delta_T(S_0) \neq \Delta_T(S_U)$. Therefore, the database must store both deltas $\Delta_T(S_0)$ and $\Delta_T(S_U)$, and if T commits before U is committed or aborted, the database knows that either the state $S_0 \oplus \Delta_T(S_0)$ is valid, or the state $S_0 \oplus \Delta_U(S_0) \oplus \Delta_T(S_U)$. Figure 2 shows the execution tree with both U and T being blocked. The leaves represent the database states that may be valid depending on the decisions for the blocked transactions U and T.

5.1. Bi-State-Termination

Let $\Sigma = \{S_0, \dots, S_k\}$ be the set of all legal possible database states for a database D. A *traditional transaction* T is a function $T : \Sigma \mapsto \Sigma$, $S_a \rightarrow S_b$, which means the resulting state S_b of T depends only on the state S_a on which T is executed on.

A *Bi-State-Terminated transaction* T is a function $BST : 2^\Sigma \mapsto 2^\Sigma$,

$$\underbrace{\{S_i, \dots, S_j\}}_{\text{Initial States}} \rightarrow \underbrace{\{S_i, \dots, S_j\}}_{T \text{ aborts}} \cup \underbrace{\{T(S_i), \dots, T(S_j)\}}_{T \text{ commits}}$$

that maps a set $\Sigma_{\text{Initial}} \subseteq \Sigma$ of Initial States to a super set $\Sigma_{\text{Initial}} \cup \{T(S_x)|S_x \in \Sigma_{\text{Initial}}\}$ of new states, where $T(S_x)$ is the state that is reached when T is applied to S_x.

This concept of Bi-State-Termination leads to the following commit decision rules for the transaction execution of a transaction T on a database DB:

DB checks for T the dependency of concurrent blocking transactions. The following situations may occur: T is independent of all currently blocked transactions. Then, T can be executed immediately.

Otherwise, T depends on a set $\{U_1 \dots U_n\}$ of blocked transactions. As T depends on each of the transactions $U_1 \dots U_n$, each of them has reached its lock point before T, and 2-Phase-Locking guarantees serializability of $\{U_1 \dots U_n\}$, i.e. for any concurrent execution of $U_1 \dots U_n$, there is an equivalent serial execution *ESE* of $U_1 \dots U_n$ on the result of which T is executed. *ESE* can always be constructed, as it only has to reflect the order in which transactions leave the lock point, as described below. Then, DB can *Bi-State-Terminate* the transactions $U_1 \dots U_n$, and executes the transaction T on all possible up to 2^n combinations of abort and commit decisions of the transactions $\{U_1 \dots U_n\}$ in *ESE*.

The serializable sequence *ESE* of the transactions $\{U_1 \dots U_n\}$, on which the T is executed, must obey the following conditions. For each pair (U_i, U_j) of the transactions for which a dependency $U_i \rightarrow U_j$ exists, U_i left its lock point before U_j left its lock point. However, in order to execute the transaction U_j that depends on the blocked

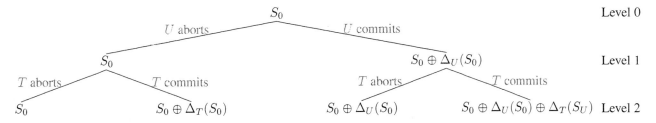

Figure 2. Possible database states if U and T conflict and block

transaction U_i, the transaction U_i must have been Bi-State-Terminated. In this case, the order $(U_i < U_j)$ is fixed.

Note that if there is no dependency $U_i \rightarrow U_j$, and no dependency $U_j \rightarrow U_i$, the execution sequence of the blocked transactions (U_i, U_j) does not matter since they are independent of each other, cf. Lemma 3.7.

This means, the transaction T must only be executed on all up to 2^n possible combinations of commit and abort of one single serializable sequence of the blocked transactions $U_1 \ldots U_n$, but not on all possible sequences (permutations) of the transactions.

If T must be executed on multiple database states, this might yield different results. Let $S_1 \ldots S_{2^n}$ be the states that can be reached by any commit/abort combination of the n transactions $\{U_1 \ldots U_n\}$ that are Bi-State-Terminated. If $\mathsf{Result}_T(S_0) = \ldots = \mathsf{Result}_T(S_{2^n})$ holds, transaction T can be committed since it has a unique result. Otherwise, the application that initiated T can choose whether

- it aborts T completely
- it commits T and deals with multiple possible results
- it aborts or commits only some transaction execution *branches* that are based on certain depending transactions. For example, the application may specify that T should only commit when U_k aborts, and that T should abort otherwise
- it waits.

When T or a single execution branch of T commits, the database merges the corresponding delta of T with the possible branch state.

Example 5.1 *Assume, T depends on U, but different from Figure 2, T should only commit when U commits, and otherwise abort. As illustrated in Figure 3, this would only affect the leftmost and rightmost branches of Figure 2. Therefore, $\Delta_U(S_0)$ in Level 1 is replaced with $(\Delta_U(S_0) \oplus \Delta_T(S_U))$ since, in this case, a commit of U means automatically a commit of T. Note that in this example, the commit decision for T is made before the decision of U is made, but the execution sequence is the other way round, namely $U < T$. Furthermore, the tree is flattened one level since only U is yet blocked.*

Figure 3. T should commit only if U commits

5.2. Complexity

It can be seen that the complexity of the execution of T depends on the number of blocked transactions b, and that our solution has a complexity of $O(2^b)$. However, our implemented solution uses a compact data structure and optimizes read and write operations in such a way that each transaction operation must only be executed once, regardless of the number of blocked transactions. Although, in the worst case, the number of tuples may grow exponentially, standard database query optimization techniques can be fully applied.

5.3. Correctness

Theorem 5.2 *Bi-State-Termination in combination with 2-Phase-Locking guarantees serializability.*

Proof As our solution uses Two-Phase Locking (2PL) and 2PL is proven to guarantee serializability according to [4], we show that Bi-State-Termination does not change the order of transactions given by 2PL: Our transaction execution involves one point, namely the lock point, where each transaction that belongs to a global transaction must hold all locks. This means, the request to vote on a transaction's commit status can only be sent by the coordinator when all databases acquired the necessary transaction locks, which the databases indicate by sending the transaction result. The sequence of transactions is fixed at that time when each transaction enters its lock point. Although Bi-State-Termination may release locks after this lock point, the release of locks does not change the order of transactions for the following reason. A transaction T that gets locks from a Bi-State-Terminated transaction U is either executed after U has been committed ($U < T$), or U is aborted.

Note that although the commit command for T may be issued before the commit command of U, the order of applying the transactions on the database is still $U < T$.

6. Implementation

We have implemented the concept of Bi-State-Termination on tuple level, i.e. our granularity level is data rows. We use version numbers for each distributed transaction and identify the private write set of a transaction by means of these version numbers. Whenever distributed transaction processing is needed, the user/application uses the Bi-State-Termination enabled distributed transaction processing API (DTP-API), the functionality of which will be explained in the following.

Our DTP-API does not only manage locking for distributed transactions, it additionally handles the private transaction spaces of distributed transactions. This gives our DTP-API the necessary functionality to terminate blocked transactions in Bi-State.

DTP-API implements BST as follows. The DTP-API stores the before image and the after image of tuples that have been modified by BST transactions. For this purpose, the DTP-API adds the two columns `Before` and `After` to each table that it uses, cf. Table 1.

6.1. Rewriting Write-Transactions

The following step is executed for each insert statement `INSERT <data> INTO ...` of a transaction T_i:

Algorithm 1 Implementing Inserts

---
1. Insert `<data>` into the corresponding table, and add T_i to the column "After" of the newly inserted data

---

For each delete statement `DELETE ... WHERE <condition>` of a transaction T_i, the following rewriting is necessary:

Algorithm 2 Implementing Deletes

---
1. Add T_i to each entry in the column "Before" of each row where `<condition>` evaluates to true.

The update operation for an update statement `UPDATE ... WHERE <condition>` is rewritten as follows.

Algorithm 3 Implementing Updates

---
1. Add T_i to each entry in the column "Before" of each row where `<condition>` evaluates to true.

2. Copy the values "ID", "Attributes", and "After" of those tuples, where `<condition>` is true, into new data tuples, and concatenate T_i to the existing entries of the "After" attribute. Update the value of "Attributes" in the columns of the newly copied tuples according to the update statement.

	ID	Attributes	Before	After
(1)	1	α_1		
(2)	2	α_2		

Table 1. Original table containing additional columns

	ID	Attributes	Before	After
(1)	1	α_1	T_1	
(2)	2	α_2	T_2	
(3)	1	α_3	T_3	T_1
(4)	2	α_4	T_3	T_2
(5)	1	α_2		T_1, T_3
(6)	2	α_2		T_2, T_3

Table 2. Content of Table 1 after Bi-State-Terminating T_1, T_2, and T_3

Example 6.1 *Assume, we execute the following sequence of three transactions T_1, T_2, and T_3, each containing only one update statement, on Table 1.*

T_1:   `UPDATE Table1 SET Attributes=`α_3
         `WHERE ID=1`

T_2:   `UPDATE Table1 SET Attributes=`α_4
         `WHERE ID=2`

T_3:   `UPDATE Table1 SET Attributes=`α_2
         `WHERE (Attributes=`α_3 `∨`
             `Attributes=`α_4`)`

Table 2 shows the result when all of the distributed transactions $T_1 \ldots T_3$ block and Bi-State-Terminate.

The DTP-API marks all tuples changed by transaction T_1 as before image (Line (1)), copies them and executes the update. The resulting row can be found in Line (3) (note that Table 2 shows the result when all transactions block, therefore it already contains the entry for T_3). The same algorithm is applied for T_2. When T_3 is executed and both transactions T_1 and T_2 block, T_3 depends on T_1 and T_2. However, our algorithm does not explicitly need to check for this dependency. In our example, T_3 only modifies data when either T_1 or T_2 commit. This dependency is maintained automatically by Step 1 of Algorithm 3 since the `<condition>` of the update statement of T_3 is only true in lines (3) and (4). Then, these two rows are copied to the rows in Line (5) and Line (6), and T_3 is added to the "After" attribute of each of these rows.

6.2. Rewriting Read-Operations

Read operations are modified in the following way: Each value of the returned result additionally contains the corresponding values of the "After" and "Before" columns. Then, the read operation must be processed by the database only a single time, regardless of the number of depending blocked transactions. However, the result R is not directly returned to the application, the DTP-API first checks whether R contains any entries in the "After" or "Before" column. If this is the case, it is the application's choice whether it handles these multiple uncertain results, or whether the application delays the read operations until the transactions listed in the "After" and "Before" column of R have been committed. If the application can handle multiple results, we can reduce the amount of transferred data by returning an object that, directly within the application, creates the different possible valid database states by means of the "After" and "Before" column.

6.3. Commit and Abort

The following rules apply, when a blocked transaction T commits or aborts:

T **commits:** Delete all rows which contain T in the attribute "Before". Delete all other entries T that occur in any attribute value of the column "After" in the table.

T **aborts:** Delete all rows which contain T in the attribute "After". Delete all other entries T that occur in any attribute value of the column "Before" in the table.

Example 6.2 *Assume, T_3 commits. In this case, the Lines (3) and (4) are deleted from Table 2. Furthermore, the string T_3 must be deleted in Lines (5) and (6) from the attribute values for the attribute "After", since a commit of T_1 or T_2 automatically implies that the changes of T_3 become valid.*

Note that the data set increases only temporarily and collapses to the original size when the commit decision for the Bi-State-Terminated transactions is known. For example, when the database receives the commit decisions for T_1 and T_3, the database knows the exact unique value for the data tuple with ID 1, which corresponds to Line (5) in case T_3 and T_1 commit, and to Line (1) in case T_3 commits and T_1 aborts.

7. Experimental Evaluation

Since the benefit of BST highly depends on the application scenario and to the authors' knowledge there is no generally accepted benchmark for distributed mobile transactions, we choose the TPC-C benchmark for generating the test data and transactions. The following questions motivate our experimental evaluation: How many transactions can be Bi-State-Terminated until the execution time and database size for following transactions is unacceptable? How does Bi-State-Termination affect the overall transaction throughput and transaction execution time, when a certain percentage of transactions block?

7.1. Experimental Setup

We have run experiments using the TPC-C benchmark for generating database content and transaction load. We used a TPC-C scaling factor of 2, which means that in total we have 139 MB for data, and a total amount of 294 transactions, 41,8% of them being update operations. Characteristic for our used implementation of the TPC-C benchmark is that the involved update transactions operate on a set of data tuples whose cardinality is low (i.e. 2 tuples), so we can expect a lot of conflicting write transactions. In order to simulate transaction blocking, a separate coordinator instance coordinates each transaction and delays the commit command based on different parameters in order to simulate blocked distributed transactions. For example, to simulate a transaction blocking of 1% of all transactions, we delayed the commit command of each 100th transaction.

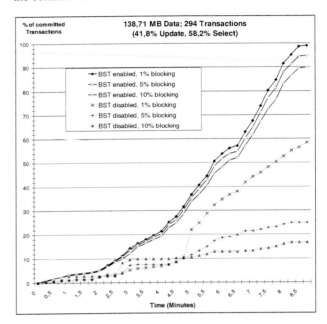

Figure 4. TPC-C simulating a hotspot

Figure 4 shows on the y-axis the sum of all successfully committed transactions. On the x-axis, the overall time is shown. The different curves indicate whether BST was enabled, and the percentage of blocked transactions. Note that due to our simulated hotspot, a huge amount of transactions depend on each other. We can see that BST enabled transaction processing is able to commit much more transactions than when disabling BST.

Note that the additional space used by BST is rather low, i.e., in our experiments, BST requires about 2% more space.

As the performance of BST highly depends on the number of blocked transactions, we additionally executed a stress test, which is illustrated in Figure 5. On the left y-axis, which applies to the black curve, the required time to process a single update transaction is shown, while the right y-axis, which applies to the gray curve with white circles, shows the resulting number of tuples that BST generates. The x-axis shows the number of blocked transactions. All of these blocked transactions depend on each other, and all of them modify exactly one tuple. This results in an exponential growth of time and space. However, as the test indicates, the processing of 10 blocked transactions does not take an extremely large overhead and is still feasible.

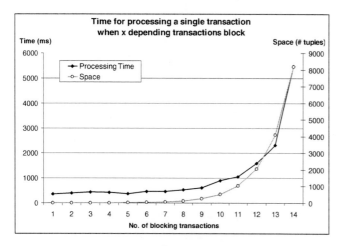

Figure 5. BST stress test

7.2. Evaluation Summary

As we have seen, BST is able to enhance the amount of committed transactions by 40% up to 70%, depending on the number of blocked transactions. Our stress test has shown that whenever a single tuple is affected by no more than 10 blocking transactions, the overhead that BST incorporates is still reasonable.

Finally, note that if no more space is available or the required processing time grows, the database can for each individual transaction decide to use BST or to wait for the commit decision, as 2PC does. In other words, our solution does not force the database to accept long execution times, and BST does never block more transactions than 2PC.

8. Related Work

Although a blocking behavior in the context of transactions has been widely studied, proposed solutions only tackle the problem of protocol blocking, as defined in Section 4.1.

Non-locking concurrency control like multiversion concurrency control [3, 22], timestamp-based concurrency control [16], or optimistic concurrency control [12, 15] omit the use of locks. However, this does not solve the infinite transaction blocking problem on concurrent transactions, since the database proposes by sending the voteCommit message that it will commit the transaction, regardless of the used concurrency control mechanism. Therefore, without Bi-State-Termination, the database cannot process a transaction U that is depending on a transaction T, while T waits for the final commit decision, even if the database uses locking-free concurrency control. This motivates the use of BST, which is a termination mechanism that supports the actually used concurrency control mechanism.

Other approaches rely on compensation of transactions. [14], for instance, proposes a timeout-based protocol especially for mobile networks, which requires a compensation of transactions. However, inconsistencies may occur when some databases do not immediately receive the compensation decision or when the coordination process fails.

In order to enhance the availability of the coordination process, some proposals rely on multiple coordinators. [10], for instance, proposes a consensus-based commit protocol that involves multiple coordinators.

However, the problem of *transaction blocking* in the sense of Definition 4.3, which occurs when the executing database disconnects from the network after sending the voteCommit message, has, to the authors' knowledge, not been studied yet. Even 1PC [1, 2], which does not require a vote message but acknowledges each operation, encounters the problem of transaction blocking since each acknowledged operation that accesses a data tuple must block this data tuple until the transaction is successfully completed.

Our solution related to three ideas that are used in different contexts: Escrow locks [11], speculative locking [18], and multiversion databases [6, 7, 13].

Escrow locks are a refinement of field calls, which are used in environments where data hotspots are frequently accessed. The escrow lock calculates by means of the currently processed updates an interval $[i, k]$ for an attribute a. The interval indicates the actual upper and lower bound that the attribute a may take. When a further transaction relies on a precondition for a, the database checks whether the precondition evaluates to *true* for each value of a that is contained in the interval $[i, k]$. Compared to escrow locks, Bi-State-Termination, which is a transaction termination mechanism in contrast to the escrow locking technique, does neither rely on numerical values, nor does it assume that an attribute may lie in an interval. BST always knows the exact values that an attribute actually can have, and even allows an application to decide that a transaction T may only be committed in a certain constellation of commit and abort decisions of transactions on which T depends.

Another related locking mechanism is Speculative Locking (SL) [18]. SL was proposed to speed up transaction processing by spawning multiple parallel executions of a transaction that waits for the acquisition of required locks. SL has in common with Bi-Sate-Termination that SL also allows a transaction T to access the after-image of a transaction U while U is waiting for its commit decision. However, unlike Bi-State-Termination, SL does not allow committing T before the final commit decision for U has been received. This means, SL cannot successfully terminate T while the commit vote for U is missing. For this reason, SL cannot be used to solve the infinite transaction blocking problem that may occur in mobile networks. Furthermore, BST can be implemented to execute read-operations in one pass even if they return multiple result values due to transactions that wait for the commit decision.

Multiversion database systems [6, 7, 13] are used to support different expressions of a data object. They are used for CAD modelling, and versioning systems. However, compared to BST, multiversion database systems allow multiple versions to be concurrently valid, while BST allows only one valid version, but lacks the knowledge which of the multiple versions is valid due to the atomic commit protocol. Whenever BST requires multiple transaction executions that all return the same result, BST is even transparent to the application. Furthermore, multiversion database systems are mostly central embedded databases that are not designed to deal with distributed transactions. Instead, the user explicitly specifies on which version he wants to work.

Our proposed BST can also be used for transaction processing within service oriented architectures, as it merges nicely with the Commit Tree proposed in [5].

9. Summary and Conclusion

We have shown that whenever an atomic commitment is necessary, two kinds of blocking may appear, namely protocol blocking and transaction blocking. Although the risk of protocol blocking can be minimized by using atomic commit protocols with multiple coordinators, the risk of infinite transaction blocking, which can appear if the database moves or disconnects, is not appropriately solved by current approaches. We have explained the concept of Bi-State-Termination, which is useful to terminate blocked transactions even without knowing the explicit coordinator decision, and have described our implementation that is based on version numbers. Finally, our experimental results have shown that Bi-State-Termination enhances the number of committed transactions, and that BST is able to deal with a large number of depending blocked transactions without experiencing significant performance loss. This justifies using BST in mobile ad-hoc networks that are exposed to the risk of transaction blocking.

To summarize, we consider Bi-State-Termination as a useful option that is usable for mobile networks in order to terminate a transaction instead of just waiting for the commit decision for a long time.

References

[1] One-phase commit: Does it make sense? In *ICPADS '98: Proceedings of the 1998 International Conference on Parallel and Distributed Systems*, page 182, Washington, DC, USA, 1998. IEEE Computer Society.

[2] Y. J. Al-Houmaily and P. K. Chrysanthis. 1-2pc: the one-two phase atomic commit protocol. In *Proceedings of the 2004 ACM Symposium on Applied Computing (SAC), Nicosia, Cyprus, March 14-17*, pages 684–691, 2004.

[3] P. A. Bernstein and N. Goodman. Multiversion concurrency control - theory and algorithms. *ACM Trans. Database Syst.*, 8(4):465–483, 1983.

[4] P. A. Bernstein, V. Hadzilacos, and N. Goodman. *Concurrency Control and Recovery in Database Systems*. Addison-Wesley, 1987.

[5] S. Böttcher and S. Obermeier. Dynamic commit tree management for service oriented architectures. In *Proceedings of the 9th International Conference on Enterprise Information Systems (ICEIS) June 12-16, 2007, Funchal, Madeira - Portugal*.

[6] W. Cellary and G. Jomier. Consistency of versions in object-oriented databases. In D. McLeod, R. Sacks-Davis, and H.-J. Schek, editors, *16th International Conference on Very Large Data Bases, August 13-16, 1990, Brisbane, Queensland, Australia, Proceedings*, pages 432–441. Morgan Kaufmann, 1990.

[7] I.-M. A. Chen, V. M. Markowitz, S. Letovsky, P. Li, and K. H. Fasman. Version management for scientific databases. In *5th International Conference on Extending Database Technology (EDBT), Avignon, France, March 25-29, 1996, Proceedings*, volume 1057, pages 289–303. Springer, 1996.

[8] K. P. Eswaran, J. Gray, R. A. Lorie, and I. L. Traiger. The notions of consistency and predicate locks in a database system. *Commun. ACM*, 19(11):624–633, 1976.

[9] J. Gray. Notes on data base operating systems. In M. J. Flynn, J. Gray, A. K. Jones, et al., editors, *Advanced Course: Operating Systems*, volume 60 of *LNCS*, pages 393–481. Springer, 1978.

[10] J. Gray and L. Lamport. Consensus on transaction commit. *ACM Trans. Database Syst.*, 31(1):133–160, 2006.

[11] J. Gray and A. Reuter. *Transaction Processing: Concepts and Techniques*. Morgan Kaufmann, 1993.

[12] T. Härder. Observations on optimistic concurrency control schemes. *Inf. Syst.*, 9(2):111–120, 1984.

[13] R. H. Katz. Toward a unified framework for version modeling in engineering databases. *ACM Comput. Surv.*, 22(4):375–409, 1990.

[14] V. Kumar, N. Prabhu, M. H. Dunham, and A. Y. Seydim. Tcot-a timeout-based mobile transaction commitment protocol. *IEEE Trans. Com.*, 51(10):1212–1218, 2002.

[15] H. T. Kung and J. T. Robinson. On optimistic methods for concurrency control. *ACM Trans. Database Syst.*, 6(2):213–226, 1981.

[16] P.-J. Leu and B. K. Bhargava. Multidimensional timestamp protocols for concurrency control. In *Proceedings of the Second International Conference on Data Engineering*, pages 482–489, Washington, DC, USA, 1986. IEEE Computer Society.

[17] P. K. Reddy and M. Kitsuregawa. Reducing the blocking in two-phase commit with backup sites. *Inf. Process. Lett.*, 86(1):39–47, 2003.

[18] P. K. Reddy and M. Kitsuregawa. Speculative locking protocols to improve performance for distributed database systems. *IEEE Transactions on Knowledge and Data Engineering*, 16(2):154–169, 2004.

[19] D. Skeen. Nonblocking commit protocols. In Y. E. Lien, editor, *Proceedings of the 1981 ACM SIGMOD International Conference on Management of Data, Ann Arbor, Michigan*, pages 133–142. ACM Press, 1981.

[20] D. Skeen and M. Stonebraker. A formal model of crash recovery in a distributed system. In *Berkeley Workshop*, pages 129–142, 1981.

[21] M. R. Stonebraker. Concurrency control and consistency of multiple copies of data in distributed ingres. pages 193–199, 1986.

[22] G. Weikum and G. Vossen. *Transactional information systems: theory, algorithms, and the practice of concurrency control and recovery*. Morgan Kaufmann Publishers Inc., San Francisco, CA, USA, 2001.

Bitmap Index Design Choices and Their Performance Implications

Elizabeth O'Neil and Patrick O'Neil
University of Massachusetts at Boston
{eoneil, poneil}@cs.umb.edu

Kesheng Wu
Lawrence Berkeley National Laboratory
kwu@lbl.gov

ABSTRACT

Historically, bitmap indexing has provided an important database capability to accelerate queries. However, only a few database systems have implemented these indexes because of the difficulties of modifying fundamental assumptions in the low-level design of a database system and in the expectations of customers, both of which have developed in an environment that does not support bitmap indexes. Another problem that arises, and one that may more easily be addressed by a research article, is that there is no definitive design for bitmap indexes; bitmap index designs in Oracle, Sybase IQ, Vertica and MODEL 204 are idiosyncratic, and some of them were designed for older machine architectures.

To investigate an efficient design on modern processors, this paper provides details of the Set Query benchmark and a comparison of two research implementations of bitmap indexes. One, called RIDBit, uses the N-ary storage model to organize table rows, and implements a strategy that gracefully switches between the well-known B-tree RID-list structure and a bitmap structure. The other, called FastBit is based on vertical organization of the table data, where all columns are individually stored. It implements a compressed bitmap index, with a linear organization of the bitmaps to optimize disk accesses. Through this comparison, we evaluate the pros and cons of various design choices. Our analysis adds a number of subtleties to the conventional indexing wisdom commonly quoted in the database community.

1. INTRODUCTION

Bitmap indexes have not seen much new adoption in commercial database systems in recent years. While ORACLE has offered bitmap indexing since 1995, other major systems such as DB2 and Microsoft SQL Server do not provide them. Microsoft SQL Server may create bitmaps during hash joins, but not for general indexing; DB2 has adopted an Encoded Vector Index [16], but this is basically an encoded projection index rather than a bitmap index. Sybase Adaptive Server Enterprise (ASE), the major Sybase DBMS, does not have bitmap indexing, although the Sybase Adaptive

Server IQ product provides quite competitive bitmap indexing for data warehousing. This situation arises in part because there is no definitive design for bitmap indexes. To investigate such a definitive design, we plan to explore different design choices through a careful study of two research implementations. Since we have control over all aspects of the research implementations, we are able to try out some new techniques for improving performances, such as new forms of compression and careful disk placement. In the process of studying their performance pros and cons, we also find some surprises.

A *basic bitmap index* (more simply, *bitmap index* in what follows) is typically used to index values of a single column X in a table. This index consists of an ordered sequence of *keyvalues* representing distinct values of the column, and each keyvalue is associated with a bitmap that specifies the set of rows in the table for which the column X has that value. A bitmap has as many bits as the number of rows in the table, and the kth bit in the bitmap is set to 1 if the value of column X in the kth row is equal to the keyvalue associated with the bitmap, and 0 for any other column value. Table 1 shows a basic bitmap index on a table with nine rows, where the column X to be indexed has integer values ranging from 0 to 3. We say that the *column cardinality* of X is 4 because it has 4 distinct values. The bitmap index for X contains 4 bitmaps, shown as B_0, B_1, ..., B_3, with subscripts corresponding to the value represented. In Table 1 the second bit of B_1 is 1 because the second row of X has the value 1, while corresponding bits of B_0, B_2 and B_3 are all 0.

To answer a query such as "X > 1," we perform bitwise OR (|) operations between successive long-words of B_2 and B_3, resulting in a new bitmap that can take part in additional operations. Since bitwise logical operations such as OR (|), AND (&) and

Table 1: A bitmap index for a column named X. Columns B_0 – B_3 are bitmaps.

RID	X	B_0	B_1	B_2	B_3
0	2	0	0	1	0
1	1	0	1	0	0
2	3	0	0	0	1
3	0	1	0	0	0
4	3	0	0	0	1
5	1	0	1	0	0
6	0	1	0	0	0
7	0	1	0	0	0
8	2	0	0	1	0

Table 2: Key differences between RIDBit and FastBit.

	FastBit	RIDBit
Table layout	Vertical storage (columns stored separately)	N-ary storage (columns stored together in row)
Index layout	Arrays of bitmaps	B-tree keyed on keyvalues (improved in project)
Bitmap layout	Continuous	Horizontally partitioned into 32K-bit Segments
Compression	Word-Aligned Hybrid compression	Sparse bitmap converted to RID-list

NOT (~) are well-supported by computer hardware, a bitmap index software could evaluate SQL predicates extremely quickly. Because of this efficiency, even some DBMS systems that do not support bitmap indexes will convert intermediate solutions to bitmaps for some operations. For example, PostgreSQL 8.1.5 has no bitmap index, but uses bitmaps to combine some intermediate solutions [10]. Similarly, Microsoft SQL Server has a bitmap operator for filtering out rows that do not participate in a join operation [5].

Let N denote the number of rows in the table T and $C(X)$ the cardinality of column X. It is easy to see that a basic bitmap index like the one in Table 1 requires $N \bullet C(X)$ bits in the bitmaps. In the worst case where every column value is distinct, so that $C(X) = N$, such a bitmap index requires N^2 bits. For a large dataset with many millions of rows, such an index would be much larger than the table being indexed. For this reason, much of the research on bitmap indexes has focused on compressing bitmaps to minimize index sizes. However, operations on compressed bitmaps are often slower than on uncompressed ones, called *verbatim bitmaps*. There is a delicate balance between reducing index size and reducing query response time, which complicates the design considerations for bitmap index implementations.

Two very different approaches to reducing index sizes are used by the research prototypes we study. FastBit implements the Word-Aligned Hybrid (WAH) compression; the WAH compressed basic bitmap index was shown to be efficient in [18][19]. RIDBit employs a combination of verbatim bitmaps and RID-lists composed of compact (two-byte) Row Identifiers (RIDS). Its unique ability to gracefully switch from verbatim bitmaps to RID-lists based on the column cardinality originated with MODEL 204 [6].

The implementations of FastBit and RIDBit were quite different at the beginning of our study, which made them ideal for contrasting the different implementation strategies and physical design choices. As our study progressed, a number of implementation ideas found to be superior in FastBit were copied in RIDBit; RIDBit software was also modified to better utilize the CPU. The lessons learned in this exercise will be covered in the

Summary section. Table 2 gives the key differences between RIDBit and FastBit. We will discuss the detailed design of the two approaches in the next two sections.

The topics covered in succeeding sections are as follows. In Sections 2 and 3, we describe the architecture of FastBit and RIDBit. Section 4 provides a theoretical analysis of index sizes for different columns. Section 5 describes the Set Query Benchmark [7], which is used to compare performance of RIDBit and FastBit. Section 6 presents the detailed experimental measurements. Finally, Section 7 provides a summary and lessons learned.

2. FASTBIT

FastBit started out as a research tool for studying how compression methods affect bitmap indexes, and has been shown since to be an efficient access method in a number of scientific applications [12][17]. It organizes data into tables (with rows and columns), where each table is vertically partitioned and different columns stored in separate files. Very large tables are horizontal partitioned, where each partition typically consisting of many millions of rows. A partition is organized as a directory, with a file containing the schema, followed by the data files for each column. This vertical data organization is similar to a number of contemporary database systems such as Sybase IQ [9], MonetDB [1][2], Kx systems [4], and C-Store [14]. Each column is effectively a projection index as defined in [9] and can sometimes be used efficiently to answer queries without additional indexing structures. FastBit currently indexes only fixed-sized columns, such as integers and floating-point numbers, although it can index low-cardinality string-valued columns through a dictionary that converts the strings to integers. Because of this restriction, the mapping from a row to a row identifier is straightforward.

FastBit implements a number of different bitmap indexes with various binning, encoding and compression strategies [13]. The index used in this study is the WAH compressed basic bitmap index. All bitmaps of an index are stored in a single file as shown in Table 3. Logically, an index file contains two sets of values: the keyvalues and the compressed bitmaps. FastBit stores both the keyvalues and

Table 3: Content of a FastBit index file.

N	Number of rows
C	Column cardinality
keyvalues[C]	Distinct values associate with each bitmap
starts[C+1]	Starting position of each compressed bit-map (final position is end of all bitmaps)
bitmaps[C]	WAH Compressed bitmaps

bitmaps in arrays on disk. Since each keyvalue is the same size, it can be located easily. To locate the bitmaps, FastBit stores another array starts[] to record the starting position of all compressed bitmaps in the index file (in bitmaps[ ]). To simplify the software, one extra values is used in array starts[] to record the ending position of the last bitmap.

FastBit generates all bitmaps of an entire index for one partition in memory before writing the index file. This dictates that the entire index must fit in memory and imposes an upper bound on how many rows a horizontal partition can hold on a given computer system. Typically, a partition has no more than 100 million rows, so that a small number of bitmap indexes may be built in-memory at once.

In general, FastBit stores the array keyvalues[ ] in ascending order so that it can efficiently locate any particular value. In some cases, it is possible to replace this array with a hash function. Using hash functions typically requires fewer I/O operations to answer a query than using arrays do, but using arrays more easily accommodates arbitrary keyvalues. FastBit uses memory maps to access the array keyvalues[] and starts[] if the OS supports it; otherwise it reads the two arrays entirely into memory. Since the index for a partition has to fit in memory when built, this reading procedure does not impose any additional constraint on the sizes of the partitions.

One advantage of the linear layout of the bitmaps is that it minimizes the number of I/O operations when answering a query. For example, to answer the range predicate "3 < KN < 10", FastBit needs to access bitmaps for values 4 through 9. Since these bitmaps are laid out consecutively in the index file, FastBit reads all these bitmaps in one sequential read operation.

The linear layout of bitmaps means that FastBit is not in any way optimized for update. An update that might add or subtract a 1-bit to one of the bitmaps would require modification of the bitmap, followed by a reorganization of all successive bitmaps in the set. In scientific applications, changes in real time between queries are unusual, so this limitation is not a serious drawback, and it is not a problem for most

commercial data warehousing applications either. Furthermore, we will see in Section 7 that the new Vertica database product [14] provides a model where a fixed index for stable data can be maintained on disk while new data is inserted to a memory resident dynamic store that takes part in all queries.

FastBit reconstitutes a C++ bitmap data structure from the bytes read into memory. This step makes it easy to use the bitwise logical operation functions implemented in C++; however, it introduces unnecessary overhead by invoking the C++ constructor and destructor. Additionally, since FastBit aggregates the read operations for many bitmaps together, a certain amount of memory management is required to produce the C++ bitmap objects.

3. RIDBIT

RIDBit was developed as a pedagogical exercise for an advanced database internals course, to illustrate how a bitmap indexing capability could be developed. The RIDBit architecture is based on index design first developed for the Model 204 Database product from Computer Corporation of America [6]. We can view bitmaps, representing the set of rows with a given value for a column, as providing an alternative form for RID-lists commonly used in indexes. The column values are represented as keyvalues in a B-tree index, and row-sets that follow each column value are represented either as RID-lists or bitmaps. Bitmaps are more space-efficient than RID-lists when the bitmap is relatively dense, and bitmaps are usually more CPU-efficient as well. To create Bitmaps for the N rows of a table $T = \{r_1, r_2, ..., r_N\}$, we start with a 1-1 mapping m from rows of T to Z[M], the first M positive integers. In what follows we avoid frequent reference to the mapping m: when we speak of the *row number* of a row r of T, we will mean the value m(r).

Note that while there are N rows in $T = \{r_1, r_2,..., r_N\}$, it is possible that the number of bits M in the bitmap representation of RIDBit is somewhat greater than N, since it associates a fixed number of rows p with each disk page for fast lookup, even when the rows are somewhat varying in size. The advantage of this is that for a given row r with row number j, the page number accessed to retrieve row r is j/p and the page slot is j%p, where % denotes the modulo operator. This usually means that rows are assigned row numbers in disk-clustered sequence during load, a valuable property. The RIDBit architecture stores the rows in an N-ary organization, where all column values of a row are stored together. Since the rows might have varying sizes and we may not always be able to accommodate an equal number of rows on

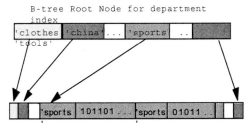

B-tree Root Node for department index
'clothes' 'china' ... 'sports' ..
'tools'

'sports' 101101 ... 'sports' 01011 ..

Figure 1: A RIDBit Index on department, a column of the SALES table.

each disk page, the value p must be chosen as a maximum; thus for a page of larger rows, some slots on a page will not accommodate the full set of p rows, and we will find that $m^{-1}(j)$ for some row numbers j in Z[M] are undefined.

RIDBit organizes its indexes as B-trees. A bitmap index for a column A with values $v_1, v_2, \ldots, v_k$, is a B-tree with entries having these keyvalues and associated data portions that contain bitmaps or RID-lists for the properties $A = v_1, \ldots, A = v_k$. Bitmaps in this index are just a different way to specify lists of RIDs, and when the density of a bitmap becomes too small to be efficient, a RID-list is used instead. Note in particular that when we speak of a bitmap index in RIDBit, we admit the possibility that some bitmaps are in fact RID-lists. See Figure 1 for an index example with low cardinality, where all row-sets are represented by verbatim bitmaps. RIDBit actually stores each verbatim bitmap as a series of successive bitmap fragments, called *segments*. Each box in Figure 1 is an illustration of multiple bitmap segments for "department = 'sports'".

Recall that bitmaps are called *dense* if the proportion of 1-bits in the bitmap is relatively large. A bitmap index for a column with 32 values will have bitmaps with average density of 1/32. In this case the disk space to hold a column index will be comparable to the disk space needed for a RID-list index in products with 32-bit RIDs. While the verbatim bitmap index size is proportional to the number of column values, a RID-list index is about the same size for any number of values (as long as we can continue to amortize the key size with a long block of RIDs). For a column index with a very small number of values, the bitmaps will have high densities (such as 50% for predicates such as GENDER = 'M' or GENDER = 'F'), and the disk savings is enormous. On the other hand, when average bitmap density for a bitmap index becomes too low, the bitmaps can be efficiently compressed. The simplest compression method, and the one used in RIDBit, is to translate the bitmap back to a RID list (albeit a special small-sized RID in the case of RIDBit). Boolean operations on these mixtures of

bitmaps and RID lists can be found in [6][11]. To account for the fact that some of the page slots are not used, we use an *Existence bitmap* (designated *EBM*), which has exactly those 1 bits corresponding to existing rows[1]. Now when RIDBit needs to performs a NOT on a bitmap B, it loops through a long int array performing the ~ operation, then AND's the result with the corresponding long int array from EBM.

In RIDBit, the sequence of rows on a table as well as the bitmaps referencing them are broken into equal-sized fragments, called *segments*, so that a verbatim bitmap segment will fit on a single disk page. In its current architecture, a RIDBit segment fits on a 4KByte page and a verbatim bitmap contains about 32K bits; thus a table is broken into segments of about 32K rows each. As for the bitmaps, there are three different ways to store them. The bitmaps with the highest densities are stored as segmented verbatim bitmaps. As the bit density decreases, the bitmaps are stored as segment-relative RID-lists, as explained in the next paragraph. At extreme low density, the segment-relative RIDs are directly stored as full-sized RIDs in the space normally used to store segment pointers to bitmaps or RID-lists in the leaf level of the B-tree. Since these RIDs are directly stored in the B-tree nodes, they are called "local" RID-lists.

RIDs used to access a row in a RIDBit segment, known as segment-relative RIDs (following the design of MODEL 204) are represented by integers from 1 to 32K - m (where m bits are used to contain a count of 1-bits in a bitmap), and thus only require two bytes each, or a short int in a typical C program. RIDBit supports verbatim bitmaps down to a density of 1/50, and a verbatim bitmap of that minimum density will thus require only 32K/50 = 655 short ints = 1310 bytes for RID-list representation. Thus several RID-lists with maximum size 1310 bytes or less are likely to fit on a single disk page. At the beginning of each segmented bitmap/RID-list pointer at the leaf level of the B-tree, the segment number will specify the higher order bits of a longer RID (4 bytes or perhaps more), but the segment-relative RIDs only use two bytes each. This is an important form of prefix compression, which greatly speeds up most index range searches.

A second implication of segmentation involves combining predicates. The B-tree index entry for a particular value in RIDBit is made up of a series of pointers to segment bitmaps or RID-list, but there are no pointers for segments that have no representative

---

1 It was pointed out by Mike Stonebraker that a "non-existence bitmap" would be more efficient, and this change is planned.

rows. In the case of a clustered index, for example, each particular index value entry will have pointers to only a small sequence of row segments. In MODEL 204, if several predicates involving different column indexes are ANDed, the evaluation begins segment-by-segment. If one of the predicate indexes has *no pointer* to a bitmap segment for a segment, then the segments for the other indexes can be ignored as well. Queries such as this can turn out to be very common in a workload, and the I/O saved by ignoring I/O for these index segments can significantly improve performance. This optimization, while present in MODEL 204, was not implemented for the RIDBit prototype product, meaning that certain queries measured for the current paper did not take advantage of it. A number of other improvements in RIDBit were implemented during the course of these experiments, but this one was considered too difficult to complete in the time allotted.

We note that a RIDBit index can contain bitmaps for some index keyvalues and RID-lists for other values, or even for some segments within a value entry, according to whether the segment's bit density falls over or under the current division point of 1/50. In what follows, we will assume that a bitmap index combines verbatim bitmap and RID-list representations where appropriate, and continue to refer to the hybrid form as a bitmap index. When we refer to the *bitmap* for a given value v in a bitmap index, this should be understood to be a generic name: it may be a bitmap or a RID-list, or a segment-by-segment combination of the two forms; the term *verbatim bitmap* however, specifically stands for a bitmap that is not in RID-list form.

To retrieve the selected values from the table data, RIDBit needs to read the disk pages containing them. Due to the horizontal data organization, the whole row is read if any value from the row is needed.

4. ANALYSIS OF INDEX SIZE

FastBit and RIDBit implement different bitmap compression algorithms. Here we look at their effectiveness in reducing index size. For FastBit, index sizes are extensively treated in [19], where Figure 6 summarizes the index size per row over various kinds of data. Here we consider only the simple uniform random case for both FastBit and RIDBit. Note that RIDBit compression efficiency is not much affected by local clusters of bits in the bitmap, so the uniform random case is a good predictor of the general case. FastBit can take advantage of local runs of bits, as shown in [19].

For FastBit in the uniform random case, we have the following index size expression which is derived from equation (4) of Section 4.2 of [19], converted

from size in words to size in bits. Here w = 32, for 32 bits per word in the current experiments.

FastBit index size per row, in bits = $(Cw/(w-1)) (1 - (1 - 1/C)^{2w-2} - (1/C)^{2w-2})$ [19]. This expression can be further simplified for small C and large C as follows:

$$
\begin{array}{ll}
(w/w-1)\,C & \text{small C} \\
(Cw/(w-1))(1 - e^{-(2w-2)/C}) \approx 2w & 1 << C << N \\
5w = 160 & C \sim N
\end{array}
$$

In the extreme case where C=N, each compressed bitmap is represented with 5 words, 3 of which are used to represent the bulk of the bits and the remaining 2 are used to represent the N%31 leftover bits.

The RIDBit implementation uses pages of size $4096 = 2^{12}$ bytes, holding 2^{15} bits (actually, 2^{15} - 16). A segment covers 2^{15} rows, using a bitmap or a segmented RID-list. The segment-relative RIDs of a segmented RID-list are 16 bits long and can start at any byte in a disk page (for current 4 KByte pages, and also for larger pages up to 8 KByte). A bitmap index has segment-relative bitmaps or RID-lists for each of C column values, ignoring cases with only one row per segment where segmentation is not used. Multiple RID-lists may share a page. If an index is composed entirely of RID-lists, the total size is 16 bits per row, for one segment-relative rid, while if it is entirely bitmaps, the total size is C bits per row, for 1 bit in each of C bitmaps. In the extreme case of C between a value on the close order of 32,000 and N: k•32,000 ≤ C ≤ N, where k is some small integer, a few rows for each column value per segment, each value requires 8 bytes for its local list entry. In summary, the number of bits per row used by RIDBit is as follows:

C   Bitmap segments; good for small C

16   Segmented RID-lists, C < k•32,000

64   Local RID-lists, k•32.000 ≤ C ≤ N

Of course an index can have a mixture of bitmaps

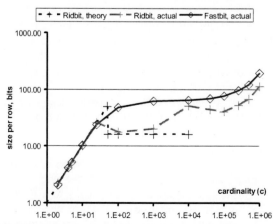

Figure 2: Index sizes vs. column cardinality.

and RID-lists, but this happens only in edge cases, since the decision is made based on a whole segment. The above simple formulas provide straight lines on both linear and log-log plots, and we use the latter in Figure 2 to cover more ground and allow easy comparison to Figure 6 in [19]. The above formula does not include the size of B-trees, which add a contribution of O(C) with a small constant of proportionality based on the number of per-key records in a leaf node.

We could minimize RIDBit index size by simply choosing the minimum of C and 16 bits per row, which suggests one to switch from bitmap to RID-list when $C \geq 16$. However, index size is not the most important criterion in deciding when to switch storage scheme. Experimentally, we have found that bitmaps are faster than segmented RID-lists for answering queries for C well above 16, even in face of the extra I/O needed. We choose to store the data in bitmaps for C up to 50. Possibly we should store the data on disk as RID-lists and construct bitmaps as we bring them into memory, but we have not tested this option.

The internal structures of RIDBit indexes for columns of various cardinalities C fall into three categories:

Low cardinality: $C \leq 16$, where segmented bitmaps are no larger than segmented RID-lists and faster.

Medium cardinality: $16 < C < 50$, where segmented bitmaps are larger than segmented RID-lists but still faster.

High cardinality: $C > 50$, where segmented RID-lists are much smaller and generally more efficient.

In the extreme case where $k \bullet 32,000 \leq C \leq N$, a few rows of each value per segment, segmentation is dropped in favor of unsegmented RID-lists of full-size local RIDs.

This analysis is easily generalized to using arbitrary p bits for segment-relative RIDs: just replace 16 with p above. With many of today's processors, including the Pentium 4 and its descendents, it is efficient to access groups of bits in memory without byte-alignment. Thus we could use p=12 bits to access any byte address in a 4 KByte page, and further compress the RID-lists.

Figure 2 shows the actual RIDBit and FastBit index sizes for the experiments reported in Section 6. The RIDBit index sizes shown here include the sizes of the B-trees, which were not included in our simple analysis, but became important for large cardinality (C = 1,000,000 for example). Similarly, the index sizes for FastBit are the total size of index files including the array starts[ ]. Overall, we see that the RIDBit indexes are never larger than FastBit indexes. When $C \leq 16$, both indexes have the same sizes; for

larger C, FastBit indexes take about 64 bits per row while RIDBit index takes about 16 bits per row; when C is close to N ($=10^6$), FastBit index takes 192 bits per row and RIDBit index takes about 113 bits per row. As noted before, when C = N, each WAH compressed bitmap takes 5 words and one word is needed to store the starting position of the bitmap, which gives the total of 6 words per row. In this extreme case, RIDBit essentially stores a B^+-tree, which takes about 3.5 words per row.

5. THE SET QUERY BENCHMARK

We use a number of queries from the Set Query Benchmark to study performance of RIDBit and FastBit. The Set Query Benchmark was designed for query-mostly applications [7][8], and predates the Star-Schema data warehouse design. Since bitmap indexes are primarily used for high-performance queries, it is a natural choice. Due to the lack of support for join operations in both FastBit and RIDBit (we expect to add join capability to both products in the future), we only implemented the first five queries from the Set Query Benchmark. This lack of join support also ruled out the well-known TPC-H Benchmark [15].

The Set Query benchmark was defined on a BENCH table of one million 200-byte rows, containing a clustering column KSEQ with unique values 1, 2, 3, ..., in order of the rows, and a number of randomly generated columns whose names indicate their cardinalities, as shown in Table 4. For example, K5 has 5 distinct values appearing randomly on approximately 200,000 times each.

Queries of the Set Query Benchmark were modeled on marketing analysis tasks. We briefly describe the five SQL queries used for our timing measurements.

Q1: SELECT count(*) FROM BENCH WHERE KN=2; KN is one of KSEQ, K500K, ..., K2. There are 13 different instances of Q1. Since it involves only one column at a time in the WHERE clause, we call Q1 a one-dimensional (1-D) query.

Q2A: SELECT count (*) FROM BENCH WHERE K2=2 and KN = 3; KN is one of KSEQ, K500K, ..., K4. There are 12 instances of Q2A.

Q2B: SELECT count (*) FROM BENCH WHERE K2=2 and NOT KN = 3;

Table 4: Set Query Benchmark columns and their column cardinalities.

Name	Cardinality
KSEQ	1,000,000
K500K	500,000
K250K	250,000
K100K	100,000
K40K	40,000
K10K	10,000
K1K	1,000
K100	100
K25	25
K10	10
K5	5
K4	4
K2	2

KN is one of KSEQ, K500K, ..., K4. Both Q2A and Q2B are two-dimensional queries since each WHERE clause involves conditions on two columns. At one time, the "NOT KN = 3" clause was difficult to support efficiently.

Since the above three queries only count the number of rows satisfying the specified conditions, we say they are *count queries*. Both FastBit and RIDBit answer count queries using INDEX ONLY.

Q3A: SELECT sum(K1K) FROM BENCH WHERE KSEQ between 400000 and 500000 and KN=3; KN is one of K500K, K250K, ..., K4. There are 11 instances of Q3A.

Q3B: SELECT sum(K1K) FROM BENCH WHERE (KSEQ between 400000 and 410000 or KSEQ between 420000 and 430000 or KSEQ between 440000 and 450000 or KSEQ between 460000 and 470000 or KSEQ between 480000 and 500000) and KN=3; KN is one of K500K, K250K, ..., K4.

Q3A0 and Q3B0: We include a variation of the above two queries by replacing the SELECT clause with "SELECT count(*)", making them count queries like Q1 and Q2.

Q4: SELECT KSEQ, K500K FROM BENCH WHERE constraint with 3 or 5 conditions. The constraints come from the Table 5. Queries Q4A selects 3 consecutive conditions from Table 5, such as, 1-3 and 2-4, and Q4B selects 5 consecutive conditions, such as 1-5 and 2-6. Our tests use 8 instances of Q4A and Q4B, where the last two instances of Q4B uses the first two conditions when there are no more conditions at the end of the list. To answer these queries, multiple indexes are needed and results from each index have to be combined.

The original Q4A and Q4B had a select clause with two columns, KSEQ and K500K. In our tests, we vary the number of columns selected from 0 (an index-only query retrieving count(*)) to 13. This creates more test cases for a better comparison between different data organizations.

Q5: SELECT KN1, KN2, count (*) GROUP BY

KN1, KN2; for each (KN1, KN2) in {(K2, K100), (K4, K25), (K10, K25)}. There are three instances of Q5.

In the following tests, this query is implemented as a set of queries of the form "SELECT count (*) WHERE KN1=x and KN2=y," where x and y are distinct values of KN1 and KN2. We choose to answer Q5 this way mainly to exercise the indexing performance of FastBit and RIDBit, even though FastBit can support this query directly [12]. Thus, this is a count query using index only.

6. INDEX PERFORMANCE EXPERIMENTS

We present the performance measurements in three parts, the time to construct the indexes, time to answer the count queries and time to answer the retrieval queries. Before presenting the timing measurements, we briefly describe the test setup.

Experiment Setup

We performed our tests on a number of different Linux 2.6 machines with ext3 file systems on various types of disk systems. Table 6 shows some basic information about the test machines and the disk systems. To make sure the full disk access time is accounted for, we un-mount the file system and then mount the file system before each query. Under Linux, this clears the file system cache. To avoid spending an excessive amount of time on mount/un-mount, we duplicated the test data four times to generate a total of five sets of the same data files. This allows us to run each query five times on different data between each pair of mount/un-mounts. Since the timing measurements are performed on five copies of the data files, we also avoid potential performance traps related to any peculiar disk placement of the files. All of these operations are repeated six times to give a total of 30 runs for each query, and the time we report is the median elapsed time for all 30 runs, measured by the function

Table 5: Range conditions used for Q4.

(1) K2 = 1
(2) K100 > 80
(3) K10K between 2000 and 3000
(4) K5 = 3
(5) K25 in (11, 19)
(6) K4 = 3
(7) K100 < 41
(8) K1K between 850 and 950
(9) K10 = 7
(10) K25 in (3, 4)

Table 6: Information about the test systems.

	CPU		disk		
	Type	Clock (GHz)	Type	Latency (ms)	Speed (MB/s)
HDA	Pentium 4	2.2	EIDE	7.6	38.7
MD0	Pentium 4	2.2	Software RAID0 (2 disks)	9.4	58.8
SDA	Pentium 4	2.8	Hardware RAID0 (4 disks)	15.8	62.2
SDB	PowerPC 5	1.6	SCSI	8.3	54.4

Table 7: Total index sizes (MB) and the time (in seconds) needed to build them.

		RIDBit	FastBit
	Size	64.2 MB	93.5b MB
time	**HDA**	75.7 sec	21.7 sec
	MD0	8.3 sec	27.2 sec
	SDA	3.5 sec	34.8 sec
	SDB	4.0 sec	41.7 sec

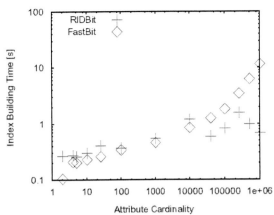

Figure 3: Time (in seconds) required to build each individual index on system MD0.

gettimeofday.

Index Building

The total time used by RIDBit and FastBit to build indexes is shown in Table 7. In Figure 3 we examine in detail how the time is spent in building different indexes, taking the **MD0** system as representative of the four systems measured. The elapsed time shown in Figure 3 is the medium value of building indexes for five separate copies of the test data. The total time reported in Table 7 is the sum of these medium values.

In Figure 3 we see that RIDBit requires slightly more time to build low-cardinality indexes and FastBit requires considerably more time to build high-cardinality indexes. In high-cardinality cases, FastBit generates a large number of small bitmap objects and spends much time in allocating memory of these bitmaps. RIDBit maintains a pre-allocated stack of page-sized buffers, and thus avoid the same pitfall.

An overview of all the timing measurements on count queries is presented in Table 8. In this table, we show the total time of all instances of each query, for example, the row for Q1 is the sum of the median elapsed time for 13 instances of Q1. The last row in the table shows the total time of all count queries. On three of the four test systems, the total time used by FastBit and RIDBit are within 10% of each other, with FastBit taking less time Q1, Q2 and Q4 while RIDBit taking less time on Q5. The performance of RIDBit was improved during this joint measurement effort by emulating some of features of FastBit, as we will explain in Section 7. On the fourth system, **SDB**, the performance difference between RIDBit and FastBit was traced to an unexpected overhead for per I/O operation at the lower levels of that I/O system apparently impacted RIDBit more than FastBit.

Both FastBit and RIDBit (modified during the joint work) have arranged index data so that most of the range predicates performed use sequential reads of a relatively large number of disk sectors; thus the total execution time of these accesses should be dominated by the time to read the disk sectors. To verify this is indeed the case, we show the number of disk sectors read in Table 9. Since the numbers of disk sectors read on different systems are nearly identical[2], we

Table 8: Total elapsed time (seconds) to answer the count queries on four test systems.

	HDA		MD0		SDA		SDB	
	RIDBit	FastBit	RIDBit	FastBit	RIDBit	FastBit	RIDBit	FastBit
Q1	0.39	0.23	0.50	0.25	0.34	0.26	0.52	0.22
Q2A	0.74	0.42	0.68	0.51	0.50	0.47	0.85	0.53
Q2B	0.71	0.42	0.66	0.49	0.53	0.46	0.88	0.52
Q3A0	2.28	2.18	2.00	1.91	1.79	1.73	1.97	2.06
Q3B0	2.08	2.46	1.76	1.90	1.49	1.41	1.87	1.81
Q4A0	1.39	0.94	1.22	0.83	0.97	0.77	2.10	1.03
Q4B0	2.20	1.46	1.75	1.31	1.67	1.21	2.98	1.65
Q5	1.13	1.44	1.09	1.46	0.81	1.21	1.03	1.50
Total	10.92	9.55	9.66	8.66	8.10	7.52	12.20	9.32

Index-Only Query Performance

Here we review the time required to answer the count queries. These timing measurements directly reflect the performance of indexing methods. We start with an overview of the timing results then drill down the details as we find various aspects of interest.

---

2 The precise number of disk sectors read may differ because there are potential differences in the number

Table 9: Number of disk sectors (in thousands) needed to answer count queries.

	RIDBit	FastBit
Q1	10.7	4.9
Q2A	15.0	9.2
Q2B	15.0	9.2
Q3A0	52.0	64.4
Q3B0	34.4	48.8
Q4A0	27.8	35.9
Q4B0	41.3	56.5
Q5	23.0	27.4
Total	219.2	256.3

only show the values from system **MD0**. We see that the indexing method that reads more disk sectors does not always uses more time, therefore we have to investigate further.

We next examine the performance on Q1 in detail. In Figure 4 the medium query response time is plotted against the number of hits for Q1. Since each instance of Q1 involves only one bitmap from one index, it is relatively easy to understand where the time is spent. The time used by FastBit is primarily for two read operations: first, to read the starting positions of the index structure shown in Table 3, and second, to read the selected bitmap. These two read operations may each incur 9.4 ms I/O latency, which leads to a total elapsed time of about 0.02 s, unless the selected bitmap happen to be in the read-ahead buffer of the first read operation, which leads to a total time of about 0.01 s. Among the 13 instances of Q1, most are either 0.01 s or 0.02 s. When the number of hits is very small and the cardinality of the column is high, it takes more time to complete the first read operation. The I/O time of RIDBit can also be divided into two parts: first to read the tablespace index blocks involved (listing the positions of pages in the tablespace), and at the same time access the B-tree root node and a few index nodes, and second (in all KN=2 cases where N is 100K 250K, 500K, and SEQ, the cases using unsegmented RID-lists) to read in the bitmap or RID-list that will determine the count to be retrieved. Since each of these operations requires at least 9.3 ms (and in fact the first one to read in the index blocks of the tablespaces requires 17 ms), the total time used by RIDBit is nearly 0.028 s (28 ms) in most cases.

The time needed to answer higher dimensional count queries is dominated by the time needed to answer each of the one-dimensional conditions. For example, the two-dimensional queries Q2A and Q2B involve two conditions of same form as Q1; we expect Q2A and Q2B to take about twice as much time as that of Q1. We see from the measurements on **MD0** in Table 8 that this estimate is accurate (a ratio

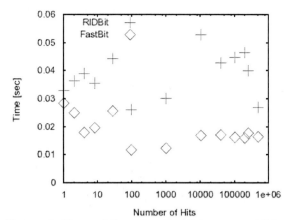

Figure 4: Elapsed time (seconds) to answer Q1 on MD0.

of 0.51/0.25 = 2.04); on the other hand, RIDBit has a much smaller increment of elapsed time (0.68/0.50 = 1.36), presumably because the initialization of a tablespace for a second index is easily combined with the initialization of the first tablespace. This observation holds for Q4A0 and Q4B0 as well. For example, the total time for Q4B0 on **MD0** is 1.31 s which is about 1.6 times of that for Q4A0. This relative difference is close to 5/3, the ratio of dimensions of the queries.

We see that the query response time for queries Q1, Q2A, Q2B, Q4A0 and Q4B0 follows our expectation. In these cases, the time used by FastBit is slightly less than that used by RIDBit. Table 10 shows the CPU time used to answer the count queries on **MD0**. Compared with the elapsed time reported in Table 8, we see the CPU time is usually $1/5^{th}$ of the elapsed time or less for queries Q1, Q2A, Q2B, Q4A0 and Q4B0. The query processing time follows our expectation partly because the I/O time is so much more than the CPU time. Next we examine the cases for Q3 and Q5.

Figure 5 shows the elapsed time to answer each instance of Q3A0 on **MD0**. We notice that the time values fall in a very narrow range; the maximum and minimum values are within 20% of each other. This is because the time to resolve the common condition on KSEQ dominates the total query response time. To resolve this condition on KSEQ, FastBit reads 100,001 compressed bitmaps of about 5 words each,

Table 10 Total CPU time (seconds) to answer count queries on MD0.

	RIDBit	FastBit
Q1	0.016	0.045
Q2A	0.028	0.059
Q2B	0.038	0.061
Q3A0	0.500	0.672
Q3B0	0.307	0.521
Q4A0	0.137	0.111
Q4B0	0.192	0.165
Q5	0.701	0.795
Total	1.919	2.429

of I/O nodes involved in different file systems. In addition, the software RAID may require additional disk accesses to resolve the file content.

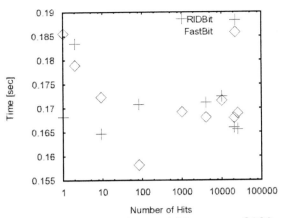

Figure 5 Elapsed Time (seconds) to answer Q3A0 on MD0.

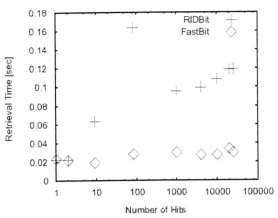

Figure 6 Time spent to retrieve the selected records to answer Q3A on MD0.

while RIDBit reads 100,001 leaf nodes of the B-tree with an average size about 3.5 words each. Even though FastBit reads more data than RIDBit, it doesn't always use more I/O time because it reads all bitmaps in one sequential read operation. Since the bitmaps selected by the conditions on KSEQ in Q3B0 can not be read in one operation, FastBit usually uses more time than RIDBit. From Table 10, we see that Q3A0 and Q3B0 also require more CPU time than Q4A0, Q4B0 and other. In FastBit, this CPU time is primarily spent on reconstructing the large number of C++ bitmap objects. On Q3A0 and Q3B0, RIDBit uses less CPU time than FastBit.

Another query where RIDBit is faster than FastBit is Q5. From Table 10 we see that RIDBit requires about 13% less CPU time on **MD0**, which again suggests that RIDBit is more CPU efficient than FastBit. The difference in elapsed time is larger (about 25% on **MD0**) than that in CPU time because FastBit indexes are larger than RIDBit indexes.

Table Retrieval Query Performance

Next we present measurements of table retrieval queries. We present the measurements on Q3 before those on Q4 because Q3 only retrieves a sum of values from one column, while Q4 retrieves a varying number of columns.

Figure 6 shows the time required to retrieve the column selected in Q3A. The time values shown are the differences between query response time of Q3A and that of Q3A0. Overall, we see that the time required by FastBit slowly rises as the number of hits increases. RIDBit uses about the same amount of time as FastBit when one or two records are retrieved; but it uses more time when the number of hits is larger. The time required to retrieve the values for Q3B has similar trend as that for Q3A.

Because of the condition on KSEQ, the records selected by Q3A and Q3B are from between row

400,000 and 500,000. The second condition in Q3A controls how many records are selected and how they are distributed. Since all columns in test data are uniform random numbers, the selected records are uniformly scattered among rows 400,000 to 500,000. The Operating Systems on our test machines all retrieve data from disk in pages (of either 4 KB or 8KB). To better understand the retrieval time, we compute how many pages are accessed assuming 4 KB pages.

Let m denote the number of rows in a data page. The RIDBit and FastBit use different organization for the table data, which leads to different number of records to be placed on a page. RIDBit uses a horizontal organization; FastBit uses a vertical data organization. The number of records per 4-KB page for RIDBit is 75. The number of records per 4-KB page for FastBit is 1024. We use m_h to denote the number of records per page for the horizon data organization, and use m_v to denote the number of records per page for the vertical data organization. Let n_h denote the number of pages for the 100,000 rows between 400,000 and 500,000 in the horizontal organization, $n_h = 100,000/m_h = 1,334$. Let n_v denote the number of pages for 100,000 records in vertical organization, $n_v = 100,000/m_v = 98$. If every page is touched, clearly, there is an advantage to use vertical data organization. Next, we examine a more general case, where s records are randomly selected. Assuming that s is much smaller than 100,000, we can use the following formulae to estimate the number of pages to be accessed [8]: $p_h = n_h (1-\exp(-s/n_h))$ and $p_v = n_v(1-\exp(-s/n_v))$.

Figure 7 shows the number of disk sectors accessed for the retrieval operation. The number of disk sectors shown is the difference of the number of disk sectors accessed to answer Q3A and that to answer Q3A0. In the same plot, we also show the number of disk sectors to be accessed using the above

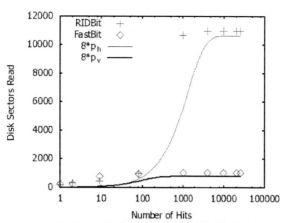

Figure 7 Number of disk sectors accessed to retrieve the records for Q3A.

formulae for p_h and p_v. The multiplying factor of 8 is to translate the 4 KB pages to 512-byte disk sectors. In general, the actual number of disk sectors accessed agrees with predictions. The actual disk sectors accessed is typically more than the prediction because the I/O system performs read-ahead.

Comparing Figure 6 and Figure 7, we see that the time used for retrieval generally follows the number of disk sectors accessed. We note two deviations. When the number of disk sectors accessed is small, the I/O overhead, in particular, the disk seek time, dominates the total retrieval time. As the number of disk sectors accessed increases, the retrieval time increases proportionally until nearly all of the disk sectors are accessed. In which case, the retrieval time may actually be less because the data file can be read into memory with large sequential read operations. This can either be accomplished by the OS or the database software.

Our modified versions of Q4 retrieve 0, 1, 3, 5, 7, 9, 11 and 13 column values. In Figure 8 and Figure 9,

we show the total query response time against the number of columns selected for Q4A and Q4B on **MD0**. In these figures, each symbol shows the total time of 8 instances of Q4A (or Q4B) with the same number of columns selected.

From Figure 8, we see that the total time used with FastBit's vertical data organization increases linearly with the number of columns selected. In Figure 8, the slope of the line form by FastBit is about 0.8, which indicates that in 0.8 seconds it can read 8 copies (8 instances of Q4Ax) of the 4-MB data file. This reading speed of about 40 MB/s is about 68% of the asymptotic reading speed of 58.8 MB/s shown in Table 6.

The timing measurements of RIDBit show the expected behavior for horizontal data organization. It takes the same amount of time as long as some columns are retrieved. In Figure 8, we see that retrieving data in the vertical data organization usually takes less time than those in horizontal organization. The line for the vertical data organization intersects that for the horizontal organization around 11. When more than 11 (out of 13) columns are retrieved, using the horizontal data organization takes less time.

The maximum number of hits from Q4A is about 1,100. In horizontal organization, there are 13,334 pages for the table data. Therefore, RIDBit does not need to access all pages. For FastBit, Each data file in the vertical data organization takes up 977 pages and nearly all these pages are accessed by FastBit. In this case, FastBit uses one sequential read on each data file. In contrast, RIDBit is reading one page at a time or a small number of pages at a time. Depending on the relative performance of random reads to sequential reads, the line for vertical data organization may cross the one for horizontal data organization at different locations. Of course, this

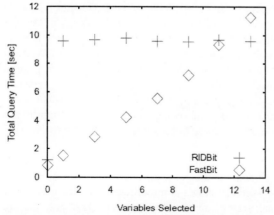

Figure 8 Total time used to answer Q4A on MD0.

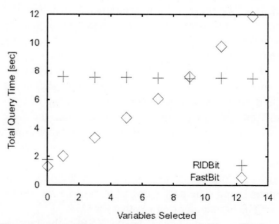

Figure 9 Total time used to answer Q4B on MD0.

cross over point also depends on the number records selected as illustrated in Figure 9.

Each Q4B query selects about 100 hits on average. In this case, RIDBit only needs to access 100 pages no matter how many columns are selected as shown in Figure 9. In contrast, FastBit accesses about 100 pages per column. We expect the horizontal data organization to have an advantage over the vertical data organization in this case. From Figure 9, we see that if less than 7 columns are selected, FastBit in fact uses less time. This is because FastBit decides to read the whole data file if more than 1/16th of the pages are randomly selected. This option reads more pages than necessary; however, because the sequential reads are much more efficient than random reads, reading more data sequentially actually take less time in this case.

7.   SUMMARY AND CONCLUSIONS

We outline what lessons we have learned from our performance tests. To be of value, these lessons should indicate how we would proceed if we were implementing a new bitmap index on a commercial database product. Though it took some time for these lessons to become clear to us, we believe the results are worth the effort.

Vertical Data Organization Has Better Performance

It seems clear that vertical data organization (columns stored separately) has an important architectural advantage over row-store for queries. Certainly, were we to make a major modification of RIDBit, the first thing we would do is to adopt this format. From Figure 8 and Figure 9, we see that the queries that retrieve one column take a much longer elapsed time than those simply counts the number of hits, even though the WHERE clause contains five different range conditions. This is the case even if as few as 100 records are retrieved as shown in Figure 9. Our tests also showed that for queries retrieving a small number of columns in a table the vertical data organization is much more efficient. Only if nearly all columns are retrieved is the row-oriented organization more efficient. Most queries that occur in commercial applications do not retrieve a large percentage of the columns in a row, for example, most queries in TPC-H retrieve two to five columns, so it seems clear that the vertical data organization is preferred.

Clustered Index Organization Has Better Performance

In terms of bitmap index organization, the linear organization of FastBit shown in Table 3 is more efficient for processing range queries because the bitmaps can be read into memory with a single sequential scan of the bitmaps[ ] array, once the starts[ ] array has determined the start and end position of the bitmaps on disk. As it stands, this approach trades flexibility of the index data structure for performance. The most severe limitation of this index organization is that any modification to the index will cause the whole index file to be reorganized, which would be exceedingly expensive.

We found in modifying RIDBit to reduce the number of disk scans for a single range query that we could read the appropriate leaf nodes of the B-tree into memory (in a single sequential scan, once the initial and terminal keyvalue leaves of the B-tree are determined), then learn the positions of the initial and terminal bitmap/RID-list in the range. This is simple because during the initial load of the index, successive keyvalues K and successive segments S within each keyvalue are placed in lexicographic order by (K,S) and the B-tree is built in left-to right order while the bitmaps/RID-lists are also placed on disk in that order. Therefore it is possible to use approximately the same approach to the RIDBit B-tree/Bitmap layout that FastBit does, performing a few long sequential scans to access all bitmaps/RID-lists. Furthermore, since the leaf level of the B-tree is present in memory, we can validate if some newly inserted rows lie outside the range and access them as well; we still cannot insert an arbitrary number of new rows in the middle of the sequence (because of the risk of a RID-list becoming too large and requiring re-positioning), but we can insert such rows up to that point and afterward place them in a new position at the end of all the segments, where this will be detected by an examination of leaf pages in the desired range. While this approach is not perfect, it is comparable to what DB2 does in terms of clustered indexes.

We note that the problems with inserts disappear entirely in the case of a product such as Vertica, where Read-Optimized Store remains unchanged and new rows are added to Write-Optimized Store until enough additions require a merge-out to form a new Read-Optimized Store.

Modifications for Modern Processors Are Needed

There are a number of ways in which older indexing methods are inefficient on modern processors. Oracle's index compression approach, known as Byte-Aligned Bitmap Code (BBC), uses a type of compression/decompression that requires a good deal of branching; this can be terribly inefficient because it causes pipeline stalls that are much more expensive on modern processors than they were when BBC was introduced. Indeed we found that using Branch-Avoiding C code on Pentium 4 to precompute conditions rather than using if-then-else forms was important for improved performance. Another change over the past fifteen years or so is that sequential scans have become much more efficient, requiring much smaller filter factors (by a factor of fifty) before a list prefetch of pages becomes more efficient than a sequential scan that simply picks up more rows. It because of this that clustering has become more important, leading to such new and important capabilities as DB2's Multi-Dimensional Clustering (MDC). All of this should be born in mind in implementing a new indexing method for today's processors.

FastBit indexes are usually larger than RIDBit indexes, but it can answer many queries in less time because it accesses the needed bitmaps in less I/O operations. Obviously, when a large fraction of the bitmaps is needed, FastBit will take more time. FastBit typically spends more CPU time in answering queries than RIDBit, though the CPU time differences are small compared with those of I/O time.

In summary, we recommend the vertical organization for base data and the linear (or packed) organization for the bitmap indexes to achieve good query performance. To insulate the indexes from changes in the base data, we suggest using separate Read-Optimized Store and Write-Optimized Store as with Vertica.

8. REFERENCES

[1] P. A. Boncz, M. L. Kersten. Monet: An Impressionist Sketch of an Advanced Database System. In Proceedings Basque International Workshop on Information Technology, San Sebastian, Spain, July 1995.

[2] P. A. Boncz, F. Kwakkel, M. L. Kersten. *High Performance Support for OO Traversals in Monet*. Technical Report CS-R9568, CWI, Amsterdam, The Netherlands, 1995.

[3] T. Johnson. Performance Measurements of Compressed Bitmap Indexes. In *VLDB,* Edinburgh, Scotland, September 1999. Morgan Kaufmann.

[4] Kx Systems. http://kx.com. 2006.

[5] Microsoft. SQL Server Database Engine: Logical and Physical Operators Reference. http://msdn2.microsoft.com/en-us/library/ms191158.aspx.

[6] P. O'Neil. Model 204 Architecture and Performance. In 2nd International Workshop in High Performance Transaction Systems, Asilomar, California, USA, September 1987. Springer-Verlag.

[7] P. O'Neil. The Set Query Benchmark. In *The Benchmark Handbook For Database and Transaction Processing Benchmarks*, Jim Gray, Editor, Morgan Kaufmann, 1993.

[8] P. O'Neil and E. O'Neil. *Database Principles, Programming, and Performance*. 2nd Ed. Morgan Kaufmann Publishers. 2001.

[9] P. O'Neil and D. Quass. Improved Query Performance with Variant Indexes. In *SIGMOD*, Tucson, AR, USA, May 1997. ACM Press.

[10] PostgreSQL: PostgreSQL 8.1.5 Documentation, Chapter 13. Performance Tips. http://www.postgresql.org/docs/8.1/interactive/performance-tips.html.

[11] D. Rinfret, P. E. O'Neil and E. J. O'Neil. Bit-Sliced Index Arithmetic. In *SIGMOD*, Santa Barbara, CA, USA, May 2001. ACM Press.

[12] K. Stockinger, E. W. Bethel, S. Campbell, E. Dart, K. Wu. Detecting Distributed Scans Using High-Performance Query-Driven Visualization. *Supercomputing 06*. 2006.

[13] K. Stockinger and K. Wu. Bitmap Indices for Data Warehouses. In *Data Warehouses and OLAP*. 2007. IRM Press. London.

[14] M. Stonebraker, D. Abadi, A. Batkin, X. Chen, M. Cherniack, M. Ferreira, E. Lau, A. Lin, S. Madden, E. O'Neil, P. O'Neil, A. Rasin, N. Tran and S. Zdonik. C-Store: A Column Oriented DBMS. *VLDB*, pages 553-564, 2005.

[15] TPC-H Version 2.4.0 in PDF Form from http://www.tpc.org/tpch/default.asp

[16] R. Winter. Indexing Goes a New Direction. 1999. http://www.wintercorp.com/rwintercolumns/ie_9901.html.

[17] K. Wu, J. Gu, J. Lauret, A. M. Poskanzer, A. Shoshani, A. Sim, and W.-M. Zhang. Grid Collector: Facilitating Efficient Selective Access from Data Grids. In *International Supercomputer Conference* 2005, Heidelberg, Germany.

[18] K. Wu, E. J. Otoo, and A. Shoshani. Compressing bitmap indexes for faster search operations. In *SSDBM'02*, pages 99-108, 2002.

[19] K. Wu, E. Otoo, and A. Shoshani. Optimizing bitmap indices with efficient compression. *ACM Transactions on Database Systems*, v 31, pages 1-38, 2006.

Boundedness of Regular Path Queries in Data Integration Systems

Gösta Grahne
Concordia University
QC, Canada
grahne@cs.concordia.ca

Alex Thomo
University of Victoria
BC, Canada
thomo@cs.uvic.ca

Abstract

In this paper we study the problem of deciding whether a regular path query over views in data-integration systems can be re-expressed without recursion. The problem becomes challenging when the views contain recursion, thereby potentially making recursion in the query uncessary. We define two related notions of boundedness of regular path queries. For one of the notions we show it PSPACE complete, and obtain a constructive method for optimizing regular path queries in data-integration systems. For the other notion of boundedness, we show it PTIME reducible to the notorius problem of limitedness in distance automata, for which only exponential time algorithms are currently known.

1 Introduction

The compile time query optimization is one of the key factors for the enormous success of database systems today. Notably, the majority of the influential work on query optimizers delt with SQL queries, which correspond to datalog queries without recursion.

Nevertheless, in the research community from the mid 1980's to the mid 1990's, another theme was the study of (recursive) Datalog (see *e. g.* [27]). Unfortunately, most decision problems related to query optimization turned out to be undecidable. One of these undecidable problems was the boundedness of Datalog, which is to decide whether a given recursive Datalog query is equivalent with one without recursion. The importance of this is that should we be able to re-express a recursive Datalog query as another query without recursion, then we could use the optimization machinery for non-recursive queries, which over the years has been proven to be very efficient and successful in commercial systems.

Notably, a well-behaved fragment of Datalog, which is both natural and quite general, did emerge in the mid 1990s, in the context of semistructured data (graph data) (see [27]).

This fragment is the class of regular queries, whose basic element is that of regular path queries.

The semi-structured data model [1] is now widely used as a foundation for reasoning about a multitude of applications, where the data is best formalized in terms of labeled graphs. Such data is usually found in Web information systems, XML data repositories, digital libraries, communication networks, and so on.

Regarding the query languages for semi-structured data, virtually all of them provide the possibility for the user to query the database through regular expressions. Fortunately, the boundedness problem for regular path queries is decidable. Simply, one has to build a finite automaton and check whether there is a cycle on a path between an initial and a final state.

This simplicity is not true anymore when the regular path queries are on an alphabet where the symbols represent views, which can in turn be recursive. Such queries are prominent today in information integration systems, where the data-sources are represented as a set of views over a *global schema*. The data is described by the *local schema*, which in the semi-structured context is the set of view names. By using the view definitions, the user query (expressed on the global schema) is rewritten in terms of the local schema. Finally, the obtained view-based rewriting is used to extract the answer from the data on the local schema. This is commonly referred in the literature as the *local-as-view* (LAV) approach for data integration (see [18]).

When it comes to decide whether a view-based rewriting is bounded, the above-mentioned simple check for recursion is not sufficient. A classical example presented in [3] is the following. Suppose that we have a single view $V = R^*$ and the query or the view-based rewriting is V^*. Clearly, this is equivalent with just V, which is more efficient than V^* to be answered on the data source.

We note here that, the view-based rewritings, generated by the method proposed in [3] always contain *all* the recursion possible, as long as the containment of the rewriting to the original query is preserved. The problem of "minimizing" a rewriting was first proposed in the same paper ([3])

but it has been open since then.

In general, the problem is more complicated than the example above, which illustrates only a case where the non-recursive rewriting reduces to a single letter word. As a more elaborated example, consider the view $V = R^+$. Now, for any given (natural) number k, take the query $Q = R^*.R^k$. The rewriting computed by [3] and [8] will be $(V^k)^+$, and clearly we need to have a way to infer that in fact the only word needed from this language is the word V^k, which has length k.

In this paper, by solving the boundedness problem for regular path queries over views, we show that for the *exact* view-based assumption in data integration, it is sometimes possible to replace a view-based rewriting with a not necessarily (purely) algebraically equivalent non-recursive one, without loosing any answers. The exact view assumption is usually the implicit assumption in a multitude of applications such as datawarehouses and enterprise data integration applications (see e.g. [11]), and has received considerable attention in the research community (see e.g. [6, 2]).

Furthermore, we obtain an optimal algorithm, which takes as input a view-based expression and a number k, and returns an equivalent expression without recursion (if such exists), in which the length of the longest word does not exceed k.

Depending on the application, we might be interested only in the *existence* of the above number k. Namely, we would like to know, for a given expression on the view definitions, whether there exists a number k, such that the sublanguage of the words of length not more than k is equivalent with the language captured by the original expression. Clearly, this amounts to deciding whether a query can be equivalently re-expressed without recursion. We show that our existential problem is polynomial time reducible to the intricate limitedness problem for distance automata, intensely investigated by Hashiguchi and others [13, 14, 15, 19, 25, 23].

2 Basic Definitions

We consider a database to be an edge labeled graph. This graph model is typical in semistructured data, where the nodes of the database graph represent the objects and the edges represent the attributes of the objects, or relationships between the objects.

Formally, let Δ be a finite alphabet. We shall call Δ the *database alphabet*. Elements of Δ will be denoted $R, S, \ldots$. As usual, Δ^* denotes the set of all finite words over Δ. Words will be denoted by $u, w, \ldots$. We also assume that we have a universe of objects, and objects will be denoted $a, b, c, \ldots$. A *database* $\mathcal{D}$ over Δ is a is a subset of $N \times \Delta \times N$, where N is a finite set of objects, that we usually will call nodes. We view a database as a directed

labeled graph, and interpret a triple (a, R, b) as a directed edge from a to object b, labeled with R. If there is a path labeled $R_1, R_2, \ldots, R_k$ from a node a to a node b we write $a \xrightarrow{R_1 R_2 \ldots R_k} b$.

A *(user) query* Q is a regular language over Δ. For the ease of notation, we will blur the distinction between regular languages and regular expressions that represent them. Let Q be a query and $\mathcal{D}$ a database. Then, the *answer* to Q on $\mathcal{D}$ is defined as

$$ans(Q, \mathcal{D}) = \{(a, b) : a \xrightarrow{w} b \text{ in } \mathcal{D} \text{ for some } w \in Q\}.$$

Let $\Omega = \{v_1, \ldots, v_n\}$ be an *outer alphabet*, frequently also called a *view alphabet*. A *view graph* is database $\mathcal{V}$ over Ω. In other words, a view graph is a database where the edges are labeled with symbols from Ω. View graphs can also be queried (by queries over Ω), and $ans(Q, \mathcal{V})$ is defined like the answer to Q on a database $\mathcal{D}$, *mutatis mutandis*.

Let h be a homomorphism from Ω to subsets of Δ^*, *i. e.* for each v_i, $h(v_i)$ is a finite or infinite regular language over Δ. The homomorphism h is applied to words, languages, and regular expressions in the usual way (see *e. g.* [16]). We shall often denote the languages $h(v_i)$ with V_i and call them *views*.

In a LAV information integration system [18], we have the "global schema" Δ, the "source schema" Ω, and the "assertion" $h : \Omega \to 2^{\Delta^*}$. The only extensional data available is a view graph $\mathcal{V}$ over Ω (see also [20, 26, 7, 5][1]). The user queries are expressed on the global schema Δ, and the system has to reason about the information it can extract from the view graph $\mathcal{V}$. In order to do this, it has to consider the set of *possible databases* over Δ that $\mathcal{V}$ could represent. Under the *exact view* assumption, a view graph $\mathcal{V}$ defines in the information integration system a set $poss(\mathcal{V})$ of databases as follows:

$$poss(\mathcal{V}) =$$
$$\{\mathcal{D} : \mathcal{V} = \bigcup_{i \in \{1, \ldots, n\}} \{(a, v_i, b) : (a, b) \in ans(V_i, \mathcal{D})\}\}.$$

(Recall that $V_i = h(v_i)$.[2]) The above definition reflects the intuition about the connection between an edge (a, v_i, b) in $\mathcal{V}$ with the set of paths between a and b in the possible $\mathcal{D}$'s, labeled by some word in V_i. The meaning of querying a view graph through the global schema in a LAV information integrations system is defined as follows. Let Q be a query over Δ. Then

$$\text{ANS}(Q, \mathcal{V}) = \bigcap_{\mathcal{D} \in poss(\mathcal{V})} ans(Q, \mathcal{D}).$$

---

[1]Regarding corresponding LAV scenarios for relational data.

[2]Furthermore, if we replace the equality sign for $\mathcal{V}$ with "$\subseteq$" then the views are considered to be *sound*.

Henceforth, we will consider only view graphs which are *valid*, that is, the view graphs for which the set of possible databases is not empty. Under the exact view assumption, not all view graphs are valid. As an example, consider a single view $V = R^*$, and the view graph $\mathcal{V} = \{(a, v, b), (b, v, c)\}$. It is easy to see that $poss(\mathcal{V}) = \emptyset$. The reason is that $\mathcal{V}$ "misses" a v-edge from a to c.

There are two approaches for computing $\text{ANS}(Q, \mathcal{V})$. The first one is to use an exponential procedure in the size of the data in order to completely compute $\text{ANS}(Q, \mathcal{V})$ (see [4]). There is little that one can better hope for, since in the same paper it has been proven that to decide whether a tuple belongs to $\text{ANS}(Q, \mathcal{V})$ is co-NP complete with respect to the size of data.

The second approach is to compute first a view-based rewriting Q' for Q, as in [3]. Such rewritings are regular path queries on Ω. Then, we can approximate $\text{ANS}(Q, \mathcal{V})$ by $ans(Q', \mathcal{V})$, which can be computed in polynomial time with respect to the size of data. In general, for a view-based rewriting Q' computed by the algorithm of [3], we have that

$$ans(Q', \mathcal{V}) \subseteq \text{ANS}(Q, \mathcal{V}),$$

with equality when the rewriting is exact ([4]). In the rest of the paper, we will assume that the data-integration system follows the second approach.

3 Query Equivalence and Boundedness

Consider two queries, Q_1 and Q_2 over an alphabet $\Sigma \in \{\Delta, \Omega\}$. We say that a query Q_1 is Σ-*contained* in a query Q_2 denoted $Q_1 \subseteq_\Sigma Q_2$ iff the answer to Q_1 is contained to the answer to Q_2, on all databases over Σ. We say that Q_1 is Σ-*equivalent* to Q_2 and write $Q_1 \equiv_\Sigma Q_2$, when $Q_1 \subseteq_\Sigma Q_2$ and $Q_2 \subseteq_\Sigma Q_1$. It is easy to see that the above query containment coincides with the (algebraic) language containment of Q_1 and Q_2, and that the query equivalence coincides with the language equality, *i. e.* $Q_1 \subseteq_\Sigma Q_2$ iff $Q_1 \subseteq Q_2$ and $Q_1 \equiv_\Sigma Q_2$ iff $Q_1 = Q_2$.

Let Q_1 and Q_2 be queries over Ω. We say that Q_1 is Ω/Δ-*contained* in Q_2, denoted $Q_1 \subseteq_{\Omega/\Delta} Q_2$, iff $h(Q_1) \subseteq_\Delta h(Q_2)$. Likewise, Q_1 is Ω/Δ-*equivalent* to Q_2 denoted $Q_1 \equiv_{\Omega/\Delta} Q_2$, when $Q_1 \subseteq_{\Omega/\Delta} Q_2$ and $Q_2 \subseteq_{\Omega/\Delta} Q_1$. It is easy to see that Ω-containment $Q_1 \subseteq_\Omega Q_2$, implies Ω/Δ-containment $Q_1 \subseteq_{\Omega/\Delta} Q_2$ but not vice-versa. As an example, if $Q_1 = v$, $Q_2 = v^*$ (where $v \in \Omega$), and $h(v) = R^*$, then Q_1 is Ω/Δ-equivalent with Q_2, although they are not Ω-equivalent.

We now have the following theorem.

Theorem 1 *Let Q_1 and Q_2 be queries over Ω. Under the exact view assumption, $Q_1 \equiv_{\Omega/\Delta} Q_2$ iff for each valid view graph $\mathcal{V}$ over Ω, $ans(Q_1, \mathcal{V}) = ans(Q_2, \mathcal{V})$.*

The importance of this theorem is that it allows us to minimize as much as possible a query on Ω (i.e. a view-based rewriting) without loosing query-power as long as we preserve Ω/Δ-equivalence, which is algebraically weaker than Ω-equivalence.

The above does not hold when we drop the exactness assumption for the views and consider them sound only. As an example, consider a view V, which is Δ-equivalent with V^*, and a view graph $\mathcal{V} = \{(a, v, b), (b, v, c)\}$. For this $\mathcal{V}$, we have that $ans(v^*, \mathcal{V}) \neq ans(v, \mathcal{V})$. Clearly, the answer of V will be equal to the answer of V^* on each database on Δ, but because the view is assumed to be sound we cannot enforce $\mathcal{V}$ to have an additional v-edge from a to c.

We give now two definitions for the boundedness of a query Q on the Ω alphabet. For this, we denote with $Q^{(k)}$ the set of *all* words in Q, which have length of not more than k. Obviously, $Q^{(0)} \subseteq Q^{(1)} \subseteq \ldots \subseteq Q^{(k)} \subseteq \ldots \subseteq Q$.

Definition 1

1. *We say that Q is k-bounded iff $Q^{(k)} \equiv_{\Omega/\Delta} Q$.*

2. *We say that Q is finitely bounded iff there exists a $k \in \mathbb{N}$, such that Q is k-bounded.*

Although related, the problems of k-boundedness and finite boundedness are different. For the k-boundedness problem, the input is a query, and a fixed number k that the user provides. Then, the question is whether the query can semantically be fully represented by the Ω query words of length at most k.

On the other hand, for the finite boundedness problem, k is not part of the input, and the question is existential. Depending on the application we could be interested in the k or the finite boundedness.

As a first observation, the problem of k-bounded-ness is decidable. For this, we can (naively) enumerate from a query Q all the words of length at most k, thereby obtaining a bloated representation of $Q^{(k)}$, and then check $Q^{(k)} \equiv_{\Omega/\Delta} Q$ by testing for the algebraic language equivalence $h(Q^{(k)}) \equiv_\Delta h(Q)$. However, by naively enumerating words and then checking Ω/Δ-equivalence, we will get an exponential space penalty.

Even if we can decide the k-boundedness more efficiently, it is still important to have a concise representation of $Q^{(k)}$, since the purpose is to run query $Q^{(k)}$ instead of Q (after testing $Q^{(k)} \equiv_{\Omega/\Delta} Q$). As it turns out, our constructive proof of PSPACE-decidability for the k-boundedness problem also gives us an algorithm for building a concise automaton for $Q^{(k)}$ (see Theorem 4).

4 Weighted Transducers

In this section, we define weighted transducers, which will help us to solve both boundedness problems.

A *weighted transducer* $\mathcal{T} = (P, I, O, \tau, S, F)$ consists of a finite set of states P, an input alphabet I, an output alphabet O, a set of starting states S, a set of final states F, and a transition relation $\tau \subseteq P \times I^* \times O^* \times \mathbb{N} \times P$.

Given a weighted transducer $\mathcal{T}$ defined as above, and a word $u \in I^*$ we say that a word $w \in O^*$ is an *output* of $\mathcal{T}$ for u through a k-*weighted path* if there exists a sequence $(p_0, u_1, w_1, k_1, p_1), (p_1, u_2, w_2, k_2, p_2), \ldots, (p_{n-1}, u_n, w_n, k_n, p_n)$ of state transitions of τ, such that $p_0 \in S$, $p_n \in F$, $u = u_1 \ldots u_n$, $w = w_1 \ldots w_n$, and $k = k_1 + \cdots + k_n$.

We denote the set of all outputs of $\mathcal{T}$ for u (regardless of the path weight) by $\mathcal{T}(u)$. For a language $L \subseteq I^*$, we define $\mathcal{T}(L) = \bigcup_{u \in L} \mathcal{T}(u)$. We will also need the notation $rel(\mathcal{T})$ to denote the set of all pairs $(u, w) \in I^* \times O^*$, where w is an output of $\mathcal{T}$ when providing u as input. Similarly, $dom(\mathcal{T})$ and $ran(\mathcal{T})$, will be used to denote the domain and range of $rel(\mathcal{T})$.

Given a weighted transducer $\mathcal{T}$, and words u and w, the $\mathcal{T}$-*cost* for u to be translated into w is defined as

$$c_{\mathcal{T}}(u, w) = \begin{cases} \inf\{k : w \text{ is an output of } \mathcal{T} \text{ for } u \\ \qquad \text{through a } k\text{-weighted path}\} \\ \infty, \text{ if } w \notin \mathcal{T}(u). \end{cases}$$

Now, we will define the $\mathcal{T}$-cost for translating one language into another. This will be needed in the formulation of a necessary and sufficient condition for the k- and the finite boundedness.

Consider a word w on I. The $\mathcal{T}$-cost for a word w to be translated into a language L_2, is

$$c_{\mathcal{T}}(w, L_2) = \inf\{c_{\mathcal{T}}(w, u) : u \in L_2\}.$$

Based on that, the $\mathcal{T}$-cost for a language L_1 to be translated into a language L_2 can be naturally defined as

$$c_{\mathcal{T}}(L_1, L_2) = \sup\{c_{\mathcal{T}}(w, L_2) : w \in L_1\}.$$

Returning to our problem, for a query Q on Ω, we construct an automaton $\mathcal{A} = (\{p_1, \ldots, p_m\}, \Omega, \tau, S, F)$ that recognizes Q (note that $S \subseteq \{p_1, \ldots, p_m\}$). Having the set $\{V_1, \ldots, V_n\}$ of view definitions, we also construct for each V_i, where $i \in [1, n]$, the (identical) automata $\mathcal{A}_{ijk} = (P_{ijk}, \Delta, \tau_{ijk}, S_{ijk}, F_{ijk})$, each recognizing V_i, whenever there is a transition $(p_j, v_i, p_k) \in \tau$, in $\mathcal{A}$, for $j, k \in [1, m]$.

Now, from the automata $\mathcal{A}$ and $\mathcal{A}_{ijk}$, for $i \in [1, n]$ and $j, k \in [1, m]$, we construct the transducer $\mathcal{T} = (P_{\mathcal{T}}, \Delta, \Omega, \tau_{\mathcal{T}}, S, F)$, where $P_{\mathcal{T}} = \{p_1, \ldots, p_m\} \cup \{\bigcup_{(p_j, v_1, p_k) \in \tau} P_{1jk}\} \cup \ldots \cup \{\bigcup_{(p_j, v_n, p_k) \in \tau} P_{njk}\}$, and

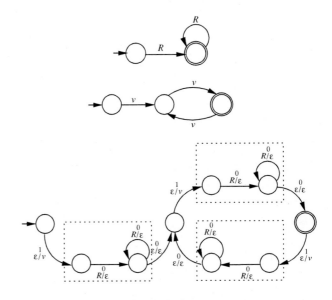

Figure 1. *Transducer construction*

$$\begin{aligned} \tau_{\mathcal{T}} = \ & \{(p_j, \epsilon, v_i, 1, s) : \\ & \quad (p_j, v_i, p_k) \in \tau \text{ and } s \in S_{ijk}\} \cup \\ & \{(f, \epsilon, \epsilon, 0, p_k) : \\ & \quad f \in F_{ijk} \text{ and } (p_j, v_i, p_k) \in \tau\} \cup \\ & \{(p, R, \epsilon, 0, q) : \\ & \quad (p, R, q) \in \tau_{ijk} \text{ for some } i, j, k\}. \end{aligned}$$

The intuition behind the above construction is that, we replace the transitions of the query automaton $\mathcal{A}$ by the view automata corresponding to the transition labels, creating so, what might figuratively be called, view-automata "pockets." Whenever the transition "jumps" into some view-automaton "pocket" there is a cost penalty of one.

An example is given in Figure 1, in which we have a single view $V = R^+$ (top) and a query $Q = (v^2)^+$ (midle) on the alphabet $\Omega = \{v\}$.[3] The resulting transducer is shown at the bottom of the figure, where the view-automata "pockets" are surrounded by dotted rectangles. By the above construction, we get a weighted transducer $\mathcal{T}$, which has $dom(\mathcal{T}) = h(Q)$ and $ran(\mathcal{T}) = Q$. Also, the transducer $\mathcal{T}$ has the following property: It associates with each word $w \in h(Q)$ all the words $u \in Q$ such that $w \in h(u)$.

Now, we give the following characterization of the k- and the finite boundedness.

---

[3]The (machine generated) $Q = (v^2)^+$ is a view-based rewriting of some user query (e.g. $R^*.R^2$).

Theorem 2

1. *Q is k-bounded if and only if $c_\tau(h(Q), Q) \leq k$.*

2. *Q is finitely bounded if and only if there is a $k \in \mathbb{N}$, such that $c_\tau(h(Q), Q) \leq k$.*

In the next section we give an algorithm for testing whether $c_\tau(dom(\mathcal{T}), ran(\mathcal{T})) \leq k$, for a given $k \in \mathbb{N}$.

5 Deciding k-Boundedness

Interestingly, deciding the k-boundedness bears some resemblance to deciding the query containment under distortions of [10]. Nevertheless, the constructions of [10] provide a mechanism for saying "yes" or "no" to a decision problem, while the constructions in this section, in addition to deciding the k-boundedness of view-based rewritings, also give a method for effectively obtaining the non-recursive equivalent rewriting if such exists. Furthermore, since it is not possible to reduce an arbitrary instance of the problem in [10] into our problem, we carefully examine and prove the complexity bounds for the k-boundedness of view-based rewritings.

We consider the transducer $\mathcal{T}$, constructed in the previous section. We will need a few simple operations on transducers. Let $\mathcal{T}_1$ and $\mathcal{T}_2$ be transducers. Then we denote with $\mathcal{T}_1 \cup \mathcal{T}_2$ the (union) transducer, obtained by the usual construction, translating $dom(\mathcal{T}_1) \cup dom(\mathcal{T}_2)$ into $ran(\mathcal{T}_1) \cup ran(\mathcal{T}_2)$. Similarly, $\mathcal{T}_1 \bullet \mathcal{T}_2$, denotes the (concatenation) transducer translating $dom(\mathcal{T}_1) \cdot dom(\mathcal{T}_2)$ into $ran(\mathcal{T}_1) \cdot ran(\mathcal{T}_2)$.

For technical reasons, we also add to the transition relation of $\mathcal{T}$ the neutral transitions $(p, \epsilon, \epsilon, 0, p)$ for each state, i.e. self-loops of weight 0, and labeled with ϵ/ϵ. Evidently, these neutral transitions do not alter any salient features of $\mathcal{T}$. However, we can now assume that any transition in the transducer $\mathcal{T}$ is always preceded by a 0-weighted transition.

Now, let's assume that all transducers have their states labeled by consecutive integers starting from 1. We denote with $\mathcal{T}_{i,j}$ the transducer obtained from $\mathcal{T}$, by shifting the set of initial states to be $\{i\}$ and the final states to be $\{j\}$.

Also, let $\mathbf{0}(\mathcal{T})_{i,j}$ be the transducer obtained from $\mathcal{T}_{i,j}$ by deleting all transitions with cost 1.

Finally, for $\{i, j\} \subset \{1, \ldots, n\}$, we consider the set of elementary transducers $\mathbf{1}_{i,j}(\mathcal{T})$, each obtained from $\mathcal{T}$ by retaining only transitions between i and j, and only those that have cost 1. Observe that, a transducer $(\mathbf{0}(\mathcal{T}))_{i,j}$ can be a full-fledged transducer i.e. it can contain loops, while an elementary transducer $\mathbf{1}_{i,j}(\mathcal{T})$ is simple in the sense that it does not contain any loops.

Given a transducer $\mathcal{T} = (\{1, \ldots, n\}, \Delta, \Omega, \tau, S, F)$ (as

constructed in the previous section)[4], we wish to compute a transducer $\mathbf{k}(\mathcal{T})$, such that

$$dom(\mathbf{k}(\mathcal{T})) = \{w \in dom(\mathcal{T}) : c_\tau(w, ran(\mathcal{T})) \leq k\}.$$

Intuitively, the $dom(\mathbf{k}(\mathcal{T}))$ would capture the set of words in $dom(\mathcal{T})$ that have a $\mathcal{T}$-cost of not more than k. Clearly, if we are able to construct $\mathbf{k}(\mathcal{T})$, then we can decide whether or not

$$c_\tau(dom(\mathcal{T}), ran(\mathcal{T})) \leq k,$$

by testing the (regular) language equality $dom(\mathbf{k}(\mathcal{T})) = dom(\mathcal{T})$. Hence, by this and Theorem 2, we cast the decision of the k-boundedness into a pure regular language equivalence test, which can be done in polynomial space. Furthermore, as we show, our construction for $\mathbf{k}(\mathcal{T})$ is such that $ran(\mathbf{k}(\mathcal{T})) = (ran(\mathcal{T}))^{(k)}$, thereby giving a constructive method for obtaining $Q^{(k)}$.

We will construct $\mathbf{k}(\mathcal{T})$ by a recursive algorithm obtained from the following equations:

$$\mathbf{k}(\mathcal{T}) = \mathcal{T}^0 \cup \mathcal{T}^1 \cup \ldots \cup \mathcal{T}^k$$

where $\mathcal{T}^0$ is an elementary transducer with self-loop transitions $(i, \epsilon, \epsilon, 0, i)$, for each state i, which is both initial and final, and for $1 \leq h \leq k$

$$\mathcal{T}^h = \bigcup_{i \in S, j \in F} \mathcal{T}^h_{i,j}$$

where

$$\mathcal{T}^h_{i,j} = \begin{cases} \bigcup_{m \in \{1, \ldots, n\}} \mathcal{T}^{h/2}_{i,m} \bullet \mathcal{T}^{h/2}_{m,j} & \text{for } h \text{ even} \\ \bigcup_{m \in \{1, \ldots, n\}} \mathcal{T}^{(h-1)/2}_{i,m} \bullet \mathcal{T}^{(h+1)/2}_{m,j} & \text{for } h \text{ odd} \end{cases}$$

for $h > 1$, and

$$\mathcal{T}^1_{i,j} = \bigcup_{\{m,l\} \subset \{1, \ldots, n\}} (\mathbf{0}(\mathcal{T}))_{i,m} \bullet \mathbf{1}_{m,l}(\mathcal{T}) \bullet (\mathbf{0}(\mathcal{T}))_{l,j}.$$

We can now show that indeed:

Theorem 3

$$dom(\mathbf{k}(\mathcal{T})) = \{w \in dom(\mathcal{T}) : c_\tau(w, ran(\mathcal{T})) \leq k\}.$$

Moreover, we have the following theorem, which provides a constructive method for obtaining $Q^{(k)}$.

---

[4]In fact our construction can be applied to any weighted transducer with a slight modification of $\mathcal{T}^0$ (see below).

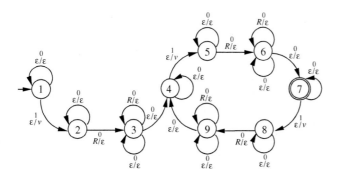

Figure 2. *Enhanced transducer*

Theorem 4 $\text{ran}(\mathbf{k}(\mathcal{T})) = Q^{(k)}$.

PROOF SKETCH. By the construction of $\mathbf{k}(\mathcal{T})$, we have captured in it all the paths of $\mathcal{T}$, which are weighted less or equal to k, and nothing else. From this, and the construction of $\mathcal{T}$, our claim follows. ∎

Continuing our example of Figure 1, we show the transducer enhanced with state labels, and 0-weighted self-loops, in Figure 2.

Let $k = 2$. In the forward direction of recursion, we will reach the point where we need to construct some of the $(\mathbf{0}(\mathcal{T}))_{-,-}$ transducers. We observe that many of the $(\mathbf{0}(\mathcal{T}))_{i,j}$ (where $\{i,j\} \subseteq \{1,\ldots,9\}$) are empty, such as $(\mathbf{0}(\mathcal{T}))_{1,2}$, $(\mathbf{0}(\mathcal{T}))_{3,2}$ etc. Considering those $(\mathbf{0}(\mathcal{T}))_{-,-}$, which are not empty, we try to compute $\mathcal{T}^1$, which results in being empty.

Next, for computing $\mathcal{T}^2$, the recursion will ask for some of the $\mathcal{T}^1_{-,-}$ to be computed. Of those, the non-empty ones are: $\mathcal{T}^1_{1,2}$, $\mathcal{T}^1_{1,3}$, $\mathcal{T}^1_{1,4}$, $\mathcal{T}^1_{2,7}$, $\mathcal{T}^1_{3,7}$, and $\mathcal{T}^1_{4,7}$.

As the recursion rewinds, based on the above transducers, we compute $\mathcal{T}^2$, which is the union of the following non-empty concatenations: $\mathcal{T}^1_{1,2} \bullet \mathcal{T}^1_{2,7}$, $\mathcal{T}^1_{1,3} \bullet \mathcal{T}^1_{3,7}$, $\mathcal{T}^1_{1,4} \bullet \mathcal{T}^1_{4,7}$.

It is easy to see that all the above three resulting transducers have *ran* equal to $Q^{(2)}$, which is v^2. Also, they have *dom* equal to $R^+.R^+$, that is equivalent to the *dom* of the full transducer, which is $(R^+.R^+)^+$. Thus, our Ω query $(v^2)^+$ is indeed 2-bounded and the equivalent non-recursive query can be obtained by the *ran* of the above transducers, which as mentioned above is v^2.

Notably, writing $\mathcal{T}^h_{i,j} = \bigcup_{m \in \{1,\ldots,n\}} \mathcal{T}^{h/2}_{i,m} \bullet \mathcal{T}^{h/2}_{m,j}$ (supposing h is even) instead of naively writing equivalently $\mathcal{T}^h_{i,j} = \bigcup_{m \in \{1,\ldots,n\}} \mathcal{T}^{h-1}_{i,m} \bullet \mathcal{T}^1_{m,j}$, makes us very efficient with respect to h (and in turn with respect to k) for computing $\mathcal{T}^h_{i,j}$ (and in turn $\mathcal{T}^k_{i,j}$). In order to see that, suppose for simplicity that h is a power of 2. Now, from our equation $\mathcal{T}^h_{i,j} = \bigcup_{m \in \{1,\ldots,n\}} \mathcal{T}^{h/2}_{i,m} \bullet \mathcal{T}^{h/2}_{m,j}$, we have that

$\mathcal{T}^2_{i,j}$ will be a union of n transducers of size $2p$ (where p, the upper bound on the sizes of $\mathcal{T}^1_{-,-}$'s, is a polynomial on n), $\mathcal{T}^4_{i,j}$ will be a union of n transducers of size $4np$, $\mathcal{T}^8_{i,j}$ will be a union of n transducers of size $8n^2p$, and so on. Hence, by using our recurrence equation we will get a resulting transducer $\mathcal{T}^h_{i,j}$, which is a union of n transducers of length $hn^{\log_2 h - 1}p$, i.e. the size of $\mathcal{T}^h_{i,j}$ will be $hn^{\log_2 h}p$. In other words, had we used the equivalent equation $\mathcal{T}^h_{i,j} = \bigcup_{m \in \{1,\ldots,n\}} \mathcal{T}^{h-1}_{i,m} \bullet \mathcal{T}^1_{m,j}$, the transducers $\mathcal{T}^h_{i,j}$ would be a union of n transducers of size pn^{h-1}, i.e. the total size would be pn^h.

We are now ready to show the following theorem.

Theorem 5 *The k-boundedness problem is in PSPACE with respect to the size of the query. Furthermore, the decision can be made in space sub-exponential with respect to k.*

PROOF. Recall that deciding k-boundedness, by Theorem 2 and Theorem 3, amounts to testing the language equality $dom(\mathbf{k}(\mathcal{T})) = dom(\mathcal{T})$. Now, from the above discussion it is clear that the size of $\mathbf{k}(\mathcal{T})$ is $\mathcal{O}(kn^{\log_2 k}p)$. So, we can test the language equivalence $dom(\mathbf{k}(\mathcal{T})) = dom(\mathcal{T})$ in space polynomial (see [17]) in the size of $\mathcal{T}$ (which is polynomial in the size of Q), and sub-exponential on k. ∎

We turn now on the lower bound for deciding the k-boundedness. Through a reduction from the universality problem for NFA's we show that

Theorem 6 *The problem of deciding k-boundedness is PSPACE-hard.*

Finally, Theorem 5 and Theorem 6 imply

Corollary 1 *The problem of k-boundedness is PSPACE-complete with respect to the size of the query.*

6 Deciding Finite Boundedness

Now, consider the weighted automaton $\mathcal{A}$, that we get if we project out the output column of the transition relation of the transducer $\mathcal{T} = (P_\mathcal{T}, \Delta, \Omega, \tau_\mathcal{T}, S, F)$, that we, in Section 4, constructed from a query Q. Formally, $\mathcal{A} = (P_\mathcal{T}, \Delta, \tau_\mathcal{A}, S, F)$, where

$$\begin{aligned} \tau_\mathcal{A} = \ & \{(p, \epsilon, 1, q) : (p, \epsilon, v, 1, q) \in \tau_\mathcal{T}\} \cup \\ & \{(p, \epsilon, 0, q) : (p, \epsilon, \epsilon, 0, q) \in \tau_\mathcal{T}\} \cup \\ & \{(p, R, 0, q) : (p, R, \epsilon, 0, q) \in \tau_\mathcal{T}\}. \end{aligned}$$

Let p and q be two states of $\mathcal{A}$, and let π be a path between them, spelling a word w. Note that there can be more than one path [5] between p and q spelling w. In reasoning about the boundedness, we will be interested in the "best" path(s) spelling w, i.e. the one(s) with the smallest weight. Let therefore

$$d_{\mathcal{A}}(p, w, q) = inf\{weight(\pi) : \pi \text{ is a path spelling } w,$$
$$\text{from } p \text{ to } q \text{ in } \mathcal{A}\}.$$

Also, for two subsets P_1 and P_2 of states, we define

$$d_{\mathcal{A}}(P_1, w, P_2) = inf\{d_{\mathcal{A}}(p, w, q) : p \in P_1 \text{ and } q \in P_2\}.$$

Now, we define the *distance* of $\mathcal{A}$, as

$$d(\mathcal{A}) = sup\{d_{\mathcal{A}}(S, w, F)\}.$$

We say that a weighted automaton $\mathcal{A}$ is *limited* if $d(\mathcal{A}) < \infty$.

Based on the these definitions, and the construction of the weighted automaton $\mathcal{A}$, the following theorem can be shown.

Theorem 7 *Q is finitely bounded iff $\mathcal{A}$ is limited.*

Hence, the finite boundedness is reducible to the limitedness of weighted automata. Since such an automaton is constructible in polynomial time on the size of Q, we have that the reduction is polynomial as well.

Now, we show how to efficiently transform the weighted automaton $\mathcal{A}$, that we obtain from the transducer $\mathcal{T}$, into one with ϵ-free transitions, is such a way that the essential features of $\mathcal{A}$ are preserved.

From the automaton $\mathcal{A}$ we will construct another "distance equivalent" automaton $\mathcal{B}$. We shall use $\epsilon\text{-}closure(p)$, similarly to [16], to denote the set of all states q such that there is path π, from p to q in $\mathcal{A}$, spelling ϵ.

Obviously, we will keep all the non-ϵ transitions of $\mathcal{A}$ in the automaton $\mathcal{B}$, that we are constructing.

Now, we will insert an R-transition ($R \neq \epsilon$) in $\mathcal{B}$ from a state p to a state q whenever there is in $\mathcal{A}$ a path π, spelling ϵ, from p to an intermediate state r and there is an R-transition, from that state r to the state q. Formally, if $\mathcal{A} = (P, \Delta, \tau_{\mathcal{A}}, S, F)$, then $\mathcal{B} = (P, \Delta, \tau_{\mathcal{B}}, S, G)$, where

$$G = F \cup \{s : s \in S, \text{ and } \epsilon\text{-}closure_{\mathcal{A}}(s) \cap F \neq \emptyset\}$$

and

$$\tau_{\mathcal{B}} = \{(p, R, 0, q) : (p, R, 0, q) \in \tau_{\mathcal{A}}\} \cup$$
$$\{(p, S, m, q) : \exists r \in \epsilon\text{-}closure_{\mathcal{A}}(p),$$
$$\text{such that } (r, S, 0, q) \in \tau\},$$

where the weight m will be the weight of the *cheapest* path from p to r in $\mathcal{A}$ spelling ϵ.

It is easy to verify about the above constructed automaton $\mathcal{B}$ that

---

[5]Such paths could have some ϵ-transitions as well.

Lemma 1 *$L(\mathcal{B}) = L(\mathcal{A})$, and $d(\mathcal{B}) = d(\mathcal{A})$.*

Hence, we are now able to use Leung's algorithm [19], which is computationally the best known algorithm for solving the limitedness problem (in single exponential time), but for which the ϵ-freeness of the automata is essential.

Regarding the lower complexity bound, it can be shown that the notorious problem of finite power property (FPP) for regular languages can be reduced to our (query) finite boundedness problem. The FPP problem was posed initially by Brzozowski in 1966 during the SWAT (now FOCS) conference. It asked whether for a given regular language, say L, there exists an $m \in \mathbb{N}$, such that

$$L^* = \{\epsilon\} \cup L \cup L^2 \cup \ldots \cup L^m.$$

Now, this can be reduced to the finite boundedness problem by considering a single view $V = L$, a corresponding alphabet $\Omega = \{v\}$, and a query v^*.

The FPP problem remained open for more than 12 years, until shown to be decidable by Hashiguchi in 1978[6] (see [12]). Through combinatorial arguments, he presented a solution which works in exponential time. Another independent solution was obtained by Simon in [24]. Simon's solution also needs exponential time. Since then, there are no new results reported for the FPP problem (see for a review [23]). Thus, it seems highly unlikely that one can do better than EXPTIME for solving the finite boundedness problem.

Finally, as shown by Weber in [28], the FPP problem is PSPACE-hard, which implies that our boundedness problem is PSPACE-hard as well.

Acknowledgment. We would like to thank Daniel Kirsten for pointing to us the [28] paper.

References

[1] Abiteboul S., P. Buneman and D. Suciu. *Data on the Web: From Relations to Semistructured Data and XML.* Morgan Kaufmann Pulishers. San Francisco, CA, 1999.

[2] Bravo L., and Bertossi L. Disjunctive Deductive databases for computing certain and consistent answers from mediated data integration systems. *J. Applied Logic* 3(1): 329–367, 2005.

[3] Calvanese D., G. Giacomo, M. Lenzerini and M. Y. Vardi. Rewriting of Regular Expressions and Regular Path Queries. *Proc. PODS '99*, pp. 194–204.

---

[6]It is before his limitedness theorem for distance automata [13].

[4] Calvanese D., G. Giacomo, M. Lenzerini and M. Y. Vardi. Answering Regular Path Queries Using Views. *Proc. ICDE '00*, pp. 389–398.

[5] Deutsch A., Y. Katsis and Y. Papakonstantinou. Determining Source Contribution in Information Integration Systems. *Proc. PODS '05*, pp. 304–315.

[6] Flesca, S., and Greco, S. Rewriting queries using views. *IEEE Trans. Knowl. Data Eng.* 13(6): 980–995, 2001.

[7] Grahne G. and Mendelzon A. O. Tableau Techniques for Querying Information Sources through Global Schemas. *Proc. ICDT '99*, pp. 332–347.

[8] Grahne G., and A. Thomo. An Optimization Technique for Answering Regular Path Queries *Proc. WebDB '00*, pp. 99–104.

[9] Grahne G., and A. Thomo. Algebraic Rewritings for Optimizing Regular Path Queries. *Proc. ICDT '01*, pp. 303–315.

[10] Grahne, G., and Thomo, A. Query answering and containment for regular path queries under distortions. *Proc. FoIKS '04*, pp. 98–115.

[11] Jonson H., and Xiaoyan Q. DB2 information integrator V8.1: Under the Hood. *ARISE '04* *http://www.scs.carleton.ca/ ~nvillanu/Presentations/IBM.ppt*

[12] Hashiguchi K. A Decision Procedure for the Order of Regular Events. *TCS* 8: 69–72, 1979.

[13] Hashiguchi K. Limitedness Theorem on Finite Automata with Distance Functions. *J. Comp. Syst. Sci.* 24(2): 233–244, 1982.

[14] Hashiguchi K. Improved Limitedness Theorems on Finite Automata with Distance Functions. *TCS* 72(1): 27–38, 1990.

[15] Hashiguchi K. New upper bounds to the limitedness of distance automata. *TCS* 233(1-2): 19–32, 2000.

[16] Hopcroft J. E., and J. D. Ullman. *Introduction to Automata Theory, Languages, and Computation*. Addison-Wesley. Reading MA, 1979.

[17] Hunt H. B. III, D. J. Rosenkrantz, and T. G. Szymanski, On the Equivalence, Containment, and Covering Problems for the Regular and Context-Free Languages. *J. Comp. Syst. Sci.* 12(2): 222–268, 1976.

[18] Lenzerini M. Data Integration: A Theoretical Perspective. *Proc. PODS '02*, pp. 233–246.

[19] Leung H. Limitedness Theorem on Finite Automata with Distance Functions: An Algebraic Proof. *TCS* 81(1): 137–145, 1991.

[20] Levy A. Y., Mendelzon A. O., Sagiv Y., Srivastava D. Answering Queries Using Views. *Proc. PODS '95*, pp. 95–104.

[21] Mendelzon A. O., and P. T. Wood, Finding Regular Simple Paths in Graph Databases. *SIAM J. Comp.* 24(6): 1235–1258, 1995.

[22] Mendelzon A. O. G. A. Mihaila and T. Milo. Querying the World Wide Web. *Int. J. Dig. Lib.* 1(1): 57–67, 1997.

[23] Pin. J. E. Tropical Semirings, *in Idempotency*, J. Gunawardena (ed.) Cambridge University Press, pp. 50–69, 1998.

[24] Simon. I. Limited Subsets of a Free Monoid. *Proc. FOCS '78*, pp. 143–150.

[25] Simon. I. On Semigroups of Matrices over the Tropical Semiring. *Informatique Theorique et Applications* 28(3-4): 277–294, 1994.

[26] Ullman J. D. Information Integration Using Logical Views. *Proc. ICDT '97*, pp. 19–40.

[27] Vardi. M. Y. A Call to Regularity. *Proc. PCK50 - Principles of Computing & Knowledge, Paris C. Kanellakis Memorial Workshop '03*, pp. 11.

[28] Weber A. Distance Automata Having Large Finite Distance or Finite Ambiguity. *Mathematical Systems Theory* 26(2): 169–185, 1993.

CINDI Robot: an Intelligent Web Crawler Based on Multi-level Inspection

Rui Chen
Department of Computer Science, Concordia University
ru_che@encs.concordia.ca

Bipin C. Desai
Department of Computer Science, Concordia University
BipinCDesai@.concordia.ca

Cong Zhou
Motorola Canada Software Center
y18519c@motorola.com

Abstract

With the explosion of the Web, focused web crawlers are gaining attention. Focused web crawlers aim at finding web pages related to the pre-defined topic. CINDI Robot is a focused web crawler devoted to finding computer science and software engineering academic documents. We propose a multi-level inspection scheme to discover relevant web pages. Through this multi-level inspection scheme, the text feature of the content contributes to the classification; furthermore other web characteristics, such as URL pattern, anchor text and so on, assist the decision process. The experiment result demonstrates this multi-level inspection method outperforms other traditional methods.

Keywords: focused web crawler, SVM classifier, Naïve Bayes classifier, multi-level inspection, revised context graph, tunneling

1. Introduction

The size of the Internet is growing exponentially; according to current estimates, the number of searchable web pages on the Internet has exceeded 8.9 billion. This volume of data makes it difficult to get targeted information from the Internet.

Two families of approaches have been proposed to better utilize the Web. One is web directories. It is often generated by web masters or directory staff. For example, Open Directory Project (ODP) [2], the biggest and most comprehensive human-edited directory of the Web, is constructed and maintained by a team of volunteers all over the world. The major advantage of this method is that it provides better content; however it requires huge human involvement.

The other method is web crawlers, automated programs, used by search engines. Web crawlers explore new pages by the hyper linked network structure and discover updates of pages the engine already knows about. This process can be done without human involvement, and has already help create many popular search engines such as Google.

Among different web search strategies, focused web crawlers are gaining attention. A focused web crawler collects relevant web pages limited to a specific topic, domain or format in traversing the Web. However, it is difficult to make the crawler remain in the topic while trying to obtain a reasonable Web coverage. Certain intelligence is required for a focused Web crawler to achieve this goal.

CINDI Robot is a focused web crawler as part of Concordia INdexing and DIscovering System (CINDI) digital library project [1]. It helps dig, collect on-topic on-line documents (research paper, technical notes, FAQs, mailing lists and so on) in the computer science and software engineering field. The topic of interest is specified by a set of user selected positive and negative web page examples.

2. System Architecture

CINDI Robot is composed of five components: Seed Finder, Web Crawler, Link Analyzer, Statistics Analyzer and File Fetcher. In addition, CINDI Robot also interacts with CINDI Document Filtering Subsystem (DFS) [3] to obtain additional statistical information used in its adaptive strategy. Figure 1 illustrates the system architecture of the CINDI Robot. And the following briefly describes these components.

2.1. Seed Finder

Seed Finder finds web sites that would most likely contain topic related documents or most likely lead to those web sites containing such documents. These sites are a good starting point for the whole crawling process. In CINDI Robot, two methods are used to detect these seed URLs.

ODP is the first source for CINDI Robot. It provides publicly accessible data files of links within each category. Using our parser, we retrieved more than 60,000 potential seed URLs from ODP UTF-8 data files. As mentioned previously, ODP provides links with higher quality. However, compared to search engines, the coverage of the Web by this way is relatively limited.

So the second method is using entries obtained from search engines to complement the above seeds. CINDI Robot incorporates searching results from Google and AltaVista to enrich seed URLs.

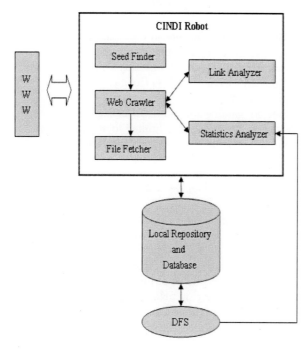

Figure 1. CINDI Robot system architecture diagram

2.2. Web Crawler

CINDI Robot web crawling infrastructure consists of four parts: frontier, preliminary filter, page fetcher and HTML parser. The frontier is a shared seed URL repository among all threads to avoid the abnormality where the threads may converge to the same domain. Seed URLs are initially retrieved from web pages discovered by Seed Finder and complemented during the crawling process. Two priority queues are set up in the frontier. Using a revised context graph and text classifiers, any web page is assigned to one of the crawling queues or discarded. Tunneling technique is used to achieve a better recall. One feature of the CINDI Robot is that it always crawls within the domain site. That is the CINDI Robot won't move to

another web site until it finishes the current one. The preliminary filter implements URL pattern inspection in order to remove useless web pages before actually crawling them. The page fetcher only fetches the web page in HTML format and stores it in a string buffer temporarily for the purpose of quick content parsing and link extraction. A HTML parser parses the text content and extracts anchor texts and outer links. Web crawler interacts with both Link Analyzer and Statistics Analyzer. Link Analyzer provides information on priority queue assignment while Statistics Analyzer provides statistical data for URL pattern inspection.

2.3. Link Analyzer

Link Analyzer is the intelligence core of the CINDI Robot and utilizes a revised context graph algorithm. It learns from the user provided training sets and evolves the knowledge base as crawling progresses. Positive and negative examples provided by the user form two categories: Computer Science and Software Engineering (CSE) category and Non-CSE category. Any web page which falls into the CSE category is considered as relevant while any web page which falls into Non-CSE category is considered as irrelevant. The Link Analyzer has two classifiers to categorize an incoming page. The first one is a Support Vector Machine (SVM) classifier [4] which works in the initial crawling phase. It classifies a web page into one of the two categories. The second is a Naïve Bayes classifier [5] which is activated after the robot has established a knowledge base. Its responsibility is also to decide the relevant category of a web page or declare it as irrelevant.

In order to increase recall, another Naïve Bayes classifier is needed to check if an irrelevant web page is still worthy to be further examined. These three classifiers work on page content text as elaborated in Section 3.2.3. In addition to these three classifiers, Link Analyzer also uses anchor text inspection to enhance CINDI Robot's performance which is defined in terms of both precision and target recall [6]. Context text classifier, anchor text inspection plus URL pattern inspection to analyze a web page form the Multi-level Inspection.

2.4. Statistics Analyzer

Statistics Analyzer works on a higher level. It analyzes at the URL level rather than at the content or anchor text level used in Link Analyzer. It not only collects the Page Relevancy Rate (PRR), the Document Download Rate (DDR) and the Accepted Document

Rate (ADR) during the crawling process, but also receives the downloaded files' filter results from DFS. The above parameters will be elaborated in Section 3.2.1. Statistic Analyzer can decide which URLs should be avoided in order to speed up the crawling process. In addition, statistic analyzer provides real-time relevance feedback for the CINDI Robot to get out of some "trap" sites on the Web. A web site with a PRR less than 5% after crawling 50 web pages will be discarded.

2.5. File Fetcher

File Fetcher uses file links discovered by Web Crawler to download files. It also eliminates duplicated files, check digital signature, filter files with undesired file names and sizes and rename files. All downloaded files are stored in temporary repository waiting for DFS processing.

2.6. DFS

DFS is not part of CINDI Robot being an off-line file filtering system. Due to the speed requirement, CINDI Robot can not perform more sophisticated operations. DFS examines documents downloaded by CINDI Robot, analyzes them and marks them as acceptable or irrelevant [3]. In this process, DFS stores the URLs from which the irrelevant documents are retrieved. This information is shared with CINDI Robot to guide the crawling process, especially for the subsequent re-crawling the sites.

3. CINDI Robot Heuristics

3.1. Revised context graph

By constructing a context graph, the crawler gains knowledge about topics that are directly or indirectly related to the target topic [7]. In a context graph, each layer is constructed using a strict link distance requirement. However, from our experiment with the CINDI Robot this link distance to target documents is of less importance. Hence we employ a revised context graph. Our aim is to identify those web pages which are irrelevant but may lead to relevant web pages in order to increase recall. Notice that in classical context graph even most of the web pages in Layer 2 are still relevant. This largely limits crawlers to find new relevant regions. Thus, we use a revised context graph. We select web pages classified as relevant by content text classifiers to form Layer 1; web pages that derived from Layer 1 web pages and classified as irrelevant but may lead to relevant web pages form Layer 2. Layer 2

web pages are manually identified. The link distances of Layer 2 web pages in the revised context graph span from 2 to 4. After construction of the revised context graph, SVM text classifier (in initial crawling phase) or Naïve Bayes classifier (after the initial crawling phase) is used to test whether a web page belongs to Lay 1. All web pages falling out of Layer 1 will be tested by another Naïve Bayes classifier to see if it belongs to Layer 2.

3.2. Multi-level inspection

Multi-level Inspection of CINDI Robot consists of URL pattern inspection, anchor text inspection and content text classification.

3.2.1. URL pattern inspection. Unlike text categorization in Information Retrieval systems in which only content texts are used in classifying a web page, for web crawlers the URL pattern can provide additional clues for web page classifications.

These clues can help us to directly identify a web site of a university's computer science department. For example, a URL such as "http://www.cs.concordia.ca" can tell us if it is worth crawling without content analysis since its name is associated with a known computer science department at a well recognized university. In some situation, this clue may rectify a wrong classification made by content text classifiers. If a web site is deemed belonging to a computer science department, it is put into the CSE category.

These clues can also accelerate the crawling process. Certain URLs will be directly ignored in the crawling process. The Statistic Analyzer maintains three parameters: PRR, DDR and ADR to achieve this goal. For a URL directory, its PRR is the ratio of the number of relevant pages over the total page number under this directory. DDR is defined as the ratio of the number of documents downloaded over the number of web pages visited for a directory and reflects the density of the links to files under a directory. From our experience, a directory with extremely low DDR (<1%) will be ignored because it is not cost effective. ADR is the ratio of the number of documents accepted over the number of documents downloaded.

PRR and DDR can be learned by Statistic Analyzer itself while for ADR the CINDI Robot has to resort to DFS. Using these three parameters, we can generate two types of lists to guide the crawling [8]. One is called stop-directory list. If DFS reports that there is no relevant document downloaded from a directory name for the first 5 distinct hosts which have this directory, this directory name is marked as a stop-directory. After that, all web pages under this directory won't be crawled. The stop-directory list applies to all web

1098-8068/07 $25.00 © 2007 IEEE

pages. If a web page URL is under one of the directories in the stop-directory list, it will not be crawled. Some stop directories are listed in Table 1.

Table 1. **A subset of stop-directory list**

Stop-directory Name
audio(s)
image(s)
section(s)
puzzle
calendar
lecturenotesweb
transparencies
contact(s)
admission(s)

The other list is called to-be-avoided directory list. For the re-crawling of a specific web site, we keep a record of directories under which there is an expectation of not finding any relevant documents. We notice that the structure of a web site is subject to change, thus new to-be-avoid directories are allowed to be added into the list. Table 2 gives an example of to-be-avoided directory list.

Table 2. **A subset of to-be-avoided directory of a web site**

Host	Directory Name
www.cs.concordia.ca	department/admissions
www.cs.concordia.ca	department/announcement
www.cs.concordia.ca	department/floors
www.cs.concordia.ca	department/policies
www.cs.concordia.ca	department/facilities
www.cs.concordia.ca	programs/ugrad/coop
www.cs.concordia.ca	search

URL pattern inspection also utilizes other heuristics obtained from our experience. For example, a URL whose directory level is greater than 7 won't be crawled [8]. In addition, the Standard for Robot Exclusion [9] is respected in URL inspection.

3.2.2. Anchor text inspection. CINDI Robot employs restrictive measures when selecting new sites from web pages. In addition to the content texts, anchor text also provides a good indication of the relevance of a target web page before actually retrieving it.

Anchor text inspection contributes to the CINDI Robot in three ways. First is to prune irrelevant outer links from a relevant page. The second one is to quickly identify a potential relevant outer links from a Layer 2 web page. It is common for two relevant web pages to be separated by some irrelevant web pages. The anchor text associated with an outer link in a Layer 2 web page can give hints to find a relevant page. For example, a homepage of a university is a typical Layer 2 web page and the anchor text "computer science department" helps CINDI Robot to discover this relevant web site. The third contribution is an off-line fast host selection algorithm after the initial crawl. By constructing an irrelevant anchor text list, we can use simple anchor text matching to filter out those web sites which are totally irrelevant or ambiguous. [8]

3.2.3. Content text classifier. The content text classification is the most important intelligent mechanism of the CINDI Robot. In our design, CINDI Robot possesses two kinds of content text classifiers, namely SVM classifier and Naïve Bayes classifier. They are used in different crawling phases and different scenarios based on their characteristics.

3.2.3.1. Preprocessing. Before extracting the web page features used for SVM Classifier and Naive Bayes Classifier, four steps of preprocessing are done. These four steps are removal of HTML tags, alphabetic characters extraction, removal of stop words [10] and stemming. Porter Stemming Algorithm is used in CINDI Robot [11]. Using terms processed by these steps, a vocabulary is constructed for the classifiers.

For vocabulary construction, we import two new concepts as Revised Keyword Function (RKF) and Revised Document Function (RDF). RKF is defined as the total occurrence frequency of a keyword in all documents in a category and it is formulated as follows:

$$lk_i^k = \sum_{j=1}^{n_k} kf_i^j$$

Where kf_i^j is the occurrence frequency of keyword i in document j; n_k is the total number of training documents in category k.

RDF is to find out the document occurrence of a keyword in a category. It can be written as follows:

$$ld_i^k = \sum_{\substack{j=1,\ldots,n_k; \\ kf_i^j \neq 0}} 1$$

Table 3 shows a subset of the vocabulary.

Table 3. **A subset of the vocabulary**

Keywords	CSE		Non-CSE	
	RKF	RDF	RKF	RDF
comput	90	638	18	26
gnu	4	6	0	0
decod	3	7	0	0
queue	4	26	0	0
hash	3	32	0	0
acm	25	71	0	0
queri	8	22	4	6
oracl	6	20	0	0
latex	2	3	0	0
perl	2	4	0	0
linux	11	41	0	0
grid	12	24	0	0
protocol	4	4	5	8
model	31	85	17	31
thesi	12	18	4	38
advertis	0	0	20	42
agricultur	0	0	14	26
film	0	0	17	105
system	20	43	38	96

* *based on 100 positive samples and 200 negative samples.*

3.2.3.2. SVM classifier. The SVM method was developed by V.N.Vapnik [12] based on structural risk minimization principle. It exhibits a desirable performance under a situation where only limited, nonlinear and high dimensional sample data are available. The SVM tries to find a hyperplane to separate positive and negative samples. Even in the worst case where these samples are inseparable, the SVM will classify these samples with the lowest error rate.

Given a training sample

$$S = ((x_1, y_1), \ldots, (x_l, y_l))$$

Where vector $x_i \in R^m$, $i = 1, \ldots, l$; y is labeled as category of +1 or -1. The corresponding classification function can be rewritten by kernel function as below:

$$f(x) = \mathrm{sgn}(\sum_{i=1}^{l} \alpha_i^* y_i K(x_i \bullet x) + b^*)$$

Where parameters with superscript * mean the optimal solutions.

Radical Basis Function (RBF) kernel function [13] is used in CINDI Robot. It is formulated as:

$$K(x_i, x) = \exp(-\gamma |x - x_i|^2)$$

Distinct words appearing in training documents constitute the feature space. Feature space reduction step is needed. According to our experiments, we select only words with total RDF (the sum of the RDF in CSE category and in Non-CSE category) bigger than 3 under which we can get a best tradeoff between processing speed and accurate classification rate. Before feature space reduction, we get 26,876 distinct words on the training set; after feature space reduction, we get 9,773 distinct words. The Term Frequency and Inverse Document Frequency ($TF \times IDF$) value [14] is widely used for term weights. It says that the importance of a word increases proportionally to the number of times a word appears in the document but is in inverse proportion to the frequency of the word in the corpus. $TF \times IDF$ value is formulated as:

$$w_{ij} = t_{ij*} \log_2 \frac{N}{n}$$

Where w_{ij} is the score of Term T_j in Document D_i; t_{ij} is the frequency of Term T_j in Document D_i; N is the number of documents in collection; n is the number of Documents where Term T_j occurs at least once. However, instead of using $TF \times IDF$ value, we use a combination of RDF and RKF. It can be formulated as:

$$RDF + \gamma * RKF$$

Where γ is a scaling factor to balance the degree of representation of RKF and RDF. It is calculated by the following formula:

$$\gamma = \frac{\sum_{k=1}^{m_c} \sum_{i=1}^{n_k} ld_i^k}{\sum_{k=1}^{m} \sum_{i=1}^{n_k} lk_i^k}$$

Where m is the number of categories and here m equals to 2. This representation gains nearly the same accurate classification rate as $TF \times IDF$ value but with less computing cost.

Practically, we use SVM^{light} [15] for the CINDI Robot. Though SVM^{light} has reasonable speed for real-time classification, the training time would still be relative long and thus not suitable for real-time application. So we only retrain our SVM classifier after we crawl every 50,000 web pages.

3.2.3.3. Naïve Bayes classifier. Naive Bayes Classifier is an intuitive and simple probabilistic classifier based on Bayes' theorem. Compared to SVM classifier, Naïve Bayes Classifier usually works well under a large training set. That's why Naïve Bayes classifier only works after the CINDI Robot collects enough training data. During the crawling course, new incoming web pages will be incorporated into our knowledge base and be used for further classifications. Usually, smoothing is needed, so the conditional probability of any word w_i can be written as:

$$P(w_i \mid category) = \frac{n_{w_i}^k + 0.5}{n^k + 0.5 \times |V|}$$

Where $n_{w_i}^k$ is the number of times w_i appears in the category k; n^k is the total number of words in the category k; $|V|$ is the number of entries in the vocabulary. To avoid arithmetic underflow, it works in log-space. In the CINDI Robot, we propose a weighted probability formula to make a decision. We assign different weight to every distinct word in a web page. Here we use $TF \times IDF$ score as the weighting scheme. Thus we can get:

$\log P(relevant \mid newPage) = \log P(relevant)$
$+ W_{w_1} \log P(w_1 \mid relevant) + \ldots$
$+ W_{w_n} \log P(w_n \mid relevant)$

and

$\log P(irrelevant \mid newPage) = \log P(irrelevant)$
$+ W_{w_1} \log P(w_1 \mid irrelevant) + \ldots$
$+ W_{w_N} \log P(w_n \mid irrelevant)$

Where W_{w_i} is the $TF \times IDF$ score of word w_i. If $\log P(relevant \mid newPage)$ is greater than $\log P(irrelevant \mid newPage)$, then the new page is relevant; otherwise it is irrelevant. The idea behind the weighting scheme is to emphasize the most "useful" words for classification.

For our Naïve Bayes classifier of Layer 2 pages, it also calculates two probabilities $\log P(inLayer2 \mid newPage)$ and $\log P(outLayer2 \mid newPage)$. However, it implements a different decision policy guided by our tunneling strategy. This is discussed in Section 3.3.2.

3.3. URL Ordering and Tunneling

3.3.1 URL Ordering. In an ideal case, one would like to retrieve pages according to the order of their relevance to the specific topic [16]. Thus we established following policies to put web pages into different priority queues of the frontier in order to crawl most relevant web pages as early as possible:

- All URLs found by Seed Finder are assigned to the high priority queue.
- All outer links extracted from web pages which are classified as relevant are assigned to the high priority queue.
- All outer links extracted from web pages which are classified in Layer 2 are assigned to the low priority queue.
- All outer links extracted from web pages which are classified out of Layer 1 and Layer 2 are discarded.

3.3.2. Tunneling. Tunneling is the phenomenon that a crawler reaches some relevant page on a path which does not only consist of relevant pages. [17] Tunneling is a technique to achieve high recall while still maintaining a high.

In CINDI Robot, we implement a simpler tunneling strategy than the one mentioned in [17].In the CINDI Robot, Layer 2 web pages won't be crawled until the CINDI Robot exhausts all Layer 1 web pages. This policy guarantees most relevant web pages are crawled first. Once all Layer 1 web pages have been crawled, tunneling is launched. In tunneling, Layer 2 Naïve Bayes classifier changes the decision policy to that as long as $\log P(inLayer2 \mid newPage)$ is greater than $75\% \times \log P(outLayer2 \mid newPage)$ it is classified as relevant; otherwise it is irrelevant. We call 75% above a bias factor. A smaller bias factor enlarges the opportunity to discover new relevant regions at the cost of the precision. Once the CINDI Robot gets more than 30 Layer 1 web sites, the bias factor will switch back to 100% in order to keep a high precision.

3.4. Additional Heuristics

Since CINDI digital library only collects academic documents such as research papers and technical reports, hence intuitively we know there should be a relationship between the document size and the acceptance probability.

To find this relationship, we did an experiment on 52,552 randomly selected PDF documents. We chose the PDF files as our test documents because they are more representative in terms of volume and diversity of document size. These test documents were processed by DFS, which has a filtering accuracy of 98%. [3] The results are summarized in the Table 4.

We perceive that the number of accepted documents increases as the size of the documents increases. A further test was made to find 8k as the cut-off point for skipping downloading since under this point all test documents are invalid.

Table 4. **Document size and document quality relationship**

Document Size	<10K	<20K	<30K	<40K	<50K
Number of Invalid	1,155	2,517	4,032	5,923	7,890
Number of Valid	8	73	155	303	486
Percentage of Valid	0.7%	2.8%	3.7%	4.9%	5.8%

4. Experiments

We consider precision and target recall as performance metrics of web crawlers. Precision is defined as the proportion of retrieved and relevant web pages to all the web pages retrieved. And target recall is the proportion of relevant web sites that are retrieved and in the target set to the target set. It is a reasonable estimate of the true recall. [6] In this section, we compare the precision and target recall among different web crawlers and also inspect the improvements due to individual heuristics. Standard Breadth-First Search crawler [18] and context graph crawler [7] are employed as comparisons.

4.1 Comparison of Precision of Web Crawlers

For all web crawlers, we use the same initial seed URLs which contains only 15 randomly selected web sites from Seed Finder. A small initial URL set ensures the performances of all web crawlers are compared fairly since for the CINDI Robot the precision is maintained during a really long crawling session due to the higher seed URL quality achieved by the Seed Finder. Figure 2 gives the precision of the crawling process for different web crawlers, where "BFS" denotes Breadth-First Search. We can observe that the CINDI Robot with multi-level inspection and other heuristics outperforms other web crawlers.

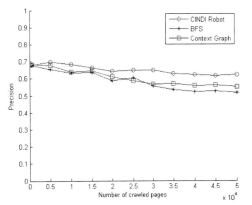

Figure 2. **The precision of web crawlers**

4.2. Comparison of Target Recall of Web Crawlers

As indicated in [6], true recall is hard to measure since we can not know the actual relevant web sites set. Thus we randomly selected 10,000 web sites from the result obtained by Seed Finder as the target set. If a page in a certain web site is crawled, we consider this web site as retrieved. The target recall comparison is given in Figure 3. The experiment result also demonstrates that CINDI Robot exhibits a more desirable target recall than BFS and context graph crawlers.

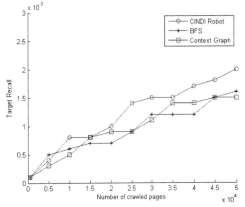

Figure 3. **The target recall of web crawlers**

4.3 Improvements due to Individual Heuristics

In this part we inspect the precision improvements obtained by URL pattern inspection and anchor text inspection along with the target recall improvements due to the revised context graph and tunneling. The content text classifier is considered as an essential part of our CINDI Robot, so we do not examine the improvements attributed to content text classifier.

Figure 4 shows the precision decrease brought by URL pattern inspection and anchor text inspection respectively, where "full-version" denotes the complete CINDI Robot, "without-upi" denotes the CINDI Robot without URL pattern inspection, and "without-ati" denotes the CINDI Robot without anchor text inspection. We can find both URL pattern inspection and anchor text inspection contributes to the precision of CINDI Robot. The contribution of URL pattern inspection here seems less attractive than anchor text inspection. However, it brings significant improvements for re-crawlings. [8]

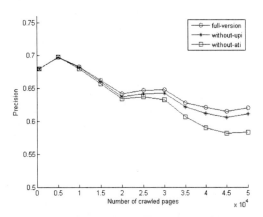

Figure 4. Improvements due to URL pattern inspection and anchor text inspection

Figure 5 gives the target recall comparison between the complete CINDI Robot and the one without the revised context graph and tunneling. This result shows that using the revised context graph and our tunneling strategy, CINDI Robot can discover more relevant regions by traversing some irrelevant intermediates.

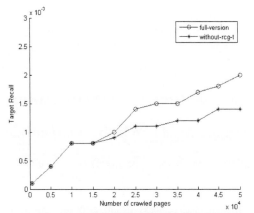

Figure 5. Improvements brought by the revised context graph and tunneling

5. Conclusion

In this paper we propose a multi-level inspection infrastructure for the CINDI Robot. This infrastructure maximally takes advantage of the characteristics of web pages rather than only focus on content text. In addition, we modify other state-of-the-art techniques to better fit the objectives of the CINDI Robot. According to our experiments, the CINDI Robot exhibits desirable precision and recall in the crawling process.

We also recognize that now the content text analysis is only applied to single words rather than phrase. Sometimes phrases give more precise semantic meaning. This will be considered in future work.

Reference

[1] CINDI digital library project, at: http://cindi.encs.concordia.ca

[2] ODP, at http://dmoz.org/

[3] Xue, F.R., "Enhancement of the CINDI system", Master Thesis, Dept. of Computer Science, Concordia University, 2003.

[4] Nello Cristianini, John Shawe-Taylor, *An introduction to Support Vector Machines and other kernel-based learning methods*, Cambridge University Press, England, 2000.

[5] Domingos, Pedro and Michael Pazzani, "On the optimality of the simple Bayesian classifier under zero-one loss", *Machine Learning*, 1997, pp.103–137.

[6] Gautam Pant and Padmini Srinivasan. "Link Contexts in Classifier-Guided Topical Crawlers", *IEEE Transactions on Knowledge and Data Mining, Vol. 18, No.1*, 2006.

[7] M.Diligenti et al, "Focused Crawling using Context Graphs", *26th International Conference on Very Large Databases, VLDB 2000*, pp.527-534.

[8] Cong Zhou. "CNDRobot: A Robot for the CINDI Digital Library System", Master Thesis, Department of Computer Science, Concordia University, 2005.

[9] A Standard for Robot Exclusion, at: http://www.robotstxt.org/wc/norobots.html

[10] Silva, Catarina and Ribeiro, Bernardete, "The Importance of Stop Word Removal on Recall Values in Text Categorization", *Proceedings of the International Joint Conference on Neural Networks, Vol. 3*, 2003, p 1661-1666

[11] C.J. van Rijsbergen, S.E. Robertson and M.F. Porter, "New models in probabilistic information retrieval", British

Library Research and Development Report, no. 5587, London: British Library.

[12] Vladimir N. Vapnik, "The Nature of Statistical Learning Theory", Springer, 1995.

[13] Rung-Ching Chen, Chung-Hsun Hsieh, "Web page classification based on a support vector machine using a weighted vote schema", Expert Systems with Applications 31, 2006, pp.427-435.

[14] Salton, G. and McGill, M. J. *Introduction to modern information retrieval*, McGraw-Hill, 1983.

[15] T. Joachims, *Making large-Scale SVM Learning Practical. Advances in Kernel Methods - Support Vector Learning*, B. Schölkopf and C. Burges and A. Smola (ed.), MIT-Press, 1999.

[16] Jyh-Jong Tsay et al, "AuToCrawler: An Integrated System for Automatic Topical Crawler", *Proceedings of the Fourth Annual ACIS International Conference on Computer and Information Science,* 2005.

[17] M. Ester, M. Gross, H.-P. Kriegel, "Focused Web Crawling: A Generic Framework for Specifying the User Interest and for Adaptive Crawling Strategies", *27th Int. Conference on Very Large Database, 2001*, Rom, Italien, 2001.

[18] M. Najork, J. L. Wiener, "Breadth-First Search Crawling Yields High-Quality Pages", *Proceedings of the 10th International World Wide Web Conference*, May 2001.

Comparison of Complete and Elementless Native Storage of XML Documents

Theo Härder   Christian Mathis   Karsten Schmidt*
University of Kaiserslautern
67663 Kaiserslautern, Germany
Email: {haerder,mathis,kschmidt}@informatik.uni-kl.de

Abstract

Because XML documents tend to be very large, are accessed by declarative and navigational languages, and often are processed in a collaborative way using read/write transactions, their fine-grained storage and management in XML DBMSs is a must for which, in turn, a flexible and space-economic tree representation is mandatory. In this paper, we explore a variety of options to natively store, encode, and compress XML documents thereby preserving the full DBMS processing flexibility on the documents required by the various language models and usage characteristics. Important issues of our empirical study are related to node labeling, document container layout, indexing, as well as structure and content compression. Encoding and compression of XML documents with their complete structure leads to a space consumption of ~40% to ~60% compared to their plain representation, whereas structure virtualization (elementless storage) saves in the average more than 10%, in addition.

1. Motivation

So far, XML research primarily focuses on the management of a few isolated documents which are typically very large (up to several GBytes). Frequently cited examples are available from [15] which reveal huge storage consumption and processing requirements. In many cases [9], [10], storage structures are optimized for specific situations and indexing schemes only support searching (say, based on XPath predicates) within a single document. For general DBMS use, it is mandatory to preserve the full processing flexibility of the "original" documents, while it is highly

advisable to provide encoded and suitably compressed storage structures to save storage space and transfer time.

What are the essential characteristics of such XML documents? An empirical study [14] gathered about 200,000 XML trees worldwide where 99% have less than 8 levels, i. e., less than depth 8 which should be the primary goal of optimization. Almost all of the remaining 1% documents range between 8–30. Only a tiny fraction of the documents gathered has more than 30 levels. To gain some insight into the structural parameters, we have empirically explored a variety of XML documents [7], for which we can only list a summary of the results. The document size is measured in the *plain* format where the XML document is stored in its external "verbose" representation without any compression technique applied (readable element and attribute names, empty spaces, etc., but without node labels used for DBMS-internal processing). The entries in Table 1 contain a representative subset of all documents, called *reference documents*, and serve as our test set in the following. These documents range from a uniform XML structure of moderate depth (4)—representing the content of a relational table—to GB-sized documents of rich XML structures and larger depths. As the last entry, *treebank* is included to show an exotic outlier used to determine the reach of our optimization efforts.

These documents are rather data-centric than document-centric, as confirmed by the column 'avg. value size per content node' in Table 1. For issues such as content compression and relative mapping overhead due to node labeling when natively stored, this kind of documents represent bad or even worst cases. As visualized in Figure 3 and 6, most space is consumed by mapping and control information (node labels, administrative data, etc.) rather than content values. In contrast, document-centric XML structures,

* *This work has been supported by the Rheinland-Pfalz cluster of excellence "Dependable adaptive systems and mathematical modeling" (see www.dasmod.de)*

Table 1: Characteristics of XML documents considered

doc name	description	size in Mbytes	# elem. & attr. nodes	# content nodes	avg. value size per content node	# vocab. names	# path classes	max. depth	avg. depth
line-item	LineItems from TPC-H benchmark	32.3	1,022,977	962,801	12.5	19	17	4	3.45
uni-prot	Universal protein resource	1,821.0	81,983,492	53,502,972	24.0	89	121	7	4.53
dblp	Computer science index	330.0	9,070,558	8,345,289	17.0	41	153	7	3.39
psd-7003	DB of protein sequences	717.0	22,596,465	17,245,756	6.5	70	76	8	5.68
nasa	Astronomical data	25.8	532,967	359,993	20.9	70	73	9	6.08
tree-bank	English records of Wall Street Journal	89.5	2,437,667	1,391,845	33.4	251	220,894	37	8.44

e.g., in digital libraries where a leaf node may host the text of a paper or even a book, have much better overhead/content ratios and would provide much more opportunity especially for content compression.

For the empirical study and all measurements in this paper, we use our prototype DBMS called XTC (XML Transaction Coordinator [8]) which stores and manages XML documents in a native way. To optimize XML storage structures, we describe the most important concepts and options in Section 2. In Section 3, we analyze the storage consumption of formats which store the complete document, i. e., structure and content. In Section 4, we develop a method to virtualize the documents' structure without loosing functionality, before we show that the use of path synopses scales and is a general method to replace the document structure in the storage format. Finally in Section 5, we wrap up with conclusions.

2. Fine-Grained XML Storage

Efficient and effective processing including concurrent read/write operations on XML documents are greatly facilitated, if we use a fine-grained, tree-like internal representation. For this reason, we have implemented in our XTC system an XML tree representation as defined in [20]. In the following, we discuss the core issues of the so-called dynamic DOM storage model exemplified by Figure 1. The structure consists of all inner nodes including the node labels, whereas the leaf nodes together with their labels capture the content of the document.

2.1. Node Labeling

After quite some practical experience, we are convinced that node labeling is the key to efficient management and compression of XML documents. Early

requirements included navigational and declarative access of *static* XML documents which put the only focus on the fast evaluation of the 13 axes (parent/child, ancestor/descendant, ...) of the XPath 2.0 and XQuery language models thereby guaranteeing the sequence semantics. Using complete k-ary trees [12] to establish a consecutive numbering scheme enabled direct and very cheap node label computation for the checking of axes predicates, but failed in case of real documents having incomplete structure of considerable breadth and depth, not to mention dynamic documents.

Substantial development effort was spent on labeling schemes supporting dynamic XML documents for which various forms of range-based and prefix-based schemes were proposed [3], [5]. Although equivalent for checking axes predicates, range-based schemes seem to exhibit some inflexibility when extensive document updates (subtree insertions) have to be accommodated. They completely fail if fine-grained document locking has to be supported. When entering inner nodes of the document via indexes, the entire ancestor path up to the root has to be protected by intention locks [13]. The required functionality to determine all ancestor node labels comes for free using prefix-based schemes, whereas range-based schemes need access to the document and/or additional indexes, thus, typically provoking disk accesses. As a consequence, prefix-based schemes are preferable for dynamic documents with multi-user read/write transactions and also for speeding up index-based processing (see Section 4.4).

An intensive comparison of labeling schemes and their empirical evaluation [7] led us to redesign the existing mechanism in XTC based on a straightforward numbering scheme. DOM trees empowered with prefix-based node labels can be considered as an abstract access model much more flexible for XML document processing; it served as a powerful and adap-

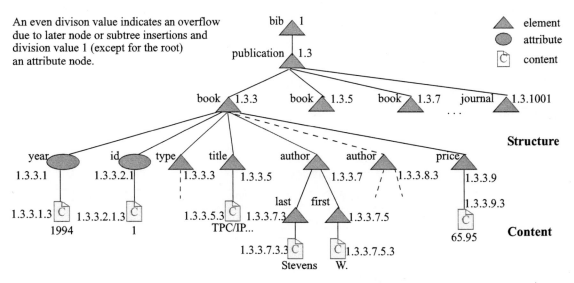

An even divison value indicates an overflow due to later node or subtree insertions and division value 1 (except for the root) an attribute node.

element
attribute
content

Structure

Content

Figure 1: A sample DOM tree labeled with SPLIDs using dist=2

tive structure to be implemented by our storage model in XTC. The prefix-based scheme for the labeling of tree nodes is based on the concept of Dewey order [4] characterized by Figure 1. The abstract properties of Dewey order encoding—each label consists of so-called *divisions* (separated by dots in the external format) and represents the path from the document's root to the node and the local order w. r. t. the parent node; in addition, optional sparse numbering facilitates node insertions and deletions—are described in [3]. Refining this idea, a number of similar labeling schemes were proposed which differ in some aspects such as overflow technique for dynamically inserted nodes, attribute node labeling, or encoding mechanism. Examples of such schemes are DLN [1] or Ordpath [17] developed for Microsoft SQL Server™. Although similar to them, our scheme is characterized by some distinguishing features and is denoted DeweyIDs [7]; it refines the Dewey order mapping: with a *dist* parameter used to increment division values, it leaves gaps in the numbering space between consecutive labels and introduces an overflow mechanism when gaps for new insertions are in short supply—a kind of adjustment to expected update frequencies. Because any prefix-based scheme is appropriate, we use the term SPLID (Stable Path Labeling IDentifier) as synonym for all of them.

Existing SPLIDs are *immutable*, that is, they allow the assignment of new IDs without the need to reorganize the IDs of nodes present. When labels degrade after weird insertion histories[1], relabeling can be pre-

planned; it is only required, when implementation restrictions are violated, e. g., the max-key length in B*-trees. Comparison of two SPLIDs allows *ordering* of the respective nodes in document order. Furthermore, SPLIDs easily provide the IDs of all ancestors, e.g., to enable intention locking of all nodes in the path up to the document root without any access to the document itself [13]. For example, the ancestor IDs of 1.3.3.7.5.3 are 1.3.3.7.5, 1.3.3.7, 1.3.3, 1.3 and 1.

2.2. Physical Node Representation

Having in the order of 10^8 nodes in large XML documents, node encoding needs careful optimization considerations. All node formats (for elements, attributes, or text) are of variable length. Element nodes and attribute nodes only consist of a *key part* and a *name part*, whereas a text node has only a key part and a value part. Because the key part consisting of a one-byte field *KL* (key length) and the encoded SPLID is the Achilles heel of the storage representation (see Figure 1 and 3), it must be reduced very efficiently.

As explored in [7], Huffman codes enable effective and efficient encoding of division values. They consist for each division of a variable-length L_i-code and a binary value O_i stored as (L_i-code | O_i). Using a specific encoding assignment such as in Table 2, a division can be encoded and decoded. Because all SPLIDs start with "1.", we do not need to store it and save 4 bits per SPLID. In addition, we can adjust the Huffman encoding scheme to typical value distributions in the SPLIDs and align codes and value representations to byte boundaries. Hence, this flexi-

1. For example, point insertions of thousands of nodes between two existing nodes can be attenuated by the dist parameter, but nevertheless may produce large SPLIDs.

Table 2: Assigning codes to divisions

L_i-code	length O_i	value range of O_i
0	3	$1 - 7$
100	4	$8 - 23$
101	6	$24 - 87$
1100	8	$88 - 343$
1101	12	$344 - 4.439$
11100	16	$4.440 - 69.975$
11101	20	$69.976 - 1.118.551$
11110	24	$1.118.552 - 17.895.767$
11111	31	$17.895.768 - 2.147.483.647$

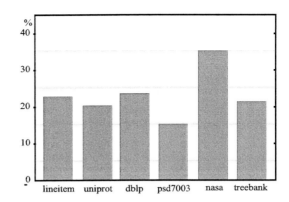

Figure 2: Efficiency of prefix compression

bility enables the tailor-made construction of Huffman codes as illustrated in Table 2.

When traversing and storing XML trees in document order (left-most depth-first order), as visualized in Figure 3, the sequence of SPLIDs lends itself to prefix compression in the key part. To exploit this observation, we designed a prefix-encoded SPLID representation consisting of a one-byte field *Rpip* (reduction of prefix inherited from predecessor) and the actually stored remainder (*Rem*) of the SPLID. Compression is achieved as follows: Within a container page, assume the SPLID sequence 1.3.3.17.33.3, 1.3.3.17.33.5, 1.3.3.17.33.7, 1.3.3.19.3, 1.3.3.19.3.3, ...; then, starting with the first SPLID 1.3.3.17.33.3, we encode the next SPLID by removing a number of divisions from the end to get the common prefix with the current SPLID and add the remainder as a new suffix division sequence: hence, (*Rpip+Rem*) entries in our example look as follows: '-1'+.5, '-1'+.7, '-3'+.19.3, '0'+.3, ... Obviously, this kind of prefix compression achieved the lion's share of space saving. Applied to all SPLIDs in the collection of our reference documents, we obtained the indicative results illustrated in Figure 2. Hence, it is safe to say that prefix compression reduces the space consumed by SPLIDs down to ~25%.

2.3. Document Storage

Document storage is based on variable-length files as document containers whose page sizes varying from 4K to 64K bytes could be configured to the document properties. We allow the assignment of several page types to enable the allocation of pages for documents, indexes, etc. in the same container. Efficient declarative or navigational processing of XML documents requires a fine-granular DOM-tree storage representation which easily preserves the so-called round-trip property when storing and reconstructing the document

(i.e., the identical document must be delivered back to the client). Furthermore, it should be flexible enough to adjust arbitrary insertions and deletions of subtrees thereby dynamically balancing the document storage structure. Fast indexed access to each document node, location of nodes by SPLIDs, as well as navigation to parent/child/sibling nodes from the current context node are important demands. As illustrated by Figure 3, we provide an implementation based on B*-trees which maintains the nodes stored in document order and which cares about structural balancing.

No matter what kind of language model is used for document modification, its operations at the storage level have to be translated into node- or record-at-a-time operations. The overwhelming share of the overhead caused by updates of nodes (names or values) or by insertions/deletions of subtrees in the XML document is carried by two valuable structural features: B*-trees and SPLIDs. B*-trees enable logarithmic access time under arbitrary scalability and their split mechanism takes care of storage management and dynamic reorganization. In turn, SPLIDs provide immutable node labeling such that all modification operations can be performed locally.

While indexed access and order maintenance are intrinsic properties of such trees, some additional optimizations are needed. Variations of the entry layout for the nodes allow for single-document and multi-document stores, key compression, use of vocabularies, and specialized handling of short documents. As shown in Figure 3 by sketching the sample XML document of Figure 1, a B-tree, the so-called *document index*, with key/pointer pairs (SPLID+PagePtr) indexes the first node in each page of the *document container* consisting of a set of chained pages. Using sufficiently large pages, the document index is usually of height 1 or 2. Because of reference locality in the B-tree while processing XML documents, most of the referenced

105

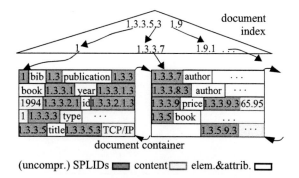

document index

document container

(uncompr.) SPLIDs ▨ content ☐ elem.&attrib. ☐

Figure 3: Stored XML document

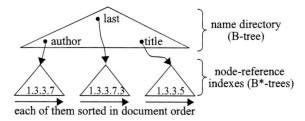

name directory (B-tree)

node-reference indexes (B*-trees)

each of them sorted in document order

Figure 5: Organization of structure indexes

tree pages are expected to reside in DB buffers—thus reducing external accesses to a minimum.

The value part of a content node is materialized (stored inline) up to a parameterized *max-val-size* together with the node as a string (of given type). When the content size exceeds *max-val-size*, then it is stored in referenced mode where it is divided in parts each stored into a single page and reachable via reference from its home page, as illustrated in Figure 4.

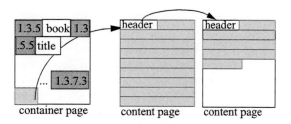

container page   content page   content page

Figure 4: Layout of long fields

2.4. Structure and Content Indexes

In addition to the document store, various indexes may be created, which enable access via structure (element or attribute nodes) or content (values of leaf nodes). An *element index* consists of a *name directory* with (potentially) all element names occurring in the XML document (Figure 5); this name directory often fits into a single page. Each specific element/attribute name refers to the corresponding nodes in the document store using SPLIDs. In case of short reference list, they are materialized in the index; larger lists of references may, in turn, be maintained by a *node reference index* as indicated in Figure 5. Content indexes are created for root-to-leaf paths, e. g., /bib/book/title, and again are implemented as B*-trees keeping for each indexed value a list of SPLIDs as references to the related locations in the document. When processing a

query, a hit list of SPLIDs is built using one or several indexes. Then, the qualified nodes together with their related path instances are located via the document index (see Figure 3). In all cases, support of variable-length keys and reference lists is mandatory; additional functionality for prefix compression of SPLIDs is again very effective.

2.5. Content Compression

There exists a large body of scientific contributions dealing with XML compression technologies [16], [18] promising enormous gains in storage saving and, at the same time, enabling a kind of query processing (restricted to very simple XPath expressions). However, all these approaches are coarse-granular thereby directly compressing the *plain*, i.e., "verbose" representation, assume static and file-based scenarios with single-user operations, are often context-dependent requiring large auxiliary data structures, and need potentially substantial compression/decompression overhead [19]. Therefore, these methods are not adequate for dynamic XML structures processed in a multi-user transactional DBMS context and, in turn, cannot be considered as candidates for our fine-grained tree-like structures.

Two of the main issues to be regarded for compression of fine-grained XML documents in databases result from the XML structure itself and its content. In contrast to the relational world, where typically column-based compression is used, the storage representation of XML paths and their uncorrelated sequence of element/attribute names complicate "simple" path-based compression algorithms such as XMill [11]. Furthermore, transactional modification applied to XML documents prevents *block-based compression* used by PPM algorithms [18]. Note, it does not seem to be helpful to separate content and structure, only to enable the concatenation of smaller values to larger text blocks and, in this way, to achieve better compression results. Such an approach would involve a complete cycle of de- and re-compression when a specific node

106

value is modified. Thus, to avoid undue limitations and overhead of XML processing, compression of single node values seems to be an appropriate and challenging choice. Therefore, we exclusively focus on single nodes and their data stemming either from text content or attribute values.

In our view, there exist two practical approaches to such kind of compression. For compressing node-based content, either *word-based* or *character-based compression* algorithms can be applied. For example, our vocabulary for element/attribute names can be considered as a specific word-based compression (applied to the structure part) used in nearly all XML databases. Due to the dynamic values of XML content nodes, it would be hard to keep a word-based dictionary for compression purposes up to date. In addition, such a dictionary would not have size limitations and, therefore, fast lookups in a memory-resident data structure could not be guaranteed. Furthermore, all our reference documents are rather data-centric having relatively short content values where word-based compression methods would cause too much overhead with limited effect. Therefore, we prefer character-based, context-free compression schemes like Huffman which also accomplish homomorphic transformations which guarantees that compressed and non-compressed documents can be processed by the same operations like parsing, searching, or validating. Hence, we provide an efficient and context-free compression/decompression algorithm called *Fixed Huffman* (FH) which seems to work sufficiently effective on data-centric documents, i. e., short node values. On a document basis, we build either a Huffman tree optimized w. r. t. the typical character distribution of the document's domain or, during an analysis run, we collect the character frequencies of the specific document and construct the optimal Huffman tree for it. To adjust for later document modifications, all 256 possible characters are considered.

3. Complete XML Documents

So far, we have outlined the essential concepts used for the optimization of native XML document storage. In our empirical study, we focus on the variability and optimization of storage structures which can be chosen by the DBMS for incoming documents. The question which secondary element/attribute indexes or content indexes should be provided is orthogonal to the choice of the native document structure and has to be answered w. r. t. the expected workload. Here, we primarily want to illustrate how much storage consumption can be reduced by applying our storage

concepts to the documents. As a comparison mark, we use the storage space needed for a document in its textual representation, i. e., a document in the format sent by the client (user) to the DBMS. We denote this as the *plain* format and normalize all results for a given document to this format (consuming 100%). In the following, we distinguish for all formats between the storage space needed for the content part and the structure part. For the collection of our reference documents, the storage consumption of 'plain' is listed in column 3 of Table 1. As illustrated in Figure 6 and presented in the Appendix in greater detail, the relative fraction of the *plain* structure part—as the prime target of our optimization—ranges between ~45% and ~81%.

The *standard* format stands for the normally chosen native XML document storage in DBMSs; it uses our structural framework: For the content part, it stores uncompressed content and SPLIDs and, for the structure part, SPLIDs, "long" VocIDs (2 bytes), and some administrative data. Storage saving as compared to *plain* is not really mind-blowing, because the reduction gained in the structure part by VocID use is partially compensated by SPLID labeling. For the content part, substantially more space is needed in all cases as compared to the *plain* content, because the relative storage space needed for content nodes due to the SPLIDs added is increased by up to ~50%. The highest reduction for *standard* obtained by *lineitem* is ~30%.

The *compressed* format tries to save storage space as much as possible and stores all structure and content nodes with prefix-compressed SPLIDs and with "short" VocIDs (1 byte), because the vocabularies for our reference documents are small (see column 7 in Table 1). Furthermore, it compresses the content nodes using the FH algorithm. In all cases, the content part is smaller than in the *plain* format, although compressed SPLIDs are added to the nodes. As summarized in Figure 6, storage saving becomes remarkable and ranges between ~40% and ~58% depending on the structure and content particularities in the collection of our reference documents.

The content part compression seems to be exhausted, because data-centric documents with relative small value sizes per content node (see col. 6 in Table 1) do not lend themselves to content compression. Hence for further optimizations, we should concentrate on the structure part. Although we have squeezed it as far as possible within the given tree context, it still consumes quite some fraction of the total compressed document, e.g., 168% of the content part of *lineitem*. Therefore, a novel approach to virtualize the structure seems appropriate, thereby reducing the space consumption further without abandoning processing functionality.

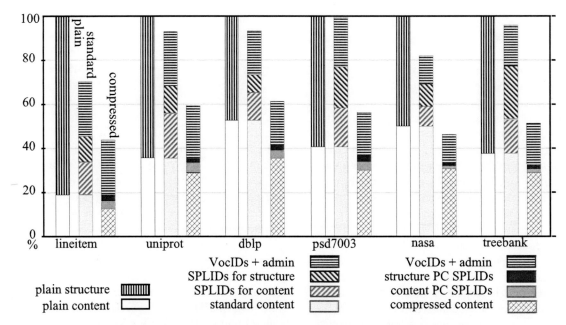

Figure 6: Storage consumption of complete XML documents

4. Virtualizing the XML Structure

So far, compression of structure has used the idea of replacing long external names by so-called VocIDs which index a vocabulary containing all distinct names of elements and attributes. Nevertheless, each structure node had to be explicitly represented and labeled by a (prefix-compressed) SPLID. Obviously with I inner nodes and L leaf nodes, $I > L$ or $I/L > 1$ always holds for all document trees (see Fig.1). To give a rough estimate of the number of structure nodes, we assume a complete tree of height h $(h > 1)$ and fanout n_i at level $1 < i < h$ and consider that each inner node at level $h - 1$ has exactly one leaf node assigned at level h. Then, we obtain

$$I = 1 + \sum_{i=2}^{h-1} \left(\prod_{j=2}^{h-1} n_j \right) \quad \text{and} \quad L = \prod_{i=2}^{h-1} n_i \quad (1)$$

Of course, I depends on the specific inner structure of the document. The relationship I/L may be unbounded $(>> 1)$, if many one-way branches occur in the structure part. In case of complete binary structure trees $(n_i = 2$ for $i = 2, ..., h - 1)$, the well-known relationship $I/L < 2$ holds. To estimate the degree of redundancy present in the structure part, we have listed indicative numbers in Table 1. By looking at columns 4 and 5, we can confirm that I/L is always less than 2. Now consider columns 7 and 8. It immediately becomes clear, that huge repetitions are buried in the names (resp. VocIDs) of the inner nodes and paths.

All paths from the root to the leaves having the same sequence of element/attribute names form a *path class*. Thus, each path in the document can be assigned to one of the relatively few distinct path classes. Reflecting these values, dramatic repetition factors become obvious: consider *uniprot*, in the average, each VocID is repeated >921,000 times and each path >442,000 times.

4.1. Path Synopsis

Our key idea is now to capture all path classes of an XML document in a small data structure [6]. Having such a separate structure, we can remove and drop the entire structure part from the physically stored document and, nevertheless, are able to reconstruct each path or the entire document, whenever needed. Note, by providing such an on-demand option, we don't want to sacrifice functionality, but only safe substantial storage space. Again, the *secret* is the SPLID mechanism with which each node carries a shorthand representation of its entire path to the root. The part missing to deliver the complete path information are the attribute/element names (resp. VocIDs) of all ancestor nodes. This task, we will "outsource" to a so-called *path synopsis*.

For this purpose, we have designed a little memory-resident data structure which maintains all path classes of a document. Cyclic-free XML schemata capture all information needed for the path synopsis; otherwise, this data structure can be constructed while

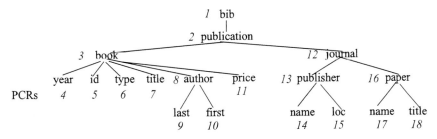

Figure 7: Path synopsis using PCRs to identify paths to the root

the document is stored. To illustrate our approach in Figure 7, we have derived a path synopsis from the document fragment sketched in Figure 1 extended by some additional nodes and path classes. Such a concise description of the document's structure is a prerequisite of effective virtualization of the structure, i.e., for an elementless storage of the document. When comparing them to the number of path instances, it becomes obvious that huge redundancy is introduced when all path instances are explicitly stored. In the popular *dblp* document, for example, one of the dominating path classes /bib/paper/author has ~570,000 instances.

Hence, when matching the right path class with a given SPLID, it is very easy to reconstruct the specific instance of this path class. In a sense, we must associate the value in a document leaf—whose unique position in the document is identified by its SPLID—with a space-saving reference to its path class. Furthermore, when document processing references an inner node—for example, by following an element index for *author* or by setting a lock on a particular *book* for some concurrency control task—, we must be able to rapidly derive the (sub-) path to the root in the virtualized structure. For this reason, by numbering all nodes in the path synopsis, we gain a simple and effective mechanism called path class reference (PCR). Such PCRs are used in the content nodes or in index structures together with SPLIDs serving as a path class encoding.[2]

The sketched usage of the path synopsis indicates its central role as a repository to be used for all structural references and operations. Although it can be stored in a little data structure residing in memory, it should provide indexed access via PCRs and via node names. Another helpful piece of information to be captured in the path synopsis is the number of instances for each path class appearing in the document or other selectivity or fan-out information supporting query optimization. Finally, the path synopsis represents a

kind of type structure which may be efficiently used for hierarchical locking protocols on the document structure.

4.2. Elementless Document Storage

Using an elementless layout of a natively stored document, we want to get rid of the structure part in a lossless way. For an XML document, only its content nodes are stored in document order using—in a similar way as for the complete document—a container as a set of doubly chained pages. The stored node format is of variable length and is composed of entries of the form (SPLID, PCR, value). Otherwise, as illustrated in Figure 8, its storage format exactly corresponds to the data structure in Figure 3. Again, the resulting B*-tree and its split/merge mechanism together with the SPLID mechanism take care of the storage management and label stability in case of modifications in the XML document.

The *elementless* format only stores the content nodes carrying prefix-compressed SPLIDs and adjusted PCRs together with some administration data (2 bytes). As shown in Figure 8, two aspects increase the content part as compared to *compressed*, a PCR (with administration data) is added to the node format and the effectiveness of our prefix compression may get worse due to the non-dense SPLID sequence. Note, both aspects only may be critical in case of data-centric documents because of the unfavorable ratio between mapping overhead (SPLID + PCR + admin) and the relatively short values in content nodes. Fortunately, both effects have only limited influence that our idea of structure virtualization pays off.

As illustrated in Figure 8, elementless storage has considerably reduced the density of the SPLID sequence, because all SPLIDs of structure nodes were removed. Obviously, the SPLID density of the complete documents caused the excellent results for prefix compression (PC). Therefore, we have checked the influence of this contra-effect to the overall space reduction. As presented in Figure 9 for the non-dense

---

2. If a node has an *empty* value, the respective node type must carry a PCR to map the empty value to the correct path.

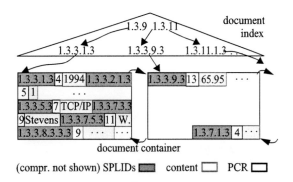

Figure 8: Stored elementless XML document

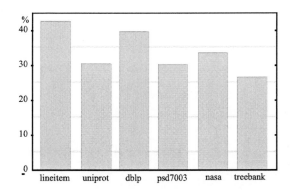

Figure 9: PC in elementless documents

case, prefix-compressed SPLIDs only decrease storage space down to ~35%, as compared to ~25% in the dense case as shown in Figure 2—a trade-off effect that is acceptable.

Figure 10 (and Table 4 in the Appendix) summarize our results gained by structure virtualization. Considering only the compressed SPLIDs and content, the space for our *elementless* reference documents does not consume more storage than the *plain* content. Of course, mapping data PCRs + admin roughly need 10% of the *plain* document size, such that the *plain* content size can not be beaten by *elementless*. However, *elementless* compared to the optimized complete document (Figure 6) is reduced once more by ~10% to ~20% of the *plain* size. Referring to *plain* format, we have achieved a reduction for the optimized document storage down to ~30% to ~50% of the *plain* size. In case of *uniprot*, this saving is 976 MByte. When directly comparing *compressed* and *elementless*, the relative saving ranges from ~15% to ~25%.

One may argue that this favorable space behavior is paid by some extra processing overhead, because coding/decoding and compression/decompression has to be performed for allocating the documents on disk and for (partially) reconstructing them for internal processing or output to the client. However, the compaction effect on the XML structures saves disk I/Os directly proportional to the reduction ratio obtained. Furthermore, it has a beneficial effect on caching effectivity, because the same cache size can host a larger fraction of the XML document in its compacted form. Therefore, there is some potential for them to win the contest also for processing times.

4.3. Comparison of Processing Times

Because the document sizes of our reference collection vary by about two orders of magnitude, the I/O-driven processing times differ by the same ratio—

ranging from ~45 secs to ~6600 secs. Therefore, it is unreasonable to compare them directly on an absolute scale. We rather normalize them to the elapsed times needed for *standard* (100%).

The characteristic processing times chosen are the costs of loading and reconstructing a document thereby preserving the round-trip property. Sent by a client in *plain* format, it is stored resp. fetched in the *standard/compressed/elementless* formats on/from disk and delivered in *plain* format to the client. As illustrated in Figure 11, all loading and reconstructing times are less than the resp. times for *standard* (loading=100%) although additional overhead for SPLID encoding and content compression had to be spent. This fact clearly confirms the dominating role of I/O in processing large XML documents. The same observation can be approved when comparing the processing times for both format optimizations with each other. By examining Figure 6 and Figure 10, we can state that the storage saving gained from choosing format *compressed* instead of *standard* resp. *elementless* instead of *compressed* translates in all cases to shorter processing times for fine-grained document storage and reconstruction back to the external format.

4.4. Using Indexes on Elementless Documents

Index support is achieved in the same way as described in Section 2.4. The various types of indexes (for content or elements/attributes) refer to the indexed nodes via SPLIDs. Location of a content node is performed via the document index, as illustrated in Figure 8, where the path instance is then recomputed. The option to include the PCR together with its SPLID in the reference lists, enables query processing often without accessing the document itself, because the path instance can be regained by using the path synopsis directly. In element/attribute indexes, this extended reference format (SPLID+PCR) is mandatory for perfor-

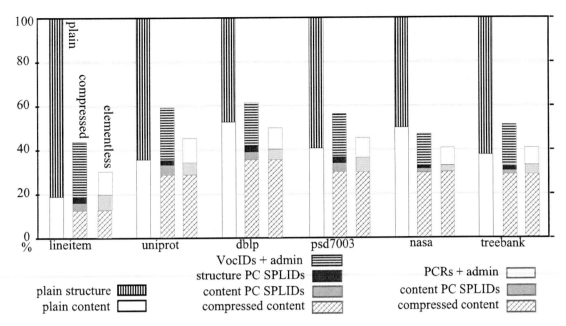

Figure 10: Storage consumption of elementless XML documents

Legend:
plain structure ▥ | VocIDs + admin ▤ | PCRs + admin ☐
plain content ☐ | structure PC SPLIDs ■ | content PC SPLIDs ▦
| content PC SPLIDs ▦ | compressed content ▨
| compressed content ▨ |

mance reasons, because an algorithmic reconstruction of the virtualized path instance in the non-existing structure part is too troublesome.[3]

In the same way, as we derive the structure or particular path class instances on demand, we can answer content-and-structure (CAS) queries only by using content indexes. Query evaluation on these indexes (B*-trees) delivers a set of SPLIDs together with the PCRs which enable the in-memory reconstruction of the paths (structure) belonging to the indexed values (content). The use of such CAS queries is particularly efficient, because our approach can often avoid expensive structural joins or twig evaluation [2] and can derive the path information from the combined use of SPLIDs and path synopsis. For specific CAS queries supported by content indexes, up to two orders of magnitude response-time reduction compared to traditional approaches were achieved with our XTC prototype DBMS [8].

4.5. Scalability of Path Synopsis Use

So far, we have tacitly assumed that the document's path synopsis is a little data structure that always can be kept in main memory. This is obviously true for most of our reference documents where less than a page is needed for maintaining all path classes.

3. Reconstruction of path instances had to be accomplished starting from the stored leaves (content nodes). SPLID checking and path synopsis use could then identify the right path instances.

However, this assumption is violated for *treebank*, a kind of exotic outlier. To check the influence of size on path synopsis use, we designed a stress test for its scalability.

Our abstract approach separated structure from content and removed all redundancy from the structure by replacing it by a much more space-economic, however, functionally equivalent path synopsis. The critical question is whether or not the processing and storage benefits will be preserved when the path synopsis grows such that eventually the size of the structure part is reached. As opposed to comparing our collection of fixed-size reference documents under *compressed* and *elementless*, we have created a synthetic document and scaled it under a specific growth pattern thereby measuring the loading and reconstruction times under both storage formats with an initial document size *IDoc*. Starting with a document root, we attached as *child-1* a (sub-) tree of IDoc=26 KB and 154 PCRs. By repeatedly attaching the same tree as *child-i* (i=2, ..., n), we enforced a linear growth of the path synopsis from 1 to 2000 occurrences of *IDoc* (>300,000 PCRs and >50 MB document size) still residing in main memory. The test runs using small growth factors (<20) are disregarded in Figure 12, because extra startup costs (creation of document container and various indexes for document, elements, and IDs) dominated the load and reconstruction cost. Apparently, all our cost measures (ms per *IDoc*) remained more or less constant in the range of >20*IDoc* to 2000*IDoc* as illustrated

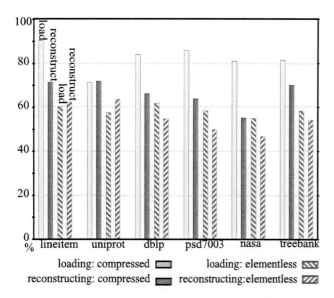

Figure 11: Comparison of processing times

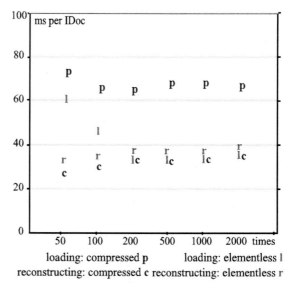

Figure 12: Scalability test for *compressed* and *elementless*

in Figure 12. This result confirms and extends our observations from the measurement of Figure 11 and states the scalability of the path synopsis as long as it can be kept in main memory (where it is designed for).

In this paper, we primarily discussed important concepts needed to obtain fine-grained storage structures for XML documents. Furthermore, we sketched the potential benefit of compression methods applied to content nodes. In a thorough empirical study, we have evaluated the storage consumption of a number of reference documents for the *standard* format and the *compressed* format. Especially, prefix compression used in the *compressed* format contributed to a large extent to the savings achieved. The still substantial storage needs for the documents' structure part gave rise to develop a path synopsis which, together with the SPLID and PCR mechanisms, enabled the design of the *elementless* format. This kind of structure virtualization really achieved impressive optimization results. Furthermore, we could show that the size of the path synopsis is insensitive to the processing times, as long as it can be kept in main memory.

5. Conclusion

What does this saving achieved by structure encoding and content compression mean? For example, assume *uniprot*: the *plain* document (in text format) arriving at the DBMS has 1821 MBytes. A straightforward encoding (VocIDs for the element/attribute names, uncompressed content, added node labels), here

denoted as *standard*, results in 1685 MBytes. Our optimizations obtain for *compressed* and *elementless* ~988 and ~845 MBytes, respectively. Using any of these models, all declarative or navigational operations can be applied with the same or improved speed. Even when storing compressed contents, the use of indexes does not pose any problem.

References

[1] Böhme, T., and Rahm, E. Supporting Efficient Streaming and Insertion of XML Data in RDBMS. *Proc. 3rd Int. Workshop Data Integration over the Web* (DIWeb), Riga, Latvia, 70-81 (2004)

[2] Bruno, N., Koudas, N., and Srivastava, D. Holistic Twig Joins: Optimal XML Pattern Matching. *Proc. SIGMOD*: 310-321 (2002)

[3] Christophides V., Plexousakis D., Scholl M., and Tourtounis S. On Labeling Schemes for the Semantic Web. *Proc. 12th Int. WWW Conf.*: 544-555 (2003)

[4] Dewey, M. Dewey Decimal Classification System. http://www.mtsu.edu/~vvesper/dewey.html

[5] Cohen, E., Kaplan, H., and Milo, T. Labeling Dynamic XML Trees. *Proc. PODS Conf.*: 271-281 (2002)

[6] Goldman, R., and Widom, J. DataGuides: Enabling Query Formulation and Optimization in Semistructured Databases. *Proc. VLDB*: 436-445 (1997)

[7] Härder, T., Haustein, M., Mathis, C., and Wagner, M. Node Labeling Schemes for Dynamic XML Documents Reconsidered. *Data & Knowl. Engineering* 60:1, 126-149 (2007)

Table 3: Sizes of Plain and Standard

doc name	Plain			Standard			
	total (MB)	structure	content	structure		content	
				SPLIDs	admin	SPLIDs	content
lineitem	32.3	26.1	6.2	3.8	8.0	4.7	6.2
uniprot	1,821.0	1152.0	669.0	204.0	433.0	379.0	669.0
dblp	330.0	156.0	174.0	29.3	65.7	41.7	174.0
psd7003	717.0	424.0	293.0	130.5	161.0	127.5	293.0
nasa	25.8	13.4	12.4	2.6	3.6	2.6	12.4
treebank	89.5	56.0	33.5	21.2	16.4	14.3	33.5

Table 4: Sizes of Compressed and Elementless

doc name	Compressed				Elementless		
	structure		content		content		
	SPLIDs	admin	SPLIDs	content	SPLIDs	PCR+admin	content
lineitem	1.03	7.0	0.96	4.39	1.98	3.84	4.39
uniprot	36.7	356.5	81.3	514.0	117.6	214.0	514.0
dblp	7.5	54.8	9.2	121.7	16.7	33.4	121.7
psd7003	21.4	138.0	18.6	216.9	39.9	69.3	216.9
nasa	0.47	3.1	0.43	8.07	0.9	1.5	8.07
treebank	2.4	14.0	1.4	25.4	3.8	7.0	25.4

[8] Haustein, M. P., and Härder, T. An Efficient Infrastructure for Native Transactional XML Processing, in *Data & Knowledge Engineering*, Elsevier, 2007.

[9] Jagadish, H. V., Al-Khalifa, S., Chapman, A., Lakshmanan, L. V S., Nierman, A., Paparizos, S., Patel, J. M., Srivastava, D., Wiwatwattana, N., Wu, Y., and Yu, C. TIMBER: A native XML database. *VLDB Journal* 11(4): 274-291 (2002)

[10] Li, H.-G., Alireza Aghili , S., Agrawal, D., and El Abbadi, A. FLUX: Content and Structure Matching of XPath Queries with Range Predicates. *Proc. XSym*, LNCS 4156, 61-76 (2006))

[11] Liefke, H., and Suciu, D. XMill: an Efficient Compressor for XML Data. *Proc. SIGMOD*: 153-164 (2000)

[12] Meier, W. eXist: An Open Source Native XML Database. *Web, Web-Services, and Database Systems*, LNCS 2593, 169-183 (2002)

[13] Mathis, Ch., Härder, T., and Haustein, M. Locking-Aware Structural Join Operators for XML Query Processing, *Proc. SIGMOD Conf.*: 467-478 (2006)

[14] Mignet, L., Barbosa, D., and Veltri, P. The XML Web: a First Study. *Proc. 12th Int. WWW Conf.*, Budapest (2003), www.cs.toronto.edu/~mignet/Publications/www2003.pdf

[15] Miklau, G. XML Data Repository, www.cs.washington.edu/research/xmldatasets

[16] Ng, W., Lam, W. Y., and Cheng, J. Comparative Analysis of XML Compression Technologies. *World Wide Web* 9(1): 5-33 (2006)

[17] O'Neil, P. E., O'Neil, E. J., Pal, S., Cseri, I., Schaller, G., and Westbury, N. ORDPATHS: Insert-Friendly XML Node Labels. *Proc. SIGMOD Conf.*: 903-908 (2004)

[18] Shkarin, D. PPM: One Step to Practicality. *Proc. IEEE Data Compression Conf.*: 202-211 (2002)

[19] Skibinski, P., and Swacha, J. Combining Efficient XML Compression with Query Processing (2007)

[20] W3C Recommendations. http://www.w3c.org (2004)

Appendix

The Tables 3 and 4 contain the numeric results of our empirical evaluation of the different storage formats for natively stored XML documents

Contrasting the Contrast Sets: An Alternative Approach

Amit Satsangi
Department of Computing Science
University of Alberta, Canada
amit@cs.ualberta.ca

Osmar R. Zaïane
Department of Computing Science
University of Alberta, Canada
zaiane@cs.ualberta.ca

Abstract

The need to identify significant differences between contrasting groups or classes is ubiquitous and thus was the focus of many statisticians and data miners. Contrast sets, conjunctions of attribute-value pairs significantly more frequent in one group than another, were proposed to describe such differences, which lead to the introduction of a new data mining technique - contrast-set mining. A number of attempts have been made in this regard by various authors; however, no clear picture seems to have emerged. In this paper, we try to address the problem of finding meaningful contrast sets by using Association Rule based analysis. We present the results for our experiments for interesting contrast sets and compare these results with those obtained from the well-known algorithm for contrast sets-STUCCO.

1. Introduction

A commonly asked question for data analysis in any discipline is: "How can several contrasting groups be compared against each other?" Depending on the context this leads to specific questions like-which categories of students are more likely to accept an admission offer from a University? What are the specific characteristics that best differentiate between patients with a specific disease and normal patients? What distinguishes between the customers that buy more than some value and those that buy less than another threshold? What is the difference between male and female managers, all other things being equal? Do postgraduate degree holders fare better in their career, than those who hold only a bachelors degree?

The differences between the contrasting groups can be described in terms of conditional probabilities (i.e. the probability of a group given some conjunctions of attribute value pairs), such as:

P(Degree=Bachelors | Income=high ∧ Position=Manager)= 34%,
and
P (Degree=Doctorate | Income=high ∧ Position=Manager) = 43%

These conditional probabilities are actually equivalent to the two association rules given by:

Degree=Bachelors → Income=high ∧ Position=Manager (34%),
and
Degree=Doctorate → Income=high ∧ Position=Manager (43%)

where the percentages represent the support for the association rule within each group and the consequent is called a contrast[1] set.

Contrast set mining was introduced as emerging pattern mining [5] by Dong et al. using the framework of Association rule-based technique introduced in [3] by Bayardo et al. in their Max-Miner algorithm. The problem was independently researched by Bay et al. [1] in the context of statistical significance of contrast sets, by employing a Max-Miner like approach in the search space; a more detailed description and evaluation can be found in [2]. The authors propose an algorithm called STUCCO (Searching and Testing for Understandable Consistent COntrasts) for determining the statistical significance of contrast-sets; they use a canonical ordering of nodes in the search space by using set-enumeration trees, and employ χ^2 testing of two-dimensional contingency tables, along with modified Bonferroni method for controlling Type I error (or false positives, i.e. finding only but not necessarily all significant contrast sets).

Later, Webb et al. [8] used rule-discovery techniques, in their algorithm called Magnum Opus, by

---

[1] The original definition of contrast set, as given in [1], has been modified here for reasons discussed later on.

employing a heuristic approach to cut down on the number of contrast sets in the search space. They conclude that contrast set mining is a special case of the more general rule-discovery task. Finally, Hilderman et al. [6] consider a different approach, whereby they employ three additional constraints to the STUCCO framework, and seek to control Type II error (or false negatives i.e. attempting to reduce the missed significant contrast sets). Using their algorithm called CIGAR (ContrastIng Grouped Association Rules), the authors find a different lot of contrast-sets from that of STUCCO; they conclude that both STUCCO and CIGAR represent valid alternative solutions to the problem of identifying contrast sets.

2. Problem Definition

Any relation with observations defined on attributes can be translated into a set of transactions D such that each example E in D is described by a vector of m attribute-value pairs A1 = V1, A2 = V2, …Am = Vm; each Vi is selected from a finite set {Vi_1, Vi_2, … Vi_n} such that the elements of this set take only discrete values. One attribute in D is such that its value V_{jk} in E is used to assign E into one of n mutually exclusive groups G1, G2, …Gn. In [1] and [2] a contrast set X is defined as a conjunction of attribute-value pairs on G_1, G_2, G_n, such that no A_i occurs more than once.

Thus we get rules of the form $(A_j = V_{jk}) \rightarrow X$, where the antecedent determines the group membership, while the consequent is called a contrast set. Contrast set mining aims to identify all contrast sets for which the support is significantly different across groups. STUCCO achieves this end by imposing two constraints

$$\exists_{ij} P(X \mid G_i) \neq P(X \mid G_j) \qquad (1)$$

$$\max_{ij} \left| \text{support}(X, G_i) - \text{support}(X, G_j) \right| \geq \text{min\_dev} \qquad (2)$$

The support of a contrast set X for a group G_k, given by support(X,G_k) is the fraction of the examples in G_k where the contrast set is true. The first constraint (equation 1) is called the significance condition; it checks for the statistical significance of the contrast-set, the second condition (equation 2) is called the largeness condition; when both the conditions are met it is called a deviation. *min_dev* is a user defined threshold called the minimum support difference.

3. Problems with Related Work

In [1], [2] and [6] the contrast sets are reported as belonging to the association rules such as *Group* $\rightarrow$ *contrast set* (for brevity we will, hence forth, refer to these kinds of contrast sets as the "first kind"). The authors do not consider other kind of contrast sets (henceforth referred to as the "second kind") that come from the rules of the type *contrast set* $\rightarrow$ *Group*. In [8], the authors consider only the second kind of contrast sets. Later, we show that only the second kinds of contrast sets exist. The second issue regarding the methodology involved in previous works is that there seems to be no consensus on the kind of filter to be used to prune the search space. In their concluding remarks in [8], the authors mention that neither STUCCO nor Magnum Opus applies a perfect filter, and that while STUCCO seemed to discard some contrasts of potential value, Magnum Opus appears to include contrast sets that were probably spurious, thus highlighting the inadequacy of the two approaches.

In [7], the authors prove that Magnum Opus actually does a within-groups comparison rather than a between-groups comparison and thus generates only a subset of the contrast sets generated by STUCCO. The claim made by Peckham *et al.* is true, at the same time it seems to be adding more confusion to the field because in [8], Webb *et al.* had claimed and reported results showing that Magnum Opus produced all the contrast sets generated by STUCCO and a few more interesting ones that STUCCO failed to produce. Thus it seems that all the approaches so far have been unable to tackle the root of the problem and there seems to be no agreement on this issue.

4. An Alternative Approach

Bay *et al.* state that employing association rules has three problems. First, there are too many rules to compare. Second, in some cases, there are rules in one group that have no match amongst any of the other groups. Third, even with matched rules, proper statistical comparison has to be made to see if the differences in the support and confidence are significant; if the contrast sets are mined separately and these comparisons are employed on them afterwards, one loses opportunities to prune the sets.

We concede that their first and third objections are true, however, that only affects the total time required and not the accuracy; also regarding their third objection we argue, later, that it can actually be a significant advantage if contrast set mining is used as an intermediate step to study certain problems. Their second argument has implications on the accuracy of the results, and rightly so, however, having found a way to overcome this issue we decided to use association rules to investigate the problem of finding contrast sets because of the inadequacies of the earlier mentioned techniques, and their conflicting conclusions.

Association rules form the backbone of all the previously mentioned approaches, and hence the accuracy of the results obtained by this approach cannot be questioned, even if this approach might be slower. Our hypothesis was that association rules, being the foundation of this problem, will generate all the "interesting" and "useful" contrast sets that were generated by STUCCO and potentially many more. While our approach still aims at identifying the contrast sets that satisfy the deviation conditions of STUCCO (i.e. to find the significant and large contrast sets), it does so using association rules, and in the process does not suffer from the same shortcomings as Magnum Opus (regarding the within-group comparison as opposed to an inter-group comparison as identified by Hilderman *et al.*)

4.1. Finding Deviations

The solution that we employed to overcome the problem regarding the presence of rules in one group that have no match amongst any of the other groups (the objection raised by Bay et al.), was to modify the largeness condition, for such cases. Consider a contrast set such as *(Income=high Λ Position=Manager Λ Sex=male)*, in the group *Degree=Doctorate* with a support of 43%. For the sake of argument let us assume that the above contrast set does **not** exist in the group *Degree=Bachelors*; we call such contrast sets α-contrast sets. The normal contrast sets, called β-contrast sets, are those for which the contrast set exists in at least two groups. In the case of α-contrast sets the largeness condition cannot *normally* be applied owing to absence of sufficient support for the second group; we propose that the minimum support used for generating the association rules for that group should instead be used, in the largeness condition. Thus the modified largeness condition is given by:

$$\left| support\left(X\middle|G_i\right) - min\_supp\_apriori \right| \geq min\_dev \quad (3)$$

The justification for this comes from the fact that if the association rule corresponding to the contrast set *(Income=high Λ Position=Manager Λ Sex=male)* is not found in the group *Degree=Bachelors*, then it must either be the case that the support for the contrast set was either much less than the minimum support used for generating the association rules or it could be, or just a shade less than the minimum support. In either case we have no way of knowing which condition was true because of the very fact that the association rule was absent, however, the minimum support forms an upper-bound in this case, and hence represents the worst case analysis in the largeness condition above. If the potential α-contrast set satisfies (3) then it should be considered as satisfying the largeness condition. By employing this condition we were able to keep a significant number of contrast sets that would have been wrongly pruned. Note that the assumption that the support for the contrast set is zero because it does not appear in the set of Association Rules ($\tilde{A}$) would be wrong; consider the case that the actual support in the dataset for a particular association rule was 1.9% (for e.g.) while the min_support used in the Apriori code was 2.0%, and hence that association rule did not appear in $\tilde{A}$. This does not imply a support of 0% for that Association Rule; had we used 1.9% as the value min_support we would have found that particular Association Rule in $\tilde{A}$ that were extracted from the dataset.

4.2. Contrast Sets: First and Second Kind

We ran an association rule program[2] on our data sets and discovered that the number of association rules generated for the first kind of *potential* contrast sets was far too less (always less than 1%) than the number of association rules corresponding to the second kind of contrast sets. In all of these cases the contrast set was composed of only single item-sets. Initially puzzling, this result was easy to interpret; consider the case where we have two groups in the data set, and assuming that they occur approximately equally in the data-thus 50% of the records belong to group 1 while the other 50% belong to group 2. The support for the rule *Group1* ➔ *A, B, C* will be: $P(A \cap B \cap C \cap Group1)/P(Group1)$.

Given that *P(Group1)* is very high (~0.5) the support for it will be very low implying that the minimum support inputted for generating association rules must be very low. We used a value of 1% for the

---

[2] Christian Borgelt's implementation of Apriori version 4.28 [4]

minimum support and found that only single item-sets on the right hand side are able to meet these conditions. On the other hand for the rules of the second kind: $A,B,C \rightarrow Group$, the denominator is the $P(A \cap B \cap C)$, which is small and hence the value of minimum support that goes into Apriori code can be relatively high. Having laid this issue to rest, we decided to consider only contrast sets (and hence association rules) of the second kind.

5. Experimental Results

In this section we present the results of our experimental evaluation and comparison of the contrast sets obtained from STUCCO and Association Rules. STUCCO was supplied by the original author-Dr. Stephen Bay. STUCCO is implemented in C++ and was compiled using g++ (version 3.4.4) run on Linux (2.6.9-42.0.3Elsmp). We implemented our code in Java 1.4.1 and ran it on a Linux (kernel version 2.6.9-42.0.3Elsmp) PC with a 2.4 GHz. AMD 64 bit Processor (4000+) and a 2 GB of memory. The Apriori code [4] is written in C. Our Java code encapsulates Apriori to extract the relevant contrast sets from the association rules results of the Apriori program.

5.1. The Datasets

We ran STUCCO and our code on different datasets and we report here three of those: Mushroom, Breast Cancer and Adult Census. The Mushroom dataset describes characteristics of gilled mushrooms; it available from the UCI Machine Learning Repository (www.ics.uci.edu/~mlearn/MLRepository.html). The Adult Census dataset is a small subset of the Adult Census Data: Census Income (1994/1995) dataset-a survey dataset from the U.S. Census Bureau. The Breast Cancer dataset, again obtained from the UCI Machine Learning Repository (as above), was collected by physicians and the data belongs to two groups: recurring and non-recurring.

The characteristics of the datasets are shown in Table 1 where the Tuples column describes the number of tuples in the dataset, the Attributes column describes the number of attributes, the Values column describes the number of unique values contained in the attributes, and the Groups column describes the number of distinct groups-as defined by the number of unique values in the grouping attribute.

Table 1. Properties of the datasets

Dataset	Tuples	Attributes	Values	Groups
Mushroom	8,142	23	130	2
Adult Census	826	13	129	2
Breast Cancer	286	9	53	2

5.2. The Algorithm

The cleaned data, for each group, is stored in a separate file and the Apriori program is run for all of these separately. Apriori generates association rules and we "grep" all those association rules of the kind $Group \leftarrow contrast\text{-}set$, and store them in separate files again. At this point we have as many files as the number of groups; we then sort these association rules and feed these files with sorted association rules to a java program. The program reads the first lines of these files initially and starts comparing the right hand side of these association rules to check if they form a contrast set. A lexicographical comparison of these "Strings" is carried out and the one that is lexicographically smaller than others is marked as zero while the rest are all ones. If more than one strings match than they are marked zero. If there is only one zero then it is a potential α-contrast sets and hence the modified largeness condition is checked for that string, while if there are more than one zeros those strings are checked for the deviation condition.

After that one more line is read only from the files(s) that has/have a zero corresponding to them; once again a lexicographical minimum is found and so on until all the lines from all the files are read. If the end of a file(s) is reached while other files still have lines to be read, then no more lines are read from that file(s).

5.3. The effect of maximal number of item-sets

Christian Borgelt's code for generating association rules using Apriori analysis requires a maximal number of items per set (**n**) where by the default value is 5. Potentially this corresponds to the maximum number of attribute-value pairs in a discovered contrast set. As we did not know of an optimal value for **n**, in advance, we decided to vary this number all the way from 2 to

13 (the maximum number of attributes) for the Adult Census dataset, and similarly for the Mushroom dataset.

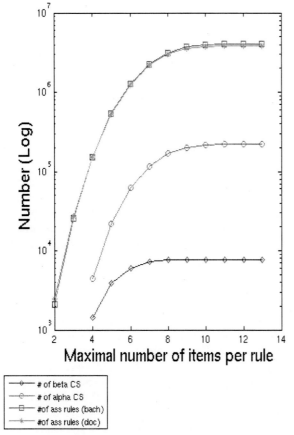

Figure 1 Behavior of association rules with contrast sets for the Adult dataset ("bach" stands for bachelor; "doc" stands for doctorate- the two groups).

We expected the number of contrast sets to increase, initially, with the increase in the value of **n**, and then we expected it to start decreasing above a certain value of **n**, however to our surprise the results were different, and at the same time interesting. They are presented in Figures 1 and 2 for the two data sets. The plot for the Mushroom dataset does not go beyond 7 maximal items per rule because we hit the limit of the maximum possible size of a file at that point (because we have more than 10 million association rules, for each group). It is clear both from Figure 1 and 2 that as the maximal number of items per rule increase, the number of association rules increase for both the groups. In Figure 1, the maximal number of items per rule at which the curve for the number of association rules become *almost* flat is approximately 9.

While the curve for the number of β-contrast sets becomes flat at 7 maximal items per association rule, corresponding number for the α-contrast sets is 9, showing that it follows the association rules. The number of α-contrast sets that are found is more than an order of magnitude higher than the number of β-contrast sets. Also the plot shows the initial rate of increase of all the curves, with the maximal number of items per rule, is much higher (e.g. from 4 to 6) than the rate of increase later (e.g. 6 to 8), thus signifying that this rate decreases with the number of maximal items per rule.

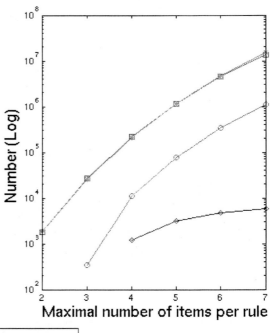

Figure 2 Behavior of association rules with contrast sets for the Mushroom dataset

For the case of Mushroom data set it is clear that the curve for the number of α-contrast sets seems to follow the curve for the number of association rules for both the groups, and also the fact that the curve for β-contrast sets seems to be close to flattening out while the other curves still have a rising trend. Figures 1 and 2 clearly show that there is a marked distinction between the α-contrast sets and the β-contrast sets.

5.4. A Comparison of the contrast sets

For the Adult data set STUCCO found 24 interesting contrast sets out a total number of 919 identified deviations. All the contrast sets found by STUCCO were also present in the interesting contrast sets that we generated with our approach. We ranked the contrast sets from our code in terms of their interestingness (i.e. confidence differential). There seemed to be many interesting contrast sets in our list that STUCCO missed. For the Breast Cancer data set STUCCO found only 18 deviations and 5 interesting contrast sets, again all of these belonged to our list of discovered interesting contrast sets and very few of STUCCO's contrast sets lie in our list of top 50. A comparative analysis for the Mushroom data set could not be performed because STUCCO's output for that dataset were garbage values, and no contrast set was discovered by it while our approach pinpointed many relevant contrast sets.

6. Conclusion and Future Work

Our analysis on the Adult Census dataset and the Breast Cancer dataset shows that Association Rule based analysis is more correct and finds all the contrast sets that are found by STUCCO, and some more potentially interesting ones that STUCCO fails to discover. We have also shown that only one kind of Association Rules make sense-the second kind. We have provided a new method for treating the α-contrast sets, which in turn finds a large number of contrast sets that would otherwise have been pruned. We found that while the number of contrast sets increases almost exponentially with the maximal number of allowed items per set (initially), and then it tapers off, this behaviour is different for α- and β-contrast sets.

We believe that our work has implications both for clustering—using the contrast sets obtained from the data, and analyzing the quality of clustering that is carried out by any of the known methods. Contrast sets can discriminate among clusters and thus help describe and label clustering results; we plan to carry out further exploration in this regard. Contrast sets can also be used to improve the accuracy of a classifier. A more systematic way to evaluate results from mining contrast sets is to study their impact on classifiers in terms of accuracy improvement.

Acknowledgements

The code for STUCCO was provided by the original author, Dr. Stephen Bay, and we would like to acknowledge his help in this regard.

References

[1] S.D. Bay and M.J. Pazzani. Detecting change in categorical data: Mining contrast sets. In Proceedings of the Fifth ACM SIGKDD International Conference on Knowledge Discovery and Data Mining (KDD'99), pages 302-306, San Diego, U.S.A., August 1999.

[2] S.D. Bay and M.J. Pazzani. Detecting group differences: Mining contrast sets. Data Mining and Knowledge Discovery, 5(3): 213-246, 2001.

[3] R. J. Bayardo, Efficiently mining long patterns from databases, In proceedings of the ACM SIGMOD Conference on Management of Data, 1998.

[4] C. Borgelt, Fast Implementation of the Apriori Algorithm available at:
http://fuzzy.cs.uni-magdeburg.de/~borgelt/apriori.html

[5] G. Dong and J. Li. Efficient mining of emerging patterns: Discovering trends and differences.

[6] R.J. Hilderman and T. Peckham. A Statistically Sound Alternative Approach to Mining Contrast Sets. In Proceedings of the 4th Australasian Data Mining Conference (AusDM), pages 157-172, Sydney, Australia, December, 2005.

[7] Terry Peckham. Contrasting interesting grouped association rules. Master's thesis, University of Regina, 2005.

[8] G.I. Webb, S. Butler, and D. Newlands. On detecting differences between groups. In Proceedings of the Ninth ACM SIGKDD International Conference on Knowledge Discovery and Data Mining (KDD'03), pages 256-265, Washington, D.C., U.S.A., August 2003.

Effective OLAP Mining of Evolving Data Marts

Ronnie Alves, Orlando Belo, Fabio Costa

Department of Informatics, School of Engineering, University of Minho
Campus de Gualtar, 4710-374, Braga, Portugal
{ronnie, obelo}@di.uminho.pt, costa_fab@hotmail.com

Abstract

Organizations have been used decisions support systems to help them to understand and to predict interesting business opportunities over their huge databases also known as data marts. OLAP tools have been used widely for retrieving information in a summarized way (cube-like) by employing customized cubing methods. The majority of these cubing methods suffer from being just data-driven oriented and not discovery-driven ones. Data marts grow quite fast, so an incremental OLAP mining process is a required and desirable solution for mining evolving cubes. In order to present a solution that covers the previous mentioned issues, we propose a cube-based mining method which can compute an incremental cube, handling concept hierarchy modeling, as well as, incremental mining of multidimensional and multilevel association rules. The evaluation study using real and synthetic datasets demonstrates that our approach is an effective OLAP mining method of evolving data marts.

1. Introduction

For a long time, organizations have been using decisions support systems to help them to understand and to predict interesting business opportunities over their huge databases. This interesting knowledge is gathered in such way that one can explore different what-if scenarios over the complete set of information available. Those huge databases are well known as data marts (DM), organizing the information and preserving its multidimensional and multilevel characteristics. OLAP tools have been used widely by DM users for retrieving summarized information, also called multidimensional data cube, through customized cubing algorithms. Since DM are evolving databases, it is necessary to have the cube updated on a useful time. Usually, traditional cubing methods compute the cube structure from scratch every time new information is available. As far as we know, almost none of them support an incremental procedure. Furthermore, those traditional cubing approaches suffer from being just data-driven oriented and not discovery-driven ones. In fact, real data application demands both strategies [1].

Therefore, bringing out some mining technique into the cubing process is an essential effort to reveal interesting relations on DMs [6, 7, 8, 10]. The contributions of this paper can be summarized as follows:

Incremental cubing. The cubing method proposed is inspired on a MOLAP approach [4], and it also adopts a divide-and-conquer strategy. We have generalized bulk incremental updating from [11]. Verification tasks through join-indexes are used every time a new cubing process is required. Thus, reducing the search space and handling new information available.

Multidimensional and multilevel mining. Since the cube is processed from a DM, the implementation of hierarchies is supported by computing several cubes. The final cube is a collection of each processed cube. This requirement is essential to guide multilevel mining through dimension selection with the desirable granularity [6, 8]. Besides, it allows discovering interesting relations at any-level of abstraction from the cubes.

Enhanced cube mining. To discovery interesting relations on incremental basis, we support inter-dimensional and multilevel association rules [6, 7]. We provide an apriori-based rule algorithm for rule discovering taking advantages of the cube structure, being incremental and tightly integrated into the cubing process. We also enhance our cube-based mining using other measure of interestingness [10].

2. Problem Formulation

Apart from the classical association rules algorithms, that usually take a flat database to extract interesting relations [9], we are interested to explore multi-dimensional databases. In this sense, the data cube plays an interesting role for discovering multidimensional and multiple-level association rules [6]. A rule of the form X→Y, where body X and head Y consists of a set of conjunctive predicates, is a inter-dimensional association rule iff {X, Y} contains more than one distinct predicate, each of which occurs only once in the rule. Considering each OLAP dimension as a predicate, we can therefore mining rules, such as: Age(X, 30-35) and Occupation (X, "Engineer") → Buys(X, "laptop").

Many applications at mining associations require that mining be performed at multiple levels of abstraction. For instance, besides finding in previous rule that 80 percent of people who age are between 30-35 and are Engineer who may buy laptops, it is interesting to allow OLAP users to drill-down and show that 75 percent of customers buy "macbook" if 10 percent are "Computer Engineer". The association relationship in the latter statement is expressed at lower level of abstraction but carries more specific and interesting relation than that in the former. Therefore, it is quite important to provide also the extraction of *multilevel association rules from cubes*.

Lets us now think in another real situation where the DM has been updated with new purchases or sales information. One may be interested to see if that latter patterns still hold. So, an *incremental procedure* is a fundamental issue on incremental OLAP mining of evolving cubes. We further present few definitions.

Definition 1 (Base and Aggregate Cells) A data cube is a lattice of cuboids. A cell in the base cuboid is a *base cell*. A cell from a non-base cuboid is an aggregate cell. An *aggregate cell* aggregates over one or more dimensions, where each aggregated dimension is indicated by a "*" in the cell notation. Suppose we have an n-dimensional data cube. Let i= (i_1, i_2, ..., i_n, *measures*) be a cell from one of the cuboids making up the data cube. We say that i is an k-dimensional cell (that is, from an k-dimensional cuboid) if exactly k (k ≤ n) values among {i_1, i_2, ..., i_n} are not "*". If k = n, then i is a base cell; otherwise, it is an aggregate cell.

Definition 2 (Inter-dimensional predicate) Each dimension value (d_1,d_2,...,d_n) on a base or aggregate cell c is an inter-dimensional predicate λ in the form $(d_1 \in D_1 \wedge ... \wedge d_n \in D_n)$. The set $\{D_1,...,D_n\}$ corresponds to all dimensions used to build all k-dimensional cells. Furthermore, each dimension has a distinct predicate in the expression.

Definition 3 (Multilevel predicate) A Multilevel predicate is a *specialization* or *generalization* of an inter-dimensional predicate. Each predicate follows a containment rule such as $\lambda \in D_i << D_j$, where "<<" poses order dependency among abstraction levels (*i to j*) for a dimension D.

Definition 4 (Evolving cube) A cube C is a set of k-dimensional cells generated from a base relation R on time instant *t*. For a time instant t_{n+1} all k-dimensional cells in C should be re-evaluated according to R' generating an evolving cube C'.

From the above definitions we can define our problem of mining evolving data cubes as: *Given a base Relation R, which evolves through times instants t to t_{n+1}, extract interesting inter-dimensional and multilevel patterns from DM, on incremental cubing basis.*

3. Cube-based Mining

3.1. Cube Structure

The cube structure will be a set of arrays. Observing the cube as an object, it is simple to realize that the cube can be split into small cubes. These small cubes, usually defined as cuboids, are each one of the arrays (partitions) that together represent the final cube. The number of cuboids in the cube is defined by the number of elements of the power set of the dimensions to be processed, which is given by 2^n, where n is the number of dimensions. Inside the cuboids, each element is represented by a pair, where the left hand side is a set of dimensions and the right hand side is the measure (usually a numeric value) resulting from the aggregation of the data.

Example1. Given the SQL-like notation for expressing a cube query is as follows:
> Select time_id, product_id, warehouse_id,
>   sum(warehouse_sales) as sum
> From inventory_fact_1997
>   group by product_id, time_id, warehouse_id
> with cube

The final array is formed by a group of eight partitions. In Figure 1, we show just the first three tuples processed from the inventory fact table of the FoodMart Warehouse provided by Microsoft SQL Server.

Partition []		Partition [product_id,time_id]	
[]	179,0982	[1, 388]	125.913
		[3, 662]	5.3452
Partition [product_id]		[6, 534]	47.84
[1]	125.913		
[3]	5.3452	Partition [product_id,warehouse_id]	
[6]	47.84	[1, 7]	125.913
		[3, 13]	5.3452
Partition [time_id]		[6, 13]	47.84
[388]	125.913		
[662]	5.3452	Partition [time_id,warehouse_id]	
[534]	47.84	[388, 7]	125.913
		[662, 13]	5.3452
Partition [warehouse_id]		[534, 13]	47.84
[7]	125.913		
[13]	53.1852	Partition [product_id,time_id,warehouse_id]	
		[1, 388, 7]	125.913
		[3, 662, 13]	5.3452
		[6, 534, 13]	47.84

Figure 1. The Complete set of partitions provided by the cube structure for the Example 1.

3.2. Cube Processing

The cubing method consists of four steps. Basically, these steps can be divided as follows:

1. Read a line from the fact table
2. Combine the dimensions
3. Insert or (update) the data in the cube
4. Update the index

Step 1. The first step is reading a line from a fact table and identifying what are the dimension(s) and the measure(s).

Step 2. Next, the dimension(s) are combined using an algorithm based on a divide and conquer strategy, in order to get the dimensions power set, each of which is per-se a cuboid. The step 2 is further explained on next section. At this point, it is required to build the temporary data structure which is used additionally for inserting or updating the cube. It is important to mention that the cubing process supports the following *distributive aggregate functions*: sum, maximum, minimum, and count.

Step 3. Following step 2, the process checks whether the set of dimensions is already in the cuboid of the cube. In this case, the information is updated with the result given by the computation of the defined aggregating function. Otherwise, the data is inserted.

Step 4. Finally, the index is built so the access to the cube information can be done quickly.

3.3. Combining Dimensions

After reading a line from the fact table, it is necessary to combine the dimensions. In this step, the power set of the dimensions is generated. However, generating power sets usually requires a great amount of resources and time. Instead of using existing cubing strategies like top-down [4] or bottom-up [5], it was developed an algorithm based on a *divide-and-conquer (DAQ)* strategy. These kinds of algorithms are recursive and proved to be extremely efficient among others algorithms, since it divides the initial problem in small ones until it reaches a trivial state which is straightforward to solve. Before presenting the algorithm, first it is explained the two trivial cases.

1. Combine a singular set X of dimensions. In this case, since there is only one element in the set, then the result is the set itself. Example, X= {A} gives [[A]].
2. Combine a set X with two dimensions. In this case, the result is given by a set containing each element of A and the set A itself. Example, X= {A,B} gives [{A},{B},{A,B}].

As it can be seen, the process has not taken into account the empty set, since it is not necessary at this time. Having presented the trivial cases, the remaining steps are discussed as follows.

Suppose we have a set of dimensions D. The main goal is to combine the items of D among them, in order to get the power set of the items.

At the start, the set D is divided in two parts (D_1 and D_2). If the number of elements of D is odd, then D_2 will have one more elements than D_1. This step is executed again, recursively for each D_i until it reaches a trivial case. Whenever a set D_i is a trivial situation, then the combination is done according to the explanation given above.

The next step consists of combining the results of the trivial cases among them, until the final solution is achieved. After solving a trivial case, the result is a set as well. At this point, the algorithm takes two resulting sets that have the same ancestor and combine its results. To execute this, it is necessary to take into consideration the position of each element in the set.

We demonstrate each step by a running example:
Given a set of dimensions to combine like X={A,B,C,D}. The temporary set T_s={{A},{B},{AB},{C},{D},{CD}} is built from the two resulting arrays A_1={{A,B}, {A,B,AB}} and A_2={{C,D},{C,D,CD}}. After the combination step, and executing a left shift operation on A_2, the results are T_s={{A},{B},{AB},{C},{D},{CD},{AC},{BD}, {ABCD}}, A_1={{A,B}, {A,B,AB}} and A_2={{ D},{CD},{C}}. Since the second set has not achieved its initial order, we repeat this combination-shift step. After more two rounds (*one*, **two**) we achieved the result set as T_s={{A},{B},{AB},{C},{D},{CD},{AC},{BD}, {ABCD},*{AD},{BCD},{ABC}*,**{ACD},{BC},{ABD}**}}
.

Applying the method (pseudo DAQ algorithm) explained above for the partition [product_id(0), time_id(1), warehouse_id(2)] = { 6,534,13} from Example 1, we get a tree representation as follow:
{6,534,13}:[0,1,2]
|--{6}:[0]
   |--{6}:[0]
|--{534,13}:[1,2]
   |--{{534}:[1], {13}:[2], {534,13}:[1,2]}
|--{{6}:[0], {534}:[1], {13}:[2], {534,13}:[1,2], {6,534}:[0,1],...,{6,534,13}:[0,1,2]}

Pseudo DAQ Algorithm.
(input: arraysOfDim[L[],I[]], output: powerset)
1. Combine array (L[], I[])
2. If sizeOf[L] = 1 or sizeOf[L]=2 *//trivial case*
   add pair (L,I) to powerset
3. If sizeOf[L]>2
   split L[] on left[] and right[]
   add each element of left[] and right[] to powerset
4. For each element in right[]
5.   For each element in left[]
    Let L[], I[]
    L[] ← *getFirst*(left[]), L[]← *getFirst*(right[])
    I[] ← *getSnd*(left[]), L[]← *getSnd*(right[])
    add pair (L,I) to powerset
    right ← *leftShift*(right)
6. *Return* powerset

4. Cubing Enhancements

4.1. Incremental

While developing a process which was able to build a cube, the cube built could also be able to be incremented by an equivalent process or by the same process itself. Therefore, the process described in Section 3.2 is itself an incremental one. The proposed method runs line by line of the fact table. Therefore, it is only required to identify the new data in the fact table, and then start the process described in Section 3.3 followed with a checking task. This checking step is achieved by using a *join-index* guided by bulk incremental updating [11].

Whenever data is inserted in that fact table, it is appended at the bottom (for instance on Oracle Databases, we can look for higher UUIDs), thus it becomes simple task to pinpoint the new lines, by saving the number of the lines that had already been evaluated.

4.2. Hierarchies

The implementation of hierarchies in the cubing process is handled by constructing several cubes instead of only one. Therefore, the final cube will be a collection of each cube processed.
Let the hierarchies be defined as follows:

$$H_1 = \{L_{1,0}, L_{1,1}, L_{1,2},...., L_{1,p}\}$$
$$H_2 = \{L_{2,0}, L_{2,1}, L_{2,2},...., L_{2,q}\}$$
$$...............................$$
$$H_n = \{L_{n,0}, L_{n,1}, L_{n,2},...., L_{n,r}\}$$

Where H_i is an hierarchy and $L_{i,j}$ is the jth level of hierarchy i. Thus, the number of cubes to be built is given by Equation 1.

N° of Cubes = (p+1) * (q+1) * ... * (r+1) **Eq.(1)**

As explained in Section 3.2, the cube is processed from a fact table. Although the process will be the same, the table used to read the data will be slightly different. Instead of having only the fact table's fields, it will have some extra fields and some others from the levels of the hierarchies, which will substitute the fields of the corresponding dimension later on. So, it will be required to construct several tables, one corresponding to each cube. These tables will be given by the combination of each and every level of the hierarchies. Once again, the algorithm described in Section 3.3 is called to combine dimensions in all hierarchies' level.

We can summarize the proposed method with hierarchies as follows:

1. First it is required the number of cubes to be processed
2. Then, the tables are generated by combining the levels of the hierarchies, using the algorithm described in Section 3.3. At this point, for each built table, apply the process describe in Section 3.2.
3. Finally, it is obtained a collection of cubes that all together form the final cube.

We provide a running example to show the total number of cubes to be calculated. Let's use Table 1 providing the dimensions and levels to compute.

Table 1: Hierarchies for Three Dimensions

Hierarchy level	Product	TimeByDay	Warehouse
		Dimensions	
0	ProdId	timeId	WarId
1		DayOMonth	WarName
2		Month	WarCountry
3		Year	

The final solution is obtained by multiplying all dimensions' levels (Product * TimeByDay * Warehouse = 1 * 4 * 3 = 12 tables). Finally, the number of tables is provided as follows.

Table 0 = {product_id, time_id, warehouse_id}
Table 1 = {product_id, day_of_month, warehouse_id}
Table 2 = {product_id, the_month, warehouse_id}
Table 3 = {product_id, the_year, warehouse_id}
Table 4 = {product_id, time_id, warehouse_name}
Table 5 = {product_id, time_id, warehouse_ctry}
Table 6 = {product_id, day_of_month, warehouse_name}
Table 7 = {product_id, day_of_month, warehouse_ctry}
Table 8 = {product_id, the_month, warehouse_name}
Table 9 = {product_id, the_month, warehouse_ctry}
Table 10 = {product_id, the_year, warehouse_name}
Table 11 = {product_id, the_year, warehouse_ctry}

5. Mining from Cubes

5.1. Inter-dimensional and Multilevel Rules

The main goal of this process is the extraction of interesting relations from a cube. This extraction is guided by an *Association Rule Mining* approach. Association Rules (AR) can extract remarkable relations, as well as, patterns and tendencies [9]. However, it can also return a great amount of rules, which makes difficult either the analysis of the data or its comprehension. In addition, traditional frequent pattern mining algorithms are single-dimensional (intra-dimensional) in nature [7], in sense of exploring just one dimension at a time. Besides, doesn't allow the extraction of inter-dimensional and multilevel association rules.

The rule extraction developed in this work is Apriori-based [9] and the most costly part, getting the frequent itemsets, is achieved by the DAQ algorithm. Each cuboid cell, along with its aggregating measure in the data cube, could be evaluated as a candidate itemset (*CI*). It is important to mention that by evaluating aggregating measures as *CIs* we are concerning to the population of facts rather than the population of units of measures of these facts. Thus, *support* and *confidence* of a particular rule is evaluated according to users' preference for a specific aggregating function (count, min, max, sum, etc...). It is clear that the cube structure provides a rich model for *rule analysis* rather than classical *count-based analysis* of ARs.

Having found all interesting cuboids, the next step is generating rules, as follows:

Pseudo Rule Algorithm.
(input: cube, output: rules)
1. For each non-singular cuboid cell T
2. Obtain the aggregate value of T (*supOfT*)
3. Generate all the non-empty cuboid Si of T, using the algorithm described in Section 2.3
4. For each cuboid Si.
   Obtain the aggregate value of Si (*supOfSi*)
5. Calculate the confidence (*conf = supOfT/supOfSi*)
   If *conf* satisfies the minimum threshold ε
      Construct rule (*Si → (T - Si)*)
      If the rule is *valid* then *store* the rule

To verify the validity of a rule it is required to check if all the subsets (cuboids) of the rule are a valid rule as well. In other words, it is necessary to generate all the subsets *Ri* of *Si* and check whether *Ri → (T - Si)* already exists. If that is true then *Si → (T - Si)* is a valid rule. Otherwise, the rule must not be stored. One particular aspect that needs to be mentioned is the fact that the process must generate the rules starting with the cuboids that have fewer dimensions and finishing with the cuboids that have more dimensions (*k-d cells*).

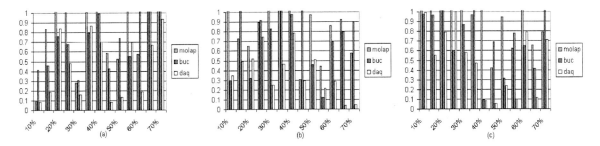

Figure 2. It Shows the Update Effects (*dg%*, X-Axis) against Cubing Speedup (*ic/rc*, Y-Axis)

Inter-dimensional association rules. Given the process explained previously, one just needs to select cube dimensions to generate valid multidimensional rules. For instance, Age(X, 30-35) and Occupation (X, "Engineer") → Buys(X, "laptop"), it is an inter-dimensional rule.

Multilevel association rules. One can also use the same process for getting multilevel association rules. Although, the granularity is controlled according to the set of pre-defined hierarchies (*selecting dimensions*) explained in 4.2. In this sense, one can explore several levels of interests in the cube to obtain interesting relations.

Even by using a cube-based mining (relying on support/confidence) approach the number of valid rules is still large to analyze. Furthermore, *what are the right cube abstractions to evaluate?* We smooth this problem by generating interesting rules according to the *maximal-correlated cuboid value* of a cuboid cell [10].

5.2. Enhancing Cubing-Rule Discovery

To avoid the generation of non-interesting relations we augment cuboid cells with one more measure called a *maximal-correlated value*. This measure is inspired on *all_confidence* measure, which has been successfully adopted for judging interesting patterns in association rule mining, and further exploited in [10] for correlation and compression of cuboid cells. This measure discloses true correlation (also dependence) relationship among cuboids cells and holds the null-invariance property. Furthermore, real world databases tend to be correlated, i.e., dimensions values are usually dependent on each other. This measure is evaluated according to the following definition.

Definition 5 (Correlated Value of a Cuboid Cell) Given a cell *c*, the correlated value *3CV* of a cuboid *V(c)* is defined as,

$maxM(c) = max \{M(c_i)|for each c_i \in V(c)\}$ **Eq.(2)**
$3CV(c) = M(c) / maxM(c)$ **Eq.(3)**,
where $M(c_i)$ corresponds to the aggregating value of this cell *c*.

By using the above definition we are able to find *infrequent cuboid cells* that may be interesting to the user but should not be obtained when using other measures of interests such as support, confidence lift, among others. In our evaluation study, we experienced the effects of correlated cuboid cells when using those measures of interestingness.

5.3. Incremental Rule Discovery

The incremental rule discovery is achieved by combining NFUP approach [12] with the incremental cube maintenance (see sections 3.3 and 4.1). The NFUP algorithm relies on Apriori and considers only these newly added transactions. Since the cubing method is devised on incremental basis, it is simple task to identify cuboid cells that are still important to the rule discovery process.

6. Evaluation Study

The complete set of tests was elaborated in a PC Pentium 4 3.0 GHz, with 1 Gb of RAM, and Windows XP. The main code was developed with Java 1.5. We have elaborated two studies with the proposed method. In the first one, we evaluate the incremental feature in presence of different cubing strategies versus re-computation. The cubing strategy DAQ was compared with one bottom-up (BUC) [5] and other top-down (MOLAP) [4] approaches. Those strategies were chosen in sense that they present the most known cubing implementations. Both algorithms were implemented to the best of our knowledge based on the published papers. The second study evaluates the cube-base mining method by incrementally maintenance of multidimensional and multilevel rules.

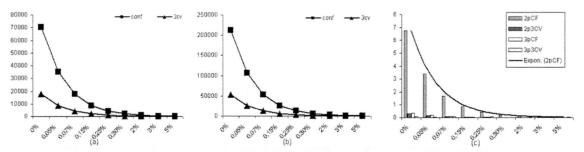

Figure 3. (a) and (b) Present OLAP Mining Performance (*Runn.time(s)*, Y-Axis) With Different Measures of Significance (%, X-Axis). (c) Presents the Number of Interesting Cuboids (*Cb*K*, Y-Axis) Against Different Thresholds.

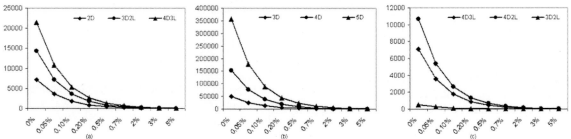

Figure 4. Illustrates OLAP Mining Performance (*Runn.time(s)*, Y-Axis) When Getting Different Patterns through Different Support Thresholds(%, X-Axis)

6.1. Incremental Cubing

In order to execute the tests for this study, it was developed a dataset generator to provide DMs in a star scheme model. Therefore, it is required to give as parameters the number of dimensions, the number of lines of the fact table, the number of lines of each dimension table, the number of levels of each hierarchy and the number of distinct elements in each column of the dimension tables. We have used three synthetics(*S*) DM, plus two real datasets(*R*). The real ones were the (F)oodMart DB provided by Microsoft SQL Server and the (W)eather Dataset (http://cdiac.esd.ornl.gov/ndps/ndp026b.html) for September 1985. The main characteristics of those datasets are presented in Table 2.

Table 2: DM's Characteristics

DS	S/R	FactSZ	NDims	HLevels
1	S-1	100,00	4	3L
2	S-2	250,00	5	4L, 3L
3	S-3	500,00	6	3L, 2L
4	R-F	164,558	5	3L, 2L
5	R-W	1,015,367	9	0L

Having generated those datasets (S-1 to S-3), we also set a degree of updating (*dg%*), meaning

insertions on fact tables. Thus, it was possible to measure the effects of each cubing strategy either by computing every fact table line-by-line from scratch or by computing it incrementally.

Figures 2(a), 2(b) and 2(c) illustrate the effects of DM updating x (re)cubing over datasets S-3, S-1 and S-2, respectively. We measure the speedup (processing time) ratio between (*rc*=re-compute cube) and (*ic*=incremental cube). This ratio (*ic/rc*), allows measuring the degree of improvement that *ic* achieves over *rc*. Although, we are working on extending the method to work with complex aggregating functions, in those experiments, just distributive ones were taken into account.

The Figure 2(a), 2(b) and 2(c) allows observe that in general *ic* performs much better than *rc*, specially when the degree of updating is low. We also notice that the speedup increases with respect to the size of the DM. Furthermore, one can see that DAQ generally shows better computational costs rather than other strategies.

6.2. Cube-base Mining

We have elaborated several experiments (observe the running time on ms) based on the value of the minimum support (%) with respect to different settings of predicates (see Figure 4). We also have

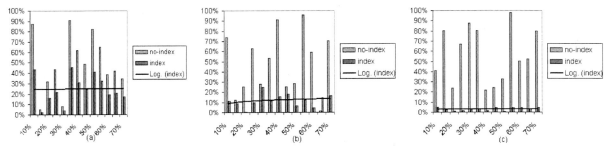

Figure 5. It Shows Update Effects (*dg%*, X-Axis) against Index Speedup of DAQ (Y-Axis) for Datasets S3(a), S2(b) and S1(c)

constrained the maximum number of levels to explore as 3, and the maximum number of dimensions to 4. Figure 4(a) and 4(c) show the performance figures of mining interesting relations through different thresholds using R-F dataset. We can see that increasing the number of hierarchies (levels) doesn't imply high costs on our incremental OLAP Mining. The other way around, increasing the number of dimensions plays few overheads. Although, we can also save cube computation when exploring the downward property of 3CV measure (Figure 3). Performance figures with R-W dataset are given in Figure 4(b) and Figure 3(b). Again, we can see the effects of mining correlated cuboids when evaluating interesting relations on each dataset. The tradeoff between cube-based mining using confidence(*conf*) and correlated-cuboids(*3CV*) are evaluated according to low and higher thresholds. Low *3CV* values will provide interesting relations regardless the high overhead provided by the *conf* measure. We can evidence this tradeoff while OLAP Mining datasets R-F and R-W on Figure 3(a) and Figure 3(b), respectively. Finally, we are able to evaluate our method with respect to update effects on a fact table. The update effects generated from S-1 dataset for a dg%=70% (Figure 2(b)) is quite exponential when OLAP Mining two or three predicates with *conf* as measure of interest, but is quite stable when using *3CV*.

7. Final Discussion

7.1. Related Work

OLAP has been taken attention of several researchers since the introduction of the cube operator [3]. There are several works on data cube computation. The closer work with our method is the metarule-guided mining approach [6, 8], but

incremental cubing issues were not mentioned in this study. To situate our work among those cubing strategies we first categorize them in three possible spots. The first one deals with data cube computation, and its many ways of cubing [2, 4, 5]. The second spot is made of the several studies which try to integrate interesting exploitation mechanisms either by using statistical approaches [1] or by integrating mining in the cube process [10]. The latter spot deals with OLAP over evolving DM. Thus, those methods basically must deal with incremental issues either when cubing [11] or when mining evolving databases [12]. Given such simple categorization we can say that:

w.r.t. **first spot**. We compute the full cube, employing a DAQ strategy. One can also make use of equivalence class from [10] to explore cube semantics and compression. DAQ also showed to be quite effective through our performance studied in presence of evolving data rather than other cubing strategies.

w.r.t. **second spot**. We use multidimensional association rules as our basis to explore interesting relations from DM. Given that traditional association rules usually work on single flat table, our method uses cube structure to extract inter-dimensional and multilevel patterns on incremental basis. Furthermore, we have enhanced this mining task extending the proposed model for exploring correlated cuboid cells.

w.r.t. **third spot**. We provide a cubing method which is per-se incremental, and it can handle effectively the addition of new information on DM fact tables; it also provides concept hierarchy modeling, as well as, integrated and incremental multidimensional and multilevel mining.

7.2. Indexing

The index strategy adopted by our method is a *join-index* on the combined (foreign key) FK columns in the fact table [11]. We provide an index for each partition (see Figure 1). In fact each cuboid has an index associated to. Therefore, if it is necessary to insert or update any information in a cuboid, first it is necessary to check if the information is already in the cube. Thus, firstly the index is analyzed to verify if there is any set of items that begins with the first item of the set of items of the information. If that is not true, then the information is not available in the cuboid and it can be inserted. Otherwise, the index will return a set of lines where the information is possibly stored. At this point, the process will go through the whole process discussed in section 3.3. If it is found, then the measure is updated based on the aggregation function used. Otherwise, the information is inserted. Figure 5, shows the effects of processing (DAQ) speed up while indexing datasets through different updating scenarios. The little overhead in Figure 5(b) is given by its multilevel properties (ranging from 3 to 4).

8. Conclusions

The updating processes on real DM applications implies that, the summarization made by cubing methods need to handle, with some incremental facility, the new information available. Furthermore, mining mechanisms should be integrated into the cubing process to improve the exploration of interesting relations on DM either before of after OLAP. Our evaluation study demonstrates that our method is quite competitive w.r.t. other known cubing strategies, also providing an effective cube-based mining method for discovering knowledge over evolving DM. We have also demonstrated that by exploring correlated cuboids during the discovery process we are able to provide an essential tradeoff between processing time and accuracy patterns. Further, we surprisingly evidenced that mining multilevel patterns with our method are less costly than inter-dimensional ones.

Acknowledgments

Ronnie Alves is supported by a Ph.D. Scholarship from FCT-Foundation of Science and Technology, Ministry of Science of Portugal.

References

[1] Sarawagi, S., Agrawal, R., Megiddo, N.: Discovery-Driven Exploration of OLAP Data Cubes. *EDBT 1998*: 168-182.

[2] Xin, D., Shao, Z., Han, J., Liu, H.: C-Cubing: Efficient Computation of Closed Cubes by Aggregation-Based Checking. *ICDE 2006*: 4.

[3] Gray, J., Bosworth, A., Layman, A., Pirahesh, H.: Data Cube: A Relational Aggregation Operator Generalizing Group-By, Cross-Tab, and Sub-Total. *ICDE 1996*: 152-159.

[4] Zhao, Y, Deshpande, P, Naughton, J: An Array-Based Algorithm for Simultaneous Multidimensional Aggregates. *SIGMOD 1997*: 159-170.

[5] Beyer, K., Ramakrishnan, R.: Bottom-Up Computation of Sparse and Iceberg CUBEs. *SIGMOD 1999*: 359-370.

[6] Kamber, M., Han, J., Chiang, J.: Metarule-Guided Mining of Multi-Dimensional Association Rules Using Data Cubes. *KDD 1997*: 207-210.

[7] Lu, H., Feng, L., Han, J.: Beyond intra-transaction association analysis: mining multidimensional inter-transaction association rules. *ACM Trans. Inf. Syst.* 18(4): 423-454 (2000).

[8] Han, J., Lakshmanan, L., Ng., R.: Constraint-Based Multidimensional Data Mining. *IEEE Computer* 32(8): 46-50 (1999).

[9] Agrawal, R., Mannila, H., Srikant, K., Toiven, H., Verkano, A.: Fast Discovery of Association Rules. *KDD 1996*: 307-328.

[10] Alves, R., Belo, O.: On the Computation of Maximal-Correlated Cuboids Cells. *DaWaK 2006*: 165-174.

[11] Feng, J., Si, H., and Feng, Y.: Indexing and incremental updating condensed data cube. *SSDBM 2003*: 23-32.

[12] Chang, C., Li, Y., and Lee, J. 2005. An Efficient Algorithm for Incremental Mining of Association Rules. *Ride-Sdma 2005*: 3-10.

Energy-Efficient Monitoring of Mobile Objects
with Uncertainty-Aware Tolerances

Tobias Farrell
*Institute of Parallel
and Distributed Systems,
Universität Stuttgart, Germany*

Reynold Cheng
*Department of Computing,
Hong Kong Polytechnic
University, Hong Kong*

Kurt Rothermel
*Institute of Parallel
and Distributed Systems,
Universität Stuttgart, Germany*

Abstract

In location-based services, continuous queries are often employed to monitor the locations of mobile objects that are determined by sensing devices like GPS receivers. Due to limited battery resources, it is important for these objects to acquire and report location data only if necessary. We study how these energy-consuming operations can be reduced with a controlled impact on query accuracy of continuous range queries (CRQs). Specifically, we develop uncertainty-aware tolerances, *which are user-defined error bounds that provide correctness guarantees, with consideration of different sources of data uncertainty: sensing uncertainty, sampling uncertainty, and communication delay. Novel algorithms are developed to control carefully when an object should acquire and update a location, while satisfying these tolerances. Extensive simulations validate the effectiveness of our methods.*

1. Introduction

Due to the rapid development of low-cost location-sensing devices, like the Global Positioning System (GPS), and wireless networking technologies, location-based services have attracted tremendous research interest lately [10],[12],[26]. In particular, long-standing, *continuous* queries are used to monitor various activities of mobile objects for an extensive period of time. A wide range of applications has been identified, including intrusion detection over security-sensitive regions, mobile advertisements for customers nearby, and traffic monitoring.

In such systems, each mobile object is equipped with a *sensing* device (e.g., a GPS receiver) to acquire location data, and a *wireless communication* interface (e.g., a GSM/GPRS transceiver) to report data to a location server. The sensing and reporting operations constitute the major fraction of energy consumed in a mobile object [23]. Since the battery resources of many

mobile objects (like cellular phones and PDAs) are precious, it is important to minimize the usage of these operations, so that the lifetime can be maximized. This issue is particularly critical for continuous queries, which require location data to be constantly sensed and reported to the server for further processing.

In order to reduce costs of continuous query processing, the idea of *object-side processing* has been utilized in various projects [3],[9],[17],[22]. These works are based on the idea that a mobile object has some processing capabilities to decide by itself whether to report a data item to the location server. Specifically, upon receiving a query request, the server sends some query information to each mobile object. The object then evaluates part of the query locally and transmits the location to the server only if the query result is affected. As an example, consider a *Continuous Range Query (CRQ)*, which returns the identities of mobile objects located inside some query region with boundary R. If this information is propagated to all mobile objects, then an object only needs to send a position update to the server if it crosses R. Since fewer items are reported to the server, the number of messages, as well as the energy costs incurred in reporting operations, can be reduced significantly.

Although object-side processing is a promising way of reducing energy use, there are two open challenges. The first is handling of *data uncertainty*, inherently associated with a location item. For example, a location value obtained by some GPS receiver is only correct within a few metres (called *sensing uncertainty*) [27]. Another source of uncertainty, known as *sampling uncertainty*, is produced when the locations are only sensed at discrete time instants. Then, the positions between adjacent samples are not precisely known [21]. Moreover, *communication delay* causes the location data to be received some time after sensing. Data uncertainty affects the accuracy of query results. In a CRQ, for instance, an object may temporarily leave the monitored region unnoticed, since it acquires a location at discrete time instants only. More importantly, the query result is usually updated late – at some time after an object crossed R. Thus, the query result cannot correctly reflect the real world at all times.

The second challenge is that energy consumption issues for *sensing* the location of a mobile object have not been well studied. While most previous works focus on communication costs [1],[3],[4],[19],[20],[22], very often the energy required for sensing at a mobile device cannot be ignored [23]. Even in low power mode, a common GPS receiver consumes no less than 75 mJoules for each position acquired [18]. The same amount of energy is required by GPRS to transmit 120 bytes of data [9]. Consequently, the design of an energy-efficient query protocol should consider the energy consumed by position sensing, too. In Section 3 we show how this factor of energy consumption can be reduced by carefully controlling the sensing rate. For example, the positioning sensor may remain in low-power mode for a longer time, if the object is located far away from R. However, this reveals an important trade-off between the frequency of sensing and accuracy of query results. A mobile object near the query boundary has to sense its position with higher frequency in order to provide better accuracy. As a result, object-side processing of CRQ requires a significant amount of energy to provide the best possible query result – while absolute query correctness cannot be guaranteed due to different sources of data uncertainty.

In this paper, we propose to overcome these two shortcomings by *relaxing* the query accuracy requirements. This is motivated by the observation that many location-aware applications do not require the highest degree of query accuracy. Instead, they can relax the correctness requirements by specifying a maximum error bound in the query results. For example, consider a CRQ used for distributing warning messages within a spatial region. It is acceptable that some users receive the notification early (before entering the queried region). In contrast, for distributing location-based advertisements to users located inside a supermarket, some users could receive it late (after entering the store). We introduce the notion of *uncertainty-aware tolerances* for CRQ, which defines the maximal acceptable error along with the query. The allowed tolerances are then guaranteed to be met in consideration of all sources of uncertainty. Furthermore, it can be utilized to reduce the energy consumption of mobile objects. We present efficient algorithms that satisfy the tolerance constraints and also consider energy usage.

The basic idea of *error-tolerant query processing* has recently been exploited by various researchers [19],[20],[4]. Based on the trade-off between the frequency of reporting operations and query correctness,

they have developed intelligent algorithms to achieve lower communication costs. However, reported sensor values were assumed to be *always* correct. In contrast, we propose a new notion of query tolerances that consider different sources of data uncertainty. Moreover, previous solutions have not considered the energy costs of *sensing* new data. As we will show, there is an important trade-off between the amount of energy spent on either sensing or reporting operations. In our paper this trade-off is controlled carefully in order to reduce the overall energy consumption.

In summary, our contributions are:
- Propose uncertainty-aware tolerances semantics for continuous range queries (CRQ);
- Show that uncertainty-aware tolerances provide correctness guarantees under three major sources of uncertainty: sensing uncertainty, sampling uncertainty, and communication delay;
- Develop efficient algorithms for processing CRQ, that satisfy uncertainty-aware tolerances and reduce the total energy consumed by sensing and reporting operations; and
- Verify the effectiveness of our approaches by extensive simulation using realistic mobility traces.

The rest of this paper is organized as follows. In Section 2 we describe our system model and detail the query model studied in this paper. Section 3 then analyzes a preliminary solution to disclose existing shortcomings of processing CRQ. Subsequently, we present how to overcome these shortcomings by introducing uncertainty-aware tolerances in Section 4. Section 5 presents our experimental results and Section 6 discusses related work. Finally, we conclude the paper in Section 7.

2. Background

We now describe the system architecture, properties of a mobile object and all basic assumptions. Then, we present the underlying principle of object-side query processing that is studied in this paper.

2.1 System Model

Our system model consists of mobile objects (MOs) and a location manager (LM). The LM processes continuous queries on behalf of location-aware applications (LAs). We do not make any assumptions on the internal organization of the LM. It might comprise multiple LM nodes, to which the MOs are mapped (dynamically) [13]. Each MO communicates with a single LM node over a wireless network, such as GPRS, UMTS or WiFi meshes.

An MO is a mobile device (e.g., cell phone, PDA) equipped with a processor, a wireless network interface and a positioning sensor to detect its geographic position. Each MO is identified by a globally unique identifier O_i, where $i=1,...,n$ and n is the total number of objects monitored by the system. To supply the LM with current position information, an MO has to perform three different operations: processing, communication and position sensing. We focus on the last two operations because they dominate energy consumption [8],[23].

(1) Communication: An MO is responsible to send update messages to the LM according to some query protocol. As all update messages will be similar in size, we assume this transmission requires a constant amount of energy W_U per message. To cope with unbounded communication delays, we assume a statistical upper bound of c_{max} for the end-to-end delay between an MO and the LM. This can be determined empirically based on the networking environment and holds with high probability [19]. Occasionally, messages may be delayed by more than c_{max} in practise. This will result in temporary violations of precision guarantees – an unavoidable effect in any distributed environment with unbounded delays.

Note that we aim at satisfying the tolerances for data stored on the LM in the following. If an LA runs on a different node, the transfer of query results causes an extra delay, which depends on the characteristics of the communication channel between LA and LM. In that case, only c_{max} must be adapted accordingly, to ensure that the tolerance constraints still hold when the LA receives the data. The algorithms proposed in this paper are not affected by that.

(2) Sensing: We adopt a generic model derived from GPS technologies [16], which is applicable to a broad class of positioning sensors. Specifically, position sensing is not performed continuously to conserve precious energy. Instead, the positioning sensor determines its current location by performing a *position fix*. Each position fix is explicitly invoked by the processor and requires some amount of time T_{sense} before the position is obtained. For example, GPS needs about 0.5 s for pseudo-range measurements of satellite signals and computing a valid position [16]. Hence, the maximum sampling rate of a positioning sensor is $1/T_{sense}$. Each position fix also requires a constant amount of energy W_S. In between two fixes the positioning sensor can operate in a low-power *sleep* mode to conserve energy.

Note that we do not consider any background energy that is not influenced by these two operations. Its consumption is independent of the reporting protocol. For instance, a GPS receiver might still wake up *periodically* to keep a lock on the satellite signals.

The real position of an MO at any time t is denoted $loc(O_i)$. However, sensing uncertainty generally causes the location data acquired by a positioning sensor to deviate from the real position. We assume that there is a maximum deviation S_{acc} from $loc(t)$ [27]. Furthermore, we assume that each MO has knowledge about its maximal velocity, denoted by v_{max}. This is a common assumption for tracking mobile objects and determining reasonable values has been discussed elsewhere, e.g., [21].

2.2 Query Model

In this paper we focus on *Continuous Range Queries* (CRQ). Given a closed region with boundary R, this query returns the identities of all mobile objects located inside R. In contrast to one-time queries, a CRQ resides in the system and is continuously evaluated for an extensive period of time. This type of query can be used to monitor objects moving into and out of a spatial region (e.g., if any child leaves a playground), which is an important building block of many location-aware systems [3],[9],[22].

Location-aware applications can *register* a CRQ at the LM. Then, the query remains *active* until it *deregistered* again. Since the locations of MOs change frequently, the result of an active query has to be refreshed timely. To do this, the LM sends a *result message* to the LA after registration and whenever the result changes. The time to refresh a result depends on the objects' movements. Specifically, the result of a CRQ must be updated whenever an MO enters or leaves the query region. That is, whenever an object crosses R, the *query boundary*.

For efficient query processing, we employ the concept of *object-side processing* [3],[9],[17],[22]. That is, the LM collaborates with the MOs to optimize query processing. It conveys query information to them over a wireless network, where it is then utilized to evaluate part of the query locally over each location item acquired. Specifically, the details of a query are first propagated to all relevant MOs in an *init message*. All MOs located inside the queried region will then respond with an *update message*. Subsequently, each MO monitors its own location and sends a new update whenever it crosses the query boundary R. In the update message, it reports its current relation to R (*inside* or *outside*). For long-running continuous queries this approach minimizes the energy spent on communication because the costs for receiving the query at the beginning are easily amortized by saving update messages throughout the query's lifetime.

In the following we focus on the local query evaluation performed by each MO (i.e., the object-side processing of CRQ). In particular, we investigate in detail when an MO must perform a position fix or generate an update message in order to meet the query requirements. Minimizing these operations is essential to reduce energy consumption.

3. Problem Analysis

In this section, we first discuss a straightforward solution to reduce the energy spent on sensing for object-side processing of CRQ. This preliminary approach will help to identify major shortcomings and motivate our solutions.

Whenever a CRQ is active, all MOs must locally monitor their position, to detect crossing the query boundary in time. But due to high energy consumption, position sensing is usually not performed continuously. Instead, an MO can use a technique called *selective sensing* to conserve more energy: After each position fix the MO computes the time it can suspend sensing without affecting the query result. This is the minimum amount of time required to reach the query boundary based on the MO's maximal velocity. If the update threshold is not yet reached after that time, the next fix can be scheduled based on the remaining distance to the query boundary.

The resulting algorithm for object-side processing is depicted in Figure 1. For a query's lifetime, the following steps are repeatedly executed: First, a new position is obtained from the positioning sensor. Subsequently, the function mustUpdate checks if the object crossed the query boundary since the last position fix. For that purpose, the MO's previous state is recorded using a boolean variable isInside (line 1). Whenever this value differs from the object's new state (line 16) the query result must be updated. Thus, a new update message is sent to the LM. Finally, the minimum amount of time

---

```
Main:
(1)   isInside := false;
(2)
(3)   while (query is active) do {
(4)       /* acquire new position */
(5)       newPos := readSensor();
(6)
(7)       /* check update */
(8)       if (mustUpdate()) {
(9)           isInside := NOT isInside;
(10)          sendUpdate(Oi, isInside);
(11)      }
(12)      /* low-power mode */
(13)      T_wait := T_max() - T_sense;
(14)      if (T_wait > 0) { sleep(T_wait) };
(15)  }

mustUpdate:
(16)  return ((newPos ∈ R) != isInside);

T_max:
(17)  d := dist(R, newPos);
(18)  return d / v_max;
```

Figure 1. Object-side processing of CRQ without tolerance.

---

to reach the query boundary is computed based on the object's maximum velocity (line 17 and 18). Since the MO cannot affect the query result during this period of time the next position fix can be deferred accordingly (line 14). Waiting any longer might, however, violate the query condition of CRQ, as the future velocity is not yet known.

As a result, the algorithm in Figure 1 generates a new update message as soon as crossing the query boundary can be discovered. While doing so, it defers each position fix as long as possible without compromising timeliness of detection. Although simple, this algorithm exhibits a number of shortcomings. First, we observe that the algorithm cannot meet the defined query semantics precisely. Ideally, the LM should always update the query result exactly at the time an MO crosses the query boundary. However, this point in time might be missed due to the limitations of current sensor technologies and communication delay. In fact, we can quantify three different sources of uncertainty for location data:

(1) Sensing Uncertainty: Since the MO's future movement is not known in advance, the best time to send an update is when the sensed position is located just beyond the query boundary. Taking limited sensing accuracy into account, however, the acquired position can deviate from the MO's real position by a maximal distance of S_{acc}. That is, at the time an update is generated, the MO could still be approaching the query boundary. If it changed its direction of movement right after the position fix, the algorithm would generate an update even though the MO has never actually crossed the boundary. In the other extreme case, the MO might be located at a distance of S_{acc} beyond the boundary at that time. As a consequence, the algorithm then generates an update late – at some time after the MO affected the query result in reality. The effect of sensing uncertainty is also illustrated in Figure 2. At the time an update is generated, the MO might actually be located anywhere inside the shaded region around its assumed position p_1.

(2) Sampling Uncertainty: Additionally, a new position is not available at all times. This is because each position fix requires some time of T_{sense}. That is, after performing a position fix, the next position will not be available until after T_{sense}. Consider a sensed position that is very close to the query boundary, but does not trigger an update yet. Although the MO might overstep the query boundary right after, it can then travel a distance of $T_{sense} \cdot v_{max}$ before the next position fix completes (depicted by position p_2 in Figure 2). In the worst case, sensing uncertainty adds into the same direction and the algorithm in Figure 1 thus generates an update message at even greater distance to R.

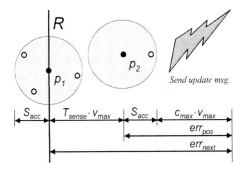

Figure 2. Error in sending an update with CRQ.

(3) Communication Delay in the network furthermore causes update messages to arrive at the LM some time after sensing. In the worst case, the MO moves away from the reported position at maximal velocity while the message is being transmitted. Recall that we assume a statistical upper bound of c_{max} for the end-to-end delay. That is, at the time the LM receives the information, the MO's real position is only known within the following distance from the acquired position (see Figure 2):

$$err_{pos} := S_{acc} + c_{max} \cdot v_{max} \quad (1)$$

By considering all three sources of uncertainty, the MO can have a maximum distance err_{next} from R at the time the query result is updated at the LM (see Figure 2), where

$$err_{next} := S_{acc} + (T_{sense} + c_{max}) \cdot v_{max} \quad (2)$$

As a consequence, the server-side result of a non-tolerant CRQ is always outdated. At any time, it suffers an error of $\pm\, err_{next}$ because the updates of both objects entering and leaving the query region arrive late. Note that this is not only a shortcoming of the presented algorithm but a technical limitation caused by limited capabilities of sensor systems and communication delay.

Next, let us examine the energy spent on position sensing. The algorithm in Figure 1 has been designed for minimizing the number of position fixes, without compromising query accuracy. In between two fixes, the positioning sensor remains in low-power sleep mode until the MO might reach R (line 14). A larger sleeping period would affect the provided accuracy, because the MO might not detect that it has crossed the query boundary on time. Consequently, the maximal error in the query result would further increase.

Figure 1 also reveals that the frequency of position fixes increases whenever the MO approaches the query boundary. This is because the sleeping time between two position fixes depends on the remaining distance to R (see line 17). The smaller this distance, the less time the sensor can remain in low-power mode. Once

the object moves close to R, position fixes have to be performed at the highest frequency in order to generate the next update message in time. Furthermore, a short sleeping time does not allow the MO to cover a large distance before the next position fix is performed. Thus, the MO is still located relatively close to the boundary after that fix. As a consequence, the power consumption may increase substantially while the MO approaches the query boundary.

This reveals a critical problem of object-side query processing: although the defined semantics cannot be met completely, an MO has to invest a lot of energy in performing frequent position sensing in order to provide the best possible accuracy. In the next section we discuss how to overcome these two shortcomings by relaxing the query semantics.

4. Distance-tolerant CRQ

The major problem of evaluating a non-tolerant CRQ is that the MO cannot deduce precisely when it reaches the query boundary. As discussed, this requires a lot of energy for position sensing, and yet uncertainty is still introduced. Let us study how these shortcomings can be overcome by introducing *uncertainty-aware tolerances*.

4.1 Definition and Semantics

Our main idea is to define the maximum allowed error related to updates along with each query. This allows applications to specify their requirements more precisely. In exchange the allowed tolerances are guaranteed to be met in consideration of all sources of uncertainty, and valuable energy of MOs can also be conserved. To achieve these goals, the boundary of R is "blurred". That is, we introduce two distinct boundaries R_1 and R_2 such that R is sandwiched between them. The query result can then be updated *while* an MO crosses the region between R_1 and R_2, which we call the *tolerance region*. Let us first look at the following definition of distance-tolerant CRQ:

Definition 1: Distance-tolerant CRQ (d-CRQ)
Given two closed regions with boundaries R_1, R_2 ($R_1 \in R_2$, $dist(R_1, R_2) > 2 \cdot err_{next}$), a d-CRQ returns a set of ids that contains all MOs located in R_1 but no MO located outside R_2. That is, it returns the set $S \cup T$, with $S := \{O_i \mid loc(O_i) \in R_1\}$ and $T \subseteq \{O_i \mid loc(O_i) \in R_2\}$ ($1 \leq i \leq n$).

In this definition, the query result must contain all objects that are located inside of R_1 (the set S). However, objects located inside the tolerance region might also be contained in the result set. These objects belong to the set T, which is any subset of mobile objects located inside R_2 – including those that are located out-

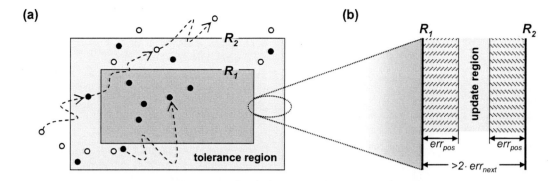

Figure 3. Definition of distance-tolerant CRQ with (a) tolerance region and (b) update region.

side R_1. However, no MO located outside R_2 is contained in the query result. This is illustrated in Figure 3a, where the tolerance region is lightly shaded. Black points depict MOs included in the result set, and the MOs not included are represented as white points.

Furthermore, note that Definition 1 is independent of the original query region R. An application can choose how to derive R_1 and R_2 thereof, depending on its requirements. For example, it can query all MOs located inside R_1 while accepting some *false positives*. The set of MOs falsely included in the result set is then bounded to MOs still located inside the larger boundary R_2. Alternatively, all MOs located inside R_2 can be queried if some *false negatives* are acceptable. Then, the smaller boundary R_1 in turn limits the set of objects missing in the query result. Balancing between these two extremes is also possible.

More importantly, Definition 1 offers well-defined bounds that can be detected in practice. The tolerance constraints are guaranteed with respect to the objects' real positions at the time a result update is received. That is, the query result contains the specified objects at all times – in spite of sampling uncertainty, sensing uncertainty and communication delay. To guarantee this, an update must be *received* while the MO is located inside the tolerance region. Consider an object initially located outside the larger region R_2 (Figure 3). The object must send an update after entering R_2, so that the update is received before it enters R_1. This ensures that the MO has already been included in the result set by the time it enters R_1. After sending an update message, the MO is free to move anywhere inside R_2 without violating the query constraint. However, it must ensure that another update is received by the LM before it leaves R_2 again. At that time it is in line with the query definition to remove the object from the result set, which must be accomplished before it actually leaves R_2.

To ensure an update can always be received in time, with consideration of uncertainty, Definition 1 requires the shortest distance between both boundaries

$dist(R_1,R_2)$ to be no less than $2 \cdot err_{next}$ (Equation 2). Let us understand this requirement by examining the object-side processing of d-CRQ.

4.2 Object-side processing of d-CRQ

For d-CRQ, the MO initially receives both query boundaries R_1 and R_2 within the query init message. In the following, we describe how to generate position fixes and updates that conform to the tolerance constraints. Let us start with the following definition:

Definition 2: Update region is the region where an update message can be generated without violating the tolerance constraints.

As shown in Figure 3b the update region is located inside the tolerance region with a distance of err_{pos} (Equation 1) to each query boundary. Recall that err_{pos} is the maximal error between a sensed position and the MO's position at the time the update is received, when taking sensing uncertainty and communication delay into account. Thus, only updates generated at a larger distance to both boundaries are definitely received within the defined tolerance bounds.

To generate update messages accordingly, the main algorithm described in the previous section (Figure 1) is extended as shown in Figure 4[1]. Consider an MO located outside R_2. As discussed before, the object must make sure that it sends an update before it enters R_1. Accordingly, the function `T_max` computes the shortest time to reach R_1 from the current position of the object (line 21). This value must be reduced by err_{pos} in order to determine the maximum distance before an update must be sent. A later update could not be guaranteed to arrive before the object enters R_1 in reality. Subsequently, the shortest time to cross that

---

[1] Let `signedDist(R,p)` be a function that returns the shortest distance to enter the region defined by R from the position p. If p is already located inside R the shortest distance to its boundary will be returned with a negative leading sign instead.

distance is computed based on the object's maximal velocity (line 23). This results in the longest time the next position fix can be deferred without violating the tolerance constraints. However, an update must be sent immediately if the subsequent position fix is not known to complete within the remaining time ($T_{max} < T_{sense}$, line 2). On that account, the defined tolerance of the query allows updating earlier – at any time the object is located inside the update region.

To assure this constraint, the function T_min calculates the time until an update might be sent at the earliest. Taking sensing uncertainty into account, the query definition would actually allow sending an update as soon as the sensed position is located inside of R_2 with a distance larger than S_{acc}. However, we also have to consider the object's situation after sending an update. Then, it has to monitor when it leaves the region R_2 again. Once the object is considered part of the query result, it must ensure another update message is *received* before it leaves R_2 again. Thus, we must ensure that the MO has sufficient time to execute at least one more position fix before this constraint is violated. Consequently, the first update message must be deferred until the distance to R_2 exceeds err_{next} (line 7). This observation also requires the minimum distance between both regions to be guaranteed. If an object was located at a distance any smaller than err_{next} to

both regions at the same time, it would be unable to fulfil the query semantics. For that reason Definition 1 required $dist(R_1, R_2)$ to exceed $2 \cdot err_{next}$ at first hand.

Finally, if none of the conditions was fulfilled yet, the object must be located somewhere in the update region with a distance larger that err_{next} to both query boundaries (line 12). In this case no update message has to be sent yet, but it is already allowed. The function updatePolicy (line 13) then decides whether the MO should send an update immediately or wait for the next position fix to complete. Regarding the energy consumption, this is an important part of the algorithm. Here, the energy costs of sensing and reporting must be balanced to reduce the total amount of energy consumed. We discuss suitable strategies to balance between these two factors of energy consumption in the next subsection.

4.3 Update Policy

The algorithm in Figure 4 always defers a position fix such that the MO could cross the update region completely before acquiring the next position. However, the MO often does not actually move at maximum velocity. Then, it is located somewhere inside the update region at the time the next position fix is performed. This situation offers an important possibility to further optimize energy use. The larger the distance tolerance defined by the query, the more room for optimization can be utilized by the update policy.

An effective update policy must balance both factors driving the energy consumption. On the one hand, a high frequency of position fixes should be avoided. Accordingly, an update should be sent whenever this extends the forthcoming sleeping time of the sensor. On the other hand, sending an update message consumes a significant amount of energy as well. To reduce this factor, a message should only be sent if absolutely required for query correctness. For example, consider an object that changes its direction of movement at some time after entering the update region and moves back to where it came from. Then, no update message is required at all. In addition, deferring an update also causes fewer changes to the query result. This can avoid an oscillating result set when an MO moves back and forth around the query boundary and applications will be relieved from rapid result updates caused by such a movement.

Often, the right time to generate an update depends on the future movement – which is usually not known in advance. For that reason, we propose two alternative policies to balance between sensing and reporting operations. Their performance is then evaluated and compared against each other in Section 5.

```
mustUpdate:
(1)   /* check upper bound */
(2)   if (T_max() < T_sense) {
(3)       return true;
(4)   } // else:
(5)
(6)   /* check lower bound */
(7)   if (T_min() > 0) {
(8)       // must not update yet
(9)       return false;
(10)  } // else:
(11)
(12)  /* between the bounds */
(13)      return updatePolicy();
(14)  }

T_max:
(15)  /* shortest time to reach upper bound */
(16)  if (isInside) {
(17)      // remaining distance to leave R2
(18)      d := - signedDist(R2, newPos);
(19)  } else {
(20)      // remaining distance to enter R1
(21)      d := signedDist(R1, newPos);
(22)  }
(23)  return (d - err_pos) / v_max;

T_min:
(24)  /* shortest time to reach lower bound */
(25)  if (isInside) {
(26)      // remaining distance to leave R1
(27)      d := - signedDist(R1, newPos);
(28)  } else {
(29)      // remaining distance to enter R2
(30)      d := signedDist(R2, newPos)
(31)  }
(32)  return (d + err_next) / v_max;
```

Figure 4. Object-side processing of CRQ with distance-tolerance.

(1) Fraction-Delay FD(*f*): This policy decides to send an update message only when a certain fraction *f* of the update region is crossed ($f \in [0,1)$). This condition depends on the boundary from which the MO entered the update region. If the distance to this boundary exceeds the fraction *f* of the distance between both boundaries, an update message is generated. The reason is that no update is required if the MO leaves the update region at the same boundary, it came from. To evaluate this condition, we can reuse the computed time spans to reach both bounds (T_{min}, T_{max}). Recall that T_{min} becomes negative inside of the update region while T_{max} is still positive. Thus, an update is sent, iff:

$$- T_{min} > f \cdot (T_{max} - T_{min}) \qquad (3)$$

With a larger update fraction, an update message is generated at a later point in time. In extreme ($f = 1$) an update is never generated in updatePolicy. Instead, it is only triggered by mustUpdate (Figure 4) when required to guarantee the tolerance constraints. Thus, less update messages are generated on average. However, a close distance to the query boundary in turn requires more position fixes.

(2) Predicted-Direction PD(*f, a*): The FD policy, although simple to implement, may not be suitable for all situations. As discussed, the best time to send an update depends on the future movement of the object. For that reason, the next policy extends FD by predicting the future direction of movement based on past position fixes in order to make a better decision. Specifically, it reports the location only if a certain fraction *f* of the update region is crossed and the movement is furthermore predicted to require an update message in the near future. This is determined by first computing the direction of reaching the respective boundary in the shortest time ($\vec{m}_{out}$). An object is considered to approach this boundary only if its predicted movement direction ($\vec{m}_{pred}$) deviates from $\vec{m}_{out}$ by an angle within $\pm a$ (where $0° \leq a \leq 180°$).

Given the MO's current location $loc(O_i)$, $\vec{m}_{out}$ can be determined as follows: let X_i denote the closest point to $loc(O_i)$, which is located on the upcoming query boundary – R_2 (R_1) if the object is currently (not) element of the result set. Then, $\vec{m}_{out}$ is the vector ($X_i - loc(O_i)$). Likewise, we compute the future direction of movement based on preceding (P_i) position fixes: $\vec{m}_{pred}$ then corresponds to the vector ($loc(O_i) - P_i$). However, more sophisticated prediction algorithms [5],[14] could be used in practice as well.

To summarize, the introduction of tolerances offers three advantages for the processing of continuous range queries. First, it guarantees query results that are always correct within well-defined, application-specific bounds. As shown in Section 3, such guaran-

tees could not be provided for non-tolerant range queries. Second, the energy spent on position sensing is reduced because the average waiting time between position fixes is increased and short sleeping times can be avoided. Finally, the amount of sensing and reporting operations can be balanced inside the update region, which can further reduce energy use. In order to identify the most effective balance, we evaluate the performance of the proposed update policies next.

5. Evaluation

In order to evaluate the performance of our approach, we have conducted various experiments based on a realistic mobility model. We will explain the experimental setup, followed by the detailed results.

5.1 Simulation Setup

We used the CanuMobiSim simulator [25] to generate movement traces of pedestrians following trip sequences through the inner city of Stuttgart. This comprises a simulation area of 2.0 x 2.0 km². Movements through the streets follow a smooth motion pattern [2]. This model uses stochastic principles to control the change of speed and direction in order to obtain a realistic movement behaviour. The target speed is chosen randomly from 0-3 m/s every 30 seconds. The sensing uncertainty is obtained from a statistical error model of GPS receivers [24] based on Gauss-Markow processes with an imprecision ≤ 6.3 m in 95 %. For each experiment we used 100 different movement traces along with five different measurement errors. Each result thus depicts the average of 500 runs. A single query is evaluated at a time with a lifetime of 3 hrs. For each object, the number of position fixes and updates is accumulated over the whole lifetime of a query. Then, we use these values to derive the overall energy consumption (of one object).

The algorithms assume a maximal sensing uncertainty of $S_{acc} = 10$ m, a maximal communication delay of $c_{max} = 1$ s and maximal velocity of $v_{max} = 5$ m/s, which reflects a pessimistic bound on actual speeds. Concerning energy costs, we assume that sending an update message consumes $W_U = 150$ mJoules. According to [9], this amount suffices to transmit about 240 bytes over GSM/GPRS. Each position fix is assumed to cost $W_S = 75$ mJoules and to take $T_{sense} = 0.5$ s. These are typical values of a low-power GPS receiver [18].

5.2 Energy consumption

To evaluate the energy consumption of d-CRQ for different sizes of the tolerance region, we varied both query boundaries (i.e., R_1 and R_2). Assume a rectangular region R with a size of 600 x 600 m² placed in the middle of the simulation area. Then, the inner region R_1 is obtained by shrinking R in each direction by d_r. Enlarging R in each direction by d_r likewise establishes the outer region R_2. The resulting width of the tolerance area is $2 \cdot d_r$. The minimal size to guarantee correct query results is $2 \cdot err_{next} = 35\text{m}$ in this setup.

Figure 5 presents the evaluation of FD(f) policy for different values of d_r. It depicts the aggregated number of (a) position fixes, (b) updates and (c) the resulting energy consumption of each object in relation to the update fraction f. Most of all, we can observe a very different performance for update fractions smaller and larger than 0.5. If f is reduced below 0.5, the number of both, position fixes and updates increases. This can be explained as follows: First, recall that lower update fractions cause updates to be sent at smaller distances to the boundary the MO crossed already. Now, consider an object is moving into the outer region R_2 and sends an update message before its distance to R_2 exceeds the remaining distance to the upcoming boundary R_1 (i.e., $f < 0.5$). After the update is performed, the waiting time T_{wait} has to be computed based on R_2 instead of R_1. As the object is still located closer to R_2 than to R_1, this reduces the waiting time till the next position fix. In consequence, the total number of position fixes increases with smaller update fractions. Additionally, the object also has to re-evaluate the update decision after that position fix based on R_2. The smaller the preceding waiting time, the higher is the chance that the object is still located close to R_2 at that time. Thus, the update policy will trigger another update message immediately. The bottom line is that a low update fraction generates a series of frequent update messages (one after each position fix) while an object traverses the update region. This causes the number of updates to increase rapidly if f is reduced below 0.5. Notice that for such low values of f even more messages are sent for higher values of d_r because an MO must cross a larger distance before this series of rapid updates ends.

For $f > 0.5$, the number of position fixes also increases again (Figure 5a). This is due to shorter waiting times at locations close to the upcoming boundary. If an update is deferred beyond $f = 0.5$, this boundary becomes closer than the boundary that was crossed already. Yet, this can sometimes prevent an update message from being sent, if the object changes its direction of movement before reaching the respective boundary. For that reason, the number of update messages simultaneously drops slightly (Figure 5b).

As a result, we can see from Figure 5c that FD(0.5) permanently performs best for all depicted values of d_r. For smaller update fractions, too many updates are generated. For larger update fractions the increase in position fixes requires too much energy and dominates the savings in update messages.

Next, we added a movement prediction to FD(0.5) to further delay updates (as described in Section 4.3). Instead of using a large update fraction, an MO should not delay an update if it has a high chance of entering R_1 soon. The resulting performance of PD(0.5, a) with varying angles of tolerated deviation a is depicted in Figure 6. Smaller values of a successfully reduce the number of updates, as shown in Figure 6b. However, the simultaneous increase in position fixes (Figure 6a) is still too high and does not outweigh the reduction of update messages. Thus, the lowest energy is consumed

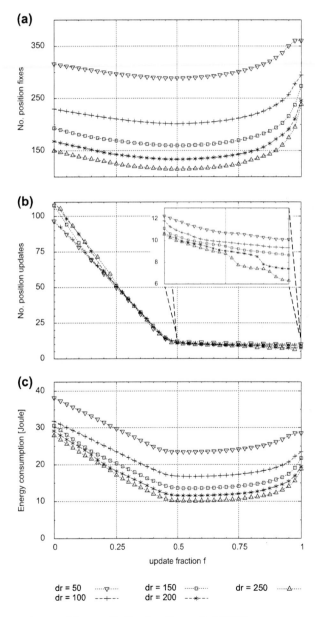

Figure 5. Evaluation of d-CRQ with FD(f) policy.

with the largest angle $a = 90°$ (Figure 6c), which in fact resembles the FD(0.5) policy. However, if sending an update is more costly – either in terms of energy or because a small number of update messages is compulsory – the direction prediction PD(0.5, a) with a small value of a offers an interesting alternative. It achieves to minimize the required communication while consuming less energy than a high update fraction.

After all, FD(0.5) is found to be the best policy for minimizing the amount of energy consumed for d-CRQ. Furthermore, Figure 5c and Figure 6c show that tolerances do help in reducing energy consumption. Increasing the update region (in terms of d_r) sig-

nificantly reduces the amount of energy consumed. For comparison, we also evaluated the preliminary algorithm from Section 3, using the initial query region R (without tolerances) and obtained an energy consumption of about 50.5 Joules. In contrast, FD(0.5) with a minimal tolerance of $d_r = 17.5$ m guarantees correct query results and requires only 42.4 Joule. This constitutes a saving of 16%. With $d_r = 50$ m another 37% of energy is saved. In fact, we can even save up to 80% in total by further increasing the tolerance to $d_r = 250$ m. In short, this evaluation approves that increasing the distance tolerances can reduce the energy consumption significantly.

6. Related Work

The approach discussed in this paper can be classified as a *data stream filtering* technique. The objective of filtering is to facilitate the efficient evaluation of continuous queries over constantly-changing data streams (e.g., locations of mobile objects, temperature). Specifically, each stream source is installed with some constraints (called *filter conditions*) derived from query requirements. A data item generated at the source is sent to the central server only if its value satisfies the conditions defined in these filters. In our approach, the MO decides when to report an update, and so it acts as a "filter". It was shown in [1],[3],[22] that significant communication effort can be saved by assigning filter conditions appropriately.

To improve the performance of filters, the concept of *tolerance* has been proposed [20]. This assumes that users can tolerate some degree of imprecision (called *tolerance*) in query results. This tolerance is incorporated into filter conditions. A well-studied tolerance is the *value-based* tolerance, which is basically a numerical value for specifying the maximum error allowed. For example, filters are developed in [19] to answer tolerant average and minimum queries. In [1], filters are designed for top-k queries. In [11] a Kalman Filter is installed at every stream. The extension of filter methods in a sensor network is studied in [7]. Filters for non-value tolerances are developed in [4].

In these works, items generated by streams are assumed to be *always* correct. However, this assumption is not always valid. As we have explained in Section 3, the data acquired by a sensing device is contaminated with different kinds of errors. If these uncertainties are not considered, stream filters can miss important events, and introduce incorrectness into query results. In fact, the tolerance definitions described in the previous work are not "uncertainty-aware". Our work, on the other hand, specifies necessary conditions in tolerance definitions to ensure that they can be enforced with consideration of data uncertainty.

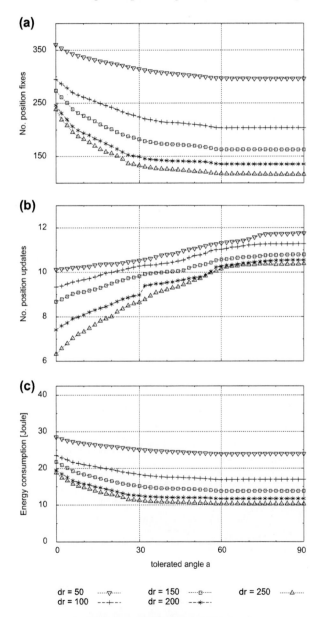

(a)

(b)

(c)

dr = 50
dr = 100
dr = 150
dr = 200
dr = 250

Figure 6. Evaluation of d-CRQ with PD(0.5, *a*) policy.

Moreover, to the best of our knowledge, none of these stream filters considers the impact of *sensing*. They assume that communication is the only relevant factor of energy consumption and thus focus on minimizing the number of update messages. However, the energy costs of acquiring new sensor data can also have a significant impact on energy use – at least for the prominent sensing technology GPS. Our results in Section 5 confirm that there is an important trade-off between the amount of sensing and reporting operations required. Deferring an update as long as possible can increase the sensing costs significantly. In our paper, we carefully control this trade-off in order to reduce the overall energy consumption.

Recently, the issues of energy consumed for sensing have been considered in sensor networks. A good overview of approaches is given in [23]. Commonly, these solutions exploit correlations between values of multiple sensors – either on the same node [8],[15], or on multiple nodes in spatial proximity [6]. The consumed energy is reduced by acquiring data from a subset of sensors only and predicting the expected value of others with some level of confidence. This differs from the problem considered in this paper.

7. Conclusion

We studied how the energy of MOs can be saved when their locations are monitored by continuous range queries. We developed object-side processing algorithms that consider both energy use and the degree of correctness (or tolerance) in query results. These tolerance definitions are "uncertainty-aware", which consider various sources of data uncertainty. Our algorithms control the sensing and reporting operations carefully so that these tolerance definitions are satisfied. Moreover, our experiments show that the algorithms developed save energy significantly. In the future, we will extend this technique to other continuous queries (e.g., nearest-neighbour queries). We will also extend our algorithms to support concurrent execution of multiple queries and consider how other kinds of tolerances can improve energy savings.

Acknowledgments

The work described in this paper was partially supported by the German Research Foundation (DFG) within the Collaborative Research Center (SFB) 627, by the HKSAR Research Grants Council (RGC) CERG grant (PolyU 5138/06E), and by the Germany/Hong Kong Joint Research Scheme (DAAD PPP D/06/00383; G_HK013/06). We would also like to thank the anonymous reviewers for their insightful comments and suggestions.

References

[1] B. Babcock and C. Olston: "*Distributed Top-K Monitoring*". In: Proc. ACM Int'l Conf. Mgmt. of Data (SIGMOD'03), San Diego, USA, June 2003.

[2] C. Bettstetter: "*Smooth is Better than Sharp: A Random Mobility Model for Simulation of Wireless Networks*". In: Proc. 4th Int'l Work. Modeling, Analysis, and Simulation of Wireless and Mobile Syst. (MSWiM'01), Rome, Italy, July 2001.

[3] Y. Cai, K. Hua, G. Cao, and T. Xu: "*Real-Time Processing of Range-Monitoring Queries in Heterogeneous Mobile Databases*". In: IEEE Trans. Mobile Comp. 5(7), July 2006.

[4] R. Cheng, B. Kao, S. Prabhakar, A. Kwan, and Y. Tu: "*Adaptive Stream Filters for Entity-based Queries with Non-Value Tolerance*". In: Proc. 31st Int'l Conf. Very Large Data Bases (VLDB'05), Trondheim, Norway, Sep. 2005.

[5] A. Civilis, C. Jensen, and S. Pakalnis: "*Techniques for Efficient Road-Network-Based Tracking of Moving Objects*". In: IEEE Trans. Know. Data Eng. 17(5), May 2005.

[6] Y. Kotidis: "*Snapshot Queries: Towards Data-Centric Sensor Networks*". In: Proc. 21st Int'l Conf. Data Engineering (ICDE'05), Apr. 2005.

[7] A. Deligiannakis, Y. Kotidis, and N. Roussopoulos: "*Processing Approximate Aggregate Queries in Wireless Sensor Networks*". In: Inf. Syst. Jour. 31(8), Dec. 2006.

[8] A. Deshpande, C. Guestrin, S. Madden, J. Hellerstein, and W. Hong: "*Model-driven data acquisition in sensor networks*". In: Proc. 30th Int'l Conf. Very Large Data Bases (VLDB'04), Toronto, Canada, Sep. 2004.

[9] B. Gedik and L. Liu: "*MobiEyes: A Distributed Location Monitoring Service Using Moving Location Queries*". In: IEEE Trans. Mobile Comp. 5(10), Oct. 2006.

[10] M. Gruteser and D. Grunwald: "*Anonymous Usage of Location-Based Services through Spatial and Temporal Cloaking*". In: Proc. 1st Int'l Conf. Mobile Systems, Applications, and Services (MobiSys'03), San Francisco, USA, May 2003.

[11] A. Jain, E. Chang, and Y. Wang: "*Adaptive stream resource management using Kalman Filters*". In: Proc. ACM Int'l Conf. Mgmt. Data (SIGMOD'04), Paris, France, June 2004.

[12] C. Jensen, A. Friis-Christensen, T. Pedersen, D. Pfoser, S. Saltenis, and N. Tryfona: "*Location-based services – A database perspective*". In: Proc. 8th Scand. Conf. Geo. Inf. Science (ScanGIS'01), Ås, Norway, 2001.

[13] A. Leonhardi and K. Rothermel: "*Architecture of a Large-scale Location Service*". In: Proc. 22nd Int'l Conf. Distr. Comp. Syst. (ICDCS'02), Vienna, Austria, July 2002.

[14] A. Leonhardi, C. Nicu, and K. Rothermel: "*A Map-based Dead-reckoning Protocol for Updating Location Information*". In: Proc. Int'l Parallel and Distr. Processing Symp. (IPDPS'02), Ft. Lauderdale, USA, 2002.

[15] S. Madden, M. Franklin, J. Hellerstein, and W. Hong. "*The design of an acquisitional query processor for sensor networks*". In: Proc. ACM Int'l Conf. Mgmt. Data (SIGMOD'03), San Diego, USA, June 2003.

[16] P. Misra and P. Enge: "*Global Positioning System: Signals, Measurements and Performance*", 2nd Ed., Ganga-Jumuna Press, 2006.

[17] K. Mouratidis, D. Papadias, S. Bakiras, and Y. Tao: "*A Threshold-Based Algorithm for Continuous Monitoring of k Nearest Neighbors*". In: IEEE Trans. Know. Data Eng. 17(11), Nov. 2005.

[18] Navman: *Jupiter 30 Data sheet*, http://www.navman.com/Documents/OEM_docs/Jupiter 30/LA000576-C_Jupiter30_DataSheet.pdf, May 2007.

[19] C. Olston, J. Jiang, and J. Widom: "*Adaptive Filters for Continuous Queries over Distributed Data Streams*". In: Proc. ACM Int'l Conf. Mgmt. Data (SIGMOD'03), San Diego, USA, June 2003.

[20] C. Olston and J. Widom: "*Efficient Monitoring and Querying of Distributed, Dynamic Data via Approximate Replication*". In: IEEE Data Eng. Bull. 28(1), Mar. 2005.

[21] D. Pfoser and C. Jensen: "*Capturing the Uncertainty of Moving-Object Representations*". In: Proc. 6th Int'l Symp. Spatial Databases (SSD'99), Hong Kong, 1999.

[22] S.Prabhakar, Y. Xia, D. Kalashnikov, W. Aref, and S. Hambrusch: "*Query Indexing and Velocity Constrained Indexing: Scalable Techniques for Continuous Queries on Moving Objects*". In: IEEE Trans. Comp. 51(10), Oct. 2002.

[23] V. Raghunathan, S. Ganeriwal, and M. Srivastava: "*Emerging techniques for long lived wireless sensor networks*". In: IEEE Comm. Mag. 44(4), Apr. 2006.

[24] J. Rankin: "*GPS and Differential GPS: An Error Model for Sensor Simulation*". In: IEEE Position Location and Navigation Symp. (PLANS'94), Las Vegas, USA, Apr. 1994.

[25] I. Stepanov, P. Marron, and K. Rothermel: "*Mobility Modeling of Outdoor Scenarios for MANETs*". In: Proc. 38th An. Simulation Symp. (ANSS'05), San Diego, USA, Apr. 2005.

[26] U. Varshney: "*Location management for mobile commerce applications in wireless internet environment*". In: ACM Trans. Internet Tech. 3(3), Aug. 2003.

[27] O. Wolfson, A. Sistla, S. Chamberlain, and Y. Yesha: "*Updating and Querying Databases that Track Mobile Units*". In: Distributed and Parallel Databases, 7(3), July 1999.

Feature Space Enrichment by Incorporation of Implicit Features for Effective Classification

Abhishek Srivastava
Dept. of Computing Science
University of Alberta
Edmonton, Canada
sr16@cs.ualberta.ca

Osmar. R. Zaïane
Dept. of Computing Science
University of Alberta
Edmonton, Canada
zaiane@cs.ualberta.ca

Maria-Luiza Antonie
Dept. of Computing Science
University of Alberta
Edmonton, Canada
luiza@cs.ualberta.ca

Abstract

Feature Space Conversion for classifiers is the process by which the data that is to be fed into the classifier is transformed from one form to another. The motivation behind doing this is to enhance the "discriminative power" of the data together with preserving its "information content". In this paper, a new method of feature space conversion is explored, wherein "enrichment" of the feature space is carried out by the augmentation of the existing features with new "implicit" features. The modus operandi involves generation of association rules in one case and closed frequent patterns in another and the extraction of the new features from these.

This new feature space is first made use of independently to feed the classifier and then it is used in unison with the original feature space. The effectiveness of these methods is subsequently verified experimentally and expressed in terms of the classification accuracy achieved by the classifier.

1. Introduction

Classifiers are computational models that have the ability to predict the class of a data item on the basis of the values of its characteristic attributes [2]. For doing this, the classifier has to be first "trained" with a set of representative data items. Once trained, the classifier has the ability to assign the most suitable class to an unlabelled data item. The accuracy of a classifier is measured by "hiding" the class labels of a set of labeled data items and monitoring the percentage of these data items that the classifier correctly classifies.

The classifier that has been used in our work is the Support Vector Machine (SVM) [3] for its reputation to be one of the best, if not the best, classifier in many real applications. The SVM separates data into classes by attempting to find a linear "maximum margin hyper-plane". If the data is linearly separable, such a hyper-plane is found and the data is classified. If the data is not separable linearly then the SVM "raises" the data to a much higher dimension making use of special functions called kernels. At a higher dimension when the data becomes separable the SVM finds the suitable hyper-plane.

The "feature space" of a classifier refers to the attributes of the data item that are made use of by the classifier for distinguishing one item from another. For example, a set of creditors at a bank may be distinguished from one another on the basis of their income, age and education level. In this case, the feature space comprises : {Income, Age, Diploma}. Feature space conversion therefore implies a *change* in the set of attributes that are thus used. This *change* may be brought about by modifying the current attributes used, by making use of an entirely new set of attributes, or a combination of the two.

Normally, the feature space that is made use of comprises the *explicit* features *i.e.* the original characteristic attributes of the data item. This paper makes an attempt to *enrich* this feature space by incorporating certain *implicit* features which are not obvious but which have to be extracted from the available attributes. We explore two possible methods of doing this: (1) a method based on generation of association rules, and (2) one based on closed frequent patterns. The first of these entails the generation of association rules which are relationships that exist between different data items in a transactional database such that the presence of one item implies the other or the presence of a combination of items implies the presence of a third item [12]. For example, weather: sunny and day: Saturday implies mood: happy.
As an association rule, this is written as:

Sunny $^\wedge$ Saturday $\rightarrow$ happy
  (antecedent)   (consequent)

The *support* of an association rule $X \rightarrow Y$ refers to the fraction of transactions that contain $(X \cup Y)$ items and the *confidence* of $X \rightarrow Y$ is the fraction of the transactions containing X that also contain Y.

Note that in this paper we are not claiming a new associative classifier [6, 14, 15] (*i.e.* a classifier based on association rules) but investigate feature space enrichment to potentially improve any classifier; in our case we use SVM.

In this paper, each data point which comprises a set of attributes and a class label, is considered a transaction and the association rules generated are those between the union of the different attribute values and the class labels. Having been generated, the rules are "filtered" to obtain only those that have the class-labels as the consequent *i.e.* the implied value. From these select association rules, two sets of features are derived: Rule Based features and Class Based features [4]. These will be discussed in detail later.

This converted feature space is subsequently made use of to train the classifier, in this case SVM, and the accuracy of the classifier is monitored.

The rule based and class based features are first used to train the SVM independently. They are further used in combination with the original feature space of the data. The variation in accuracy of the classifier is studied over different values of minimum support threshold (*i.e.* by using features generated from association rules whose support is above the minimum support threshold).

In addition to this, closed frequent patterns are also made use of, to generate new features [13]. A group of items X in a transactional database is a closed frequent pattern if X occurs in the database more frequently than the minimum support threshold and there is no *proper* super-set of X that has the same support as X.

All the frequent patterns for the concerned dataset are generated and from these patterns, a new feature vector is fabricated for each original data vector. The new feature space thus obtained, like in the case of the association rules ones, is first used independently to train the SVM and then in combination with the original features.

Some work on feature space augmentation or enrichment has been done but limited and not necessarily related to our focus of study. For instance feature space augmentation was investigated in the context of classification with taxonomies [16]. The authors of [17] investigating image clustering highlight the need for feature space augmentation in the context of image datasets but do not exploit the possibility.

Relatively less work has been done on feature space augmentation of the kind we are dealing with. Rather most of the related work concentrates on the "trimming" of the feature space so as to effectively handle large volumes of high dimensional data. It is referred to as feature selection. This has especially been done in text categorization. Yang *et al.* reduce the dimensionality of the feature space of text documents

by quantitatively expressing the relevance of terms using Information Gain and the χ^2-test methods and expressing the content using the highly relevant terms only [9]. Koller *et al* . in their work attempt to transform the feature space of text documents by first creating a hierarchy of topics and then merging sufficiently *close* topics to each other [10]. From this reduced number of modules, representative terms are chosen as features. Scott *et al.* explore the "syntactic and semantic" relationships that exist between words in a text, rather than the morphological relationship as was normally done [11]. All synonymous terms were mapped to one feature. This way, they were able to substantially reduce the feature space. One recent work that does concentrate on feature space augmentation is that of Cheng *et al.*[8]. They map a relationship between minimum support threshold and information gain, and modify the original feature space by generating closed frequent patterns corresponding to the optimal support threshold and combining them with the original features.

2. Feature Space Conversion

As mentioned, two broad methodologies of feature conversion are made use of in this paper. The new features are mainly used to enrich the feature space *i.e.* they are used in combination with the original features although we also briefly analyze their respective independent influence on the classifier accuracy. The two categories of feature conversion being dealt with here are:

- Association rules based features.
- Closed frequent patterns based features.

2.1. Association Rules based Features

The methodology followed to carry out feature space conversion involves first the generation of association rules from the data-set, followed by filtering out irrelevant rules, and finally the construction of the rule-based and class-based features.

2.1.1. Generation of the Relevant Association Rules. The data-set that is made use of for classification usually consists of a set of data points each represented by a unique *vector*. This vector comprises the attribute values of the data-point as also the class to which the data point belongs. This is illustrated in the following:

$$X: x_1, x_2, x_3, \ldots x_n \quad C_x$$

x_i (i = 1-n) represents the values of n attributes of data point X and C_x represents the class to which X belongs.

The association rules are generated by considering each data vector to be a transaction, and the attributes and class labels as the data items. Let us consider a simple example of a very small data-set:

$$2, 12, 1, 67, 3, 6, 7, 23, 9, 8, C_1$$
$$54, 7, 8, 22, 1, 9, 78, 12, 91, C_1$$
$$7, 1, 89, 4, 22, 12, 3, 9, 54, 2, C_2$$
$$1, 123, 7, 8, 3, 35, 65, 2, 9, 66, C_3$$
$$2, 1, 4, 6, 89, 3, 56, 3, 88, 9, C_2$$
$$7, 12, 95, 16, 9, 1, 56, 78, 70, C_1$$

The attributes C_i are the class labels.

From this data-set, the association rules are generated. Further, from these rules the only rules that are relevant are the ones that have a class label as the consequent. All other rules are "filtered" out. Below is a simple example of a possible set of relevant rules.

Table 1. Example of a set of relevant rules

$9 \wedge 78 \wedge 12 \rightarrow C_1$ Sup. = 33.33%, Conf. = 66.67%
$7 \wedge 1 \wedge 9 \rightarrow C_1$ Sup. = 50%, Conf. = 60%
$3 \wedge 89 \rightarrow C_2$ Sup. = 33.33%, Conf. = 100%

The more practical approach however is to make use of tools that directly generate association rules with the constraint that the consequent should be a class label rather than generating all the association rules and filtering out the irrelevant ones.

2.1.2. Construction of the New Feature Space. This portion of the methodology is the *crux*. Based on the selective association rules obtained in the previous two steps, two new feature spaces are generated:

(i)   Rule Based feature Space.
(ii)   Class Based Feature Space.

2.1.3. Rule Based Features. In the rule based feature conversion method, for every data point in the data set, a new feature vector is generated. The steps followed in doing this are simple. All the relevant association rules obtained in the previous steps are scanned. The rules whose antecedent is *contained* in the original attributes of the data point are checked. In the new feature vector every relevant rule generated is assigned two fields. The first field takes a value of 1 if the rule is marked (*i.e.* its antecedent is contained in the attributes of the data point) otherwise it takes a value 0. The other field is assigned the confidence value of the respective rule. A simple example follows: Let us consider the set of relevant rules in Table 1.

Let the data points be :

$$23, 45, 8, 1, 3, 54, 7, 123, 89, 9, 17, C_3$$
$$1, 4, 3, 12, 78, 9, 7, 52, 654, 89, 90, C_2$$

The rules whose antecedents are contained in the attributes of the first data point are the second and the third rule in Table 1 whereas the antecedents of all 3 rules are contained in the second data point.

The rule based feature vectors for these data points thus become:

Rule 1		Rule 2		Rule 3	
Conf.	Marked	Conf.	Marked	Conf.	Marked
66.67	0	60	1	100	1

Rule 1		Rule 2		Rule 3	
Conf.	Marked	Conf.	Marked	Conf.	Marked
66.67	1	60	1	100	1

2.1.4. Class Based Features. The methodology for obtaining the class based feature vector is similar to the rule based one. Here, too the rules are scanned and those rules whose antecedents are contained in the data point are marked.

The feature vector in this case, however, has a different construction. All the rules that are marked are examined for their respective consequents (*i.e.* class labels in this case). The new feature vector constructed, has two fields allocated for each *unique* class that the marked rules have as their consequents. The first field is given the value of the number of rules that have that class label as their consequents, and the other field is allocated the average confidence values of all the rules to which that class applies.

Continuing with our example :

Two rules are contained in the first data point, the second rule and the third rule. Each of these rules has a unique class label in its consequent, rule 2 has class C_1, and rule 3 has class label C_2. Therefore there would be four fields in the new feature vector, two corresponding to class C_1 and two to C_2. Whereas in the second data point, all three rules are contained. The first two rules have the same class label C_1, therefore the "Avg. Conf." field in this case becomes 63.33 (average of 66.67% and 60% of the first and second rules respectively) . The third rule is the only rule with the label C_2 and therefore the Average Confidence is equal to the confidence of the rule.

The feature vectors obtained are shown below :

Class 1		Class 2	
No of rules	Avg. Conf.	No of rules	Avg. Conf,
1	60	1	100

Class 1		Class 2	
No of rules	Avg. Conf.	No of rules	Avg. Conf,
2	63.33	1	100

2.2 Closed Frequent Patterns based Features

This approach of generating features is more straightforward. Here, the first step is the generation of all the closed frequent patterns corresponding to the set minimum support threshold. The patterns generated are then numbered from 1 to n (n being the number of closed frequent patterns). Next, given a data vector, all the generated patterns are scanned to see if they exist within the data vector. If a certain pattern does exist within the data point, its corresponding number is assigned a "1" in the new feature vector, else it is assigned a "0".

Again, considering a simple example. Let the set of closed frequent patterns generated that are subsequently numbered be:

1.	7,9
2.	23,48,2
3.	1,7,17
4.	53,49,78,61

Let the original data vector be:

23, 45, 8, 1, 3, 54, 7, 123, 89, 9, 17, C_3

The patterns numbered 1, and 3 exist in the data vector whereas pattern number 2, and 4 are absent. Therefore the new feature vector becomes as shown below. Here the first field corresponds to the first pattern. Since it does exist within the data vector, the field is assigned a "1". The other fields similarly correspond to the numbered patterns and are assigned relevant values.

1	0	1	0

3. Experiments

The experiments were conducted on 4 datasets: Pima, Glass, Hayes-Roth, and Lymphography obtained from the UCI Machine Learning Repository [5]. The association rules corresponding to the closed frequent patterns for these datasets were generated using an 'in-house' software. Several groups of association rules were generated corresponding to different minimum support thresholds within a restricted range (15 – 25% for Glass dataset, 1-51% for Lymphography, and 1-11% for the others). The range was restricted because beyond the upper-bound, very few rules were generated to be of relevance. The same software was also made use of to generate the closed frequent patterns. The minimum support threshold was deliberately kept the same as that for the association rules.

The rule based and class based feature conversion was carried out using the association rules generated from the closed frequent patterns only and the closed pattern based feature conversion was carried out using the closed frequent patterns generated.

The classifier made use of was LIBSVM [7]. 10-fold cross validation (which is performed by the classifier itself) was considered and the accuracy was calculated on the training data. The kernel used was the linear kernel.

All the new feature spaces obtained were first used independently to train the classifier and then combined with the original features and the combined features were used to train the classifier. Subsequently, the following combinations of features were also used:
1. Rule-based + Class-based
2. Rule-based + Class-based + Original Features
3. Closed Frequent Patterns based features + Rule-based + Class-based + Original features (*i.e.* all features)

The classification accuracy achieved is plotted against the different minimum support thresholds used for the 4 datasets.

3.1 Experimental Results

The results are plotted as the classification accuracy achieved as a percentage against the minimum support threshold also expressed as a percentage. The plots in Figures 1, 2, 3, and 4 are the accuracy versus support threshold for the four datasets respectively. The accuracy achieved using all the combinations mentioned above are plotted *i.e.* the new features independently, the new features in combination with the original features, and the three combinations indicated explicitly above. The accuracy achieved by the original features is also indicated in each of the graphs as a reference by a straight dotted line (above the line indicates an improvement in accuracy)

Figure1 shows the plot for the Glass dataset. Here, a demarcation is clear between the new features in combination with the original (which return a much higher accuracy) and the new features taken alone. Figures 2 and 3 show the plots for the Hayes-Roth, and the Pima datasets respectively. In these cases the difference between the two groups is not as marked as in Glass but broadly, the combined (*i.e.* the new features + original) perform better than the new features alone. Figure 4, for the lymphography dataset is a contrast, with the new features taken alone returning better accuracy results than when taken in combination with the original features. There is therefore no clear 'winner'. The only point that is consistent is the fact that the augmented features usually perform better.

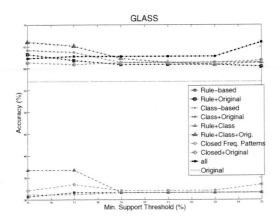

Figure 1. Accuracy versus min. support threshold for the Glass dataset

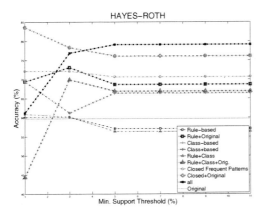

Figure 2. Accuracy versus min. support threshold for the Hayes-Roth dataset

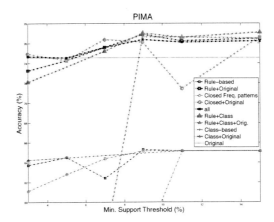

Figure 3. Accuracy versus min. support threshold for the Pima dataset

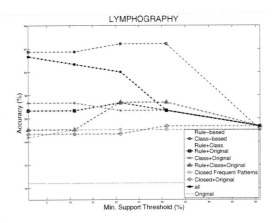

Figure 4. Accuracy versus min. support threshold for the Lymphography dataset

Studying the behaviour of the accuracy achieved by the original features augmented by the various feature spaces, reveals certain notable points. The average (over the four data-sets) variation of the (rule-based + original) feature space is interestingly almost identical to the average variation of the original feature space augmented by the closed frequent patterns based features. The other feature spaces when combined with the original features have a tendency to gradually improve the accuracy achieved, with increasing minimum support threshold. This is illustrated in Figures 5, 6, 7, 8, 9. This behaviour of the feature spaces would compel us to conclude that the best accuracy results may be obtained using the features generated keeping the minimum support threshold as high as practicably possible, and using this feature space in combination with the original features.

Our approach is found to better the accuracy achieved by the original feature space in all the data-sets. It is to be however noted that most of the time the improvement in accuracy is achieved only when new features generated enrich the original feature space. Independently each of the feature spaces falls short of the original features.

Figure 10 compares the best accuracy results obtained by each of the feature spaces in different combinations as also the original feature space.

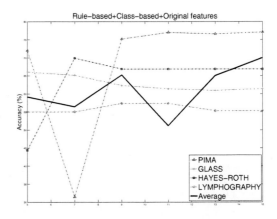

Figure 7. Behaviour of the Original features when augmented together with the Class-based and the Rule-based features.

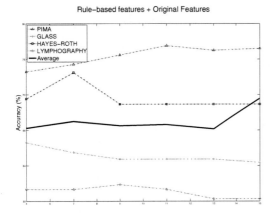

Figure 5. Behaviour of the Original features when augmented with the Rule-based features.

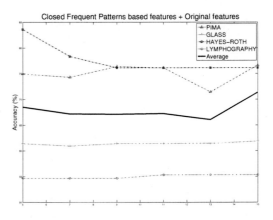

Figure 8. Behaviour of the Original features when augmented with the Frequent Closed Patterns based feature space.

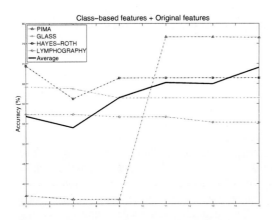

Figure 6. Behaviour of the Original features when augmented with the Class-based features.

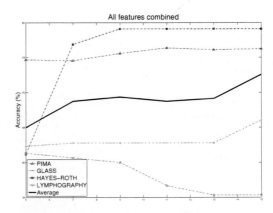

Figure 9. Behaviour of the Original features when augmented with all the new Feature Spaces together.

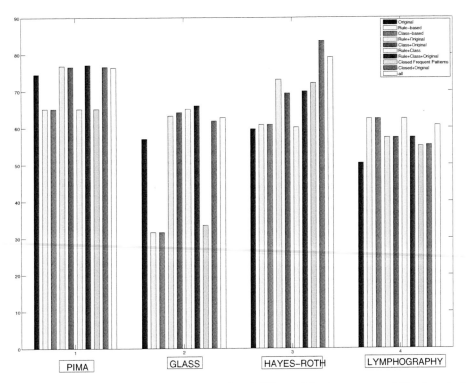

Figure 10. A comparative chart of the results of different feature spaces (all values in %)

Table 2: Accuracy values for different combinations of feature spaces

	O	R	C	R+O	C+O	R+C	R+C+O	Cl	Cl+O	Cl+O+R+C
Pima	74.56	65.15	65.15	76.88	76.62	65.15	77.11	65.15	76.62	76.36
Glass	57.00	31.63	31.63	63.26	64.19	65.15	66.05	33.49	61.86	62.79
Hayes.	59.70	60.90	60.90	73.13	69.40	60.15	69.92	72.18	83.58	79.10
Lymph.	50.42	62.42	62.42	57.33	67.33	62.42	57.38	55.03	55.33	60.67

R: Rule –based; C: Class-based; O: Original ; Cl: Closed Freq. Pat. based

5. Conclusion

A new approach to feature space conversion for classifiers was proposed and subsequently tested on a few datasets in this paper. It was found to substantially improve upon the accuracy achieved by the original feature space alone. In spite of this we were unable to determine one clear 'clear' amongst the methodologies, and were able to more broadly conclude that the enrichment of the original feature space with the new features returned better results than considering either of the features separately.

More important however was the fact that this paper has opened doors to a fresh approach to feature conversion using association rules and frequent patterns. Future work could concentrate on the

1098-8068/07 $25.00 © 2007 IEEE

incorporation of further "implicit information" from these rules and patterns into the feature vector.

Studying the behaviour of the classification accuracy achieved by using the various transformed feature spaces, against minimum support threshold , we were able to conclude that the best results would be returned using the features generated from a small number of highly frequent association rules or patterns in combination with the original features.

6. References

[1] R. Agrawal, T. Imielinski, and A. Swami, "Mining association rules between sets of items in large databases", In *Proc. of SIGMOD*, 1993, pp. 207-216.

[2] J. Han, and M. Kamber, "Data Mining: Concepts and Techniques", *Morgan Kaufmann*, 2001.

[3] Vladimir N. Vapnik, *The Nature of Statistical Learning Theory*. Springer, 1995.

[4] M. –L. Antonie, O. R. Zaiane, and R. C. Holte, "Learning to use a learned model: A two-stage approach to classification", The Sixth IEEE *International Conference on Data Mining (ICDM'06)*, 2006.

[5] C. Blake and C. Merz, "UCI repository of machine learning databases", http://www.ics.uci.edu/~mlearn/MLRepository.html, 1998.

[6] Maria-Luiza Antonie, Osmar R. Zaiane, Alexandru Coman, Application of Data Mining Techniques for Medical Image Classification, in *Proc. of Second Intl. Workshop on Multimedia Data Mining (MDM/KDD'2001)* in conjunction with *Seventh ACM SIGKDD*, pp. 94-101, San Francisco, CA, August 26, 2001

[7] C. C. Chang, and C. –J. Lin, "LIBSVM: a library of support vector machines", http://www.csie.ntu.edu.tw/~cjlin/libsvm, 2001.

[8] H. Cheng, X. Yan, J. Han, C. –W. Hsu, "Discriminative frequent pattern analysis for effective classification", In *Proc. of ICDE*, 2007.

[9] Y. Yang, and J. O. Pedersen, "A comparative study on feature selection in text categorization", In *Proc. of ICML*, 1997.
[10] D. Koller, and M. Sahami, "Hierarchically classifying documents using very few words", In *Proc. of ICML*, 1997.

[11] S. Scott, and S. Matwin, "Feature engineering for text classification", In *Proc. of ICML*, 1999.

[12] Agrawal R, Srikant R. "Fast Algorithms for Mining Association Rules", VLDB. Sep 12-15 1994, Chile, 487-99.

[13] N. Pasquier, Y. Bastide, R. Taouil, L. Lakhal, "Discovering frequent closed itemsets for association rules", In *Proc. of ICDT*, 1999.

[14] Bing Liu, Wynne Hsu, Yiming Ma, "Integrating Classification and Association Rule Mining." *Proceedings of the Fourth International Conference on Knowledge Discovery and Data Mining (KDD-98)* New York, USA, 1998.

[15] W. Li, J. Han, J. Pei, "CMAR: Accurate and Efficient Classification Based on Multiple Class-Association Rules" , In *Proc. of IEEE-ICDM*, 2001.

[16] Flavian Vasile, Adrian Silvescu, Dae-Ki Kang, Vasant Honavar, "TRIPPER: Rule learning using taxonomies", In *Proc. of Tenth Pacific-Asia Conference on Knowledge Discovery and Data Mining (PAKDD'06)*, pp. 55-59, Singapore, April 9-12, 2006

[17] Jacob Goldberger, Shiri Gordon, and Hayit Greenspan, Unsupervised Image-Set Clustering Using an Information Theoretic Framewor, *IEEE Transactions on Image Processing*, pp 449-458, February, 2006

Foreign Superkeys and Constant References

Jon Heggland
Norwegian University of Science and Technology
Department of Computer and Information Science
jon.heggland@idi.ntnu.no

Abstract

A foreign superkey *in relational database theory is a set of attributes referring to a superkey of some relation variable. In this paper, the notion of* constant references *is introduced: foreign superkeys with constant elements, which lead to simplified constraint formulation and integrity enforcement when implementing entity subclassing in relational databases.*

Keywords: *Relational theory, integrity constraints, entity subclassing, foreign keys.*

1. Introduction

A common approach to database design is to describe the structure and constraints of the problem domain in a semantic, conceptual data model; and subsequently translate this into a logical, relational data model by means of some mapping technique. However, the mapping of the entity subclassing (or generalization) structure of the Extended Entity-Relationship (EER) model [19] to the relational model is not trivial. Existing literature on this ([14], [15], [12], [2]), including database textbooks (e.g. [8], [9], [6]) is rather cursory with regard to the constraints necessary to ensure the integrity of the corresponding relational design. Such constraints are needed in all but the most trivial cases, but are not very well supported by existing techniques and tools, as the following example shows.

Figure 1 shows a very simple EER-style data model, with arrows indicationg subclassing. The entity class (or set) S has three subclasses (or subsets): A, B and C. That A is a subclass of S means that each entity of class A is also an entity of class S, and has a superset of S's attributes and relationships.

There are many ways of transforming this conceptual model into a relational schema; [8] and [9] present five different approaches. We shall initially consider only the most straightforward, general and (by not requiring NULLs) uncontroversial technique: Create a relation variable (relvar

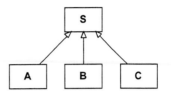

Figure 1. Example entity class hierarcy

[6]) S with the attributes of entity class S; denoting its key attribute by K.[1] For each subclass, create a relvar consisting of K in addition to the subclass-specific attributes. K is (a) key for these relvars as well, and also a foreign key from each subclass-relvar to S.

The key constraints and foreign key constraints make sure that each member of a subclass is also a member of the superclass; and that a member of S does not occur multiple times in a given subclass (speaking loosely). However, there are often other constraints that must be enforced. Let us consider the requirement that the subclasses must be disjoint, i.e. each entity is either a member of A, B or C, but just one of them. A straightforward implementation of this requires $n(n-1)/2$ constraints (given n subclasses, i.e. one constraint for each pair of them) of the form CREATE ASSERTION AB_DISJOINT CHECK NOT EXISTS (SELECT * FROM A NATURAL JOIN B) if using SQL[2] [16]. An alternative might be a single constraint of the form CREATE ASSERTION DISJOINT_SUBCLASSES CHECK (SELECT COUNT(*) FROM A) + (SELECT COUNT(*) FROM B) + (SELECT COUNT(*) FROM C) = (SELECT COUNT(*) FROM ((SELECT K FROM A) UNION (SELECT K FROM B) UNION (SELECT K FROM C))). These are not very good

---

[1]For notational simplicity, we assume that the key is not compound; i.e. it consists of the single attribute K. Also, we will often refer to K as a key, even though it really is the set {K} that is the key. This has no significant impact on the discussion; neither has the fact that a relvar may in general have more than one key.

[2]For reasons of familiarity, we use SQL for examples; noting that the non-relational aspects of SQL are not relevant for the subject at hand.

solutions, for several reasons:

- The constraints are numerous and/or long-winded and unintuitive.

- Constraints of this type (SQL ASSERTIONs, or—in more technology-neutral terms—*database constraints* as opposed to relvar, tuple, attribute or type constraints [6]) are not supported by any of the major SQL DBMSs [20].

- Such constraints are not trivial to implement efficiently. (This may be related to the previous point.) A naive implementation of the constraints above would evaluate them fully each time one of the involved relvars changed; it is not so simple to (say) infer from the COUNT-based constraint that the deletion of a tuple will never cause a violation. A different kind of constraint may offer better opportunities in this regard.

Our contribution is to simplify the specification and enforcement of constraints (primarily) related to entity subclassing, by proposing a straightforward extension to the way foreign keys work. Through the use of foreign superkeys and constant references, the integrity of subclass structures such as the one above can be ensured with both fewer and simpler constraints (conceptually, logically and implementation-wise) than would otherwise be possible.

The remainder of the paper is organised as follows: Section 2 presents foreign superkeys and introduces the notion of constant references, explaining how it greatly simplifies integrity maintenance in entity subclassing contexts. In sections 3, 4 and 5, we discuss the uses of constant references in various other situations, most related to entity subclassing. Section 6 presents related work, while we give our concluding remarks and suggestions for further work in section 7.

2. Foreign superkeys and constant references

2.1. Foreign superkeys

An *inclusion dependency* (IND) [3] is a constraint stating that a certain projection of a relvar S must be a subset of a certain projection of relvar T (with S and T not necessarily distinct). A *foreign key* (FK) is a special case of an IND, where the attributes projected over in the "target" relvar (T) constitutes an irreducible key.

A *superkey-based inclusion dependency* [13], or *foreign superkey*, is likewise an IND where the set of attributes projected over in T is a superset of a key for T. A foreign superkey will usually imply some redundancy in the "source" relvar, but can be useful nonetheless.

As an example of such usefulness, consider the relvar R(A,B,C), with the functional dependencies (FDs)

$\{A,B\} \rightarrow C$ and $\{C\} \rightarrow B$. This is the classic example of a relvar that is not in Boyce-Codd normal form (BCNF), but cannot be decomposed into independent parts [18], i.e. without losing the first FD. Thus we are left with either keeping the relvar as is, with the obvious anomalies that result from that, as well as the relatively complicated constraint necessary to enforce the FD $\{C\} \rightarrow B$; or, to decompose it into CB(C,B) and AC(A,C), and enforcing the first FD by a relatively complicated constraint involving the join of the two.

A third alternative is using a foreign superkey: We keep the relvar R(A,B,C), but introduce the relvar CB(B,C) as well, with a foreign "key" on the attributes B,C from R to CB. Note that C is the key of CB, so the FK is in fact a foreign superkey. This solution preserves both dependencies, and it removes the anomalies: tuples can be inserted into CB and deleted from R without problems. The cost is some redundancy—R is of course still not in BCNF—but the redundancy is controlled; there is no possiblity for inconsistence.

2.2. Entity subclassing and integrity

Now reconsider the example in figure 1. A helpful technique when creating relational schemas based on subclassing, is to include a *defining attribute* or *discriminator* [8] in the superclass—that is, an attribute that determines or records which subclass each entity belongs to. Such attributes may or may not have direct counterparts in the real world situation that is modelled by the database, but may be desirable regardless. For instance, a query to determine the subclass of a given entity need only consult the defining attribute in the superclass, instead of checking whether the entity occurs in each subclass-relvar. Some methodologies, e.g. [17], require such attributes whenever entity subclassing is used.

Let us consider such an attribute for our superclass relvar S: Call it T (for "Type"), and let its domain be the set { 'a', 'b', 'c' }, with the obvious interpretation. On the face of it, this seems only to complicate the integrity issue: The attribute is redundant, since the same information is also represented as the presence or absence of tuples in A, B and C, and we now have to ensure consistency between these two representations. However, this can be done with one constraint per subclass-relvar, of the form CREATE ASSERTION A_TYPE CHECK NOT EXISTS (SELECT * FROM A NATURAL JOIN S WHERE T <> 'a')—and this also takes care of the disjointness requirement, since each tuple in S necessarily has but one T value.

This reduces the number of constraints, but the other problems remain: Commercial SQL DMBSs do not support ASSERTIONs; and a naive implementation of such a constraint would be expensive if the entire join had to be performed each time either relvar changed. It is a difficult task for a mechanical optimiser to figure out when a cheaper algorithm can be used.

2.3. Constant references

This is where foreign superkeys come in. The attribute set { K, T } is a superkey of S, and might be referred to by a foreign superkey from (say) A. Now, A has no T attribute—but such an attribute would be redundant, because all the tuples in A would necessarily have the value 'a' for it. Therefore, we suggest a small extension to the notion of foreign (super)keys (FSKs): that some of the "source" attributes of an FSK may be specified as constant expressions instead of as actual attributes.[3] For definiteness, we suggest the following SQL-based syntax for such an FSK from A to S: FOREIGN KEY (K, 'a') REFERENCES S (K, T).[4] The precise meaning of this is that the projection A[K], extended with an attribute T with the value 'a', must be a subset of the projection S[K,T]—or in SQL terms: the table expression SELECT K, 'a' as T FROM A must be a subset of SELECT K, T FROM S. We refer to this special case of FSK as a "constant reference" (CR).

The advantages of such a construct in this context are obvious:

- A foreign key from subclass to superclass is required anyway. An FSK/CR like this implies both the conventional foreign key and the join-based constraint(s) discussed earlier; thus, only one constraint instead of two (or more) is needed.

- An FSK/CR will most likely be cheaper to implement and easier to optimise than general multi-relvar database constraints. Most DBMSs already support foreign (super)keys; adding support for CRs does not seem very difficult. The techniques for maintaining referential integrity presented in [4] and [10] are not materially affected by FSK/CRs: The main difference is that in addition to checking for the presence of the superclass relvar's key in the index one assumes is present, one must also check the value of the discriminating attribute—by reading the tuple pointed to by

the index entry, or possibly by including the discriminator in the index.

Note also that despite being a (proper) foreign superkey, the FSK/CR in this case does not entail any redundancy, since the constant T attribute associated with each subclass is not actually stored, neither at the logical nor physical level (except once as part of the constraint definition, of course).

3. Non-disjoint subclassing

Our original motivation for FSK/CRs was disjoint subclassing, but they are useful for overlapping subclassing (i.e. each entity may belong to more than one subclass) as well. In such cases, a single discriminating attribute in the superclass is not sufficient. Instead, we need a boolean attribute for each class, e.g. IS_A, IS_B and IS_C. The FSK/CRs would then be of this form (using subclass B as the example this time): FOREIGN KEY (K, true) REFERENCES S (K, IS_B).

With unconstrained overlapping among subclasses, constraints are obviously not all that important; the FSK/CRs suggested above merely make sure that the tuples in the subclass-relvars agree with the IS_ attributes in S. However, the technique shows its strength when the disjointness/overlapping characteristics are more complicated. Consider the case where an entity may be in *either* subclass A, *or* in subclass B or C or both. That is, B and C overlap with each other, but not with A. This rule can be enforced simply by stating a tuple constraint (i.e. not an ASSERTION) on relvar S; in this case CONSTRAINT S_TYPE CHECK IS_A XOR (IS_B OR IS_C). The FSK/CRs in the subclasses will take care of the rest.

4. Alternative subclassing mappings

As mentioned earlier, there are several other techniques for mapping subclass structures to relational schemas, and we will now consider some of them in connection with FSK/CRs.

One approach, presented in [8], is to create one relvar for each subclass with the subclass-specific attributes and *all* the attributes from the superclass, and not create any superclass relvar. This works well only when the subclassing is disjoint, and the superclass does not have any many-to-many or many-to-one relationships—since there would be no single relvar for the foreign keys associated with such relationships to refer to. We consider such cases degenerate, with very little reason to use the subclassing construct at all, and thus do not discuss this technique further.

[9] presents a technique called "the object-oriented approach". The idea is to create a relvar for each possible

---

[3]For orthogonality's sake, if nothing else, *all* of the components might be specified as such expressions; and not only constants but arbitrary tuple-based expressions (of which constants and plain attribute names are but two special cases) might be allowed. However, we do not consider the possible issues or uses of this further in this paper.

[4]"FOREIGN KEY" is a misnomer here, since it is in fact a foreign *super*key, but it seems an unnecessary burden on the user to require the use of different keywords for these two closely related concepts. A better solution might be to replace the term/keyword "foreign key" by something more generic, e.g. "reference", but we will stick with "foreign key" for now.

combination of classes, with all the attributes that appear in that combination. Each entity is then represented by a tuple in exactly one relvar. In addition to leading to a combinatorial explosion of relvars, this approach suffers from problems analogous to the previous technique with regard to superclasses with relationships, so we do not consider it viable in the general case.

A more common approach is to create just one single relvar for the class hierarchy, include all the attributes from all the classes in this relvar, and use NULLs for the non-applicable attributes for each entity. The use of FSK/CRs from subclass-relvars to superclass-relvar is obviously not applicable here, but is still useful for another purpose. Figure 2 shows a more elaborate version of our example model, where the subclass A has a one-to-many relationship with an entity class P. With our original mapping, where each (sub)class corresponds to a relvar, this would simply entail an ordinary foreign key from relvar P to relvar A. However, with the single-relvar subclassing approach, there is no relvar A, only a big relvar S(K,T,X,Y,Z) (assuming a discriminating attribute T). Thus, the foreign key from P needs to be constrained to refer to tuples that represent members of class A only, i.e. those where the discriminating attribute T has the value 'a'. A FOREIGN KEY (K, 'a') REFERENCES S (K, T) from relvar P takes care of this. Overlapping subclassing are handled analogously.

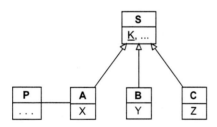

Figure 2. Example class hierarchy with attributes and (many-to-one) relationship, UML-like notation

5. Other uses

FKS/CRs also have another benefit with regard to the multiple-relvar subclassing approach. Consider the case where a subclass (say A) has no subclass-specific attributes, just subclass-specific many-to-many or one-to-many relationships. Without FSK/CRs, a relatively useless A relvar (with just the key attribute K) would still have to be created in order to act as "target" for the foreign keys corresponding to the A subclass' relationships. With FSK/CRs, this relvar can be omitted, simplifying the schema; instead can FSK/CRs refer directly to the superclass relvar while still

enforcing the constraint that they only refer to instances of subclass A.

FSK/CRs also have utility in situations not normally considered applications of subclassing. Figure 3 shows a model where an entity class E has a "status" attribute S. The relationships to entity classes P and Q are intended to be "conditional" in the sense that a relationship between P and E may only occur if E's status is 'x', and between Q and E only if S is 'y'. These constraints are handled gracefully by FSK/CRs; in the case of P by FOREIGN KEY (K, 'x') REFERENCES E (K, S). Note that this example corresponds to E having two subclasses with no subclass-specific attributes (except that the class of an entity is not supposed to change).

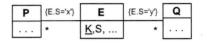

Figure 3. Conditional relationships

6. Related work

Techniques for mapping entity subclass structures to the relational model are presented in [14], [15], [12] and [2], but the integrity issues we have discussed here are not covered. The challenge of disjoint subclasses is mentioned in [1], but it is claimed that relational databases lack the capabilities to adequately deal with it.

The SQL standard [11] permits foreign superkeys, provided that the superkey is declared UNIQUE (or PRIMARY KEY). At the logical level, the declaration of uniqueness for a set of attributes is of course redundant when a subset has also been declared unique, but SQL still requires it.

Dataphor by Alphora[5] is a relational database not based on SQL. It supports foreign superkeys without circumlocution; a "reference" (as Alphora calls it) must refer to a superset (not necessarily proper) of a key of the target relvar.

Celko [5, chapter 10] presents a technique very similar to constant references to handle integrity in entity subclass schemas. However, his solution involves actually storing the constant discriminating attributes in the subclass relvars. This leads to obvious redundancy: If the subclass relvar A(K, T) is constrained to have the same value for T in all tuples, there is a functional dependency $\emptyset \rightarrow T$, and the relvar (having key K) is not in second normal form. However, the redundancy is controlled, and the technique has the advantage of being usable in current SQL systems.

Date and Darwen [7] advocate that it should be possible to enforce constraints on derived/virtual relvars (views). This would provide an alternative to constant references:

---

[5]http://www.alphora.com/

We could, given the subclass relvar `A(K)`, define a view `A_WITH_T(K,T)` as `SELECT A.*, 'a' AS T FROM A`, and thus use a "regular" foreign superkey from `A_WITH_T` to the superclass relvar `S`. This has the advantage of not requiring any extension to the way foreign (super)keys work. However, enforcing constraints on views efficiently is likely no trivial matter.

It should in any case be noted that the FSK/CR functionality suggested by this paper, is not *required* in order to enforce the relevant integrity constraints—as long as general database constraint facilities [6] are provided. To draw an analogy: A key constraint on the relvar `R(K,A1, ... ,AN)` can in SQL be expressed as `CONSTRAINT MANUAL_KEY_K CHECK NOT EXISTS (SELECT * FROM R AS R1, R AS R2 WHERE R1.K = R2.K AND (R1.A1 <> R2.A1 OR ... OR R1.AN <> R2.AN))`—but it is better, for the sake of both usability and performance/optimisability, to state it as `UNIQUE (K)`. Likewise, FSK/CRs can simplify both the expression and implementation of a certain class of useful integrity constraints.

7. Conclusion and further work

We have presented constant references, a straightforward extension to foreign (super)keys, as a lightweight alternative to heavy SQL `ASSERTION`-type constraints. In contrast with "regular" non-key based inclusion dependencies, FSK/CRs typically do not cause any redundancy in the database.

Our proposal is based on the assumption that FSK/CRs are easier to implement efficiently than equivalent join-based constraints. The implementation techniques described in [4] and [10] seem to confirm this assumption, but further study is needed. SQL's requirement that foreign keys refer to a set of columns that have been declared as `UNIQUE` or `PRIMARY KEY` might indicate that an index on the target columns is required for satisfactory performance of the constraint enforcement—and (proper) foreign superkeys thus less efficient in the absence of a complete index. Efficient implementation and optimisation of `ASSERTION`-type constraints should also be examined more closely.

References

[1] M. R. Blaha and W. J. Premerlani. Observed idiosyncracies of relational database designs. In *Proceedings of 2nd Working Conference on Reverse Engineering*, pages 116–125, 1995.

[2] M. R. Blaha, W. J. Premerlani, and J. E. Rumbaugh. Relational database design using an object-oriented methodology. *Commun. ACM*, 31(4):414–427, 1988.

[3] M. A. Casanova, R. Fagin, and C. H. Papadimitriou. Inclusion dependencies and their interaction with functional dependencies. In *Proceedings of the ACM Symposium on Principles of Database Systems, March 29-31, 1982, Los Angeles, California*, pages 171–176. ACM, 1982.

[4] M. A. Casanova, L. Tucherman, and A. L. Furtado. Enforcing inclusion dependencies and referential integrity. In F. Bancilhon and D. J. DeWitt, editors, *Fourteenth International Conference on Very Large Data Bases, August 29 - September 1, 1988, Los Angeles, California, USA, Proceedings*, pages 38–49. Morgan Kaufmann, 1988.

[5] J. Celko. *Joe Celko's Trees and Hierarchies in SQL for Smarties*. Morgan Kaufmann, 2004.

[6] C. J. Date. *An Introduction to Database Systems*. Addison-Wesley, eighth edition, 2004.

[7] C. J. Date and H. Darwen. *Databases, Types and the Relational Model—The Third Manifesto*. Addison-Wesley, third edition, 2006.

[8] R. Elmasri and S. B. Navathe. *Fundamentals of Database Systems*. Addison-Wesley, third edition, 2000.

[9] H. Garcia-Molina, J. D. Ullman, and J. Widom. *Database Systems—The Complete Book*. Prentice Hall, third edition, 2002.

[10] T. Härder and J. Reinert. Access path support for referential integrity in sql2. *VLDB J.*, 5(3):196–214, 1996.

[11] International Organization for Standardization. *ISO/IEC 9075-2:1999: Information technology — Database languages — SQL — Part 2: Foundation (SQL/Foundation)*. International Organization for Standardization, Geneva, Switzerland, 1999.

[12] D. C. Kung. Object subclass hierarchy in sql: A simple approach. *Commun. ACM*, 33(7):117–127, 1990.

[13] M. Levene and M. W. Vincent. Justification for inclusion dependency normal form. *IEEE Trans. Knowl. Data Eng.*, 12(2):281–291, 2000.

[14] V. M. Markowitz and A. Shoshani. On the correctness of representing extended entity-relationship structures in the relational model. In J. Clifford, B. G. Lindsay, and D. Maier, editors, *Proceedings of the 1989 ACM SIGMOD International Conference on Management of Data, Portland, Oregon, May 31 - June 2, 1989*, pages 430–439. ACM Press, 1989.

[15] V. M. Markowitz and A. Shoshani. Representing extended entity-relationship structures in relational databases: A modular approach. *ACM Trans. Database Syst.*, 17(3):423–464, 1992.

[16] J. Melton and A. R. Simon. *SQL:1999—Understanding Relational Language Components*. Morgan Kaufmann, 2002.

[17] G. M. Nijssen and T. A. Halpin. *Conceptual Schema and Relational Database Design*. Prentice Hall, 1989.

[18] J. Rissanen. Independent components of relations. *ACM Trans. Database Syst.*, 2(4):317–325, 1977.

[19] T. J. Teorey, D. Yang, and J. P. Fry. A logical design methodology for relational databases using the extended entity-relationship model. *ACM Comput. Surv.*, 18(2):197–222, 1986.

[20] C. Türker and M. Gertz. Semantic integrity support in sql: 1999 and commercial (object-)relational database management systems. *VLDB J.*, 10(4):241–269, 2001.

Implementing Physical Hyperlinks for Mobile Applications Using RFID Tags

Joachim Schwieren, Gottfried Vossen

ERCIS, Leonardo Campus 3, 48149 Muenster, Germany

E-mail {schwieren, vossen}@ercis.de

Abstract

Hyperlinks are a well understood and widely used concept in many applications. Particularly the Web has promoted the concept of "clickable" links to users. Typically, hyperlinks are only used to interact with applications and content in the "virtual" sphere of information systems. However, the basic idea of a hyperlink, which is creating an inviolable link between two resources, can be extended to the physical world as well and then allows a much closer and more intuitive interaction with information systems in many scenarios. We describe how RFID tags can be used to implement physical hyperlinks that establish a direct connection between a physical object and a mobile information system. Any kind of mobile, object-centered information system, such as the PDA-based visitor information system for museums MoVIS presented in this paper, provides a richer experience for users when it is extended into the physical world with physical hyperlinks.

1. Introduction

Hypertext and hypermedia in general have become probably the most widely used and accepted type of media for human interaction with information systems (IS) [1], [3], following a suggestion that has originally been made in [2]. The paradigm of clickable links is very common for users nowadays because it is so intuitive, simple, and effective. The largest hypertext application today is the Web: Content (mostly text) is organized in a loosely coupled, non-linear way that allows users much freedom when interacting with an IS. A major characteristic of hyperlinks is, however, that they are strictly limited to the "virtual" sphere of an IS. Physical resources usually cannot point to "virtual" resources in the information system such as text or images. In order to bridge the gap between the physical world, in which we exist, and the virtual world of IS, a lot of efforts have been made so far, such as the design of innovative and more ergonomic user interfaces. However, porting the simple and successful concept of hyperlinks directly into the physical world tends not to be easy, the reason being that a physical resource like an object or a location cannot directly be connected or interrelated to an IS without considerable effort; we try to remedy this situation in this paper.

The concept of physical hyperlinks has many beneficial applications: For example, a mobile visitor information system that makes use of physical hyperlinks can offer a new dimension of experience to visitors of museums, parks and other similar tourist sites. Visitors can easily access relevant information and services about exhibits simply by touching physical hyperlinks with a PDA guide system; such a system, under development in our group, will be presented later in this paper. Another application of physical hyperlinks allows consumers, while shopping in a supermarket, to get information about certain products. Simply by touching the product with his or her mobile phone or PDA, access to the related information is provided like detailed descriptions, price-comparisons or community generated content about experiences other consumers made with this product. Another example are scenarios where URLs or e-mail addresses are printed on business cards, advertisement flyers, billboards or in newspapers and magazines. In order to access them, the user has to manually enter the URL into the web browser of his computer. But touching parts of the printed text with a mobile device and directly accessing the resources and services that are referenced would be much more comfortable, intuitive and also more reliable since unnecessary, manual steps are avoided. In mobile healthcare or mobile maintenance, where a user needs to access content or services that are related to a physical object or location, physical hyperlinks offer a simple and easy to use functionality.

In this paper, we present an approach that systematizes the relevant aspects that have to be taken into account when leveraging the hyperlink concept from the virtual to the physical world; this extension is achieved via a proper incorporation of RFID (*Radio*

Frequency Identification) tags. Clearly, also other implementations are possible, including infra-red beacons, (2D-) barcodes or (often imprecise) location-sensing techniques [8], [10]. Since these alternatives all require tremendously complex technical installations to work properly, RFID tags tend to be the optimal way for implementing physical hyperlinks; indeed, they are cheap, maintenance-free, and available in almost any form factor and size (even ultra-small to be integrated into normal paper[1]). To navigate a physical hyperlink, some kind of mobile computing device like a smart phone, a PDA or an UMPC (Ultra Mobile PC) with an integrated RFID reader is required. Yet not only the "hardware perspective" is relevant for implementing physical hyperlinks; from a database or IS perspective questions such as where and how the URL is stored that is referenced by the physical hyperlink and what influence the availability of network access of the mobile device has on the whole concept as well as aspects such the incorporation of user-context.

The paper is organized as follows: An overview of existing research on physical hyperlinks is given in Section 2. The basic aspects of RFID technology are briefly explained in Section 3. Then a new scalable and flexible concept for physical hyperlinks is introduced in Section 4. Section 5 gives an example that shows how physical hyperlinks can enrich the functionality and the experience for the user of a mobile PDA-based visitor information system for museums. Finally, Section 6 concludes the paper.

2. Related Work

Up to now there have been several approaches to find ways for implementing or designing physical hyperlinks, mostly focusing on specific aspects such as a close integration into the existing WWW infrastructure or the consideration of user context when navigating a hyperlink. Also, different experimental approaches[2] using 2D-barcodes as physical hyperlinks that are photographed with the build-in camera of a mobile phone and then decoded by special image recognition software have been made, and the use of RFID tags has already been proposed [9].

One of the first approaches to physical hyperlinks has been made in the context of HP's *Cooltown Project* [9]. There the main focus was put on identifier resolution in order to map the IDs of physical objects to simple Web URLs. Since Cooltown has been

discontinued, this approach has not been developed any further. Another approach has been made by the NFC Forum[3], a non-profit industry association that promotes the use of NFC (*Near Field Communication*) short-range wireless interaction in consumer electronics, mobile devices, and PCs. Companies like Nokia, HP, Microsoft, Sony and others have founded this organization to overcome one of the most problematic aspects of mobile, user-centered RFID applications: missing or highly heterogeneous standards and limited applications of RFID technology in certain domains. The NFC specification does not only define technical standards for the air interface and the tags, but also application-specific standards for different usage scenarios of NFC such as micro-payment, wireless communication, wireless synchronization, and also Web links. The basic idea of the latter is to encode the URL of a Web link as space saving as possible into the data block of an RFID tag. Since a lot of RFID tags only contain identification code and no additional data block for user-defined raw data, this limits the use of possible tag types for NFC applications. Currently the NFC standard is being defined and ratified, therefore only prototypical applications exist so far. Nokia has presented a device called *NFC shell*[4] which is attached to a mobile phone in order to add NFC capabilities. Additionally, the first mobile phone by Nokia with build-in NFC support has been announced lately[5].

Another approach that makes use of RFID tags is presented in [15], where it is proposed to request pervasive services by touching RFID tags. Thus, RFID tags are regarded as some kind of "button" that can be "pressed" by reading the tag with a mobile RFID reader in order to invoke a service that is associated with the tag (e.g., launch a specific application on the mobile device). The authors suggest storing the information about the service to be invoked in the tag using the NFC data block format. This has the advantage that new tags do not have to be registered globally in the system in advance. On the other hand, this approach is also limited by the relatively small data storage capacity of today's tags. Choosing tags with more data storage capacity also rapidly increases the costs of such an application.

Another aspect that has been considered is the fact that many applications that use physical hyperlinks require to adapt to the user and his current context. Kindberg [9] proposes that location, static personal user preferences, and the choice of application should

---

[1] Hitachi's μ-chip is only 0.4mm2 in size, see http://www.hitachi-eu.com/mu/products/mu_chip.htm.
[2] Semapedia.org, Physical Hyperlinks to Wikipedia articles with 2D barcodes, see http://www.semapedia.org/

[3] Near Field Communication (NFC) Forum, see http://www.nfc-forum.org/
[4] http://www.nokia.com/A4136002?newsid=966879
[5] http://www.nokia.com/A4136001?newsid=1096858

have an influence on the resolution process of a hyperlink. How this could be accomplished and what needs to be considered for this functionality is not explained by the author.

Millard et al. [12] apply existing hypertext models such as OHP/FOHM [11] to physical hyperlinks and study the differences between hypermedia systems that only exist in a computer and those that can occur in mixed reality. They also regard physical hyperlinks that point from within an information system to an external, physical object or location. A similar approach is made by Romero et al. [16] who present *HyperReal*, a hypermedia model for mixed reality that tries to integrate "classical" hypermedia with physical interactions. Another hypermedia framework is *HyCon* [6] which also has a strong focus on physical hypermedia. It is a framework for context-aware hypermedia systems and offers features such as geo-based browsing, geo-based search, location-based link trails, and location-based annotations. The term *"Physical Hypermedia"* is also used in [5]. Rukzio at al. [17] regard physical hyperlinks as a possible from of mobile interactions with the physical world and therefore integrate this into their more general framework.

Since physical hyperlinks need to be navigated actively by a user (in contrast to location based services [18], [13] that usually announce themselves to the user), the first step always is to discover a tag visually in the physical world. To this end, Välhhynen et al. make suggestions for visualizing physical hyperlinks [19]. They also follow the idea that different tags are used to invoke different services, and they propose specific pictograms that are printed on tags in order to give the user an idea of the service or functionality that can be invoked by reading the tags. This often leads to the situation that multiple tags need to be attached to the same object or location in order to provide different services. We will return to this issue in the next section.

3. RFID Basics

RFID is a technology that has recently become popular due to the fact that its components (mainly tags) have become so cheap that large-scale, economic production and usage are possible today. An RFID system consists of three basic components as shown in Fig. 1: *RFID transponders* (usually referred to as tags), *RFID readers/writers* for accessing the tags over the air interface, and an information system that handles the tag data in the desired way. Often an additional layer between reader and information system is implemented which is referred to as *RFID middleware*.

This middleware (although the term does not quite fit here) abstracts from the hardware interface of the reader and handles typical problems of RFID applications such as duplicate or erratic reads and reduces complexity for the linked-up information system. In simple (e.g., mobile) applications the "middleware" is often no more than a driver API (application programming interface) provided by the manufacturer of the reader hardware.

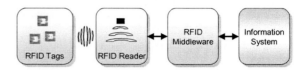

Fig. 1. Basic components of an RFID system.

Tags are small microchips comprising (a small amount of) data storage (e.g., a few bytes; read-only as well as rewritable versions exist) and a build-in antenna. Most tags do not have a power-source (e.g., a battery) and are therefore referred to as *passive tags*. *Active tags*, in contrast, include a build-in battery which increases the communication range. All RFID tags contain at least an identification code. The memory of a tag can be used to store raw user-defined data directly on the tag. There is no general standard for RFID transponders and readers. Especially the frequency bands that are used vary between America, Europe, and Asia due to different regulatory terms for radio applications. The intended type of application has an important influence on the choice of the proper frequency band. [7] has proposed an RFID taxonomy that surveys all relevant aspects and parameters (including frequency band) of an RFID system.

The GEN-2 standard represents a first attempt towards a global standardization and has been made by EPCglobal[6], an non-profit organization that was set up to achieve a world-wide adoption and standardization of Electronic Product Code (EPC) technology. EPC can be regarded as the advancement of UPC (the Universal Product Code) for usage with RFID technology. A major focus of EPCglobal is to develop a world-wide standard for RFID and sharing data about RFID-tagged trading goods via the EPCglobal Network. Other popular standards [4] include ISOCARD, CLAMSHELL, FeliCa, Mifare and I-Code. Some of them have also become ISO standards.

Most RFID systems are currently used in logistics and supply chains, where a contact-less identification of objects or containers offers a new level of automation and efficiency. In these scenarios the

---

[6] EPCglobal : http://www.epcglobalinc.org

identification of objects is the main focus, and since many RFID applications deal with moving objects around, tracking and tracing is one of their main functionalities. However, RFID technology is not limited to these applications. Indeed, by leveraging RFID technology beyond supply chains and towards applications that are more consumer oriented, it can also be applied in a number of innovative scenarios such as ubiquitous computing applications. For example, clothes can be made interacting with a laundry cleaner in order to prevent improper handling. Location sensing of people or equipment with RFID tags in a building can be used to support many applications. Another major use case for RFID technology is the implementation of physical hyperlinks, which will be discussed in the next section.

4. Physical Hyperlinks

In order to provide a general framework for physical hyperlinks, a concise definition of what physical hyperlinks are and what the exact differences between physical hyperlinks and ordinary ones are is needed. To this end, a comparison with traditional hyperlinks is helpful.

Hyperlinks are a fundamental concept of hypermedia applications, as they support an *associative* style of reading a document as opposed to a strictly sequential one; they originally go back to [2]. Parts of a given text (e.g., words) or images, usually referred to as "anchor", are the visible occurrence of a hyperlink that can be invoked by a user (e.g., by clicking on it with a mouse). This causes an immediate navigation to the referenced resource (referred to as "target resource"). Since also parameters can be included when navigating a hyperlink, dynamic services and applications can be invoked in that way. This is how most Web applications work today. So the basic components of a hyperlink are the *link base* that contains the *anchor* which visually represents the hyperlink within the link base and finally the *reference* that points to the *target resource*; this is illustrated in Fig. 2.

Fig. 2. Basic concept of a (traditional) hyperlink.

A characteristic aspect of hyperlinks is the fact that any resource referenced is identified by a unique identifier. Furthermore, in order to navigate to the referenced resource, information about the location of this resource is required which is either encoded in the unique identifier itself or available in a separately supplied resolution table. In the case of the Web with its underlying HTTP (protocol), the content is both identified and referenced by URLs (Universal Resource Locator)[7]. The URL is resolved by the DNS (Domain Name System) into a global IP address of the machine holding the target resource. Additionally, a local part in the URL specifies the exact position and the local name of the resource inside the (file) system of the referenced machine.

We turn to physical hyperlinks next. Any physical object or even a location such as a place or room inside a building can be regarded as "link base" for a physical hyperlink. An RFID tag that is attached to or near the object or location in question acts as "anchor". This of course requires the tag to be visible to a user. The presence of a physical hyperlink can be indicated by printing a special pictogram on the RFID tag. In contrast to [19], we propose to use a single pictogram as shown in Fig. 3 that only indicates the presence of a physical hyperlink. All other information about the referenced resources or the services provided by this link can be displayed and selected on the user's mobile computing device. This gives more flexibility when focusing on context aware functionality and helps to keep the physical user interface (mobile computing device with RFID reader + RFID tag) simple.

Fig. 3. Pictogram indicating the presence of an RFID tag acting as physical hyperlink.

In the tag a reference to the target resource(s) needs to be encoded. Basically there are two different ways how this can be done. If the tag has an internal memory, the URL of the referenced resource can be stored in the tag itself. The disadvantages of this include that tags with integrated memory are quite expensive and that memory space is very limited (often only a few bytes). Furthermore, a standard needs to be defined how a URL is encoded in a tag's memory. Storing a URL in a tag's memory complies with the concept that is used by the NFC application "Web link". In order to save space when encoding the URL into the tag, the NFC standard defines a special, space-saving notation for URLs: Substrings that appear in

---

[7] http://www.ietf.org/rfc/rfc3986.txt

almost any URL (like *"http://"* or *"www"*) are encoded with shortcuts that have only the size of a few bits. Moreover, memory on the tag is partitioned into "data blocks". Thus, a tag can even store multiple Web links, as long as enough memory is available. The advantage is that no resolution process is needed to retrieve the target's URL and that the tag does not need to be registered before using it. All information needed for the hyperlink application is stored on the tag.

A more flexible way of assigning reference(s) to a physical hyperlink is to map the unique identifier of the tag to URL(s). This requires the tag identifiers to be truly unique identifiers (at least in a global scenario), and the mobile device that is used to navigate the physical hyperlink needs access to a resolution service that performs the identifier-to-URL-mapping. Most tag types (especially the cheap ones) come with a factory-defined, read-only identifier that can be regarded as globally unique. By using the native hexadecimal representation of this identifier together with an application-specific namespace prefix, a URN (uniform resource name)[8] can be generated. If the tag identifier is, for example, "FF03D5BF", the URN could be "urn:phid:ff03d5bf," where "phid" refers to the "physical hyperlink identifier" namespace identifier. The URN can then be translated into a URL by a resolution service for the "phid" namespace.

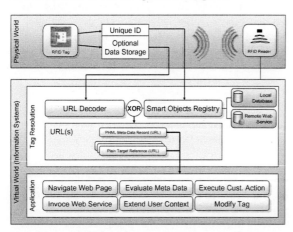

Fig. 4. Architecture for resolving physical hyperlinks.

Fig. 4 shows an architecture for handling both physical hyperlinks that store the referenced URLs in the tag memory (like NFC) or that require an additional resolution service for resolving referenced URLs. If URLs are stored in the tag memory, they are simply extracted by the reader and decoded. If only a tag identifier can be read, this tag identifier is transformed

into an application specific URN (in this case for the physical hyperlink application). This URN is then resolved by a *Smart Objects Registry* which can be either a remotely available web service or a locally available database (in case of closed scenarios like the museum application presented in Section 5). The *Smart Objects Registry* returns the URLs that are associated with the URN of the tag that has been read. After that, the application can handle the URL returned in the desired way (e.g., by accessing Web pages in a simple scenario).

In many scenarios, it is helpful to not only get a set of URLs but also meta-data about the physical object and the referenced resources. So instead of returning a set of plain URLs that need to be handled by the application, the Registry may also return a single URL only that refers to an XML file containing meta-data about the object to which the physical hyperlink is attached to, as well as a semantically enriched list of the referenced target resources of the hyperlink. We propose the simple, yet (due to extensibility) powerful language *PHML (Physical Hyperlink Markup Language)* to this end. PHML is used to wrap meta-data about an object and its referenced resources. This is helpful because in the physical context an adaptation to the specific context of the user is necessary. Also, in the case that a physical hyperlink references multiple resources, the mobile application needs to know more in order to present a proper interface to the user or to invoke the navigation of the appropriate target resources autonomously depending on the current context of the user. Fig. 5 shows an example of how a PHML file may look.

The basic concept of PHML, which can be regarded as *"meta-meta language"*, is to bind meta-data to the object itself and to the referenced resources. The meta-data can be provided in many different ways. The example of Fig. 5 shows meta-data that conforms to the Dublin Core standard which is also used to annotate Web pages and the Geotag[9] micro format to include geographic meta-data. Geographic meta-data cannot always be specified because objects to which physical hyperlinks are attached might be movable and frequent updates of geographic metadata are in most cases not realistic or even possible. Currently, PHML is still under development. A similar approach in a different context is followed with *PML (Physical Markup Language)* proposed by the EPC standard. However, since EPC is limited to very specific tag and reader types (UHF) and the entire EPC infrastructure is more focused on supply chain management and B2B communication, an application in a more end-user-

[8] http://tools.ietf.org/html/rfc2141

[9] http://geotags.com/

oriented ubiquitous computing scenario does not derive much value from PML. Especially the tight and limited annotation with meta-data which is often context-specific in ubiquitous computing scenarios limits the application of PML in this field.

```xml
<?xml version="1.0" encoding="utf-8" ?>
<phml:PhysicalHyperlink
xmlns:phml="http://dbms.uni-
muenster.de/phml/0.1/PhyscialHyperlink.xsd"
xmlns:xsi="http://www.w3.org/2001/XMLSchema-
instance"
xmlns:dc="http://purl.org/dc/elements/1.1/"
xmlns:dcterms="http://purl.org/dc/terms/">

  <phml:id>urn:phid:ff03d5bf</phml:id>

  <phml:metadata xsi:type="phml:dc">
    <dc:title>Office of Database Group at the
ERCIS Institute"</dc:title>
  </phml:metadata>

  <phml:metadata xsi:type="phml:geotag">
    <phml:meta name="geo.position"
content="51.976514;7.601155" />
    <phml:meta name="geo.placename"
content="ERCIS Institute, Münster, Germany" />
    <phml:meta name="geo.region" content="de-
nw" />
  </phml:metadata>

  <phml:reference xsi:type="phml:weblink">
    <phml:target
xsi:type="phml:url">http://dbms.uni-
muenster.de</phml:target>
      <phml:metadata xsi:type="phml:dc">
        <dc:format
xsi:type="dcterms:IMT">text/html</dc:format>
        <dc:type
xsi:type="dcterms:DCMIType">Text</dc:type>
      </phml:metadata>
  </phml:reference>

  <phtml:reference xsi:type="phml:weblink">
      <phml:target
xsi:type="phml:email">vossen@uni-
muenster.de</phml:target>
  </phtml:reference>

</phml:PhysicalHyperlink>
```

Fig. 5. Sample PHML file describing a physical hyperlink.

As already stated, physical hyperlinks can be navigated by using a mobile computing device with an integrated RFID reader. The interaction paradigm of touching the tag with the device in order to activate the hyperlink emulates the traditional hyperlink invocation mechanism of clicking. Depending on the implementation of the mobile application and the capabilities of the integrated RFID reader, the tag is read automatically if it comes within reading range. If no polling mode for the reader is supported (i.e., if the reader autonomously scans for all tags within range),

the software will have to provide some kind of "navigate link" button that activates the reader to scan for a nearby tag.

Finally, network connectivity is an important issue for mobile IS. In order to work properly, mobile IS that use physical hyperlinks need permanent network access to perform identifier resolution tasks or to access referenced resources and meta-data. If the mobile IS does not have network access when navigating a physical hyperlink, it can only "bookmark" the tag identifier or the encoded URL in order to invoke it later (this also shows that there is no direct advantage in storing the URL in the tag). The only exception for this are closed scenarios where all tags that can be accessed are known in advance by the application and the referenced resources are also locally available on the mobile device. This is the case in the mobile visitor information system that is described as a sample application for physical hyperlinks in the next section.

5. An Application for Physical Hyperlinks

A typical example for an application where physical hyperlinks are very useful is a mobile PDA-based visitor information system for museums, parks, or other tourist sites, as will be described in this section. A museum visitor wants to get information about exhibits while exploring a museum, or wants to do a guided tour in the museum. A PDA is a good choice for enabling both tasks, since content can be dynamically adapted to a user's needs (e.g., concerning the level of detail or the background of the user), and also rich multimedia content such as photos, videos, animations, or audio tracks can be included. These are features that traditional, printed guide books cannot offer. An overview of existing PDA-based applications for museums has been arranged by Raptis et al. [14]. Most applications use infra-red beacons to interact with the physical world, which leads to higher costs for the solution and requires intensive maintenance. Other approaches that use Bluetooth technology face the same problem.

Apart from the advantages that PDAs can generally offer for this kind of application, there are also some limitations: Due to the small screen and the limited input methods, a user has to spend a lot of time on browsing catalog or directory structures in order to find the desired content, which is not very convenient and even unsuited for inexperienced users. As a result, one of the most important aspects of a PDA-based guide system is that it must be very easy and intuitive to use in order to provide a pleasant experience, even if the application itself is quite complex and offers a lot of functionality. This also explains why many attempts towards PDA-based guide systems did not meet their expectations [14] or simply are nothing more than expensive audio guide systems offering only little extra functionality.

In order to have users make most of their time during a museum visit, some existing guide systems require the user to enter numbers that are associated with exhibits. While this speeds up content lookup, it also makes the user interface more complex since the user has to call up a screen with the number pad on it before the desired information can be accessed. It is not acceptable to waste space on a small screen for an additional soft-button that activates a number pad. Reassigning hardware keys for this purpose is also not a good idea, since this requires additional explanation to the user.

Physical hyperlinks implemented with RFID tags can help to solve these problems in a pragmatic way. By attaching RFID tags to the exhibits and by equipping PDAs with RFID readers, it is possible to make use of physical hyperlinks as proposed above. However, in order to provide advanced features such as guided tours or content adaptation to the user's needs and context, it is not sufficient to just use physical hyperlinks for linking to static content in the respective IS. The system must be capable of adapting the content to a users' needs and must be able to intuitively guide a user through the museum.

Another major aspect that influences the design of an application that uses physical hyperlinks is connectivity. An easy solution would be an always-on WiFi connection. Most of today's PDA guide systems [14] rely on that. Often, the PDA is actually nothing more than a mobile Web browser that serves as thin client, while the actual application is running on a remote Web server. However, this requires a full coverage of the museum with a wireless network. Since many museums are housed in either old buildings with massive walls or in very modern buildings constructed with lots of steal in the buildings structure, a complete wireless coverage is a challenging task and therefore hardly realized. Moreover, wiring multiple access points is also a matter of cost. Since many museums face a rather difficult financial situation, a mobile visitor information system must be designed with economical aspects in mind.

MoVIS (Mobile Visitor Information System), currently under development at the University of Münster in cooperation with the *Geologic-Paleontologic Museum of Münster* and *Elatec GmbH*, a German RFID- and electronics company, is based on a multi-channel client-server architecture as shown in Fig. 6. The mobile units (PDAs) are equipped with an integrated Compact Flash (CF) 125 kHz RFID reader that runs in a power-saving polling mode, in order to detect RFID tags within a range of 5-10 cm without requiring the user to press an extra button on the device when accessing a physical hyperlink. On the mobile unit an instance of *Microsoft SQL Server Compact Edition*, a light-weight database system stores all data about tags, exhibits, tours, and the museum environment. Tracking data, implicitly generated by a user while interacting with the system, is also stored in this local database. Because all data is stored on the device itself, there is no need for a permanent network connection to the backend system. This makes the system more reliable and easier to maintain. Only when updating data on the device or when writing tracking data into the database of the backend system, a network connection needs to be established. This can either be done by accessing any WiFi hotspot or by connecting the PDA to an ordinary PC with Internet access.

The backend system runs on a central server that does not have to be exclusively setup for a specific museum. Since the backend system can manage multiple clients (= museums) at the same time, this service is hosted by a central provider. Again this allows the museum to save unnecessary costs for maintenance and the operation of the server. The backend system basically consists of a *Microsoft SQL Server Express* database system and an *IIS Web Server* instance that provisions an *SQL Server Compact Edition Server Agent*. This agent is the interface that is accessed by mobile clients. Communication is done using *RDA (Remote Data Access)*, a data access and replication mechanism for distributed systems[10]. Since RDA is a very light-weighted protocol that can easily be implemented and works over an ordinary HTTP(S) connection, it is well-suited for this kind of application where multiple remote clients need to synchronize partitioned data with a central database server from time to time. RDA synchronizes data on a per-table-basis between the backend database and the local database of the mobile clients and offers two basic concepts for this task: "RDA Pull" transfers a specific table containing data from the backend database to the mobile client. While acting as an autonomous device, all changes that are applied to the local database instance are tracked by the database management system. After connection to the backend server is reestablished, "RDA push" is used to propagate the changes that have been recorded since the last "RDA pull" back to the backend database.

---

[10] http://msdn2.microsoft.com/en-us/library/ms172917.aspx

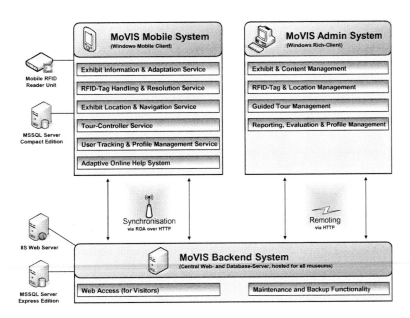

Fig. 6. Basic architecture and functional decomposition of MoVIS.

Additionally, MoVIS offers the museum operator a fully-fletched GUI application that can be run on any computer with Internet access to administer content and exhibits. The MoVIS Admin System uses *.NET Remoting[11]*, a Web-Service-based middleware to communicate with the backend server. A mobile client can also be put into a special administration mode that allows the museum operator to easily register new tags to the system's database. Since all tags are known to the system in advance, new tags need to be registered before they can be used. Only the unique ID of each tag is registered in the database and then associated with the matching content that is supposed to be displayed when accessing the physical hyperlink. Every content object is annotated with meta-data in the administration application, in order to display and adapt the content to the specific needs and context of the visitor. Before starting the visit a short survey is presented to the user to generate an initial user profile. This profile is then refined during the visit by the user's interaction with the system. User profiles and tracking data are also used for evaluation and reporting purposes in the backend system, as well as for a special Web-based service: Back at home, a visitor can review his visit on a personalized Web site of the museum. Optionally, the tour taken by the visitor with all exhibits is also available as an RSS feed.

The system basically offers two modes of operation: In *Explorative Mode*, a user can request information about exhibits randomly. The *Tour Mode* guides a user through the museum after having chosen a specific tour to take. In tour mode the invocation of physical hyperlinks is used to verify that the user is standing in front of the proper exhibit. A simple navigation component of the system helps the user to find the various locations of the exhibits in the museum. While MoVIS is currently being developed as a system that requires PDAs with special hardware (i.e., an integrated RFID reader), the server-centered architecture also allows an integration of other client devices such as private mobile phones that come with an integrated NFC reader.

MoVIS is an application that shows how physical hyperlinks can be used to enhance a user experience in a museum (or a related scenario) when using a PDA-based guide system. Since high reliability of the system is required in order to provide a pleasant experience for users, the system implements physical hyperlinks in a scenario where no constant network access is available, but the content of the system can still be updated dynamically by the museum operator, using an efficient data replication mechanism.

6. Summary and Conclusion

Physical hyperlinks as presented in this paper can simplify and enrich the interaction of human users with mobile IS in many scenarios where object-centered and context-specific information is required directly at the physical location of an object. If an easy and simple

---

[11] http://msdn2.microsoft.com/en-us/library/ms973857.aspx

interaction paradigm is required, physical hyperlinks turn out to be a valuable solution. Apart from using complex location sensing techniques, physical hyperlinks can also be implemented easily by using passive RFID tags. This is an economic approach since passive RFID tags are cheap and completely maintenance-free. However, many aspects need to be considered in a mobile scenario where RFID tags are used to implement physical hyperlinks, such as the availability of network access, the type of tags used, or the way references on the tag are resolved into target URLs. Therefore, we have proposed a general framework that provides an orientation when designing an application that is supposed to make use of physical hyperlinks.

We have presented MoVIS, a PDA-based visitor information system that uses physical hyperlinks in a scenario where a highly intuitive handling is required. In order to provide a reliable system, permanent network access is not required. Because the application is running in a closed scenario, this leads to a solution where a tag ID is resolved locally on the device into a URL to a locally available resource. The data both for the resources and the resolution service is maintained in a central database that is replicated to the mobile device.

The next step will be an implementation of MoVIS that will allow getting detailed insights on how users react on a truly mixed-mode reality application that extends the virtual sphere of a classical PDA-based information system into the physical world. Furthermore, we will soon release a first draft of the PHML specification. PHML adds the necessary flexibility that is required to support the specific demands on meta-data of mobile and ubiquitous computing applications when dealing with physical hyperlinks in a user-centered way to provide contextual adaptation and a rich and intuitive user experience.

References

[1] Bieber, M. (2000), "Hypertext", *Encyclopedia of Computer Science* (4th Edition), Ralston, A., Edwin Reilly and David Hemmendinger (eds.), Nature Publishing Group, 2000, 799-805.

[2] Bush, V. (1945), As We May Think, *The Atlantic Monthly*, July issue (176).

[3] Chen, C., and Rada, R. (1996), Interacting with Hypertext: A Meta-Analysis of Experimental Studies, *Human-Computer Interaction*, 1996, v. 11, 125-156.

[4] Finkenzeller, K. (2003), *RFID Handbook*: Fundamentals and Applications in Contactless Smart Cards and Identification, John Wiley & Sons, Inc., New York, USA.

[5] Grønbæk, K.; Kristensen, J.F., Ørbæk, P. & Eriksen, M.A. (2003), "Physical hypermedia": organising collections of mixed physical and digital material, in *'HYPERTEXT '03: Proc. 14th ACM Conf. on Hypertext and Hypermedia'*, ACM Press, New York, 10-19.

[6] Hansen, F.A.; Bouvin, N.O.; Christensen, B.G.; Grønbæk, K.; Pedersen, T.B. & Gagach, J. (2004), Integrating the web and the world: contextual trails on the move, in *'HYPERTEXT '04: Proc. 15th ACM Conf. on Hypertext and Hypermedia'*, ACM Press, New York, NY, USA, 98-107.

[7] Hassan, T. & Chatterjee, S. (2006), A Taxonomy for RFID, in *'HICSS '06: Proc. 39th Annual Hawaii Int. Conf. on System Sciences'*, IEEE Computer Society, Washington, DC, USA, 184.2.

[8] Hightower, J. & Borriello, G. (2001), Location Systems for Ubiquitous Computing, *IEEE Computer 34(8)*, 57-66.

[9] Kindberg, T. (2002), Implementing physical hyperlinks using ubiquitous identifier resolution, in *'WWW '02: Proc. 11th Int. Conf. on World Wide Web'*, ACM Press, New York, NY, USA, 191-199.

[10] Ladd, A. M., Bekris, K. E., Rudys, A. P., Wallach, D. S. and Kavraki, L. E. (2004), On the Feasibility of Using Wireless Ethernet for Indoor Localization, *IEEE Trans. Robotics And Automation*, 20(3), 555-559.

[11] Millard, D.E.; Moreau, L.; Davis, H.C. & Reich, S. (2000), FOHM: a fundamental open hypertext model for investigating interoperability between hypertext domains, in *'HYPERTEXT '00: Proceedings of the eleventh ACM on Hypertext and hypermedia'*, ACM Press, New York, NY, USA, pp. 93-102.

[12] Millard, D.E.; Roure, D.C.D.; Michaelides, D.T.; Thompson, M.K. & Weal, M.J. (2004), Navigational hypertext models For physical hypermedia environments, in *'HYPERTEXT '04: Proc. 15th ACM Conf. on Hypertext and Hypermedia'*, ACM Press, New York, NY, USA, 110-111.

[13] Munson, J.P. & Gupta, V.K. (2002), Location-based notification as a general-purpose service, in *'WMC '02: Proc. 2nd Int. Workshop on Mobile Commerce'*, ACM Press, New York, 40-44.

[14] Raptis, D.; Tselios, N. & Avouris, N. (2005), Context-based design of mobile applications for museums: a survey of existing practices, in *'MobileHCI '05: Proc. 7th Int. Conf. on Human Computer Interaction with Mobile Devices & Services'*, ACM Press, New York, NY, USA, 153-160.

[15] Riekki, J.; Salminen, T. & Alakarppa, I. (2006), Requesting Pervasive Services by Touching RFID Tags, *IEEE Pervasive Computing 5(1)*, 40.

[16] Romero, L. & Correia, N. (2003), HyperReal: a hypermedia model for mixed reality, in *'HYPERTEXT '03: Proc. 14th ACM Conf. on Hypertext and Hypermedia'*, ACM Press, New York, USA, 2-9.

[17] Rukzio, E.; Wetzstein, S. & Schmidt, A. (2005), A Framework for Mobile Interactions with the Physical World, in *'Wireless Personal Multimedia Communication (WPMC'05)'*.

[18] Spiekermann, S. (2004), General Aspects of Location Based Services, *'Location-Based Services'*, 9-26.

[19] Välkkynen, P.; Tuomisto, T. & Korhonen, I. (2006), Suggestions for Visualizing Physical Hyperlinks, in *'PERMID 2006: Pervasive Mobile Interaction Devices - Mobile Devices as Pervasive User Interfaces and Interaction Devices-'*

Integration of Patent and Company Databases*

Matteo Magnani
Dept. of Computer Science,
University of Bologna
Via Mura A.Zamboni, 7
40127 Bologna, Italy
matteo.magnani@cs.unibo.it

Danilo Montesi
Dept. of Computer Science,
University of Bologna
Via Mura A.Zamboni, 7
40127 Bologna, Italy
danilo.montesi@unibo.it

Abstract

In this paper we describe an activity of information integration performed on databases with patent data and company indicators. In particular, we present a detailed case study on company name matching. We show how to choose and tune existing methods to work on the domain object of this paper, and describe an efficient implementation to process large volumes of data. The integration activity involves the application of approximate string matching techniques. Then, we show the experimental results obtained on real data sets, highlighting the pros and cons of approximate string matching in this specific domain, and analyze the impact of domain knowledge on the results of the matching activity.

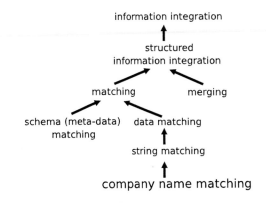

Figure 1. Relationships between company name matching and other aspects of information integration

1. Introduction

This paper is a case study in the area of information integration. In particular, we describe a **company name matching** activity. Information integration consists of two phases [13, 10, 12]: matching, i.e., finding relationships (mappings) between the elements of the data sources [17, 15, 5, 11, 9], and merging, where the aforementioned relationships are used to build a unified view of the data sources. The more studied kind of **matching** regards structured data sources, e.g., relational databases, which can be separated into two parts: schemata (meta data) and instances (data). In the former case, we usually speak of schema matching, in the latter of instance matching, data matching or record/tuple matching. Differently

from schema matching, tuple matching is characterized by a higher cardinality and by the need of specific data manipulation and comparison techniques, depending on the kind of data we want to match. A sub-problem of tuple matching is field matching, the most typical case being **string matching**. Depending on the data represented by the strings, the approaches to compare them may vary, because of different features of the data and different domain knowledge to include into the matching algorithms. The two best known examples of string matching are biological string matching, which is a basic activity in bioinformatics, and personal name matching, which is widely used in managing company databases and counterterrorism [16, 7]. The object of this paper is a third kind of string matching that is becoming more and more relevant. In Figure 1 we have represented the relationship between company name matching and the other aspects of information integration mentioned in this paragraph.

The company name matching activity described in this

*This work has been supported by projects Prin 2005 "Middleware basato su Java per la fornitura di servizi interattivi di TV digitale" and CIPE 4/2004 "Innovazione e centri di ricerca nelle Marche", and has been developed in the context of the European project *Study on the effects of allowing patent claims for computer-implemented inventions*, EC-DG Information Society

paper has been performed on two databases of patent data and company indicators. During the past three years the OECD (Organization for Economic Co-operation and Development) patents statistics task force has been engaged in a project to develop a world-wide patent database, called Patstat [18]. Among the planned applications of this important resource there is the integration of patent data with company level data, like R&D expenditures, profits and investments. The database with company indicators that we matched against Patstat is Amadeus, a European database containing financial information on about 9 million public and private companies in 38 countries [1]. From it, we have extracted a subset of more than 200,000 enterprises of interest. These have been matched with patent assignees from about 300,000 patents of the Patstat database version September 2006.

Although data matching is already used in a number of important applications, there is still a gap between general approaches and practical solutions. This is the main motivation of this case study, that is aimed at partially filling this gap. Some techniques that we apply in this study have already been investigated in general, but their effectiveness and applicability to the domain object of this paper are still untested. In addition, it is valuable to investigate the "integration" of these techniques into a complete approach to efficiently solve a real problem. The contributions of this paper are the following:

- We describe a complete case study in the area of data integration, performed on real datasets.

- We show how to choose and apply existing techniques to a very specific domain and to large volumes of data.

- We analyze the impact of domain knowledge on the results of the matching.

Matching string fields usually involves two main steps: harmonization and the actual matching phase. These procedures can be preceded by some **preprocessing**, which in many cases has relevant consequences on the results of the integration. In addition, these activities can be inserted inside a learning procedure, to tune their parameters and to correct unwanted behavior (Figure 2). **Data harmonization** is a cleansing activity involving several steps, like punctuation standardization (e.g., from FERRARI⎵,& C. to FERRARI,⎵& C.) and company name standardization (from FERRARI, & C. to FERRARI, **AND COMPANY**) [14]. A specific kind of company name harmonization is the one that produces the legal name of the company, which is a valuable activity in general but is not necessary in our case. Name harmonization can also be used as an independent process, to produce a harmonized name reflecting the original names from which it has been obtained. This is important if for each cluster (set of names relative to the same

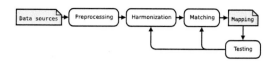

Figure 2. Generic string matching

company) we want to choose one representative name. With regard to our integration problem, this is not necessary: we only need that after the harmonization different names of the same company become similar enough to be matched. The second step, **string matching**, may range from a simple character-to-character comparison to complex approximate string comparison techniques, that may increase the number of matches at the cost of decreasing their precision.

The paper is organized as follows. The next three sections concern the phases of data preparation, harmonization and matching. In Sections 5 and 6 we discuss the implementation of a tool to perform the matching and show some experimental results. In particular, we describe the techniques we used to improve the efficiency of our implementation, and compare our results with an exact string matching approach and with a method that does not use domain knowledge. Finally, we draw some conclusions.

2. Data preparation and analysis

The input data sets of our integration activity have been a set of text files containing different versions of the Amadeus database (relative to different years), and a text file with a table of the Patstat database containing patent assignee names and countries. Before harmonization and matching, the input files have been preprocessed to check and correct the character encoding, normalize the format and remove redundancies. Even if these processes are not conceptually difficult, they are necessary to obtain correct results, and even very good matching algorithms may fail if the input data has not been prepared appropriately.

2.1. Data preparation

The first thing to check was that the input data used an appropriate **character encoding**. In our case, we needed to support all European languages, and used UNICODE and its UTF-8 serialization [4]. To work with UNICODE data we first checked if our operating system, text editors and integrated development environments were configured to understand it. This could be easily verified opening an example file from the UNICODE website. Then, we checked the input files provided by the owners of the data. The first version of the files we received had been exported from the source database using a wrong encoding, and many special characters had been lost. Therefore we asked for new data, and again some of the data had encoding errors, which were present in old versions of the original data source. At the end, these errors could not be avoided.

After the encoding had been checked, we had to be sure that the data was in the correct **format**. In general, if the data is stored in text files, it must be imported into a relational database system, or we need to know the characters used to separate different columns and be sure that they do not appear inside the data. In fact, in our case the different input files had different schemata (number and order of columns) and different data separators, sometimes mixed with the data.

Then, we had to select the columns and rows required for the matching, i.e., remove **unnecessary columns** and **duplicate rows**. For example, we did not need company indicators for the matching phase, where only company names were involved. In general, the reduction of the data size may discriminate between main memory and secondary memory executions — which was not the case in our problem. On the contrary, the second operation reduced the number of rows from Amadeus data from more than $600,000$ to a few more than $200,000$, with a significant impact on the execution time of the subsequent matching phase.

2.2. Data analysis

As we have previously mentioned, the kind of integration activity object of this paper strongly depends on the specific data set we manipulate, and requires a clear understanding of it, which may be acquired by a **manual analysis** of a sample of the data, an **automatic analysis** of all the tuples, to find markup, punctuation symbols, special text characters and non-text characters, and an **evaluation of string comparison** methods on the specific data set. This analysis was therefore necessary to choose and tune the activities of harmonization and matching.

The characters automatically extracted from the data have been listed in Table 1, where we have not represented non textual characters related to the aforementioned encoding errors. From the manual analysis, we identified the presence of many company specific names, like AND COMPANY or LTD, often written in several different variations, e.g., AND CO. and & C.. This information has been useful to tune the string edit distance and harmonization procedure, that we discuss in the next section.

An important part of the analysis phase was aimed at choosing the most appropriate string similarity function(s) for our data. String similarity functions compare two strings and produce a number between 1 and 0, where 1 means that they are very similar and 0 that they are unrelated. This value refers to the characteristics of the strings analyzed by the function. Existing functions can be classified into four

Table 1. Result of character analysis

Class	Characters
Markup	*no markup found*
Punctuation	! " # $ % & ' ( ) * + , - . / : ; < = > ? @ [ ] _ ` { |
Special chars	À Á Â Ã Ä Å Æ Ç È É Ê Ë Í Ì Î Ï Ð Ñ Ó Ô Õ Ö Ø Ú Ù Û Ü Ý ß ã é ô õ ö ü

main classes.

The first class uses **edit distances** to evaluate the similarity of two strings. To define an edit distance function we must choose a set of operations on strings, like character substitution and deletion, assign a cost to each operation and compute the minimum cost transformation to change the first string into the second. In particular, an edit distance can be defined using a function $c(s1, s2)$ that returns the cost to pay if we substitute the substring $s1$ with $s2$ — deletion and insertion can be specified using empty strings respectively as the second or first argument. When we know how to compute an edit distance between two strings, we can map it to the interval $[0, 1]$ to obtain their similarity. As an example, consider the edit distance defined by $c(c1, c2) = 1$, where $c1$ and $c2$ can be any character or the empty string (ϵ). The distance between HOME and DOG is $c(\text{H,D}) + c(\text{M,G}) + c(\text{E},\epsilon) = 3$. At this point, the similarity can be computed as 1 minus the ratio between the distance and the length of the longest string, that is $1 - \frac{3}{4} = \frac{1}{4}$ (other similarity functions can be obtained using other mappings). The best known edit distances are the Levenstein and the Smith-Waterman distances, which assign respectively unit costs and variable costs to the allowed operations. The second class of similarity functions uses the concept of **token-based distance**, and methods in this class tackle the following aspect not captured by edit distances. If we compare the strings Matteo Magnani and Magnani Matteo their edit distance is high, while the two strings are very similar. If we cut the strings into two tokens Matteo and Magnani and compare these sets of strings, we see that they are equal. Many different functions belong to this class, changing the way in which tokens are produced (white-space separated substrings, or N-grams) and the way in which sets of tokens are compared (for example the Jaccard distance and TF-IDF distance). Different functions can be used together to create **hybrid methods**, like the recursive evaluation of Monge and Elkan or the SoftTF-IDF method. Finally, there is a fourth class of **ad-hoc methods**, that have been defined to solve specific problems like the phonetic comparison of personal names, e.g., Phonex and Soundex. The methods mentioned in this paragraph are referenced in [8, 6, 7].

The approach we used to choose the functions to apply to our data sets is the following. First, we applied two very general functions from the first two basic classes to a small sample of data, to be able to manually check their results. Then, we tuned them, choosing from each class the most appropriate version of the function.

Using a very general edit distance, allowing substitution, deletion, insertion and character swapping, and assigning very small costs to them, we found the following potential matches (among many others):

1. HILLE & M**UE**LLER GMBH & CO. /
   HILLE & M**U**LLER GMBH & CO KG /
   HILLE & M**Ü**LLER GMBH & CO KG

2. AB ELECTRONIK GMBH /
   AB Elektronik GmbH

3. B**HLER AG / BAYER** AG

The first example highlights the presence of **spelling variations** and the second of **spelling errors**, showing that edit distances may in fact increase the number of true positive matches. However, case 3 shows two strings with a low distance that are not related at all. In fact, the distribution of company names does not allow an automatic application of edit distances — starting from many unrelated company names we can transform them into each other with only one or two operations. However, while **spelling errors** could not be automatically identified without significantly reducing the precision of the method, **spelling variations** could be easily tackled using edit distance functions with 0 cost transformations from one variation to the other.

Then, we applied a trivial Jaccard token distance, breaking the strings on white spaces and computing the fraction of common tokens. Using this method, we obtained the following potential matches (among many others):

1. **AAE** HOLDING /
   AAE TECHNOLOGY INTERNATIONAL

2. Japan as represented by the
   president of the **university** of **Tokyo**
   / **President of Tokyo University**

3. AAE **HOLDING** / AGRIPA **HOLDING**

4. VBH **DEUTSCHLAND GMBH** /
   IBM **DEUTSCHLAND GMBH**

Cases 1 and 2 show the high potential of this kind of distance. However, case 3 highlights the necessity to assign different weights to significant tokens, like AAE, and non-discriminating tokens that should not contribute to the matching, like HOLDING. Case 4 suffers from the problems of both kinds of similarity functions.

Table 2. Harmonization procedures (with ellipses and explicit white spaces where necessary)

	FELINO- Fundiçao e Construçoes Mecânicas, S.A.
#1	FELINO- FUNDICAO [...] MECANICAS, S.A.
#7	FELINO-␣FUNDICAO [...] MECANICAS
#9	FELINO␣␣FUNDICAO [...] MECANICAS
#10	FELINO FUNDICAO [...] MECANICAS
	S.F.T. SERVICES SA
#7	S.F.T. SERVICES
#8	S.F.T. SERVICE
#9	SFT SERVICE

3. Harmonization

The harmonization procedure we adopted has been partially taken from [14], and applies the following manipulations to each company name: (1) **replace accents**, (2) replace multi spaces, (3) replace double quotation marks, (4) replace trailing non alphanumeric chars, (5) correct commas and periods, (6) replace company names, (7) remove company names, (8) replace spelling variations, (9) **purge** and (10) replace multi spaces.

The details of the harmonization steps 2—8 and 10 may be found in the aforementioned work, therefore we will not discuss them here. However, their names should be self-understandable, and in Table 2 we have shown the effect of some of these operations on two company names taken from one of our databases. Activities #1 and #9 differ from [14] because of the different matching techniques we applied later. First, during step #1 we did not replace all accented characters with their unaccented versions, because we could subsequently use a tailored edit distance function to manage them. In particular, we replaced all characters with only one possible variation with their unaccented form (like È and E) and kept all characters with alternative spellings (like Ü, which can be written as U or UE). Second, our *purge* function replaces punctuation symbols, but keeps the distinction between different tokens inside each name — it does not remove white spaces. This enables the matching of similar names in which the order of words is different. As indicated in Table 2, this function keeps together the acronyms it recognizes, but separates different tokens (words) to enable further analysis.

4. Matching

This is the most interesting and difficult part of the integration. Character-to-character comparison of harmonized strings is very precise, but tends to have a very small recall.

Table 3. 0-cost operations

$c(\ddot{A},AE)$	$c(\dot{A},A)$	$c(\ddot{O},OE)$	$c(\dot{O},O)$	$c(\emptyset,OE)$
$c(\ddot{U},UE)$	$c(\dot{U},U)$	$c(\text{\AE},AE)$	$c(\mathring{A},AA)$	$c(\text{ß},SS)$

Table 4. Number of occurrences of some tokens in distinct parent companies

TOKEN	#
INTERNATIONAL	2183
HOLDING	1628
DEUTSCHLAND	691
THE	773
...	...
AAE	1

Table 5. Weights of the tokens used in our example

Token	Weight
AAE	1
HOLDING	.12
TECHNOLOGY	.12
INTERNATIONAL	.12
AGRIPA	1

As shown after the analysis phase, the application of string distance functions may increase the recall, but may also reduce the precision. The objective is to balance these two phenomenons.

As we have already mentioned, the first function we used is a simple edit distance where the cost of substituting a character or set of characters with one of its spelling variations is 0, and all other costs are 1. For example, the cost of substituting the character $\ddot{A}$ with the characters AE is 0. In addition, when we find the character A we may think of it as an alternative spelling for $\ddot{A}$. Therefore, we have assigned a lower cost (α) also to the substitution of As with AEs (and similar sequences). 0-cost operations are indicated in Table 3.

The second function weights each token proportionally to its significance. Let us notate $s1$ the set of tokens obtained from a string S1, and w_t the weight of token t, given by $w_t = \frac{1}{\log(occ_t)+1}$, where occ_t is the number of occurrences of the token inside different parent companies. The similarity function we used is:

$$\sim(S1,S2) = \frac{2\sum_{t \in s1 \cap s2} w_t}{\sum_{t \in s1} w_t + \sum_{t \in s2} w_t} \quad (1)$$

In Table 4 we have indicated the number of occurrences of some tokens. When all the weights are set to one, this function reduces to the Jaccard similarity function:

$$J(S1,S2) = \frac{2|s1 \cap s2|}{|s1| + |s2|} \quad (2)$$

As an example of application of this measure, consider the strings S1: AAE HOLDING, S2: AAE TECHNOLOGY INTERNATIONAL and S3: AGRIPA

HOLDING. Their sets of tokens and common tokens are: $s1$ = {AAE, HOLDING}, $s2$ = {AAE, TECHNOLOGY, INTERNATIONAL}, $s3$ = {AGRIPA, HOLDING}, $s1 \cap s2$ = {AAE}, $s1 \cap s3$ = {HOLDING}. Without token weighting, their similarities would be $J(S1,S2) = \frac{2 \cdot 1}{2+3} = .4$ and $J(S1,S3) = \frac{2 \cdot 1}{2+2} = .5$. The second comparison returns a higher result because the percentage of common tokens is higher. However, the common token of the second comparison (HOLDING) is not significant, and the same is true for the uncommon tokens of the first comparison (TECHNOLOGY and INTERNATIONAL). We have indicated in Table 5 the weights of these tokens evaluated on the Amadeus data set. With token weighting, we obtain the following similarities: $\sim(S1,S2) = \frac{2 \cdot (1)}{(1+.12)+(1+.12+.12)} = .85$, and $\sim(S1,S3) = \frac{2 \cdot (.12)}{(1+.12)+(1+.12)} = .11$. As it appears from this example, this similarity function is tuned on the specific relevance of single tokens inside the data sets object of this paper.

5. Testing and Experimental Results

In this section we present another relevant aspect of our case study. As we have already mentioned, a specific feature of data integration is the high cardinality of the input data. While the integration of schemata often regards tenths to hundreds of (schema) objects in each input data source, data integration problems like ours usually involve hundreds of thousands to millions of (data) objects. Therefore, efficient techniques are necessary to enable the matching.

The time complexity of the naive comparison of all company names from one database with all the other company names is $ct \cdot ntp \cdot nta$, where ntp and nta are the cardinalities of the two data sources (**n**umber of **t**uples in **p**atstat/**a**madeus) and ct represents the time needed to compare a single pair of names. The fact that we are dealing with instances, and not with schemata, makes the naive implementation unusable. In particular, after preprocessing we had $ntp = 290,956$ and $nta = 211,253$. In Table 6 we

Table 6. Execution time of alternative implementations of the matching phase, including the generation of indexes. DE refers to German companies — the second largest partition, and the execution time of the whole data set (ALL) using the naive implementation has only been estimated

Data set	Task	CPUs	Time
ALL	Naive Matching	1	(est.) 1962h
DE	Naive Matching	1	30h55m53s
DE	Naive Matching	~70	27m17s
DE	Indexed Matching	1	55s
DE	Indexed Matching	~70	7s

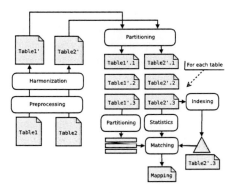

Figure 3. Detailed integration process

have estimated the time needed to match the two databases using the naive comparison and a single computer[1]. To improve the efficiency of the integration process we applied three strategies, that are described in the following: partitioning, parallelism, and indexing. In addition to them, we also used efficient implementations of the input methods and of the distance functions. In fact, it was not necessary to compute the distance between each pair of strings: whenever the distance equaled the maximum allowed value (1, with regard to the edit distance) we could stop the computation. Although this is only a detail with respect to the techniques we describe in the following, it may determine a very significant improvement of the efficiency of the integration activity. In Figure 3 we have illustrated how we implemented the general process shown in Figure 2.

The first approach to reduce the matching time was to identify pairs of data sets that had not to be compared with each other. This technique is already used in some rela-

tional implementations of the Join operator, and is usually called **partitioning**. To partition the data, we used country codes not to compare companies from different countries with each other, and obtained $N_p = 189$ pairs of subsets of data, one for each different country. At this point, we could compare each subset with only one of the others, reducing the time complexity to N_p times the time needed to integrate each subset. In particular, using the naive implementation on each subset the execution time would reduce to $N_p(\mathrm{ct} \cdot \frac{\mathrm{ntp}}{N_p} \cdot \frac{\mathrm{nta}}{N_p}) = \frac{\mathrm{ct \cdot ntp \cdot nta}}{N_p}$ in case of equal-size partitions, saving a factor N_p. However, in practice each subset had a different size. In particular, the cardinalities of the data sets relative to big countries were much higher than $\frac{\mathrm{ntp}}{N_p}$. In Table 6 we have indicated the execution time on one of the largest pairs of data sets, the German one, containing 38, 925 entries from Patstat and 24, 983 entries from Amadeus. After partitioning, we obtained only six pairs of data sets with more than 10, 000 entries, with a significant reduction of the execution time. In addition, notice that different partitions can be easily processed in parallel, being independent on each other.

In fact, a second technique we used, that can be applied with or without partitioning, is **parallelism**. We used a cluster of about $N_{\mathrm{PC}} = 70$ computers[2] to additionally reduce the execution time. It is important to notice that each computer had its own CPU, RAM and HD, but we fetched the data from a single remote database. However, this did not influence the execution time of the matching phase, because we fetched all the data at the beginning and performed the matching locally to each computer. Adding parallelism to this implementation is straightforward, and the execution time can be additionally reduced to $\mathrm{ctrl} + N_{\mathrm{PC}} \cdot \mathrm{fetch} + \frac{\mathrm{match}}{N_{\mathrm{PC}}}$, where ctrl is the time to assign the sub-tasks to the nodes (not significant), fetch is the time needed to fetch the data from a single computer and match is the time needed to perform the matching, which depends on the actual implementation. We have indicated the new experimental execution time in Table 6.

While the last two techniques were already sufficient to make our problem tractable, they would not scale to larger volumes of data. Therefore, we also implemented an **index** on the tokens of the company names. For example, the company name AAE HOLDING would be indexed under AAE and HOLDING. This is a traditional token-based index, that can be used to retrieve all the company names from the other data set with at least one token in common with the search key. However, we could further improve the efficiency of the index. Consider that we only want to keep pairs of names whose similarity is above a certain threshold th. Therefore, given a string $S1$ from the non-indexed data

---

[1]Linux Ubuntu 2.6.15-27-686, 1GB RAM, Intel[R] Pentium[R] 4 CPU (3.00GHz), as for all the following experiments

[2]The exact number depended on the actual availability, because we used a shared cluster

set, we may not consider all indexed strings for which:

$$\sim (S1, S2) = \frac{2\sum_{t\in s1\cap s2} w_t}{\sum_{t\in s1} w_t + \sum_{t\in s2} w_t} < \text{th} \qquad (3)$$

The problem is that for each string S1 we only know its tokens, and not those on all the possible matches from the other data set. Therefore, to separate the tokens in S2 but not in S1 we need to rewrite (3) as

$$\frac{2\sum_{t\in s1\cap s2} w_t}{\sum_{t\in s1\setminus s2} w_t + 2\sum_{t\in s1\cap s2} w_t + \sum_{t\in s2\setminus s1} w_t} < \text{th} \quad (4)$$

and

$$2(1-\text{th}) \sum_{t\in s1\cap s2} w_t < (\sum_{t\in s1\setminus s2} w_t + \sum_{t\in s2\setminus s1} w_t)\ \text{th} . \quad (5)$$

This condition gives us a precise idea of the strings that would match $S1$, where we have separated the tokens that do not belong to $s1$. Now, we can define the more stringent condition:

$$2(1-\text{th}) \sum_{t\in s1\cap s2} w_t < \sum_{t\in s1\setminus s2} w_t\ \text{th} \qquad (6)$$

that implies (5). Using this condition, we can partition the tokens of $S1$ into two subsets ($s1 \cap s2$ and $s1 \setminus s2$) and find the sets of tokens that must necessarily be present also in $S2$, i.e., in $s1 \cap s2$, to *allow* the matching — the fact that the two string match depends on the additional tokens of $S2$, and can be checked only on the retrieved company names.

Let us consider again our previous example: we want to match AAE HOLDING with all the other (indexed) data set, and retrieve only those pairs that are at least .7 similar. The weights of AAE and HOLDING are respectively 1 and .11. We have four possible situations, that we have indicated in Table 7. Notice that if the token AAE does not belong to $s2$ the condition in (6) is satisfied, meaning that the similarity of the two strings will be necessarily under the threshold. As a consequence, we may discard all company names from the indexed data set not containing the token AAE. It is worth noticing that the tokens that we must search in the index are those that discriminate more, i.e., the ones contained inside less company names.

There are many ways to choose a set of tokens satisfying (6). In our implementation we used a greedy approach, which is very fast even if it finds only one of the possible combinations of tokens satisfying (6). We ordered the tokens by their weights, and considered all of them in the intersection, as if they were present in both strings. Then we started moving the heaviest tokens from $s1 \cap s2$ to $s1 \setminus s2$, until the equation was satisfied. In our example this happens as soon as the token AAE is moved to $s1 \setminus s2$, meaning that if

Table 7. Alternative sets of common tokens ($s1 \cap s2$), where we have indicated when they satisfy (6)

$s1 \cap s2$	Condition
	Yes
HOLDING	Yes
AAE	No
AAE, HOLDING	No

it does not belong to $S2$, $S2$ will not be matched against $S1$ independently of the other tokens. We are therefore ready to collect all company names containing at least one of these tokens. With regard to the other company names in the indexed data set, we are sure they will not match $S1$.

The impact of this index on the execution time is expressed by the following formula: idx_build + ntp(idx_acc + ct · nta$_{\text{idx}}$). We need some time to build the index (idx_build), then for each tuple in the first data set (ntp tuples, or less if we are matching a partition) we must access the index (idx_acc) and compare it with the number of tuples from the other data set filtered by the index (ct · nta$_{\text{idx}}$). We have indicated the practical time reduction obtained by using this index in Table 6. Notice that the time for the parallel indexed implementation is not exactly $1/N_{\text{PC}}$ of the time needed for the local implementation, because we built a local index for each node of the cluster.

6. Evaluation

In this section we discuss the effect of approximate string matching and domain knowledge on the precision and recall of the matching.

In Figure 4 we have plotted precision and recall on the data relative to companies from Great Britain. This is the largest partition among the ones we have analyzed. The analysis has been manually performed by two economists, that have checked the matches found by the tool and indicated false and true matches. Notice that we could not compute the set of all true matches — otherwise we would not need an automated tool! Therefore we have specified the number of matches and not the normalized recall in the interval $[0, 1]$. In the x axis we have the confidence level, i.e., the threshold on the results of the string similarity function. For example, with confidence level 100 (exact matching) we could retrieve $2,423$ matches with a precision of 1, meaning that all of them were correct. With confidence level 70 we accepted all strings with a similarity degree of at least .7. In this case we could find $3,734$ matches, but only less than

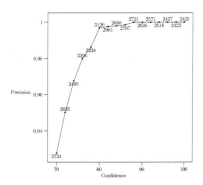

Figure 4. Precision and absolute recall varying the confidence level

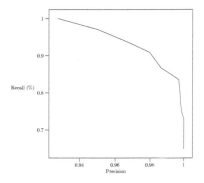

Figure 5. Precision and relative recall (recall 1 corresponds to the maximum recall obtained in our experiments)

Table 8. Comparison of the matching quality with (W) and without (W/O) domain knowledge during harmonization, on sample data

	Log				Linear			
	W DK		W/O DK		W DK		W/O DK	
thres.	P	R	P	R	P	R	P	R
1	1	.47	1	.39	1	.47	1	.38
.9	1	.51	.96	.59	**.97**	.66	.96	.57
.8	1	.51	.88	.61	.92	.70	.91	.62
.7	<u>1</u>	<u>.69</u>	<u>.86</u>	<u>.67</u>	**.92**	**.74**	.89	.68
.6	**.92**	**.74**	.83	.76	<u>.86</u>	<u>.77</u>	<u>.86</u>	<u>.77</u>
.5	.87	.83	.78	.78	.85	.83	.80	.79

without significantly decreasing the precision.

In Table 8 we have analyzed the impact of domain knowledge on the quality of the matching. In particular, we have manually analyzed two samples of the data (about 200 items) with and without applying the harmonization procedures that standardize and remove company specific names and known spelling variations (items 6, 7 and 8, page 4). If we focus on the Log column of the table we can appreciate the significant improvement of the quality of the matching using external domain knowledge: we reach a recall of .69 without decreasing the precision, where without using domain knowledge we must reduce it of about 15% (underlined numbers, Log column).

In the column labelled Linear we have described a different test where we have substituted the inverse logarithmic function previously used to weight the tokens with an inverse linear function. In particular, the weight w_t of a token t has been computed as $\frac{1}{occ_t}$, where occ_t is the number of occurrences of t inside different parent companies. Basically, this function gives more importance to the distribution of tokens, trying to capture the non-significance of company specific names. This function has two main effects on the results of the matching. First, the quality of the matching when we use domain knowledge decreases. More specifically, to increase the recall we must reduce the precision at once. Second, and most important, the difference between the test that uses domain knowledge and the one where it has not been used is less significant. In particular, a precision of .86% corresponds to the same recall in both cases (underlined numbers, Linear column). This comes from the fact that common terms like LTD or COMPANY are not removed from company names during harmonization, but are considered less during the matching phase because the linear weighting makes them less significant.

In Figure 6 we have plotted the data indicated in Ta-

93% were correct. To better highlight the increase of recall, in Figure 5 we have plotted precision and recall, where recall 1 corresponds to the recall obtained with confidence level 70. Therefore, if we call R the recall at 70, a recall x in the graph corresponds to the absolute recall $x \cdot R$.

From the figures the advantage of using approximate matching techniques is evident. If we decrease the confidence level of 20%, the precision is still about 1, meaning that we find only true matches, but the recall increases of 35%. Lowering again the confidence level we decrease the precision and increase the recall, as expected. This means that above this confidence we start finding a significant amount of false matches, and the threshold to choose depends on the impact of these errors on the specific application. In particular, the graph gives us an estimation of the probability of finding a correct match depending on the confidence level. The important result highlighted by the graph is that using well tuned approximate matching algorithms we can increase the recall up to a relevant percentage

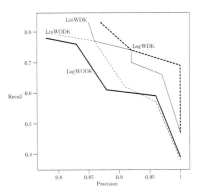

Figure 6. Graphical comparison of the data in Table 8: Log = logarithmic, Lin = linear, WDK = with domain knowledge, WODK = without domain knowledge

ble 8. Domain knowledge improves the results of the integration, and works better with a logarithmic weighting scheme. If we do not use domain knowledge, a linear weighting scheme is preferable.

7. Conclusion

In this paper we have described a case study in the area of information integration. The matching of company names is a complex task, because of the specificity of the data, requiring the use of domain knowledge, and because of its cardinality, that must be managed using efficient implementations. In addition, the quality of a data integration process depends on many small activities (during preprocessing and harmonization) that we have been presenting in detail.

In addition to the techniques described in the paper, there are some other existing approaches that we have not discussed. The first is to allow human intervention: our tool has already been developed to allow users to specify lists of significant and insignificant tokens and stop words. However, by design we tried to minimize and (where possible) avoid human intervention. The second addition would be to use an acronym identification sub-procedure, as in existing commercial systems [3]. This would enable the matching of strings like ABB and Asea Brown Boveri, that cannot be managed otherwise. In our case this was not a primary goal, because we had a lot of redundant information — patents with different versions of the same company name, and several versions of the company database with many alternative spellings. For example, both ABB and Asea Brown Boveri were present in our databases. In addition, human intervention would be unavoidable when using acronyms of hundreds of thousand companies from tenth of countries. Finally, some existing works deal with learning

the weights of the tokens. However, this was not applicable to our problem, where we did not have test data sets, and anyway the weights directly computed from the input data sets have shown excellent performances. In addition to these approaches, there is a large literature on name matching in different fields, where it takes different names like co-reference resolution or record linkage, and general text processing systems, like [2], but to the best of our knowledge there are no publicly available applications to the specific context object of this paper.

References

[1] Amadeus database. www.bvdep.com/en/amadeus.html.
[2] Gate. http://gate.ac.uk.
[3] Intelligent search technology. www.intelligentsearch.com.
[4] The unicode standard. www.unicode.org.
[5] P. A. Bernstein, S. Melnik, and J. E. Churchill. Incremental schema matching. In *VLDB Conference*, pages 1167–1170. VLDB Endowment, 2006.
[6] M. Bilenko, R. Mooney, W. Cohen, P. Ravikumar, and S. Fienberg. Adaptive name matching in information integration. *IEEE Intelligent Systems*, 18(5):16–23, 2003.
[7] P. Christen. A comparison of personal name matching: Techniques and practical issues. In *ICDM Workshops*, pages 290–294, 2006.
[8] W. W. Cohen, P. Ravikumar, and S. E. Fienberg. A comparison of string distance metrics for name-matching tasks. In *IIWeb*, pages 73–78, 2003.
[9] H.-H. Do and E. Rahm. Matching large schemas: Approaches and evaluation. *Information Systems*, 2007. to appear.
[10] A. Doan and A. Y. Halevy. Semantic-integration research in the database community. *AI Mag.*, 26(1):83–94, 2005.
[11] A. Gal. Why is schema matching tough and what can we do about it? *SIGMOD Rec.*, 35(4):2–5, 2006.
[12] A. Halevy, A. Rajaraman, and J. Ordille. Data integration: the teenage years. In *VLDB Conference*, pages 9–16. VLDB Endowment, 2006.
[13] M. Lenzerini. Data integration: a theoretical perspective. In *PODS Conference*, 2002.
[14] T. Magerman, B. van Looy, and X. Song. Data production methods for harmonized patent statistics: Patentee name harmonization. Technical report, K.U. Leuven FETEW MSI, 2006.
[15] M. Magnani, N. Rizopoulos, P. McBrien, and D. Montesi. Schema integration based on uncertain semantic mappings. In *International conference of conceptual modeling, LNCS 3716*, 2005.
[16] G. Navarro. A guided tour to approximate string matching. *ACM Computing Surveys*, pages 31–88, 2001.
[17] E. Rahm and P. A. Bernstein. A survey of approaches to automatic schema matching. *The VLDB Journal*, 10(4):334–350, 2001.
[18] J. Rollinson and R. Heijna. Epo worldwide patent statistical database. In *EPO-OECD Conference on Patent Statistics for Policy Decision Making*.

Managing Uncertain Expressions in Databases

Nauman A. Chaudhry, Moginraj Mohandas
Department of Computer Science, University of New Orleans,
2000 Lakeshore Drive, New Orleans, LA 70148, USA

E-mail: {nauman,mogin}@cs.uno.edu

Abstract

Expressions are used in a range of applications like publish/subscribe, website personalization, etc. Integrating support for expressions in a database management system (DBMS) provides an efficient and scalable platform for applications that use expressions. Additionally, in many cases these applications can benefit from support for uncertain data and expressions. Current DBMS lack such support. In this paper, we investigate how expressions with uncertainty can be integrated in a DBMS and processed like other data stored in the DBMS. We describe the underlying theory and implementation of UNXS (UNcertain eXpression System), a system that we have developed to handle uncertainty in expressions and data. We first develop a theoretical model to compare previous efforts in supporting uncertainty in DBMS and publish/subscribe systems. We propose new techniques for matching uncertain expressions to uncertain data. We then describe an implementation that integrates this support in the PostgreSQL DBMS.

Keywords: Uncertain data management. Expressions in database management systems. User-defined data types. Emerging database technologies. Publish/subscribe systems.

1 Introduction

In many application domains, such as publish/subscribe systems [17], website personalization [5], etc., users' interest in expected data is specified in terms of expressions. The application then needs to persistently maintain these expressions and match data with these expressions to inform users of items of interest.

Example 1. In a publish/subscribe system for a Real Estate application, publications correspond to houses being sold and subscriptions correspond to users' interests

defined over various attributes of houses. Consider a user is interested in houses with price less than 40,000 that have a garage and have more than two bedrooms. The user's interest can be modeled by the following expression:

```
price < 40000 AND garage = yes AND
rooms > 2
```

This expression, as well as expressions defined by other users, would be matched with publications given by information providers, e.g., real estate agents.

Most existing systems support expressions outside a database management system (DBMS). It has been noted that integration of expressions in a DBMS would provide a powerful platform for building applications requiring support for expressions [24]. This integration requires adding an expression datatype to the DBMS, along with relevant operators that can be used in SQL statements. Such integration would facilitate the management of large number of expressions in an efficient and scalable manner. It will also allow seemless integration of expressions with all the other data stored in the DBMS, since operators on expressions can be composed with operators on all the other data stored in the DBMS.

Current support for expressions in DBMS though is limited to crisp data models [1]. There is no support for uncertainty in the expressions, the data or in how expressions and data are matched. However, as noted in [17], in many situations users find it easier to express their interest in uncertain or vague terms, rather than in precise terms.

Example 2. In a real estate application a user may be certain that he can pay up to 40,000 for a house and that house must have more than 2 bedrooms. Additionally, he would like the house to have a garage, but is willing to consider houses without one.

Similarly, many times lack of exact knowledge about the state of the world may imply that the information provider is not absolutely certain about some attributes

---

[1]Other terms used for *crisp* data include *precise* and *certain* data.

of the data items. This scenario is particularly common when databases are automatically curated from unstructured sources using tools for structure extraction that are imperfect [14].

A motivation to support uncertainty in matching expressions and data comes from the fact that lay users many times do not clearly define their interest [19]. This means that some queries are so overly specific that they return no results (*empty answers problem*), while some other queries are so general that they return too many results (*many answers problem*). It would be beneficial if the data management system would handle the empty answers problem by returning data which while not completely matching the user's specified interest is still likely to be of relevance to the user. Similarly, for the many answers problem, a numerical ranking of the results would be useful [1].

Support for uncertainty in expressions and data requires that the underlying data management system extend the traditional crisp data model. Additionally, matching uncertain data with uncertain expressions requires that we have an appropriate theoretical model for determining the match. There is a large body of work in supporting uncertainty in data management systems as well as in automatic ranking of results. We build on this work and in this paper, we describe the underlying theory and implementation of UNXS (UNcertain eXpression System), a system that we have developed to handle uncertainty in expressions and data. The major contributions of this paper are as follows:

- We develop a theoretical model that enables comparison of uncertainty support in very different data intensive systems that have been previously developed. We achieve this by developing a framework to describe the matching of individual predicates with individual attributes, and then another framework to describe the matching of complete expressions with complete tuples.

- We extend the existing approaches to propose new techniques for matching uncertain expressions to uncertain data.

- We then describe an implementation that integrates support for uncertain expressions in a DBMS via a new **Expression** data type. To the best of our knowledge, this is the first integration of uncertain data and expressions within a DBMS.

The rest of this paper is organized as follows. In Section 2, we describe the formal syntax for modeling expressions. In Section 3, we discuss research in managing uncertain data. In Sections 4 and 5 we introduce a

Table 1. `Customer`

ID	Zipcode	Interest
1	70122	price < 40000 AND rooms = 2
2	70123	price < 50000 AND garage = yes AND rooms > 2

theoretical model for describing the semantics of matching uncertain expressions and uncertain data. We use this theoretical model to compare various existing techniques to handle uncertainty and to explain how we handle uncertainty in UNXS. Section 6 describes the implementation we carried out to add expression support to the PostgreSQL DBMS. In Section 7, we give conclusions and outline future work.

2 Expression Syntax and Terminology

In this section, we describe the expression data type as it is currently supported in DBMSs and its relationship to queries in conventional relational database applications. We then describe the syntax of the expression data type in UNXS.

2.1 Expression Support in DBMS

The idea of adding an Expression data type to support expressions inside the DBMS was proposed in [24] and such support has been available in Oracle 10G Server [21]. In Oracle, expressions are stored in a column of type VARCHAR or CLOB and the expression data type is not a full-fledged data type. A special *expression constraint* enforces the validity of the expressions stored in a particular column by constraining the attributes and functions that can appear in that column. Oracle also introduced an EVALUATE operator that compares stored expressions to incoming data items. For a given data item, this operator returns 1 if the expression matches the data item and 0 otherwise. EVALUATE operator takes two arguments: the column in which expressions are stored and the data item to which the expressions are to be matched.

Example 3. In the `Customer` table, the interest of a particular customer in houses is stored in the `Interest` column. The query
```
SELECT ID FROM Customer WHERE
EVALUATE(Customer.Interest, rooms=>2,
price=>36000) = 1
```
returns the value of ID for tuples in which the expression in the `Interest` column and the given data item match. For the given table this query will return the tuple with ID 1.

Support for expressions in the DBMS allows for seamless integration of expressions with other data stored in the DBMS. For example, the above query can be easily modified as below to identify customers in a specific zip code whose are interested in the specified data item.

```
SELECT ID FROM Customer WHERE
EVALUATE(Customer.Interest, rooms=>2,
price=>36000) = 1 AND Zipcode = 70122.
```

2.1.1 Mapping Expressions to Queries

The format of each expression corresponds to the WHERE clause of a SQL query. The evaluation of an expression against a data item is equivalent to a conventional SQL query, that has the expression as its WHERE clause, against a table that contains just one tuple, corresponding to the data item [24]. This mapping of expressions to queries and of data items to tuples allows us to use ideas from systems that use queries and tuples (e.g., [3], [1]) in developing a system to support uncertain expressions and data. In the rest of the paper, we use the terms *data item* and *tuple* interchangeably. Similarly, *data term* and *attribute* are used interchangeably, as are the terms *query* and *expression*.

2.2 Syntax of Expressions & Data Items in UNXS

Oracle supports crisp expressions and data. To model uncertainty, we use the notion of confidence values from Trio [3]. The formal syntax of an UNXS Expression in BNF notation is given below:

Expression ::= Predicate | Predicate AND Expression
Predicate ::= Identifier Operator Constant : Confidence
Operator ::= < | > | = | ≤ | ≥

Expressions are evaluated against *data items*. A data item is composed of one or more *data terms*. The formal syntax of a data item is given below:

Data Item ::= Data Term | Data Term AND Data Item
Data Term ::= Identifier Operator Constant : Confidence
Operator ::= =

Each confidence is a value in the interval (0,1], excludes 0 but includes 1. In a predicate, confidence value 1 represents that user is absolutely certain about the predicate. Similarly, for a data term value of 1 indicates an attribute whose value is known with certainty. In crisp expressions all predicates have confidence value 1. Similarly, in a crisp data item all data terms have confidence value 1.

Example 4. Consider the following uncertain expression and uncertain data item.

Expression: price<40000 : 0.5 AND rooms=2 : 0.6 AND garage=yes : 0.6

Data Item: price=50000 : 0.6 AND rooms=3 : 0.4 AND garage=yes : 0.8

The first predicate of the expression models the user's interest in those houses for which there is at least 50% surety that the price is less than 40000. In the data item, the data term *price = 50000* has the confidence value 0.6 implying that the information provider is 60% sure that this price is indeed 50000.

We note here that the focus of this paper is on how to integrate processing of uncertain expressions and data in the DBMS. The confidence values for expressions can be specified by a user utilizing a high-level interface or mined from past user interaction with the system, as in A-ToPSS [18]. The confidence values for the data may be determined by information extraction systems [14]. Discussion of how the uncertainty is specified is thus outside the scope of this paper.

3 Uncertainty Support in Data-Intensive Systems

The need for supporting uncertainty in data-intensive systems has been of interest for a long time [2]. This includes research in incomplete databases (e.g., [15], [13]), fuzzy databases (e.g., [4], [23]), probabilistic databases (e.g., [2], [9], [16], [10]), as well work in integration of information retrieval and database systems (e.g., [11]). To gain insight into how uncertainty can be supported in expressions, data and matching expressions with data, we decided to focus in depth on the support for uncertainty provided by one recent representative system from each of three very different types of data-intensive systems. One of these systems (A-ToPSS) uses fuzzy theory, another (Trio) is motivated by incomplete and probabilistic databases, and the third system (Auto Rank) utilizes information retrieval approaches. In later sections, we present a theoretical framework to compare the approaches taken in these three specific systems and the UNXS system created by us. In future, we plan to broaden the scope of our theoretical framework and extend it to encompass other research efforts that provide support for uncertainty.

Uncertainty in Publish/Subscribe Systems

Most publish/subscribe systems only support crisp data model. However, a publish/subscribe system, called A-ToPSS, that supports uncertainty in publications as well as subscriptions is described in [17]. A-ToPSS uses fuzzy set theory to model uncertainty in subscriptions. A

---

[2]We use the term *data-intensive systems* instead of *DBMSs* because one of the systems we consider (A-ToPSS) is a middleware system, rather than a DBMS.

Table 2. Saw

ID	(Witness, Car)
1	(Cathy, Ford) : 0.4 ‖ (Cathy, Honda) : 0.6

fuzzy set M on a universal set U specifies for each element x of U a degree of membership in the fuzzy set M. It is defined by a membership function $\mu(M) : U \rightarrow [0,1]$. To model uncertainty in publications, A-ToPSS uses possibility distribution, $\pi_A(x)$, to quantify the uncertainty that x is A.

Example 5. In a subscription, a predicate *size is large* for House can be given by the following membership function:

$\mu_{medium}(x) = \{0 \ if \ x < 1500, \ 0.5 \ if \ 1500 \leq x \leq 2500, \ 1 \ if \ x > 2500\}$

A publication attribute *(price, cheap)* may have the possibility distribution:

$\pi_{cheap}(x) = \{1 \ if \ x < 30000, \ 0.5 \ if \ 30000 \leq x \leq 50000, \ 0 \ if \ x > 50000\}$

Uncertainty Support in DBMS

Uncertainty management in DBMS has long been of interest. Recently this area has attracted a lot of interest [12]. The Trio system developed at Stanford University is a prominent example of recent work [3]. In Trio, uncertainty is modeled via *alternatives*, *maybe annotations* and *numerical confidence values*. Alternatives represent uncertainty about the contents of a tuple and are modeled via an *X-tuple*. Each X-tuple consists of one or more alternative crisp tuples. Uncertainty about the existence of an X-tuple is denoted by a *?* annotation on that tuple. This indicates that the entire tuple may or may not be present. To specify the confidence with which the user thinks the tuple value is true, *numerical confidences* can be attached to the alternatives of an X-tuple. Trio has a query language called TriQL which extends SQL to support queries with confidences.

Example 6. The table Saw contains one X-tuple that signifies that Cathy either saw a Ford or a Honda. If she saw a Ford, she was 40% sure it was a Ford, and if she saw a Honda, she was 60% sure that it was a Honda. An example query in TriQL is:

```
SELECT Saw.Witness as person INTO
RESULT FROM Saw
WHERE Saw.Car = 'Ford' AND conf(Saw)
> 0.3.
```

Automated Ranking in Databases (Auto Rank)

A-ToPSS and Trio explicitly support uncertain data. However, certain DBMS with no provision for uncertain data use approximate matching to automatically rank results of crisp queries on crisp data. A representative work in this area is described in [1]. Using ideas from infor-

mation retrieval a similarity function for ranking query results called QF (Query Frequency) is proposed. The *QF* similarity function uses the intuition that the frequent appearance of *a particular data value in many queries* implies that the data value should lead to a higher similarity value. The *QF* similarity function is computed using the frequency of occurrence of an attribute value in the workload [3].

Let $RQF(q)$ be the raw frequency of occurrence of value q of attribute A in the query strings of the workload. Let RQF_{max} be the raw frequency of the most frequently occurring value in the workload for this attribute. Then $QF(q) = RQF(q)/RQF_{max}$. For an attribute t in a tuple and a predicate value q in the query, the similarity coefficient $S(q,t) = \{QF(q) \ if \ q = t, \ and \ 0 \ otherwise\}$. The similarity value for the query against the tuple is the average of the similarities of individual attributes. Using the same technique, the similarity values of other tuples can be computed and the results of this query are ranked.

Example 7. Consider the following query and tuple.

Query: rooms=3 AND garage=yes.

Tuple: rooms=3 AND garage=no.

For *rooms*, values in the query predicate and tuple match, $S(q,t) = S(3,3) = QF(3) = RQF(3)/RQF_{max}$. For *rooms*, let $RQF_{max} = 100$ and $RQF(3) = 40$. Then $QF(3) = 40/100 = 0.4$. For *garage*, the values in the tuple and the query don't match. $S(yes, no) = 0$. The similarity value for the query and the tuple $= (0.4 + 0)/2 = 0.2$.

Another ranking technique introduced in [1] uses the concept of *missing attributes* and their *global importance*. Missing attributes are those attributes in a tuple that are *not* mentioned in the query. The global importance of a missing attribute with value t_k is $QF = QF(t_k)$. Thus for missing attributes QF function uses the value in the tuple, rather than the one in the query.

4   Matching Predicates & Data Terms

Different systems discussed in Section 3 have different semantics for matching predicates and data terms. We now introduce a framework to describe, in a uniform fashion, the semantics for evaluating predicates and data terms already used in these existing systems. We also define two new evaluation semantics for UNXS. The semantics of evaluating a predicate against a data term will be denoted by $match_p$. $\{0,1\}$ denotes the set that con-

---

[3][1] also introduces another similarity function, IDF, which uses the conventional information retrieval notion of assigning *smaller similarity values* to *frequently occurring values*. We only discuss the QF similarity function in this paper. IDF and its relationship to UNXS is discussed in [20].

tains 0 and 1, while [0,1] denotes the set that contains all real numbers between 0 and 1, including 0 and 1. *crisp* refers to an exact match between the predicate and the data term, while an approximate match between the predicate and the data term is denoted by *approx*. We denote the confidence of a data term by α and that of a predicate by β.

$match_{p1}$
crisp(pred, data term) $\rightarrow$ {0,1}
Use: Crisp DBMS. In a Crisp DBMS, if the attribute in the tuple matches the predicate, the result is 1; otherwise 0.

$match_{p2}$
crisp(pred, data term) * $Bool(\alpha \geq \beta) \rightarrow$ {0,1}
Use: Trio [3]. Trio extends the Crisp DBMS match, by additionally checking if the confidence of the data term is $\geq$ than that of the predicate. If so, the result is 1; otherwise 0.

$match_{p3}$
$Bool(approx(pred, data term) \geq threshold) \rightarrow$ {0,1}
Use: A-ToPSS [17]. Using fuzzy set theory, an approximate match between the predicate and the data term is computed and returns a value in [0,1]. This value is then compared with user-specified threshold to decide whether the predicate and data term match or not. The end result is a value in {0,1}[4].

$match_{p4}$
crisp(pred, data term) * *QF(pred, data term)* $\rightarrow$ [0,1]
Use: Auto Rank [1]. In this case, the match is crisp. But a similarity function, QF is used to map the crisp result into the interval [0,1]. Intuitive justification of QF function is given in [1] [5].

$match_{p5}$
crisp(pred, data term) * $Bool(\alpha \geq \beta)$ * *QF(pred, data term)* $\rightarrow$ [0,1]
Use: UNXS. Unlike Auto Rank, in UNXS confidence values are attached to data terms and predicates. We use the concept of comparing confidences of the data term and the predicate in Trio to extend the semantics of the predicate level match in Auto Rank [1]. First a crisp match is computed between the predicate and the data term. If this returns *true*, then we check if $\alpha \geq \beta$. If yes, then we compute the QF similarity function for the given predicate and data term. The evaluation result is thus in the interval [0,1].

---

[4] In A-ToPSS the approximate match results in two values, a possibility measure and a necessity measure, and there are two corresponding threshold comparisons. Details of these measures can be found in [17].
[5] [1] also supports approximate match between predicates and *numeric* attribute values. Discussion of this can be found in [20].

Example 8. Consider predicate $pred_1$: *rooms = 3 : 0.4* and data term dt_1: *rooms = 3 : 0.6*. $crisp(pred_1, dt_1) = 1$ and $Bool(\alpha \geq \beta) = 1$. For attribute *rooms* let $RQF_{max} = 1000$ and $RQF(3) = 40$. Then $QF(3) = 40/100 = 0.4$ and $match_{p5}(pred_1, dt_1) = 1 * 1 * 0.4 = 0.4$. Now consider predicate $pred_2$: *price < 30000 : 0.5* and data term dt_2: *price = 40000 : 0.8*. $crisp(pred_2, dt_2) = 0$ and therefore, $match_{p5}(pred_2, dt_2) = 0$.

$match_{p6}$
crisp(pred, data term) * $Bool(\alpha \geq \beta)$ * *average(α, β)* $\rightarrow$ [0,1]
Use: UNXS. We have also developed an alternative match semantic which does not use QF, and thus does not require statistics on the workload and is cheap to compute. The difference from $match_{p5}$ is that if the predicate and data term crisp match returns 1 and also $\alpha \geq \beta$ is true, then the evaluation result is the average of the α and β values. Note that the semantics of $match_{p6}$ imply that if both α and β are 1.0 and the predicate and data term match, then the evaluation result is 1, just as it is for crisp predicates and data terms in crisp DBMS. In fact, provided $\alpha \geq \beta$, the closer α and β are to 1.0, the closer is the evaluation result to 1.0, which is also the intuitive result.

Example 9. Let us consider the evaluation of $pred_1$ against dt_1 from Example 8. $match_{p6}(pred_1, dt_1) = 1 * 1 * average(\alpha, \beta) = average(0.6, 0.4) = 0.5$.

5 Matching Expressions & Data Items

We now turn our attention to the semantics of matching expressions and data items. Determining the evaluation result of expression-data item match requires defining how the evaluation results for individual predicate-data term match are combined to obtain the result for the expression-data item level match. We describe these semantics by first introducing certain variables to define cases of predicate-data term evaluation. Using these variables, we can identify interesting categories of expression-data item match. As we show, the categories proposed by us enable an easy comparison of the evaluation semantics of different systems.

5.1 Variables to Describe Cases of Predicate-Data Term Evaluation

Example 10. Consider the evaluation of the following crisp expression against the given crisp data item. To simplify the notation, we have left out the confidence values, all of which are 1.0.

Expression: price>40000 AND rooms=2 AND garage=yes

Data item: price=50000 AND rooms=3 AND area=300

There are four interesting cases of evaluation of predicates in an expression against data terms in the data item as illustrated by Example 10.

1. Predicates that can be evaluated against data terms in the data item and $match_p(pred, data\ term) > 0$. In Example 10, the predicate *price > 40000*.

2. Predicates that can be evaluated against data terms in the data item and $match_p(pred, data\ term) = 0$. In Example 10, the predicate *rooms = 2*.

3. Predicates that cannot be evaluated against any data term in the given data item. In Example 10, the predicate *garage = yes*. In conventional DBMS this case arises whenever a query predicate cannot be evaluated because a tuple has a NULL value for the corresponding attribute.

4. Data terms that do not get evaluated against any predicates in the expression. In Example 10, the data term *area = 300*. Such data terms correspond to *missing attributes* in Auto Rank [1] as discussed in Section 3. Conventional relational theory though ignores this case and uncertain DBMS have also ignored this case.

We define the following variables that allow us to describe the results of all the predicate-data term level evaluations that occur when an expression is matched against a data item.

P Total number of predicates in the expression.

D Total number of data terms in the data item.

P_t Number of predicates that can be evaluated and for which $match_p > 0$.

P_f Number of predicates that can be evaluated and for which $match_p = 0$.

P_{ne} Number of predicates that couldn't be evaluated against any data term.

D_{nu} Number of data terms that did not get evaluated against any predicate.

Example 11. The expression in Example 10 has 3 predicates, and hence $P = 3$. One of the 3 predicates ($garage = yes$) cannot be evaluated, hence $P_{ne} = 1$. For one of the 2 remaining predicates, $match_p(pred, data\ term) > 0$ and for the other $match_p(pred, data\ term) = 0$. Hence $P_t = 1$ and $P_f = 1$. The data item has 3 data terms and $D = 3$. Only one of the data terms $area = 300$ does not get evaluated against any predicates and therefore $D_{nu} = 1$.

5.2 Categories of Expression-Data Item Evaluation.

We see that 8 interesting categories of evaluation of expressions against data items can be defined based on different combinations of the variables P_f, P_{ne} and D_{nu}.

Table 3. Categories of Expression-Data Item Evaluation

Category	Variable Combination
1	$P_{ne}=0\ P_f=0\ D_{nu}=0$
2	$P_{ne}=0\ P_f=0\ D_{nu}>0$
3	$P_{ne}>0\ P_f=0\ D_{nu}=0$
4	$P_{ne}>0\ P_f=0\ D_{nu}>0$
5	$P_{ne}=0\ P_f>0\ D_{nu}>0$
6	$P_{ne}>0\ P_f>0\ D_{nu}>0$
7	$P_{ne}=0\ P_f>0\ D_{nu}=0$
8	$P_{ne}>0\ P_f>0\ D_{nu}=0$

These categories are shown in Table 3. Note that Example 10 falls into Category 6.

5.3 Evaluation Semantics for Different Systems

We can now use the formal model introduced by us to compare and contrast the semantics of matching expressions and data items in Crisp DBMS, Trio, A-ToPSS, Auto Rank and UNXS. The possible values of expression-data item evaluation result for various systems for the eight categories identified in Table 3 are listed in Table 4. In the rest of this subsection we explain each row of Table 4.

Crisp DBMS Crisp DBMS don't support uncertainty in data or queries. The predicate-attribute match is done using $match_{p1}$. A tuple matches a query only if all predicates in the query evaluate to 1. This corresponds to Cat_1 and Cat_2. For the rest of the categories, the result is 0, since either $P_{ne} > 0$ implying at least one predicate can't be evaluated because of NULL value in the corresponding attribute of the tuple, or $P_f > 0$ implying that at least one predicate-attribute level match returned 0.

Trio In Trio, confidence values are considered in computing the predicate-attribute match using $match_{p2}$. However, if $match_{p2} = 0$ for any predicate or if any predicate can't be evaluated, the tuple doesn't match the query. Thus, for each category at the query-tuple level, the result is the same as Crisp DBMS.

A-ToPSS In A-ToPSS the predicate-attribute match is done using $match_{p3}$. If the result of each match is 1, then the tuple (i.e., the publication) matches the query (i.e., the subscription). However, if $match_{p3} = 0$ for any predicate or if any predicate can't be evaluated, the tuple doesn't match the query. Again, for each category at the query-tuple level, the result is the same as Crisp DBMS.

Auto Rank Auto Rank uses a crisp data model and does not support uncertainty in data or queries. However,

Table 4. Result of Expression-Data Item Evaluation in Different Systems

System	Cat_1 P_{ne}=0 P_f=0 D_{nu}=0	Cat_2 P_{ne}=0 P_f=0 D_{nu}>0	Cat_3 P_{ne}>0 P_f=0 D_{nu}=0	Cat_4 P_{ne}>0 P_f=0 D_{nu}>0	Cat_5 P_{ne}=0 P_f>0 D_{nu}>0	Cat_6 P_{ne}>0 P_f>0 D_{nu}>0	Cat_7 P_{ne}=0 P_f>0 D_{nu}=0	Cat_8 P_{ne}>0 P_f>0 D_{nu}=0
Crisp DBMS	1	1	0	0	0	0	0	0
Trio	1	1	0	0	0	0	0	0
A-ToPSS	1	1	0	0	0	0	0	0
Auto Rank	[0,1]	[0,1]	n/a	n/a	[0,1]	n/a	[0,1]	n/a
UNXS ($match_{p5}$)	[0,1]	[0,1]	[0,1]	[0,1]	[0,1]	[0,1]	[0,1]	[0,1]
UNXS ($match_{p6}$)	[0,1]	[0,1]	[0,1]	[0,1]	[0,1]	[0,1]	[0,1]	[0,1]

as described in Section 3, evaluation result for a crisp tuple against a crisp query can result in a value other than 0 or 1.

Cat_1 corresponds to the *many answers problem*. This problem occurs when a query is very unselective and returns too many results, most of which may not be of interest to the user. In such cases the tuples in the results are ranked using QF and only the best matching tuples are returned to the user.

Cat_2 corresponds to the *missing attributes* scenario. Missing attributes are the ones that contribute to $D_{nu} > 0$. QF for these attributes is computed using the value in the tuple rather than the query (as described in Section 3) and then used in computing the query-tuple similarity value.

Cat_5 and Cat_7 correspond to the *empty answers* problem. This problem occurs when the query is so selective that the result is empty. For both these categories the crisp match of at least one predicate in the query results in a 0 value, i.e., $P_f > 0$. Thus the contribution of these predicates to the query-tuple similarity value is 0.

In the other 4 categories $P_{ne} > 0$, and hence at least one predicate cannot be evaluated because the corresponding attribute in the tuple is NULL. This case is not discussed in [1].

UNXS ($match_{p5}$) When using $match_{p5}$, UNXS combines similarity values for the predicate-data term match in the same manner as in Auto Rank, i.e., by computing the average of all these values. For the other four categories, where $P_{ne} > 0$, the predicates that cannot be evaluated are taken into account by computing QF using the value in the predicate.

Example 12. Consider the following expressions and data item.

exp_1: *rooms=3 : 0.4 AND price=30000 : 0.5*
exp_2: *price=40000 : 0.6 AND garage = yes : 0.9*
di_1: *rooms=3 : 0.6 AND price=40000 : 0.8*

For attribute *rooms*, let $QF_{rooms}(3) = 0.4$. In the evaluation of exp_1 against di_1, for *rooms*, $match_{p5}(3,3) = crisp(3,3) * Bool(0.6 \geq 0.4) * QF_{rooms}(3) = 1 * 1 * 0.4 = 0.4$. For *price*, $match_{p5}(30000, 40000) = 0$. At the expression-data item level, $P_f > 0$, $P_{ne} = 0$ and $D_{nu} = 0$. This corresponds to Cat_7 and $eval(exp_1, di_1) = (0.4 + 0)/2 = 0.2$.

When evaluating exp_2 against di_1, the predicate on *garage* cannot be evaluated and the data term on *rooms* is not used. For the predicate on *price*, $match_{p5}(40000, 40000) > 0$. This evaluation thus corresponds to Cat_4. Therefore, $eval(exp_2, di_1) = (QF_{price}(40000) + QF_{rooms}(3) + QF_{garage}(yes))/3$.

UNXS ($match_{p6}$) $match_{p6}$ does not use QF similarity function. Thus a non-zero match value cannot be computed for attributes corresponding to $D_{nu} > 0$ and predicates corresponding to $P_{ne} > 0$. In UNXS, when $match_{p6}$ is used, we ignore attributes corresponding to $D_{nu} > 0$. The expression-data item evaluation result is obtained by taking the average of $match_{p6}$ over all the predicates, with $match_{p6} = 0$ for predicates that cannot be evaluated (corresponding to $P_{ne} > 0$).

6 Supporting Uncertain Expressions in a DBMS

In this section we describe the implementation we carried out to manage uncertain expressions and data items inside a DBMS. The implementation was done on PostgreSQL 8.1.5 DBMS [22] on Ubuntu Linux platform. PostgreSQL is an extendible DBMS and allows the addition of new User Defined Types (UDTs) and user defined functions. The first step in the addition of a new UDT in PostgreSQL is definition of two functions: the input function, which converts the external representation of the UDT to an internal representation, and the

```
postgres@salman-uno:/root
File  Edit  View  Terminal  Tabs  Help
postgres@salman-uno:/root$ psql testdb
Welcome to psql 8.1.5, the PostgreSQL interactive terminal.

testdb=# create table customer(custno int, interest expression);
CREATE TABLE
testdb=# insert into customer values(1, 'p=20000 : 0.4 AND bedrooms=3 : 0.6');
INSERT 0 1
testdb=# insert into customer values(2, 'p=30000 : 0.6 AND bedrooms>2 : 0.5 AND garage=yes :0.4');
INSERT 0 1
testdb=# insert into customer values(3, 'p>28000 : 0.7 AND garage=yes : 0.5 AND bedrooms=3 : 0.6');
INSERT 0 1
testdb=# insert into customer values(4, 'p>30000 : 0.7 AND bedrooms>2 : 0.7 AND garage=yes : 0.6');
INSERT 0 1
testdb=# select * from customer;
 custno |                          interest
--------+-----------------------------------------------------------
      1 |  p=20000 : 0.4 AND bedrooms=3 : 0.6
      2 |  p=30000 : 0.6 AND bedrooms>2 : 0.5 AND garage=yes : 0.4
      3 |  p>28000 : 0.7 AND garage=yes : 0.5 AND bedrooms=3 : 0.6
      4 |  p>30000 : 0.7 AND bedrooms>2 : 0.7 AND garage=yes : 0.6
(4 rows)
```

Figure 1. Inserting and Querying Expressions.

output function which converts the internal representation of the UDT back to the external representation. These two functions were added to PostgreSQL for the `Expression` data type. This allows us to perform basic `INSERT` and `SELECT` statements, as shown in Figure 1.

To support evaluation of uncertain expressions over uncertain data items, we implemented an `EVALUATE` operator with the semantics of $match_{p6}$. Additionally, using the idea of a confidence threshold from TriQL (see Example 6), the `EVALUATE` operator in UNXS can be provided with a *threshold* value along with a comparison operator ($>, <, =, \geq, \leq$). Only those expressions for which the match with the data item satisfies the comparison with the threshold are returned in the result. A screenshot showing the result for two different values for the threshold is shown in Figure 2 [6].

7 Conclusions and Future Work

Integrating support for expressions in a DBMS provides an efficient and scalable platform for many application domains that use expressions. Current DBMS though only support crisp data model and cannot support uncertainty in expressions or data. To provide such support, we first developed a theoretical framework to compare popular schemes to handle uncertainty in DBMS and publish/subscribe systems. Our theoretical framework provided us with the ability to easily compare support for uncertainty provided by three recent data intensive systems. It also enabled us to combine and extend the ideas from these disparate systems to develop UNXS, a system to manage uncertain expressions and data. We have implemented UNXS by adding a new expression data type to PostgreSQL. We have thus integrated support for uncertainty within the DBMS, as opposed to implementing this functionality in a layer outside the DBMS, as has been done in, e.g., Trio [3]. To the best of our knowledge, this is the first integration of uncertain expression support within a DBMS.

In future, we plan to extend UNXS by investigating the following items:

- In the current paper, we focussed on three recent uncertain data intensive systems. We plan an in-depth examination of other data management systems and models that support uncertainty, e.g., [4], [23]), [2], [9], [16], [10], [11], and extend our theoretical model to encompass these systems.
- The current UNXS uncertainty model allows only a single confidence value for each predicate and for each data term. Supporting a probability distribution, as in ORION [6], instead of a single value, can add substantial power to UNXS data model.
- Our underlying uncertainty model is an extension of [1]. The match for the expression is computed without considering any effect of the match of one predicate on the match of other predicates in the expressions. This independence assumption may not be always justified. We plan to investigate a more sophisticated formal model that considers statistical dependence.
- Current expression syntax in UNXS is limited to the use of conjunction (AND) of predicates. Disjunction of predicates, as well as negation are not supported. A potential extension is to support more powerful expressions. However, the benefit of increased expressive power must be weighed against the increase in computational complexity that comes with more expressive models [8].
- To enable efficient processing of expressions in UNXS, we plan to investigate query optimization as

[6] In future, alternative match semantics can be tested in UNXS by implementing additional user defined operators in PostgreSQL.

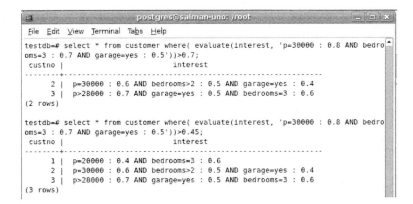

Figure 2. Evaluation of Expressions against Data Items using Evaluate Operator.

well as indexing techniques for uncertain data and expressions, possibly by extending techniques for indexing crisp expressions [24] and for query optimization of probabilistic data [6], [7].

References

[1] Agarwal, S., et. al. Automated Ranking of Database Query Results. In *Proc. of CIDR* (2003).

[2] Barbara, D., Garcia-Molina, H., Porter, D. The Management of Probabilistic Data. In *IEEE TKDE*, vol. 14, no. 5, (Oct. 1992), 487–502.

[3] Agrawal, P., et. al. Trio: A System for Data, Uncertainty, and Lineage. In *Proc. of VLDB Conf.* (2006), 1151–1154.

[4] Buckles, B. and Petry, F. A Fuzzy Model for Relational Databases. Int. Journal of Fuzzy Sets and Systems, vol. 7, (1982), 213–226.

[5] Ceri, S., Fraternali, P., and Paraboschi, S. Data driven one-to-one web site generation for data-intensive applications. In *Proc. of VLDB Conf.* (1999), 615–626.

[6] Cheng, R., Kalashnikov, D., and Prabhakar, S. Evaluating Probabilistic Queries over Imprecise Data. In *Proc. of SIGMOD Conf.* (2003), 551–562.

[7] Cheng, R., et. al. Efficient Indexing Methods for Probabilistic Threshold Queries over Uncertain Data. In *Proc. of VLDB Conf.* (2004), 876–887.

[8] Das Sarma, A., et. al. Representing Uncertain Data: Models, Properties, and Algorithms. *Stanford University Infolab Technical Report 2007-3.* (2007).

[9] Dey, D. and Sarkar, S. A Probabilistic Relational Model and Algebra. In *ACM TODS*, vol. 21, no. 3, (Sep. 1996), 339–369.

[10] Dey, D. and Sarkar, S. Generalized Normal Forms for Probabilistic Relational Data. In *IEEE TKDE*, vol. 14, no. 3, (May/June 2002), 485–497.

[11] Fuhr, N., and Roellke, T. A Probabilistic Relational Algebra for the Integration of Information Retrieval and Database Systems. In *ACM TOIS*, vol. 15, no. 1, (1997), 32–66.

[12] Garofalakis, M., Suciu, D (co-editors) Bulletin of IEEE Technical Committee on Data Engineering. Special Issue on Probabilistic Data Management (March 2006).

[13] Grahne, G. Horn Tables – An Efficient Tool for Handling Incomplete Information in Relational Database. In *Proc. of ACM PODS*, (1989), 75–82.

[14] Gupta, R., and Sarawagi, S. Creating Probabilistic Databases from Information Extraction Models. In *Proc. of VLDB Conf.*, (2006), 965–976.

[15] Imielinski, T., and Lipski, W. Incomplete Information in Relational Databases. In *Journal of the ACM*, vol. 31, no. 4, (Oct. 1984), 761–791.

[16] Lakshmanan, L., et. al., Probview: A Flexible Probabilistic Database System. In *ACM TODS*, vol. 22, no. 3, (Sep. 1997), 419–469.

[17] Liu, H., and Jacobsen, H-A. Modeling Uncertainties in Publish/Subscribe Systems. In *Proc. of ICDE* (2004), 510–522.

[18] Liu, H., and Jacobsen, H-A. A-ToPSS: A Publish/Subscribe System Supporting Imperfect Information Processing. In *Proc. of VLDB Conf.* (2004), 1281–1284.

[19] Kambhampati, S., et. al., QUIC: Handling Query Imprecision and Data Incompleteness in Autonomous Databases. In *Proc. of CIDR* (2007), 263–268.

[20] Mohandas, M. Evaluation of Expressions with Uncertainty in Databases. Master's Thesis, Dept. of Computer Science, Univ. of New Orleans (2007).

[21] Oracle 10G Expression Filter Overview. Oracle White Paper (March 2005).

[22] PostgreSQL. http://www.postgresql.org.

[23] Raju, K and Majumdar, A. Fuzzy Functional Dependencies and Lossless Join Decomposition of Fuzzy Relational Database Systems. In *ACM TODS*, vol. 13, no. 2, (June 1988), 129–166.

[24] Yalamanchi, A., Srinivasan, J., and Gawlick, D. Managing Expressions as Data in Relational Database Systems. In *Proc. of CIDR* (2003).

Multiple Entry Indexing and Double Indexing *

Victor Teixeira de Almeida, Ralf Hartmut Güting, and Christian Düntgen
Database Systems for New Applications, Faculty of Mathematics and Computer Science
University of Hagen, D-58084 Hagen, Germany
{victor.almeida, rhg, christian.duentgen}@fernuni-hagen.de

Abstract

Traditional indexing techniques are not well suited for complex data types such as spatial, spatio-temporal, and multimedia data types, where an instance is a composite of multiple components. In this paper we propose two indexing techniques that allow the parts of a composite object to be indexed separately, called multiple entry indexing and double indexing. We present the implementation of these approaches in the SECONDO extensible database system. The improvements in terms of performance of both approaches presented in this paper are shown in an experimental evaluation.

1 Introduction

Non-conventional database systems support complex data types such as spatial, spatio-temporal, and multimedia data types such as lines, regions, moving objects, texts, images, audio data, etc. One common property of such data types is that they have variable length size, but their size is unpredictable, it can be very small, e.g. a 16 colors 16x16 pixels icon, or very big, e.g. a high resolution satellite image. Another important property of these data types is that sometimes they contain multiple components. A line is composed by a set of segments, a moving object by a set of units with linear movement, an audio by a set of tracks, etc.

Indexing mechanisms are crucial for efficient query processing coping with these complex data types. Approximations are used to index such attributes, e.g. minimum bounding rectangles (MBR) for spatial data types. We will use spatial and spatio-temporal data types as examples in the rest of this section. The MBR of an object is the minimum rectangle aligned with the coordinate axes that totally encloses the object.

Figure 1. The MBR of Germany.

Figure 1 shows the region of Germany and its MBR. The dark color represents the so-called dead space, which is the difference between the area of the MBR and the object area. It is well known that the amount of dead space in a data set deteriorates the performance of a query on such indexes.

In some cases, the amount of dead space can be unacceptable. Figure 2 shows some of these cases using a data set containing the world countries as regions, which we call the world data set. The regions of France, Russia, and the USA contain several components and a huge dead space is introduced by their MBRs, shown in Figure 2(a), 2(b), and 2(c), respectively.

The data set contains 239 tuples and the MBR of France has intersection with 207 other MBRs, but the region of France just intersects 15 other regions. The following query: "Return the neighbor countries of France" can use a spatial index to improve its efficiency, i.e. before checking the intersection between the real representation of the countries, a search in the spatial index is done to retrieve the entries that have MBR intersection with France's MBR. However, in this case, this step is not very restrictive, given that it returns 86,61% of the data set.

The dead space would be significantly reduced if every component is considered separately by the index, which means every component of a country is separately indexed. We call this approach *multiple entry indexing*, because every tuple in the data set may contain several entries in the index.

Table 1 shows the improvement achieved to answer the query: "Find the countries that intersect country X" where

---

*This work was partially supported by the grant Gu 293/8-2 from the Deutsche Forschungsgemeinschaft (DFG), project "Datenbanken für bewegte Objekte" (Databases for Moving Objects)

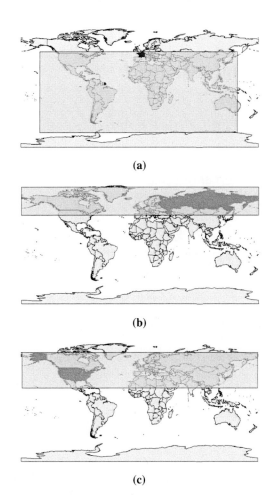

(a)

(b)

(c)

Figure 2. The MBRs of (a) France, (b) Russia, and (c) USA.

Table 1. Intersections between all countries and France, USA, and Russia.

Country	France	Russia	USA
MBR intersections	207	110	60
Component MBR intersections (with duplicates)	21	42	33
Component MBR intersections (without duplicates)	17	4	25
Real intersections	15	2	13

the gain we achieve with multiple entry indexing.

Multiple entry indexing is similar to partial indexes ([13, 14]) in the PostgreSQL DBMS. However, with partial indexes it is possible to restrict the tuples in the relation to be indexed to a subset with the help of a SQL query but it is not allowed that the index contains multiple entries for each tuple of the corresponding relation.

However, there is still place for optimization. In traditional query processing with indexes, every leaf entry in the index points to the corresponding tuple of that entry and, once the entry's approximation satisfies the query predicate, the object inside the tuple is retrieved and then the query predicate is applied to it. In our case, where objects can contain several components, we also want to avoid reading the whole object, but only the components of the object that satisfied the query predicate. With this approach the gains are twofold: we do not read the whole object (I/O), which can span into several disk pages, and we do perform the predicate in complex objects only containing the components that satisfied the approximation test (CPU).

The technique is then the following: when inserting an entry for a component into the index we carry additional information about the position of that component in the composite object. An interval storing the starting and ending position of the component in the whole object is stored together with the leaf entries in the index. In query processing, after performing the query in the index, the result is then sorted by tuple identifiers and by the intervals. In order to retrieve the tuples, the set of intervals of the same tuple is used to retrieve only a restricted portion of the complex object. We call this approach *double indexing*.

In our example of the world data set, if we check whether the USA and Russia intersect each other using the double indexing approach dividing the regions by component, only a few islands of the USA MBRs intersect the MBR of the bigger component of Russia. In this case, only a few pages will be read for the USA components (maybe only one) and the complexity of the intersection predicate is lowered given that the representation of the reduced USA instance is much smaller.

we used France, USA, and Russia as X. The first line with data presents the number of MBR intersections using the whole country MBRs, the second and third ones present the number of MBR intersections using component MBRs without and with an additional step to remove duplicates, respectively. The fourth line shows the expected result of the query, i.e. the number of intersections using the real representation of the objects. We can see that the number of computations of intersections using the real representation of the countries is reduced by approximately a factor of 12 for France, 27.5 for the USA, and 2.5 for Russia using the multiple entry indexing approach with duplicate removal.

With multiple entry indexing it is possible, for these composite data types, to perform queries more efficiently. Obviously, not in every case multiple entry indexing is better than traditional approaches, because it needs an additional duplicate removal step after the execution of the query in the index. The more selective the query the bigger

In this introduction, we used a spatial data set to demonstrate the motivation to our work. However, this approach is general and is not limited to spatial databases. Every composite data type can be indexed using the two approaches presented in this paper. As an example, the works in [10,11] present an approach to splitting a moving object trajectory into pieces before indexing it, without considering that this is not possible using traditional indexing approaches.

In this paper we present an integrated approach in the SECONDO extensible database system implementing both multiple entry indexing and double indexing. The paper is organized as follows: Section 2 presents a brief overview of SECONDO. Section 3 presents the operators for both indexing approaches in the paper. In Section 4 we present an experimental evaluation comparing the techniques presented in this paper against traditional indexing approaches. Finally, Section 5 concludes the paper.

2 SECONDO Overview

In order to explain the implementation of our indexing approach proposed in this paper, we first need to present a brief overview of the SECONDO extensible database system, which is done in this section. The goal of SECONDO is to provide a "generic" database system frame that can be filled with implementations of various DBMS data models. For example, it should be possible to implement relational, object-oriented, temporal, or XML models and to accommodate data types for spatial data, moving objects, chemical formulas, etc.

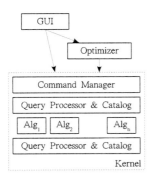

Figure 3. The SECONDO architecture.

SECONDO has been demonstrated at some conferences, such as ICDE'05 ([2, 8]) and MDM'06 ([4]).

The SECONDO system consists of three major components shown in Figure 3:

- The SECONDO kernel implements specific data models, is extensible by algebra modules, and provides query processing over the implemented algebras. It is written in C++.

- The optimizer provides as its core capability conjunctive query optimization, currently for a relational environment, and also implements the essential part of SQL-like languages. It employs a novel algorithm for query optimization described in detail in [7], based on shortest path search through a predicate order graph. It is written in Prolog.

- The graphical user interface (GUI) is an extensible interface for an extensible DBMS such as SECONDO, where new data types or models can provide their own viewers or extend an existing viewer by display methods. It is written in Java.

Since the discussion of the techniques presented in this paper will be restricted to the SECONDO Kernel, we present a more detailed description of this component of the system.

2.1 The SECONDO Kernel

A very rough description of the architecture of the SECONDO kernel is shown in the bottom of Figure 3. A data model is implemented as a set of data types and operations. These are grouped into *algebras*. For example, there is an algebra called *Relational Algebra* with tuples and relations as data types and operations like projection or hashjoin. Traditional indexing techniques are supported on SECONDO with algebras for B-trees and R-Trees.

The kernel can evaluate a query plan, also called an executable query, or a query at the executable level, which is just a term of the implemented algebras. Query processing is performed as follows: the Command Manager receives an executable query, parses it and passes the result to the Query Processor. The Query Processor then evaluates the query by building an operator tree and then traversing it, calling operator implementations from the algebras. More details about this process can be found in [5]. SECONDO objects are stored (and retrieved) by the Storage Manager into a database and managed by the Catalog.

A collection of algebras is available in the SECONDO Kernel, such as the *Standard Algebra* containing standard data types like *bool*, *int*, *real*, and *string*; the *Relational Algebra* containing the data types for tuples (*tuple*) and relations (*rel*); the *BTree Algebra* and the *RTree Algebra* containing implementation of B-Trees and R-Trees indexes, respectively; the *DateTime Algebra* with the implementation of the *instant* and *duration* data types; the *Spatial Algebra* containing 2-dimensional data types like *point*, *line*, and *region*; the *Temporal Algebra* providing moving object data types (e.g. *moving(point)*).

An important feature of SECONDO is that it offers a specific concept for the implementation of persistent attribute data types, where they are represented as a *root record* and

183

can contain some *database arrays*. Database arrays are basically persistent arrays of elements with fixed size, and are implemented on top of a concept called FLOB (Faked Large Object) described in [6], which means that they are automatically either represented inline with the tuple representation, or outside in a separate list of pages, depending on their sizes. FLOBs are read paged from disk. As an example, the *line* data type could contain some aggregate information in the root record such as its length, its MBR, the number of disconnected components, etc. and a database array of line segments.

3 Indexing

In this section, we give detailed information about the implementation of the indexing approach presented in this paper. As said in the previous sections, SECONDO already has algebras for indices such as B-trees and R-trees. These algebras contain data types for such indices and some operators mainly for creating the index and querying it. We focus this paper on the R-tree family indexing ([1, 9, 12]), since we use spatio-temporal data sets in our experiments. Everything that is presented here can be, and actually is, extended to indexing of standard data types with B-trees ([3]).

During the operators syntax description, we will follow our discussion with some examples in order to clarify the explanations. In the examples, we use the Berlin data set, graphically seen in Figure ??, which contains several relations with spatial objects in the city of Berlin, Germany — such as streets, underground train lines, green and water areas, sightseeing spots, restaurants, etc. — and a relation containing several lines of underground trains as moving points. This relation containing moving points is the one that will be mainly used in our examples and is described as

```
Trains(Id: int, Line: int, Up: bool, Trip: mpoint)
```

where *Id* is a numeric identifier (primary key), *Line* contains the line number of the train, *Up* identifies the direction of the movement of the train in the line, and *Trip* contains the moving point object.

The presentation of the operators is divided into three steps containing the operators to create and query standard indexes, the operators for multiple entry indexing, and finally the operators for double indexing.

3.1 Operators for Traditional Indexing

A traditional query processing with the help of an index runs in the following steps:

1. Send the query condition to an index and receive some result candidates

2. Retrieve the tuples pointed to by the candidates from their respective relations

3. Apply the query condition to these tuples and return the result (this step is needed if the index search cannot decide the predicate, as in filter and refine techniques).

Indices are directly connected to relations and every tuple of the relation has a corresponding entry in the index. Otherwise, the query processing will not work.

The operator called **creatertree** which performs the index creation needs a relation as one of the arguments and the attribute on that relation that needs to be indexed as the second argument. In the case of our examples, the attribute must be of a spatial type, e.g. *point*, *points*, *line*, or *region*, or of a spatio-temporal type, e.g. *mpoint* (*mpoint* is the abbreviation of *moving*(*point*) which is the data type for moving points). MBR approximations of the values of this attribute are indexed in a R*-Tree. Here is the description of the **creatertree** operator:

$$rel(\underline{tuple}(X)) \times attrname$$
$$\rightarrow \underline{rtree}(\underline{tuple}(X)\ attrtype\ Std) \quad \textbf{creatertree}$$

One should note that this operator creates a standard R-tree, which can be seen in the third parameter in the R-tree data type description (*Std*).

Using the *Trains* relation we can then create a standard R-tree index using the following command:

```
let trains_Trip = Trains creatertree[Trip];
```

This operation creates a 3D R-Tree indexing the 3D MBRs (2D MBR + time) of the attribute *Trip* of the *Trains* relation.

The following operation, called **windowintersects**, is available for querying:

$$rtree(\underline{tuple}(X)\ attrtype\ Std) \times rel(\underline{tuple}(X)) \times rect\langle dim\rangle$$
$$\rightarrow stream(\underline{tuple}(X)) \quad \textbf{windowintersects}$$

This operator receives an R-Tree, a relation and a $<dim>$-dimensional query rectangle (window) as arguments — where *dim* is the dimensionality of the indexed attribute type —, searches in the R-Tree all entries that intersect the query rectangle and retrieves the corresponding tuples in the relation, returning them as a stream. Streams of tuples are used internally in the SECONDO system in order to pipeline the operators of the relational algebra.

The **windowintersects** operator only performs the steps (1) and (2) of the query processing scheme for retrieving the tuples given the approximation in the index. Step

(3) of performing the query predicate on the candidate tuples must be executed later. The following query example counts the MBRs that intersect the MBR of the Mehringdamm Station (object *mehringdamm*):

```
query trains_Trip Trains
    windowintersects[ bbox(mehringdamm) ]
    count;
```

If we want to retrieve the objects that really pass the Mehringdamm Station, the predicate filter needs to be added after the index query.

```
query trains_Trip Trains
    windowintersects[ bbox(mehringdamm) ]
    filter[ .Trip passes mehringdamm ]
    count;
```

This query completely represents all steps (1), (2), and (3) of traditional query processing scheme stated in the beginning of this sub-section.

3.2 Operators for Multiple Entry Indexing

To support multiple entries in the index we must get rid of the relation argument in the **creatertree** operator and allow a stream of tuples as input. This stream of tuples must contain one and only one attribute of type $\underline{tid}$, which stores tuple identifiers.

$$stream(\underline{tuple}([X, id : \underline{tid}])) \times attrname$$
$$\rightarrow \underline{rtree}(\underline{tuple}(X) \; attrtype \; Std) \qquad \textbf{creatertree}$$

The type of this R-Tree created is the same as the one created in Section 3.1 (*Std*). The following command creates the same R-Tree as in the previous example.

```
let trains_Trip =
    Trains feed addid creatertree[Trip];
```

Here we make use of the **feed** and **addid** operators. **feed** converts a relation into a stream of tuples and **addid** extends the tuple with its tuple identifier, an internal number that uniquely identifies a tuple in the relation.

With this new way of creating an R-tree index we have much more flexibility. The following example creates an index only for those objects that pass the Mehringdamm Station, which is not possible to be done with the traditional R-Tree creation operator.

```
let trains_Trip =
    Trains feed addid
    filter[ .Trip passes mehringdamm ]
    creatertree[Trip];
```

The following operator, called **windowintersectsS** ('S' comes from *stream*), allows us to query a multiple entry index without directly specifying the relation, from which

the tuples should be retrieved. The result is a stream of tuples containing only one attribute of $\underline{tid}$ type containing the tuple identifiers of the entries in the index that satisfy the query condition.

$$\underline{rtree}(\underline{tuple}(X) \; attrtype \; Std) \times \underline{rect}\langle dim \rangle$$
$$\rightarrow stream(\underline{tuple}([id : \underline{tid}])) \qquad \textbf{windowintersectsS}$$

In order to later retrieve the tuples from the corresponding relation, the **gettuples** operator is provided. This operator receives a stream of tuples containing an attribute of type $\underline{tid}$ with tuple identifiers and a relation, and retrieves the tuples from the argument relation appending their attributes (Y) to the end of the tuple received as argument (X). The attribute with the tuple identifiers is removed from the resulting tuple type. The result of this operator is still a stream of tuples.

$$stream(\underline{tuple}([X, id : \underline{tid}])) \times \underline{rel}(\underline{tuple}(Y))$$
$$\rightarrow stream(\underline{tuple}([X, Y])) \qquad \textbf{gettuples}$$

As an example, with this new query operator, to simply count the number of MBR intersections we have between the trips and the Mehringdamm Station, we do not need to load the tuples from the *Trains* relation as follows:

```
query trains_Trip
    windowintersectsS[ bbox(mehringdamm) ]
    count;
```

If we want to know the trips that really passed the Mehringdamm Station, the query is then

```
query trains_Trip windowintersectsS[bbox(mehringdamm)]
    Trains gettuples
    filter[ .Trip passes mehringdamm ]
    count;
```

However, this query does the same as the standard one. The power of this approach comes from the fact that we have more flexibility on indexing and retrieving tuples.

As an example of this flexibility we will now create an R-tree containing entries for every piece of movement of the trips in the *Trains* relation. One should note that now we (possibly) have multiple entries for the same tuple of the *Trains* relation in the index.

```
let trains_Trip_unit =
    Trains feed addid
    extendstream[Unit:  units(.Trip)]
    creatertree[Unit];
```

For this query, we make use of the operators **extendstream** and **units**. The **units** operator takes a moving object, a $\underline{mpoint}$ in this example, and returns a stream of temporal units, which are the linear pieces of the movement, in this case of type *upoint*. The operator **extendstream** combines the tuples coming from the outer stream with the ones coming from the inner stream. With the combination of these two operators we expand the units inside the temporal data type, indexing them into the resulting R-tree.

Now, the query to find the trips that passed the Mehringdamm Station is

```
query trains_Trip_unit
  windowintersectsS[ bbox(mehringdamm) ]
  sort rdup
  Trains gettuples
  filter[ .Trip passes Mehringdamm ]
  count;
```

Note that we added a duplicate removal after the index query (step (2) in the new query processing scheme below), with the usage of the **sort** and **rdup** operators, to eliminate possible duplicate results for the same tuple. The query processing scheme can now be stated as

1. Send the query condition to the index and receive some result candidates

2. Remove duplicates

3. Retrieve the tuples pointed to by the candidates from their respective relations

4. Apply the query condition to these tuples and return the result (this step is needed if the index search cannot decide the predicate, as in filter and refine techniques).

3.3 Operators for Double Indexing

In the last sub-section, we showed how to change the traditional query processing with the help of an index to allow multiple entries in the index. However, there is still place for optimization, because we still need to retrieve the entire tuples in order to perform the last query condition check.

It would be perfect if we could load only the parts of the tuples that conform with the query condition in the index retrieval. This is done with our last approach called double indexing. With double indexing, we are not only able to store multiple entries in the index but also to store an interval for every entry in order to, when retrieving the tuples, restrict the object loading only to the components that are of interest for the query, i.e. to retrieve only the components that satisfy the query predicate in the index retrieval.

In order to achieve this, the **creatertree** operator is again modified to receive the *low* and *high* attributes in the stream of tuples, which represent the interval.

$$stream(\underline{tuple}([X, id : \underline{tid}, low : \underline{int}, high : \underline{int}])) \times attrname$$
$$\rightarrow \underline{rtree}(\underline{tuple}(X) \ attrtype \ Dbl) \qquad \textbf{creatertree}$$

One should note that the R-Tree index description is now different, i.e. of type *Dbl* (from double).

Following our examples using the Berlin data set, we can create an R-tree index with one entry for every piece of movement of the trips in the *Trains* relation.

```
let trains_Trip_unit =
  Trains feed addid
  filter[seqinit(0)]
  extendstream[Unit:  units(.Trip)]
  extend[Box:  bbox(.Unit), Low:  seqnext()]
  extend[High:  .Low]
  project[Box, TID, Low, High]

  creatertree[Box];
```

In this first index, the values of *high* and *low* are always the same, informing to the index that there is only one entry indexed by this value in the trip. The operator **seqinit** initializes a counter to its argument's value and return 'TRUE', while the operator **seqnext** returns the counter's current value and post-increment it.

The same **windowintersectsS** operator as for multiple indexing is available, but it returns not only the tuple identifier, but also the *low* and *high* values for every entry in the candidate result.

$$\underline{rtree}(\underline{tuple}(X) \ attrtype \ Dbl) \times \underline{rect} < dim >$$
$$\rightarrow stream(\underline{tuple}([id : \underline{tid}, low : \underline{int}, high : \underline{int}]))$$
$$\textbf{windowintersectsS}$$

To later retrieve the tuples, a new version of the **gettuples** operator is provided, called **gettuplesdbl**. This operator expects a tuple in the format that is returned from the latter operator, but it also expects that the tuples are sorted by *tid*, *low*, and *high* in ascending order.

The operator combines all intervals of the same tuple identifier into an interval set. Then it retrieves the tuple corresponding to the tuple identifier, restricting the reading of the attribute named by the operator's third argument to only those components given by this interval set.

$$stream(\underline{tuple}([X, id : \underline{tid}, low : \underline{int}, high : \underline{int}]))$$
$$\times \underline{rel}(\underline{tuple}(Y)) \times attrname$$
$$\rightarrow stream(\underline{tuple}([X, Y])) \qquad \textbf{gettuplesdbl}$$

The query that counts the number of objects that pass through the Mehringdamm Station is now

```
query trains_Trip_unit
  windowintersectsS[ bbox(mehringdamm) ] sort
  Trains gettuplesdbl[Trip]

  filter[ .Trip passes Mehringdamm ] count;
```

The tuples retrieved by the **gettuplesdbl** are restricted to the components that satisfy the query predicate in the index. This approach improves the performance of the query processing in two ways. First, it allows one to retrieve only parts of the object, which means it reduces the number of disk accesses. Second, as far as the object passed to the last filtering condition is (possibly) reduced, the filtering condition step can also be performed faster, which means less CPU time.

The query processing scheme of the last two sub-sections can now be stated as

1. Send the query condition to the index and receive some result candidates

2. Sort the entries on the candidate set by *id*, *low*, and *high* attributes

3. Retrieve the tuples pointed to by the candidates from their respective relations, restricting the query attribute to only those parts in the intervals represented by the *low* and *high* values.

4. Apply the query condition to these tuples and return the result (this step is needed if the index search cannot decide the predicate, as in filter and refine techniques).

4 Experimental Evaluation

In this section we aim to show the advantages of both multiple entry and double indexing approaches. We use two data sets for this purpose:

- **TrainsL.** We translated the Berlin database explained in Section 3 five times in all directions: x, y, and *time*. We then have a database that is 125 times larger than the Berlin database. The translated *Trains* relation we call *TrainsL*, where 'L' comes from *large*. This relation contains a relatively large number of tuples with moving objects (*TripL* attribute) of small trajectories, consequently of small size.

- **U1lin.** This data set is similar to *Trains* relation in the Berlin data set explained in Section 3. The *U1lin* relation contains only one train line (*U1*) with 13 trains performing 11 two-way trips per day for 6 months. The trains with even identifiers stop on weekends and the ones with odd identifiers run on weekends as they do on weekdays. This relation contains a small number of tuples with moving objects (*TripL* attribute) with large trajectories.

Some statistics about both data sets are provided in the Table 2.

For creating the indexes we have the following variables:

- **dimensionality**: spatial (dS), temporal (dT), or spatio-temporal (dST)

Table 2. Statistics about the data sets.

	TrainsL	U1lin
Size in MBytes	673.80	429.56
# of tuples	70,250	13
Avg. # of units per tuple	82,025	309,355
Avg # of pages per tuple	3	8594

- **entry type**: one entry per object (eO), one entry per temporal unit (eU)

- **index type**: standard (iS) and double index (iD)

As an example, the temporal double index with one entry per unit for the relation *TrainsL* is called *trainsl_dT_eU_iD*. We simply call *trainsl* the approach that sequentially scans the whole relation directly applying the query predicates, bypassing the index filtering step.

4.1 Temporal queries

For temporal queries we used the **atinstant** operator receiving a moving point (*mpoint*) and an instant i as arguments. This operator restricts the movement to the position at time instant i. We performed the following query with five different values of i: the first instant of the data set, the last instant, the first and third quartiles, and the middle instant.

The query in SQL-like format is written below. We use a SQL-like format to write the query to avoid presenting all queries for all approaches in the SECONDO executable format.

```
select val(trip atinstant i) as pos
  from trainsl
  where trip present i;
```

We added the predicate with the operator **present** in the *where* clause in order to use the index in the query. The **present** is the corresponding predicate to the **atinstant** operator.

Tables 3 and 4 present the results of the temporal query for the various approaches in terms of number of disk accesses for the *U1lin* and *TrainsL* data sets, respectively. Both **present** and **atinstant** operators perform a binary search in the movement. In the *U1lin* data set, since we have 8,594 pages per tuple in average we could expect to have 13 reads per tuple, which is $\log_2(8594)$, which gives us 169 reads for the query without using an index. We achieve numbers similar to this analytical expectation.

When using standard indexing approaches, only for the queries with lower selectives, the number of disk accesses is reduced. For the times in the middle of the data set, all tuples return in the query. However, with double indexing, we could reduce considerably the number of disk accesses also for the non-selective queries, given the fact that the selectivity inside the complex object is high, which means that the size of the returned object is considerably smaller than the original one.

Table 3. Performance of the temporal queries for the U1lin data set.

Selectivity (# of tuples)	1	13	13	13	1
	Disk accesses				
u1lin	173	173	167	168	180
u1lin_dT_eO_iS	13	174	168	169	14
u1lin_dT_eU_iS	19	179	175	187	20
u1lin_dT_eU_iD	7	19	21	33	7

For the *TrainsL* data set we have a higher selectivity even for the query time instants in the middle of the data set. In this case, even the traditional indexing approach reduces considerably the number of disk accesses. With the double indexing approach we could reduce the number of disk access by a factor close to 2.

Table 4. Performance of the temporal queries for the TrainsL data set.

Selectivity (# of tuples)	100	2.250	2.400	2.400	50
	Disk accesses				
trainsl	106.787	118.232	131.333	144.286	155.978
trainsl_dT_eO_iS	108	4.237	4.646	4.593	154
trainsl_dT_eU_iS	110	4.246	4.644	4.598	156
trainsl_dT_eU_iD	110	2.412	2.568	2.566	57

4.2 Spatial queries

For spatial queries we used the **at** operator receiving a moving point and a point p as argument. We performed the following query with different values of p, which correspond to some positions at the five values of i chosen in the last sub-section.

```
select val(trip at p) as pos
  from trains
  where trip passes p;
```

As done before, we added the **passes** operator in the *where* clause, since it is the corresponding predicate for the **at** operator.

Tables 5 and 6 present the results of the spatial query for the various approaches in terms of number of disk accesses for the *U1lin* and *TrainsL* data sets, respectively.

Table 5. Performance of the spatial queries for the U1lin data set.

Selectivity (# of tuples)	13	13	13	13	13
	Disk accesses				
u1lin	110.466	110.466	110.466	110.466	110.466
u1lin_dS_eO_iS	110.467	110.467	110.467	110.467	110.467
u1lin_dS_eU_iS	111.803	111.803	114.281	111.803	111.803
u1lin_dS_eU_iD	19.752	19.752	35.251	19.752	19.752

Table 6. Performance of the spatial queries for the TrainsL data set.

Selectivity (# of tuples)	505	290	290	290	400
	Disk accesses				
trainsl	203.192	203.192	203.192	203.192	203.192
trainsl_dS_eO_iS	4.682	3.176	3.176	3.176	2.008
trainsl_dS_eU_iS	2.073	1.171	1.171	1.171	2.008
trainsl_dS_eU_iD	685	312	312	310	428

For the *U1lin* data set, all queries are non-selective and standard indexing techniques cannot improve the performance of the queries, just adding extra overhead in the query processing. This non-selectivity occurs because all the trains pass through the Mehringdamm Station lots of times during their journeys. The double index approach could reduce the number of disk accesses by a factor of 5, because only a portion of the movement must be read from disk.

For the *TrainsL* data set, the query is selective and the index approaches give a good improvement. But even in these cases, the double indexing is still perform at least 3 or 4 times better.

4.3 Spatio-temporal queries

For spatio-temporal queries we combine a spatial and a temporal predicate. Internally, a spatio-temporal index is used under such combination. We performed the following query with different values of p and i, corresponding to the ones from the two last sub-sections.

```
select val(trip atinstant i) as pos
  from trains
  where (val(trip atinstant i) = p)
```

Tables 7 and 8 present the results of the spatio-temporal query for the various approaches in terms of number of disk accesses for the *U1lin* and *TrainsL* data sets, respectively.

For these queries performed in the *U1lin* data set, their selectivity in terms of number of tuples returned is the same

Table 7. Performance of the spatio-temporal queries for the U1lin data set.

Selectivity (# of tuples)	1	13	13	13	1
	Disk accesses				
u1lin	173	185	205	181	181
u1lin_dST_eO_iS	13	187	206	182	15
u1lin_dST_eU_iS	19	198	146	114	21
u1lin_dST_eU_iD	9	26	112	20	9

as for the temporal queries and their selectivity in terms of the size of the moving objects' trajectories is similar. Therefore, these results are quite similar to the ones achieved for the temporal queries.

Table 8. Performance of the spatio-temporal queries for the TrainsL data set.

Selectivity (# of tuples)	1	10	12	12	2
	Disk accesses				
trainsl	106885	122051	135199	148258	156076
trainsl_dST_eO_iS	9	157	162	177	13
trainsl_dST_eU_iS	9	11	11	12	13
trainsl_dST_eU_iD	9	9	9	9	9

Given the high selectivity of these queries in the *TrainsL* data set, the standard index approaches are enough, reducing considerably the number of disk accesses. However, the double indexing approach still gives an improvement in performance of 20% in some cases.

It is important to note that the double indexing approach was never worse than the standard indexing approaches.

5   Conclusions

In this paper, we aimed to show the need for the multiple entry and the double indexing approaches. The operators in SECONDO that allow one to create and query such indexes are presented. Following the presentation of the operators, examples on how to use them are also provided. Finally, an experimental evaluation of the proposed approaches is done in order to show their improvements in terms of efficiency with some spatial, temporal, and spatio-temporal queries. The double indexing approach showed the best overall performance in this comparison. Moreover, in our experiments the double indexing approach was never worse than any of the other ones.

As future work, we plan to provide optimization rules that take into consideration not only the selectivity in terms

of the number of tuples, but also the selectivity in terms of the tuple size. These rules would enable the optimizer to better decide when to use the multiple entry and the double indexes present in the database.

References

[1] N. Beckmann, H. P. Kriegel, R. Schneider, and B. Seeger. The R*-tree: An efficient and robust access method for points and rectangles. In *Proc. of the ACM SIGMOD Intl. Conf. on Management of Data*, pages 322–331, 1990.

[2] T. Behr and R. H. Güting. Fuzzy spatial objects: An algebra implementation in SECONDO. In *Proc. of the 21st Intl. Conf. on Data Engineering (ICDE)*, pages 1137–1139, 2005.

[3] D. Comer. The ubiquitous B-tree. *ACM Comput. Surv.*, 11(2):121–137, 1979.

[4] V. T. de Almeida, R. H. Güting, and T. Behr. Querying moving objects in SECONDO. In *Proc. of the 7th. Intl. Conf. on Mobile Data Management (MDM)*, page 47, 2006.

[5] S. Dieker and R. H. Güting. Plug and play with query algebras: SECONDO – a generic DBMS development environment. In *Proc. of the Intl. Database Engineering and Applications Symposium (IDEAS)*, pages 380–392, 2000.

[6] S. Dieker, R. H. Güting, and M. R. Luaces. A tool for nesting and clustering large objects. In *Proc. of the 12th Intl. Conf. on Scientific and Statistical Database Management (SSDBM)*, pages 169–181, 2000.

[7] R. H. Güting, T. Behr, V. T. Almeida, Z. Ding, F. Hoffmann, and M. Spiekermann. SECONDO: An extensible DBMS architecture and prototype. Technical Report 313, Fernuniversität Hagen, Fachbereich Informatik, 2004.

[8] R. H. Güting, V. T. de Almeida, D. Ansorge, T. Behr, Z. Ding, T. Höse, F. Hoffmann, M. Spiekermann, and U. Telle. SECONDO: An extensible DBMS platform for research prototyping and teaching. In *Proc. of the 21st Intl. Conf. on Data Engineering (ICDE)*, pages 1115–1116, 2005.

[9] A. Guttman. R-trees: A dynamic index structure for spatial searching. In *Proc. of ACM SIGMOD Intl. Conf. on Management of Data*, pages 47–57, 1984.

[10] M. Hadjieleftheriou, G. Kollios, V. J. Tsotras, and D. Gunopulos. Indexing spatiotemporal archives. *VLDB Journal*, 15(2):143–164, 2006.

[11] S. Rasetic, J. Sander, J. Elding, and M. A. Nascimento. A trajectory splitting model for efficient spatio-temporal indexing. In *Proc. of 26th Intl. Conf. on Very Large Data Bases (VLDB)*, pages 934–945, 2005.

[12] T. K. Sellis, N. Roussopoulos, and C. Faloutsos. The r+-tree: A dynamic index for multi-dimensional objects. In *VLDB'87, Proceedings of 13th Intl. Conf. on Very Large Data Bases, September 1-4, 1987, Brighton, England*, pages 507–518, 1987.

[13] P. Seshadri and A. N. Swami. Generalized partial indexes. In *Proc. of the IEEE International Conference on Data Engineering (ICDE)*, pages 420–427, 1995.

[14] M. Stonebraker. The case for partial indexes. *SIGMOD Record*, 18(4):4–11, 1989.

On the Use of Semantic Blocking Techniques for Data Cleansing and Integration

Jordi Nin[1], Victor Muntés-Mulero[2], Norbert Martínez-Bazan[2], Josep-L. Larriba-Pey[2]

[1]IIIA, Artificial Intelligence Research Institute
CSIC, Spanish National Research Council
Campus UAB s/n 08193
Bellaterra, Catalonia, Spain
Email: jnin@iiia.csic.es

[2]DAMA-UPC
Computer Arch. Dept. Campus Nord. UPC
C/Jordi Girona, 1-3. Módul D6. 08034 Barcelona
Email: {vmuntes, nmartine, larri}@ac.upc.edu
http://www.dama.upc.edu

Abstract—Record Linkage (RL) is an important component of data cleansing and integration. For years, many efforts have focused on improving the performance of the RL process, either by reducing the number of record comparisons or by reducing the number of attribute comparisons, which reduces the computational time, but very often decreases the quality of the results. However, the real bottleneck of RL is the post-process, where the results have to be reviewed by experts that decide which pairs or groups of records are real links and which are false hits.

In this paper, we show that exploiting the relationships (*e.g.* foreign key) established between one or more data sources, makes it possible to find a new sort of semantic blocking method that improves the number of hits and reduces the amount of review effort.

Keywords: Semantic information, blocking algorithms, record linkage, data integration, data cleansing.

I. INTRODUCTION

The amount of information stored about individuals has increased dramatically in the recent years [17]. The ubiquitous presence of computers causes this information to be distributed and represented in a large amount of heterogeneous ways. Resolving the different instances of one entity among different heterogeneous data sources is, thus, a requirement in many cases.

As a consequence, the importance of tools and techniques that contribute to the process of data cleansing and data integration [20] has increased in the recent years. Among these, *Record Linkage* (RL) has gained relevance. The purpose of RL is to either identify and link different record instances of one entity that are distributed across several data sources, or to identify records from a single data source with similar information.

In practice, since the size of the source files is usually very large, comparing all the records among them becomes unfeasible. Therefore, RL resorts to blocking methods that are meant to gather all the records that present a potential resemblance, only allowing comparisons between records within each block. Typically, the traditional blocking methods for RL, like standard blocking [9] or sorted neighborhood [8] are based on the syntactic information of each record.

However, the quality of the results provided by these methods is very dependant on the data chosen to classify records in blocks and the quality of this data. A solution to this problem is to relax the creation of a block, by building larger blocks that allow for the comparison of a larger number of records. However, this has three clear drawbacks: (i) the number of unnecessary comparisons increases, (ii) the probability of RL to relate records belonging to different entities also increases and (iii), the review effort of the results grows and becomes a problem.

In this paper, we propose a new blocking method that builds groups of records based on the relationship among them in the data sources, as opposed to the use of the syntactic information of its attributes, as in other classic methods. In order to find the relationship of a record with other records, we build a collaborative graph [12] that contains all the entities that are related to the record under analysis up to a certain degree, using, for instance, foreign key relationships. The records included in the graph are the building units of each block and we link them using regular record comparison strategies. With the results presented in this paper, we show that, for environments where the connectivity between entities is low, our blocking method can clearly improve the quality of the results by significantly reducing the number of false hits while maintaining and, in the best cases, improving the number of returned real hits.

The structure of the paper is as follows. In Section II we introduce the basics of RL and standard blocking methods. Then, in Section III we present our approach based on semantic blocking. Section IV describes the experiments. The paper finishes with the description of some preliminary work, some conclusions and a description of future work.

II. RECORD LINKAGE: PRELIMINARIES

Record Linkage processes a set of files obtaining a list of record groups that can be considered similar. For our work, we consider that the RL process is formed by different phases, as shown in Figure 1. To start the process, data sources are cleaned or pre-processed in such a way that the attributes in the record files are normalized individually to allow a simpler comparison with other data in the following steps [3].

1098-8068/07 $25.00 © 2007 IEEE

190

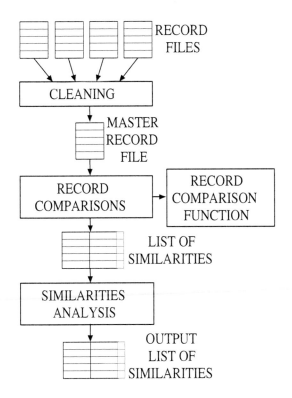

Fig. 1.   Record Linkage processing model.

Once the pre-processing is done, we proceed with the RL analysis. There are two kinds of RL algorithms for record comparison. The first type is based on probabilistic methods and the second type is based on distance functions [19], [20]. During the record linkage process, the records are compared following a strategy that may have several objectives, like reducing the number of comparisons as with the Standard Blocking or Sorted Neighborhood methods, or finding the largest groups of similar records with the lowest comparison cost as in RAR [18]. Usually, the proposed blocking techniques build the blocks using the information obtained from the values in one or more attributes (syntactic information).

In order to avoid possible errors induced by the blocking methods, it is usual to perform several passes using different criteria. In any of those cases, a record comparison function is used, which returns a similarity weight W between pairs or groups of records.

After the RL process delivers the result, it is necessary to analyze the similarities. This last step usually requires the human intervention by means of expert individuals. If the number of pairs produced by RL is large, the time necessary to allow human experts to review all the pairs may be really significant leading also to extra unnecessary review errors.

In order to obtain a good result from the RL process, it is necessary to obtain the maximum number of real groups in the result, but it is also necessary to minimize the number of false positives, so that the manual process is also minimized.

The phase where records are compared is the most expensive in the RL computational process, with a quadratic complexity ($O(N^2)$) in the number of records N, as opposed to the linear complexity of the other phases. However, the analysis of similarities may be even more costly in time and budget because there may be different human reviewers involved in it during a considerable amount of time.

Blocking methods

In this subsection, we describe the most frequently used blocking methods: *Standard Blocking* (SB) and *Sorted Neighborhood* (SN). We explain the basics of these two classical methods and describe their main drawbacks.

1) Standard Blocking: The Standard Blocking method (SB) groups records that share the same *Blocking Key* (BK) [9]. An exhaustive comparison of all the records among them is performed within each group.

A BK is defined based on information extracted from one or more attributes. Usually, a BK can be either a common categorical attribute, *e.g. marital status* {single, married, divorced or widowed}, or a common numerical attribute, *e.g. age*. When files do not have common categorical or numerical attributes, a BK can be also a part of a string attribute, *e.g.* the first four characters of a *surname* attribute. The cost-benefit trade-off of the BK selection is studied in [19].

Note that using SB the size of the blocks is not constant. Therefore, in some situations the final blocks may contain a large number of records, in which case, the amount of work will not be reduced much from the comparison of all the records without using blocks, but the possibility to match really similar records will grow. However, the amount of false positives will most probably be large.

2) Sorted Neighborhood: The Sorted Neighborhood (SN) method [8] sorts the records based on a sorting key (SK) and then moves a so called Sliding Window (SW) of fixed size l sequentially over the sorted records. At every step, the oldest record is removed from the window and a new record is inserted, which is compared to all the records in the window.

An important problem with SN arises if a certain number of records, larger than the window size, have the same value in a SK. For instance, let us suppose that we are using SN with two similar files based on a SK extracted from an attribute 'surname'. Typically, if the data sources are large enough, there will be thousands of records containing the value 'Williams' or 'Smith' in that attribute and, therefore, not all the records with the same value in a SK will be compared.

Another problem with SN occurs when there is a significant error rate where the differences among data may cause the sorting algorithm to separate the values enough to avoid their comparison.

III. SEMANTIC BLOCKING FOR RL

We propose a new family of blocking algorithms that substitute the blocking or sorting key used by typical blocking methods by another type of block building method based on the *context*. This method is not based on the values of one or more attributes of the records but on the relationship established between the records in the source files. We refer to this relationship as *context or semantic information*. As stated by the *Context Attraction Principle* presented in [10], the basic idea is that two occurrences that could belong to the same individual are more likely to refer to a single individual if they are closely related, in the context established by their relations with other entities in the data set.

The method used to relate the entities of a database will vary depending on the data sources. For example, if we have a relational database as data source, we are able to obtain some context information from the foreign keys of the database, which is the case studied in this paper. If we have a plain text file as a data source, we can relate the entities based on the relationships between all the records that contain values with the same contextual meaning in one or more textual attributes. Or even, if we turn to graph databases [7] [11] [16], we can use the edges between entities to infer similarities between the text items in the nodes.

This approach is very useful in databases that contain a lot of information about the relationship of an individual with the rest of the database, specially when the connectivity between entities is not very high, as we will show below. There are several examples of databases that have this kind of information. Bibliographic databases like Citeseer [5] or social network databases that proliferate in the web nowadays are examples of data sources that contain a large quantity of information about the relationship between entities.

The Semantic Blocking that we propose allows to avoid the problems caused by spelling errors in the classic blocking approaches described above, by only allowing comparisons between records that have a relationship among them. This reduces the chances to gather in the same block records that are similar but do not have any relation.

A. Semantic Graph Blocking

The Semantic Graph Blocking (SGB) proposed in this paper is based on the capabilities that collaborative graphs offer in order to extract the information about the relationship between the records in the source files. Collaborative Graphs are a common method for representing the relationships among a set of entities [12]. Nodes represent the entities and edges capture the relationships between entities.

The main idea of our approach is to build up a graph, exploring the relationships of the entity that we want to deduplicate or merge. We denote our graph as $G = (V, E)$, where V is the set of nodes and E is the set of edges. Each element in V represents an entity and each element in E represents a relationship established between two entities, e.g., the information inferred from the foreign keys in the database.

In order to build the graph, we create a first node $v_0 \in V$ that represents the current record to be compared to other records to find pairs corresponding to the same entity. Following we create a new node v_i for every record that is directly related to the first one. From this first level of nodes, we explode their relationships again, adding all those records

that did not previously exist in the graph. This process is repeated until there are no more nodes to explode. However, since theoretically all the nodes could be connected and, therefore, all the records would be included in the same block, we reinforce the stop condition either by predefining the maximum depth of the graph or by specifying a maximum number of nodes.

Once the block is created, we use regular record and attribute comparison functions to detect similarities between records, comparing all the records in a block between them. Note that, with our technique, we only need to execute this process once. More passes would be unnecessary because SGB does not depend on possible misspelling in the data.

Figure 2 shows a small graph built from a toy database containing three relations in a star schema [4]. Relation *AUTHORS* is a table containing a set of authors. For each author, the relation contains an identifier, the name and other attributes that are not important for this example. Relation *PAPERS* is a table that contains a set of publications. Analogously to *AUTHORS*, each paper has an associated identifier. Finally, the table *WRITES* relates the authors to all those papers written by them. In this example, the purpose is to identify duplicated authors in the database. There are three possible authors that could be considered the same entity in a record linkage process based on the edit distance: *Smith, John*; *Smith, Jehn* and *Xmith, Jhon*. However, suppose that there are two real authors whose names are *Smith, John* and *Smith, Jean*.

In order to find the duplicated information, we start the record linkage process. For each author, a graph is created by following the relations established by the foreign key attributes in table *WRITES*. In Figure 2, we have limited the depth of such a graph to distance 2. Of course, the size of this graph is very small because of the size of this toy example. In a real system, a graph might contain hundreds of nodes. The four-nodes graph obtained by the first author in relation *AUTHORS*, *Smith, John*, is marked in a darker area. We can observe that the other three authors included in the graph are those with identifiers 4, 5 and 6 respectively. The remaining nodes are *too far* in this domain to be considered related to *Smith, John*. Once the block is created by obtaining the nodes included in the graph, we compare all the names in this block. In this case, the record linkage process would consider *Smith, John* and *Xmith, Jhon* to be the same entity, while *Smith, Jehn* would be discarded as a possible duplicated value of the same entity.

Note that, using a traditional record linkage process based on standard blocking or sorted neighborhood, we would not have any information that would help us to understand whether these three names refer to the same unique author. Thus, when they are sorted by name, *Smith, John* and *Smith, Jehn* would probably be considered to refer to the same author (and they are not). On the other hand, *Xmith, Jhon* would never be compared to the other two using SB or SN, since there is a mistake in the first character, which would most probably place the first two occurrences in a different block from that of this third occurrence.

RELATIONAL DATABASE

CONTEXT GRAPH

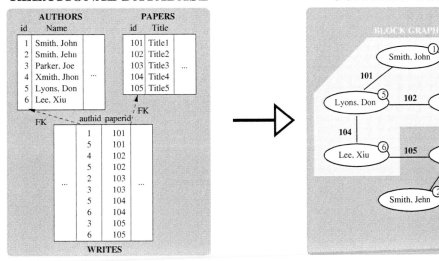

Fig. 2. Toy example of Semantic Blocking.

IV. EXPERIMENTS

In order to test our approach in a wide variety of scenarios, we have divided our experiments into two parts. First, we test the quality of our approach compared to other traditional approaches using a set of synthetically created databases. This experiment allows us to test different conditions such as the size of the data set or the degree of connectivity between entities. Second, we test our entity resolution technique using the Citeseer database [5], presenting a real scenario to run our new RL blocking technique.

All the experiments have been performed on a 64 bit Intel Core2 Duo, at 2.6 GHz, using 2 GB of RAM.

A. Metrics

For each experiment performed in this paper, we analyze the quality of the results using the typical quality measures: recall, precision and F-measure [15]. Precision is defined as:

$$precision = \frac{|\{real\ pairs\} \cap \{retrieved\ pairs\}|}{|\{retrieved\ pairs\}|} \quad (1)$$

Recall is defined as:

$$recall = \frac{|\{real\ pairs\} \cap \{retrieved\ pairs\}|}{|\{real\ pairs\}|} \quad (2)$$

Sometimes it is desirable to have one single number for the performance of an algorithm instead of two. In such cases, the F-measure is frequently used [14]. It can be parameterized to give a higher weight to either precision or recall. The neutral parametrization, where precision and recall are weighted equally, is used throughout this work. Thus, F is defined as the weighted harmonic mean of precision and recall:

$$F = \frac{2 \cdot precision \cdot recall}{precision + recall} \quad (3)$$

Name	Standard Blocking (SB)	Sorted Neighborhood (SN)	Semantic Graph Blocking (SGB)
Par1	substring(Full name,0,4)	l=200	S=200
Par2	substring(Full name,0,3)	l=500	S=500
Par3	substring(Full name,0,2)	l=1000	S=1000

TABLE I

DIFFERENT PARAMETERIZATIONS FOR BLOCKING (SB), SORTED NEIGHBORHOOD (SN) AND SEMANTIC GRAPH BLOCKING (SGB).

B. Parameterizations of the methods

We have tested the three blocking methods using three different parameterizations for each one. We show the parameterizations in Table I. We consider small, medium and large blocks. The second column in the table shows the three different BK selected for each parametrization. As we can observe, the BK in the first parametrization is expressed as $substring(Full\ name, 0, 4)$ meaning a substring containing four consecutive characters of attribute *Full name* starting at string position 0. The other two parameterizations correspond to those strings containing the first three and the first two characters, respectively. In the third column of the same table, we show parameter l that defines the window size in the SN blocking. The fourth column defines the values selected for S, that defines the maximum size in terms of nodes of the collaborative graph.

We use two different thresholds to accept the similarity of a pair of records using their edit distance [13]:

- **Strict RL:** we force RL to classify as a hit only those pairs of records that differ less than 25% in their full name, i.e., it is necessary to change less than 25% of the characters of one of the strings in the pair to let it be equal than the other string in the pair.
- **Weak RL:** we force RL to classify as a hit all the pairs

of records that differ less than 50% in their full name.

The reason for using different thresholds for RL is that we want to see the influence of such parameter on the quality of the result and, therefore, on the reviewing effort, for the different methods.

C. Synthetic Data Experiments

First, we will test our blocking technique through a variety of bibliographic data sets generated synthetically. The synthetic data sets contain information about authors and papers, and the relationship between them, following the schema used in the toy example of Figure 2. This will allow us to understand the effects of our technique when different properties in the data set are modified. We test the different blocking approaches for data sets of different sizes. Specifically, we have generated data sets containing 10000, 100000 and 250000 authors. For each of these sizes, we try different author duplicate percentages, namely 50%, 20% and 5% of authors are duplicated in each case. The number of erroneous characters for each case is calculated using a normal distribution $N(2, 1)$ with mean $\mu = 2$ and standard deviation $\sigma = 1$. The number of duplicates per each original duplicated entity is distributed following a $N(3, 1)$ distribution. We control the degree of connectivity by changing the average number of papers per author. Specifically, we build data sets were the number of papers per author is distributed as $N(2, 1)$ for a first set of experiments and $N(20, 1)$ for a second set of experiments. The number of authors per paper is normally distributed following a distribution $N(3, 1)$. The distance between an original entity and its duplicates follows a normal distribution $N(3, 1)$.

In order to create a realistic scenario, we have used names and surnames extracted from a frequency dictionary containing 1564 names and 13068 surnames.

Following, we analyze the effect of varying the different factors studied on the three measures used to evaluate the blocking methods, namely recall, precision and F-measure.

1) Effect of the data set size: Figure 3 shows the effect of the variations of the data set size on the different quality measures. The figure is divided into two rows of plots. The upper row shows the results when applying the strict RL, while the lower plot shows the results for the weak RL. The leftmost plot in the upper row shows the effect of the size of the data set on the recall for the three methods and the three parameterizations for each method. First of all, we can observe that the average recall of SGB is higher than that using other blocking methods, independently of the size. In addition, as the size of the data set increases, SN tends to decrease in terms of recall. This is because, the size of the window is fixed and the number of elements with the same value for a certain attribute increases. These two effects reduce the chances to find different instances of the same entity in a certain window. For SB, increasing the size of the data set does not have a radical effect since all the instances within a block are compared among them. Note that although the recall is not affected, the size of the blocks will increase significantly. On the other hand, using SGB, even keeping the size of the block, the recall is kept similar. Note that the fact that new authors (different entities that can have small edit distances with existing authors in the data set) are introduced into the database will not prevent the SGB blocking algorithms to find the closest relations in the graph. Also note that we are not increasing the connectivity of the existing entities, but just adding new entities and preserving the average degree of connectivity. The effect of altering the connectivity is studied later in this section. The leftmost plot in the lower row shows the same results for weak RL. As expected, we can observe that the recall slightly increases, since we accept a larger number of pairs. Of course, this will have a negative effect on the precision, as we will see later on.

If we focus on the two plots in the middle, we observe the effect of the size on the precision. We can clearly see that, while precision using SB and SN is clearly reduced when the size of the data set increases, it is kept constant for SGB. Again, having a larger number of authors but keeping the average degree of connectivity between them does not prevent SGB from finding the same relationships as with a smaller data set. Therefore, precision and recall are preserved. For weak RL the differences are even more noticeable. Strings in SB or SN are compared because they are relatively close in terms of the blocking key or the sliding window, while for SGB they are compared because they are related somehow in the data, even though they are completely different. Therefore, relaxing the record linkage acceptance condition will have a big impact for SB and SN, accepting a clearly larger set of pairs, and naturally reducing precision. On the other hand, it will not affect so clearly SGB since the strings to be compared in this case are in general clearly different and are not accepted as pairs even using weak RL.

In general, the differences between the three methods are summarized by the F-measure, shown in the rightmost plots in the figure. Again we can see that an increase in the size of the data set does not affect significantly our technique, while it degrades the quality of the results obtained by SB and SN. As we have seen previously, this effect is more marked when we relax the restrictions to accept a pair as valid.

2) Effect of the percentage of duplicated entities in the data set: Next, we study the effect that the portion of entities with duplicated entries has on recall, precision and the F-measure for the three studied techniques. Our experiments show that the portion of entities having duplicates does not have a significant effect on the quality of the results obtained. Figure 4 shows the average F-measures for different percentages of duplicated entities for strict RL. As we can observe, there is not a clear trend in the quality indicator. Other experiments not plotted in this figure show that we can extract the same conclusions by observing recall and precision separately for both the strict and the weak RL.

3) Effect of the connectivity of the entities in the data set: Finally, in Figure 5 we study the effect of the average connectivity of an author on recall, precision and the F-measure. As we explained in the experiments setup, we study two different situations. In the first case, we assume that the

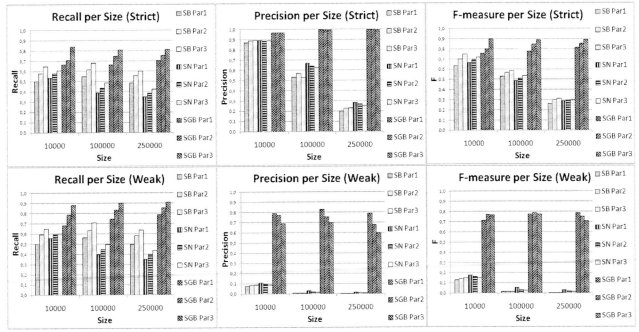

Fig. 3. Effect of the data set size on the recall, precision and F-measure.

distribution of the number of papers per author is centered in 2, while in the second case it is centered in 20. Note that the average number of papers per author in a real database like Citeseer is 2.76, therefore, the first scenario is an example closer to the reality and the second scenario aims at simulating an unrealistic highly connected scenario to extend our study.

In the two leftmost plots in Figure 5, we can observe the effect of the connectivity between entities in the graph on the recall. Both for strict RL and weak RL, we can see that the recall is clearly better when the connectivity between authors is not very high, i.e., when the number of papers per author is reduced. On the other hand, when we increase the connectivity, in this case by increasing the average number of papers per author, the recall for SGB is reduced and

cannot be considered significantly better than that for SB or SN. Since in a bibliographic database two duplicates of an entity would never be connected directly, because they cannot coauthor a paper together, if the connectivity is high, a large part of the blocking graph, which has a limited size, will consist of all those entities directly connected to the explored entity, therefore reducing the probabilities of SGB finding real matches.

However, the precision is not affected as clearly as the recall. The two plots in the middle show us that SGB achieve better precision than the other two methods both when the connectivity is low and high. The F-measure in the rightmost plots, show that combining recall and precision, SGB would still be the blocking method of choice.

Note that, in our work, we are focused on a bibliographic database-like scenario. In other words, we are assuming an scenario were the entities in the graph are not highly connected. In other situations where the connectivity between the entities in the graph would be higher, SBG would not be suitable. We have tested an unrealistic scenario where we had 10000 authors and each paper had an average of 1000 authors to simulate a highly connected environment. In this situation, the number of authors directly connected to the entity we are trying to deduplicate will be, in general, larger than the number of nodes included in the block graph and, therefore, SGB will be unable to find most of the real pairs, having a very low recall. Therefore, the technique we are presenting must be used in those scenarios were the connectivity is low.

D. Citeseer Experiments

Now, in order to test our approach in a real scenario, we have performed some experiments on the Citeseer database [5].

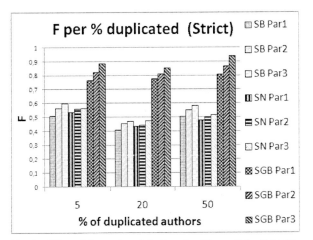

Fig. 4. Effect of the portion of duplicated entities on F for Strict RL.

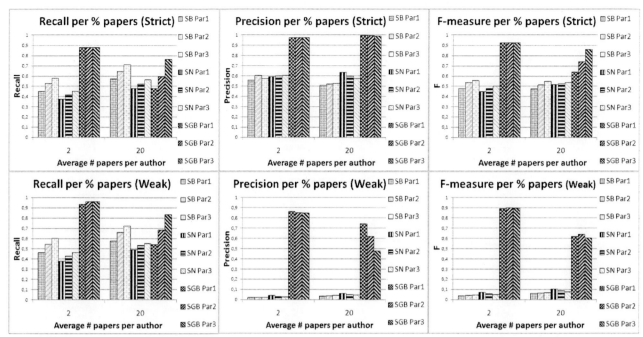

Fig. 5. Effect of the average number of duplicates author with duplicates on the recall, precision and F-measure.

Citeseer is one of the most used scientific databases with more than 1,6 Million scientific papers and more than 750,000 authors. We have only downloaded a part of all the attributes stored in Citeseer: the full name of the authors and the identifier of the papers. Table II shows a sample of the downloaded file. As we can see, our approach only needs two attributes to exploit the semantic information stored in the Citeseer database. We are able to construct a collaborative graph using the author full name as the node and the paper identifier as the relationship between two individuals (or records).

The Citeseer database presents a scenario where data are automatically extracted from a set of heterogeneous data sources presented in different formats. In this kind of scenarios, it is very difficult to preserve data consistency and, therefore, the probability of having mistakes in the integrated data set is very high. We can observe this in Table III, where we present all the occurrences of the ten full professors of the department of Computer Architecture at UPC, and the different names introduced in the database for each of them.

In order to compare the quality of the methods that we are working with, we focus exclusively on the names appearing in Table III. For each name we create a block and analyze the

quality of the results obtained for that block, namely the recall and the precision.

We observed that there are several occurrences of the same individual differing in more than 25%, *e.g.* J.M. Llaberia is the same author than Mara Llabera[1]. This allows to study two scenarios by using weak and strict RL.

Results: We have used recall and precision as the metrics to assess the methods evaluated. In addition, we take into consideration the absolute values of the number of pairs provided by the different methods in order to assess the real amounts both in terms of quality and in terms of review work needed by human experts.

Table IV shows the accumulated results for Citeseer of the experiments run for the full professors of the Computer Architecture Department at UPC shown in Table III. The real total number of duplicates for our data set is 38 and the recall (R) in Table IV is calculated based on this figure. Both the recall and the precision (P) are calculated as percentages and the strict and weak RL are separated into two groups of columns in the table.

We can observe two different trends in the figures of Table IV. First, weak RL improves the recall of SGB over strict RL. The reason is clear, the number of records with a small edit distance per block created with SGB is relatively reduced, and with high chances, if they are similar syntactically, they will most probably be the same, confirming what we observed in the synthetic experiments. Thus, relaxing the RL from strict

Full name	Paper identifier
Gabriele Scheler	1
Xianshu Kong	2
Hazel Everett	2
Godfried Toussaint	2
Helge Frauenkron	3
Peter Grassberger	3

TABLE II

SAMPLE OF THE FILE DOWNLOADED FROM CITESEER [5].

[1]The real name is *José María Llabería*. In the first case *José María* has been abbreviated to *J.M.* In the second case *José* has been removed possibly due to a parsing error and the fact that the vowels contain an stress sign (í), that has been omitted, generating a significantly different name (*Mara Llabera*)

Full Professor	Duplicated Records
Eduard Ayguade	E. Ayguade, E. Ayguad, Eduard Ayguad, Eduard Ayguad E
	Eduard Ayguad Parra*, Eduard Ayguade Parra*, Eduardo A. Parra
Jordi Domingo-Pascual	J. Domingo-pascual*, Jordi Domingo Pascual
Jordi Garcia	J. Garcia, Jorge Garca, J. Garcia-vidal*, Jorge Garcia-vidal*
Antonio Gonzalez	Antonio Gonz Alez*, Antonio Gonzlez, A. Gonzlez*, Antonio Gonzz*
Jesus Labarta	J. Labarta, Jess Labarta, Jes Us Labarta, Jesffs Labarta*, Jes Labarta*
J. M. Llaberia	Jos Mara Llabera, Jos M. Llabera, Mara Llabera*, J. M. Llabera
Manel Medina	Manuel Medina
Juan J. Navarro	J. J. Navarro, Juanjo Navarro*, Juan J. Navarroy*
Mateo Valero	Andmateo Valero, M. Valero, Larriba-pey Mateo Valero,
	Advisor Mateo Valero*, Mateo Valeroy
Miguel Valero Garcia	Miguel Valero-garc, Miguel Valero-garca, M. Valero-garca*

TABLE III

DUPLICATED RECORDS FOR FULL PROFESSORS OF THE COMPUTER ARCHITECTURE DEPT. OF UNIVERSITAT POLITÈCNICA DE CATALUNYA. *THESE AUTHORS ONLY APPEAR IN ONE DOCUMENT.

Method		Strict RL				Weak RL			
Type	Parame-trization	Pairs provided	True matches	R	P	Pairs provided	True matches	R	P
SB	Par1	18	12	31.6%	66.7 %	435	16	42.1%	3.7%
SB	Par2	22	17	44.7%	77.3 %	808	17	44.7%	2.1%
SB	Par3	22	17	44.7%	77.3 %	1669	21	55.3%	1.3%
SN	Par1	14	11	28.9%	78.6%	241	15	39.5%	6.2%
SN	Par2	15	12	31.6%	80.0%	393	16	42.1%	4.1%
SN	Par3	21	16	42.1%	76.2%	480	20	52.6%	4.2%
SGB	Par1	16	14	31.6%	87.5%	24	20	52.6%	83.3%
SGB	Par2	16	14	31.6%	87.5%	27	21	55.3%	77.8%
SGB	Par3	16	14	31.6%	87.5%	32	22	57.9%	68.8%

TABLE IV

ACCUMULATED RESULTS OF THE TWO METRICS FOR THE EXPERIMENTS PERFORMED.

to weak, we have more chances to catch similar records with a lower probability of finding false positives. Specifically, the number of false positives is very small, less than 33% with strict RL, which amounts to only 10 elements, a very insignificant effort for an expert human reviewer.

On the contrary, for SB and SN, the weak RL improves the recall, while it reduces the precision over strict RL significantly. Note in this case that the precision is reduced because the number of similar records found by the methods grows significantly to hundreds of pairs, at least, while the number of real similarities is still kept low. This larger number of false positives implies a large number of cases for the expert human reviewer, leading to a larger effort and number of possible human errors compared to strict RL.

If we compare the methods, we find that SGB is able to capture a larger number of true matches when relaxing the RL than SB and SN. Also, it can be compared in terms of recall to the other methods even for strict RL situations. This makes us think that semantic blocking (i.e. SGB) is better than SB and SN if there are such relationships present in the data set. Also, the review effort imposed by SGB is significantly smaller (two orders of magnitude in some cases) than the review effort imposed by SB and SN. This makes us state that SGB is significantly better than SB and SN because of the smaller chances to accept false positives, both in an automated review effort and in a manned review process. As an example of the benefits obtained by SGB, if an expert needs 10 seconds on average to decide whether a hit is real or false and we

are interested in obtaining as many real hits as possible, (i.e. we choose Par3 for the three methods using a Weak RL), the whole RL plus reviewing process would take around 4.6 hours using SB, 1.3 hours using SN and 5.33 minutes using hour approach. In addition, with our approach we would obtain a slightly larger amount of real hits than with the other two approaches. Note that the record linkage process using SGB takes less than a second to be executed.

Finally, the computational effort of using SGB might be similar to that imposed by SB or SN. The former requires the traversing of relationships by means of foreign keys in a database or a set of tables. The latter impose the sorting of the data set to create the blocks. Again, note that while we must typically perform several passes with SB or SN, only one pass is necessary when using SGB. Of course, this will finally depend on the size of the blocks created by each blocking technique. A detailed performance analysis and the implications on the precision and recall are out of the scope of this paper.

V. RELATED WORK

Among the large amount of work done in the area of Record Linkage, there is also a considerable effort in the use of graphs and relations to relate entities and disambiguate references. Apart from the references cited in the previous chapters which give a taste of the work done in the area of standard blocking for Record Linkage, in this section we give a short description of a few pieces of research that are related to the use of graphs or relationships for the disambiguation task.

Among the many different pieces of work in the area, we can distinguish Kalashnikov and Mehrotra's [10], who analyze the inter-object relationships to improve the quality of reference disambiguation. In some other work by Ananthakrishna et al. [1], the authors use the similarity of directly related links to solve record deduplication that can be applied to hierarchical relationships. Bhattacharya and Getoor [2] use an object consolidation method that goes beyond that of [1] allowing other types of relationships. Our work differentiates from the other works that take into account relationships for data disambiguation or record linkage in that we use the inter-object relationships, no matter how distant they are, to build blocks. The records in those blocks are compared among them with record comparison functions as in a standard blocking strategy.

VI. Conclusions and future work

In this paper, we have presented a new sort of blocking methods based on the context information extracted from the relation among entities in the database. We present an specific method called Semantic Graph Blocking (SGB) oriented to reduce the expert review time in the RL process, using a collaborative graph to build blocks based on contextual information. We show the results of our SGB in comparison to the classic blocking and sorted neighborhood blocking methods using a synthetically created set of databases and the Citeseer reference database.

We have shown that our approach tackles the most important problem in data integration and cleansing: the time consumed in the post-process of RL and, at the same time, it improves the amount of hits (recall) compared to the classic blocking methods, when the connectivity between entities in the data set is low. We show in our experiments that we can drastically reduce the false hit ratio and, in the best cases, we reduce the number of false positives by two orders of magnitude. In addition we improve the quality of the RL process when we relax the hit acceptance threshold.

As future work we want to explore different approaches for the SGB, using strategies that allow to prune the graphs obtained without reducing the hit ratios. In particular, we want to explore the differences between creating blocks based on levels or number of nodes included. Also, we want to explore the possibility of using comparison weights based on the distance between the nodes compared. Finally, we want to explore the combination of syntactic and semantic blocks in order to improve the recall and the precision measures.

Acknowledgments

The authors want to thank Generalitat de Catalunya for its support through grant number GRE-00352 and Ministerio de Educación y Ciencia of Spain for its support through grant TIN2006-15536-C02-02. Jordi Nin wants to thank the Spanish Council for Scientific Research (CSIC) for his I3P grant.

References

[1] Ananthakrishna, R., Chaudhuri, S., and Ganti, V. Eliminating Fuzzy Duplicates in Data Warehouses. In Proc. of the VLDB Conference, 2002.

[2] Bhattacharya, I. and Getoor, L. Iterative record Linkage for Cleaning and integration. In Proc. of the DMKD Workshop, 2004.

[3] Bilenko, M., Basu, S., Sahami, M., Adaptive Product Normalization: Using Online Learning for Record Linkage in Comparison Sopping. Proceedings of the 5th Int'l. Conference on Data Mining 2005. Pages 58–65.

[4] Surajit Chaudhuri and Umeshwar Dayal. An overview of data warehousing and olap technology. SIGMOD Record, 26(1):6574, 1997.

[5] Citeseer database, http://citeseer.ist.psu.edu

[6] Goffman, Casper (1969). "And what is your Erdos number?". American Mathematical Monthly 76

[7] M. Gyssens, J. Paredaens, van den Bussche, J. and D. van Gucht. A graph-oriented object database model. IEEE Transactions on Knowledge and Data Engineering, 6(4). Pages 572-586. 1994

[8] Hernandez, M., Stolfo, S., (1998), Real-world data is dirty: Data cleansing and the merge/purge problem. Data Mining and Knowledge Discovery, 1(2), 1998.

[9] Jaro, M. A., (1989), Advances in Record Linkage Methodology as Applied to Matching the 1985 Census of Tampa, Florida. Journal of the American Statistical Society, 84(406):414-420, 1989.

[10] Kalashnikov, D. and Mehrotra, S.. Domain-Independent Data Cleaning via Analysis of Entity-Relationship Graph, ACM TODS, Vol. 31, No. 2, June 2006, pp. 716-767.

[11] N. Kiesel, A. Schuerr and B. Westfechtel. GRAS, a graph-oriented (software) engineering database system. Information Systems, 20(1). Pages 21-51. 1995.

[12] Kubica, J., Moore, A., Cohn, D., Schneider, J., (2003) Finding Underlying Connections: A Fast Graph-Based Method for Link Analysis and Collaboration Queries. Proceedings of the Twentieth International Conference on Machine Learning (ICML-2003), Washington DC, 2003.

[13] Levenshtein, Vladimir I. Binary codes capable of correcting deletions, insertions, and reversals. Soviet Physics Doklady. Pages 707-710. 1966.

[14] C. J. van Rijsbergen, Information Retrieval, London, Butterworth, 1979, pp. 174 ff.

[15] G. Salton and M. McGill. Introduction to Modern Information Retrieval. McGraw- Hill, New York, NY, 1983.

[16] Srinath Srinivasa, Martin Maier, Mandar R. Mutalikdesai, Gowrishankar K. A. and Gopinath P. S. LWI and Safari: A New Index Structure and Query Model for Graph Databases. COMAD, pages 138-147. 2005.

[17] Sweeney, L., (2001), Information explosion, in Confidentiality, Disclosure, and Data Access: Theory and Practical Applications for Statistical Agencies, eds. P. Doyle, J. I. Lane, J. M. Theeuwes and L. M. Zayatz, Elsevier, 43–74.

[18] Sung, S. Y., Li, Z., and Peng, S.. A Fast Filtering Scheme for Large Database Cleansing. International Conference on Information and Knowledge Management (CIKM), McLean, Virginia, USA, 2002.

[19] Torra, V., Domingo-Ferrer, J., (2003), Record linkage methods for multidatabase data mining, Information Fusion in Data Mining, Springer, 101-132.

[20] Winkler, W., (2003), Data Cleaning Methods, Proc. SIGKDD 2003, Washington.

Scalable Query Dissemination in XPeer

Giovanni Conforti
Dipartimento di Informatica - Università di Pisa
Largo B. Pontecorvo 3 - 56127
Pisa - Italy
confor@di.unipi.it

Giorgio Ghelli
Dipartimento di Informatica - Università di Pisa
Largo B. Pontecorvo 3 - 56127
Pisa - Italy
ghelli@di.unipi.it

Paolo Manghi
ISTI - CNR
via G. Moruzzi 1 - 56124
Pisa - Italy
paolo.manghi@isti.cnr.it

Carlo Sartiani
Dipartimento di Informatica - Università di Pisa
Largo B. Pontecorvo 3 - 56127
Pisa - Italy
sartiani@di.unipi.it

Abstract

This paper presents XPeer, a data sharing system for massively distributed XML data. XPeer allows users to publish and query heterogeneous information without any significant administration efforts. XPeer tries to dispatch any given query to all and only the potentially relevant peers, exploiting a superpeer network to this aim.

1. Introduction

In today's world, the Internet affirmed as a powerful communication *medium*, allowing people from distant places to share and exchange information, as well as to interact. The Internet offers users many ways to communicate, such as forums, blogs, email, instant messages, voip and conference applications. In a similar way, complex global-scale applications can be built by composing services dispatched by single sites (e.g., web services), so to provide new and sophisticated tools to large and geographically distributed organizations.

While much emphasis is posed on the role of the Internet as a communication medium, this vision is someway limiting. Indeed, the Internet can also be seen as a formidable, massively distributed data repository, containing user-supplied information about near all knowledge fields. This repository is characterized by some ground properties, mostly induced by the behavior of data providers (typically, net-users) and by the characteristics of data being provided. These properties can be described as *heterogeneity*, *autonomy*, and *no administration*.

Heterogeneity   Data published on the Internet and, more generally, information exchanged on the Net are by nature heterogeneous. Not only they span over completely unrelated domains (e.g., espresso machines reviews and discussions about LaTeX), but also data referring to the same domain are represented in quite different ways.

With only a few notable exceptions, heterogeneity is definitely not avoidable, and it is common to data published by single net-users as well as to data exported by applications. Even though some application fields have very well defined standard data representation formats (e.g., the logs of SMTP servers can be assumed to be homogeneous), the same does not happen for some very popular applications. Consider, for instance, multimedia players like iTunes, WinAmp, and MediaPlayer: although they manage essentially the same kind of information (usually mp3 or AAC music files), they organize their internal *metadata* database in very different and usually incompatible ways.[1]

When building an Internet-scale application, managing heterogeneity is, to some extent, an inevitable (and disturbing) issue. In particular, heterogeneity plays a significant role in any large scale data sharing system, where users are allowed to share information without a superimposed global schema. For instance, in the above example of multimedia players, one can think of a system allowing users to *transparently* share descriptions, comments, and ratings about the multimedia files they legally own: as each kind of player represents its internal database according to a different schema (differences spread from field names to data nesting), some efforts for managing heterogeneity are nec-

---

[1] We are still wondering why simple information can be modeled in so many different ways.

essary for making data available to all users.

Autonomy Strictly related to heterogeneity, a second ground property of the Internet as massively distributed repository is data providers' and data sources *autonomy*. As data providers are (almost) free to publish whatever kind of information they want, they are also free to add new contents, as well as to modify and even drop existing contents they already published. For instance, a blogger has usually the full control on the information she is publishing, hence she can add new posts, modify existing posts, or delete old ones whenever she wants.

Of course, autonomy is someway limited by replication and gossiping phenomena that are intrinsic to the nature of the Internet.

No administration A key factor in the success of the Internet as global communication medium and global-scale repository is that publishing new information (or using even sophisticated Internet services) requires no or little administration efforts by a net-user. For instance, setting up a new blog can be done in a few minutes by a non-expert user and requires only a few and non-technical information about the new blog. Furthermore, popular file sharing systems currently being used for sharing large amounts of video and/or music files do not even require significant administration efforts, as they are able to self-manage their distributed architecture and their configuration.

1.1. Our Contribution

We emphasized the role of the Internet as a massively distributed, global-scale data repository. Till now, database technology has not been able to replicate the success of the Internet in building large or global-scale databases. As pointed out in [5], the reasons of this failure are mostly related to common features of current database systems, such as ACID transactions, that are not adequate to a global-scale environment (and they are sometimes even an obstacle).

The main objective of this paper is to present XPeer [11], a data sharing system for massively distributed XML data, and, in particular, its query dissemination and compilation techniques. XPeer allows users to publish and query *heterogeneous* information without any significant administration efforts. To this end, XPeer is based on a p2p architecture that is able to *self-organize* and *self-manage* its own administrative layers without the intervention of a database or system administrator.

Unlike similar projects like PIER [5], XPeer recognizes that heterogeneity is unavoidable and assists the user in *surviving* heterogeneity, i.e., XPeer assumes that data are potentially heterogeneous and tries to dispatch any given query to any potentially relevant peer, while retaining a good degree of selectivity in query dissemination. The technique used is based on automatic extraction of schematic information from peers and use of a *query-to-schema* matching technique to identify the potentially relevant peers.

The contribution of XPeer is twofold. First, XPeer offers very selective query dissemination solutions, that allow the system to deliver a query only to a small superset of the peers containing relevant data, hence reducing both communication and execution costs. Second, its architectural design is scalable and fault-tolerant, and can be easily adapted to more sophisticated data integration techniques based on schema mappings and query reformulation.

1.2. Paper Outline

The paper is structured as follows. Section 2 outlines the design choices on which XPeer architecture is based. Section 3 describes the architecture of the system. Section 4 illustrates the solutions used in XPeer for query dissemination, while Section 5 describes the query execution strategy. Section 6 presents some experimental results validating the XPeer approach. Sections 7 and 8, finally, discuss related work and future research.

2. Architectural Choices

XPeer main objective is the management of global-scale XML data repositories, allowing users to share and query heterogeneous data without the need for any administration activity.

These goals require the adoption of architectural solutions enhancing both the scalability and the reliability/availability properties of the system. In particular, the architectural design of XPeer was inspired by the goal of *distribution scalability*, i.e., the system performance should not deteriorate when the number of nodes in the system increases. As the number of peers increases, both the degree of data distribution and the magnitude of the query workload increases, hence the system must cope with an increasing data tracking and query processing load.

In order to design a scalable data management system for heterogeneous XML data, we made some architectural choices that depart from the tradition of centralized and distributed databases, but can also be regarded as heretic wrt usual p2p design criteria.

Query Compilation vs Query Execution A *selective* and efficient query dissemination is critical for the scalability of the XPeer system. To this end, query processing is split in two distinct phases of query compilation and query execution. During query compilation, a *superpeer network* cooperatively tries to identify the peers containing relevant data, so to provide the issuing peer with a quite precise query plan. During query execution, then, the issuing peer deploys the query at the peers identified in the previous step, and coordinates the execution of the distributed query.

Separation between query compilation and query execution is unusual in p2p systems. Much more frequently, queries are disseminated or routed while being executed [7], hence dissemination choices are taken at query runtime. The reason of this departure from the p2p tradition is twofold. First, we see in this separation a way for improving query optimization: once received the compiled access plan from the superpeer network, the issuing peer can apply distributed query rewriting rules [9] so to decrease query execution costs; this in turn leads to a significant enhancement of system scalability.

Second (and most important), effectiveness and selectivity of query dissemination can be significantly improved by exploiting a wider knowledge of the system properties, managed by a specialized network, while the dissemination of queries on the basis of local information may lead to decisions that are only locally promising. We validate this claim in Section 6, where several experimental results show that XPeer performs query dissemination in a quite selective way.

Non-DHT Superpeer Network Supporting an effective and efficient query compilation phase requires the adoption of an adequate architecture for the superpeer network. In our vision, the superpeer network should track the peers connected to the system and store some form of summary of the content of each peer (describing both the structure and the data distribution); indeed, any peer joining the system submits such a summary of its data to the superpeer network, and should refresh it every time a local update of its data leads to a change in its schema or in the data distribution. By aggregating and manipulating these summaries, the superpeer network is able to identify those peers having potentially relevant data, even if their schemas are not homogeneous.

A key point of this vision is that complex schema manipulations are necessary for surviving heterogeneity and identifying query-relevant peers. To lower both communication and processing costs during schema manipulation, schemas and synopses should be stored in a very *localized* way, i.e., without any fragmentation. Hence, we decided to drop architectures based on *Distributed Hash Tables* (DHTs) in favor of a *dynamically hierarchical* organization of the superpeer network, allowing the superpeer network to store schemas without fragmentation. We understand that this choice is somewhat unusual and, to some extent, heretic. Despite the very good scalability properties of DHTs, we believe that DHTs are not adequate to our aims. Indeed, DHTs fragment data in a very fine way, so to maximize load balancing and parallelism; unfortunately, this aspect

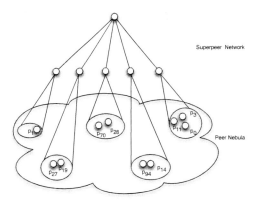

Figure 1. Peer and superpeer network.

significantly increases communication and processing costs of any activity with limited parallelism, including schema manipulation.

3. System Architecture

The starting point of our architecture is a set of autonomous peers. To make this nebula act as a distributed repository and query system, XPeer builds an *hierarchical tree-shaped* superpeer network over it, as shown in Figure 1.

On the leaves of the superpeer tree, each node (called superpeer) can *spot* a distinct fragment of the nebula, i.e., it keeps track of the schemas and synopses of peers in that fragment, so that the whole nebula is covered by leaf superpeers. The summaries managed by these nodes are then tracked by superpeer nodes in the upper level; in this way, nebula spots are aggregated to allow superpeers to have a wider view of the peer network. This aggregation introduces some form of approximation in the combined summaries, to balance the larger set of information to be managed. This aggregation process is repeated recursively until the root of the tree hierarchy is reached. The superpeer network root, hence, has a high level vision of the whole peer network.

An important issue in this hierarchical process is given by summary (schemas and synopses) representation and aggregation. The current implementation of XPeer uses a DataGuide-like structure (called *treeguide*) [3] for representing peer schemas, which are automatically inferred by the system. Data distribution inside XML simple elements is captured by means of *equi-depth* histograms and Bloom filters: histograms are used for numeric (integer/floats) element only, while Bloom filters come into play for string-valued elements. Histograms, Bloom filters, and treeguides are integrated by endowing each treeguide leaf with the corresponding histogram or Bloom filter, if any.

Based on these representations, summary aggregation is quite straightforward: treeguides are merged, while histograms are combined to lower the space requirements. In particular, buckets are reshaped to preserve equi-depth. As usual, Bloom filters are combined through disjunction.

Hierarchical structures in p2p systems, with only a few exceptions [6], are known to be prone to scalability, reliability, and adaptivity issues. To overcome these problems and make XPeer scale with the size of the peer network, XPeer adopts a technique called *cloning*, which is essentially farm-like replication, with weak synchronization requirements.

The basic idea of cloning is that a superpeer is not a physical entity, but, instead, a *virtual* entity consisting of several nodes cooperating in managing queries and updates. Each of these nodes is called a *clone*, as it replicates the information managed by the virtual superpeer where it resides. It is important to notice that a clone is not a dedicated machine or supercomputer; instead, any peer in the system may become a clone, once it has expressed its willing to perform administrative tasks. A superpeer, hence, is a virtual entity consisting of heterogeneous and geographically distributed clones.

From outside a superpeer, clones are invisible and each of them is able to handle both query compilation requests and summary update requests. Each request to a superpeer is routed to a randomly chosen clone by an enhanced communication and transport layer, which is *clone-aware*, and which is an essential part of the communication infrastructure on top of which XPeer is built.

A relevant issue for the proper work of clones is summary synchronization. As superpeer information is fully replicated among clones, and, as each clone can independently handle summary update requests, a synchronization algorithm among clones, ensuring (some sort of) consistency and scalability, is necessary. We chose to favor scalability on consistency by adopting a synchronization algorithm based on a best-effort linear synchronization scheme, where, every time a clone receives an update request, it forwards the request to all its sibling clones. Retransmission mechanisms based on version numbers and hash signatures are employed for dealing with synchronization message failure.

We can now see how cloning helps both reliability and scalability. For what concerns reliability, a superpeer failure requires that *all* clones fail, which is quite infrequent.

For what concerns scalability, the number of clones in a superpeer is continuously modified to match the load of incoming and outgoing messages. In particular, each clone in a superpeer periodically monitors the length of its message queues: when they exceed a given threshold the clone tries to recruit a new peer to join the superpeer.[2] This process is performed by the system with no human intervention.

4. Query Compilation

Query compilation in XPeer aims at transforming a query in an algebraic expression where each leaf is a *location operator*, identifying a data source that is found in a specific peer. The core step of this process is *distributed compilation*, where the superpeer network tries to identify interesting peers on the basis of their summaries, so that only such peers appear in the compiled query.

4.1. Query Language and Query Algebra

XPeer supports a significant fragment of XQuery [2], roughly equivalent to the FLWR core of the language. The XPeer query algebra [9] contains operators for evaluating path and twigs, for filtering variable bindings according to predicates, for building new XML fragments, and for incorporating peer information inside query plans. This algebra is an extension of that described in [10], and is close to other algebras for semistructured and XML data [8].

4.2. Local Compilation

Local compilation translates a query into an *incomplete* algebraic expression, i.e., an algebraic expression without location operators. The query is first translated, by the issuing peer, into an *intermediate* representation based on *query blocks*; on this representation standard rewriting techniques are applied, like, for instance, the factorization of common subexpressions. Finally, the intermediate representation is used for generating the algebraic expression corresponding to the query.

4.3. Distributed Compilation

Once a peer p_x issuing a query q has locally compiled the query into an *incomplete* algebraic expression, it submits the algebraic representation of q to the superpeer network. The superpeer network, hence, fills the holes in the algebraic expression by identifying a set of peers containing potentially relevant data; this process is guided by the summary information stored in the superpeer network.

For an example, we will refer to the query shown below, assuming that the query is satisfied by peers p_1, p_{13}, and p_{17}, and that the superpeer network has the structure shown in Figure 2. This query retrieves the titles of all undergraduate courses from a university courses database.

```
for $c in $db//course,
```

---

[2]Clone failures are managed essentially in the same way, as they impact the messaging load of the remaining clones.

```
    $l in $c/level
where $l = "U"
return $c/title
```

The distributed compilation step is then organized in two phases: the *ascending* phase, and the *descending* phase.

Ascending phase p_x submits the query q, by sending its compiled version to its superpeer (sp_1, in this case). Once received the query, this superpeer i) *propagates* the query to its father in the hierarchy, and ii) *matches* the query against schemas and synopses locally hosted, as shown in Figure 2(a). Any positive match (p_1) is then directly communicated to p_x.

As the father of sp_1 (sp_{19}) receives the query from sp_1, it recursively forwards the query to its father (the *root* of the hierarchy, in this case) and matches the query against its schemas and synopses. Unlike the match performed by leaf superpeers, which can directly identify interesting peers, the match at an intermediate level serves the purpose of finding hierarchy subtrees that may contain information about peers with relevant data. In the case of our example, sp_{19} finds that sp_{27} children may comprise interesting peers, hence sp_{19} forwards the query to sp_{27} (see Figure 2(b)). sp_{27} will perform exactly the same actions as sp_1, with the only difference that it will not resend the query to its own father.

Descending phase When the root of the tree hierarchy receives a query from one of its children, the ascending phase for this query ends, and the descending phase starts. The purpose of this phase is to explore the fragment of the hierarchy that has not been touched by the ascending phase. This exploration is performed on a *summary-driven* basis, hence only the subtrees that track potentially relevant peers are actually explored. In the case of our example, the root finds that the subtree rooted by sp_{90} is worth a further exploration, hence it propagates the query to sp_{90} (Figure 2(c)). sp_{90}, in turn, discovers that sp_{99} may have information on interesting peers, while sp_{94} does not match the query; hence, sp_{90} sends the query to sp_{99} (Figure 2(d)). sp_{99}, finally, identifies p_{17} as a potential data supplier, and sends this information directly to p_x.

Two important things must be noted about distributed compilation. First, each query must reach the root of the hierarchy, as the root only has some knowledge about the whole peer network. This, in turn, means that the superpeer load increases while moving from the bottom to the top of the hierarchy. This is not a problem, since each superpeer just recruits as many clones as necessary to perform its task.

Second, the superpeer network sends the information about any interesting peer as soon as it is found. This allows for an improvement in the compilation response time.

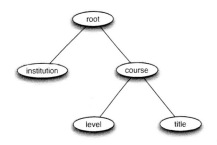

Figure 3. p_1 **treeguide.**

4.4. Query-to-schema Match

A key aspect of the query compilation approach of XPeer is represented by the algorithm being used for *matching* a query against a schema and a set of synopses. This algorithm guides the compilation process and allows the system to identify peers that may satisfy the query as well as to avoid the traversal of fragments of the superpeer network that do not contribute to the compilation result.

The *query-to-schema match* algorithm works in two main steps. During the first step, the algorithm extracts the twigs (i.e., the "tree patterns") from a given query (after clause normalization), and "evaluates" the twigs over the schema: if the result of this evaluation is not empty, there may exist some instance of the schema that contains data satisfying the structural requirements of the query. To improve the selectivity of the matching process, the algorithm then compares the predicates specified in the `where` clauses of the query with the statistical synopses associated with the schema, so to discard those peers that give no contribution to the query result. The following Example illustrates the algorithm and the use of synopses.

Example 4.1 *Consider the query of the previous Section, and assume that p_1 data are described by the schema shown in Figure 3.*

Suppose that sp_1 checks whether p_1 may contain relevant data. To this purpose, sp_1 interprets p_1 treeguide as a data tree, and executes the binding fragment of the query on it. In our case, sp_1 evaluates `for $c in $db//course, $l in $c/level` *on the treeguide, and returns a non-empty tuple where $c and $l are bound to the matching schema nodes.*

This tuple tells sp_1 that p_1 data satisfy the structural requirements of the query; however, p_1 data may not comprise level *elements whose content is "U". As a consequence, a supplementary check is needed to enforce the satisfaction of the* `where` *clause predicate. To this end, sp_1 accesses the Bloom filter associated to the* level *node of the schema, and just verifies if the set of strings described by the filter includes "U".*

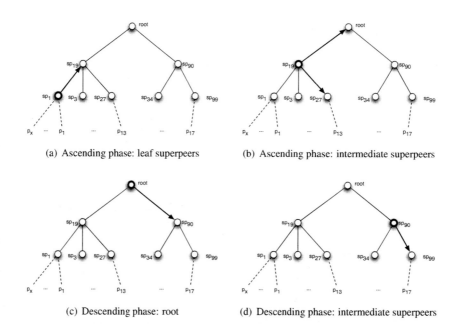

(a) Ascending phase: leaf superpeers

(b) Ascending phase: intermediate superpeers

(c) Descending phase: root

(d) Descending phase: intermediate superpeers

Figure 2. Distributed compilation.

5. Query Execution

Query execution strategy of XPeer is quite simple, as it involves no other nodes but the query issuer and the data sources, and it exploits the simplest communication pattern. The input of this phase is an algebraic expression, where every data source has been identified during the distributed compilation phase. The peer issuing the query decomposes this algebraic expression into subexpressions, called *pipes*, to be delivered to and executed by remote peers, and coordinates remote peer execution. As usual, XPeer tries to minimize network traffic by pushing selections and twig evaluation down the tree, exploiting canonical algebraic rewriting rules [9].

The decomposed query is then formed by several *pipes*. Each given pipe contains an algebraic expression describing the query fragment that a given remote peer must execute. Any operation involving data coming from multiple peers is executed by the issuing peer: the corresponding pipe, which essentially *coordinates* the execution of the whole query, is called the *host* pipe.

After query decomposition, pipes are sent to remote peers and executed. When a remote peer receives a pipe $\mathcal{P}$, it compiles the algebraic expression inside $\mathcal{P}$ into a physical plan and waits for a *start-execution* message.

Execution inside a given pipe follows the iterative model, where new results are requested by means of `next` messages. Interaction among pipes, instead, follows an *asynchronous buffered* iterative model. To avoid deadlocks and to be resilient to node and network failures, interactions are asynchronous and subject to *time-outs*: indeed, the operator used for managing communications with children pipes sends asynchronous `next` requests to the children pipes; if no response is given after a certain period of time, it assumes that the corresponding pipe is blocked or that no more data are available, hence it stops contacting the remote peer.

6. Experimental Results

A crucial feature of XPeer is its ability to dispatch a given query to a relatively small superset of the peers with relevant data, avoiding dissemination policies based on broadcast or flooding. In this Section we will present experimental results validating this claim; these results show that, by relying on the query-to-schema match algorithm, the superpeer network of XPeer is able to discard a significant fraction of peers containing irrelevant data.

6.1. Experimental Setup

Experiments were performed on a 100-node peer network, running on a cluster of Linux machines. We simulate an application where a set of universities publish information on their courses, and the data of each university is structured according to one among three different schemas. To this aim, we started from the three files in the University Courses XML dataset, available at http://www.cs.washington.edu/research/xmldatasets/; these XML documents have been randomly fragmented and each fragment has been assigned to a peer. This setup exemplifies a typical situation where a number of sites publish information with a limited degree of heterogeneity.

The behavior of the system was controlled and observed through XOrch, a global orchestration tool that we developed inside the XPeer project. XOrch can control the behavior of peers and superpeers by means of *scores*, i.e., scripts represented in a CSP-based language and describing the actions a single peer or superpeer must execute; scores are sent by the *Orc* (i.e., the central monitoring component) to local *proxies*, which execute them by interacting with the attached peers.

6.2. Query Workload

The test query workload is formed by 10 XQuery queries, shown in Figure 4, divided into four classes on the basis of a qualitative selectivity estimation. The first class contains queries with rather selective twigs, while the second class focuses on selective predicates; the third class comprises queries where both twigs and predicates are deemed as selective; the fourth class, finally, contains negative queries only, i.e. queries with no answer.

We assembled our test workload with the aim of mimicking "real life" workloads, hence the test queries contain both / and // operations, union paths, and multiple predicates connected by *and/or* logical connectors.

6.3. Experiments

In our experiments, we measured *precision* and *recall* of compilation for positive queries, as well as the absolute compilation error for negative queries, i.e., the difference between the number of peers deemed as interesting by the compilation process and the number of peers actually hosting relevant data; we performed these evaluations for four different compilation configurations. In the first configuration, we did not use synopses (Bloom filters and histograms) at all, hence limiting the query-to-schema match to a purely structural one; in the remaining configurations we used synopses of increasing dimensions: 96-bit, 480-bit, and 4800-bit Bloom filters, and histograms containing up to 15, 30, and 70 values, respectively.

Results of our experiments are shown in Figures 5 and 6. Since both schemas and synopses are upper approximations of the actual peer data, the *recall* should always be 100% when data is neither updated nor lost; the experiments confirm this, hence we only plot *precision*. As it can be noted, compilation is quite precise even in the absence of synopses; only query Q6 showed poor results, probably related to some issues concerning partial match string predicate.

```
Q1:   for $c in $db//course,
          $l in $c/level
      where $l = "U"
      return $c/title
Q2:   for $c in $db//course,
          $en in $c/enrolled
      where $en >= 5
      return $c/title
Q3:   for $c in $db//course,
          $cr in union($c/credits, $c/credit)
      where $cr > 6
      return $c
Q4:   for $r in $db/root,
          $inst in $r/institution,
          $c in $r/course,
          $cr in $c/credits
      where $c/credits > 4 and $inst = "wsu"
      return $c
Q5:   for $c in $db//course,
          $p in union($c/prefix, $c/subj)
      where $p = "CHEM"
      return $c
Q6:   for $c in $db//course
      where $c/instructor = "Parker"
      return $c
Q7:   for $c in $db//course,
          $l in $c/lab,
          $li in $c/limit
      where $li <= 25
      return $c
Q8:   for $r in $db/root,
          $inst in $r/institution,
          $c in $r//course,
          $en in $c/enrolled
      where $inst = "reed" and $en >= 25
      return $c
Q9:   for $r in $db/root,
          $inst in $r/institution,
          $c in $r/course
      where $inst = "Stanford"
      return $c
Q10:  for $c in $db//course,
          $l in $c/level,
          $en in $c/enrolled
      where $l = "U" and $en >= 25
      return $c
```

Figure 4. Query workload.

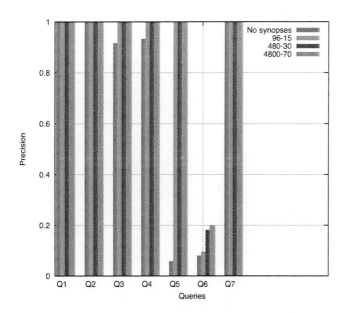

Figure 5. Precision of compilation.

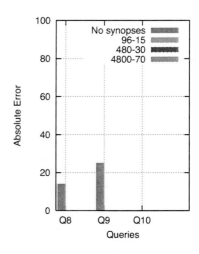

Figure 6. Absolute compilation error on negative queries.

Synopses really come into play on negative queries; while the no-synopses configuration generates significant compilation errors, the use of synopses allows the system to correctly recognize negative queries.

7. Related Works

Several projects focus on the problem of evaluating structured and complex queries in p2p systems. Among these projects, Pier [5] is definitely the closest system to XPeer. Pier is based on the use of a DHT, where relational, homogeneous data are cached. Pier queries are executed by adapting techniques from parallel databases to a DHT-based storage, hence exploiting the inner parallelism of DHTs. As Pier is focused on homogeneous data and parallelizable queries, it should be regarded as complementary wrt XPeer, which, instead, focuses on heterogeneous, hierarchical data and mostly hierarchical query operators. The only significant limitation of Pier wrt XPeer is query dissemination, which, in most cases, requires a broadcast on the whole peer network.

Heterogeneity management is, instead, the focus of the Piazza project [4]. Piazza is essentially a p2p-structured data integration system for XML data, where the data integration task is dispersed across the whole network. Peers (which may represent data sources) are connected through schema mappings, and query processing is based on a *flooding* algorithm that broadcasts queries among peers. Piazza, hence, suffers from severe scalability and query dissemination problems, that greatly limit its applicability.

A different way of supporting heterogeneity is adopted in the system described in [7], where a *coordinator-free* architecture for distributed XML query processing is presented. By assuming that peers contain semantically related data, the system uses a multi-hierarchic organization of the domain space to route queries (in the form of *mutant query plans*, i.e., query plans containing materialized data too). This approach does not seem adequate when data are semantically heterogeneous, and it makes query dissemination quite expensive.

An interesting hybrid between structured and unstructured p2p systems is represented by KadoP [1]. In KadoP a DHT is used for storing a distributed full-text index about documents and web services; this index, together with ontologies, is used during query processing for locating interesting data and services. Resource location, hence, requires the system to perform several key lookups in the DHT index, with a significant messaging cost, which depends on the dimension of the query, as well as on the data and services involved by the query.

8. Conclusions

The wide diffusion of the Internet has greatly increased the number of datasources publicly available as well as the amount of available data. As a consequence, a need for query systems able to match the scalability properties of the Internet emerged. This paper presented XPeer, a query system for massively distributed and heterogeneous XML data. XPeer allows users to perform structured queries on globally distributed data, without the hassles of any administration activity and while preserving full control on their own data. We described the principles on which XPeer is based, as well as its architectural paradigm, relying on a tree-shaped superpeer network; we also illustrated how a virtualization technique called *cloning* can be used for ensuring both robustness and scalability of the architecture.

We showed in detail the techniques used for disseminating queries inside the network: indeed, we illustrated how a query-to-schema matching technique can be exploited for making query dissemination smart and precise, as confirmed by the experimental results we provided.

In the near future, we plan to perform extensive experiments about compilation, so to evaluate the selectivity of query dissemination in the presence of massive network or node failures. We also plan to enhance the class of supported predicates at compilation time, as well as to study the behavior of the system on very large networks.

References

[1] S. Abiteboul, I. Manolescu, and N. Preda. Constructing and querying peer-to-peer warehouses of XML resources. In *ICDE*, pages 1122–1123, 2005.

[2] S. Boag, D. Chamberlin, M. F. Fernandez, D. Florescu, J. Robie, and J. Siméon. XQuery 1.0: An XML Query Language. Technical report, World Wide Web Consortium, Jan 2007. W3C Recommendation.

[3] R. Goldman and J. Widom. DataGuides: Enabling query formulation and optimization in semistructured databases. In *VLDB'97, Proceedings of 23rd International Conference on Very Large Data Bases, August 25-29, 1997, Athens, Greece*, pages 436–445. Morgan Kaufmann, 1997.

[4] A. Y. Halevy, Z. G. Ives, P. Mork, and I. Tatarinov. Piazza: data management infrastructure for semantic web applications. In *Proceedings of the Twelfth International World Wide Web Conference, WWW2003, Budapest, Hungary, 20-24 May 2003*, pages 556–567. ACM, 2003.

[5] R. Huebsch, B. N. Chun, J. M. Hellerstein, B. T. Loo, P. Maniatis, T. Roscoe, S. Shenker, I. Stoica, and A. R. Yumerefendi. The architecture of PIER: an Internet-scale query processor. In *CIDR*, pages 28–43, 2005.

[6] H. V. Jagadish, B. C. Ooi, and Q. H. Vu. Baton: A balanced tree structure for peer-to-peer networks. In *VLDB*, pages 661–672, 2005.

[7] V. Papadimos, D. Maier, and K. Tufte. Distributed Query Processing and Catalogs for Peer-to-Peer Systems. In *CIDR 2003, First Biennial Conference on Innovative Data Systems Research, Asilomar, CA, USA, January 5-8, 2003*, 2003.

[8] S. Paparizos and H. V. Jagadish. Pattern tree algebras: Sets or sequences? In *VLDB*, pages 349–360, 2005.

[9] C. Sartiani. A query algebra for XML p2p databases. In *Proceedings of the 11th International Workshop on Foundations of Models and Languages for Data and Objects (FMLDO). In conjunction with the 10th Int. Conference on Extending Database Technology (EDBT 2006).*, 2006.

[10] C. Sartiani and A. Albano. Yet Another Query Algebra For XML Data. In M. A. Nascimento, M. T. Özsu, and O. Zaïane, editors, *Proceedings of the 6th International Database Engineering and Applications Symposium (IDEAS 2002), Edmonton, Canada, July 17-19, 2002*, 2002.

[11] C. Sartiani, G. Ghelli, P. Manghi, and G. Conforti. XPeer: A self-organizing XML P2P database system. In *Proceedings of the First EDBT Workshop on P2P and Databases (P2P&DB 2004), 2004*, 2004.

Semantic Interoperability Between Relational Database Systems

Quang Trinh, Ken Barker, Reda Alhajj
Computer Science Department
University of Calgary
Calgary, Alberta, Canada
qtrinh, barker, alhajj@cpsc.ucalgary.ca

Abstract

Relational DataBase Systems (RDBSs) are well-known and widely used in many organizations, however, semantic conflicts between the participating RDBSs must be resolved before data can be exchanged between them. Semantic resolution between the RDBSs is extremely difficult to address mainly because participating RDBSs are designed and built independently. Furthermore, individual RDBSs are likely to evolve over time and the changes must be reconciled dynamically. In this paper, we describe an approach to resolve the semantic conflicts between RDBSs automatically while allowing the individual RDBSs to evolve. Relational DataBase Ontology (RDBO) is created and used to ensure the semantic descriptions of the individual RDBSs are conformed to a set of vocabularies, structures, and restrictions. We show how a modified reasoning engine is used to validate and infer additional semantic relationships from the existing relationships. We also show how terms defined in different database ontologies are compared to each other semantically using semantic weights and our modified reasoning engine. As a result, RDBSs can interoperate with each other seamlessly and at the correct level of semantics defined in their ontologies.

1 Introduction

In general, each RDBS is designed to store a particular data set and is described by the terms commonly used and understood by its local users. Since the individual RDBSs are designed and built independently, many challenges arise when two or more RDBSs must interoperate with each other. One of the main challenges is semantic conflict, which include [12]: (i) naming conflict, such as homonyms and synonyms; (ii) generalization and specialization conflicts; (iii) atomic and composite conflicts; *etc.* Over the past two decades, many different approaches have been proposed in the literature for resolving the semantic conflicts

between RDBSs. These different approaches, ranging from resolving the semantic conflict at the data level, schema level, and application level, all have two things in common: (i) no deduction of additional semantic relationships from existing ones; (ii) no mention of semantic comparisons between terms defined in different RDBSs. For example, (a) given "Term A is semantically equivalent to Term B" (denotes by $T_A \equiv T_B$) and $T_B \equiv T_C$. Previously we cannot derive $T_A \equiv T_C$ from $T_A \equiv T_B$ and $T_B \equiv T_C$; or (b) given T_A and T_B from two different systems, what can we say about T_A and T_B? Is T_A more general, more specific, or equivalent to T_B? Without some semantic reference, no such comparisons can be done.

Other approaches such as the unified global schema and multidatabase language approaches also have limitations. The unified global schema approach brought with it many challenges since the individual RDBSs are designed and built independently so it is difficult for them to agree on a single schema. The multidatabase language approach gives users the ability to perform queries across multiple databases but semantic reconcilations are left to the users to resolve manually.

Recently, motivated by the Semantic Web [1], some approaches make use of ontologies to resolve semantic conflicts between participating systems [9, 10, 16]. Weihua and Shixian [19] presented a layered model approach that combined agents and ontologies to address the semantic interoperability problem in large-scale environments. The model has three layers: (i) a syntax layer that deals with syntactic interoperability; (ii) a semantic layer that deals with semantic interoperability; and (iii) an agent layer that deals with information interoperability. Suwanmanee *et al.* [13] propose a mediator-wrapper approach with OWL ontologies to enable semantic interoperability between relational or object data sources. Each data source is described by an OWL ontology and it is assumed that these ontologies are created manually. Mappings between ontologies are defined manually and only atomic mappings are mentioned. The mediator uses the Racer reasoner engine [5] to check for consistency of the "integrated" ontology and RICE (Racer Interactive Client Environment) to allow users to pose queries over the "integrated" ontology. These approaches can be applied to RDBSs but no standardization on how RDBS semantics are described and no semantic comparisons between terms are mentioned.

Similar to the web, semantic conflicts between RDBSs should be validated and resolved dynamically while allowing participating RDBSs to have full control to their data. In this paper, we describe an approach to resolve the semantic conflicts between RDBSs using database ontologies and a modified reasoning engine. Database ontologies provide the semantic information of the participating RDBSs and mappings between them indicate how data in different RDBSs are related to each other. The modified reasoning engine is used to: (i) compare and rank terms defined in different database ontologies; (ii) validate relationships or mappings between the related terms defined in different database ontologies to ensure that they are semantically and correctly stated; (iii) deduct additional semantic relationships from existing relationships. The modified reasoning engine carries out these operations automatically based on the semantic information provided. This enables RDBSs to interoperate with each other semantically and at the correct levels of granularity regardless of their structures and how their semantic information is stated.

The rest of the paper is organized as follows: Section 2 describes the general requirements for enabling semantic interoperability between RDBSs. Section 3 describes how RDBS semantics are presented while conforming to a standardized structure that supports reasoning. Section 4 describes how semantic mappings are defined between the individual RDBSs, shared domain ontologies, and shared global ontologies. This section also describes a mapping scheme that supports transformations/translations. Mappings with translations are necessary for data instances of concepts that are semantically the same but defined in different formats. Section 5 describes how mappings between ontologies are validated and compared using a modified reasoning engine called Pellet. Finally, Section 6 concludes the paper and provides a brief discussion of the future work.

2 Semantic Interoperability Between RDBSs

In general, semantic interoperability between RDBSs requires: (i) a common set of vocabularies and their semantic relationships and constraints for describing the RDBSs; (ii) standardized database ontologies that describe the semantics of the individual RDBSs; (iii) a set of mappings state the semantic relationships between the database ontologies (hence RDBSs); and (iv) a reasoning engine that validates, compares, and deduce semantic relationships between database ontologies. T-Box and A-Box reasoning

(reasoning about concept definitions and their instances respectively) ensure inferences between input ontologies can be made automatically. Figure 1 shows our framework for enabling semantic interoperability between RDBSs. The following sections describe our framework in details.

3 Representing RDBS Semantics

Since there are many different types of DataBase Management Systems (DBMSs), a common language for representing the RDBS semantics is necessary. It is also important that the common language chosen is rich and expressive enough to accommodate the dynamic and heterogeneous nature of the individual RDBSs. OWL, Web Ontology Language [18], is designed for such purposes so we choose OWL as the common language for representing the RDBS semantics. Furthermore, a common way of describing the RDBSs in OWL is also needed because without it, different RDBSs are likely to describe themselves differently so it would be difficult to relate, validate, and compare the semantic definitions of terms defined and used in different RDBSs. Trinh et al. [14] have described such a common model in OWL called the Relational DataBase Ontology (OWL-RDBO). OWL-RDBO is a set of common vocabularies and their semantic relationships and constraints for describing RDBSs. OWL-RDBO preserves the underlying structural constraints of the RDBSs and guarantees user applications work with data instances that conformed to a set of vocabularies and structures. Using the common vocabularies defined in OWL-RDBO, database ontologies are created for the individual participating RDBSs (see Figure 1). Database ontologies can be created manually, however, even for the domain experts, this task can be error-prone and time-consuming. To ease the burden on users, we have developed a tool for generating and publishing database ontologies automatically from the metadata of the RDBSs while maintaining their structural constraints [15]. The generated database ontologies are instances of the OWL-RDBO and are independent of the underlying RDBSs they described. Database ontologies are necessary for a number of reasons: (i) they provide an explicit and common semantic description of the underlying RDBSs that both human and computers can understand; (ii) there are many existing domain ontologies available that database ontologies can map to and facilitate the data exchange with other existing systems; and (iii) there are many existing reasoning engines available that can be used to validate the semantic mappings between the database ontologies and to infer additional semantic relationships from existing ones. For example, the following OWL mapping states that the term Employee, a rdbo:Table object, is semantically equivalent to the term Staff in another database ontology with the namespace URI of cs:

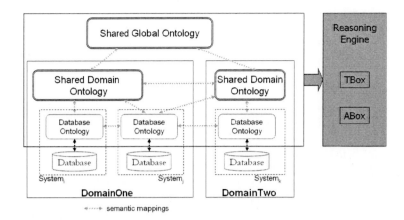

Figure 1. A framework for semantic interoperability between the RDBSs.

```
<rdbo:Table rdf:ID="Employee">
  <owl:equivalentClass rdf:resource="cs:Staff"/>
</rdbo:Table>
```

If `cs:Staff` is not of type `rdbo:Table`[1] then Employee and `cs:Staff` are not equivalent because they are not the same type. A database schema can be considered as an ontology for a mini-world but it lacks formal semantics and reasoning supports. For example, $umcs:Employee \equiv cs:Staff$ and $cs:Staff \equiv cs:Employee$ then by *transitivity*, $umcs:Employee \equiv cs:Employee$. Using the database ontologies and a reasoning engine, such conclusions can be extracted automatically from the knowledgebase of the reasoning engine. We will describe how this is done in Section 5.

4 Semantic Mappings Between RDBSs

Database ontologies and semantic mappings between them are the key to success for semantic interoperability between RDBSs. Semantic mappings between the database ontologies are stated independent of the underlying RDBS's logical and physical structures so changes can be made to the underlying RDBS's structures without effecting the semantic relationships between the database ontologies. Semantic mappings between the database ontologies can be defined in three ways [17]:

- between the individual database ontologies.

- between the individual database ontologies and shared domain ontologies.

- between the individual database ontologies, shared domain ontologies, and shared global ontology.

The first approach is flexible but the main drawback is there will be a large number of mappings between the database ontologies (i.e., each term in one database ontology must explicitly map to all other equivalent terms in other database ontologies) [6, 8]. Compared to the first approach, the second approach is better in the sense that shared domain ontologies are used so the number of mappings between the database ontologies is reduced. A shared domain ontology is an ontology that describes a set of common terms, properties, and their relationships used in a domain. Shared ontologies are created by their domain experts. The third approach reduces the number of mappings between the database ontologies even more since both shared domain ontologies and a global ontology are used. Similar to a shared domain ontology, a shared global ontology contains a set of common terms, properties, and their relationships agreed and shared by all participants. In our approach, mappings can be stated between the database ontologies, shared domain ontologies, and shared global ontologies (see Figure 1). Shared global ontology is created and agreed by experts in the community.

Semantic mappings between the ontologies can be created manually or semi-automatically as described by Doan *et al.* [3]. Given any two terms T_i and T_j in any two database ontologies, there are four types of semantic relationships between T_i and T_j:

i. T_i is equivalent to T_j (denoted by $T_i \equiv T_j$)

ii. T_i is not equivalent to T_j (denoted by $T_i \neq T_j$)

iii. T_i is a generalization of T_j (denoted by $T_i \sqsupseteq T_j$)

iv. T_i is a specialization of T_j (denoted by $T_i \sqsubseteq T_j$)

The first two relationships are obvious. Generalization and specialization describe the hierarchy structures in RDBSs. For example, if Employee IS_A Person then

---

[1]In OWL, `owl:Thing` is the parent class of all classes, however, we have explicitly excluded this case when we validate mappings between the ontologies.

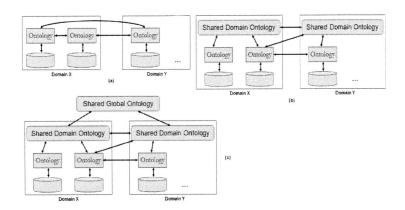

Figure 2. Three approaches of how ontologies can be used for enabling semantic interoperability between RDBSs (adopted from [17]): (a) mappings between the individual ontologies; (b) mappings between the individual ontologies and shared domain ontologies; (c) mappings between the individual ontologies, shared domain ontologies, and shared global ontologies.

`Person` is more general than `Employee` (denoted by `Person ⊒ Employee`).

Semantic mappings must be defined at both the conceptual and data levels and OWL supports mappings at both levels. Semantic mapping at the conceptual level maps one *concept* to another. A concept is a term or a phrase that is used to represent an object that exists in the real world, that has certain properties, and that is distinguishable from other objects. Similarly, semantic mapping at the data level maps an instance of one concept to an instance of another concept. The following describes how semantic mappings are defined at both levels.

4.1 Semantic Mappings At The Conceptual Level

Semantic mappings at the conceptual level state the semantic relationships between terms defined in different database ontologies. For example, the mapping:

$$umcs:last \equiv cs:lastName$$

states that `umcs:last` is semantically equivalent to `cs:lastName` (where `umcs` and `cs` are namespace URIs for two database ontologies). Since they are equivalent, we can now compare and combine instances of these two terms together. In this mapping, we assume that both terms are defined with the same data format (e.g., string) so no additional work is needed. However, if one of the terms is defined in a different data format, then in addition to the mapping, a translation is also needed before the data instances of the two terms can be compared to each other. For example, the mapping:

$$umcs:hiredDate \equiv cs:startDate$$

states the semantic equivalent between `umcs:hiredDate` and `cs:startDate`, yet, if the formats of `umcs:hiredDate` and `cs:startDate` are in short date format (i.e., MM/DD/YYYY) and long date format (i.e., MM DD,YYYY), then we either need to convert them to a common format or convert one format to the other before comparing their instances. This leads us to *semantic mappings with translations*, which is described next.

4.2 Semantic Mappings With Translations

Semantic mappings with translations state the semantic relationships at the conceptual level with *one or more translational operations* on the data instances of the participating term(s). Similar to mappings at the conceptual level, mappings with translations are defined in the form:

$$<uri:term_i> \equiv uri:\Im(<uri:term_j>)$$

where $uri:\Im$ is an aggregate function that applies to the instances of its argument and can be provided as a Web Service. For example, to address the previous date mapping problem, we can define a mapping with translation as follows:

$$umcs:hiredDate \equiv$$
$$ws:\Im_{Long2ShortFormat}(cs:startDate)$$

where $\Im_{Long2ShortFormat}$ is an aggregate function provided by the namespace `ws:` that takes a long date format and converts it to a short date format. With the translation provided, instances of the two dates are now in the same format and can be compared to each other. Semantic mappings with translations do not state the equivalent relationships between the data instances. Instead, they state the *equivalent formats* of data instances that belongs to equivalent concepts. This ensures the same format is used when comparing data instances of equivalent concepts. Alternatively, if mappings are stated directly between the data instances, they may also include relationships that are not used in the same context. For example, short format instances for `cs:birthdate` and `cs:startDate` are both dates but they are not used in the same context so they should not be compared to each other.

Semantic mappings with translations can also be used to address composite/atomic mapping problems. For example, we can now define a mapping that merges `firstName` and `lastName` together and maps the result to `fullName`:

$$fullName \equiv$$
$$ws:\Im_{merge}(name, ``,", firstName, lastName)$$

where $ws:\Im_{merge}$ merges instances of `firstName` and `lastName` together with the token ","," separation. Likewise, we can also define a translational mapping that splits a term into multiple terms and maps one of the terms to another. For example, we can define a mapping that splits `fullName` into the two terms `first` and `last` and maps the term `last` to the term `cs:lastName`:

$$ws:\Im_{project}(last, ws:\Im_{split}(fullName, ``,", first, last)) \equiv$$
$$lastName$$

where $ws:\Im_{split}$ takes `fullName` and splits it into two terms based on the ","," token and $ws:\Im_{project}$ projects out only instances of the term `last`.

5 Semantic Mapping Validation and Ranking

Semantic mappings between the database ontologies state the semantic relationships between the RDBSs they described. However, before they are used, it is necessary to validate the mappings to ensure they are semantically correct. For example, if the terms `cs:Employee` and `cs:Staff` are disjoint from each other, then we cannot have another term that have both of these terms as generalization. It is also necessary to deduct additional semantic relationships from existing relationships between the database ontologies. This reduces the number of redundant and unnecessary mappings users need to define. For example, given the following mappings:

$$umcs:Employee \equiv cs:Staff$$
$$cs:Staff \equiv cs:Faculty$$

then, by the *transitivity property*, it is true that:

$$umcs:Employee \equiv cs:Faculty$$

Previously, we could not deduct such relationships and they all have to be defined explicitly. Using a reasoning engine, we can derive such relationships automatically from the knowledgebase and there is no need for users to define such mappings. Alternatively, without using a reasoning engine, such mappings must be stated explicitly. Similarly, other properties such as *functional property*, *inverse functional property*, *symmetric property*, *etc.* are all supported and can be used to derive additional relationships from existing ones. It is also necessary to be able to compare the semantics of terms defined in different database ontologies. For example, given the three ontology hierarchies in Figure 3 and the mappings defined between `umcs:Faculty` and `Professor` and `Employee` and `cs:Staff`, can we define an equivalent mapping between `umcs:TeachingStaff` and `cs:Lecturer`? Before we can do so we first need to compare the semantics of these two terms based on the semantics provided. We will show how this is addressed later using *semantic weights*.

Manual validation, deduction, and comparison of mappings between the database ontologies is extremely difficult if not impossible. We have modified a reasoning engine called Pellet (version 1.3) to automate the validations, deductions, and comparisons of semantic mappings between ontologies. Pellet supports both reasoning over the terminologies (TBox) and their instances (ABox) (see Figure 1). TBox and ABox reasoning ensure concept definitions and their instances are consistent. Pellet generates a semantic knowledgebase automatically from the input ontologies and their semantic mappings. We then query the knowledgebase for relationships that are stated explicitly and those derived from the existing relationships. If Pellet produces "clashes" for a relationship, then the relationship does not entail or follow from the semantic information in the knowledgebase. Alternatively, if Pellet does not produce "clashes", then the relationship is consistent with the semantic information provided.

Comparing between terms defined in different database ontologies requires a quantitative measurement of the semantic relationships between terms. This measurement indicates how far or close two terms are to each other semantically. We refer to this the quantitative measurement as *semantic weight*. Table 1 shows the semantic relationship types and their corresponding semantic weights. A weight of 1.0 means the two terms are semantically the same (i.e., they have the same intensional meaning). Alternatively, a weight of 0 means the two terms are not equivalent to each other. Finally, a weight of $1-0.1^{\lceil log(h) \rceil}$ means one term is more generalized than the other (where h is the height of the ontology tree).

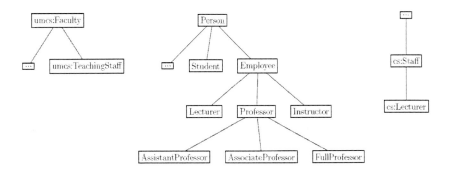

Figure 3. Three sample database ontology trees.

In general, the semantic weight of any two terms $term_i$ and $term_j$ is calculated as follows:

$$weight(term_i, term_j) = (1 - 0.1^{\lceil log(h) \rceil})^k$$

where k is the height differences in the same generalization/specialization hierarchy path between $term_i$ and $term_j$. If the two terms do not share the same generalization/specialization path, then their semantic weight is 0.0 since they do not participate in a generalization/specialization relationship. The value $1 - 0.1^{\lceil log(h) \rceil}$ is chosen for the generalization relationship because $(1 - 0.1^{\lceil log(h) \rceil})^k$ shows a slow linear decrease as k increases. This implies the more specialized a term is, the further away it is from its generalization. Castano *et al.* [2] used 0.8 as the weight for generalization/specialization relationships but this value is not a good value because as k increases, $(0.8)^k$ converges very quickly to 0. For example, since the height of the middle ontology tree in Figure 3 is 4, the generalization weight of any two terms is 0.9 (i.e., $1 - 0.1^{\lceil log(4) \rceil}$). Thus, `weight(Person, Employee)` is 0.9 since `Person` is a direct generalization of `Employee`. Similarly, `weight(Person, FullProfessor)` is 0.729 because:

```
weight(Person,Employee) = 0.9
weight(Employee,Professor) = 0.9
weight(Professor,FullProfessor) = 0.9
```
and
```
weight(Person,FullProfessor)=0.9*0.9*0.9=0.729
```

To evaluate whether or not we can define a mapping between `umcs:TeachingStaff` and `cs:Lecturer` mentioned in the previous example, we first evaluate and assign semantic weights to the existing semantic relationships that relate `umcs:TeachingStaff` and `cs:Lecturer`. From Figure 3, starting with `umcs:TeachingStaff`, we derive the following semantic weights:

Relationships	Semantic Weights
`equivalent`	1.0
`not equivalent`	0.0
`generalization`	$1 - 0.1^{\lceil log(h) \rceil}$

Table 1. Semantic relationships and their semantic weights (where `h` is the height of the ontology tree).

```
weight(umcs:Faculty,umcs:TeachingStaff) = 0.9
weight(umcs:Faculty,Professor) = 1.0
weight(Employee,Professor) = 0.9
```
and
```
weight(Employee,umcs:TeachingStaff)=0.9*1.0*0.9
```

Similarly, starting with `cs:Lecturer`, we derive the following semantic weights:

```
weight(cs:Staff,cs:Lecturer) = 0.9
weight(cs:Staff,Employee) = 1.0
```
and
```
weight(Employee,cs:Lecturer) = 0.9*1.0 = 0.9
```

Since `Employee` is the common generalization in the same hierarchy path for both `umcs:TeachingStaff` and `cs:Lecturer`, we compare their semantic weights with respect to `Employee`. According to the semantic weights calculated, `weight(Employee,umcs:TeachingStaff)` is 0.81 and `weight(Employee,cs:Lecturer)` is 0.9 thus we can conclude that `umcs:TeachingStaff` and `cs:Lecturer` do not have the same semantic granularity so an equivalent mapping should not be defined between them. The semantic weight function added to Pellet is described in Algorithm 5.1.

The weights calculated by the three update functions are accumulative. Initially, weights are set to a value of 1 and when the conditions are satisfied, Pellet updates the weights

Algorithm 5.1 (Semantic Weight Calculation)

```
Input:
        domain ontology DO
        ontology O1
        ontology O2
        a list of mapping statements stmts between O1, O2, and DO

Output: a list of semantic weights added the input stmts

1    build knowledgebase KB from DO, O1, and O2
2    check KB for consistency
3        if not consistent, exit
4    for each statement st in stmts do
5        check satisfiability of st
6        unfold Ti and Ts to use only primitive T's
7        if Ti is a subclass of Tj then
8            update_subclass_weight(Ti, Tj)
9        if Ti is equivalent to Tj then
10           update_equivalent_weight(Ti, Tj)
11       if Ti is disjoint from Tj then
12           update_disjoint_weight (Ti, Tj)
13   end for
```

according to their semantic weights.

6   Conclusion and Future Work

RDBSs are designed and built independently. Database ontologies provide standardized and semantic descriptions of the underlying RDBSs. Semantic mappings between the database ontologies and/or shared ontologies enable semantic interoperability between the RDBSs described by the database ontologies. Mappings between ontologies can be defined manually or semi-automatically and validation is necessary to ensure their correctness. Semantic comparison of concepts defined in different ontologies is also necessary because mappings with different granularity are possible and we want to be able to detect such such mappings. Manually validate and compare mappings is not the solution. In this paper, we modified the Pellet reasoning engine and showed how it can be used to validate and compare mapping between ontologies automatically. The result ensures RDBSs interoperate with each other at the correct level of semantics regardless of how the individual RDBSs are constructed. Using a reasoning engine, such as Pellet, also has other advantages such as: (i) additional mappings can be deduced from existing mappings thus reducing the number of unnecessary and redundant mappings users need to define; (ii) when new mappings are added, the new knowledge is added automatically to the knowledgebase by the reasoning engine there is no additional work required.

In the future, we would like to investigate the following: (i) apply the semantic weight concept to the three reasoning engines RACER [4], KAON2 [7], and OWLJessKB [11] and compare their results with that produced by Pellet. Regardless of their implementation, the results produced should be based on the semantics; (ii) semantic mappings between ontologies are the key to enable semantic interoperability between systems. Mapping management between ontologies must be managed dynamically since evolutions of the individual RDBSs must be supported. We plan to associate *contracts* with mappings and use a shared memory model to manage semantic mappings between ontologies. This allows mappings to be added or removed dynamically.

References

[1] T. Berners-Lee, J. Hendler, and O. Lassila. The Semantic Web: A New Form of Web Content that is Meaningful to Computers Will Unleash a Revolution of New Possibilities. *Scientific American*, (51), May 2001.

[2] S. Castano, A. Ferrara, S. Montanelli, and G. Racca. Semantic Information Interoperability in Open Networked Systems. In *Proceedings of Int. Conference on Semantics of a Networked World (ICSNW), in cooperation with ACM SIGMOD*, pages 215–230, Paris, France, June 2004.

[3] A. Doan, J. Madhavan, P. Domingos, and A. Halevy. Learning to Map Between Ontologies on the Semantic Web. In

WWW '02: Proceedings of the eleventh international conference on World Wide Web, pages 662–673, New York, NY, USA, 2002. ACM Press.

[4] V. Haarslev and R. Möller. Racer: A Core Inference Engine for the Semantic Web. In *EON*, 2003.

[5] V. Haarslev and R. Moller. Racer: An OWL Reasoning Agent for the Semantic Web. *Proc. of the International Workshop on Applications, Products and Services of Web-based Support Systems, in conjunction with 2003 IEEE/WIC International Conference on Web Intelligence, Halifax Canada*, pages 91–95, October 2003.

[6] A. Y. Halevy, Z. G. Ives, D. Suciu, and I. Tatarinov. Schema Mediation in Peer Data Management Systems. In *Proceedings of International Conference on Data Engineering*, March 2003.

[7] KAON2. http://kaon2.semanticweb.org. December 2006.

[8] N. F. Noy. What Do We Need for Ontology Integration on the Semantic Web (Position Statement). In *Proceedings of the Semantic Integration Workshop, Collocated with the Second International Semantic Web Conference (ISWC-03)*, volume 82, October 2003.

[9] N. F. Noy. Semantic Integration: A Survey of Ontology-Based Approaches. *SIGMOD Record*, 33(4):65–70, 2004.

[10] N. F. Noy and D. L. McGuinness. Ontology Development 101: A Guide to Creating Your First Ontology. Technical Report Stanford Knowledge Systems Laboratory Technical Report KSL-01-05 and Stanford Medical Informatics Technical Report SMI-2001-0880, Stanford University, March 2001.

[11] OWLJessKB. http://edge.cs.drexel.edu/assemblies/software/-owljesskb. December 2006.

[12] E. Pitoura, O. Bukhres, and A. Elmagarmid. Object Orientation in Multidatabase Systems. *ACM Computing Surveys*, 27(2):141–195, 1995.

[13] S. Suwanmanee, D. Benslimane, and P. Thiran. OWL-Based Approach for Semantic Interoperability. In *AINA*, pages 145–150. IEEE Computer Society, 2005.

[14] Q. Trinh, K. Barker, and R. Alhajj. Relational Database Definition in Web Ontology Language. Available at http://white.cpsc.ucalgary.ca/ontologies/rdbo/, August 2005.

[15] Q. Trinh, K. Barker, and R. Alhajj. RDB2ONT: A Tool for Generating OWL Ontologies From Relational Database Systems. *Advanced International Conference on Telecommunications (AICT 2006)*, February 2006.

[16] M. Uschold and M. Gruninger. Ontologies and Semantics for Seamless Connectivity. *SIGMOD Record*, 33(4):58–64, 2004.

[17] H. Wache, T. Vögele, U. Visser, H. Stuckenschmidt, G. Schuster, H. Neumann, and S. Hübner. Ontology-Based Integration of Information - A Survey of Existing Approaches. In H. Stuckenschmidt, editor, *IJCAI-01 Workshop: Ontologies and Information Sharing*, pages 108–117, 2001.

[18] Web Ontology Language (OWL). http://www.w3.org/2004/owl. December 2006.

[19] L. Weihua and L. Shixian. Improve the Semantic Interoperability of Information. *2nd IEEE International Conference on Intelligent Systems*, 2:591–594, June 2004.

Stream Processing in a Relational Database: a Case Study

Andrzej Hoppe   Jarek Gryz

Department of Computer Science and Engineering
York University
{ahoppe,jarek}@cse.yorku.ca

Abstract

A consensus seems to have emerged that streams cannot be processed efficiently by relational database engines. This point has been strongly advocated by Michael Stonebreaker, whose StreamBase [19] offers two orders of magnitude better performance in stream processing than a standard DBMS. We faced the challenge and investigated how much improvement in stream processing can be achieved in a standard DBMS just by appropriate tuning and use of features already available there. In this paper, we describe some of the techniques useful for stream processing and show how dramatic performance improvements they can provide. We tend to agree with Stonebreaker that the idea "One Size Fits All" in no longer applicable to all data-centric applications. However, we also believe that dismissing DBMS as irrelevant in stream processing applications is premature. We hope to show that relational database systems are sufficiently flexible to make the idea "One Size May Fit You" worth looking into.

1. Introduction

During the last few years, the stream processing market has been growing rapidly. Research community investigates solutions which could handle data streams better than when they are processed by relational databases. Many new dedicated stream processing engines [1] [7] [8] [23] have been designed and built, some of them as full-fledged commercial products. A consensus seems to have emerged – both in research as well as in industry - that streams cannot be processed efficiently by relational database engines. It is claimed that relational databases were not designed to process data dynamically on a continuous basis, hence stream processing requires a novel, different approach. This point has been strongly advocated by Michael Stonebreaker, whose StreamBase [19] offers two

orders of magnitude better performance in stream processing than a standard DBMS. It is quite likely, however, that the comparison was made with DBMS at its default settings, without any special adjustments made for the new type of data. We accepted the challenge and decided to investigate how much improvement in stream processing can be achieved in a standard DBMS just by appropriate tuning and use of features already available there. We used a commercial database system, DB2 UDB version 8.21 (the setup's details are provided in Section 4). The results we achieved by tuning and the use of standard DB2 features were dramatic: a twenty-fourfold improvement over the performance of a relational database reported in [19]. Although our best result reached only 13% of the processing rate of StreamBase, we should emphasize that it does not represent the limit of DB2's performance (for example, we have not done any hardware tuning). Moreover, we believe that there are many applications where the rate achieved in our experiments would be perfectly acceptable. We tend to agree with Stonebreaker that the idea "One Size Fits All" in no longer applicable to all data-centric applications. However, we also believe that dismissing DBMS as irrelevant in stream processing applications is premature. We hope to have shown that relational database systems are sufficiently flexible to make the idea "One Size May Fit You" worth looking into.

The paper is organized as follows. In Section 2 we discuss the reasons why the relational databases have difficulty handling efficiently data streams. Section 3 provides an overview of some solutions we believe can improve DBMS's stream processing performance. We describe in detail the solutions we implemented and the performance results in Section 4. We conclude in Section 5.

---

[1] The choice of this particular product was entirely accidental; we believe that similar results can be achieved with other commercial database systems.

216

2. Bottlenecks for stream processing in relational databases

To the best of our knowledge, there is no work addressing the specific issue of tuning a standard relational database system for stream processing. Information on research in stream data processing can be found in several surveys [4] [17] [22] [24]. We start our work by a short overview of bottlenecks for stream processing.

The relational databases were originally designed to support the "outboud" model. However, in many situations the stream market requires the "inbound" model. The "outbound" model can be described: store first, then possibly process. The "inbound" model can be described: process, possibly store, possibly process. In many situations of data stream processing, it is not required to store the entire incoming stream of data in a database. Writing into or reading from a disk is one of the critical paths in databases, because of the I/O cost. Hence, the gain can be significant if the incoming data is not stored. This situation is typical when a database deals with the stream from which customers want to get some statistics, for instance moving average or outliers, rather than the actual data.

Multi-users access is one of the most important features of databases systems. The implementation of it has various aspects. Each relational database is implemented in the client-server architecture. Every client connected to the database has its independent environment. Those issues introduce overhead and should prompt a redesign for a single-user DMBS. Transaction management is one of the most important issues correlated with multi-user access. Assurance of ACID properties for transaction execution is a must. However, it comes with a significant cost. The recovery and backup utilities are heavy-weight parts of a database [16]. They are responsible for assurance of durability of the system and the possibility to return the system to some previous version. However, in the stream market they are often superfluous, as customers may accept approximate answers and temporary inconsistencies. It should be possible to turn them off completely or implement lighter solutions (for instance, as in BerkeleyDB [18]).

The database systems suffer from a lack of business logic or from its inefficiency. DBMS has a seamless integration of logic (SQL) with conventional programming facilities. Using the embedded procedural language such as SQL-PL for DB2 or PL-SQL for Oracle is limited. They are not full-fledged languages. They are the second-class users [6]. Many customers would like to see in DBMS a lightweight combination of C++ and query language as was done in StreamBase [19]. Moreover, there are several technical problems in applications development in the procedural languages; for instance, lack of correlation between procedural languages and rollback systems.

Queries over data streams have much in common with queries in DBMS. However, there is an important distinction peculiar to the data stream model. It is the distinction between one-time queries and continuous queries. One-time query is evaluated once as a point-in-time snapshot of a database and the answer is returned. On the other hand, continuous queries are evaluated continuously as the data stream arrives; their computation is incremental. The incremental computation can be faster than computations from scratch each time, because of the possibility of work reuse. Moreover, computation of one-time queries periodically is not equivalent to the continuous query idea. DBMSs do not support continuous queries and the computation of one-time queries each time a new tuple arrives is unacceptable [4] for performance reasons.

Performance requirements are the reason why blocking algorithm and multi-pass algorithms are not acceptable for stream processing. If a data set does not fit into main memory, algorithms have to be multi-pass. However, if approximate answers are acceptable, then one-pass algorithms should be feasible. The majority of one-pass algorithms are designed to support very specialized queries. Examples include quantile and order statistics computation, estimating correlated aggregates and simple statistics over sliding windows [2]. One-pass algorithms are the best in the specific aggregations queries [3]. Solutions based on sampling, implemented in traditional databases such as row-level sampling and block-level, are too slow or too sensitive on data partitioning [14]. One novel issue, which is implemented in some stream databases, for instance in Aurora [6], is load shedding. The difference between traditional sampling and load shedding is that the latter makes decision on discrediting a tuple dynamically, when the size of the query answer or the temporary table exceeds a definite limit. This is very useful during joins, and can protect against cross products. Moreover, it can be used to assure Quality of Service (QoS) during an overload of a database [21].

3. Tools and Techniques Used to Improve Stream Processing Performance in DB2

3.1 Data Stream Management System architecture

Schema design is very important for any type of workload. A bad design can not only reduce understanding of the data, but may also introduce unnecessary joins, hence a decrease in performance. Schema design for stream data processing in relational database and its impact on performance was not much investigated. Our schema design is influenced by general Data Stream Management System architecture [17]. A slightly different architecture (shown in Figure 1) is proposed in [25], where much attention is turned to the scheduler, which is responsible for scheduling queries being computed interchangeably. The data is typically stored in three partitions: temporary working storage (for example, for sliding window queries), summary storage for stream synopses and static storage for meta-data and the rest of information. The results are streamed to the users or temporarily buffered. Different parts of this architecture are clearly separated, so that different privileges and resources can be assigned to them (for instance different tablespaces). We follow some the recommendations from this architecture for our prototypes as well.

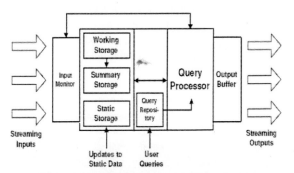

Figure 1. Architecture for a data stream management system.

3.2. Indexes

The typical bottleneck for most databases is disk access. Although stream processing usually does not require storing the whole data on disk, a database engine must do it to be able to process it. The I/O cost can be reduced by either keeping as much as possible of the processed data in memory or by accessing as little as possible of redundant data from disk. There are great many solutions to achieve these goals both at the

hardware (e.g. size of memory) as well as the software level (e.g. page replacement strategies). A database administrator also has a few tools at his/her disposal, for instance, memory management. Indexes and materialized views (Materialized Query Tables or MQTs in the DB2 terminology) are one of the most widely used and powerful techniques to significantly speed up query processing. DB2 supports only one type of index, a B+ tree index, which has several parameters and settings. A few of them were found useful for our workload:

Unique This keyword prevents the table from containing two or more rows with the same value of the index key. This introduces a small overhead, because it has to be verified each time the index is modified. However, in our scenario it never happened after applying include clause. The uniqueness of the key increases the possibility of generating a better plan by the optimizer.

Include This keyword is unique for DB2 in the context of index creation. It allows the extension of the leaf page to contain additional columns. Such an approach has several advantages. First, it increases the fan out of nodes in the B-tree. This diminishes the depth of the tree and the number of pages read during the search of a particular node. Second, it decreases the overall size of an index. This can reduce the page flushing. Third, it eliminates the necessity of checking the uniqueness of the key if the unique word is also specified and the value of the include column has changed. Last but not least, for traditional workloads the include clause makes index much more universal and increases the possibility of creating an index-only access plan. We illustrate this feature with an example:

Table definition:
CREATE TABLE TAB1 (A integer, B integer, C integer, D BLOB);

Indexes definitions:
CREATE UNIQUE INDEX I1_TAB1 ON (A, B, C);
CREATE UNIQUE INDEX I2_TAB1 ON (A) include (B,C);

Queries:
SELECT A FROM TAB1 WHERE A=5 and B>6;
SELECT A FROM TAB1 WHERE A=5 and C>6;

In this scenario, only the second index can allow both queries to use index only scan. The second index improves the performance significantly for the first query, but is not as useful for the second one. The plan generated for the second query using first index can be much faster if the condition is very selective. Hence, usage of the include keyword requires an analysis of the workload.

Clustered The order of tuples in a table and keys in the index is similar and is maintained dynamically as the data is inserted into the table. This property adds some overhead during the delete, update, and insert operations, because matching between order in the table and the index has to be maintained. However, in our scenario it comes free, because we do not have any delete or insert statement and the update statements do not change the keys of the index column. They change only values in the included columns. This property can significantly increase the performance of some queries, since there is a good chance that matched rows found in one index leaf pages are on the same or sibling pages in the hard disk.

Pcfree This parameter defines what percentage of each index page can be left as free space when building the index. It is another way to compress and reduce the size of the index. The default value was decreased to reduce the size of the index. The disadvantage of reducing this parameter is a possibly higher cost of maintenance of the index. It increases the chance of reorganization of the tree structure of the index. In our workload, it does not happen, because the key value of the index is not changed.

Disallow reverse scan This feature allows index scan only with increasing values of keys (that is, in one direction only). The following example shows such a situation.

Table definition: the same as above. Indexes definitions:
CREATE UNIQUE INDEX I3_TAB1 ON (A,B) ALLOWS REVERSE SCAN;
CREATE UNIQUE INDEX I4_TAB1 ON (A,B) DISALLOWS REVERSE SCAN ;

Queries:
SELECT min(A) FROM TAB1 WHERE A>5;
SELECT max(A) FROM TAB1 WHERE A<5;

The first index is useful for both queries, whereas the second one, only for the first query. The advantage of disallowing reverse scan is index compression.

3.3. Multi users access

Concurrency control causes deadlocks. In a stream processing environment, where data is often processed in real time, this is unacceptable. Moreover, long waits between concurrent transactions are also undesirable. There are a few techniques, such as operation policy, commit policy, and schema design that reduce the cost

of concurrency control. Each of them has advantages and disadvantages. These trade-offs are described below.

Modification of the isolation level can have significant impact on performance. The isolation has to be set to the strictest level for the majority of workloads. In DB2 the strictest level is called repeatable read (RR) (serializable in ANSI SQL terminology). RR prevents access to uncommitted data, non-repeatable reads and phantom reads. However, the isolation level can be decreased if the gain of the performance is significant and customers' scenarios allow it. This is often the case in the data stream environment, where approximate answers are usually acceptable. We should point out, however, that the decrease of isolation level does not necessarily increase the performance significantly. In our study we found it useful only in one of our prototypes.

Data redundancy is not used often in the traditional workloads, because the maintenance of the duplicated data is difficult and expensive. The situation is different for the majority of stream data processing. Even if the database schema is large, the isolation of the module responsible for stream processing is possible and the application of this method is feasible. Data duplication enables users to access the same data in parallel. This can protect against deadlocks and waiting. The data consistency has to be ensured, but the data, which does not change very often and is accessed frequently can be duplicated.

Another method to reduce deadlocks and waiting problem is through commit policy. The commit statement causes transaction to be accepted by the database and frees locks on resources such as tables, indexes, materialized views. However, the commit statement is an expensive operation and introduces significant overhead. The trade–offs between deadlock and waiting problems and overhead of the commit statement has to be considered. Unfortunately, there are no straightforward solutions to this problem and the literature [11] [14] contains few guidelines for the general workload.

3.4. Triggers

A trigger defines a set of actions executed by a delete, insert, or update operation on a specified table. When such an SQL operation is executed, the trigger is said to be activated. The trigger can be activated before the SQL operation or after it. For any operation, many different triggers can be activated [11]. Trigger is an obvious tool to use to process streaming data as it allows immediate execution of side effects (for example, aggregation computation) at the time of data arrival. Another advantage of the triggers is their expressiveness and implementation on the server-side.

3.5. Data-change-table-reference clause

Data-change-table-reference-clause (DCTRC) was originally designed to support data warehousing [5]. DCTRC allows the execution of a select statement from an intermediate table which can be the result of insert, update, or delete statement. The intermediate table can be represented as old table, new table, or final table described in more detail below.

Old table: Specifies that the rows of the intermediate result table represent the set of rows that are changed by the SQL data change statement, as they existed prior to the application of the data change statement.

New Table: Specifies that the rows of the intermediate result table represent the set of rows that are changed by the SQL data change statement prior to the application of referential constraints and AFTER triggers. Data in the target table at the completion of the statement might not match the data in the intermediate results table because of additional processing for referential constraints and AFTER triggers. It is different from Old Table, because BEFORE trigger are applied.

Final Table: Specifies that the rows of the intermediate result table represent the set of rows that are changed by the SQL data change statement as they appear at the completion of the data change statement. Unfortunately, the table is not allowed to have AFTER triggers [13] [10].

There are a few reasons for performance improvement with DCTRC. The first one is that DCTRC locks data only once. Second, the select statement does not have to search in the whole table; it can search only in the modified part of it (internal results). The necessary part of the table is already found in the buffer pool. Moreover, it can be directly pipelined to the select statement without usage of the buffer pool. Last but not least, it reduces overhead generated by every individual statement: each statement has to be initialized, return results, and return SQLSTATE.

3.6. Temporary tables

A temporary table is another feature introduced into the relational database engine. It is not well standardized between different vendors. DB2 has different types of temporary tables depending on the type of the operating system. DB2 for Unix, Windows has only a declared global temporary table, but DB2

for z/OS has a created global temporary table. The main differences between those types are:
- Logging: no logging for created table, limited logging for declared
- Locking: no locking for created table, limited locking for declared

In the latest versions of DB2, the declared tables can turn off locking. The created global temporary tables are not available in our systems and have not solved more technical issues. For instance, one cannot create indexes on them. However, the declared global temporary tables are more useful.
- Declared temporary tables do not have descriptions in the DB2 Catalog. They are defined in the program, prior to the program execution.
- Declared temporary tables can have indexes and CHECK constraints defined on them.
- One can issue UPDATE statements and position DELETE statements against them.
- One can implicitly define the columns of a declared temporary table and use the result table from a SELECT statement.

The biggest performance advantages of declared temporary tables come from reduction of locking, logging, and recovery mechanisms. They are not thrown away as it was in created temporary tables, but, they are implemented with a lighter approach. Our performance tests show that operations on temporary tables are twice as fast as with ordinary tables. Unfortunately, not all features are available to them, for instance, index cannot contain include clause and it is impossible to create trigger on them. This is because declared tables are not stored in system catalogs.

From the technical point of view the usage of declared temporary tables is not easy. It requires setting options and to create a new bufferpool and a temporary tablespace to store the temporary tables. Another problem is that they are outside the system, which prevents the use of bulk loading utilities to populate temporary tables.

3.7. Database tuning and data loading

Database tuning in DB2 is split between a database manager configuration and a database configuration [20]. The former changes parameters for DB2 instance. The latter modifies settings for each individual database. In our problem, the database tuning did not give as much improvement as we expected at the outset. In the final solutions, the problem of swapping buffer pools turned out to be irrelevant. The problem of deadlock and wait times was not burdensome. Hence, the parameter modification correlated with those issues did not improve anything. Moreover, no advantage can be taken of parallelism. In the database where hardware allows parallelism, good setting can leverage the performance. There are different levels of parallelism: disks-RAID, processors, machines; we did not try any of them. Changes of a few parameters from automatic to precise numbers were made and unnecessary resources were freed. Furthermore, DB2 has different levels of query optimization, but the changes of this parameter did not have any influence on the results. In the end, database tuning increased the performance by 4%, which was much less than expected. The performance difference was more pronounced in the first prototypes, where the swapping problem occurred but still it was a marginal factor in comparison with other solutions.

Our initial approach to data loading was to explore various types of bulk loading rather than use a sequence of simple insert operations. Each single operation causes a small overhead, but if the number of operations is large, amortizing the overhead over all operations can potentially provide significant performance improvement. Moreover, the load utility does not check integrity constraints and triggers calling. It also uses smarter policy of commit statements. The load utility has implemented SMP (Symmetric Multiprocessor Machines) to increase intra-partition parallelism. After a short study of possible utilities to move the data in bulk [15], we performed a few simple experiments testing their performance. Unfortunately, our experimental results show that load and import utilities are not very useful for a single processor and a single disk machine.

4. Experimental Evaluation

Our experimental evaluation of the stream processing in DB2 has been done using a benchmark described in [19]. We describe the benchmark first, and then present several distinct solutions implemented on the top of DB2. A comparison of performance results follows.

The benchmark presented in [19] is a good reflection of financial-feed processing. It describes a scenario, where a broker office receives stock rates from NASDAQ and Dow Jones Industrial Average. The goal is to monitor feeds and late ticks. The broker's office needs to be informed, when it has received incomplete information. The company orders services from two independent suppliers A and B. Each of them supplies both stock rates. There are 4,500 securities, 500 of which are "fast moving". A stock tick on one of these securities is late if it occurs more than five seconds after the previous tick from the same security. The other 4,000 symbols are slow moving,

and a tick is late if 60 seconds have elapsed since the previous tick. The customer wants to receive an alert message when (a) there is a late tick; (b) there are 100 late ticks from either provider; (c) there are 100 late ticks from either exchange through either feed vendor. In this benchmark, StreamBase is able to serve 160,000 messages per second.

In our implementation, we simulate the scenario described above. There are two applications, which supply data. They simulate tick stream suppliers. Each stream contains stocks rates from two stock exchanges. The stock rate contains id, to distinguish between stock exchanges. The time stamp is taken from a system. The applications are very light. For example, the prices are taken from previously generated table that are stored inside the application and send cyclically. This is necessary to avoid calling expensive random function frequently. In all of the prototypes described in this case study, client-side and server-side terms are used as if the supplying applications were on a different machine. Each prototype has four tables to store the counters. They are all single row, single column tables and each of them stores information about errors (late ticks) described above. Such atomization reduces the concurrency and deadlocks problem in the critical path. In addition, the database has a table (tables), which store and process the incoming stream. The requirements in [19] do not assume that the whole stream needs to be stored.

Following the design of a stream processing architecture shown in Figure 1, we separated working, summary, and statistic storage. The working storage is stored in separate table (tables) and has only the most recent data. Since it is relatively small, it can stay in the buffer pool at all times making all operations performed on it relatively inexpensive. That working storage represents a moving window, because all operations are performed on the recent data only. The summary storage does not exist in the final design, because it is not required by the benchmark. The four error counter tables can be considered statistics storage.

Our testing environment is similar to the one described in [19] (both are shown in Table 1). StreamBase has a somewhat slower processor and less memory, but has a faster disk.

Table 1. System Configuration Comparison.

	StreamBase Environment	DB2 Environment
Processor	2.8Ghz Pentium	Intel Pentium 4 CPU 3.00GHz.
Main memory size	512 Mbytes	896 Mbytes
Disk	single SCSI disk	single IDE disk
Operating system	Unknown	Linux
Database	Unknown	DB2 UDP v8.2.6

We present our solutions as 8 prototypes below, each implemented with C++ and embedded static SQL. Each prototype introduces a new feature that provides some performance improvement. The order of the introduction of the features is from simple to more elaborate ones. We do not present experiments with each of the features introduced separately as the optimizations provided by each feature are not additive (that is, if features A and B provide 50% improvement each, then it does not follow that both of them together will improve performance by 125%). On the other hand, we cannot provide results for all combinations of features as this would require 2^8 experiments.

Prototype 1: Stock ticks from both suppliers are stored in one table. No indexes are defined. The business logic is implemented on the client side. This approach is applied in all prototypes excluding the fifth and the seventh prototype. Commit statement is invoked for each tick, which is handled by at least two statements: select and update. Additional operations to update counters are required, if the tick is late.

Prototype 2: It is similar to the first prototype, but it contains indexes. The basic indexes (without any of the features discussed in Section 3.2) are defined on tables populated by suppliers. The indexes on errors counter tables are not created, because they are one tuple, one column tables. The introduction of indexes doubles the performance. A big advantage of indexes is their ability to work in combination with other techniques introduced in the following prototypes.

Prototype 3: In this prototype, the data is duplicated to reduce the concurrency problem and to allow a better use of internal parallelism. Each supplier populates a different table. This prototype uses similar basic indexes and commit policy as the second prototype. After the duplication, only the errors counter tables are common resources for two data-generating applications. This technique introduces the largest

performance improvement: seven times over the previous version.

Prototype 4: In this prototype, we change the commit policy, which is used in the first three prototypes. In this, and the following prototypes, the statements are grouped together and commit statement is invoked once per group. The indexes now take full advantage of features such as unique, include, clustered, pcfree, disallow reverse scan.

The performance increases three times over Prototype 3. Unfortunately, this technique is not neutral with respect to other solutions (for example, it cannot be used together with the observer application introduced in Prototype 7).

Prototype 5: In addition to all improvements added in the fourth prototype, we now implement business logic on the server side by means of after triggers as described in Section 3.4. The trigger presented below shows some fragment of the business logic necessary to implement our fifth prototype.

```
CREATE TRIGGER FIRST_SUPPLIER
  AFTER UPDATE OF time ON Quotations
  REFERENCING OLD AS oldrow NEW AS newrow

            FOR EACH ROW MODE DB2SQL
BEGIN ATOMIC
  IF( newrow.idCompany < 4000 ) THEN
    IF (newrow.time - oldrow.time > 60 ) THEN
      UPDATE slow_error_counter SET
                COUNTER = COUNTER + 1;
      UPDATE first_supplier_error_counter SET
                COUNTER = COUNTER + 1;
    END IF;
  ELSEIF ( newrow.time - oldrow.time > 5 ) THEN
    UPDATE fast_error_counter SET
                COUNTER = COUNTER + 1;
    UPDATE first_supplier_error_counter SET
                COUNTER = COUNTER + 1;
  END IF;
END @
```

Its goal is to modify suitable error counters if the conditions for on-time arrival of ticks are violated. It is activated, when a timestamp is modified for a company. The old version tuple (before modification) is stored as an old row and new (after modification) is stored as a new row. The old timestamp is retrieved from the first one and the new timestamp from the second one. The difference between timestamps allows us to classify the stock tick as late. Additional information (idCompany) is used to distinguish between stock exchanges. It defines the admissible delay (5 or 60 seconds). If an unacceptable delay happens, the two errors counters are modified.

Similarly, another trigger is defined for the second supplier. Moreover, four more triggers are created on fast_error_counter, slow_error_counter, first_supplier _error_counter, second_supplier_error_counter tables to check the number of errors and signal that the limit (100) has been reached.

Performance gain is modest (around 25%). Also, triggers cannot be used together with any of the solutions introduced below.

Prototype 6: This prototype moves back to implementation of the business logic on the client side (it is an alternative to Prototype 5). We introduced DCTRC clause described in Section 3.5. One data-change-table-reference clause is used instead of a pair of select and update statements for each tick. We used one DCTRC per a pair of select and update statement for example.

```
SELECT time INTO :oldTime
FROM quotations
WHERE idCompany=:id; newTime=:newTime;
(UPDATE quotations
SET time=:newTime price=:newPrice
WHERE idCompany=:id );

SELECT time INTO :oldTime
FROM OLD TABLE
(UPDATE quotations
SET price=newPrice, time=:newTime
WHERE idCompany=:id);
```

The first two statements implement a service of one incoming tuple. The first one gets the old timestamp as oldTime for a company, and the second one updates a price and sets the new timestamp for the company. The third statement makes exactly the same as the first two, but takes an advantage of doing so in one operation using DCTRC. The internal part (update) modified the table and the outer part (select) queries the old version of the table. In other words, the select statement has access to the table, before modifications. The idea of old table is similar to the old row in triggers.

The performance improvement is 73% over Prototype 4 and 23% faster in comparison with the trigger implementation.

Prototype 7: In this solution, the business logic is shifted to the server side once more. We introduce an additional application, which is called the observer that is running on the server side continuously. Its purpose is to monitor the timing of arriving ticks. If a tick is late, then the error tables are updated and late message generated by the observer. It posts one time-queries continuously. The isolation level has to be changed to increase the performance. The data duplication and commit policy do not protect against deadlocks and

waiting, because the supplying applications do not have any common resources together, but the observer accesses populated tables simultaneously with the supplying applications. Such overlapping is unacceptable with the default isolation level. Hence, it is changed from RR to uncommitted read (UR) only for the observer application. It allows the observer application to access tables without exclusive locks. Fortunately, the observer reads only common resources and rollback operations do not occur in the system. Hence, an access to uncommitted data is not a problem, because the new uncommitted timestamps should be considered correct. Moreover, non-repeatable reads and phantom reads do not cause problems either.

Performance gain is modest (around 20%). This shows that the performance of many one-time queries instead of long-running queries is sometimes acceptable. The observer cannot use the techniques described in the next subparagraph.

Prototype 8: This prototype moves back to implementation business logic on the client side. It has used similar approaches and solutions as the sixth prototype, but it takes advantage of global declared temporary tables as described in Section 3.6. The supplier tables are stored in the temporary tables. The error counters are stored as in all previous prototypes in the traditional tables. This is the fastest prototype. However, the previous one has an advantage over this one, because the business logic is implemented on the server side, which can be desirable or even required by the customer and the performance is only slightly worse.

The results of the experiments using the prototypes described above are shown in Figure 2. Our default configuration, Prototype 1, performs even worse (256 messages/sec) than in the test reported in [19], where a commercial relational DBMS could serve 900 messages per second. However, each introduced feature increases the performance significantly.

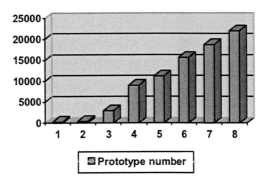

Figure 2. Experimental results (messages/sec).

5. Conclusions

Two points should be emphasized as conclusions. First, the tools and techniques presented in this case study are by no means complete or most effective: there are plenty of other opportunities to improve performance of stream processing in a relational database system (hardware tuning, intra and inter parallelism, introduction of new features, to name a few). Some of these new features would be relatively easy to add. For example, the ability to modify tables in before triggers (currently not available in DB2) would allow the DBMS to process an incoming tuple and store (possibly) only a fragment of the incoming stream. This would strongly improve the support for the "inbound" model. Second, the results achieved by applying just a few, relatively simple techniques were astounding: two orders of magnitude difference between a naïve approach and our top-performing solution. We believe that there is still more that can be done in this area.

6. References

[1]   A. Arasu, B. Babcock, S. Babu, M. Datar, K. Ito, I. Nishizawa, J. Rosenstein, and J. Widom, "STREAM: The Stanford Stream Data Manager", SIGMOD 2003, 665.

[2]   A. Dobra, M. Garofalakis, J. Gehrke, and R. Rastogi, "Processing complex aggregate queries over data streams", SIGMOD 2002, 61-72.

[3]   A. Gilbert, Y. Kotidis, S. Muthukrishnan, and M. Strauss "Surfing Wavelets on Streams: One-Pass Summaries for Approximate Aggregate Queries", VLDB 2001, 79-88.

[4]   B. Babcock, S. Babu, M. Datar, R. Motwani, and J. Widom, "Models and Issues in Data Stream Systems", PODS 2002, 1-16.

[5]   B. Devlin, and B. O'Connell, "Information Integration: New capabilities in data warehousing for the on demand business", January 2005.

[6]   D. Carney, U. Çetintemel, M. Cherniack, C. Convey, S. Lee, G. Seidman, M. Stonebraker, and N. Tatbul, S. B. Zdonik, "Monitoring Streams - A New Class of Data Management Applications", VLDB 2002, 215-226.

[7]   D. J. Abadi, D. Carney, U. Çetintemel, M. Cherniack, C. Convey, C. Erwin, E. F. Galvez, M. Hatoun, A. Maskey, A. Rasin, A. Singer, M. Stonebraker, N. Tatbul, Y. Xing, R. Yan, S. B. Zdonik, "Aurora: A Data Stream Management System", SIGMOD 2003, 666.

[8]   D. J. Abadi, W. Lindner, S. Madden, and J. Schuler, "An Integration Framework for Sensor Networks and Data Stream Management Systems", VLDB 2004, 1361-1364.

[9]   DB2 Everyplace 9.1 for Lotus Expeditor 6.1: DB2 Everyplace 9.1 for Lotus Expeditor Toolkit 6.1, 2006.

[10]   G. Birchall, DB2 UDB V8.2 SQL Cookbook, November 2004.

[11]   IBM DB2 Universal Database Application Building Guide.

[12]   IBM DB2 Universal Database Call Level Interface Guide and Reference, Volume 1 Version 8.2.

[13]   IBM DB2 Universal Database SQL Reference Volume 1 Version 8.2.

[14]   IBM DB2 Universal Database Administration Guide: Performance Version 8.2.

[15]   IBM DB2 Universal Database Data Movement Utilities Guide and Reference Version 8.2.

[16]   L. Gu, T. Bhatnagar, and Y. Ha, DB2 UDB Backup and Recovery with ESS Copy Services, August 2002.

[17]   L. Golab, and M. T. Özsu, "Issues in data stream management", SIGMOD 2003, 5-14.

[18]   M. I. Seltzer, and M. A. Olson, "Challenges in Embedded Database System Administration", USENIX 1999.

[19]   M. Stonebraker, and U. Çetintemel, ""One Size Fits All": An Idea Whose Time Has Come and Gone", ICDE 2005, 2-11.

[20]   N. Alur, P. Farrell, P. Gunning, S. Mohseni, and S. Rajagopalan, DB2 UDB ESE V8 non-DPF Performance Guide for High Performance OLTP and BI, April 2004.

[21]   N. Tatbul, U. Cetintemel, S. Zdonik, M. Cherniack, and M. Stonebraker, "Load Shedding in a Data Stream Manager", VLDB 2003, 309-320.

[22]   R. Stephens, "A Survey of Stream Processing" Acta Inf. 2007, 34.

[23]   S. Madden, and M. J. Franklin, "Fjording the Stream: An Architecture for Queries Over Streaming Sensor Data", ICDE 2002, 555-566.

[24]   S. Muthukrishnan, "Data streams: algorithms and applications", SODA 2003, 413-413.

[25]   W. Lindner, and J. Meier, "Towards a Secure Data Stream Management System", TEAA 2005.

Streaming Random Forests

Hanady Abdulsalam, David B. Skillicorn, and Patrick Martin
School of Computing
Queen's University
Kingston, ON Canada, K7L 3N6
{hanady,skill,martin}@cs.queensu.ca

Abstract

Many recent applications deal with data streams, *conceptually endless sequences of data records, often arriving at high flow rates. Standard data-mining techniques typically assume that records can be accessed multiple times and so do not naturally extend to streaming data. Algorithms for mining streams must be able to extract all necessary information from records with only one, or perhaps a few, passes over the data. We present the* Streaming Random Forests *algorithm, an online and incremental stream classification algorithm that extends Breiman's Random Forests algorithm. The Streaming Random Forests algorithm grows multiple decision trees, and classifies unlabelled records based on the plurality of tree votes. We evaluate the classification accuracy of the Streaming Random Forests algorithm on several datasets, and show that its accuracy is comparable to the standard Random Forest algorithm.*

Keywords Data mining, Classification, Decision trees, Data-stream classification, Random Forests.

1. Introduction

Many applications such as internet traffic monitoring, telecommunications billing, near-earth asteroid tracking, closed-circuit television, and sales tracking produce huge amounts of data to be analyzed. It is not usually cost-effective to store all of this data. Such data is a conceptually endless, real-time, and ordered sequence of records and so is modelled as a *stream*. In order to extract knowledge from stream data, existing data-mining algorithms must be adapted to reflect the properties of streams.

Data stream mining algorithms face several issues that are not critical for ordinary data-mining algorithms:

- Algorithms must be online and incremental, so that re-

sults can be produced at any time (perhaps after some initial starting period). In particular, the relationship of the accuracy of the model to the amount of data seen must be understood.

- Algorithms must be fast enough to handle the rate at which new data arrives (which means effectively amortized $\mathcal{O}(1)$ time for both learning and prediction/clustering).

- Algorithms should be adaptive to changes in the distribution of values in the underlying stream as the result, for example, of concept drift, since they may run for long periods of time.

- Results that depend on observing an entire data set cannot be computed exactly, so the results of stream mining must necessarily be an approximation.

Data-stream mining has attracted a great deal of attention, with research in, for example, detecting changes in data streams [15, 16], maintaining statistics of data streams [7, 20], data-stream classification, and data-stream clustering [3, 11]. In this paper, we consider the problem of classification for stream data.

Classification is normally considered as requiring three phases, each with its associated data. In the first phase, a model is built using labelled training data; in the second phase, the model is tested using previously-unseen labelled data (test data); and in the third phase, the model is deployed on unlabelled data. In stream classification, there is only a single stream of data, so the problem must be formulated in a different way. We assume a setting in which some records in the stream are labelled, which are used for building or testing the model, while others are not, and the goal is to predict the class of the unlabelled records.

Within this setting there are several different scenarios, depending on how the (labelled) training examples are distributed through the stream. Some possibilities are shown in Figure 1. In Scenario 0, labelled data records occur only in some initial segment of the data stream. In this case, the only new issues are related to performance. The classifier can be built in a standard (offline) way, but must be built quickly enough to keep up with the arrival rate of the labelled records. Similarly, classification must be fast enough to keep up with the arrival rate of unlabelled records. Some subset or suffix of the labelled records can be used as test data. In this scenario, there is no way to respond to changes in the underlying distribution of the records such as concept drift.

In Scenario 1, labelled records occur regularly in the stream but, when they occur, there are enough of them to build and test a robust classifier. This classifier can then be used to classify the subsequent unlabelled records. However, after some time, new labelled records arrive in the stream, and the existing classifier must take these into account, either building a new model to reflect the structure of the new labelled data, or altering the existing model (if necessary) to reflect the new information. The decision about which approach to take depends on how much variability is expected, but a full range of responses are available.

In Scenario 2, labelled records again occur regularly in the stream, but there are not enough of them in each batch or block to build and test a robust classifier. Classification of unlabelled records could begin very early, with appropriate caveats about accuracy, or might be postponed until the classifier is observed to be working well, which might require several batches of labelled records. However, in this scenario, the classifier can be very sensitive to changes in the labelled data, and reflect them in classification of unlabelled records very rapidly. In both Scenarios 1 and 2, the known frequency of labelled records enables the algorithm to amortize the cost they induce to train the classifier more efficiently.

In Scenario 3, labelled records occur at random in the stream. This is the most challenging, but also the most realistic, situation since the classifier must be able to keep up with using the labelled examples to build or modify the classifier, even when they appear close together in the stream.

Classification of unlabelled records could be required from the beginning of the stream, after some sufficiently long sequence of labelled records, or at specific moments in time and for a specific block of records selected by an external analyst.

In many situations, records are able to be labelled because the passage of time has revealed the appropriate class labels for each one. For example, a classification system for approving mortgage applications is based on historical data about which applicants previously granted mortgages repaid them without problems. Clearly, the problem is a two-class classification problem, that is either the application is approved or not. Another example for stream classification is spam detection, where an incoming stream of emails (unlabelled records) could be supplemented by

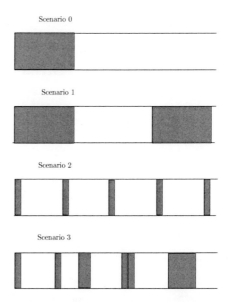

Figure 1. Possible scenarios for the embedding of labelled records in streams

emails that have already been delivered to users' mailboxes and have been (implicitly) labelled as spam or not based on whether the user deleted them unread or read them. These labelled records could help to improve the spam classification model continuously based on user feedback.

In other situations, *some* records are labelled because only *some* people or objects participate. For example, traffic delays in congested areas are beginning to be predicted based on the transit time of cell phones from tower to tower (or from specialized traffic direction systems available in some cars). Only a small percentage of cars provide this information, but the resulting data can be used to classify particular routes as free-flowing or congested. The data used to provide these predictions matches Scenario 3, since the labelled records (cars with known transit times along a particular route) arrive at random compared to the requests from cars for route classification.

Some applications, for example spam detection, do not require that unlabelled records are classified all the time. There may be periods where it is possible to ignore the unlabelled records and only consider the labelled ones to train the classifier. Such situation matches Scenario 1.

Decision trees have been widely used for data-stream classification [9, 13]. These are typically based on Hoeffding bounds, which indicate when enough data have been seen to make a robust decision about which attribute and which split value to use to construct the next internal node.

Tree ensembles have also been used for stream classification [8, 10, 12, 18, 19]. The Random Forest algorithm by Breiman [5] is a classification algorithm that grows multiple binary decision trees, each from a bootstrap sample of the data. The splitting decision at each node selects the best attribute on which to split from a small set of attributes chosen randomly. Classification is based on the plurality of votes from all of the trees. The use of bootstrap samples and restricted subsets of attributes makes it a more powerful algorithm than simple ensembles of trees.

The contribution of this paper is to define a new algorithm, *Streaming Random Forests*, a classification algorithm that combines techniques used to build streaming decision trees with the attribute selection techniques of Random Forests. We demonstrate that the streaming version of random forests achieves classification accuracy comparable to the standard version on artificial and real datasets using only a single pass through the data. Our Streaming Random Forest algorithm handles only numerical or ordinal attributes for which the maximum and minimum values of each attribute are known, but it can be easily extended to handle categorical attributes. It also handles multi-class classification problems, in contrast to many stream classification techniques that have been designed and/or tested only on two-class problems [8, 9, 13, 18, 19].

This paper is organized as follows: Section 2 describes some background and related work. Section 3 defines the Streaming Random Forest algorithm. Section 4 describes experiments and results. Finally, Section 5 draws some conclusions.

2. Related work

2.1. Attribute selection for standard decision trees

Each internal node of a decision tree is built by determining the attribute whose values are most discriminative among the target classes, based on one of a number of criteria such as information gain or Gini index importance [6]. For numeric attributes, each internal node is an inequality involving the selected attribute and the best split point for the inequality must also be determined.

The Gini index is one example of a measure of impurity among the data records that are considered at a node of the tree. For a dataset D that contains n records from k classes,

$$Gini(D) = 1 - \sum_{i=1}^{k} p_i^2$$

where p_i is the ratio of the number of records in class i to the total number of records in the set D. If the set D is split into two subsets D_1 and D_2, each having a number of records n_1 and n_2 respectively, then

$$Gini(D)_{split} = \frac{n_1}{n} Gini(D_1) + \frac{n_2}{n} Gini(D_2)$$

The best attribute on which to split is the one that maximizes $Gini(D) - Gini(D)_{split}$.

2.2. Decision trees for data streams

The biggest problem in extending decision trees for data streams is that the measures of attribute importance used to determine the best choice of attribute require counts or probabilities computed over all of the training data. Clearly this is not possible when the data is a stream.

A tree under construction consists of internal nodes, containing an inequality on one of the attributes, *frontier nodes*, nodes that have not yet been either split or turned into leaves, and leaf nodes. Initially, a tree consists of a single frontier node. As each frontier node is considered, a mechanism is needed to decide when to make a selection of the 'best' attribute, or perhaps to not split this node further and convert it to a leaf. The solution is to let each new training record flow down the tree according to the inequalities of the existing internal nodes until it reaches a frontier node. When a frontier node has accumulated 'enough' records that the standard technique for splitting will give a robust result, it is split and its descendants become new frontier nodes. Alternatively, if a frontier node has accumulated records that are predominantly from one class, it may become a leaf.

The Hoeffding bound provides a way to estimate when the number of records accumulated at a node is 'enough' for a robust decision [9]. The Hoeffding bound states that, given a random variable r in the range R, and n independent observations of r having mean value $\bar{r}$, the true mean of r is at least $\bar{r} - \epsilon$, where

$$\epsilon = \sqrt{\frac{R^2 \ln(1/\delta)}{2n}}$$

with probability $1 - \delta$, where δ is a user-defined threshold probability [9]. The Hoeffding bound ensures that no split is made unless there is a confidence of $1 - \delta$ that a particular attribute is the best attribute for splitting at the current node.

The Hoeffding bounds is used in following way. Assume that we have a general function G that checks an attribute's goodness for splitting at a specific internal node of the decision tree. At each point in tree construction, G is calculated for all attributes and the best and second best attributes are chosen to calculate $\Delta G = G_{highest} - G_{second\_highest}$. The algorithm then recalculates G for all attributes as each new record arrives, and updates ΔG continuously until it satisfies a stopping condition, $\Delta G > \epsilon$. At this point, the true value of the largest G is within ϵ of the approximated G with probability $1 - \delta$ and therefore the attribute with the highest G is the best choice for splitting at the current node with confidence $1 - \delta$.

2.3. The standard Random Forest algorithm

The Random Forests algorithm is a classification technique developed by Breiman [5]. Superficially, random forests are similar to ensembles of binary decision trees. Suppose that a dataset contains n records, each with m attributes. A set of decision trees are grown, each from a subset of the n records, chosen from the dataset at random with replacement. Hence the training dataset for each tree contains multiple copies of the original records. Random selection with replacement ensures that about $n/3$ of the records are not included in the training set and so are available as a test set to evaluate the performance of each tree.

The construction of a single tree uses a variant of the standard decision tree algorithm. In the standard decision-tree algorithm, the set of attributes considered at a node is the entire set of attributes that have not yet been used in parent nodes. By contrast, in the Random Forest algorithm, the set of attributes considered at each internal node is a randomly chosen subset of the attributes, of size $M \ll m$. Trees are not pruned. A random forest is deployed as if it was an ensemble classifier, that is the classification for each new record is the plurality of the votes from each of the trees.

The Random Forest algorithm classification error depends on two things:

- The correlation among the trees: the smaller the correlation among the trees the more variance cancelling takes place as the trees vote, and therefore the smaller the error rate.

- The strength of each individual tree: the more accurate each tree is, the better its individual vote, and therefore the smaller the error rate.

The value of M is a parameter to the algorithm and must be chosen with care. A small value for M decreases the correlation between the trees, while a large value increases the strength of each individual tree.

3. The Streaming Random Forest algorithm

We extend the standard Random Forest algorithm so that it can be applied to streaming data. The difficulty in doing this is that the Random Forest algorithm makes multiple passes over the training data, in two different ways. First, a pass through the data is made to create the training data for each tree that will be built. Second, for each tree, a pass is made through (some columns of the data) for each internal node of the tree, to generate the counts that are used to decide which attribute and split point to select for it.

A streaming algorithm does not have the luxury of multiple passes over the data. To build each tree, a separate batch or block of labelled records is used. As a result, the Streaming Random Forest algorithm requires substantially more labelled data than the standard algorithm to build a set of trees. It would be conceivable to use a separate batch of labelled data to make the decision about each internal node, but this would require an even larger amount of labelled data, and would increase the time before robust classifications could be made for unlabelled records. Instead, we adapt ideas from streaming decision tree algorithms [9, 13] to route every labelled record to an appropriate node of the tree under construction, so that every labelled record contributes to a decision about one node.

The Streaming Random Forest algorithm builds a set of trees, just as the standard Random Forest algorithm does. For the time being, the algorithm takes the required number of trees as a parameter, but extensions in which the number of trees is derived from the classification accuracy, or the set of trees has new members added and old ones deleted to respond to changes in the labelled data are straightforward.

As a new labelled record arrives, it is routed down the current tree, based on its attribute values and the inequalities of the internal nodes, until it arrives at a frontier node. At the frontier node, the attribute values of the record contribute to *class counts* that are used to compute Gini indexes. To be able to maintain information about the distribution of attribute values and their relationship to class labels, attributes are discretized into fixed-length intervals. The boundaries between these intervals are the possible split points for each attribute.

The procedure for deciding when and how to change a frontier node into another kind of node is somewhat complex. A parameter, n_{min}, is used to decide how often to check whether a frontier node should be considered for transformation.

Whenever a node accumulates n_{min} labelled records, the Gini index and the Hoeffding bound tests are applied. If the Hoeffding bound test is satisfied, then the frontier node has seen enough records to determine the best attribute and split value. The Gini index test is then used to select the best attribute and split point, and the frontier node is transformed into an internal node with an inequality based on this attribute and split point [5]. The two children of this node become new frontier nodes.

If the number of records that have reached the frontier node exceeds a threshold called the *node window*, and the node has not yet been split, the algorithm checks to see if this node should instead be transformed into a leaf. If the node has accumulated records that are predominantly from one class, then it is transformed into a leaf. Otherwise, the node is transformed to an internal node using the best attribute and split point so far.

The size of the node window threshold depends on the depth of the node in the tree, because fewer records will reach deeper nodes. We therefore define the node window as a function of the tree window and the node level:

$$\frac{1}{\alpha}(\text{tree window}/(2^{nodelevel}))$$

so that the node window shrinks linearly with depth in the tree. The value of the parameter α is determined empirically.

The construction of a tree is complete when a total of *tree window* records have been used in its construction. The algorithm then begins the construction of the next tree, until the required number of trees have been built.

A limited form of pruning is necessary, because a node may have generated two descendant frontier nodes that do not see enough subsequent records to be considered for splitting themselves. If two sibling nodes have failed to receive enough records when the *tree window* is reached, the node purity is calculated for both. Node purity is the ratio of the number of instances of records labelled with the most frequent class label to the total number of records. If both siblings' node purity is less than *1/number of classes*, then both nodes are pruned and their parent node is labelled as a leaf rather than an internal node. Otherwise, the sibling nodes become leaf nodes labelled with the majority class among the records in their parent that would have flowed down to them.

The entire tree building procedure for the Streaming Random Forest is shown in Figure 2.
This algorithm handles a single phase of learning and classification in Scenario 1. It can be extended to multiple phases by growing new trees from subsequent batches of labelled records, and discarding the oldest trees from the previous phase.

The standard Random Forest algorithm relies on samples chosen using random selection with replacement, both to guarantee attractive properties of the learned models and to provide a natural test set. Sampling with replacement is not possible when the data arrives as a stream, so we must consider whether this affects the properties of the new algorithm.

For an infinite stream of data drawn from the same distribution, the results produced by sampling with replacement and sampling without replacement are not distinguishable, since each outcome is independent of the previous one. This is because the covariance between two records x_i and x_j, where $i \neq j$, sampled without replacement, depends on the dataset size: $cov(x_i, x_j) = -\frac{\sigma^2}{n-1}$, where σ^2 is the population variance and n is the set size. As n becomes large, the covariance tends to zero, and sampling is effectively independent, exactly as if sampling with replacement had been used. Part of the motivation for sampling with replacement

```
procedure BuildTree
/*grow tree*/
  while more data records in the tree window
    read a new record
    pass it down the tree
    if it reaches a frontier node
      if first record at this node
        randomly choose M attributes
      find intervals for each of the M attributes
      update counters
      if node has seen n_min records
        if Hoeffding bounds test is satisfied
          save node split attribute
          save corresponding split value
      if no more records in the node window
        if node records are mostly from one class
          mark it as leaf node
          assign majority class to node
        else
          save best split attribute seen so far
          save corresponding split value
  end while
/* prune tree */
  while more frontier nodes
    if node has records arrive at it
      mark it as leaf node
      assign majority class to it
    else /* node has zero records */
      if sibling node is frontier with no records
        calculate purities of both sibling nodes
        if purities < pre-defined threshold
          prune both nodes
          mark parent node as a leaf
          assign majority class to it
      else
        mark node as leaf node
        assign dominant class to it
  end while
end
```

Figure 2. Building a tree in Streaming Random Forest algorithm

is also to increase the effective size of the training and test sets, and this is clearly not necessary for infinite datasets.

However, during the very early stages of tree construction, only a very small number of records have been seen, and the covariance will not be close to zero. To make sure that sampling without replacement does not have a noticeable effect, perhaps distorting the behaviour of the first few trees, we performed experiments simulating sampling with replacement. We did this by randomly retaining labelled records, with probability 1/3, and applying them as training examples twice (by double incrementing the counts), until the observed covariance values become small. The results of these experiments show that, in practice, sampling without replacement does not decrease the accuracy of the constructed forest.

4. Experimental Results

Our implementation of the Streaming Random Forest algorithm is based on the open-source Random Forest Fortran code by Breiman and Cutler [1]. We implement Scenario

1 from Figure 1. The labelled records at the beginning of the stream are used as training records, with later labelled records used as test records.

We evaluate the performance of the Streaming Random Forests algorithm by comparing its classification accuracy with that of the standard Random Forest algorithm using the same datasets. The training set for standard Random Forests is, however, a small randomly chosen subset of the training set for Streaming Random Forests. The reason is, as mentioned before, that the streaming algorithm observes data records only once, and therefore requires much more data than the standard algorithm, which can use data records many times for building different nodes. We also consider the classification time per unlabelled record for different forest sizes to estimate the flow rate that the algorithm can handle.

Results for each dataset are averages over 50 runs, selecting different random subsets of attributes for each run. The number of attributes considered at each internal node is M, chosen as suggested by Breiman to be $M = int(\log_2 m + 1)$.

4.1. Classification accuracy

Synthetic data

We generate synthetic data sets using the DataGen data-generation tool [17]. Each dataset has 1 million records, 5 numeric attributes, and 5 target classes. We vary the noise to generate 6 datasets containing 1%, 3%, 5%, 7.5%, 10%, and 15% noise, respectively. Each dataset is used by both the standard and streaming random forest algorithms. The training set for the standard random forest is 1% of the records randomly chosen from the original data set, giving about 10,000 records. The test set for both the standard and streaming algorithms is 0.2% of records randomly chosen from the original dataset, giving about 2000 records. There is no overlap between the training sets and the test set. The training set for the Streaming Random Forest algorithm is therefore the remaining 99.8% of the original data set, about 998,000 records.

For the Streaming Random Forest algorithm, we discretize each attribute's values into 200 intervals, and set $n_{min} = 200$ and $\alpha = 8$. The tree window is set to be the total number of training records divided by the number of desired trees, giving around 19,960 records to be used for growing each tree. This is a much smaller number of records than the number used in other streaming decision tree construction [9, 13, 14].

For each of the synthetic datasets, both algorithms grow 50 trees with $M = 3$ attributes considered at each node. Figure 3 shows the classification error rates of both algorithms for the six synthetic datasets.

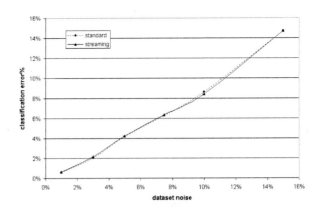

Figure 3. Classification error rates for standard and streaming random forest algorithms

The algorithms have comparable classification error rates. The confidence intervals for each test point at a confidence level of 99% overlap except for the dataset with 3% noise. The confidence intervals for this dataset are [2.02%–2.08%] and [2.09%–2.19%] respectively.

Real data

We use the Forest CoverType dataset from the UCI repository [2]. The dataset has 12 attributes (10 numerical and 2 categorical), 581,012 records, and 7 classes with frequencies of about 37%, 48.5%, 6%, 0.5%, 1.5%, 3%, and 3.5%, respectively. This dataset has been widely used in experiments reported in the literature. The classification error rates reported by Blackard [4], for example, are 30% using a neural network and back propagation, and 42% using linear discriminant analysis.

We first test the standard Random Forest algorithm by randomly sampling 0.2% of the data records for training, and 0.1% for testing. This gives a classification error of 23%. Deleting the 2 categorical attributes increases the error slightly to around 26%. Since the current implementation of the Streaming Random Forest algorithm handles only numerical attributes, we deleted the two categorical attributes. We also deleted the records for target classes 3 through 7, since they have very low frequencies compared to target classes 1, and 2. The resulting dataset has two target classes with frequencies of 43% and 57%, respectively, and ten attributes. This new dataset is used in our comparative experiments.

The training set for the standard Random Forest algorithm contains about 1000 records and the test sets for both algorithms contains about 500 records. The training set for the Streaming Random Forest algorithm therefore contains about 496,000 records.

For both standard and streaming algorithms, we grow

Table 1. Classification errors and confusion matrices for the Forest CoverType data set

	Standard Random Forest		Streaming Random Forest	
Classification Error%	24.73%		24.96%	
Test Set	219 from class 1			
	285 from class 2			
Confusion Matrix	*True* class		*True* class	
	1	*2*	*1*	*2*
1	147	53	149	56
2	72	232	70	229

150 trees using $M = 4$ attributes for building each node. The value of α used is 4, the value of n_{min} is 300, and the number of intervals into which each attribute is discretized is 300, since the ranges are quite large. As before, the tree window is the total number of training records divided by the number of trees, about 3300 records per tree, and errors are averages over 50 runs.

Table 1 presents the classification errors and confusion matrices of both algorithms for the Forest CoverType date set. Both algorithms have a classification error of approximately 25%, with a confidence interval of ±0.4% at a confidence level of 99%. The two algorithms have equivalent confusion matrices as well. This demonstrates that the Streaming Random Forest algorithm is as powerful as the standard Random Forest algorithm on real data.

4.2. Classification time per record

In the scenario we have been considering, the per-record classification time is the rate-limiting step because each new record must be evaluated by all of the trees (although in other scenarios, the per-record training time will also be important).

We base our classification time measurements on the synthetic dataset with a noise level of 15%. We use a Pentium 4 system with 3.2 GHz processor and 512MB RAM, and consider the effect of different forest sizes, that is different numbers of trees. The forest sizes use are 5, 50, 100, 150, 200, 250, 300, 350, 400, 450, and 500 trees.

The per-record classification times are shown in Figure 4. The times are averaged over 50 runs, and measured in microseconds. The increase in per-record classification time with number of trees in the forest is no worse than linear. The average flow rate of a stream that this implementation of the Streaming Random Forest algorithm can handle is 1.7×10^4 records/sec for forests with up to 500 trees. A more typical number of trees used in a random forest is perhaps 50 to 200 trees (according to Breiman's experiments [5]) which would allow a stream rate of up to 2.8×10^4 records/sec.

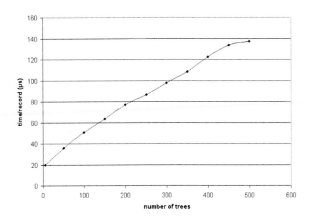

Figure 4. Per-record classification time

5. Conclusion

This paper has defined the *Streaming Random Forest* algorithm, an online and incremental stream classification algorithm. It is an extension of the standard Random Forest algorithm due to Breiman [9]. The algorithm gives comparable classification accuracy to the standard Random Forests algorithm despite seeing each data record only once. Because stream algorithms can never see 'all' of the data, our algorithm uses node windows and tree windows to decide when to begin constructing new trees, transform frontier nodes, or carry out a limited form of pruning. These refinements mean that the algorithm requires many fewer labelled records for training than other stream-based decision tree algorithms. The Streaming Random Forests algorithm is fast enough to handle streams in many applications. Its per-record classification time complexity is $\mathcal{O}(t)$, where t is the number of trees in the forest.

References

[1] Random Forest FORTRAN Code. Available from http://www.stat.berkeley.edu/breiman/RandomForests/cc_software.htm/.

[2] Forest CoverType data set. Available from http://kdd.ics.uci.edu/.

[3] C. Aggarwal, J. Han, J. Wang, and P. Yu. Sa framework for clustering evolving data streams. In *Proceedings of 29th International Conference on Very Large Data Bases(VLDB)*, pages 81–92. Berlin, Germany, 2003.

[4] J. Blackard. *Comparison of Neural Networks and Discriminant Analysis in Predicting Forest Cover Types*. PhD thesis, Department of Forest Sciences. Colorado State University, Fort Collins, Colorado, 1998.

[5] L. Breiman. Random forests. Technical Report, 1999. Available at www.stat.berkeley.edu.

[6] L. Breiman, J. Friedman, R. Olshen, and C. Stone. *Classification and Regression Trees*. Wadsworth International, Belmont, Ca., 1984.

[7] A. Bulut and A. Singh. A unified framework for monitoring data streams in real time. In *Proceedings of the 21st International Conference on Data Engineering (ICDE)*, pages 44–55. Tokyo, Japan, 2005.

[8] F. Chu, Y. Wang, and C. Zaniolo. An adaptive learning approach for noisy data streams. In *Proceedings of the 4th IEEE International Conference on Data Mining (ICDM)*, pages 351–354. Brighton, UK, November 2004.

[9] P. Domingos and G. Hulten. Mining high-speed data streams. In *Proceedings of the 6th ACM SIGKDD International Conference on Knowledge Discovery and Data Mining (KDD)*, pages 71–80. Boston, MA, August 2000.

[10] W. Fan. A systematic data selection to mine concept-drifting data streams. In *Proceedings of the 10th ACM SIGKDD International Conference on Knowledge Discovery and Data Mining (KDD)*, pages 128–137. Seattle, Washington, August 2004.

[11] M. Gaber, S. Krishnaswamy, and A. Zaslavsky. Cost-efficient mining techniques for data streams. In *Proceedings of the 1st Australasian Workshop on Data Mining and Web Intelligence (DMWI)*, pages 81–92. Dunedin, New Zealand, 2003.

[12] J. Gama, P. Medas, and R. Rocha. Forest trees for on-line data. In *Proceedings of the 2004 ACM Symposium on Applied Computing (SAC)*, pages 632–636. Nicosia, Cyprus, March 2004.

[13] G. Hulten, L. Spencer, and P. Domingos. Mining time-changing data streams. In *Proceedings of the 7th ACM SIGKDD International Conference on Knowledge Discovery and Data mining (KDD)*, pages 97–106. San Francisco, CA, August 2001.

[14] R. Jin and G. Agrawal. Efficient decision tree construction on streaming data. In *Proceedings of 9th International Conference on Knowledge Discovery and Data Mining (SIGKDD)*, pages 571–576. Washington, DC, August 2003.

[15] D. Kifer, S. Ben-David, and J. Gehrke. Detecting change in data streams. In *Proceedings of the 30th International Conference on Very Large Data Bases (VLDB)*, pages 180–191. Toronto, Canada, 2004.

[16] B. Krishnamurthy, S. Sen, Y. Zhang, and Y. Chen. Sketch-based change detection: methods, evaluation, and applications. In *Proceedings of the 3rd ACM SIGCOMM Internet Measurement Conference (IMC)*, pages 234–247. Miami Beach, FL, 2003.

[17] G. Melli. Scds-a synthetic classification data set generator. Simon Fraser University, School of Computer Science, 1997.

[18] H. Wang, W. Fan, P. Yu, and J. Han. Mining concept-drifting data streams using ensemble classifiers. In *Proceedings of the 9th ACM SIGKDD International Conference on Knowledge Discovery and Data Mining (KDD)*, pages 226–235. Washington, DC, August 2003.

[19] X. Zhu, X. Wu, and Y. Yang. Dynamic classifier selection for effective mining from noisy data streams. In *Proceedings of the 4th IEEE International Conference on Data Mining (ICDM)*, pages 305–312. Brighton, UK, November 2004.

[20] Y. Zhu and D. Shasha. Statistical monitoring of thousands of data streams in real time. In *Proceedings of the 28th International Conference on Very Large Data Bases (VLDB)*, pages 358–369. Hong Kong, China, 2002.

Structural Semi-Join: A light-weight structural join operator for efficient XML path query pattern matching

Seokhyun Son, Hyoseop Shin, and Zhiwei Xu
Department of Advanced Technology Fusion
Konkuk University
Seoul, Korea
{myviki, hsshin, xuzhiwei}@konkuk.ac.kr

Abstract

Optimal evaluation of structural relationships between XML nodes is crucial for efficient processing of XML queries. Though stack-based structural join algorithms showed improved performance over the merge-based algorithms, the algorithms still suffer potential overhead in processing XML path expressions. This is mainly because the existing structural join algorithms have been designed for returning (ancestor, descendant) node pairs even when the actual processing of the XML path queries requires the structural join operators to return either descendant nodes only or ancestor nodes only, which makes a query processor further compute for elimination of unnecessary nodes from the results. To address this problem, this paper proposes a new operator called structural semi-join and the algorithms for efficient processing XML path queries. The experiments show that the proposed algorithms improve the performance of the XML path processing by up to an order of magnitude.

1. Introduction

In processing XML queries, efficient evaluation of structural relationships between XML nodes such as ancestor-descendant and parent-child is a very important issue. This is because the most fundamental building block of XML queries is the path expression that is a combination of such structural relationships. For example, the XPath query *"Paper[Title='XML']/Author"* contains as conditions two parent-child relationships among *'Paper'* and *'Title'*, and *'Paper'* and *'Author'*. When representing XML data as a tree structure, the node numbering scheme can be used to show the structural relationship

among the XML nodes. Each XML node can be represented with (*docid, start_pos, end_pos, level*) information [12,13]. The *docid* is the document identifier to identify each input XML document, and *start_pos* and *end_pos* are the starting and ending offset of the XML nodes within a document, and *level* is the depth of the node starting from the root node. For the sample XML document in Fig. 1-(a), Fig. 1-(b) shows the (*start_pos, end_pos, level*) value for each XML node of the document. *docid* values are omitted under the assumption that all the nodes are in the same document. When two XML nodes are provided with a node numbering information, their structural relationship can be determined by comparing the attributes of the nodes. Specifically, given two nodes r and s, they are in the ancestor-descendant relationship if and only if ($r.docid = s.docid$) and ($r.start\_pos < s.start\_pos$) and ($r.end\_pos > s.end\_pos$). And, they are in the parent-child relationship if the condition ($r.level=s.level$-1) is added to the above conditions. If we consider the (*start_pos, end_pos*) pair alone, an XML node can be interpreted as an *interval*. And, the structural relationships between XML nodes can be interpreted as the locational relationships between intervals. Note that the intervals of arbitrary two XML nodes in a same document are in one of the two relationships: containment or disjoint. For example, if the interval of an XML node, r, contains the interval of another XML node, s, then r is an ancestor of s. Fig. 1-(c) shows an interval representation for Fig. 1-(a). Structural join[1] has been introduced as a primitive operator for evaluation of structural relationships between a large number of XML nodes.

In general, the XML path $n_1//n_2// \ldots //n_k$ may be processed in forward manners or in backward manners. In forward processing, structural join operations for (n_i, n_{i+1}) are cascaded in increasing order of i, and in backward processing, they are cascaded in decreasing

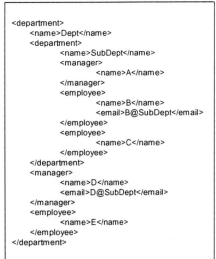

(a) an XML document

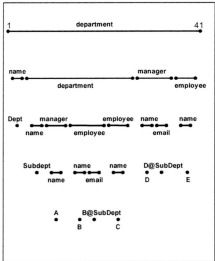

(c) interval representation

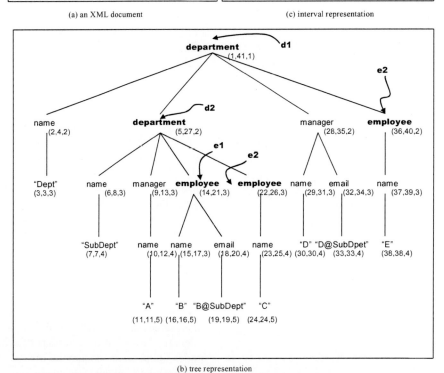

(b) tree representation

Fig.1. An XML document and its tree and interval representation

order of *i*. In either case, in processing XML paths, ancestors or descendants are required. However, the existing structural join algorithms[1] have been designed for returning (ancestor, descendant) node pairs, which makes a query processor further compute for elimination of unnecessary nodes from the results. In this paper, in order to address the problem, we define novel structural semi-join operators and the efficient algorithms for them.

The rest of this paper is organized as follows. Section 2 gives preliminaries and the motivation of the paper. Section 3 presents the proposed structural semi-join algorithms. Section 4 shows the experimental results. In Section 5, related work is described. Section 6 concludes this paper.

2. Preliminaries and Motivation

To clarify the problem, we summarize the structural join operators proposed by Srivastava et al[1].

Definition 1 (Structural-Join) Given the two XML node list *AList* and *DList* in which the nodes are in increasing order of *start_pos*, **Structural-Join(AList, DList)** is defined to return the list of the node pairs $<a, d>$ such that $(a \in AList) \wedge (d \in DList) \wedge (a.docid = d.docid) \wedge (a.start\_pos < d.start\_pos) \wedge (a.end\_pos > d.end\_pos)$.

The structural join has two specializations:

Definition 1.1(Structural-Join-Desc) *Structural-Join-Desc(AList, DList)* is a specialized version of *Structural-Join* in that the list of the node pairs $<a, d>$ in the resulting list are in increasing order of *d.start_pos*.

Definition 1.2(Structural-Join-Anc) *Structural-Join-Anc(AList, DList)* is a specialized version of *Structural-Join* in that the list of the node pairs $<a, d>$ in the resulting list are in increasing order of *a.start_pos*.

Example 1. For the XML example in Fig. 1-(c), the result of the *Structural-Join-Desc* between the *department* and the *employee* node lists in processing the XPath query, "*department//employee*," is as follows:

Structural-Join-Desc(department, employee)
= {<d1,e1>,<d2,e1>, <d1,e2>,<d2,e2>,<d1,e3>}

Note that the result above is not complete as the answer of the given XPath query, but the final one should be {<e1>,<e2>,<e3>}. To obtain the final query result from the structural join result, *employee* nodes from each <*department, employee*> node pair should be extracted, and then, duplicated *employee* nodes should be eliminated from the result. We define this operation as *ProjectNode*.

Definition 2 (NodeProject) Assume that *SList* represents a list of *n*-tuples and the structure of each tuple corresponds to the combination of the node names $<s_1, s_2, ..., s_n>$ and *PNodes* represents a combination of the node names $<s_{k1}, s_{k2}, ..., s_{km}>$ extracted from the *SList* node name combination such that $1 \leq k_1 < k_2 < ... < k_m \leq n$, then **NodeProject(SList, PNodes)** is defined to return the list of *m*-tuple $<a_{k1}, a_{k2}, ..., a_{km}>$ such that $(<a_1, a_2, ..., a_n> \in SList) \wedge$

$(a_i.nodename = s_i (1 \leq i \leq n))$ and no duplicated tuples exist in the resulting list.

The output when applying the *ProjectNode* operator to the result of the *Structural-Join-Desc* in the Example 1 is as follows:

NodeProject(Structural-Join-Desc(department, employee), <employee>)
= {<e1>,<e2>,<e3>}

, which is the final answer set for the given XPath query.

In summary, in order to get the correct results for XPath queries, *Structural-Join* opeartors alone are not enough but an additional operator (*ProjectNode* in the above) is required. Also, in terms of query processing efficiency, considerable parts of the intermediate results produced by structural joins can be redundant when compared with the final query results. From this observation, we propose a new operator, *structural semi-join*, in order to efficiently process XML queries of a path type

3. Structural Semi-Joins

To begin with, we define a new operator, structural semi-join.

Definition 3 (Structural SemiJoin) Given the two node list *AList* and *DList* both of which are in sorted order of *start_pos*, **Structural-SemiJoin(AList, DList)** is defined to return the list of $<a> \; or \; <d>$ such that $(a \in AList) \wedge (d \in DList) \wedge (a.docid = d.docid) \wedge (a.start\_pos < d.start\_pos) \wedge (a.end\_pos > d.end\_pos)$ and no duplicated nodes exist in the resulting list.

The *Structural-SemiJoin* also has two specializations like the *Structural-SemiJoin*.

Definition 3.1(Structural-SemiJoin-Desc) *Structural-SemiJoin-Desc(AList, DList)* is a specialized version of *Structural-Join-Desc* in that the resulting list of $<d>$ is in sorted order of *d.start_pos*.

Definition 3.2(Structural-SemiJoin-Anc) *Structural-SemiJoin-Anc(AList, DList)* is a specialized version of *Structural-Join-Anc* in that the resulting list of $<a>$ is in sorted order of *a.start_pos*.

For ease of demonstration of the algorithms, from now on, we will use an XML document tree with symbolic nodes in Fig. 2. In the figure, the answer sets are {D2, D3, D4, D5, D6} and {A1, A2, A3} for

Structural-SemiJoin-Desc and *Structural-SemiJoin-Anc*, respectively.

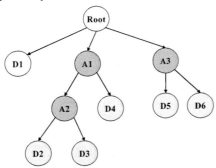

Fig.2. A symbolized XML document tree

3.1 Stack-based Naive Algorithms

In designing the algorithms for the structural semi-join operators, we first introduce naive versions composed by direct adaptation of the stack-based structural join algorithms[1].

Like *StackTree-Desc* algorithm[1], the algorithm of the stack-based structural semi-join for descendants (*Naive-SSJoin-Desc*) maintains a stack to store ancestor nodes. Whenever an incoming descendant matches with any of the stack nodes, the descendant is returned as a result unless it is equal to the previously returned node. The algorithm of the stack-based structural semi-join for ancestors (*Naive-SSJoin-Anc*) employs the *self* and *inherit* lists for each ancestor node in the stack that have been used in the *StackTree-Anc* algorithm[1]. When an ancestor is popped from the stack, all the nodes in its lists should be moved to its below stack node, Also, As soon as a matching descendant node comes, any ancestor node is returned as a result unless it is equal to the previously returned node.

Figure 3-(a) and 3-(b) demonstrates the process of the naive algorithms.

Input Node	Ancestor Stack	Output
D1		
A1	A1	
A2	A2 A1	
D2	A2 A1	D2
D3	A2 A1	D3
D4	A1	D4
A3	A3	
D5	A3	D5
D6	A3	D6

(a) Naive-SSJoin-Desc

Input Node	Ancestor Stack	Self List	Inherit List	Output
D1				
A1	A1			
A2	A2 A1			
D2	A2 A1	{D2} {D2}		
D3	A2 A1	{D2,D3} {D2,D3}		
D4	A1	{D2,D3,D4}	{(A2,D2),(A2,D3)}	
A3	A3			{A1, A2}
D5	A3	{D5}		A3
D6	A3	{D5,D6}		

(b) Naive-SSJoin-Anc

Fig. 3. Demonstrations of Naive Structural Semi-Join Algorithms

3.2 *NStack-SSJoin-Desc*: Non-Stack Structural-SemiJoin for Descendants algorithm

In this section, we propose a more efficient algorithm for the *Structural-SemiJoin-Desc* operator. The proposed *Structural-SemiJoin-Desc* algorithm retrieves the nodes in sorted order of *start_pos* from each node list. However, the *Structural-SemiJoin-Desc* algorithm becomes more efficient in using memory than the *Naive-SSJoin-Desc* algorithm in that no stack is required in the middle of processing. Instead, an in-memory variable called *ancestor indicator* is employed, which is supposed to point to an ancestor node having the biggest *end_pos* value among the ancestor nodes examined so far.

The ancestor indicator corresponds to the bottom node in the stack within the *Naive-SSJoin-Desc* algorithm. The rest of the nodes in the stack are not necessary for qualifying incoming descendant nodes. This is from the observation that the differentiation of each ancestor node is not necessary for the *Structural-SemiJoin-Desc* operator. If an ancestor indicator is not null, then it implies that an ancestor node exist for qualifying the incoming descendant node. Fig. 4 represents the proposed *NStack-SSJoin-Desc* algorithm.

In summary, the proposed *NStack-SSJoin-Desc* algorithm is more efficient in computation cost and memory usage than the naive algorithm, *Naive-SSJoin-Desc*. First, in the proposed algorithm, each descendant does not have to be compared with all its ancestor nodes, but is compared only with the node pointed by the ancestor indicator. Also, the maximum memory usage of the proposed algorithm is constant, while the naive algorithm uses memory up to the depth of the ancestor stack.

```
1   Algorithm Semi-Structural-Join-Desc (AList, DList)
2   a = AList->firstNode; d = DList->firstNode; OutputList =
3   NULL;
4   ancestor_indicator = NULL;
5   while ( (AList->isempty() == false) || (DList->isempty() ==
6   false)
7           || (ancestor_indicator != NULL) ) {
8               if ( (ancestor_indicator != NULL) &&
9                   (a.startpos > ancestor_indicator.endpos) &&
10                  (d.startpos > ancestor_indicator.endpos) )
11                  ancestor_indicator = NULL;
12              else if (a.startpos < d.startpos) {
13                  if ( ancestor_indicator == NULL )
14                      ancestor_indicator = a;
15                  a = a->nextNode;
16              }
17              else {
18                  if ( ancestor_indicator != NULL )
19                      append d to OutputList;
20                  d = d->nextNode;
21              }
22  }
23  Return OutputList;
```

Fig. 4. NStack-SSJoin-Desc algorithm

For the Fig. 2 example, the process of the NStack-SSJoin-Desc algorithm is demonstrated in Fig. 5. The execution of the proposed algorithm for the example is as follows: At first, D1 node is ignored because the ancestor indicator is null. Then, A1 is stored as the ancestor indicator, but the next coming A2 is ignored because A1 has the bigger end_pos value than A2. Next, D2, D3, and D4 are qualified as the output nodes. Similarly, A3 becomes the new ancestor indicator and D5 and D6 are qualified as output nodes.

Input Node	Ancestor Indicator	Output
D1		
A1	A1	
A2	A1	
D2	A1	D2
D3	A1	D3
D4	A1	D4
A3	A3	
D5	A3	D5
D6	A3	D6

Fig. 5. Demonstration of NStack-SSJoin-Desc Algorithm

3.3 NList-SSJoin-Anc: Non-List Structural-SemiJoin for Ancestors algorithm

In this section, we propose an efficient algorithm for the *Structural-SemiJoin-Anc* operator. In the *StackTree-Anc*[1] algorithm, the *self* and *inherit* list have been used in order to remember the order of the output ancestor nodes because each output ancestor node can be matched with one or more descendant nodes and thus the output ancestor nodes are not generated to be returned in increasing order of *start-pos*. As far as the structural seim-join for ancestors is concerned, however, while we still need to output ancestor nodes in increasing order of *start_pos*, we do not have to identify each descendant node as the counter part. So, if we make sure that each ancestor node is output at most once, then the *self* and *inherit* lists are no longer required. From this observation, as soon as we find a matching descendant node, we return all the ancestor nodes in the stack as outputs. Furthermore, making the stack empty can reduce the cost of the comparison between the ancestor nodes in the stack and the incoming descendants. Fig. 6 represents the *NList-SSJoin-Anc* algorithm.

```
1   Algorithm Semi-Structural-Join-Anc (AList, DList)
2   a = AList->firstNode; d = DList->firstNode; OutputList =
3   NULL;
4   stack->setempty();
5   while ((AList->isempty() == false) || (DList->isempty() ==
6   false) || (stack->isempty() == false) ) {
7           if ((a.startpos > stack->top.endpos) &&
8               (d.startpos > stack->top.endpos))
9               /* time to pop the top element in the stack */
10              stack->pop();
11          else if (a.startpos < d.startpos) {
12              stack->push(a);
13              a = a->nextNode;
14          }
15          else {
16          /* append ancestors to OutputList and make stack empty */
17              for (a1 = stack->bottom; a1 != NULL; a1 = a1->up)
18                  append a1 to OutputList;
19              stack->reset();
20              d = d->nextNode;
21          }
22  }
23  Return OutputList;
```

Fig. 6. NList-SSJoin-Anc algorithm

In summary, the proposed *NList-SSJoin-Anc* algorithm saves the cost for maintaining the *self* and *inherit* list for each ancestor node by immediately returning ancestor nodes in the stack and resetting the stack as soon as a matching descendant is available. The size of *self* and *inherit* list for each node can be up to the number of sibling nodes against a node.

Therefore, the effect will become larger if a given XML document contains more tags of same names.

For the Fig. 2 example, the process of the proposed algorithm is demonstrated in Fig. 7. The execution of the proposed algorithm for the example is as follows: *D1* node is ignored because the stack is empty. Then, *A1* and *A2* are stored in the stack. When *D2* arrives, *A1* and *A2* are qualified as the output nodes and the stack becomes empty again. *D3* and *D4* are ignored because the stack is empty. Next, *A3* is qualified as the output when *D5* arrives. *D6* is ignored again because the stack is empty.

Input Node	Ancestor Stack	Output
D1		
A1	A1	
A2	A2 A1	
D2	A2 A1	{A1, A2}
D3		
D4		
A3	A3	
D5	A3	A3
D6		

Fig. 7. Demonstration of the NList-SSJoin-Anc Algorithm

4. Experimental Results

We evaluate the performances of our proposed algorithms for the *Structural-SemiJoin* operator, and compare them with the stack-based structural join algorithms proposed by Srivastava et al. [1] and the naïve semi-join algorithms presented in this paper. We use a synthetic XML document of about 200M byte size. The DTD of the document for the experiments is described in Fig. 8. The *department* element can have *name*, *email*, *manager*, *employee*, and *department* in recursive way as sub-elements. The *manager* and *employee* element can have *name* and *email* as sub-elements. The number of each element is specified in Table 1. Table 2 lists up the XPath queries used in the experiments. The return type indicates whether each query is processed by the *Structural-SemiJoin-Desc* operator or *Structural-SemiJoin-Anc* operator. The table also specifies the number of query results.

```
<?xml version="1.0" encoding="UTF-8"?>
<!ELEMENT department (name+, email?, manager*,
employee+, department*)>
<!ELEMENT manager (name+,email?)>
<!ELEMENT employee (name+,email?)>
<!ELEMENT name (#PCDATA)>
<!ELEMENT email (#PCDATA)>
```

Fig5. DTD used in the experiments

Table 1. Database statistics

Tag Name	Number of Tags
department	397,947
manager	597,302
employee	796,671
name	3,383,862
email	895,957

Table 2. XPath queries used in the experiments

Query No.	Query	Return Type	No. of Results
1	department//employee	Descendant	796,671
2	department[.//employee]	Ancestor	397,947
3	department//manager	Descendant	597,302
4	department[.//manager]	Ancestor	397,947
5	department//email	Descendant	895,957
6	department[.//email]	Ancestor	376,930
7	employee/name	Descendant	1,592,063
8	employee[name]	Ancestor	796,671

The *Structural-SemiJoin* operator is implemented in three ways in the experiments: 1) the stack-based *Structural-Join* algorithms[1] (*StackTree-Desc* and *StackTree-Anc*) plus *NodeProj* algorithm, 2) the naïve *Structural-SemiJoin* algorithms (*Naïve-SSjoin-Desc* and *Naïve-SSjoin-ANC*) presented in this paper, 3) the proposed *Structural-SemiJoin* algorithms (*NStack-SSjoin-Desc* and *NList-SSjoin-Anc*).

Fig.8 depicts the experimental results. For each query identified by the number on the X axis of the graph, the response time of each algorithm is represented with bars in the Y axis direction. The proposed *NStack-SSjoin-Desc* algorithm is compared with other four algorithms (Fig. 8-(a)) and the proposed *NList-SSjoin-Anc* algorithm is compared with other four (in Fig. 8-(b)). As the graphs show, the proposed *Structural-Semi-Join* algorithms perform better than *Stack-Tree+ProjectNode* combinations or *Naïve Structural SemiJoin* algorithms for all the tested queries. The *Structural-SemiJoin* costs less than even the *Stack-Tree* alone without *NodeProj*. This is because the *Semi-Structural-Join* algorithms reduce the redundant intermediate results that exist in structural join algorithms, thus reducing the cost of computation as well. We also observe that the relative performance gain of the *Structural-SemiJoin* algorithms gets larger as the number of descendant nodes per ancestor node increases. For the query 2, the average ratio between the number of *department* versus the number of *employee* is three and the performance gain is over an order of magnitude.

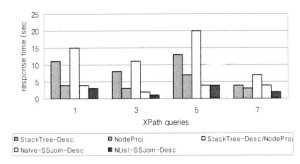

(a) The performances of Structural SemiJoin-Desc

algorithms

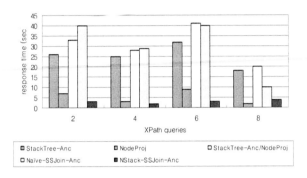

(b) The performances of Structural SemiJoin-Anc

algorithms

Fig. 8. Comparison of response times of five algorithms: structural join only, project node only, combination of structural join and project node, naive structural semi-join, proposed structural semi-join

5. Related Work

Srivastava et al. [1] initially proposed the structural join as a primitive operator for XML query processing. The paper introduced two merge-based join algorithms and proposed two new stack-based join algorithms. In their analyses and experiments, stack-based algorithms have been shown better in performance.

There have been a variety of related papers on structural joins: indexing schemes for structural joins[2,3], structural join size estimation[4], structural join order selection[5], hash-based algorithm for unordered node lists[6], locking-aware algorithm[7], aggregates over structural joins[8,9], and so on. Meanwhile, the holistic approach for XML twig matches by Bruno et al. [10] has the advantage that it is not necessary to stitch several structural joins for more than one structural relationship shown in XPath queries. As a result, the approach requires less intermediate results and less cost. However, the

approach can be less applicable because it assumes only ancestor-descendant or parent-child relationship. Complex XML queries including diverse structural relationships, aggregates, group-by operations can be difficult to process with the holistic approaches alone.

Node numbering schemes for storing large amounts of XML documents have been proposed. Zhang et al. [11] suggested to use the offsets of the beginning and ending word of each node to represent the 'containment' relationship between nodes in an XML document. The node numbering scheme proposed by Li et al. [12] provides flexibility and efficiency when updating XML documents.7. Main text

6. Conclusion

In this paper, we proposed a novel operator, structural semi-join, for efficient evaluation of XML path queries. The operator is defined to return either ancestor or descendant nodes only for (ancestor, descendant) node pairs having structural relationships. It can make the additional operator like duplicate node elimination unnecessary which was necessary for the previous structural join operator in processing XML path expressions. Also, compared with the naïve version algorithms based on the stack-based structural join algorithms, the proposed algorithms of implementing the semi-structural join operator are relatively light-weight and efficient in terms of memory usage and computation cost as well. From the experimental results, it was observed that the proposed algorithm performed even faster than the previous stack-based algorithms, especially when many duplicated nodes occurred.

7. References

[1] Divesh Srivastava, Shurug Al-Khalifa, H. V. Jagadish, Nick Koudas, Jinesh M. Patel, and Yuqing Wu. Structural joins: A primitive for efficient XML query pattern matching. In Proc. of the 2002 IEEE conference on Data Engineering, San Jose, USA, Feb. 2002.

[2] Shu-Yao Chien, Zografoula Vagena, Donghui Zhang, vassilis J. Tsotras, and Carlo Zaniolo. Efficient structural joins on indexed XML documents. In Proc. of the 28th VLDB conference, pages 263-274, Hong Kong, China, Aug. 2002.

[3] Kun-Lung Wu, Shyh-Kwei Chen, and Philip S. Yu: Efficient structural joins with on-the-fly indexing. In Proc. of WWW 2005: 1028-1029, Chiba, Japan, May 10-14, 2005.

[4] Cheng Luo, Zhewei Jiang, Wen-Chi Hou, Feng Yan, and Chih-Fang Wang. Estimating XML Structural Join Size Quickly and Economically. In Proc. of ICDE 2006, Atlanta, GA, USA, 3-8 April 2006.

[5] Christian Mathis and Theo Härder. Hash-Based Structural Join Algorithms. In Proc. of EDBT Workshops 2006: 136-149, Munich, Germany, March 26-31, 2006.

[6] Christian Mathis, Theo Härder, and Michael Peter Haustein, Locking-aware structural join operators for XML query processing. In Proc. of SIGMOD Conference 2006: 467-478, Chicago, Illinois, USA, June 27-29, 2006.

[7] Yuqing Wu, Jignesh M. Patel, and H. V. Jagadish, Structural Join Order Selection for XML Query Optimization. In Proc. of ICDE 2003: 443-454, Bangalore, India, March 5-8, 2003.

[8] Priya Mandawat and Vassilis J. Tsotras: Indexing Schemes for Efficient Aggregate Computation over Structural Joins. In Proc. of WebDB 2005: 55-60, Baltimore, Maryland, USA, June 16-17, 2005.

[9] Kaiyang Liu, Frederick H. Lochovsky: Efficient Computation of Aggregate Structural Joins. In Proc. of WISE 2003: 21-30, Rome, Italy, 10-12 December 2003.

[10] Nicolas Bruno, Nick Koudas, and Divesh Srivastava: Holistic twig joins: optimal XML pattern matching. In Proc. of SIGMOD Conference 2002: 310-321, Madison, Wisconsin, June 3-6, 2002.

[11] Chun Zhang, Jeffrey F. Naughton, Qiong Luo, and David J. DeWitt, and Guy M. Lohman. On supporting containment queries in relational database management systems. In Proc. of the 2001 ACM-SIGMOD conference, Santa Barbara, CA, USA, May 2001.

[12] Quanzhong Li and Bongki Moon. Indexing and querying XML data for regular path expressions. In Proc. of the 27th VLDB conference, Rome, Italy, Sep. 2001.

The LBF R-tree: Efficient Multidimensional Indexing with Graceful Degradation

Todd Eavis
Department of Computer Science
Concordia University
Montreal, Canada
eavis@cs.concordia.ca

David Cueva
Department of Computer Science
Concordia University
Montreal, Canada
david.cueva@yahoo.com

Abstract

In multi-dimensional database environments, we typically require effective indexing mechanisms for all but the smallest data sets. While numerous such methods have been proposed, the R-tree has emerged as one of the most common and reliable indexing models. Nevertheless, as user queries grow in terms of both size and dimensionality, R-tree performance can deteriorate significantly. In some application areas, however, it is possible to exploit data and query specific features to obtain dramatic improvements in query performance. We propose a variation of the classic R-tree that specifically targets data warehousing architectures. The new model not only improves performance on common user-defined range queries, but gracefully degrades to a linear scan of the data on pathologically large queries. Experimental results demonstrate reductions in disk seeks of more than 50% relative to more conventional R-tree designs.

1 Introduction

Within contemporary data warehousing environments, the scale of many systems is now exceeding tens of terabytes or more. Typically, such databases are constructed as a series of data marts, each designed around a heavily denormalized logical model known as a Star Schema (or its normalized counterpart, the Snowflake Schema). In its simplest form, the Star schema consists of a central *fact table* and a series of peripheral dimension tables connected via standard foreign key relationships. Within the fact table, we refer to the foreign keys as *feature* attributes, while fields identifying the aggregate values for the underlying organizational process are known as *measures*. Standard Decision Support queries generally require a traversal of the fact table, coupled with a join on one or more dimension tables.

In practice, the dimension tables are relatively small, with their record counts equivalent to the cardinality of the related entity (e.g., date, customer or product). The fact tables, by contrast, can be extremely large and comprise the bulk of the data warehouse. In commercial settings, it would not be unusual to see such tables holding hundreds of millions of records. Since data warehouse queries specifically target the fact table, it is imperative that efficient indexing mechanisms be available. Otherwise, standard user queries would result in unacceptable performance.

Beyond this, it is important to note that the majority of Decision Support queries are *multi-dimensional* in nature. In other words, the most common access pattern tends to be some form of *range query*, in which the user (or a graphical interface working on their behalf) submits a request that specifies a range restriction on one or more dimensional columns. Such a request is, in fact, not well supported by traditional single-dimensional indexes such as the b-tree. Instead, true multi-dimensional indexes are often used to more effectively support data warehousing workloads.

While a significant number of such techniques have been presented in the literature, the R-tree has emerged as perhaps the most rigorously studied and consistently implemented model. As was the case with the b-tree, numerous variations on the basic R-tree have been presented over the years, each with possible advantages when applied in selected environments or with specific data distributions. To our knowledge, however, none fully support all three of the simple but crucial features of the data warehousing fact table; namely, that it supports medium dimensionality range queries, that it is relatively *static*, and that it is extremely large in practice. The third point, in particular, tends to be under-appreciated in theoretical treatments on the topic.

In this paper, we present the Linear Breadth First R-tree. The LBF R-tree builds directly upon the traditional R-tree model but optimizes its construction and tree traversal in order to consistently reduce the number of costly seeks associated with arbitrary user-defined range queries on large data sets. Specifically, we utilize a space filling curve to pre-pack the R-tree and then carefully arrange the associated blocks on disk to allow a breadth first traversal pattern to map directly to the physical storage layout. Perhaps more importantly, this *linearization* model also provides graceful performance degradation in the face of arbitrarily large queries. As such, it is not necessary to rely upon selectivity estimators (e.g., multi-dimensional histograms) to determine whether linear scans are in fact more cost effective than index traversal. We also identify compression and update techniques that support the use of the LBF R-tree in practical environments. Experimental results demonstrate a 30%-50% reduction in the number of seeks relative to existing R-tree packing and query strategies, without the unacceptable memory requirements often associated with breadth first tree traversals.

The remainder of the paper is organized as follows. In Section 2 we discuss related work. Section 3 presents relevant supporting material while Section 4 describes the new algorithms for index construction, searching, compression and updates. Experimental results are presented in Section 5. Finally, Section 6 offers concluding remarks.

2   Related Work

Gunter and Gaede provide a comprehensive survey of multi-dimensional indexing methods in [5]. However, while many of these techniques are quite interesting, few have actually found their way into practical systems. Of this latter group, the R-tree and its numerous variations have been targeted by commercial vendors and academics alike. The seminal R-tree paper was presented by Guttman [8], who described the structure, processing model, and algorithms for node splitting. The r^+-tree [23] alters the basic model by prohibiting box overlap at the same level of the tree, while the r^*-tree [2] uses an object re-insertion technique to reduce overlap during node splitting. In static environments, R-tree *pre-packing* has been proposed in order to improve storage utilization and object clustering properties. The original packing technique, based upon *lowX* coordinate order, was proposed by Roussopoulos and Leifker [22]. An improved method utlizing the Hilbert curve was presented by Kamel and Faloutsos [12], while Leutenegger et al. discuss an alternative known as Sort Tile Recursion [16].

In terms of R-tree traversal patterns, most implementations employ the more resource efficient depth first (DF) approach. Nevertheless, researchers have also used breadth first (BF) searches to exploit optimizations not possible with DF search. In [14], Kim and Cha describe a *sibling clustering* technique that tries to at least partially order spatially related nodes so that a breadth first traversal can more efficiently retrieve query blocks. Breath first traversal is also employed by Huang et al. to globally optimize the join processing for pairs of spatial data sets [11].

Subsequent to the early work on node splitting and packing, researchers turned to the creation of theoretical models for analyzing performance and predicting worst case behaviour. Kamel and Faloutsos used the idea of fractals to identify a lower bound for multi-dimensional point data [13]. In terms of spatial data, Theodoridis and Sellis describe a model for predicting optimal R-tree range query performance in dynamic environments [25], while Pagel et al. provide a similar result for static data [20]. In each case, the models' estimates are shown to fall within 10%-20% of actual results. Arge et al. also define an asymptotic lower bound on the number of blocks retrieved, and provide the PR-tree as a mechanism for improving the I/O efficiency of hyper-rectangular objects [1]. In all of these cases, the underlying assumption is that performance is strictly a function of the number of blocks retrieved, rather than a function of the number and size of the *seeks* required.

In the data warehousing context, fact table indexing is of crucial importance. In [7], Gupta et al. propose a simple indexing model composed of a collection of b-trees. Roussopoulos et al. [21] describe the cube tree, a *data cube* indexing model based upon the concept of a packed R-tree [22]. The data cube, first described by Gray et al. [6], refers to an OLAP (Online Analytical Processing) data model representing the materialization of the $O(2^d)$ group-bys or *cuboids* in a d-dimensional space. In addition to identifying the R-tree as a powerful indexing model for data warehousing applications, the cube tree paper is significant in that it also describes a very efficient *bulk incremental* update method, a key benefit given the size and fluidity of today's data warehouses. In commercial environments, designers often utilize *join* or *bitmap* indexes [18, 19]. In the former case, multi-table joins are pre-computed and stored as $< key, rowID >$ pairings. In the latter case, we use bit strings to represent low cardinality domains so that fact table record locations can be resolved by way of standard binary operators. Wu and Buchanon [26] extend the bitmap mechanism for higher cardinalities, though the general technique can still require an excessive number of binary operations for higher dimension and cardinality counts.

Finally, we note that more recent research in the data warehousing context has focused on the development of structures for the compact representation of the data cube [24, 15]. For example, Sismanis et al. present the Dwarf cube [24], a tree-based data structure that reduces attribute redundancy in order to minimize the cost of cube materialization. However, while the Dwarf is certainly an interesting option when data cube queries are heavily utilized, it may still be significantly larger than the original fact table due to the considerable information that it must store. Moreover, its complex structure represents a measure of *overkill* since few users actually query the high dimensional group-bys that the Dwarf so efficiently represents.

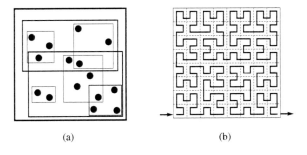

Figure 1. (a) R-tree partitioning for a maximum node count of four. (b) A $\mathcal{H}_3^2$ Hilbert curve.

3 R-trees and bulk loading

Before presenting the details of the new methods, we first briefly review the R-tree model, particulary as it relates to the concept of bulk loading for static data. To begin, the R-tree is a hierarchical, d-dimensional tree-based index that organizes the query space as a collection of nested, possibly over-lapping hyper-rectangles [8]. The tree is balanced and has a height $H = \lceil \log_M n \rceil$, where M is the maximum *branching factor* and n is equivalent to the number of points in the data set. A user query Φ may be defined as $\{r_1, r_2, \ldots, r_d\}$ for ranges $(r_{min(i)}, r_{max(i)})$, $1 \leq i \leq d$, and is answered by comparing the values on $\{r_1, r_2, \ldots, r_d\}$ with the coordinates of the rectangle $\aleph$ that surrounds the points in each data page. The search algorithm descends through levels $l = 1, 2, \ldots, H$ of the index until valid leaf nodes are identified. Because the boxes may overlap (at least in the original R-tree), multiple path traversals may be necessary. A simple R-tree hyper-rectangle decomposition can be seen in Figure 1(a).

For static environments, it is possible to improve space utilization by *packing* points into disk blocks. Here, we use some form of bulk insertion method, rather than the standard point-by-point technique. As such, it is possible to avoid the half-filled boxes that often result from dynamic node splitting. Run-time query performance may also be improved as the packing process typically reduces box overlap and improves point clustering. Regardless of the packing strategy employed, the basic approach is as follows:

1. Pre-process the data — usually by sorting — so that the n points are associated with m pages of size $\lceil \frac{n}{M} \rceil$. The page size/branching factor is chosen so as to be a multiple of the disk's physical block size.

2. Associate each of the m leaf node pages with an ID that will be used as a file offset by parent bounding boxes.

3. Construct the remainder of the index by recursively packing the bounding boxes of lower levels until the root node is reached.

Clearly, the sort order is the key requirement and, in fact, several approaches have been taken. Previous research has shown that both STR [16] and Hilbert ordering [12] appear to outperform the original lowX method [22], though there does not appear to be a clear winner amongst the first two when evaluated across a variety of data sets.

The Hilbert order employed in [12] is particularly interesting in the current context as it can be used to provide a linear ordering of points in a d-dimensional space. We note that while no single ordering can perfectly preserve locality in d dimensions, the Hilbert curve has been shown to be among the most effective in this regard. First proposed in [10], the Hilbert curve is a non-differentiable curve of length s^d that traverses all s^d points of the d-dimensional grid having side length s, making unit steps and turning only at right angles. The curve can be visualized as an interval I existing within the unit square S. If we decompose S into equivalent sub-squares S_i, for $1 \leq i \leq 4$, then with a series of reflections and rotations, we may concatenate the sub-intervals I_i to satisfy the requirements of the linear mapping. We say that a d-dimensional cubic space has order k if it has a side length $s = 2^k$ and use the notation $\mathcal{H}_k^d$ to denote the k-th order approximation of a d-dimensional curve, for $k \geq 1$ and $d \geq 2$. Note that *order* should not be confused with *dimension* as it is possible, for example, to have an order four curve in two dimensions. Figure 1(b) illustrates a $\mathcal{H}_3^2$ curve.

4 A new I/O efficient model for DW environments

As noted, R-trees have been used in one form or another for the indexing of multi-dimensional data. Extensions to the basic model have been used to minimize bounding box overlap and/or reduce bounding box size, thereby reducing the number of blocks retrieved from disk. In the absence of any additional information regarding the structure or characteristics of the data set, this would appear to be a reasonable strategy to take. For this reason, previous work in the area of disk-based indexing has focused on blocks retrieved as a metric of index performance [16, 12, 1, 22].

However, a "raw" count of accessed blocks can be quite misleading since the true response time is dependant not just upon the number of accesses but upon the *type* of access. This same point was also made in [17] with respect to Hash-Join performance. In particular, we must be able to distinguish between (i) blocks that are read following an independent seek — denoted here as *intra-file* seeks — and (ii) blocks that are read following an access of the previous (contiguous) physical block. While the *read ahead* caching mechanism employed on modern disks tends to hide the penalty associated with very short seeks, intra-file movements can, and do, have a tangible effect upon query performance in production scale environments. Moreover, because DW systems typically have a smaller number of users than OLTP system, the I/O for individual queries is often processed as a single operation. Again, this tends to exaggerate the effect of seeking during query resolution.

4.1 The Linear Breadth First R-tree

We now present the LBF R-tree model. Our primary objective is to reduce the occurrence of intra-file seeks by structuring the blocks of both index and data set so as maximize the number of contiguous blocks associated with an arbitrary query. Conceptually, this is similar to the B^+-tree model, where records of the data set are maintained in sorted order so that the index is able to identify contiguous record clusters. In fact, this notion of building upon the strength of the B^+-tree was also discussed in [14], where the authors construct an R-tree for dynamic spatial environments. There, pre-allocated blocks are used to form *sibling clusters*. As nodes reach capacity they are split, so that points are distributed into the pre-allocated cluster blocks. Of course, there are limits on the degree of pre-allocation and, in practice, sibling clustering in dynamic environments deteriorates with increased query size and complexity.

In effect, our model employs an extreme form of linear clustering for static environments. Like other R-trees frameworks targeting such spaces, we exploit a packing strategy to improve storage and run-time query performance. In our case, we utilize the Hilbert curve so as to most effectively map the multi-dimensional points to a linear order. Algorithm 1 describes the construction technique. Though similar to the basic packing strategies previously discussed, the key feature in our method is the combination of the WHILE loop in Step 4 and the concatenation of temporary files in Step 7. As each successive level R_{tmp}^i, $1 \leq i \leq H$, in the index tree is constructed, its blocks are written in a strictly linear fashion to disk (i.e, a logical left-to-right traversal). A series of H temporary *level indexes* is created. Once the root level R_{tmp}^H is reached, we produce a final index by arranging the levels of the indexes by reverse order of creation, $R_{tmp}^H, R_{tmp}^{H-1}, ... R_{tmp}^1$. Note that this process is composed of a series of streaming operations and therefore can be executed with minimal buffer space.

Figure 2 illustrates the final structure of a small LBF R-tree, with $n = 15$, $M = 3$, and $H = \lceil \log_M n \rceil = 3$. In Figure 2(a), we see how the ordering of data points (B3–B8) is dictated by the order of the $\mathcal{H}_4^2$ Hilbert curve. Index boxes (B0–B2) are then constructed as per the creation order of their children (note that B0 is simply the

---

Algorithm 1 LBF R-tree Construction

Input: An arbitrarily ordered multi-dimensional data set S of size n, with branching factor M
Output: A packed R-tree index R_{ind} and associated Hilbert-ordered data set R_{data}.
1: Sort records of S as S' in terms of their Hilbert ordinal index
2: In a linear pass, partition the n records of S' into $\lceil \frac{n}{M} \rceil$ blocks
3: Write the base level to disk as R_{tmp}^1
4: **while** we have not reached the index root **do**
5:     Linearly partition the q blocks of R_{tmp}^i into the $\lceil \frac{q}{M} \rceil$ parent boxes at level $i + 1$
6:     Write the blocks of level $i + 1$ to disk as R_{tmp}^{i+1}
7: Concatenate the H temporary index files into R_{ind} in the order $R_{tmp}^H, R_{tmp}^{H-1}, ... R_{tmp}^2$.
8: R_{tmp}^1 becomes R_{data} and may be appended to R_{ind} or written separately

---

box that encloses the full d-dimensional space). However, as we shall see in Section 4.2, the motivation here isn't the minimization of storage or box overlap (though these are certainly beneficial), but is instead the manipulation of a purely linear $[R_{ind} + R_{data}]$ combination. In Figure 2(b) we see the physical disk arrangement, consisting of an independent index and data set. Note the purely sequential block ID sequence represented by the direct concatenation of index and data components. Specifically, let us assume that for R_{ind} and R_{data} we have block counts C_{ind} and C_{data} respectively. We can therefore guarantee a disk resident mapping of the consecutive block ID sequence $ID_{ind(0)}, ID_{ind(1)}, \ldots, ID_{ind(C_{ind}-1)}, ID_{data(C_{ind})}, ID_{data(C_{ind}+1)}, \ldots, ID_{data(C_{ind}+C_{data})}$.

4.2 The Search Strategy

In all previous R-tree clustering algorithms, the primary motivation has been a reduction in the number of blocks *touched* by a user query (this is true of the Hilbert packing algorithm as well). As such, implementations rely upon a conventional Depth First Search (DFS) and seek to measure performance via a count of accessed blocks. However, the application of DFS is poorly suited to data warehousing fact tables. Specifically, by repeatedly moving between index and data set in order to resolve multi-block range queries, we introduce dramatic growth in intra-file seek time. As the size of the underlying data set increases, the growing number of random head movements can lead to a significant degree of *thrashing*. Because the previous packing algorithms were evaluated (i) on very small data sets (100,000 records or less), and (ii) with the unrealistic assumption that all indexes would be entirely cached in memory, this fact would

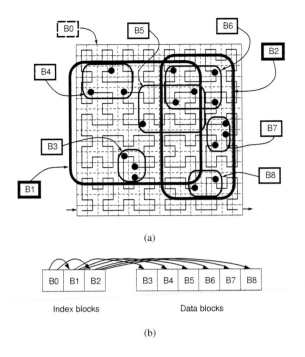

(a)

<table>
<tr><td>B0</td><td>B1</td><td>B2</td><td></td><td>B3</td><td>B4</td><td>B5</td><td>B6</td><td>B7</td><td>B8</td></tr>
</table>

Index blocks   Data blocks

(b)

Figure 2. (a) The logical partitioning of a small $\mathcal{H}_3^2$ Hilbert space and (b) The physical layout on disk.

Algorithm 2 Linear Breadth First Search

Input: A packed R-tree index, its associated data, and a user query ϕ.

Output: Fully resolved query.

1:   Initialize $pageList$ with ID of first index block
2:   **while** not at the leaf level **do**
3:     $childList$ = new empty list
4:     **for** each range node k in the $pageList$ **do**
5:       **for** each page ID $i \geq pageList[k]_{min}$ AND $\leq pageList[k]_{max}$ **do**
6:         Using i as a block offset, read the relevant disk block B into memory.
7:         **for** each child block j of B that intersects ϕ **do**
8:           **if** for the current range node l in the $childList$, we have $childList[l]_{max} = j - 1$ **then**
9:             set $childList[l]_{max} = j$
10:          **else**
11:            create new range node $l + 1$ and set $childList[l + 1]_{min} = childNode[l + 1]_{max} = j$
12:     $pageList = childList$
13: **for** each page ID i in the current $pageList$ **do**
14:     Using i as an offset, read the relevant disk block B into memory.
15:     Process B for records matching ϕ.

have been completely obscured. In Tera-scale data warehousing environments, it would certainly not be.

Algorithm 2 describes an alternative search strategy that is tailored to the unique structure of the packed R-tree. We refer to this strategy as Linear Breadth First Search, where the term "linear" denotes the fact that the logical BFS strategy in fact maps directly to a physical linearization on disk. In general, the algorithm follows the standard BFS technique of traversing the tree level-by-level in a left-to-right fashion. Queries are resolved as follows. For the current level i of the tree, the query engine successively identifies the j nodes at level $i - 1$ whose bounding boxes intersect the query $\Phi = \{r_1, r_2, \ldots, r_d\}$. It places these page IDs into a *working list* W. We note that because of the way the LBF R-trees are built, the page IDs of W are, by definition, sorted in ascending order. Using the list of j page IDs, the query engine traverses the blocks at level $i - 1$ and replaces the current working list W with a new child list $W\prime$ containing the relevant blocks for level $i - 2$. It repeats this procedure until it has reached the data blocks (R_{data}) at the base of the tree. At this point, the algorithm simply identifies and returns the d-dimensional records encapsulated by Φ.

We note that one of the primary reasons for the use of a Depth First search strategy in most R-tree implementations is its more modest memory requirements. Specifically,

it must store no more than $O(\lg_M n) = H$ nodes to traverse the length of a path from root to leaf, while for an m-block data set a standard Breadth First traversal is $O(m)$ in the worst case (i.e, Φ fully encapsulates block $B0$). Recall, however, that the primary purpose of the Hilbert order is in fact to identify point and/or box clusterings in the d-dimensional space. As such, hyper-rectangular range queries consist primarily of one or more *contiguous* clusters of disk blocks. In this context, it is extremely inefficient to store individual block IDs. Instead, the *monotonically increasing* ID lists (i.e., $pageList$ and $childList$) for Linear BFS consist of a sequence of min/max *range nodes* that identify contiguous block clusters in the linearized disk layout. The lists themselves are constructed in lines 7–11 as a given level is sequentially accessed. Figure 3 provides an illustration of how the combination of range nodes and Linear BFS would be utilized. Note how the selected nodes of the index and data set consist of a strictly increasing set of block IDs, a sequence that maps directly to the physical disk ordering.

In the case of a query that encloses the entire space, for example, the total memory requirement for Linear BFS is just one range/node. Asymptotically, of course, the worst case complexity remains $O(m)$ as we could have every other leaf node included in the result. We note, however,

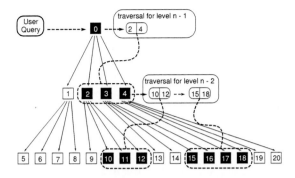

Figure 3. Mapping Linear Breadth First search to the physical block order.

that this is clearly a pathological case and is quite difficult to actually produce with a linearized Hilbert-ordered space.

4.3 Analysis of Performance Degradation

In [4], Faloutsos and Roseman provide a theoretical model for the estimation of R-tree query cost based upon the notions of *fractals*. Again, however, the assumption is that all block retrievals are equally costly, a notion that is simply not accurate for large data sets. In fact, for queries of sufficient size (typically 5% - 15% of the data set), a straight sequential scan of the data set will outperform a multi-dimensional index due to the degree of disk thrashing introduced by the latter. It is therefore useful to look at the practical impact for the LBF R-tree for very large queries. In fact, it is possible to show that the worst case I/O of a packed R-tree using Linear BFS is equivalent to $LS(r\text{-}tree_{ind}) + LS(r\text{-}tree_{data})$, where LS implies a linear scan.

Recall that the construction mechanism of the LBF R-tree implies that block IDs run consecutively from $ID_{ind(0)} \dots ID_{data(C_{ind}+C_{data})}$. Moreover, the blocks of the data set explicitly obey this same linear ordering. Consequently, while traversing $[R_{ind} + R_{data}]$, we can guarantee for a given level l that (i) a block $b_{l(i)}$ *must* be visited before $b_{l(j)}$ for $i < j$, and (ii) any block $b_{l(i)}$ *must* be visited before $b_{l-1(j)}$ for any i, j. The implication is that the disk head moves in one logical direction only. The worse case I/O performance is therefore equivalent to the time taken to sequentially scan the index, followed by the time taken to sequentially scan the data set.

To illustrate the impact of the previous observation, we issued a query on a pair of ten dimensional data sets, the first containing one million records (43,479 blocks) and the second housing 10,000,000 records (434,783 blocks). The hyper-rectangle of the query was designed to encapsulate the full space. A sequential scan on the first set resulted in

43,478 contiguous read and a resolution time of 1.04 seconds. The time for the LBF search on the same set was 1.17 seconds, with the 12.9% increase associated with the additional scan of the R-tree index. A standard Depth First strategy, however, ran in 1.33 seconds, with the 28.3% increase being generated by 3925 non-contiguous reads. One might expect the results on the larger set to follow a similar pattern. However, it is important to note that the non-contiguous intra-file seeks in larger tables are much more likely to cross cylinders. As such, intra-file seek time becomes much more of an issue in practice. With the sequential traversal, read time on the larger file was 11.2 seconds. Linear BFS — gracefully degrading to a linear scan of the index and the data file — was once again competitive with an I/O time of 12.8 seconds. The standard Depth First Traversal, on the other hand, generated 39,228 non-contiguous reads and caused the read time to explode to 61.73 seconds, a 550% increase over the sequential scan.

As a final point, it should be obvious that Linear BFS is only effective if the logically linearized order of disk blocks is equivalent to the physical ordering of blocks. This would not be true in the general R-tree/b-tree case because the dynamic updates of the tree would permute the original order of the blocks. In the data warehousing context, however, this is not the case. Recall that bulk loading/updating is typically used in such environments. This is essentially a streaming operation that writes blocks to disk during a single phase. We briefly review the process below.

4.4 Updating the tree

While we have referred to the target environment as static, it is quite likely that periodic "batch" updates will be required. As such, an efficient mechanism for updating the LBF R-tree is required. In particular, we must avoid resorting the fact table data, as Hilbert sorting is the dominant cost in the construction of the LBF R-tree. Here, we can in fact adapt a bulk update technique first proposed by Roussopoulos et al. for lowX data sets [21]. The basic LBF update algorithm can be expressed as follows:

1. Sort the records of the update set U in Hilbert order. Note that $|U| \ll |r_{data}|$.

2. In a single sequential pass, merge the records of U with the records of r_{data}, which are already sorted in Hilbert order. Write the result $r\prime_{data}$ to fresh storage.

3. Repeat Steps 4–7 of Algorithm 1 to rebuild $r\prime_{ind}$. Space permitting, the old index $[R_{ind} + R_{data}]$ may remain online during this process.

The LBF update effectively reduces the batch update to a streaming merge operation that can be performed quite efficiently even for large data sets. Should there be a need to further reduce the update schedule, it is also possible to trade-off a small amount of r_{data} storage for reduced merged frequency. Specifically, the default packing method defined in Algorithm 1 assumes that R-tree nodes are to be filled to capacity. In fact, this is not required. For example, we might fill the original r_{data} blocks to 90% capacity, thereby leaving space in each block for future update records. A series of direct, in-place updates can therefore be performed before a full merge is actually required.

4.5 Compressing the tree

Since the LBF tree is designed for very large data warehousing environments, it is quite likely that compression of the underlying tables may have to be performed. Compression not only reduces the footprint of the core fact tables, but increases the storage available for materialized groupbys and summary tables. In a related research project, we have developed a series of Hilbert-based compression methods for both our indexes and data sets [3]. While the details of those methods are outside the scope of this paper, we briefly describe the compression model in terms of its relationship to the current work.

Recall from Step 1 of Algorithm 1 that data records are first sorted in terms of their relative position in the $\mathcal{H}_k^d$ space. Specifically, for a d-dimensional space of side-length s, the s^d-length curve identifies a unique, strictly increasing order on the s^d point positions. We refer to the numeric representation of a point position as a Hilbert *ordinal*. In fact, the LBF R-tree can work exclusively with ordinals, rather than the more intuitive (and costly) multi-attribute record form. Moreover, in the low to medium dimensionality spaces common to data warehouse environments, we may efficiently represent a pair of *adjacent* points $< i, j >$ along the curve as the integer difference value $|ordinal_i - ordinal_j|, i < j$. When coupled with a bit compaction technique that strips away leading zeros, differential compression can produce significant savings in storage. Figure 4(a) provides a simple example in which points are located 6 and 9 steps from the $\mathcal{H}_3^2$ origin. With the first point serving as the *anchor*, the second point is stored as $9 - 6 = 3$, or 11 in binary form. This is 62 bits less that the default encoding for a 2-d value (assuming 32-bit integers).

The compression framework is completely integrated with the LBF R-tree, and includes both the data sets (r_{data}) and the associated indexes (r_{ind}). Experimental evaluation demonstrates compression ratios of 80%–90% on both uniform and skewed data, and 90%-98% on the indexes.

4.6 Linear Depth First R-trees

While we have described an R-tree linearization that supports a breadth first traversal strategy, it is in fact possible

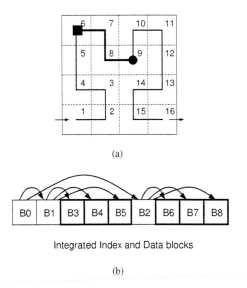

(a)

Integrated Index and Data blocks

(b)

Figure 4. (a) Compressing a $\mathcal{H}_2^2$ Hilbert space (b) The physical layout on disk for a LDF tree.

to linearize the index and data files so as define a depth first traversal as well. For example, given the current LBF R-tree as input, we can perform an *in-order* traversal of the $[r_{ind} + r_{data}]$ pair, serializing the blocks to disk in the order in which they are read. A subsequent depth first search would allow the query engine to again reduce disk head movement by following a strictly increasing block order on a range query $\Phi = \{r_1, r_2, \ldots, r_d\}$.

Note, however, that unlike the LBF R-tree we cannot create separate storage for the index and data components for the LDF R-tree. Doing so would require the query engine to repeatedly transition (i. e., seek) between the index and data set to obtain the leaf data, thereby destroying any potential performance gains. Instead, in an LDF R-tree, we must integrate the index and data set blocks into a single composite storage structure. Figure 4(b) illustrates how the blocks of the running example would be reorganized into a new $r_{ind+data}$ structure in order to support depth first search. Note how Block B2, for example, is stored between a pair of contiguous leaf level blocks. Unfortunately, single-store integration negatively affects any operations that directly process the data points themselves. In the current context, this would increase the complexity and degrade the performance of the streaming compression and update methods.

5 Experimental Results

In this section, we provide experimental results that assess the performance of the LBF R-tree relative to a number of practical alternatives. All tests are conducted on a 3.2 GHz workstation, with 1 GB of main memory and a 160

GB disk drive operating at 7200 RPM. The majority of individual tests utilize synthetic data sets so that we may vary key test parameters in a precise fashion. For completeness, results for a real data set that is commonly employed in the DW literature are also provided. For the performance evaluations, we use the standard approach of timing queries in batch mode. In our case, an automated query generator constructs batches of range queries, in which high/low ranges are randomly generated for each of k attributes, randomly selected from the d-dimensional space, $k \subseteq d$. To more closely reflect the characteristics of real world query environment, queries are restricted to subsets of 3 attributes or less (users tend not to use a large number of attributes in the same query). To minimize the interference of OS caching, we utilize the page deletion mechanism offered by the 2.6.x line of the Linux kernel to completely clear the page caches between individual queries.

5.1 Data Set size

To assess the impact of data set size on index performance, we ran a series of tests on synthetically generated data sets with record counts from 100,000 to 10 million records. The data sets consist of 6 dimensions, with cardinalities randomly chosen in the range 4–400 and a data distribution skewed with a zipfian value of one. Batches of 50 queries per run were used, with the results averaged across five independent runs. In total, five distinct index forms were created: a linear breadth first R-tree (LBF), a linear depth first R-tree (LDF), a standard depth first Hilbert packed R-tree (HDF), a bitmap index on unordered data (U-BMP), and a bitmap index on the Hilbert ordered data set (H-BMP). In Figure 5(a), we see a count of the total number of blocks accessed during the query runs (note the logarithmic y axis). The results are as expected, with a close to linear increase in blocks processed as the data set grows in size. Counts are virtually identical for each of the Hilbert ordered data sets, with a small increase for the unordered Bitmap index. Note that we do not plot the values for the bitmaps at 10 million records due to the excessive memory requirements in larger spaces.

In Figure 5(b), we examine the actual seek counts on the same queries. Here, the "seek count" refers to the total number of seeks across the full query set. The results paint a clear picture of the effect of linearization on both R-trees and the bitmap models. The new LBF form produces the lowest seek counts, followed closely by LDF. In contrast, the conventional packed R-tree, HDF, generates almost twice as many seeks on the largest data set. H-BMP is comparable to the standard R-tree (it is using the same underlying data set and its index must be paged from disk), while the unordered U-BMP bitmap produces almost 3 times as many seeks due to its lack of point clustering.

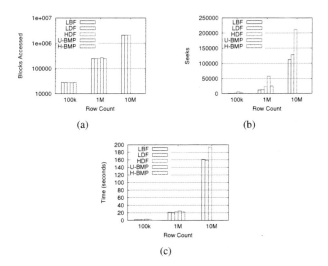

Figure 5. (a) Blocks accessed (b) seeks performed (c) run time for data sets of 100K to 10M records

Finally, Figure 5(c) provides a partial illustration of the effect of seek count on run-time performance. Again, we can see that the linearized r-tress, LBF and LDF, produce the lowest query times. In fact, LDF is about 1% faster on ten million records, a result attributable to the fact that it's *average seek length* is slightly smaller that that of LBF even though its total count is marginally higher. Performance for the standard R-tree and the bitmaps are demonstrably slower. For example, the bitmaps are 10%-20% slower than LBF at 1 million records, while at 10 million records, we see that the run-time of the standard R-tree is approximately 20% higher than that of LBF. We note that this is smaller than the gap for the raw seek count. There are two reasons for this. First, due to the interleaving of I/O and post processing (e.g., sorting, aggregation, presentation) our query times include both components. In fact, post processing costs typically account for close to half of total query resolution costs and, moreover, are identical for all methods. Consequently, if post processing contributions were removed, we would expect the relative difference in run-time to almost double for the data set with 10 million records.

Second, as noted previously, smaller seeks can be "absorbed" by the read-ahead caching mechanism of modern disks, thereby partially hiding the degree of improvement we would expect to see on the Terabyte-scale fact tables found in production environments. To demonstrate how this issue might affect larger tables, we created a data set of 70 million records with the same basic parameters of our previous test. This data set was approximately 2 GB in size, and is the largest fact table that we can create on a 32-bit file system. LBF and HDF indexes were then created. Figure 6(a) displays the head-to-head comparison for the run-time of the two methods. Note that the run-time does not represent a seven-fold increase over the times for 10 million records. Due to the fact that an external memory version of the index methods was required, we utilized our full framework which includes the R-tree compression algorithms. As a result, the final data set is only 28% larger than the set of 10 million records. Still, we can see an increase of almost 30% in run-time for the HDF index relative to LBF, a significant difference versus the smaller data sets. Again, we would expect this growth to be far more dramatic on data sets that might in practice be an order of magnitude larger.

5.2 Dimension Count

Figure 6(b) and Figure 6(c) illustrate the impact of an increase in dimensions on seek count and performance, respectively. We specifically evaluate the R-trees in this test, using data sets with 10 million records, mixed cardinalities and a zipfian skew of one. In Figure 6(b), we clearly see that as dimensions increase, there is rapid growth in seek count. In fact, by 8 dimensions, the seek count for HDF has more than tripled that of LBF. This is reflective of the fact that higher dimension spaces tend to produce shorter clusters, thereby producing frequent tree traversals for HDF. The same general trend is illustrated in the performance results of Figure 6(c). By 8 dimensions, the HDF query stream takes about 25% longer to execute than the linearized trees. Again, the relative penalty will grow significantly in practical environments where we see much larger data sets.

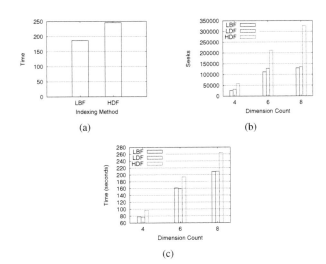

(a)

(b)

(c)

Figure 6. (a) Run-time for 70 million records (b) seeks by dimension count (c) run-time by dimension count

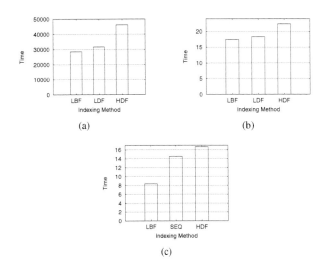

(a)

(b)

(c)

Figure 7. (a) seek count, real data (b) run-time, real data, time versus sequential scans

5.3 Real Data

While we have utilized a zipfian skew in all of our synthetic tests, real data sometimes has skew patterns that are difficult to mimic programmatically. We have therefore evaluated the R-tree methods on a weather pattern data set that is regularly used in the DW literature [9]. It consists of 1.2 million records, nine dimensions, and cardinalities ranging from 2 to 7,037. Figure 7(a) depicts the growth in seek times for the three tree methods, demonstrating a 60% rise in seeks in HDF relative to LBF. The associated query times are shown in Figure 7(b), with a 29% increase in cost for HDF. The results for the real data set are therefore consistent with those of the synthetic data sets of comparable size.

5.4 LBF versus sequential scans

Recall that as the size of a query relative to the underlying data set increases, there comes a point at which no index can improve upon a sequential scan. In our testing this occurred when the query set exceeded 10% to 15% of all of the records in the data set. However, because of the use of Linear BFS, the penalty associated with unusually large queries is so small that sequential scans would almost never be necessary. Figure 7(c) illustrates the relative cost of LBF and HDF versus sequential scans of the real data set described above (again with random query batches). Here, the queries have been defined so as to represent "large" result sets, in this case averaging approximately 7% of the full data set. The results are quite interesting. First, we see here a more extreme difference between the linearized LBF R-tree and the standard HDF R-tree. In fact, the cost of HDF is essentially twice that of LDF. Second, we see that since the average query size is about half that of the "index usefulness threshold", the LBF indexes do indeed significantly outperform a simple sequential scan. Specifically, the scan requires about 75% more time on the same queries. Note as well, however, that the sequential scan actually outperforms the standard packed R-tree in this query range. As a final conclusion, it should be clear that the use of an LBF R-tree provides an attractive alternative to the use of complex and error prone multi-dimensional query size estimators (e.g., histograms) that might be employed in order to decide between a sequential scan and a standard R-tree search.

6 Conclusion

In multi-dimensional environments, R-trees have been used extensively and successfully to provide efficient access to point and spatial data. Researchers have also shown great interest in the R-tree and have identified packing methods that reduce the total number of blocks accessed per query. Still, these techniques do not optimize (or even assess) the number or size of the seeks required to retrieve relevant disk blocks. For large data sets, such as those found in data warehousing systems, this disk head movement can have a significant impact on overall query performance. In this paper, we discuss the linearization of R-tree indexes and data, a technique that dramatically reduces the number of seeks required for common range queries. Though it is actually possible to linearize both depth first and breath first searches, we have been able to incorporate the breadth first strategy into an integrated indexing framework that includes compression, external memory support, and efficient batch updates. Experimental results support our design decisions and suggest that even more pronounced improvements are likely in production environments, where the scale of the core fact tables would significantly exaggerate the impact of intra-file seeks.

References

[1] L. Arge, M. de Berg, H. Haverkort, and K. Yi. The Priority R-tree: A practically efficient and worst case optimal R-tree. *ACM SIGMOD*, pages 64–75, 2004.

[2] N. Beckmann, H. Kriegel, R. Schneider, and B. Seeger. The r-tree: an efficient and robust method for points and rectangles. *ACM SIGMOD*, pages 322–331, 1990.

[3] T. Eavis and D. Cueva. A Hilbert Space compression architecture for data warehouse environments. In *DaWaK*, 2007.

[4] C. Faloutsos and S. Roseman. Fractals for secondary key retrieval. *ACM PODS*, pages 247–252, 1989.

[5] V. Gaede and O. Gunther. Multidimensional access methods. *ACM Computing Surveys*, 30(2):170–231, 1998.

[6] J. Gray, A. Bosworth, A. Layman, and H. Pirahesh. Data cube: A relational aggregation operator generalizing group-by, cross-tab, and sub-totals. In *ICDE*, pages 152–159, 1996.

[7] H. Gupta, V. Harinarayan, A. Rajaraman, and J. Ullman. Index selection for OLAP. *ICDE*, pages 208–219, 1997.

[8] A. Guttman. R-trees: A dynamic index structure for spatial searching. *ACM SIGMOD*, pages 47–57, 1984.

[9] C. Hahn, S. Warren, and J. Loudon. Edited synoptic cloud reports from ships and land stations over the globe. Available at http://cdiac.esd.ornl.gov/-cdiac/ndps/ndpo26b.html.

[10] D. Hilbert. Ueber die stetige abbidung einer line auf ein flchenstck. *Mathematische Annalen*, 38(3):459460, 1891.

[11] Y. Huang, N. Jing, and E. Rundensteiner. Spatial joins using r-trees: Breath first traversasl with global optimizations. *VLDB*, pages 322–331, 1997.

[12] I. Kamel and C. Faloutsos. On packing r-trees. *CIKM*, pages 490–499, 1993.

[13] I. Kamel and C. Faloutsos. Hilbert R-tree: An improved r-tree using fractals. *VLDB*, pages 64–75, 1994.

[14] K. Kim and S. Cha. Sibling clustering of tree-based indexes for effcient spatial query processing. *CIKM*, pages 322–331, 1998.

[15] L. Lakshmanan, J. Pei, and Y. Zhao. QC-trees: An efficient summary structure for semantic OLAP. *ACM SIGMOD*, pages 64–75, 2003.

[16] S. Leutenegger, M. Lopez, and J. Eddington. STR: a simple and efficient algorithm for r-tree packing. *ICDE*, pages 497–506, 1997.

[17] M. Lo and C. Ravishankar. Towards eliminating random i/o in hash joins. In *ACM PODS*, pages 64–75, 1995.

[18] P. O'Neil and G. Graefe. Multi-table joins through bitmapped join indices. *SIGMOD Record*, 24(3):8–11, 1995.

[19] P. O'Neil and D. Quass. Improved query performance with variant indexes. In *ACM SIGMOD*, pages 38–49, 1997.

[20] B. Pagel, H. Six, and M. Winter. Window query-optimal clustering of spatial objects. *ACM PODS*, pages 64–75, 1995.

[21] N. Roussopoulos, Y. Kotidis, and M. Roussopoulos. Cubetree: Organization of the bulk incremental updates on the data cube. *ACM SIGMOD*, pages 89–99, 1997.

[22] N. Roussopoulos and D. Leifker. Direct spatial search on pictorial databases using packed r-trees. *ACM SIGMOD*, pages 17–31, 1985.

[23] T. Sellis, N. Roussopoulos, and C. Faloutsos. The r+-tree - a dynamic index for multidimensional objects. *VLDB*, pages 507–518, 1987.

[24] Y. Sismanis, A. Deligiannakis, N. Roussopoulos, and Y. Kotidis. Dwarf: Shrinking the PetaCube. *ACM SIGMOD*, pages 464–475, 2002.

[25] Y. Theodoridis and T. Sellis. A model for the prediction of r-tree performance. In *ACM PODS*, pages 161–171, 1996.

[26] M. Wu and A. Buchmann. Encoded bitmap indexing for data warehouses. In *ICDE*, pages 220–230, 1998.

XPath Selectivity Estimation for a Mobile Auction Application

Sebastian Obermeier
University of Paderborn
Fürstenallee 11
33102 Paderborn, Germany
so @ upb.de

Stefan Böttcher
University of Paderborn
Fürstenallee 11
33102 Paderborn, Germany
stb @ upb.de

Thomas Wycisk
University of Paderborn
Fürstenallee 11
33102 Paderborn, Germany
thwycisk @ upb.de

Abstract

Whenever nodes in a mobile network try to access an XML database server, the offered data must be somehow queried and transported by a mobile network to the querying node. For this purpose, two mechanisms are possible: query shipping and data shipping. Which one is better depends among other aspects on the query result size, more precisely on the overhead that data shipping incorporates compared to query shipping.

In this paper, we present a query result size estimator that allows each mobile user to estimate the resulting size and cardinality of an XPath query by means of special distributed metadata in order to decide between query shipping or data shipping by comparing the estimated size of the result with the data that must be requested for data shipping. We show how the metadata is generated for certain query classes, how the metadata can be used to predict the result size and cardinality, and we give experimental results on the deviation of the predicted results.

1 Introduction

Whenever nodes in a mobile network query for data which is stored on an XML database server and partially cached on mobile clients, estimations about query result size and query result cardinality are helpful for a lot of reasons.

Data caching speeds up query processing, e.g. when a device that already stores a part of the data and can reuse it for certain operations instead of accessing the network again and again. However, the reuse of query results is limited to a very small class of queries fulfilling certain conditions (cf. [9]).

Data shipping is an approach, where the database is split into handy parts, and each device detects which parts it needs to request in order to answer a query locally. This approach does not limit data reuse to certain query types, it works for all kinds of queries that access the cached part of the database. As the data shipping approach requests to locally store all data necessary to answer the query, it has the advantage of better cache usability if parts of the needed data are located directly in the neighborhood. In such cases, local data can be transferred faster and with lower costs than receiving data from a remote database, which is many hops away. However, data shipping may result in much more overhead than query shipping, which sends a query to the database and gets only the result in return.

The decision of doing query shipping – i.e. to send the query to the database – or data shipping – i.e. to request the data that is needed to execute a query locally – mostly depends on the estimated result size. For instance, the fraction $\frac{queryResult}{requestedData}$ is a means for the overhead that applies when doing data shipping and executing the query locally. In order to be able to mathematically reason about this trade-off, the device must know how much more data is requested when demanding previously defined parts of the XML document instead of sending the query to the database.

The rest of the paper is organized as follows: In Section 2, we identify requirements for a query result and cardinality estimator usable for mobile networks. In Section 3, we compare the requirements with existing related work and explain the shortcomings of current approaches. Section 4 shows our solution and Section 5 gives experimental results. Finally, Section 6 concludes the paper.

1.1 Example Scenario

Current online auction web-applications are very popular due to a lot of reasons, e.g. easy searching, bidding and offering. However, like every other virtual online application, these approach does not allow users to view and inspect the goods before purchasing them. In contrast, traditional auctions and flea markets allow prospective buyers to touch and inspect the offered goods, and take them home after the successful transaction. An approach to combine the advantages of the classical flea market with the virtual internet auctions is the use of mobile devices in a classical flea market. Each offerer sends the data of his offered goods to the flea market server, and buyers may use both the internet and their mobile devices to find and locate desired items. In addition, the amount of mobile devices allows multi-hop ad-hoc communication.

A solution for the above scenario would require the following query classes to be supported:

Q_1 simple path expressions, e.g. list product title, current price, description, etc.

Q_2 simple path expressions containing existential filters, e.g. return only items with picture.

Q_3 queries containing category filters, e.g. return items of the category music or DVD.

Q_4 queries containing range filters, e.g. return items of a certain price range.

Furthermore, filters containing functions, e.g. a substring function for returning items containing a certain keyword, must be supported. We assign to these filters the query class Q_f. Specific for Q_f is that the concrete query instances are not known in advance.

In our mobile auction scenario, a mobile user with a query q can either send the query directly to the data server, or the user can use mechanisms to locate and request those parts of the XML database that are needed to answer the query locally within its neighborhood. Furthermore, requested parts can be offered to other participants. Which approach should be used depends mostly on the estimation of the query size.

2 Requirements

Within a scenario explained in Section 1.1, we can identify the following requirements concerning a query *size and cardinality estimator* (SCE). The SCE must

- estimate size and cardinality of the nodes returned by a given query
- support the query classes Q_1 to Q_4, explained in Section 1.1
- support filter functions Q_f that are dynamically invoked during the application execution
- support queries containing a wildcard ($*$) or a descent-or-self axis location step ($//$)
- be based on metadata that is distributable to the mobile clients in order to avoid DB access.
- limit metadata size to a predefined constant, e.g. 15kB
- be adaptable to frequent query patterns such that the accuracy increases for frequent queries.

3 Related Work

Query result size estimators are proposed for two database types: relational databases and XML databases. However, estimators are used for different purposes. In the context of relational databases, estimators are especially used for optimizing the sequence of applying join and select operators in order to work with small interim results. For this purpose, histograms are a good means to represent the cardinality of the database [6]. However, when XML databases are used, the concept of histograms cannot be directly transferred since XML documents are not "flat" like relational tables are.

XML data is far more complex than relational tables for the following reason. Normally, XML represents data as trees being deep and wide. XML documents are not necessarily balanced and elements with the same name may appear in different depths with different semantics. Furthermore, elements can encapsulate other elements.

[1], for instance, suggests the use of two data structures, namely *Path Trees* and *Markov Tables*. The concept of *Path Trees* is inspired by methods for estimating selectivity of substring predicates, e.g. [7]. A *Markov Table* contains all sub paths with a defined in addition with their frequency. A similar concept was described in [10] for the *Lore* DBMS. Both datastructures allow a selectivity estimation of *simple path expressions*. However, query class Q3 containing category filters is not supported by this approach.

XPATHLEARNER [8] uses the *Markov Table* and extends it to a *Markov Histogramm*, which additionally stores the distribution of values for data nodes. This data structure is maintained by query feedback. However, for the use in mobile networks, the information that is needed to do selectivity estimation must be distributed in advance.

XSKETCH [11, 12] and FXSKETCH [4] use the idea of the *Path Tree* and extend it by using `id/idref` constructs (cf. XLink [14]) to generate a graph like data structure. The use of this approach is mainly to estimate selectivity of structural joins (`X/Y`: how many child nodes `Y` have a parent node `X`), but not to give precise estimation on the result size.

STATIX [5] allows to estimate the selectivity of XQuery. It assigns each element during the validation of an XML document a unique ID, and generates a structure histogram (how many parent nodes exist within a certain ID range for a given node) and a value histogram (how many nodes fall into a certain value range). However, this approach does not allow a dynamic adaption to frequent query filters.

[15] introduces a *Bloom Histogram* which gathers all possible paths in a *path count table*. Then they are grouped by the number of selected nodes by means of bloom filters. Compared to this approach, our metadata size is still small but allows a perfect estimation for simple path expressions.

In [3] the *Correlated Subpath Tree (CST)* is introduced as

a means to statistically collect information about an XML-document. The approach is based on a suffix tree like data structure that stores frequently occurring sub paths together with their frequency. Furthermore it uses set hashing signatures to determine the dependency of sub paths in path queries containing branches. However, the *CST*s may grow extremely. Furthermore, *Markov Tables* give a more precise estimation for *Simple Path Expressions* [1].

Another approach is used in DB2 [2]. It generates path-value pairs for all possible paths of a DTD. The selectivity estimation is based mainly on the *fanout*, which represents the average number of XML elements per context element. However, the DB2 approach assumes an uniform distribution of nodes and predicates, e.g. for `/axisX::testX[Y]` holds: those X that fulfill Y are spread uniformly through all X.

4 Solution

Our SCE consists of two modules: an offline static module M_s and an online function module M_f. The offline module M_s generates metadata about the underlying database that is necessary to estimate size and cardinality for query types Q_1 to Q_4. Whenever the database content changes significantly, the module can be invoked to update the metadata.

The online module M_f is triggered whenever queries of the type Q_f, i.e. queries that contain functions, are passed to the database. The module identifies frequent functions and generates metadata about these functions. Before we explain both modules in detail, we first give some definitions.

Definition 4.1 *We call the* cardinality *of an XPath query q the number of elements returned by q.*

The cardinality corresponds to the result of the following XPath expression:

$$\texttt{fn:count}(q)$$

Definition 4.2 *We call the* selectivity *of a query filter* [P] *of a query q the amount of result nodes that are selected by a query* q^* *which is the same as q except that* q^* *does not contain* [P].

The selectivity corresponds to the following XPath expression:

$$\frac{\texttt{fn:count}(q)}{\texttt{fn:count}(q^*)}$$

with $q^* = q$ without filter [P]

4.1 Module M_s

The offline module M_s is used to generate statistics in terms of metadata about the data guide for the XML database. After a client has received this metadata, it can use it to estimate the size and cardinality of a given query. We select a list of all possible paths for M_s as follows. If there is a non-recursive DTD, we select a set S of all paths from the DTD as described below. Otherwise, we inspect the given real XML data to select a set S of paths. If a query q_w contains wild-cards or the descendant-or-self axis location step, all possible element names and paths according to the DTD are looked up, and the query is decomposed into n queries that subsume q_w and do not contain wild-cards or the descent-or-self axis.

4.1.1 Metadata for Querytype Q_1

To estimate the size and cardinality of queries belonging to the class Q_1, module M_s first determines the size and cardinality of every valid path, which may be indicated by a given, non-recursive DTD.

Figure 1 shows an example that is used by the auction application described in Section 1.1. The DTD is analyzed and a list of all possible paths is generated:

- `/auctions`
- `/auctions/auction`
- `...`
- `/auctions/auction/articleDesc/desc`

This list is enriched with paths that end up in text nodes:

- `/auctions/auction/title/text()`
- `/auctions/auction/price/text()`
- `...`
- `/auctions/auction/articleDesc/desc/text()`

We call each of these paths a *base path* and determine the cardinality of each base path by determining how many nodes of the database are selected by each of these base paths. Furthermore, we determine the size of the result set. To calculate the *average size* of a returned base path node, we divide the size of the base path result by its cardinality.

Storing these base paths does not need a large amount of bytes. Each base path corresponds to an exploration step of the traversal of the DTD tree. Therefore, if the DTD is known, we can leave out the concrete base path and put only the size and cardinality information into the metadata. For example, line 1 of the metadata corresponds to base path 1, line 2 to base bath 2 and so on.

4.1.2 Metadata for Querytype Q2

In order to get metadata for queries containing existential filters, we add to each base path i *conditional car-*

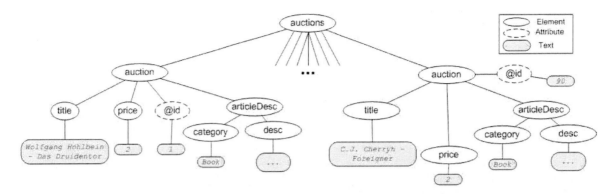

Figure 1. Example document of the auction database

dinalities, which are cardinalities that are generated by transferring the last $1\ldots i$ location steps of a given query q in a filter. For $i = 2$ and the given base path `/auctions/auction/articleDesc/desc`, we additionally store the average size and cardinality of the following queries:

$i = 1$: `/auctions/auction/articleDesc[./desc]`

$i = 2$: `/auctions/auction/[articleDesc/desc]`

4.1.3 Metadata for Querytype Q3

Our algorithm first identifies, which text nodes contain categories, i.e., a limited universe of possible entries. For such identified category nodes, a list is created that stores the cardinality and size of the contained textual data `/node₁/.../nodeₙ/text()`. The list contains besides the most frequent $k - 1$ entries an additional entry "rest" which summarizes the *arithmetic means* of the *remaining* entries, therefore its sum is not 100%. An example for $k = 5$ can be seen in Table 1, which consists of the values of Figure 2.

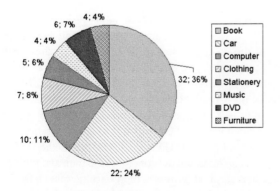

Figure 2. Example for category distribution

4.1.4 Metadata for Querytype Q4

Whenever text nodes contain solely numerical values like price information or dates, range queries can

Category	Amount
Book	36%
Car	24%
Computer	11%
Clothing	8%
Rest	5%

Table 1. List for category text

be formulated, e.g. `price ≥ 2`). For such paths `/node₁/.../nodeₙ/text()`, we determine by means of the XPath functions `fn:min` and `fn:max` the smallest and largest value. In addition, we determine the average by `fn:avg`. Furthermore, to calculate the standard deviation for n entries x_1 to x_n, we apply the following formula

$$\frac{n \sum_{i=0}^{n} x_i^2 - \left(\sum_{i=0}^{n} x_i\right)^2}{n(n-1)}$$

Finally, an equi-depth-histogram is created as Algorithm 1 shows. The algorithm requires that the data field numbers is sorted in ascending order (line 1). The breadth of a class is at least 1, and the histogram contains only integer numbers indicating the number of elements falling in each class. An example can be seen in Figure 3, which was generated with XMark data.

A histogram is a series of tabulated frequencies which refer to non-overlapping integer intervals $[min, max]$ like $[1, 2]$, $[3, 5]$ or $[6, 6]$. The combination of frequency and interval is called a "bucket". At the beginning of the algorithm the first bucket is initialized with the first entry of the *numbers* array (lines 2 - 2). The rest of the numbers is distributed in the loop (line 3. *frequency* is incremented for each number until the next higher number is encountered (line 4. Then the algorithm checks whether the frequency of this bucket is already high enough (line 5). If it is then current bucket will be added to the histogram and a new bucket is opened for the current nr by adjusting the min value and resetting the frequency. Should the frequency still be too

Algorithm 1 Create static Equi-Depth-Histogramm

Require: num is sorted in ascending order
```
 1: procedure CREATEHISTOGRAM(num)
 2:     currentValue = min = max = num[0]; frequency := 1
 3:     for all currentValue in num do
 4:         if currentValue > max then          ▷ New value
 5:             if frequency > MIN_BUCKET_DEPTH then
 6:                 STOREBUCKET(min, max, frequency)
 7:                 frequency := 0; min := currentValue   ▷ Open
    new bucket
 8:             end if
 9:             max := currentValue
10:         end if
11:         frequency := frequency + 1   ▷ Put into current bucket
12:     end for
13:     if frequency > 0 then               ▷ "Close" final bucket
14:         STOREBUCKET(start, max, frequency - 1)
15:     end if
16: end procedure
```

low, then interval is simply extended (line 9). Finally, the algorithm checks whether the last bucket is still open and closes it in a similar manner (line 13).

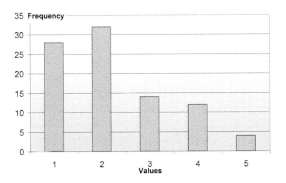

Figure 3. Example histogram

4.2 Module M_f

M_f handles cardinality and result size estimation for Q_f queries. It is called online module as it gains most of data by query feedback. M_f can be initialized with a short list of queries which the user is expected to pose (in our online auction scenario this may be queries that check the item description for terms like "warranty", "slightly damaged" etc.). Although this step is optional, it can significantly improve the performance at the beginning of the runtime.

The behavior (and performance) of M_f is controlled by two parameters: *defaultSelectivity* and *accessThreshold*. *defaultSelectivity* is returned when there is no data available for an accurate estimation. This value has to be determined by experiments for a specific scenario in order to minimize over- and underestimation. *accessThreshold* states how many times the database must see a filter f before the correct values for cardinality and result of size f

are computed.

4.3 Using Metadata for Estimating Size and Cardinality

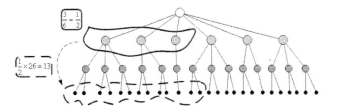

Figure 4. Selectivity Propagation

In this section we explain how to use the statistics that we gathered in Section 4.1 to estimate the result size and cardinality of the query classes Q_1 to Q_4 and Q_f. First, we describe a general assumption that is common to all following estimation techniques. It is called *selectivity propagation* and is illustrated in Figure 4.

Suppose there is a query q which contains a filter with an estimated selectivity of 0.5 that applies to nodes with depth 1 (light grey). q selects and returns nodes with depth 3 (black). To estimate the cardinality of q, the selectivity 0.5 is propagated downwards and multiplied by the number of black nodes. In our example this results in an estimated cardinality of 13 which is actually an overestimation as the two rightmost nodes do not belong to the result set. The more balanced the XML tree and the shorter the propagation path is, the better the estimation accuracy will be.

4.4 Estimation of Q_2

In this section, we show how to estimate queries containing filters like the following example query $q_2 = $ `/auctions/auction[./articleDesc/desc]`. If the length of filter is less or equal to the previously defined value i that indicates the path length of conditional cardinalities stored in the metadata, then the selectivity can be determined by a simple lookup (cf. Section 4.1.2). However, if the filter length is greater than i, then the metadata does not contain selectivity data that can be directly used for estimations on this query. In such a case, the selectivity must be approximated by decomposing the query into two subqueries of which the conditional cardinalities are available in the metadata. Assume, the metadata contains only selectivity for conditional cardinalities of path length 1, i.e. $i = 1$. Then, a decomposition of our example query q_2 would look like this:

$$\frac{\text{/auctions/auction[./articleDesc]}}{\text{/auctions/auction}} \times$$

$$\frac{\text{/auctions/auction/articleDesc[./desc]}}{\text{/auctions/auction/articleDesc}}$$

255

If all cardinalities in the numerator and denominator are greater then 0, the lower bound for a selectivity that is computed with our approximation technique is $\frac{1}{\texttt{/auctions/auction}}$.

4.5 Estimation of Q_3

The following example query q_3 with q_3 =/auctions/auction[./articleDesc/category/text() = 'Book'] illustrates the selectivity estimation of category filters. The only action to do is to lookup the entry in the corresponding selectivity table (see Table 1). Therefore the result is 36%.

4.6 Estimation of Q_4

By means of the example query q_4 with q_4 =/auctions/auction[./price/text() >= 2], we will explain how the selectivity of interval filters is estimated. At first the filter interval has to be normalized as the histogram does not support lookups for intervals like $[2, \infty]$. The normalized interval is determined by the expression $[max(min_{filter}, min_{HG}), min(max_{filter}, max_{HG})]$, where min_{filter} and max_{filter} are the minimum value and the maximum value of the current filter, and min_{HG} and max_{HG} are the minimum value and the maximum value stored in the histogram. For the example query q_4, this results in $[2, 5]$. According to the histogram in Figure 3, there are $33 + 14 + 13 + 4 = 64$ nodes in this interval which corresponds to a selectivity of $\frac{64}{91} = 70\%$.

4.7 Estimation of Q_f

The selectivity of a query q_f with q_f = /auctions/auction/desc[contains(text(), "guarantee")] is estimated the following way. If there is a metadata entry then a lookup will be sufficient. If such an entry does not exist, then a *default* value is returned. This value has to be determined before-hand in such way that overestimation as well as underestimation is minimized for all Q_f queries. Should a client pose a certain query more often than a threshold value k, the real selectivity is computed by sending this query to the database. Furthermore, if the *default* value must be used at some point during the estimation, the returned estimation will contain this fact.

5 Experiments

We have evaluated the performance of our query result estimation technique on two different datasets: a 100MB document generated by the synthetic XML benchmark XMark [13] and a 100MB excerpt of the DBLP dataset.

XMark documents, which represent the database of an Internet auction site, are very deep and consist of a large amount of different tags, whereas the DBLP document is mostly flat and contains information about various scientific publications.

The following metric was used for performance evaluation:

$$Dev_{avg} := \frac{1}{n} \sum_{i=0}^{n} \left(||QR_i| - \widetilde{|QR_i|}| \right) \qquad (1)$$

where $|QR_i|$ is the actual result size and $\widetilde{|QR_i|}$ is the estimated result size of some query q_i. The experiments were conducted on a Intel PIV-2.6GHz machine running Windows XP (Service Pack 2) with 1GB main memory.

5.1 Test query generation

For each query set mentioned in Section 1.1 (Q_1-Q_4), 10,000 test queries were constructed using schema information and the content of the actual documents. The generation of test queries for Q_1 was done by choosing n base paths at random. For testing queries belonging to Q_2, we first choose a filter length k (Pareto-distributed between 1 and 4) and then pick a base path /node$_1$/node$_2$/.../node$_m$ in which the filters are inserted. This is accomplished by either transforming the last k location steps into a filter expression (/node$_1$/.../node$_{m-k}$[./node$_{m-k+1}$/.../node$_m$]) which we call query class Q_{2a}, or appending a branching filter expression on a suitable location step (/node$_1$/.../node$_j$ [./node'$_{j+1}$/.../node'$_{j+k}$]/.../node$_m$), which we call query class Q_{2b}.

Test queries for Q_3, Q_4 and Q_f are created by varying elements in the base queries. For example, in the DBLP dataset the journal of an article can be reached by the path /dblp/article/journal/text(). To analyze how well our estimation technique performs on Q_3, we generate a variety of queries /dblp/article[./journal/text() = 'X'] in which the category X is a randomly chosen possible category. Test queries for Q_4 are created in a similar manner but now we vary min and max in a query which might look like this: /dblp/article[./year/text() >= min and ./year/text() <= max].

Finally there are test queries for Q_f. Elements, to which functions (e.g. the substring function) are applied are e.g. /dblp/article/title/text(). The corresponding base query would look like this: /dblp/article/title[contains(text(), X)]. In this base query, we chose X as a random word which is contained in at least one of all possible titles. We chose the parameter *defaultSelectivity* to be 0.005, and *accessThreshold* to be 2.

5.2 Results

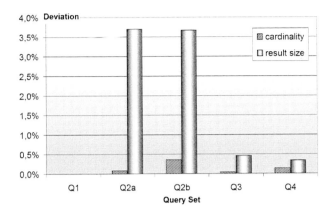

Figure 5. Results for Q_1 - Q_4 (XMark)

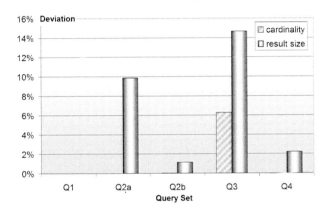

Figure 6. Results for Q_1 - Q_4 (DBLP)

dataset	metadata size for Q_1 to Q_4
XMark	3kB
DBLP	4kB

Table 2. Metadata sizes for evaluated data

Table 2 shows the resulting metadata size (Q_1 to Q_4) for each evaluated data set. The resulting sizes are very small, therefore the use of this metadata in mobile networks is possible.

In Figure 5 and 6, the deviation of the size and cardinalities of the offline module M_s are shown. We have compared each estimated value with the size and cardinality of the result of the executed query. On the $x-axis$, two bars are shown for each query class, one indicating the cardinality deviation, the other one the deviation of the estimated result size, while the $y-axis$ shows the average deviation. For the query classes Q_1 to Q_4, the estimated results are quite

precise: the average deviation from the real values is below 4% (XMark) and below 15% (DBLP).

Q_1 is estimated perfectly as the metadata contains precise estimations for all possible simple paths.

While Q_2's cardinality results are very precise, the size estimations depend on an average size which is not applicable to all elements. Furthermore, queries containing shorter filters return a more precise estimation than queries containing longer filters.

Estimations for query type Q_3 are more precise for the XMark document than for the DBLP. This can be explained by structural reasons of the document, one of the DBLP categories (`author`) appeared more than once per parent whereas all XMark categories (`location`, `privacy`) did not. This results in a reverse selectivity propagation problem. If we look at Figure 4, this means that there is a filter referencing the black nodes, but the query is actually selecting the light grey ones. If the black nodes are not distributed equally among their parents this can either increase or decrease the selectivity. In other words, our estimator does not keep track of correlations like "author name" ⇔ "number of publications".

The estimation of queries belonging to query class Q_4 is also very precise due to the used histogram technique.

Furthermore, the metadata configuration has an effect on the precision. Whereas the XMark categories are made up of a relative small set of distinct values (categories with $\geq$ 10% exist) the average DBLP categories has a selectivity of 10^{-4}. Therefore to improve to estimation accuracy, we have to increase the number of categories as seen in figure 7.

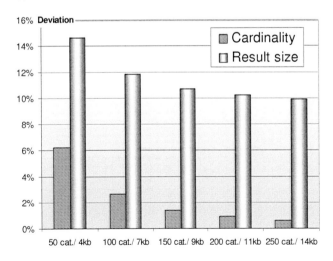

Figure 7. Category Tradeoff for DBLP dataset

Finally the performance of the online module M_f has to be evaluated. Figure 7 shows the result of the experiments. The $x-axis$ shows the number of processed queries, while the $y-axis$ shows the deviation for each bar. Again, we use two bars, one indicating the deviation of the cardinality, one the deviation of the estimated size. Furthermore, a line indicates the number of misses, i.e. how often did the estimator not find a corresponding entry in the metadata. The scale for the number of misses if plotted on the right $y-axis$. As we can see, the deviation for cardinality and size is high at the beginning but gradually decreases during the runtime. Q_f exhibits the highest deviations as the it consists of completely random queries. If you took locality principles of real life queries into account there would be less misses which would decrease the deviation.

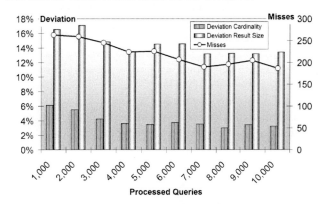

Figure 8. Results for Q_f (Xmark)

5.3 Main Result

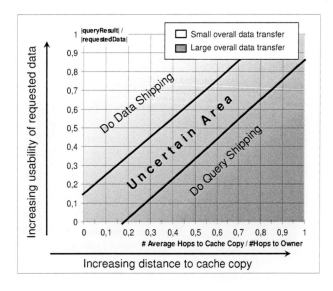

Figure 9. Query vs. Data Shipping

Figure 9 shows a decision map considering the total amount of transferred data. It does not take energy consumption for powering up transmitter, lookup costs for the

cache copy etc. into consideration, but these device dependent parameters can be integrated into the decision map for each application case. The $x-$axis shows the fraction $\frac{\#HopsToCacheCopy}{\#HopsToOwner}$, which is a metric for the distance to the cache copy. The $y-$axis shows the amount of overhead a data shipping approach has for a given query. A low y value means that only a small fraction of the requested data is usable. Light fields indicate a small overall data transfer when data shipping is used, while darker fields indicate that data shipping require more overall data transferred than query shipping. As we have seen in our experimental results, our query size estimator has a maximum average error of 16% for the used data sets. Therefore, we can identify uncertain area, where we do not favor one or the other approach regarding the total amount of transferred data. However, for queries that lie outside of this uncertain area, our approach allows precisely to determine if query shipping or data shipping results in smaller amount of total data transferred.

6 Summary and Conclusion

We presented an estimator for predicting size and cardinality of XPath queries, which can be used in mobile networks for distinguishing between query and data shipping. Furthermore, we showed how the estimator treats several query classes, and how it adapts to dynamically changing filters. We evaluated experimentally how precise the estimator works, and how small the resulting metadata is. Therefore, we consider our contribution as a good means for answering the question "is data shipping favorable to query shipping".

References

[1] A. Aboulnaga, A. R. Alameldeen, and J. F. Naughton. Estimating the Selectivity of XML Path Expressions for Internet Scale Applications. In *VLDB '01: Proceedings of the 27th International Conference on Very Large Data Bases*, pages 591–600, San Francisco, CA, USA, 2001. Morgan Kaufmann Publishers Inc.

[2] A. Balmin, T. Eliaz, J. Hornibrook, L. Lim, G. M. Lohman, D. Simmen, M. Wang, and C. Zhang. Cost-based optimization in DB2 XML. *IBM Systems Journal*, 45(2):299–326, 2006.

[3] Z. Chen, H. V. Jagadish, F. Korn, N. Koudas, S. Muthukrishnan, R. T. Ng, and D. Srivastava. Counting Twig Matches in a Tree. In *ICDE '01: Proceedings of the 17th International Conference on Data Engineering*, pages 595–604, Washington, DC, USA, 2001. IEEE Computer Society.

[4] N. Drukh, N. Polyzotis, M. N. Garofalakis, and Y. Matias. Fractional XSketch Synopses for XML Databases. In *XSym*, pages 189–203, 2004.

[5] J. Freire, J. R. Haritsa, M. Ramanath, P. Roy, and J. Siméon. Statix: Making XML Count. In *SIGMOD '02: Proceedings of the 2002 ACM SIGMOD international conference on Management of data*, pages 181–191, New York, NY, USA, 2002. ACM Press.

[6] Y. E. Ioannidis. The History of Histograms (abridged). In *VLDB 2003, Proceedings of 29th International Conference on Very Large Data Bases, September 9-12, Berlin, Germany*, pages 19–30, 2003.

[7] H. V. Jagadish, R. T. Ng, and D. Srivastava. Substring Selectivity Estimation. In *PODS '99: Proceedings of the eighteenth ACM SIGMOD-SIGACT-SIGART symposium on Principles of database systems*, pages 249–260, New York, NY, USA, 1999. ACM Press.

[8] L. Lim, M. Wang, S. Padmanabhan, J. S. Vitter, and R. Parr. XPath-Learner: An On-line Selftuning Markov Histogram for XML Path Selectivity Estimation. In *VLDB '02: Proceedings of 28th International Conference on Very Large Data Bases*. Morgan Kaufmann Publishers Inc., 2002.

[9] B. Mandhani and D. Suciu. Query caching and view selection for xml databases. In *VLDB '05: Proceedings of the 31st international conference on Very large data bases*, pages 469–480. VLDB Endowment, 2005.

[10] J. McHugh and J. Widom. Query Optimization for XML. In M. P. Atkinson, M. E. Orlowska, P. Valduriez, S. B. Zdonik, and M. L. Brodie, editors, *VLDB'99, Proceedings of 25th International Conference on Very Large Data Bases, September 7-10, 1999, Edinburgh, Scotland, UK*, pages 315–326. Morgan Kaufmann, 1999.

[11] N. Polyzotis and M. Garofalakis. Statistical Synopses for Graph-Structured XML Databases. In *SIGMOD '02: Proceedings of the 2002 ACM SIGMOD international conference on Management of data*, pages 358–369, New York, NY, USA, 2002. ACM Press.

[12] N. Polyzotis and M. N. Garofalakis. Structure and Value Synopses for XML Data Graphs. In *VLDB '02: Proceedings of 28th International Conference on Very Large Data Bases*, pages 466–477, 2002.

[13] A. Schmidt, F. Waas, M. Kersten, M. Carey, I. Manolescu, and R. Busse. Xmark: A benchmark for xml data management, 2002.

[14] XML Linking Language (XLink). `http://www.w3.org/TR/xlink/`.

[15] W. Wang, H. Jiang, H. Lu, and J. X. Yu. Bloom Histogram: Path Selectivity Estimation for XML Data with Updates. In *VLDB 2004, Proceedings of 30th International Conference on Very Large Data Bases*, pages 240–251, 2004.

IDEAS 2007
Short Papers

A Framework for Outlier Mining in RFID data

Elio Masciari
ICAR-CNR
Via P. Bucci 41/C
87030 Rende, Italy
masciari@icar.cnr.it

Abstract

Radio Frequency Identification (RFID) applications are emerging as key components in object tracking and supply chain management systems. In next future almost every major retailer will use RFID systems to track the shipment of products from suppliers to warehouses. Due to RFID readings features this will result in a huge amount of information generated by such systems when costs will be at a level such that each individual item could be tagged thus leaving a trail of data as it moves through different locations. We define a technique for efficiently detecting anomalous data in order to prevent problems related to inefficient shipment or fraudulent actions. Since items usually move together in large groups through distribution centers and only in stores do they move in smaller groups we exploit such a feature in order to design our technique. The preliminary experiments show the effectiveness of our approach.

1 Introduction

Datastreams are potentially infinite sources of data that flow continuously while monitoring a physical phenomenon, like temperature levels or other kind of human activities, such as clickstreams, telephone call records, and so on. Datastreams could be generated in different scenario by different devices, in this paper we will focus on Radio Frequency Identification(RFID) data streams as these applications are emerging as key components in objects tracking and supply chain management systems. Sometimes RFID tags are referred to as electronic bar codes. Indeed, RFID tags emit a signal that shares basic identification information about a product. Such tags can be used to track a product from manufacturing through distribution and then on to retailers. These features of RFID tags open new perspective both for hardware and data management. In fact, RFID is going to create a lot of new data management needs[1]. In particular, RFID applications will generate a lot of so called "thin" data, i.e. data pertaining to time and location[6]. In addition to providing insight into shipment and other supply chain process efficiencies, such data should also prove valuable for determining product seasonality and other trends resulting in key information for the companies plans. Moreover, companies are already exploring more advanced uses for RFID. For example, tire manufacturers plan to embed RFID chips in tires to determine the tire deterioration. Many pharmaceutical companies are embedding RFID chips in drug containers to better track and avert the theft of highly controlled drugs. Airlines are considering RFID-enabling key onboard parts and supplies to optimize aircraft maintenance and airport gate preparation turnaround time. A further key application is the following. USA Department of defense recognizes the value of expanding the global RFID infrastructure and sees a RFID-capable supply chain as a critical element of defense transformation[5]. These scenarios entail different systems generating varying data sets. This is because different systems tend to value similar attributes of a product line differently or track some attributes, such as price and not others, such as color. For example, Point of Sale systems typically emphasize price and quantity, while a warehouse distribution system can focus on weight and size. These differences pose new problems when attempting to analyze performance in making, selling and stocking products. Thus an interesting challenge is an effective and efficient management of such a huge amount of data generated by RFID. In particular systems for monitoring data streams could benefit of the definition of a suitable technique for detecting anomalies in the datastreams being analyzed. Such a problem is relevant to a huge number of application scenario that make impossible to define an absolute notion of anomalies (in the follow we refer to anomalies as outliers). In this paper we propose a framework for dealing with the outlier detection problem in massive datastream environment. The main idea is to provide users a simple but rather powerful framework for defining the notion of outlier for almost all the application scenarios at a higher level of abstraction, separating the specification of data being investigated from the specific outlier characterization. We introduce a suitable encoding strategy that represents the (huge) sequence of readings as a time series and then computing its Fourier Transform in order to exploit only a small amount of information to compare different Rfid streams. As an anomalous data is detected we signal it in order to quickly recover the possible error. We point out that such a technique is flexible and can be applied in different scenario in order to monitor very different systems independently of their spatial extension.

2 Problem Statement

An RFID stream is composed of an ordered set of n sources (i.e. tag readers) located at different positions, denoted by $\{r_1, \ldots, r_n\}$ producing n independent streams of data, representing tag readings. Each data stream can be viewed as a sequence of triplets $\langle id_r, epc, ts \rangle$, where: 1) $id_r \in \{1, .., n\}$ is the tag reader identifier(observe that it implicitly carries information about the spatial location of the reader) ; 2) epc is the product code read by the source identified by id_r; 3) t_r is a *timestamp*, i.e. a value that indicates the time when the reading epc was produced by the source id_r. In our model id_r represents the location of the reader. The data streams produced by the sources are caught by a *RFID Data Stream Management System* (Rfid-DSMS), which combines the RFID readings into a unique data stream in order to support data analysis. As objects move through the network they can be traced using the spatio-temporal information generated by RFID readers. As time goes by we collect the stream of readings. Our goal is to identify anomalies in the flow of the data. Possible anomaly can be an object that is planned to pass through a series of checkpoint but some check is missing, so it could be the case that someone with fraudulent intentions modified the path. Another relevant information that we want to extract is the continuous stay of an object in the same place since it could be the case that the object is damaged or some shipment problem occurred.

As a running example consider the following sequence of readings being collected at the $RfidDSMS$ assuming for the sake of simplicity that the system is composed of 3 readers (r_1, r_2, r_3), 5 tagged objects$(o_1, o_2, o_3, o_4, o_5)$ and the initial time is 0. A possible sequence of readings could be: $Seq = (r_1, o_1, 1), (r_2, o_1, 2), (r_3, o_1, 3), (r_2, o_2, 4), (r_2, o_2, 5), (r_1, o_2, 6), (r_3, o_3, 7), (r_3, o_2, 8), (r_2, o_5, 9), (r_1, o_5, 10), (r_2, o_4, 11)$. In order to quickly identify the kind of anomalies described above we need to define a way to continuously compare the streams generated by the reader with the original shipment plan. To accomplish this task we need to define a measure of similarity between the two sequences. Intuitively, two sequences are said to have a similar structure if they correspond in the type of readings

they contain and in the way these elements appears. Observe that, even if it is easy to detect whether the structure of two streams is almost the same (the item has been scanned by the same set of readers), this information is rarely useful for our aims. Indeed we would like to quantify the similarity between the structures of two stream, also emphasizing the differences that are more relevant. For instance, we consider as similar two streams that exhibit the same features with different regularities since this could be due to a simple shipment delay as will be clear in next section. Much attention has been devoted to the problem of detecting similarity between time series using approaches such as time warping. In this paper we propose a different approach, which is essentially based on the idea of associating each stream of readings with a time series representing its structure, and checking the structural similarity by looking at the Fourier transformation of the corresponding time series. As we shall see, this approach is both efficient and effective.

3 Mining RFID Data

In this section we will introduce a technique for encoding the input datastream into a time series and define a suitable similarity function that will be used to identify outlier data. We will give the intuition first and then we will give the details of the technique. Given an RFID stream we encode it as a time series by means of some encoding functions that will encode in a suitable way the information contained in the stream by first assigning a proper value to the source of every simple event (i.e the location where the reading has been originated for every EPC) and then obtaining the overall signal by considering the complete sequence of reading. Applying such a strategy we obtain a signal that represent the "history" of each item being monitored. Once obtained such signal we can continuosly compare it with the original one available at the RfidSMS. Unfortunately, comparing two such signals can be as difficult as comparing the original streams since comparing streams having different lengths requires costly resizing and alignment operations, and stretching (or narrowing) signals is not a suitable solution since such operations heavily affect the corresponding stream structure. These drawbacks can be avoided if the signals are compared by examining their *Discrete Fourier Transforms DFT* [4], which reveal much about the distribution and relevance of signal frequencies and can be computed incrementally as new readings arrive avoiding the problem of recomputing at each step the signal for each epc.

Reader Encoding Given a set R of RFID tag readers, a function E from R to N is an *encoding function* for R. We can assign a number n to each reader in several different ways: for instance, by generating it randomly, or using a hash function. Obviously, a good encoding function should at least ensure to be injective w.r.t. reader location. The encoding functions presented in the following differ in the way in which they capture information about each reader neighbors. The simplest encoding function we consider is named *Simple encoding* (S_E) and works as follows. Given a set R of readers, we build a sequence of distinct reader $[r_1, r_2, \cdots, r_k]$ by considering a (randomly chosen) linear order on the location of the readers in R. Given an element $r \in R$, the direct encoding simply associates each reader r with the position n of the reader r in the previously built sequence. For our running example the encoding will be the following(assuming the sequence of reader is r_1, r_2, r_3 according to some ordering criteria): $S_E = \{(r_1, 1), (r_2, 2), (r_3, 3)\}$. An interesting extension of the Simple encoding consists in assigning a value to each reader by relating such value to the one of some neighbor reader. We denote by C the pairs of tag readers $< r_i, r_j >$ such that they appear consecutively in a possible routing. We associate an integer number $P_{<r_i,r_j>}$ with each pair of different reader $< r_i, r_j >$ by considering a randomly chosen linear order on C. Given a pair of readers r_i, r_j appearing consecutively in a shipment plan S, the *Pairwise encoding* function (P_E) associates with r_i the number $P_{<r_i,r_j>}$. We report the pairwise encoding of the running example (for completeness reason we encode here every possible pair of readings even if they not appear in our example): $P_E = \{(r_1, r_1, 1), (r_1, r_2, 2), (r_1, r_3, 3), (r_2, r_1, 4), (r_2, r_2, 5), (r_2, r_3, 6), (r_3, r_1, 7), (r_3, r_2, 2), (r_3, r_3, 3)\}$

Stream Encoding Let I be a set of tagged items being monitored in the system. A stream encoding is a function enc that associates each $epc \in I$ with a sequence of real numbers, i.e. $Enc(epc) = \{h_0, h_1, \cdots, h_n\}$. Given a sequence of tag readings $\{r_1, r_2, \cdots, r_n\}$ and a reader encoding function E, a *trivial encoding* of epc ($Tr_{enc}(epc)$) is a sequence $[R_0, R_1, \cdots, R_n]$, where $R_i = E(r_i)$. This encoding simply applies S to each tag reading being received. More precisely such an encoding build the sequence of readers being crossed by the item. Consider in our running example the sequence of readings produced for object o_2 the resulting sequence will be: $S = \{2, 2, 1, 3\}$ (remember that $S_E(r_1) = 1$ and so on).A *linear encoding* of epc ($L_{enc}(epc)$) is a sequence $[R_0, R_1, \cdots, R_n]$, where $R_0 = E(r_0)$ and $R_i = \sum_{k \leq i} E(r_k)$. Here, each element of the time series associated with an item should encode the information corresponding to more than a single tag reading. Indeed, it computes a linear combination of the tag encodings, in order to take into account the travelled "path" to reach the current reader. Consider in our running example the sequence of readings produced for object o_2 the resulting sequence will be: $S = \{2, 4, 5, 8\}$.

Building the overall signal In the following we evaluate the encoding functions proposed above, with the main objective of measuring their impact in detecting dissimilarities among RFID streams. Even if all possible combination of reader encoding and stream encoding could be considered, we shall focus for the sake of simplicity only on the following combinations (in the experimental section we refer to it as encoding schemes): 1) *Trivial encoding*, consisting in the adoption of the Direct Reader encoding and the Trivial Stream encoding; 2)*Linear encoding*, in which we combine Simple Reader encoding and Linear Stream encoding; 3) *Pairwise Linear encoding*, in which we adopt the Pairwise Reader encoding combined with the Linear Stream encoding. The idea underlying the above combinations is the following. Trivial and Linear encoding schemes allow to evaluate the effectiveness of a reader encoding function when the main focus is on the traversed readers. The Pairwise encoding summarizes both the reader and stream features, but in addition performs a look-ahead of the reader that appear in the stream. Hence, it is expected to resume the peculiarities of a sequence of readings with high precision. Even if the idea of encoding the stream using the above reported combination of reader and stream encoding could seem rather obscure it has been proved really effective in many application context dealing with very different kind of data [2]. In our case the approach results more effective since we deal with numerical value that allow a perfect match with signal since we can interpret each reading as an impulse whose amplitude is given by the corresponding encoding value. Once obtained this discrete signal we can apply the Discrete Fourier Transform as will be clear in next section.

Computing Similarity Encoding a document provides a particular view of the structure of the time RFID datastream, that can be seen as a time series. For each reading, there is an impulse whose amplitude is determined by the encoding function; as a result of this physical simulation, the flow of readings related to a given epc produces a signal $h_d(t)$ that varies in the time interval being monitored.As mentioned above comparing two such signals can be as difficult as comparing the original streams so we compare them examining their *Discrete Fourier Transforms (DFT)* [4]. Given a stream s, we denote as $DFT(enc(s))$ the Discrete Fourier Transform of the time series resulting from its encoding. To compare two signals, we consider the difference in the magnitude of the corresponding frequency components, that allows (*i*) to abstract from the length of the streams, and (*ii*) to know whether a given subsequence (representing for example a set of repeated readings) exhibits a certain regularity, no matter where it is located within the signal. Let epc_1, epc_2 be two streams of readings relative to objects being monitored, and enc be a document encoding, such that

$h_1 = enc(epc_1)$ and $h_2 = enc(epc_2)$. We define the *Discrete Fourier Transform distance* of the documents as an approximation of the squared difference of the magnitudes of the two signals.

4 Outlier Identification

Once defined a technique to state the similarity between Rfid time series we need to define a strategy that exploits such a technique in order to identify anomalies in the data flow. To better understand such a problem we define two possible scenario on our running example. Consider a container (whose epc is $p1$) containing dangerous material that has to be delivered through check points c_1, c_2, c_3 in the given order and consider the following sequence of readings: $Seq_A = \{(c_1, 1), (c_1, 2), (c_2, 3), (c_2, 4), (c_2, 5), (c_2, 6), (c_2, 7), (c_2, 8), (c_2, 9), (c_2, 10), (c_2, 11), (c_2, 12)\}$. Sequence A correspond to the case in which the pallet tag is read repeatedly at the check point c_2. This sequence may occur because: i) the pallet (or the content) is damaged so it can no more be shipped until some recovery operation has been performed, ii) the shipment has been delayed. Depending of the anomaly different recovery action need to be performed. In our encoding strategy this situation will be reported in the frequency spectrum as a single impulse repeated many times that cause only the frequency corresponding to c_1 and c_2 to be observed. Consider now a different sequence of readings: $Seq_B = \{(c_1, 1), (c_1, 2), (c_1, 3), (c_1, 4), (c_3, 5), (c_3, 6), (c_3, 7), (c_3, 8), (c_3, 9), (c_3, 10), (c_3, 11), (c_3, 12)\}$. Sequence B correspond to a more interesting scenario, in particular it is the case that the pallet tag is read at check point c_1, is not read at check point c_2 but is read at checkpoint c_3. Again two main explanation could be considered: i) the original routing has been changed for shipment improvement, ii) someone changed the route for fraudulent reason (e.g. in order to robber the content or to modify it). In our encoding strategy this case will produce two different signals exhibiting low similarity since the structure is significantly changed. The two situation described above have an intuitive explanation but we point out that our encoding strategy allow us to detect all anomalies that cause the signals representing the streams to be different. Based on the above examples we can now define our notion of outlier. Given a sequence of readings $R = \{r_1, \cdots, r_n\}$ for an object epc being traced whose planned sequence is R^P and a threshold value T, we say that R is an outlier sequence if $dist_{DFT}(R, R^P) > T$. The threshold value can be chosen depending on the stream being monitored and as we will show in the experimental section it can be easily tuned. Once defined our notion of outlier we can design an effective method for object tracking. In particular

as objects enter our RFID environment the readings are collected by the $RfidDSMS$. At the $RfidDSMS$ the signal corresponding to the original shipment plan is stored (s_o) along with its DFT. As readings are generated the DFT of the signal corresponding to the actual plan is computed(s_a) by using one of the previously described encoding strategy. If $dist_{DFT}(s_o, s_a)$ is greater than a predefined threshold T (suitable for the context being analyzed) the *signaling service* will notify the detected outlier in order to allow a proper recovery action. The algorithm is really naive and is not reported due to space limitations. More in details, as new readings arrives their contributions to the DFT of the proper epc is computed. This task can be accomplished very efficiently since the computation of the DFT can be performed incrementally without recomputing it from scratch. If the computed distance between the original signal and the actual one is greater than T a *signaling service* will notify the detected anomaly, the location and the epc to be checked. The running time of the algorithm is $O(M \log(M))$ and can be trivially computed by observing that for each reading being produced we have to compute the proper encoding of the signal and this operation costs $O(M)$ where M is the maximum number of readings for each epc, then we have to compute the Fourier Transformation and this operation is performed in $O(M \log(M))$ time.

5 Results Evaluation

In this section, we present some experiments we performed to assess the effectiveness of the proposed approach in detecting outliers in RFID data streams. The direct result of each test is a similarity matrix S representing the degree of similarity for each pair of streams. The evaluation of the results relies on some *a priori* knowledge about the data streams being used. In fact, the streams are related to a set of container of tinned foods being tracked from the farm to the distribution center through all stages of the productive chain; a group of streams related to the same category (e.g. tinned tuna fish) is said to be a *class*. We analyzed about 100 streams, belonging to 4 classes: 1) Tuna Fish, whose readings are generated by 26 tagged containers storing 500 cans each; 2) Tomato, whose readings are generated by 23 tagged containers storing 400 cans each;3) Syrupy Peach, whose readings are generated by 20 tagged containers storing 350 cans each;4) Meat, whose readings are generated by 35 tagged containers storing 600 cans each. As said before, we refer to a combination of a reader- and a stream-encoding function as to an *encoding scheme*. In particular, we will show some results concerning the three above mentioned schemes: *Trivial*, *Linear* and *Pairwise Linear*. and we discuss the similarity measures obtained over the data streams described above. Average values of intra- and inter-class similarities are summarized into a matrix CS, with the objective of supporting a simple quantitative analysis. In particular, given a set of streams belonging to n prior classes and a similarity matrix S defined on those streams, a $n \times n$ matrix CS is produced, where each element is computed as the sum of the similarity of objects belonging to the class weighted by the the number of elements in the class. Due to space limitation we report a brief summary of the results and give the interpretation of them. Elements on the diagonal states the degree of similarity between the streams belonging to the same class thus stating if the actual shipment plan match the scheduled one, while elements outside the diagonal states the degree of overlap between shipment plan belonging to different classes. Note that even if the containers travel through the same shipment center thus causing the encoding of different readings to be quite similar the overall signal is enough different to allow effective detection of outlier data as will be clear by the following results.

	Tuna Fish	Tomato	Syrupy Peach	Meat
Tuna Fish	0.9608	0.8039	0.8068	0.8094
Tomato	0.8039	0.9053	0.7045	0.6039
Syrupy Peach	0.8068	0.7045	0.9095	0.7065
Meat	0.8094	0.6039	0.7065	0.9536

Figure 1. Results for the Trivial encoding scheme

The quantitative results shown in Fig. 1 reveal that the Trivial scheme performs surprisingly well. Indeed, for all classes, the intra-class similarity values are sufficiently higher than the inter-class ones, allowing for separating all classes from one another and thus stating that the containers follows the predicted plan.

	Tuna Fish	Tomato	Syrupy Peach	Meat
Tuna Fish	0.9650	0.8047	0.8064	0.8056
Tomato	0.8047	0.9076	0.8044	0.8042
Syrupy Peach	0.8064	0.8044	0.9108	0.8051
Meat	0.8056	0.8042	0.8051	0.9779

Figure 2. Results for the Linear encoding scheme

The results shown in Fig. 2 demonstrate a slight improvement in recognizing the prior classes which the Linear scheme gains with respect to the Trivial one. As in the previous case, the last class is the most homogeneous, while the second one exhibits the minimum average intra-class similarity. Finally, the similarity matrix in Fig. 3 looks better than the one produced by the previous encoding scheme. Furthermore, high similarities among most of the documents can still be noticed, even when they belong to different classes. This behavior is due to the combination of the Linear reader encoding with the Pairwise stream encoding, that considers all the pairs of consecutive readers, and is

	Tuna Fish	Tomato	Syrupy Peach	Meat
Tuna Fish	1.0000	0.9997	0.9998	0.9997
Tomato	0.9997	0.9998	0.9996	0.9997
Syrupy Peach	0.9998	0.9996	0.9999	0.9995
Meat	0.9997	0.9995	0.9996	0.9999

Figure 3. Results for the Pairwise encoding scheme

therefore prone to produce a high number of codes, emphasizing the differences of readers located at different stages of the productive chain. This combination hence makes the similarity between two streams essentially depend on the readings being collected at the later stages. However, even in this case, the results are globally satisfactory since all the classes can be distinguished from one another, in spite of the high inter-classes similarities and the quite low homogeneity of class $Tomato$.

6 Conclusion

In this paper we addressed the problem of detecting outliers in RFID readings stream. The technique we have proposed is mainly based on the idea of representing a stream of readings as a time series. Thereby, the structural similarity between two series can be computed by exploiting the Discrete Fourier Transform of the associated signals. Experimental results showed the effectiveness of our approach, with particular regard to some of the encoding schemes defined in the paper. The current work is subject to further significant extensions, that we plan to address in future works, in particular we plan to use more robust methods (e.g. non parametric-ones) for determining outliers, like the ones shown in [3].

References

[1] H. Gonzalez et al. Warehousing and analyzing massive rfid data sets. In *ICDE*, 2005.

[2] S. Flesca et al. Fast detection of xml structural similarity. *IEEE TKDE 17(2)*, pages 160–175, 2005.

[3] S. Subramaniam et al. Online outlier detection in sensor data using non-parametric models. In *VLDB*, pages 187–198, 2006.

[4] A.V. Oppenheim and R.W. Shafer. *Discrete-Time Signal Processing*. Prentice Hall, 1999.

[5] D. Shuping and W. Wright. Geo-temporal visualization of rfid providing global visibility of the dod supply chain. *Directions Magazine*, 2005.

[6] F. Wang and P. Liu. Temporal management of rfid data. In *VLDB*, pages 1128–1139, 2005.

A Generalized Model for Mediator Based Information Integration

Ali Kiani
Computer Science & Software Engineering
Concordia University
Montreal, Quebec, Canada
ali_kian@cse.concordia.ca

Nematollaah Shiri
Computer Science & Software Engineering
Concordia University
Montreal, Quebec, Canada
shiri@cse.concordia.ca

Abstract

Heterogeneity of schema and data in information integration complicates metadata management and query processing. We consider a mediator-based approach (MI) to information integration and propose a model theoretic approach to describe integration. In this model, we view the schema of the integration as a 3D space, and assume it is a complete lattice. The first dimension in the model specifies the concepts (e.g., entity sets, relations, classes, etc), the second dimension indicates the data model in which a concept is represented (e.g., relational, semi-structured, object-oriented, etc), and the third dimension gives the application domain. We also introduce three basic transformations, called X-transform, Y-transform, and Z-transform, to all of which we refer as primitive queries and show how user queries can be expressed using primitive queries. We show a typical architecture and illustrate usefulness of this model as it generalizes the mediator based information integration in which the global schema is basically the least upper bound of all the points in the 3D space.

1 Introduction

Mediator based information integration (MI) as an approach of integration has been the subject of numerous studies in both database and AI communities. Its aim is to provide a uniform access to multiple (possibility heterogeneous) information sources [5, 4, 12]. Even though there has been much progress in this area, more work is required to overcome the challenges, including: (1) lack of a generic model for MI, and (2) availability of the global schema. In this paper we attempt to address these issues and develop a generalized model for MI that helps understand better the metadata management and query processing tasks, by relaxing on the presence of a global schema and work instead with partial global schemas.

For this, we first review the primary elements in MI systems and provide a suitable abstraction/extension of these elements to serves as a generic model. An information system has three main elements: metadata management, query processing, and the actual data. Similarly, our model of integrated framework has metadata management, generic query processing, and information sources. Each element in our model is an abstraction/extension of the corresponding element in a single information system.

Metadata management in a general heterogeneous framework relies on the presence of some *operators* such as "Match" [11], whose implementation is application dependent and labor intensive [11]. In order to abstract away such details in our model, we define the required such operators and use them in the metadata management component. This allows us to plug in and use any desired realization of such operators that satisfies the requirements of the abstract operators employed.

Based on these abstract operators, we define our uniform query processing component which provides access to information in the integrated framework. Considering schema and/or data heterogeneity of sources in general, we may further consider our query processing to be polymorphic. As a result, our model allows querying information sources that are heterogeneous in both schema and data model.

Our model is inspired by and relies on the abstraction in generic model management (GMM) proposed in [2]. GMM focuses on metadata issues and provides abstract operators such as "Match" (used in schema matching [11]) and "Merge" (used in schema integration). [2, 3, 9] also illustrate applicability and effectiveness of GMM in describing several applications. The idea of the 3D model was first introduced in [6]. In this work, we provide technical details of rewriting and processing queries in the proposed framework.

While we use some of the abstract operators introduced by GMM, our work differs from GMM in its focus being on information integration while dealing with metadata management issues. Further, we propose a corresponding algebra for query processing. Other issues such as handling inconsistencies that are important in this context are not discussed in this paper.

The rest of this paper is organized as follows. Next, we study metadata management, review basic concepts and present a 3D conceptual space. Using the abstraction provided for metadata management, section 3 introduces an algebra for query processing in our model. We present a typical architecture for the proposed model in section 4, and conclude the paper in Section 5 with a list of possible future work.

2 Our Conceptual 3D Space

In this section, we introduce our 3D model of conceptual space and discuss the issues of metadata management in an information integration with heterogeneous sources.

A homogeneous information system works based on a number of assumptions including unique data model, unique name, unique schema, and so on. However, in an information integration with heterogeneous sources, not all of these assumptions are valid. While information sources may have different data models, for example, relational, semi-structured, object oriented, it is also possible to have different schemas from different sources for the same concept, and/or the same name refer to different concepts in different sources.

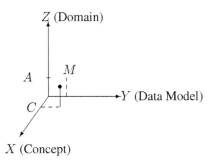

Figure 1. The 3D Conceptual Space

In order to represent such heterogeneity, we consider two dimensions: the data model and the domain (which are fixed in standard, homogeneous systems) and propose a 3D conceptual schema. Fig. 1, illustrates our model in which the X, Y, and Z axes represent concepts, data models, and domains (application), respectively. A point (C_i, M_j, S_k) in this space indicates that C_i is a concept represented in data model M_j in domain S_k. Different points along the X dimension represent different concepts. Similarly, different points along the Y and Z dimensions represent different data models and different domains, respectively. We refer to the collection of points in the 3D space as the "Conceptual Space." To provide a better insight of the conceptual space, we may compare it to the *conceptual level* in conventional relational databases where there is no Z axis as the application domain is fixed. There is also no Y axis since the only

data model is the relational data model. In fact, the 3D space reduces to the conceptual level in conventional databases if we restrict the domain to a single source and the data model to the relational model.

The concepts in an application domain may have different data models, e.g., both relational and semi-structured. Therefore, in our 3D model, a schema S is represented as a point (X, Y, Z) in a *plane* where the first and the second arguments denote the concepts in S and their corresponding data model. The third argument represents the domain to which S belongs. Since the schema of an information source is unique, in the rest of this paper, we use the terms schema, domain, and source interchangeably.

Let $Y = y_R$ and $Y = y_X$ denote the relational model and XML model, respectively. Furthermore, assume that a conventional relational database and an XML database are defined at domains A and B, respectively. Let S_A and S_B denote respectively the schema of source A and B. Therefore, the concepts of database in domain A are shown on the line (X, y_R, A). Also queries over these concepts are defined over the same line. Similarly, line (X, y_X, B) represents the concepts defined in domain B and queries in domain B work on the points located on line (X, y_X, B).

Since the result of a query is a new concept, every query defines a new point. In other words, a query defines a new point which is temporary and removed after the query is executed.

We can also see that in our model, (X, y_R, Z) is a plane which includes all the relational schemas in the integrated framework. This could be viewed as the surface containing all the concepts in relational model (from different domains). Also $(Student, Y, Z)$ contains all the definitions of the concept *Student* in different domains expressed possibly in different models. Note that if domains A and B both include a concept "Student", there would be two points $(Student, y_R, A)$ and $(Student, y_X, B)$ in the conceptual space. A question which may arise at this point is: how these two points contribute to a query about *Student*.

To answer this question, we need to define some basic transformations in our model. The idea intuitively is to "Match" (find the mappings between) $(Student, Y_A, A)$ and $(Student, Y_B, B)$ and "Merge" them based on the result of Match to get $(Student_I, Y_I, I)$, where I is a new domain obtained by integrating these two point from domains A and B. We refer to such new domains as *partial global schema*.

2.1 Types of Transformations

Queries in our 3D model may refer to possibly heterogeneous concepts in both schema and data model. To simplify query processing, we define three primitive types of transformations. Given a query we break it into a set of basic transformations that would be more manageable. The *basic types* of transformations are defined as follows.

1. X-transform (*Diagonal Transform*): An X-transform is a query over a schema S in a data model M, represented by line (X, M, S). It corresponds to queries over the concepts of the same domain that have the same data model, i.e., concepts located on a line parallel to the X axis.

2. Y-transform (*Horizontal Transform*): A Y-transform is a transformation which converts data in a data model M_1 to data model M_2. A Y-transform is a directed line segment connecting (C, M_1, S) to (C, M_2, S), where C is a concept and S is a source (schema). For example, the Y-transform from $(Student, y_X, s_A)$ to $(Student, y_R, s_A)$, transforms the XML students data into a relation student in the same source.

3. Z-transform (*Vertical Transform*): A vertical mapping is a transformation which transforms data in a source schema to the target schema.

   Assume we need to transform data in a relation associated with concept (R, M, S_1) to its corresponding concept in schema S_2 in the same data model, (R', M, S_2). Note that this transformation requires a mapping between (R, M, S_1) and (R', M, S_2). In fact, Z-transform is generated by query rewriting using the concepts in the query. This issue has been the subject of numerous studies [8, 10, 7].

In order to define these transformations, we define the notion of "Default" data model and "schema lattice" as the basis for Y-transforms and Z-transforms, respectively. Note that applying Z-transforms on the set of concepts in a query in our model unifies them into an integrated domain, then applying Y-transforms would transform concepts in different data models into a unified/default data model. As a result, all concepts would be transformed into the same domain and data model. Evaluating the query in this situation would be the same as evaluating a query in a single information system (i.e., X-transform).

2.2 Default Data Model

Let $\mathbb{D} = \{D_1, \dots, D_k\}$ be the set of data models. We assume that $\mathbb{D}$ is a poset, where $D_i \preceq D_j$ means there is a transformation from D_i to D_j. We consider the relational model as the top ($\top = Relational$), since from every data model we used in our practice, there is a transformation to relational model. Moreover, relational model and its algebra are well understood.

Definition [*Default Data Model*] *Let* $\mathbb{D}' \subseteq \mathbb{D}$, *then, we define the least upper bound of* $\mathbb{D}'$ *as the default data model*

for $\mathbb{D}'$ *and denote it as* $D_{def} = \bigvee(\mathbb{D}')$. Semantics of the default data model is given as follows. A default data model among some data model D_is is a data model D_{def} where from every D_i there exists a formula for transforming data in D_i into D_{def}. Note that existence of a default data model is a necessary condition for our model to work.

Example Let $\mathbb{D} = \{Relational, \ Object \ Oriented, \ XML\}$ be the set of data models in an integration. Then, $D_{def} = \bigvee(\mathbb{D}) = Relational$, i.e., *Object Oriented* $\preceq Relational$, and $XML \preceq Relational$. Note that we can always transform an XML data file into some relations.

Default data model would support horizontal or Y-transforms. Next, we will define the schema lattice which would support Z-transforms.

2.3 Conceptual Schema Lattice

We introduce the notion of conceptual schema lattice of a set S of schemas in an information integration system. That would be a basis for our Z-transforms (vertical queries) defined in the previous section.

For that, we first review the definition of the "Merge" operator. This operator returns all the elements of the operands, however, those elements that match are collapsed and will be shown by just one representative [2].

Definition [*Sub-type*] *Let* s_1 *and* s_2 *be two schema sets where* $s_1 = \{s_{1i}\}$ *and* $s_2 = \{s_{2j}\}$. *If* $Merge(s_1, s_2) = s_2$, *then we write* $s_1 \preceq s_2$. *Intuitively, this indicates that* s_1 *is a sub-type of* s_2.

Definition [*Conceptual Schema Lattice*] *We define the Conceptual Schema Lattice* $\mathcal{CSL} = <S, \preceq>$, *where* S *is the conceptual space ordered by* $\preceq$.

For every two schema sets s_1 and s_2, the least upper bound (*SLUB*) denoted $\oplus\{s_1, s_2\}$ is defined as follows.

$$\oplus\{s_1, s_2\} = Merge(s_1, s_2)$$

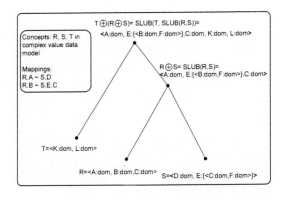

Figure 2. Example Conceptual Schema Lattice

For example, Fig. 2 includes three concepts R, S, and T, shown in Complex Values data model [1]. Also, there is a mapping between elements of R and S expressing that $R.A = S.D$ and $R.B = S.E.C$. With no loss of generality, we simply considered schemas instead of schema sets. In the *SLUB* of R and S, we get all attributes of both except $S.D$ and $S.E.C$, as that they are represented by $R.A$ and $R.B$, respectively.

Note that in our model, we require that the least upper bound of every non-empty subset of schemas to exist. Next, based on the concept of schema lattice, we define the notion of "partial global schema" for a set of concepts used in a query.

Definition *[partial global schema (PGS)] A partial global schema S is a set of points (X, Y, Z_{int}) defined by integrating some points in the conceptual space.*

In this model, there is no fixed global schema, however, one should know the concepts in the query, using which we create the partial global schema to formulate the query. So, in order to pose a query, the user will be first provided with a collection of concept notions from which s/he selects the relevant ones. Using this selection, we identify all the concepts from different information sources and use the Merge operator to build the corresponding partial global schema. The merge operation returns the least upper bound of the input concepts.

For example, at the integrated level, we provide the user with some concept notions related to "Student", "GradStudent", "Teacher", etc. Assuming user selects "GradStudent", then the system finds all corresponding concepts, e.g., $(Grad, y_R, S_1)$, $(Student, y_R, S_2)$, and $(Supervisor, y_R, S_2)$, and then uses Merge to build a PGS which will be available to the user to compose his/her queries. In this view, we define integration system as follow.

Definition *[Integration System] An integration system $\mathcal{I}$ is a triple (S, Q, A) where S is a PGS, Q is a query over S, and A is the answer to the query Q, provided by $\mathcal{I}$.*

3 Proposed Query Processing

In previous section, we explained how metadata is modeled in our integration model. Here, we propose a corresponding algebra for query processing, which has the following operators.

1. $Rewrite(Q, S)$: this operator implements Z-transforms in our 3D model. It takes a query Q posed at the integration level and uses the set $S = \{s_i\}$ of corresponding concepts to rewrite it. Since this is an abstract function, depending on the query language used at integration, we should use the proper rewriting algorithm.

2. $Transform(r, D)$: Denoted as Θ, this operator implements horizontal transforms (Y-transforms). It

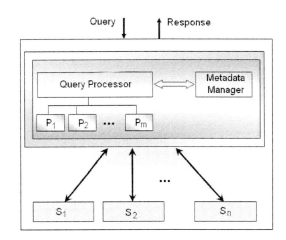

Figure 3. Proposed Architecture

takes a concepts r and a data model D as parameters, and transforms tuples of r into the data model D.

Let $r_1, \ldots, r_n$ be the concepts in the conceptual space (CS) at the integrated level used to define a query. Furthermore, assume $V = \{v_1 \cdots v_j \in CS\}$ includes the concepts related to some r_is defined through some mappings. Based on this, the steps in our algebra is as follows.

Using "Rewrite(Q, V)", we first unify the schema. This would generate Q_{XY}, a new query, with some embeded Z-transforms. Then, we unify data models for which we replace every concept v_j in Q_{XY} by $\Theta(v_j, y_R)$ and generate a new query Q_X. This new query includes both Y and Z transforms. Now that heterogeneity of schema and data model is resolved, we can evaluate this query.

4 Proposed Model Architecture

As shown in Fig. 3, our model consists of two layers: integration layer as the top layer and information sources as the lower layer. In general, an information source might have concepts in different data models, e.g., some in relational model, and some semi-structured.

The top layer consists of several components including metadata manager, query processor, and primitive operators. Our metadata manager exploits the idea of GMM [2] which provides a platform independent metadata management. That is supporting heterogeneous information sources with respect to both schema and data model. As explained in previous section, before formulating the query, user will be prompted to select the concepts required to express the query. This can be done by providing a list of loosely defined concepts though a user interface. Having this set of selected concepts, metadata manager construct the corresponding PGS and makes it available to the user. The user then may formulate the query accordingly.

The query processing engine embedded in the integration layer gets the query from the user and uses metadata information to rewrite and evaluate the query. The tasks of the query processor includes 4 steps. (1) identifying the concepts in the query together with their corresponding mapping to concepts (views) in the information sources; (2) rewriting the query based on the available concepts (views) found in previous step; (3) deciding the required transformations to unify the data model; and (4) evaluate the resulting query. Note that steps 2, 3, and 4 correspond to Z-transform, Y-transform, and X-transform, respectively.

Primitive operators that support metadata management and query processing modules include, e.g., *Match, Merge, Rewrite, and Transform.*

Example Assume the user has selected the concepts r and s from the list and wants to formulate a query using them. Metadata manager then considers all related concepts, namely, V_1 and V_2 for r, and V_1 and V_3 for s, and constructs the PGS which would include $r(A, B, C)$ and $s(D, E)$ in this case. Now, consider the following simple example of a user query in relational algebra, with the mapping between concepts in the query and their correspondences:

$$Q : \pi_{A,E}(\sigma_{B>10}(r \times s)).$$
$$V_1 : \pi_{A,B}(\sigma_{B>15 \wedge c=D \wedge D=E}(r \times s)).$$
$$V_2 : \sigma_{A=C}(r).$$
$$V_3 : \pi_D(\sigma_{E='123'}(s)).$$

Note that the above mappings, view definitions, show how concepts are mapped, and each of the views V_1, V_2, and V_3 might have their own data model, and have come from different sources. The first step is to apply the Z-transform and *rewrite* the query Q with respect to the views. The result of the rewriting is Q_{XY}, defined as:

$$Q_{XY} : \pi_A(V_1) \cup \pi_A(\sigma_{B>10 \wedge C=D}(V_2 \times V_3)).$$

This new query is based on the concepts V_1, V_2, and V_3 from the information sources. Assuming that their default data model is relational, we define Q_{YZ} as follows:

$$Q_X : \pi_A(\Theta(V_1, y_R) \cup$$
$$\pi_A(\sigma_{B>10 \wedge C=D}(\Theta(V_2, y_R) \times \Theta(V_3, y_R)),$$

where $\Theta(V_i, y_R)$ denotes transformation of V_i into relational model. Here, Y-transform and Z-transform are embedded in Q_X. To find the answer to Q, we can evaluate Q_X using the function *execute* to perform X-transform.

5 Conclusion

We identified two important issues in the context of mediator based information integration:(1) lack of a generic model for mediator based integration, and (2) availability of the global schema. We proposed a generic framework for MI based on our conceptual space and exploited the idea of partial global schema. Conceptual space is 3D world of concepts, data models, and domains and corresponds to the conceptual schema in conventional relational model. Furthermore, we defined default data model and schema lattice based on which we introduced 3 types of primitive queries, X-transform, Y-transform, and Z-transform. Accordingly, we defined a generic algebra for query processing in this context. Based on the proposed MI model, we have developed a running prototype which contains a metadata manager and a query processor to support heterogeneous schema, in say relational and XML data models.

As for future work, we will investigate ways to incorporate different schema matching techniques, and ways to extend the proposed query rewriting algorithm to support queries with constraints.

Acknowledgments: This research was supported in part by NSERC Canada and Concordia University.

References

[1] S. Abiteboul, R. Hull, and V. Vianu. *Foundations of Databases.* Addison-Wesley, 1995.

[2] P. Bernstein. Generic model management: A database infrastructure for schema manipulation. In *Proc. of Int'l Conf. on Cooperatice Information Systems.* Springer-Verlag, LNCS-2172, 2001.

[3] P. A. Bernstein, L. M. Haas, M. Jarke, E. Rahm, and G. Wiederhold. Panel: Is generic metadata management feasible? In *The VLDB Journal*, pages 660–662, 2000.

[4] S. Cluet, C. Delobel, J. Simeon, and K. Smaga. Your mediators need data conversion. In *Proc. of ACM SIGMOD Int'l Conf. on Management of data*, Seattle, WA, 1998.

[5] H. Garcia-Molina, Y. Papakonstantinou, D. Quass, A. Rajaraman, Y. Sagiv, J. Ullman, and J. Widom. The TSIMMIS project: Integration of heterogenous information sources, March 1997.

[6] Kiani, Ali and Shiri, Nematollaah. A unified model for information integration. In *Proc. of Int'l Conf. on Cooperative Information Systems (CoopIS)*, pages 8–9, 2006.

[7] Kiani, Ali and Shiri, Nematollaah. Answering queries in heterogenuous information systems. In *Proc. of ACM Workshop on Interoperability of Heterogeneous Information Systems*, Bremen, Germany, Nov. 4, 2005.

[8] Levy, Alon Y. Answering queries using views: A survey. *The VLDB Journal*, 10(4):270–294, 2001.

[9] S. Melnik, E. Rahm, and P. A. Bernstein. Rondo: a programming platform for generic model management. In *Proc. of ACM SIGMOD Int'l Conf. on Management of data*, pages 193–204. ACM Press, 2003.

[10] Pottinger, Rachel and Levy, Alon Y. A scalable algorithm for answering queries using views. *The VLDB Journal*, pages 484–495, 2000.

[11] E. Rahm and P. A. Bernstein. A survey of approaches to automatic schema matching. *The VLDB Journal*, 10(4):334–350, 2001.

[12] Ullman Jeffrey D. Information integration using logical views. In *Proc. of Int. Conf. on Database Theory (ICDT)*, Delphi, Greece, 1997.

A Theoretical Framework for Customizable Web Services Description, Discovery and Composition

Yacine Sam, Omar Boucelma

LSIS, Aix-Marseille Université.

Avenue Escadrille Normandie-Niemen, 13397 Marseille, France

E-mail: {yacine.sam, omar.boucelma}@lsis.org

Abstract

In this paper we are interested in offering customizable Web services : we present a theoretical framework for customizable Web services description, discovery and composition. In our approach, each Web service is described at a high level of abstraction and can be seen as a "black box" labeled by its name and input/output parameters. Complementary to this formalism, we define a set of mechanisms for customizable Web services discovery and composition.

1 Introduction

The exponential proliferation of the number of services offered via the Web and the cosmopolitan aspect of this last justify the adoption of the mass customization paradigm – which means that products and services must be conceived under various configurations in order to satisfy the preferences of various customers categories (see [8] and [11]) – to Web services. The concept of "Web service" means primarily an application put online in the Internet by a service supplier, and can be accessible by services customers through Internet standards protocols [3]. Examples of Web services currently available relate to weather forecasting, online trip reservation, banking services, etc. Essentially, Web services are autonomous and self-descriptive software components and constitute by this fact a new paradigm for application integration known under the name of "Service Oriented Computing" (SOC [7, 1]).

Application of the mass customization paradigm to Web services led to the concept of "Web services customization", which will refer to a Web service being able to be offered under various alternatives. As an example, in the case of online trip reservation previously quoted, it will be smart to advertise the service prices with various currencies and to describe the service itself in various languages. This will enlarge certainly its spectrum of use by extending its accessibility to customers being able to handle different currency units and various languages. This offer diversification is valid for any service characteristics being able to be offered under various alternatives : currency, language, measuring unit, etc.

In order to catch all the facets of Web services diversification, a clear and abstracted representation of customizable Web services is mandatory. However, such representation can certainly not be carried out while being expressed in terms of low level concepts attached to Web services, that is standards such as WSDL, UDDI or SOAP. Web services basics (languages, protocols) are implementation oriented, while we need to address (high level) functional integration problems such as they emerge in the context of intra or inter-organizational processes.

We present in this paper a theoretical framework for customizable Web services description, discovery, and composition. This framework is based on the atomic model [2] for the description of Web services, in which each Web service is seen like an atomic entity, or a "black box" represented by its name and input/output parameters, and realizing a specific functionality specified by its name. In Section 2, we introduce the class of Web services studied in this article (customizable Web services (CWS)), as well as the approaches described in the literature regarding *Web services customization* (WSC). Section 3 is devoted to our theoretical framework for customizable Web services description, while we present the mechanisms of customizable Web services discovery and composition in Section 4, and we conclude in Section 5.

2 Overview of the Approach

In this section, we will be using an example where a CWS is described by a set of pairs (attribute : value). We consider a WS as an abstract entity, and we perform reasoning on abstract representations of WS. In other words, a CWS is a class described by a set of attributes, and from which the instances are distinguished by the various values that some of its attributes can receive, said customizable attributes. Each request seeks however a particular variant of such a class if the required customizable Web service is simple or the aggregation of the instances of two classes (services) or more if the required Web service is composite. A given request is thus also a set of pairs (attribute : value), that represent the constraints seeking a particular variant of a given simple or composite Web service.

2.1 Motivating Example

Figure 1 illustrates a simple Web service on hotels' prices, with four attributes : *service* (its name), *city* (localization of the required hotel), *price* (for one night) and *money* (accepted currency), expressed in several currency units. This is an abstract description of the informational customizable Web service on hotels in Paris, which can be offered under three different variants, in *euro*, *dollar*, and *yen*.

Attribute	Value
service	hotel
city	Paris
price	numbers
money	euro, usd, yen

FIG. **1.** Abstract customizable Web service

To answer a simple query, i.e., one targeting a particular variant of the simple service described above, a simple matchmaking operation is needed between the description of that query and that of each variant of the service. However, if the answer to a given request is obtained by combining two services or more, the answering process requires the exploitation of the detailed knowledge resulting from the relations between the Web services descriptions implied in the answering process. This knowledge exploitation has for objective to ensure the consistency of the Web services compositions turned over in the answering processes.

In order to provide a theoretical framework for an abstract description of customizable Web services and to reason on such descriptions in the Web services answering processes, our approach is mainly inspired from the knowledge engineering domain. In the essence, our contribution here is nothing more than the idea that some results from the configuration of knowledge based systems domain, starting from reusable components, can directly be applied to customizable Web services. Indeed, our approach to Web services modeling and discovery/composition is very close to that used for complex systems composition starting from reusable components [6].

2.2 Comparison with other Approaches

The idea of WSC appears also in many other works, with various instances : it is presented in the form of "generic procedures customizable by users' requests" in [5], instantiation of BPEL preset process models in [4], coordination patterns in [10] and as the parametrization of predefined composite Web services in [9]. However, unlike the approaches [5], [4], and [10], where the services specifications are generic and where *planning* is the main metaphor behind the Web services composition (i.e., general reasoning based only on the components specifications), our approach, like the one in [9], is based on Web services descriptions in a specific knowledge domain, and the metaphor behind the Web services composition is called *mediation* (i.e., reasoning with the knowledge specialized in a restricted domain). Indeed, a planner is supposed to be domain independent, it is supposed to work for any set of components, given their descriptions. A mediator exploits specific knowledge about the objects (services) it manipulates, it is domain directed, therefore it is more specialized.

Our approach provides more genericity than the one proposed in [9] where answers to the requests consist in a set of predefined composite Web services customizable by user requests. In our approach, the response to a given request can be supplied by a simple (basic) service or by any combination of simple services available in the domain. In our approach, each WS domain is built from a restricted set of services ; hence, when answering a given request, if a composition of Web services is necessary, knowledge (descriptions) of the services involved in the composition are used to ensure the consistency of the obtained customizable composite Web service. For instance, in the example of Figure 1, it is not allowed to use the variant in *euro* with a variant in *dollar* of the informational WS trips' fares. A resulting new composite WS may enforce constraints expressed in the local knowledge (descriptions). Example of such constraint is "an attribute appearing in several services of a given composition should have identical values".

3 Framework

Having defined the concept of *Web services customization* (WSC), we present in this section a theoretical framework for describing customizable Web services.

3.1 Customizable WSs Description

As a basis for our knowledge model we start with the domain components model presented in [6]. In this model, a set of components may be selected, composed and parameterized ; which means that each domain is described by an exhaustive/complete set of components. The term "components model" refers to the knowledge used to describe the parts (sets of components — sets of simple Web services in the framework proposed here) composing a given system. This knowledge must be mandatory and sufficient to perform query processing ; it may also guide the Web services composition process in order to answer complex requests. However, this knowledge should describe the Web services only at a high level of abstraction, i.e., ignoring implementation details. It appears to us that functionalities-based model (FBM) [6] – descriptions consist of a set of functionalities, i.e., a set of pairs ("attribute :value"), the values being symbolic or numerical – is very appropriate to model WSs which are characterized by their very dynamic behavior. In fact, services can show up/hide at any time from a WSs directory. In this case, implicit descriptions of the relations that hold between domain specific WSs can be applied. The FBM is stable with respect to addition/removal of WSs : one does not need to update the model each time a WS is added or removed.

With FBM, each domain is represented as a network of dependencies ; a dependence is called a *common functionality*. The composition of components is carried out then by the instantiation of the model. Thus, connections between WSs are expressed in a canonical form similar to the one used for components in KBS, that is :

Web Service ⟷ Functionality ⟷ Web Service

In using FBM, maintaining the knowledge (model) is made easy : addition/removal of a service does not lead to the update of relations between services. More than this, a service can be "added/removed" simply by the creation/suppression of link(s) between functionalities.

3.2 Formalization of the WSC Problem

Given a domain and its Web services directory, and a customer request, finding the set of services that match the request's requirements aims to discover the Web service(s) able(s) to satisfy such a request. We call the set made up of the Web services of a given domain in one side, and a customer request in another side, *Web service customization problem*. It is what we present in this Sub-section.

In order to well formalize and understand the Web services customization problem, various sets of elements and operators must be defined : (i) a set of simple Web services (which constitute the domain or the community) ; (ii) a set of functionalities which are used to characterize the simple services of the domain ; (iii) a set of properties which establish the pairs "attribute :value " of the simple services ; (iv) some operators defining the calculation rules on the attributes describing the services ; and finally (v) some test predicates for the attributes of the services.

As an example, if we deal with the tourism domain, one

can find services concerning the tariffs of the hotels, the tariffs of the trips from a city to another, etc, like services belonging to (i) the set of the services constituting the community of the tourism domain. The (ii) attributes set can consist on elements like the name of a service, the currency used, the price, etc. Moreover, the informational Web service on the hotels prices can contain for example the (iii) set of the following properties : {(service :hotel), (money :euro), (price :45) }. The rule (iv) of calculation on the attribute *price* can be the addition "+". A useful test predicate (v) to compare a request with the offers (services offered in a domain) on the basis of the attribute "price" can be "$\leq$".

For the specification of the various variants of a given service, no constraint is imposed on the significance of its attributes, however, there must be at least an attribute which can have several possible values in order to be able to customize the service. Also, to associate the several variants of the same service (to describe a service by its several variants), there must be at least a common attribute to all the variants (the name of the service for example). The latter point makes it possible to ensure that each given service variants set can be identified in a single way through an identifying attribute named "service". The attribute "service" represents the name of the service (name of the class), and the name of all its variants consequently. We now present a formal definition of the Web services customization problem.

Definition 1 *(WSC problem)*.
A WSC problem Π *is a tuple* $(\mathcal{S}, \mathcal{F}, \mathcal{V}, \mathcal{P}, \mathcal{A}, \mathcal{T}, \mathcal{D})$ *where :*

- $\mathcal{S}$ *is a finite set of services, those delimiting the WSC space (that is to say the set services of the domain).*

- $\mathcal{F}$ *is a finite set of functionalities (attributes). For each functionality* $f \in \mathcal{F}$*, there exists a finite set* v_f *of values for* f*.* $\mathcal{V} = \{v_f \mid f \in \mathcal{F}\}$ *is the set of values.*

- *For each service* s*, there exists a set of properties* p_s*, which contains the pairs* (f, x)*, where (i)* $f \in \mathcal{F}$ *et* $x \in v_f$*, and (ii) each functionality* f *appears at most one time in* p_s*. A set of properties defines the values of the functionalities of a given service. The set* $\mathcal{P} = \{p_s \mid s \in \mathcal{S}\}$ *contains the set of all services' properties of* $\mathcal{S}$*.*

- *For each functionality* f*, there exists an addition operator* a_f*, which is a partial function* $a_f : v_f \times v_f \to v_f$*. An addition operator specifies how two values of a functionality will be combined to give a new value if a new service is added to a given collection of services which constitutes part of the services able to answer the customer request (Web services composition).* $\mathcal{A} = \{a_f \mid f \in \mathcal{F}\}$ *is the set of all addition operators.*

- *For each functionality* f*, there exists a test* t_f *which is a partial function* $t_f : v_f \times v_f \to \{True, False\}$*. A test* t_f *specifies under which conditions a request is satisfied.* $\mathcal{T} = \{t_f \mid f \in \mathcal{F}\}$ *is composed of all the tests.*

1. $\mathcal{S} = \{\text{hotel1, hotel2, hotel3, trip1, trip2}\}$

2. $\mathcal{F} = \{\text{service, city, departure, currency, price}\}$

3. $v_{service} = \{\text{hotel,trip}\}$, $v_{city} = \{\text{paris,rome, } \cdots \}$, $v_{departure} = \{\text{paris,rome, } \cdots \}$,
   $v_{currency} = \{\text{euro,yen, } \cdots \}$, $v_{price} = \mathcal{R}$.
   $\mathcal{V} = \{v_{service}, v_{city}, v_{departure}, v_{currency}, v_{price}\}$

4. $p_{hotel1} = \{(\text{service :hotel}),(\text{city :paris}),(\text{currency :euro}),(\text{price :45})\}$
   $p_{hotel2} = \{(\text{service :hotel}),(\text{city :paris}),(\text{currency :euro}),(\text{price :50})\}$
   $p_{hotel3} = \{(\text{service :hotel}),(\text{city :paris}),(\text{currency :yen}),(\text{price :1000})\}$
   $p_{trip1} = \{(\text{service :trip}),(\text{departure :rome}),(\text{city :paris}),(\text{currency :euro}),(\text{price :150})\}$
   $p_{trip2} = \{(\text{service :trip}),(\text{departure :rome}),(\text{city :paris}),(\text{currency :yen}),(\text{price :15000})\}$
   $\mathcal{P} = \{p_{hotel1}, p_{hotel2}, p_{hotel3}, p_{trip1}, p_{trip2}\}$

5. $a_{service}(x,y) = \{x,y\}$, $a_{price}(x,y) = x+y$
   $a_{city}(x,y) = a_{currency}(x,y) = a_{departure}(x,y) = \begin{cases} a & \text{if } x = y = a \\ \perp & \text{otherwise} \end{cases}$
   $\mathcal{A} = \{a_{service}, a_{city}, a_{currency}, a_{departure}, a_{price}\}$

6. $t_{price}(x,y) = \begin{cases} True & \text{if } x < y \\ False & \text{otherwise} \end{cases}$
   $\mathcal{T} = \{t_{price}\}$

7. $\mathcal{D} = \{(\text{service :}\{\text{hotel,trip}\}), (\text{departure, rome}),(\text{city, paris}),(\text{currency :euro}),(\text{price :200})\}$

FIG. **2. Formalization of a simple WSC problem in the tourism domain**

- $\mathcal{D}$ *is a finite set of requests (set of properties). Each request d is a pair (f,x), where $f \in \mathcal{F}$ and $x \in v_f$.*

Remark 1 *An addition operator is either an aggregation, a subsumption or a unification, etc.*

Figure 2 illustrates a simple WSC problem in the tourism domain. For illustration purposes, the set of services is limited to two services : a hotel trade service and a trip service. The former is offered under three variants (hotel1, hotel2, and hotel3), and the latter in two variants (trip1 and trip2).

4 Customizable WSs Discovery and Composition

Stated in an informal way, the (candidate) solution to the WSC problem is the set of WSs that match a request. In the following subsections we give a more formal description of this solution by means of its structure (Subsection 4.1) and its processing mechanisms (Subsection 4.2).

4.1 Structure of a (candidate) solution for a WSC problem

Definition 2 (*Solution Structure*).
Let $\Pi = (\mathcal{S}, \mathcal{V}, \mathcal{F}, \mathcal{P}, \mathcal{A}, \mathcal{T}, \mathcal{D})$ be a WSC problem. The structure of a (candidate) solution for Π is a pair $\mathcal{C} = (\mathcal{I}, \mathcal{Q})$ where $\mathcal{I}$ is a set of items of the form (k,s), and $\mathcal{Q}$ is a set of properties of the form (f, x). An item (k,s) denotes the fact that the service s is used k times in the solution ; although in general, each Web service is invoked only once (thus often k = 1). $\mathcal{Q}$ is a set of simple or composite properties ; $\mathcal{Q}$ may contain composite properties if the answer to a given request requires the invocation of more than one service. In this case the services' properties involved in the composition need to be composed, leading to another kind of properties – those of a complex service, named qualities.

Definition 3 (*Properties composition*). *Let (f,x) and (g,y) be two properties and a_f a defined addition operator. The formula*

$$\varphi((f,x),(g,y)) = \begin{cases} \{(f, a_f(x,y))\}, & if \quad f = g; \\ \{(f,x), (g,y)\}, & otherwise. \end{cases}$$

is called the composition of the properties (f,x) and (g,y).

The structure of a (candidate) solution $\mathcal{C}$ for a problem Π presented in Fig. 2 can be instantiated as follows : $\mathcal{C} = (\mathcal{I}, \mathcal{Q})$ with $\mathcal{I} = \{(1, \text{hotel1}), (1, \text{trip1})\}$ and $\mathcal{Q} = \{(\text{service :}\{\text{hotel, trip}\}), (\text{departure :rome}), (\text{city :paris}), (\text{currency :euro}), (\text{price :195})\}$. We provide in Figure 3 an inductive definition of such a possible solution.

Remark 2 *Although qualities and properties are syntactically (synonymously) the same, one distinguishes between them since a property is a "attribute :value" couple of a simple service whereas a quality (f, x) is the result of the*

1. $\mathcal{C} = (\emptyset, \emptyset)$.

2. If $\mathcal{C} = (\mathcal{I}, \mathcal{Q})$ is a Web service (simple or composite) and s a service of $\mathcal{S}$, then $\mathcal{S}' = (\mathcal{I}', \mathcal{Q}')$ is also a service, which in this case is composite, if the following conditions are met.

   (i)   for each $(f,x) \in p_s$ and for each $(g,y) \in \mathcal{Q}$, the composition $\varphi((f,x),(g,y))$ is defined or $\mathcal{Q} = \emptyset$.

   (ii) $\mathcal{I}' = \begin{cases} \mathcal{I} \setminus \{(k,s)\} \cup \{(k+1,s)\}, \exists (k,s) \in \mathcal{I}; \\ \mathcal{I} \cup \{(1,s)\}, \quad otherwise. \end{cases}$

   (iii) $\mathcal{Q}' = \begin{cases} \bigcup \varphi((f,x),(g,y)) \mid (f,x) \in p_s, (g,y) \in \mathcal{Q}\}, & if\ \mathcal{Q} \neq \emptyset; \\ p_s, & if\ \mathcal{Q} = \emptyset \end{cases}$

FIG. 3. Structure of a possible solution for a Web services personnalisation problem

composition of various services having the functionality f in their sets of properties.

4.2 Effective solution for a WSC problem

We introduced above the structure of a (candidate) solution to a WSC problem, we now define the effective solution of such a problem. However, because of space constraint, we omit here the WSC problem resolution algorithm.

Definition 4 *(Effective solution for a WSC problem)*
A set $\mathcal{C}$ (a candidate solution for a WSC problem $\Pi = (\mathcal{S}, \mathcal{F}, \mathcal{V}, \mathcal{P}, \mathcal{A}, \mathcal{T}, \mathcal{D})$) is effective if and only if for each request $d = (f,x) \in \mathcal{D}$ there exists a quality $q = (g,y) \in \mathcal{Q}$ so that $f = g$ and $t_f(x,y) = True$. The set $\mathcal{S}ol(\Pi) = \{\mathcal{C} \mid \mathcal{C} \text{ is an effective solution for } \Pi\}$ is called solutions space of Π. The condition above means that all the requests for $\mathcal{D}$ must be satisfied before a candidate solution becomes effective.

5 Conclusion

The heterogeneity of the Web services customers profiles often constrain suppliers to offer customizable Web services, targeting the satisfaction of several different categories of customers. In this article we have presented a theoretical framework for customizable Web services description, discovery, and composition. Our Web services description approach is domain dependent, a dependence materialized by the concept of model which represents all knowledge (set of Web services) necessary for the description of a given domain. We were interested more precisely by the functionalities based model, a knowledge representation formalism well established in the field of complex systems configuration. In this model, each Web service has a conceptual representation from an external point of view, therefore by disregarding all internal detail of its implementation. In other words, each Web service is seen as a "black box" represented by its name and input/output parameters. On this Web services description formalism, we introduced a set of mechanisms for cuwtomizable Web services discovery and composition.

Références

[1] G. Alonzo, F.Casati, H.kuno, and V.Machiraju. *Web Services. Concepts, Architecture and Applications.* Springer, 2004.

[2] D. Berardi. *Automatic Composition Services : Models, Techniques and Tools.* Phd thesis, 2003.

[3] G. Hohpe. *Web services : Pathway to a Service Oriented Architecture.* Thought Works, Inc., 2002.

[4] D. J. Mandell and S. A. McIlraith. Adapting bpel4ws for the semantic web : The bottom-up approach to web service interoperation. In *International Semantic Web Conference*, pages 227–241, 2003.

[5] S. A. McIlraith and T. C. Son. Adapting golog for composition of semantic web services. In *KR*, pages 482–496, 2002.

[6] O. Najmann and B. Stein. A theoretical framework for configuration. In *IEA/AIE*, pages 441–450, 1992.

[7] M. E. Orlowska, S. Weerawarana, M. P. Papazoglou, and J. Yang, editors. *Service-Oriented Computing - ICSOC 2003, First International Conference, Trento, Italy, December 15-18, 2003, Proceedings*, volume 2910 of *Lecture Notes in Computer Science*. Springer, 2003.

[8] B. PineII and S. Davis. *Mass Customization : The New Frontier in Business Competition.* Harvard Business School Press, 1993.

[9] A. ten Teije, F. van Harmelen, and B. J. Wielinga. Configuration of web services as parametric design. In *ECAI*, pages 1097–1098, 2004.

[10] S. van Splunter, M. Sabou, F. M. T. Brazier, and D. Richards. Configuring web services, using structuring and techniques from agent configuration. In *Web Intelligence*, pages 153–160, 2003.

[11] B. P. B. Victor and A. Boynton. Making mass customization work. In *Harvard Business Review*, pages 109–119, Sept/Oct 1993.

A Web Database Security Model Using the Host Identity Protocol

Xueyong Zhu
Network Information Center
University of Science and Technology
of China
Hefei, Anhui, China
zhuxy@ustc.edu.cn

J. William Atwood
Department of Computer Science and
Software Engineering
Concordia University
Montreal, Quebec, Canada
bill@cse.concordia.ca

Abstract

*Web database security is a very important issue in E-commerce. This paper presents a new Web database security model. It utilizes the Host Identity Protocol (HIP), which is being defined by the IETF, and a proposed User Identity exchange, to achieve authentication of **Host Identity** and **User Identity**, and combines it with the database system itself and encryption to guarantee Web database security and confidentiality of the data. For these purposes, we define a new concept of the **User Identity** namespace for the user, and using it to realize the binding-authentication of the **Host Identity** and **User Identity** of the client, and build a relationship between the host and the user. In the new Model, we set up a high strength shell of security for the database.*

Keywords: Web Database, Security, HIP, Host Identity, User Identity, Model.

1. Introduction

With the development of E-commerce and end-user services, it becomes imperative to ensure that access to secure Web-based databases is limited to authorized users. In E-commerce, the fact that partners and customers must access corporate data means that the Web databases cannot simply be hidden behind a firewall. While the use of traditional network security mechanisms—firewalls, Intrusion Detection Systems (IDSs), Https over SSL and other products—remains vital, data theft remains alarmingly common and shows no signs of abating, in spite of the large amounts of money spent each year on IT security. Reports about the retrieval of credit records from some E-commerce sites and about defaced corporate websites are frequent. The attacks on Internet sites are increasing in sophistication, and now attackers can easily cut across protecting devices such as firewalls.

So it is imperative to properly secure web database against attacks from the outside world.

A web-based interface is generally open to the public. (This is a widely used "feature" of the web.) As such, there is little control over the clientele who can access the interface. As noted above, strong security measures are available for the database itself, and for the part of the network owned by the database provider. However, an additional problem is the relatively weak forms of access control "in front of" the database itself—a database can be attacked simply by sending it a sufficient number of bogus requests. This puts a load on the database server, and reduces its ability to serve legitimate requests.

One way to alleviate this problem is to control access to the database, using the web server as a strong filter. Also, since many of the applications will choose to encrypt the query and the response, it is an advantage if the procedures used to authenticate an end user and/or the accessing host can also provide for the establishment of a secure connection with little or no increase in cost.

Finally, in the context of the increased use of mobile terminals, a mechanism that retains the validity of a host and/or a user in spite of a change in IP address is highly desirable.

In this paper, we show how to make use of the Host Identity Protocol (HIP) for host authorization, and how to extend HIP to allow for identification of the end user, and (more importantly) how to bind the user to a particular host for a specific transaction.

In this paper, we do not consider various factors such as software bugs, mis-configurations, or incorrect usage, and we concentrate on the factors of the architecture and Internet environment.

2. The architecture of the new proposed Web database security model

A common architecture for offering a relatively open access to a database is to provide a web server that accepts requests in an easy-to-use format, and passes them to the database, possibly through some form of application server. Since the parameters used for authenticating the requestor are simply passed to the database, this leaves the database open to attacks based on invalid requests or invalid requestors. If a method can be developed to validate user identities in the web server, then part of the load on the database can be alleviated, and all packets originated by invalid users can be discarded before they arrive at the database. If the user is required to register both his identity and the host that he is tied to, then theft of a user identity is not useful, because its use by an attacker on a different host will result in a host/user mismatch, which can be used to reject the request. When the exchanged data must be encrypted as part of the application requirements, a secure connection must be ultimately established between the database and the requesting user.

While these steps can be achieved independently, it is also true that to validate the identity of the host or the end user, it is essential to establish a secure connection between them. This secure connection can then be used for the data exchange. This is part of our motivation for the use of HIP.

Additional motivation comes from the fact that the Host Identity validated through the use of HIP is independent of the IP address of the host, which is known to be easy to spoof.

Finally, the Protocol Rendezvous Extensions to HIP provide for mobility—the end user can change the IP address of his host, while maintaining the Host Identity, which will become increasingly useful in the future.

The Host Identity Protocol (HIP) is used to authenticate the Host Identity of an end system and to set up a limited relationship of trust between two hosts on the Internet [3]. The core of HIP is a new namespace HI (Host Identity). The HI is independent of the location (IP address) of the host. In the HIP architecture, the end-point name and locator are separated from each other. The IP address continues to act as locator. The Host Identifier takes the role of end-point identifier. There are two main representations of the *Host Identity*, the full *Host Identifier* (HI) and the *Host Identity Tag* (HIT). The HI is a public key and directly represents the Identity. Since there are different public key algorithms that can be used with different key lengths, the HI is not good for using as a packet identifier or as an index into the various operational tables needed to support HIP. Consequently, the *Host Identity Tag* (HIT) is used as one representation of the HI. It is obtained by taking the output of a secure hash function applied to the HI, truncated to the IPv6 address size. It is 128 bits long and is used in the HIP payloads and to index the

corresponding state in the end host. The complete HIP protocol consists of three key elements: HIP Initiator (I for short), HIP Responder (R for short) and HIP Base Exchange. The HIP realizes authentication between two hosts (I and R) via the HIP Base Exchange, which includes four packet exchanges (packet I1, R1, I2, and R2) [3], [4]. The last three packets constitute a Diffie-Hellman exchange that permits the establishment of a pair of IPsec security associations between the two hosts. In addition, using the mechanism of Host Identity Protocol Rendezvous Extensions, the HIP is also designed to support mobile hosts and multi-homed hosts [5], [6], [7].

The authenticating and security features of HIP are then available to protect Web database systems and applications from most attacks. To ensure host legality, the Host Identity of the client must be authenticated by the database owner (the same as it is necessary that a bank authorizes an Automatic Teller Machine); on the other hand, the database owner must also authenticate the User Identity of the client using that host. This means that we must realize a binding-authentication of the Host Identity and User Identity of the client, and build a relationship between the host and the user. So, we can guarantee that the Host Identity of the client (below call it host for short) and the User Identity of the client using the host (below call it user for short) are legitimate simultaneously. That will not permit an arbitrary combination of the user and the host, which can stop hackers using the User Identity in an unauthorized host, and reinforce manageable function of the Web database to the users. In this way, we can know who does the actions, where he does them and what he does at any time. It is also possible to limit the accesses of one user to specific authorized hosts, or set one host to be accessed by only certain users. Thus, even if a credit card is lost, the thief cannot use it on the illegal hosts.

Because the standard HIP only authenticates the Host, for authenticating the User, it is necessary to extend the standard HIP. We define a new concept for the user: the User Identity namespace. Similar to the Host Identity [1], there are two main representations of the User Identity, the full User Identifier (UI) and the User Identity Tag (UIT). The UI is normally a public key of the user.

So, the topology of the new model of Web database security to implement above functions is shown in Figure 1.

Figure 1 shows a scenario for accessing the Web database with m hosts and n users in the new model, which is based on the extended HIP with Rendezvous Server (RVS). The HIP Responder lies in the Web server and logically in front of it. The clients (hosts and users) accessing the Web database act as the HIP

Initiators. They constitute a complete extended HIP authentication system with the Rendezvous Server (RVS) and DNSsec Server. Its HIP authenticating functionality is located within the Web server of the Web database system. The RVS also cooperates with the Web server to authenticate the User Identity and Host Identity, register User Identity and Host Identity, and set up a binding relationship between the hosts and the users.

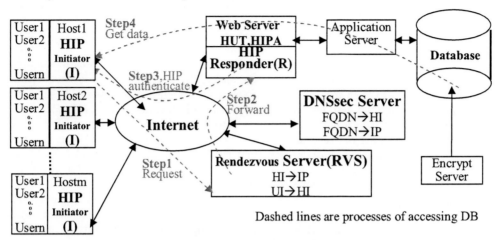

Figure 1   Architecture of new model of Web database security

Here, the processes of a client accessing the Web database include two phases: the first is the client gets the extended HIP authentication of the Web server (step1, 2, 3); the second is the Web server starts actually accessing the database (step4).

Let HI(R)   represent the HI of R (Responder);
      HI(I)   represent the HI of I (Initiator);
      IP(R)   represent the IP address of R;
      →   represent the corresponding relation;
      (HI,UI) represent the binding relation.
Then:

Before the client accesses the Web database, the Responder must have registered its Host Identity and created HI(R)→IP(R) records in the RVS, and registered its domain namespace and created FQDN→IP(RVS) and FQDN→HI(R) records in the DNSsec Server in advance. The Initiator must have registered its two Identities (HI,UI) and created HI(I)→IP(I) and binding--UI(I)→HI(I) records (manual or on line) in the RVS, and registered its domain namespace and created FQDN→HI(I) and FQDN→IP(I) records in the DNSsec Server in advance. If the IP address of the host is changed for various reasons that include mobility of user or host, the host (I or R) must re-register the above records. Then, the registered client can start an extended HIP authentication with UI and access the Web database. Firstly, the client (Initiator) sends packet I1 to the RVS starting the extended HIP authentication. After validating it, the RVS forwards I1 to the Responder (in the Web server). Later on, the extended HIP exchange with UI operates directly between the Initiator (the

client) and the Responder (in the Web server). Finally, the authentication finishes and the real accessing of the database begins.

In the new model, we combine the HIP Responder with the Web Server. This allows the Web server to work under the control of the HIP Responder. If the client wants to access the Web server and database, the HIP Responder must authenticate it. However, the HIP Responder can also be separate from the Web server and be located in front of it. Given that the functionality of database server may not be a good match to the likely applications of the clients, the application server may be used to provide additional information processing or application-specific responses. The encryption server is for encrypting the sensitive data in the database and is responsible for security of the database source itself. Neither one participates in the HIP authentication. The DNSsec Server and RVS serve the HIP authentication, and they can be located anywhere on the Internet. In general, the DNSsec Server and RVS should belong to the owner of the database; besides, they may also belong to an authentication organization of the network or an ISP.

3. The operation of the new Web database security model with extended HIP with UI

For accessing a Web database, a registered client must start an extended HIP Exchange with UI for getting HIP authentication. The process of an extended HIP Exchange with UI is basically the same as the standard HIP Exchange that includes packets I1, R1,

I2, and R2. A difference is that we add the UI item to the packets of the HIP exchange. Firstly, a client (Initiator) gets IP(RVS), IP(R), HI(R) from the DNSsec Server, and sends a trigger packet, I1, to the RVS. The packet I1 contains the HIT of the Initiator, the UIT of the User and possibly the HIT of the Responder (in the Web server), if it is known. Upon receiving I1, the RVS will check it. If the HI and UI items in the I1 have been registered and been bound in the RVS, then the RVS adds UI→HI binding flag to the packet I1, and relays the I1 to the Responder. If the RVS does not find the registered binding UI to HI of the Initiator, then it drops the packet I1 silently. So the non-registered client cannot access the Web server (Responder). Receiving packet I1, the Responder will check I1, if it finds the packet I1 without a UI→HI binding flag or not coming from the RVS, it drops the packet I1 silently. The UI→HI binding flag in the I1 can protect the Responder from attacker directly sending a forged I1 to it but not via the RVS.

After checking the packet I1, if I1 has a UI→HI binding flag added by RVS, the Responder (in the Web server) directly sends packet R1 to the Initiator, and starts the actual extended HIP exchange with UI. It is noticed that the next three packets of the exchange, R1, I2, and R2, will not pass through the RVS. The R1 contains a challenge puzzle to HI and UI, that is, a cryptographic challenge that the Initiator must solve before continuing the exchange. In addition, it contains the initial Diffie-Hellman parameters and a signature.

In the packet I2, the Initiator (client) must display the solution to the received challenge puzzle. Without a correct solution, the Responder (in the Web server) discards the I2 message. The I2 also contains a Diffie-Hellman parameter that carries needed information for the Responder. The packet R2 finalizes the 4-way handshake, containing the SPI (Security Parameters Index) value of the Responder.

If above the extended HIP Exchange with UI is successful, then the client (Initiator) has been authenticated by the Web server, else the authentication failed and all the messages are dropped silently. After the client (host bound user) has been authenticated, the Responder will set up the HIP Association (HIPA) and a binding HI→UI --authenticated Table (HUT) in the Web server and pass the client (host and user) to the Web server. The Web server just accepts the clients in the HUT to access the database according to the original database security policies. When a client logs out, the Web server must update the HIPA, HUT and stop the client. The authenticating process guarantees that the client who obtains the right to access the database is the legitimate user on the legitimate host, and does not affect the Web server itself and the database.

In general, after a client registers its HIs and UI in the RVS, the following tables must be stored in the RVS:

[HI(R)→IP(R)], [HI(I)→IP(I), UI(I)→HI(I)].

These messages can also dynamically decide the IP address or location of a host and a user. So the client (host and user) can roam through different IP addresses or locations, and the user can roam on different hosts, as long as it can be reachable to the RVS. The Responder (in the Web server) can also be permitted to change its own IP addresses or locations. However, it is more important that a client (Initiator) can roam through different IP addresses, locations or hosts. This indicates the provider of database services is only concerned with the client Identity instead of its IP address or location. Of course, these addresses, locations, hosts and users must have been registered in the Rendezvous Server (RVS) and DNSsec Server; and they have to get the authorization of coming from the provider of database services. The operating processes of the new model are shown in Figure 2 (Step #1---#10). The common FQDN registers are omitted.

Now, whenever a client wants to access the Web database, the client will become the HIP Initiator and will start a process of the extended HIP authentication between the client (Initiator) and the Web server (Responder). If the Web server has successfully authenticated the User Identity and Host Identity of the client, then the accessing request of the client is accepted, the HIPA and HUT are set up, and the Web server starts to access really the database. Otherwise, the accessing request of client is dropped silently.

4. Analysis of security of the new model

The Web database security depends on limiting actual access to the Web server and database itself. In the new model, we have limited the access to the Web server and database to the greatest extent. Its database server only exchanges information with the Web server; and only allows connections from the Web server. Anyone accessing the database via the Web server must be authenticated by the extended HIP with UI. Anyone who is permitted to access the Web server surely is a real and legitimate client. If an attacker attempts to directly connect to the Web server and access the database bypassing the HIP Responder, then his request will be dropped silently by the Web server, because he is not in the HUT and does not have the HIPA. If an attacker wants to connect to the Web server via the HIP Responder, he will not be authenticated, because he has not registered the HI, UI in the RVS, and does not have a UI→HI binding flag in the packet I1, and he also cannot answer the correct solution to the puzzle challenge. In general, the RVS will drop all messages except I1; the Responder will drop all request messages except I1 coming from its RVS. The application server is optional for applying functions and is not involved in security authentication. The encryption server is for guaranteeing that sensitive data in the database will not be exposed on the Internet and for the security of the database itself. Consequently, the whole security of the Web database system in the new model depends on two aspects: the security of authentication of the extended HIP with UI and the security of database system itself behind the Web server.

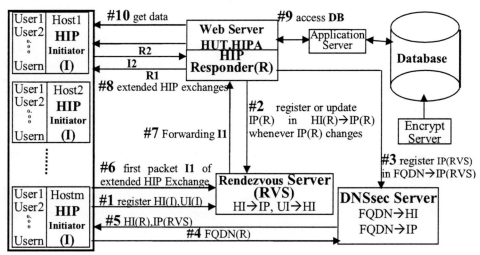

Figure 2   The processes of HIP Exchange and access DB of the new model

The extended HIP authentication with UI has inherited whole security of the standard HIP [3], [4]. It can limit attacks such as sniff, spoof, snoop, and so on. It also limits the exposure of the host to various denial-of-service (DoS) and man-in-the-middle (MitM) attacks. In addition, due to introducing the RVS, it also reinforces the security of the standard HIP. First, for using packet I1 attacks, the attacker has no UI or HI registered; the I1 will be dropped by the RVS silently. If the I1 is directly sent to the Responder, due to lack of UI→HI binding flag in the packet and because it does not come from the RVS, it will be dropped by the Responder silently. Therefore this attack cannot bring too much effect. For resource exhausting denial-of-service attacks, the RVS only checks the UI and HI items and does not do more processing, so the load on the RVS is small too. Consider the DoS attack that is emulating the restart of state after a reboot of one of the partners in state ESTABLISHED. An attacking host would send a starting packet I1 to the RVS or Responder. However, this I1 has no UI, HI, and UI→HI flag registered in the RVS, so the I1 will be dropped by the RVS or Responder.

Because the users that reach database system behind the Web server surely are authenticated and are legitimate, the database system only needs to verify their identity in the database and authorize to them appropriate rights for accessing the data. In fact, the most current database systems such as Oracle, Sybase, and SQL server will suffice for these requirements of security. They have a wealth of access control methods for legitimate users.

In order to ensure the sensitive data security further, the encrypting server is set up in the new model. It can encrypt data using different encryption algorithms, according to different application requirements. It is very convenient and flexible to fit into different requirements of security.

5. Analysis of performance of the new Model

Upon introducing HIP with UI, we just add four packets to the Web server (Responder), in which I1 is simply checked, R1 is pre-created. After I2 arrives, the Web server will calculate some data and verify the solution, but not compute too many items. R2 finalizes the 4-way handshake. Most of work of HIP with UI will be done by the Initiator (User's host or Attacker). The structure of the extended HIP packets is as follows:

I1: HIT(I), HIT(R),UIT, Host-User-bind_flag.

R1: HIT(I), HIT(R),UIT, Puzzle(N,K), (DH(R), HI(R),UI, HIP Transforms, ESP Transforms, Echo_Request)sig.

I2: HIT(I), HIT(R), UIT, (Solution(N,K,J), SPI(I), DH(I), HIP Transforms, ESP Transforms, {HI(I), UI}, Echo_Response)sig.

R2: HIT(I), HIT(R), UIT, (SPI(R), HMAC)sig.

In above puzzle and solution, N is the puzzle nonce, K is the difficulty level, and J is the solution. The Web server can easily verify a puzzle solution:

First, concatenate N, the Host Identity Tags HIT(I) and HIT(R), UIT, and the solution J. Then, compute the SHA-1 hash of the concatenation. Finally, check that the K low-order bits of the hash are all zeros.

$$\text{Ltrunc}(\text{SHA-1}(N \mid \text{HIT(I)} \mid \text{HIT(R)} \mid \text{UIT} \mid J), K) == 0.$$

In general, the client or attacker must do a brute-force search for the value of J, which takes $O(2K)$ trials. The Web server, on the other hand, can verify the solution by computing a single hash. On receiving R1, the client checks whether it had sent a corresponding I1 and verifies the signature using the public key HI(R). If the signature is ok, it solves the puzzle and creates the message I2. I2 includes the puzzle and its solution, the client's Diffie-Hellman key, the HIP and ESP transforms proposed by the Initiator, a security parameter index (SPI) for the Web server-to-User IPsec SA (HIPA), the client's public key (HI(I)) and UI encrypted using the new session key, and the Echo_Response. A signature covers the entire message. Key material for the session keys is computed as a SHA-1 hash of the Diffie-Hellman shared secret Kij:

$$\text{KEYMAT\_k} = \text{SHA-1}(Kij, \mid \text{sort}(\text{HIT(I)} \mid \text{HIT(R)} \mid \text{UIT} \mid k) \text{ for } k = 1, 2,...$$

On receiving I2, the Web server simply verifies the puzzle solution. So, for the Web server, the load of authentication is not heavy, and does not overload the Web server. The cost of the key generation is also not too heavy.

The Rendezvous Server (RVS) introduced in the new model is a first watchdog of the Web database system. It not only can register and bind the user and host, but it also shares the attacks of hacker to the Web server. It will reduce opportunity of directly attacking the Web server. As mentioned before, the workload of RVS is not too heavy.

The architecture that we have introduced has two novel features. The first is the prior association of the User Identity and the Host Identity; this allows the RVS to reject any invalid combinations. The use of HIP extended with the UI permits associating the two identifiers, thus restricting the scope for undesirable attacks. The second is the use of HIP to bring together an authentication mechanism and the security associations that would (in most cases) be necessary. This allows achieving savings in processing time and overall complexity. Essentially, a highly secure shell surrounds the whole Web database system.

Behind the Web server, we can freely set up the elements of database system and optimize the structure of the database system according to the application and performance requirements. Since the database accepts queries only from the Web server, and since these queries have been authenticated, the task of the database is much smaller, and the ease of attack is substantially reduced.

6. Validation of the new Model

We have used the formal validation language PROMELA to specify the validation for the new Web database system model and used the verifier tool SPIN to validate that validation model. In simulation experiments, we embedded C code fragments inside PROMELA models for accessing the database and simple encryption.

The validation model consists of 32 Initiator processes, some Intruder processes, an RVS process, a Web and Responder process, and a Database accessing process. The logical structure of the validation for the new model is shown in figure 3.

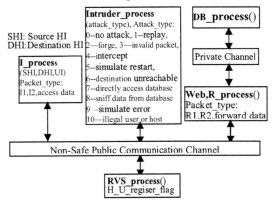

Figure 3 The logical structure of Validating processes

The running environment is Pentium (M) 1.5GHz CPU, 512MB memory, Windows XP OS, and SPIN v4.25. Firstly, we validate violation of system. Then we print all running information of the system, and trace processes of communication of the system. Finally we analyze the statistic results of running information and get some conclusions.

The result shows that the new model of Web database system is free from assertion violation, invalid end-state and unreachable state. We did not find any real, successful or valid attack to the Web database system.

In the simulation experiments, we adjusted the sending rate of attacking packets of the intruder, and observed as follows results: When the sending packet rate of the intruder is not more than that of normal users, there is negligible effect on the authentication of extended HIP and the accessing of the database. It also almost does not result in re-transmission of the authenticated packets. If the sending packet rate of the intruder is much more than that of normal users, then it delays time of authentication and access database for about 10 times of normal condition. The frequency of re-transmission of authenticated packets is about 7 times of normal condition. However, the authentication and the accessing of the database are still successful.

As the ratio of the intruder's sending rate over the user's sending rate increases, the ratio of the actual delay to the delay for the case of no attack will change. Figure 4 shows this relationship.

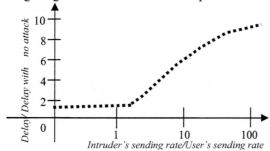

Figure 4   The statistical results of delay time

As the ratio of the intruder's sending rate over the user's sending rate increases, the frequency of re-transmitted packets will increase. It is shown in Figure 5.

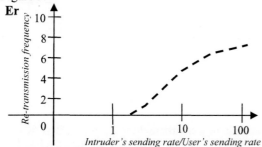

Figure 5 The statistical results of re-transmission

The results of experiments showed that our new model is valid and correct. It is clear that attacking packets interfered in the process of the extended HIP authentication, and resulted in re-transmission of HIP packets and accessing packets. Then it delayed the time of authentication and accessing database.

7. Conclusion

It is shown that the new model is feasible. It provides robust security due to the strong authentication of extended HIP with UI. It also has good scalability, and high availability for the most demanding environments. It is believed that the new model realizes a relatively complete solution for Web database security. It would appear to have particular advantages in military systems or in important financial systems.

8. Acknowledgements

X. Zhu acknowledges the support of the Department of Computer Science and Software Engineering of Concordia University, during his sabbatical visit, and the provision of the environment for verification and validation. J.W. Atwood acknowledges the support of the Natural Sciences and Engineering Research Council of Canada, through its Discovery Grants program. We are also both grateful to the anonymous reviewers for their comments.

References

[1] Ingrian Networks, Inc. Encrypting Critical Data in Databases with Ingrian Networks, 2004.12.
[2] Ingrian Networks, Inc. Ensuring Compliance with Credit Card Security Policies, 2004.12.
[3] R. Moskowitz, Nikander, P. Jokela, T.Henderson, "Host Identity Protocol" (draft-07), 2007. 02.
[4] R. Moskowitz, P. Nikander, "Host Identity Protocol Architecture", (RFC 4432), 2006.05.
[5] J. Laganier,Host Identity Protocol (HIP) Rendezvous Extensions, (draft-05), 2006.06.
[6] P. Nikander, Host Identity Protocol (HIP) Domain Name System (DNS) Extensions, (draft-07), 2006.09.
[7] P. Nikander, "End-Host Mobility and Multi-Homing with Host Identity Protocol", (draft-04), 2006.06.
[8] S. Kent, "IP Encapsulating Security Payload (ESP)", (RFC 4303), 2005.12.
[9] NIST, "FIPS PUB 180-1: Secure Hash Standard", 1995.04.
[10] Madson, C. and R. Glenn, "The Use of HMAC-SHA -1-96 within ESP and AH", RFC 2404, 1998.11.
[11] H. Krawczyk, "HMAC: Keyed-Hashing for Message Authentication", RFC 2104, 1997.02.
[12] Vixie, P., Thomson, S., Rekhter, Y. and J. Bound, "Dynamic Updates in the Domain Name System (DNS UPDATE)", RFC 2136, 1997.04.
[13] Wellington, B., "Secure Domain Name System (DNS) Dynamic Update", RFC 3007, 2000. 11.
[14] P. Jokela, R. Moskowitz, et al. "Using ESP transport format with HIP", (draft-04), 2006.10

An SLA-Enabled Grid Data Warehouse

Rogério Luís de Carvalho Costa and Pedro Furtado
University of Coimbra - Departamento de Engenharia Informática
Pólo II - Pinhal de Marrocos - 3030-290 - Coimbra - Portugal
rogcosta@dei.uc.pt pnf@dei.uc.pt

Abstract

Database servers typically offer a best-effort model of service to submitted commands, that is, they try to process every command as fast as possible. Hence, they are not prepared to provide differentiation for quality of service. In this paper we consider the distributed Grid-DWPA architecture context, which fragments and replicates data into several sites to provide an efficient grid data warehouse solution. Instead of offering best-effort service to every query, we propose the use of a performance predict model that is used in conjunction with QoS oriented scheduling to enable the establishment of Service Level Agreements (SLA).

1 Introduction

Data warehouses are repositories of large amounts of historical data from multiple sources and are used primarily for decision support purposes. They must ensure acceptable response time for complex analytical queries.

Many works have been done in order to provide high performance for data warehouses. These works involve special structures such as materialized views [2], special operators [7] and the use of distributed data and parallelism [4].

In fact, recently works on parallel and distributed computing have mostly focused on grid and peer-to-peer technologies. These technologies could lead to high levels of flexibility, scalability, reliability and efficiency. Grid-based data warehouses are especially interesting for enterprises that operate in a highly distributed fashion.

In this work, we present Grid-DWPA (*Grid-Data Warehouse Parallel Architecture*), a new architecture for the implementation of a parallel data warehouse in the Grid. We are especially concerned on the management of user specified Quality of Service (QoS) parameters.

Our discussion in this paper centers around implementing a grid data warehouse which could consider different QoS requirements, like query deadline and query priority. We consider the heterogeneity and unpredictability of the grid environment, besides using good data partition and placement policies.

This paper is organized as follows: in the next Section we present a general overview of the Grid-DWPA architecture. In Section 3 we discuss SLA negotiation and QoS level prediction in Grid-DWPA. Then, we present task execution process. Section 5 overviews related work. Finally, on Section 6, we conclude and discuss future work.

2 GRID-DWPA Architecture

In this Section, we present the most important components of Grid-DWPA. We also present a general view of data allocation and intra-query parallelism in Grid-DWPA.

2.1 System Components

Nodes in Grid-DWPA could be grouped into 3 major groups: clients, data loaders and executors.

Executors and Executor Coordinators: We call Executor Site to each group of nodes that has a replica or a fragment of the data warehouse's database. Each Executor Site has an Executor Site Coordinator and some Executor Nodes. The Executor Nodes are the nodes that actually access the database and execute queries. The Site Coordinator is responsible to coordinate data slicing and replication at its site nodes. All the communication with the outside nodes is done by the Executor Site Coordinator. It is also responsible to negotiate the Quality of Service level that the site can deliver on any incoming query.

Clients and Clients Coordinators: Queries are submitted to the system in Client nodes. When a client node submits a query, it is sent to a Client Site Coordinator. Client Site Coordinators evaluate if intra-query parallelism can be applied to each incoming query. They also verify which sites have the data necessary to answer the query and if cached data may be used. Client Site Coordinators transform queries into tasks (new queries whose results must be combined to obtain the same results from the original query) and negotiate QoS levels with Executor Site Coordinators.

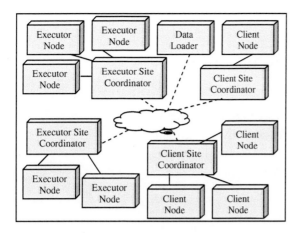

Figure 1. Grid-DWPA Architecture

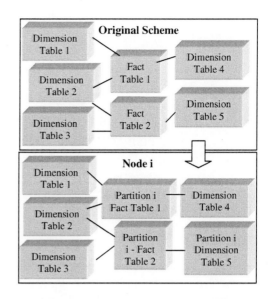

Figure 2. Data allocation in NPDW

Data Loaders: In data warehouses, the data update process is usually based on periodic loads. In Grid-DWPA, these loads are done by nodes called Data Loaders. These nodes also control the data loading propagation into other nodes, coordinating the data slicing and replication between executor sites. Discussing data loading process is out of this paper's scope.

A general view of Grid-DWPA is presented in Figure 1.

2.2 Data placement in Grid-DWPA

Data Warehouses are usually deployed in relational databases using star schemas. These schemas are comprised of a few huge central fact relations and several smaller dimension relations [3], as shown in Figure 2. Each fact references a tuple in each dimension. For instance, facts may be sales measures and dimensions may include time, shop, customer and product the sales fact refers to.

In Grid-DWPA, data placement is done according to the Node-Partitioned Data Warehouse (NPDW) strategy [4]. It is a strategy to process those star schemas' tables efficiently in parallel shared-nothing systems. In NPDW each relation can be partitioned (divided into partitions or fragments) or copied entirely into processing nodes (Figure 2). Very large fact relations are workload-based partitioned and dimensions (which are typically small) are replicated into all sites. In this case most of the query processing can proceed in parallel between the nodes with only modest amounts of data being exchanged between nodes [4].

One can organize the processing nodes by groups, which allows some nodes to go off line simultaneously. The idea is that partitions of all nodes participating in one group should always be (sliced and) replicated into nodes of a different group. No replicas of large table's data should be done in nodes of the same group. This strategy is called PRG (Partitioned Replica Groups) [6]. With this simple constraint,

a whole group can be offline without stopping the whole system.

In order to implement PRG in Grid-DWPA, we consider that, in grid environment, it is more susceptible that a link from a site to another site goes down (WAN link) than to have a link failure between nodes within a single location (LAN link). This way, each executor site is a PRG group: all the nodes in each geographical location (Executor Site) should have its database sliced and replicated into other executor sites. No replica of large table's data is done in nodes of the same executor site. Hence, if a link to an executor site goes down, the system continues to work.

2.3 Intra-query Parallelism and Task Generation

When a query is submitted at a Client Node, it sends the query to its site coordinator. The Client Site Coordinator node must verify if intra-query parallelism may be applied and rewrite the query accordingly.

Consider a query that executes a *SUM* operation [1]. In order to execute this query in Grid-DWPA, one can execute a *SUM* operation at each executor node and, then, aggregate the results from each node. When doing query rewrite, some operators must be replaced by others (e.g. the STD-DEV expression must be replaced by *SUMs* and *COUNTs*).

In general, intra-query parallelism is achieved by processing different fragments using different tasks (new queries), which implies that the data should be partitioned in the first place. Nodes are "natural" partition boundaries, but

---

[1]It is one of the most common operations in data warehouses queries. Other common operations are *AVG*, *COUNT*, *MAX* and *MIN*.

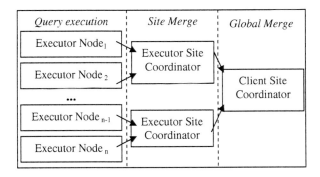

Figure 3. Merging results

in order to better adapt the amount of data to be processed to dynamic performance features, the number of fragments may be much larger than the number of nodes, so that there will be many more tasks than nodes and the system will be able to adapt the scheduling.

As soon as the query rewrite is done, the Client Site Coordinator will known all the tasks that should be executed in order to answer a submitted query. The system must verify if the user-specified QoS requirements can be met: tasks are allocated to executor sites by a negotiation between the Client Site Coordinator and Executor Site Coordinators, as it will be presented in Section 3.1. Each Executor Site Coordinator allocates the site's tasks to site's Executor Nodes.

2.4 Merging Results

The results from the tasks executed by each Executor Node must be merged in order to represent the results from the original query. This could be done by Client Site Coordinator, in a centralized way. But, in order to improve performance, one can apply Hierarchical Aggregation [5], which is represented in Figure 3. It can both reduce the network traffic and do a better use of processing parallelism.

Executor Site Coordinators will merge the results obtained by the executor nodes from its site, obtaining a site merge (in some cases, it is necessary that the Executor Site Coordinator receives all tasks' results in order to do a site merge). Then, each Executor Site Coordinator sends the result of its site merge to Client Site Coordinator, which does a global merge.

3 QoS Verification

When a query is submitted at a Client Node, it sends the query to its site coordinator. The Client Site Coordinator must verify if the required levels of QoS can be achieved. For each incoming query, a tasks list is generated. Then, The Client Coordinator must negotiate QoS levels with Executor Site Coordinators.

3.1 QoS Negotiation

The next 6 steps resume the actions that should be done during QoS negotiation.

Step 1. Sending Tasks to Sites: First of all, the Client Coordinator sends the query's tasks list to each executor site for QoS requirements evaluation (some sites that do not achieve some special QoS requirements, like data freshness, can be easily discarded).

Step 2. Verifying QoS Requirements at each Site: Each Executor Site Coordinator must evaluate if the site can execute the requested tasks with the QoS levels that were specified (this process will be illustrated in the next Section). Then, each Executor Coordinator sends to Client Coordinator the list of tasks (called L_{Site}) its site nodes can execute by the specified QoS levels. When including a task in its L_{Site} list, the Executor Site Coordinator makes a commitment to execute the task according to the specified QoS levels.

Step 3. Reviewing Sites' Lists: The Client Site Coordinator will decide which site executes each task. In case more than one site has agreed to execute a task with the specified QoS levels, Client Coordinator must review such sites' lists, removing the repeated tasks. Each task must remain in only one L_{Site} list. Client Coordinator never includes tasks in L_{Site} lists, it can only remove tasks. Only Executor Coordinators can include tasks in L_{Site} lists.

Step 4. Verifying complete allocation: After Client Coordinator has revised sites' lists, three situations can happen: (i) each task is assigned to only one site list - it means the incoming query can be executed within the specified QoS level → Client Coordinator will establish a SLA; (ii) there exist unassigned tasks but no L_{Site} list was reviewed by Client Site Coordinator → Client Coordinator will decide that the incoming query cannot be executed by the required QoS level; (iii) there exist unassigned tasks and some L_{Site} lists were revised by Client Site Coordinator → Client Coordinator will try to allocate remaining tasks to sites, as presented bellow.

Step 5. Allocating Remaining Tasks: Unassigned tasks are sent for evaluation by sites that had their L_{Site} list altered by Client Coordinator. Client Coordinator also sends to sites their new (modified) L_{Site} lists. Executor Site Coordinators should verify if they can execute the unassigned tasks together with L_{Site}'s tasks according to the desired QoS levels. Then, Executor Site Coordinators should send a new L_{Site} list to Client Site Coordinator. Client Site Coordinator must review lists again (Step 3).

Step 6. Establishing a SLA: If all the tasks are assigned, then Grid-DWPA will be able to execute the query according to the specified QoS levels. A SLA is established. Client Site Coordinator will inform the user that the query will be executed according to the specified QoS requirements.

It also sends to Executor Coordinators the final version of their L_{Site} tasks lists. Each Executor Coordinator should inform the final task allocation to its site Executor Nodes and reserve the necessary resources to execute tasks according to the QoS level it has agreed to provide.

3.2 Verifying QoS Requirements at each Site

After a query is submitted to a Client Site Coordinator, it is transformed into tasks. These tasks are submitted to Executor Site Coordinators, who should verify it its site can execute or not the incoming tasks according to the desired QoS levels. This process is highly dependent on the used QoS parameters. In this work, we consider the use of *Query Deadline* as a QoS parameter. This is used to illustrate the actions Executor Coordinators should take.

Generating L_{Site}

To evaluate if a task may be executed according to a desired deadline, Executor Site Coordinators must estimate the task execution time. Unfortunately, this is not a common functionality in current DBMS. So, the Executor Site Coordinator must have a way to estimate the task execution time.

Each Executor Site Coordinator knows the tasks that are currently assigned for each node of its site. In order to evaluate a task execution time, the Executor Site Coordinator may have a local DBMS with all or at least a representative set of the data fragments, partitioned in the same way as they are in the executor nodes[2].

This DBMS will be used to estimate the execution cost of a task (query). First of all, the task is submitted to the DBMS with a common EXPLAIN PLAN command. Then, a *"query costs conversion factor"* (γ) is used. This factor represents the ratio between the query cost estimated by the local DBMS (by the use of the EXPLAIN PLAN command) and the real execution time (at Executor Node). It should be calculated for each node and recomputed at the end of each task's execution. γ is determined by Equation 1.

$$\gamma_i = \frac{\gamma_{i-1} + (\alpha * \frac{task's_i \ execution \ time}{task's_i \ estimated \ cost})}{\alpha + 1} \quad (1)$$

In Equation 1, α is a factor that should be adjusted according to the system overall workload fluctuation. When using α greater than 1, one considers that the relation between the measured execution time and the estimated cost of the most recently executed task is more important than γ_{i-1} (which is the last calculated value of γ) in order to calculate a new value for γ. This is generally true in grid environment, as the environment is susceptible to constant

changes, and the former relation represents the most recently changes.

Therefore, in order to estimate the executing time of a task, the Executor Coordinator carries through the following operations:

1. Gets the estimated execution plan for the task in the local DBMS by using the EXPLAIN PLAN command (some important information that should be acquired: total query cost, CPU cost, necessary memory and the expected number of bytes in the results);

2. Allocates an executor node for the task;

3. Multiplies the task estimated cost (obtained in the local DBMS) by chosen node's γ_{i-1} factor. As a result, it will obtain the estimated *Site Execution Time* (SET) for the task;

4. Collects a *Sleep Time* (ST) parameter of the executor node that is expected to execute the task. A task's *Sleep Time* is the time that a task will have to wait until its execution starts (a task execution may have to wait due to the existence of other tasks whose execution is already scheduled or whose execution has already started - ST will only exists if one limit the number of tasks the DBMS can execute concurrently). The executor node estimates this parameter considering its current task schedule and the task's QoS requirements.

5. Estimate the elapsed time (ET) until the task execution is finished. ET is calculated as the sum of SET and ST. By comparing ET with the desired deadline, the Executor Coordinator can estimate if the site can execute the query by the desired deadline.

Then, each Executor Site Coordinator sends to the Client Site Coordinator the list of tasks (L_{Site}) its site could execute according to the specified QoS levels.

Total time for each task

For simplicity, we will consider (Δ_{Msg}) as the time spent in message communication between the client coordinator and each executor coordinator and (Δ_{Data}) the time spent to transfer result data sets between nodes. We call Δ_{Merge} the elapsed time from merge operations. This way, one can provide a rough estimate for the time to finish a task execution ($\Delta_{TaskTime}$):

$$\Delta_{TaskTime} = \Delta_{Msg} + SET + ST + \Delta_{Data} + \Delta_{Merge} \quad (2)$$

Given the $\Delta_{TaskTime}$, the Client Coordinator will decide who executes which tasks and remove the tasks from Site's task list for those that will not execute them. If there are tasks unassigned at this step, it will redistribute those tasks (as discussed in Section 3.1).

---

[2]A set of statistics (e.g. number of tuples, the distribution of the data) for the data stored at each node may be sufficient in some DBMS implementations.

4 Task Execution

After the establishment of the SLA, the Client Site Coordinator should direct to each Executor Site Coordinator the final version of the site's tasks list (L_{Site}) and a *start execution* command. Therefore, task execution may begin.

Each Executor Site Coordinator will place the received tasks in the corresponding Executor Node Task list. Besides each task, the task list also includes the estimated task execution beginning time, the estimated task execution ending time, and the estimated CPU and memory resources that are necessary in order to execute the task according to specified QoS levels. The Executor Site Coordinator sends to each executor node of its site the list of tasks the node should execute. It also sends the estimated number of bytes that the task query would return. This will be necessary in order to allocate network resources.

Whenever an Executor Node completes a task, it sends task's results for the Site Coordinator. Executor Node also sends the task's execution time to its Site Coordinator. The Executor Coordinator must use the task's execution time to adjust the corresponding γ value. The execution time will also be used to verify if it is still possible to end waiting tasks within the expected deadline. One must verify if the new estimated finish time for the hanging tasks surpasses their deadlines. If any tasks estimated end time surpasses its deadline, the Executor Coordinator should notify the Client Coordinator a QoS requirement may not be achieved.

5 Related Work

There have been some related works on distributed data warehouses. Usually, these works consider totally controlled environments, like clusters environment. On the other hand, grid technology is becoming more and more popular. Although today's typical data intensive science Grid application still uses flat files to process and store data [8], there are some works on the integration of database technology into the Grid. They consider different database related aspects, like distributed query processing and data replication strategies.

The use of the QoS in databases and related applications is discussed in more recent works. In [9] the authors discuss QoS management in web-based real-time Data Services. The work deals with two kinds of QoS requirements: deadline miss ratio of user transactions and data freshness. Data freshness is divided into database freshness and perceived freshness. The proposed approach tries to provide the perceived freshness guarantee while managing the database freshness internally.

In [1] a main memory real-time database model is considered. The paper presents a framework consisting of a model for expressing QoS requirements in terms of data and transaction preciseness. The imprecision is applied at data object and/or user transaction level. For a data object stored and representing a real-world variable, a certain degree of deviation compared to the real world is allowed. A metric called Data Error is used to indicate how much the value of a data object stored in the database deviates from the corresponding real-world.

6 Conclusions and Future Work

In this work we present Grid-DWPA, architecture for deploying large data warehouses in grid with high QoS levels. Not only the architecture provides high availability and scalability, but it also enable to deal with user-specified QoS parameters, like deadline marked queries.

We present a model to enable that the system predicts if user specified QoS requirements could be reached before executing incoming queries. We believe that the user should know in some seconds that the query will not be done by its deadline, instead of waiting many minutes to discover that.

As future work, we plan to evaluate the proposed strategies and to expand the proposed architecture by incorporating data caching mechanisms, besides enabling the use of user-defined data freshness requirements.

References

[1] M. Amirijoo, H. Hansson, and S. H. Son. Specification and management of qos in imprecise real-time databases. *ideas*, 00:192, 2003.

[2] E. Baralis, S. Paraboschi, and E. Teniente. Materialized views selection in a multidimensional database. In *VLDB*, pages 156–165. Morgan Kaufmann, 1997.

[3] S. Chaudhuri and U. Dayal. An overview of data warehousing and olap technology. *SIGMOD Record*, 26(1):65–74, 1997.

[4] P. Furtado. Experimental evidence on partitioning in parallel data warehouses. In *DOLAP '04: Procs. of the 7th ACM Internat. workshop on Data warehousing and OLAP*, pages 23–30, 2004.

[5] P. Furtado. Hierarchical aggregation in networked data management. In *Euro-Par*, volume 3648 of *Lecture Notes in Computer Science*, pages 360–369, 2005.

[6] P. Furtado. Replication in node partitioned data warehouses. In *VLDB Workshop on Design, Implementation, and Deployment of Database Replication (DIDDR)*, 2005.

[7] J. Gray, A. Bosworth, A. Layman, and H. Pirahesh. Data cube: A relational aggregation operator generalizing group-by, cross-tab, and sub-total. In *ICDE*, pages 152–159, 1996.

[8] M. A. Nieto-Santisteban, J. Gray, A. Szalay, J. Annis, A. R. Thakar, and W. O'Mullane. When database systems meet the grid. In *CIDR*, pages 154–161, 2005.

[9] S. H. Son and K.-D. Kang. Qos management in web-based real-time data services. In *WECWIS '02: Procs. of the Fourth IEEE Internat. Workshop on Advanced Issues of E-Commerce and Web-Based Information Systems (WECWIS'02)*, page 129, 2002.

Examining the Performance of a Constraint-Based Database Cache

Andreas Bühmann   Joachim Klein

Databases and Information Systems, Department of Computer Science
University of Kaiserslautern, P. O. Box 3049, 67653 Kaiserslautern, Germany
buehmann@informatik.uni-kl.de   jklein@informatik.uni-kl.de

Abstract

Constraint-based database caching aims at correctly answering SQL query predicates from a local cache database by exploiting constraints that have previously been used in selecting sets of records to be cached from a remote database.

In this paper, we take our first steps in looking at performance aspects of our prototype Adaptive Constraint-based Cache (ACCache), which is realized in a middleware manner on top of regular databases. Within our measurement setup, the initial focus is on two central ACCache functions: query processing and cache loading. To demonstrate their time behavior and interaction, we have chosen a scenario based on the TPC-W specification. We conclude with a discussion of our first measurement results.

1. Motivation

Applications that interact with real-world users typically strive for good (or at least acceptable) response times. This is a particular challenge if the application routinely relies on the services of a central backend database (DB) system that is located far from the application, e. g., in a Web scenario where application servers have been spread around the world at the "edge" of the Web to reduce their (network) distance to the users. In this scenario with usually a large number of users, relieving the backend system of some of its load becomes equally important.

Caching is a means to approach these two aims: By intercepting requests to a remote system component and constructing responses locally (from earlier responses or prefetched data), communication costs to and processing costs on the remote component can be saved. Caching can be performed on various levels within an information-system infrastructure: For example, generated Web pages (or fragments thereof) can be cached, persistent objects within an application server, or pages of a database in a DB buffer.

Database caching is located at the level of logical data structures (such as tables and records in a relational DB) and higher query languages (such as SQL). The goal is to have a cache in the path from the application to the backend DB that is as transparent as possible and that is able to process SQL queries locally based on locally stored parts of the backend DB. The constraint-based approach to database caching maintains a selection of cache tables, each containing a subset of records of the corresponding backend table. Cache constraints restrict what constitutes a valid state of the cache such that deciding what is in the cache and which predicates can be answered becomes easy.

2. Constraint-based Database Caching

In the general database-caching scenario, there are a backend (BE) database, which holds all data, and one or more cache databases, which contain varying subsets of that data. Ideally, the cache databases would contain data needed often in the nearer future.

With our model of constraint-based DB caching, *cache groups* are used to describe what data is to be kept in the cache and what constraints the cache contents have to fulfill at any time. These constraints can later be utilized to reason about whether a query can be (partly) answered from the cache.

For selected backend tables T_B, a cache group includes a corresponding cache table T with the same schema, i. e., for each column $T_B.c$ in the backend table there is a column $T.c$ of same type (incl. unique constraints) in the cache table. (Foreign key constraints are not copied into the cache.)

2.1. Completeness and Constraints

For DB caching, *completeness* is a most important concept: Having all the records that are needed to evaluate a certain predicate in the cache is known under the term *predicate completeness* [4]. Completeness of more complex predicates is achieved by starting with completeness of very simple equality predicates and extending them with the help of cache constraints.

Equality predicates (EPs) of the type $T.c = v$, where v is a value of column $T.c$, are supported by the completeness of v. This value v is *complete* in a cache column $T.c$ if all records from T_B that have this value in c are in the cache (in T).

A *referential cache constraint (RCC)* is a value-based relationship between two columns: a source column $S.a$ and a target column $T.b$. An RCC $S.a \rightarrow T.b$ guarantees that every value in $S.a$ (in the cache!) is complete in $T.b$. This allows an equi-join (EJ) $S.a = T.b$ to be performed in the cache, once it has been verified that the needed S records (specified by other predicates such as $S.b = v$) are in the cache.

Basically, this procedure allows us to deal with predicates of the form $EP \wedge EJ_1 \wedge EJ_2 \wedge \cdots \wedge EJ_n$ in the cache, where all of the equi-joins EJ and the equality predicate EP_i are connected via some tables. More complex predicates that can be constructed from this simple type by con-/disjunction and by further restrictions could also be processed in the cache.

2.2. Probing and Query Execution

When a query reaches the cache, it has to be decided whether the query can be answered partially in the cache and what part of the query result must be fetched from the backend. Deciding on the completeness of a (partial) predicate in the cache is done in two phases:

1. For each equality predicate $T.c = v$, which compares a column $T.c$ to a value v, completeness of v is decided by *probing* the cache.
2. Starting from complete values providing entry points for the query into the cache, RCCs $S.a \rightarrow T.b$ matching equality predicates of type $S.a = T.b$ in the query predicate are then used to extend the completeness to the largest predicate possible.

Probing works by issuing simple existence queries for values in some columns: You might know from prior analysis that all values in a cache column are complete (column completeness [4]), or you can leverage the RCCs by probing in their source columns. Either way, the existence of a value implies its completeness in a (possibly different) column.

Once the partial predicate that is complete in the cache has been found, it is clear that, for the tables referenced in that predicate, their cache counterparts can be used for executing the query. For the remaining tables, the original table at the backend must be accessed.

2.3. Loading and Unloading

Records are loaded into the cache whenever there is a hint that they will be needed in the future. *Filling columns* are responsible for providing these hints: As soon as specific value v of a filling column f is referenced in a query, v is made complete in the cache and fulfilling RCCs make sure that a "neighborhood" of related records becomes available in the cache, too.

Loading is guided by the graph of RCCs: The sets of records to be inserted in the cache can be determined by following the RCCs Usually, records inserted into the source table of an RCC demand matching records to be loaded into the target table. The actual insertion of those record sets into the cache tables may be performed in the reverse order (bottom-up) to provide more consistent cache states during the loading and thus better concurrency with readers [2].

Unloading aims at reversing the process of loading but has to cope with added difficulties due to records being required via multiple RCCs.

2.4. Prototype ACCache

Our prototype implementation of the techniques just sketched is called ACCache (Adaptive Constraint-based Cache) [2]. It employs a middleware strategy to realize the behavior of the database cache on top of two regular databases (backend and cache) that are accessed via JDBC: Probing, (un)loading, and maintenance of RCCs are done via (prepared) SQL statements. Query processing leverages the federated-query functionality of the underlying database management system to be able to access backend as well as cache tables within a single SQL query that is a rewrite of the original user query. (To the outside, ACCache implements a JDBC interface.)

Data to be unloaded from the cache is chosen based on access statistics, but the unloading itself is not performed yet. At our current stage, we start out with an empty cache and consider only a number of loading operations and their influence on query performance.

Adaptiveness comes in two facets in ACCache: First, ACCache adapts its contents to the query workload on the instance level, i. e., only useful sets of records that will be used in the future are kept in the cache. Second, we are planning to make ACCache adaptive on the schema level: The cache group definition may be adapted, i. e., cache tables or RCCs may be added or dropped if monitoring the workload provides hints at often used join directions or at data that is often used together (either in the same query or in multiple queries that occur closely together in time).

291

In the current implementation, the cache system is responsible for initiating the necessary loading actions and for deciding what data has to be loaded. This approach guarantees that the backend is not additionally burdened. Besides, for each incoming query, the probing has to be performed. In the following sections, we would like to check the behavior and the performance aspects of these two main cache functions. This allows us to reflect on our design decisions later on.

3. Measurement Setup

It is a well-known fact that caching dramatically improves the performance of query processing under heavy workloads and high network latency. Therefore, our main goal is not to prove this fact again, even though this is observable in our measurements, of course. We want to measure the behavior and the overhead of the main functions implemented in our cache system (probing and loading). It is not overly urgent to verify the overhead of these functions separately. On the contrary, we should look at them together and especially at the interactions between the backend and cache database under the anticipated high latency.

Measurements with a setup where there is almost no latency give us only a feeling of how much overhead the cache system generates. The more interesting part is to analyze how much time the loading process takes to enable a significant caching effect as soon as the needed data is available in the cache: Such results can help to improve the way data is loaded into the cache. In addition, the results can assist us in finding optimization rules so that we can improve the adaptivity of the cache system. For example, assuming we implement advanced loading methods, it will be possible to switch the loading method automatically to the appropriate implementation dependent on the observed latency.

3.1. Capturing Measured Values

For performing measurements in the ACCache system, we use a framework developed in-house [5]. It supports a developer in setting up and executing measurements for a distributed system. The framework's components offer a wide range of functionality for measuring distributed structures.

In our measurement framework we use a *working node* to represent an application within the distributed system we want to measure: For our first measurement, we have built three working nodes representing the backend database system, the ACCache system, and a simulated client, which generates the workload during the measurement (see also Fig. 1). To capture values from an application represented by a working node, an observer needs to be defined. The captured values are associated with *execution contexts* that model their semantics and dependencies among each other.

For our ACCache measurements, our overall setup including the measured components (square boxes) as well as the measuring components (curved boxes), which are spread over four separate network nodes, is shown in Fig. 1. It also sketches two of our parameters that will be explained in the following: network delay and cache bypass.

3.2. Parameters

As it is difficult for us to actually maintain and use a backend DB in some remote part of the world, we employ a network emulator to approximate the characteristics of the network between backend and cache: NetEm is an enhancement of the traffic control facilities of the Linux kernel that allows adding delay, packet loss and other scenarios. [3]

The round-trip delay inherent in our real network between backend and cache node is about 0.2 ms. During our measurements we raised this round-trip delay by an amount of $\mu \pm \sigma$ according to a normal distribution with a standard deviation of $\sigma = \mu/10$ and a correlation $\rho = 25\%$. The mean round-trip delay μ was chosen from 0, 40, and 100 ms.

3.3. Backend Schema and Cache Group

As a baseline, we performed all measurements a second time with our cache still in the path from client to backend but with the main caching functionality bypassed (i. e., no query analysis, probing, rewriting, etc., were performed but every query was immediately executed at the backend). In this case, our cache acted as a kind of forwarding proxy.

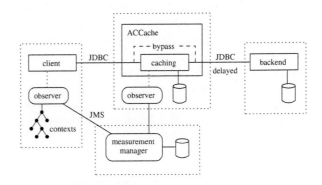

Figure 1. Measurement setup on four nodes: client, ACCache, backend, and measurement manager

The scenario for our measurements is loosely based on the TPC-W benchmark [8], which models an online store. We use its database schema (with tables for customers, orders, items, etc.) and data in the backend DB (100000 items).

As a cache group, we use the one given in Fig. 2, which ensures that for any order loaded into the cache the corresponding order lines, addresses, and items are loaded, too. Furthermore, every item loaded into the cache will be accompanied by its author. Orders and items get into the cache only if referenced specifically by their primary keys (*id* columns).

3.4. Queries: Order Display

The queries that we pose to the cache are inspired by the web interaction "order display" of TPC-W. First of all, we display the details of a selected order including the referenced addresses:

```
select O.id, O.c_id, O.status, O.date,
       O.total, bill.*, ship.*
from orders O, address bill, address ship
where (O.bill_addr_id = bill.id)
  and (O.id = ⟨order id⟩)
  and (O.ship_addr_id = ship.id)
```

We then need a listing of all order lines belonging to that order where we include some basic information on the ordered items:

```
select OL.id, OL.qty, OL.discount,
       OL.comments, I.id, I.title, I.desc
from order_line OL, item I
where (OL.o_id = ⟨order id⟩)
  and (OL.i_id = I.id)
```

Finally, we simulate the user requesting the item details for each displayed order line in turn with multiple instances of the following statement.

```
select I.*, A.*
from item I, author A
where (I.id = ⟨item id⟩) and (I.a_id = A.id)
```

3.5. Measured Values

We designed two observers (for the client and cache), which transmit measured values to the manager. On the client, we have only a single execution context for executing a query. For each query, we capture three timestamps: before the query processing starts, when the first row of the query result has been fetched (first-row time), and after fetching and printing all resulting rows (all-rows time).

For the cache, we built the execution contexts "query", "analysis", and "load". In the query context, we capture the start and end timestamp of the query

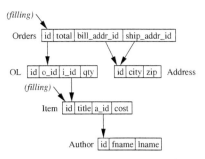

Figure 2. A cache group for the TPC-W schema [8] (with five cache tables, two filling columns $O.id$ **and** $I.id$**, and five RCCs)**

processing and a reference to the client query execution context that caused the execution on the ACCache system. One of the parts of processing a query is the analysis phase (probing, query rewriting). Therefore, an analysis context is created as a child context of the query and the start and the end of this phase are captured. Furthermore, the analysis phase might decide that tuples should be loaded into the cache: Each loading job created within our system is mirrored into a load execution context. This execution context captures the start and end timestamps and, additionally, the pair of column and value that is the starting point for the loading job.

Timestamps are retrieved with Java's `nanoTime` method, which has an accuracy of about ± 3 µs on our nodes. This means that the error in calculated durations will be twice that much and thus is negligible (compared with durations of about 30 ms and more).

4. Results

In our concrete setup, we executed the work unit "order display" five times in a row per measurement run without any delays between the queries: After displaying an order (O) and the retrieval of the corresponding order lines (OL), all of the related five items (I) were accessed. This work unit was then repeated for the very same order id.

As described above, we varied the round-trip delay between backend and cache and enabled or disabled our cache bypass: The six resulting configurations were repeated three times each, resulting in 18 measurement runs in total.

Figure 3 shows the average times spent on reading and displaying the query results in all measurement runs. The actual measured values lie within about ± 10 ms around this average. Figure 4 shows the timing and the duration of client queries and load operations at

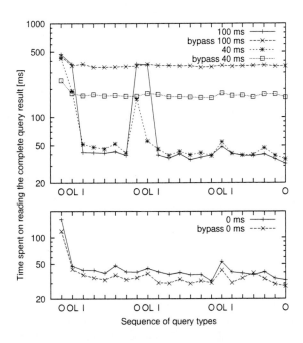

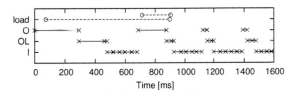

Figure 3. Query execution times as perceived by the client

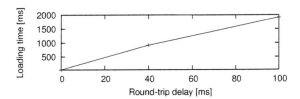

Figure 5. Cache loading times (for an order plus dependent records)

(and usable) in the cache before the order itself does. As can be seen in Fig. 4, the loading is complete shortly after the second O query (which corresponds to the second set of peaks in Fig. 3); from then on, all following queries benefit from the cache contents.

For reference, the lower part of Fig. 3 shows the measurement runs with no latency (0 ms). The difference between the runs with and without bypass clearly identifies the overhead inherent in our cache processing steps: Without delay (i. e., with a non-remote backend database), the cache needs 5 to 10 ms more time to answer a query than in the bypassing scenario. This is caused by the analysis phase and in particular the probing, which is always performed if a query could potentially be executed in the cache. When the delay increases, the costs involved in the probing are more than compensated by the savings due to the avoidance of remote accesses to the backend.

Figure 5 shows how the time needed to load the requested order into the cache and to fulfill the RCCs by loading dependent records changes with the (network) distance between cache and backend DB. As can be seen, the loading time increases almost linearly with the round-trip delay. With 0 ms delay, the cache is loaded almost instantly (after 37 ms); with a delay of 100 ms, it takes 2 s. This might mean that in some cases the cached data could be available too late to answer queries that have occurred in the meantime.

You might wonder why there are two loading operations in Fig. 4, which actually refer to the same order. The second loading operation is initiated at a time (ca. 700 ms) when the first operation has not yet succeeded in loading the order into the cache. When this first operation finishes at about 900 ms, a quick check suffices to see that there is not any work left. (Loading operations are executed strictly sequentially at the moment.)

From this behavior, we can draw the conclusion that we should look into other ways of performing the cache loading. Moreover, we need to know or make assumptions about typical workloads and the delay between queries associated to each other via data locality; only then can we decide whether our loading is fast enough or whether loading should be coupled with

Figure 4. Query execution/loading times and sequence of events (round-trip 40 ms, no bypass)

the cache in a selected measurement run with a round-trip delay of 40 ms where the cache is not bypassed. The crosses mark significant points of time within the processing of a query, namely start of the query, the first-row time, and the all-rows time. However, these are only visible separately in the case of an order-line query (OL). The other queries deliver only one row, which makes first-row time and all-rows time almost coincide.

As expected, the cache dramatically improves the response time of the queries if the cache loading for the order under consideration has finished. Interestingly, the cache can already be used to process the first five item queries when the loading has not yet finished (compare Figs. 3 and 4). This is due to the fact that, in the current implementation, loading is performed bottom-up (as sketched in Sect. 2.3). That is, with our cache group, loading starts at the author and address tables and proceeds to the orders table. Therefore, the items related to the order requested become available

query execution (i. e., data would simultaneously be used to answer a query and load the cache).

5. Related Work

Meanwhile, the most important database vendors IBM, Microsoft and Oracle have developed their own approaches to database caching in addition to existing replication methods. Recent development has shown that using cache groups is one of the standard approaches. IBM and Oracle both allow sub-table-level caching via cache groups in their prototypes/products (DBCache from IBM, Times Ten In-Memory Database from Oracle). IBM measured its prototype's functionality [1] and showed that the overhead of probing and loading has low significance: The response time increases only by up to 6 % for join queries. This result compares to our observation (with a latency of 0 ms). But the influence of high latency between backend and cache on the loading process is not discussed.

For the Oracle In-Memory Database TimesTen, we did not find any significant measurements. For the timing values given in the technical whitepaper [7], it is unclear to which tested functionalities they refer exactly.

Microsoft has built a caching solution called MT-Cache [6]. This solution does not use the concept of cache groups as its basis. Instead, materialized views are used together with standard replication methods to build a cache mechanism. Keeping subsets of base tables in the cache in a way similar to a cache group can be modeled via stacking views. Since the presented measurements of the MTCache system aim at the performance of the entire system, they cannot be directly compared with our measurements. Anyway, there is no description of the cache functions' behavior when a significant latency to the backend database exists.

6. Conclusion

We have subjected our ACCache prototype to a first series of measurements to get an indication of its potentials. Our results are encouraging: Already with small delays to the backend database server, our constraint-based cache is able to save query processing time, even for queries that are only related to an initiating query: Expected locality in database accesses can be conveniently modeled through cache groups, especially with cache constraints like RCCs that define an environment of related tuples.

The observed time spent on loading all needed data into the cache, which depends linearly on the latency between cache and backend, could become a problem if the latency is too high. Because we can expect a

high bandwidth, another possibility to load data into the cache is, for example, to compose a single package of data related to a cache miss at the backend database: Then the backend database is responsible for resolving all RCC dependencies. But as an advantage, all of the data dependent on a cache miss can be transferred at once (perhaps bundled with the result of the initiating query) and just a notification of the cache miss may be sent to the backend.

This idea of improving the loading process, which directly results from our measurements, shows that analyzing the effects of latency cannot be neglected as earlier analyses of caching products tended to do (cf. Sect. 5). High latency is one of the fundamental assumptions in scenarios that caching is designed for; hence, there is no point in performing measurements in no-delay setups.

We also learned from these measurements that setting up a general, automated measurement environment for a distributed system is a complex and time-consuming task. But after all, the possibility of designing well-suited execution contexts for tracing the work performed on the working nodes and their dependencies will assist us in setting up future measurement runs more quickly.

References

[1] M. Altinel, C. Bornhövd, et al. Cache tables: Paving the way for an adaptive database cache. In *VLDB*, 718–729, 2003.

[2] A. Bühmann, T. Härder, et al. A middleware-based approach to database caching. In Y. Manolopoulos, J. Pokorný, et al., eds., *ADBIS 2006*, vol. 4152 of *LNCS*, 182–199. Thessaloniki, 2006.

[3] S. Hemminger. Network emulation with NetEm. In *Proceedings of linux.conf.au (LCA)*. Canberra, 2005.

[4] T. Härder, A. Bühmann. Value complete, column complete, predicate complete – Magic words driving the design of cache groups. *VLDB Journal*, 2007. Online First, http://dx.doi.org/10.1007/s00778-006-0035-9.

[5] J. Klein. Development of an automated measurement environment for the constraint-based database caching (in German). Master's thesis, TU Kaiserslautern, 2006. http://wwwdvs.informatik.uni-kl.de/pubs/DAsPAs/Kle06.DA.html.

[6] P. Larson, J. Goldstein, et al. MTCache: Transparent midtier database caching in SQL server. In *ICDE*, 177–189. IEEE Computer Society, 2004.

[7] Oracle. Oracle TimesTen Product and Technologies. White paper, 2007. http://www.oracle.com/technology/products/timesten/pdf/wp/wp_timesten_t%ech.pdf.

[8] TPC. TPC benchmark W (web commerce) specification. http://www.tpc.org/tpcw/spec/tpcw_V1.8.pdf, 2002. Version 1.8.

Kruskal's Algorithm for Query Tree Optimization

Pryscila Barvik Guttoski
Universidade Federal do Parana
Departamento de Informatica
Curitiba, Brazil
guttoski@gmail.com

Marcos Sfair Sunye
Universidade Federal do Parana
Departamento de Informatica
Curitiba, Brazil
sunye@c3sl.ufpr.br

Fabiano Silva
Universidade Federal do Parana
Departamento de Informatica
Curitiba, Brazil
fabiano@c3sl.ufpr.br

Abstract

This paper describes an implementation of Kruskal's algorithm in query optimization process for generation of a near optimal execution query tree. The open source PostgreSQL DBMS was used in the experiments since its query optimization is performed by Dynamic Programming and Genetic algorithm, which allows a concrete comparison with our approach. Kruskal's algorithm presents some advantages like its simplified code, its polynomial-time execution and the reduced search space to generate only one query tree, that will be the optimal tree. In most experiments, Kruskal's algorithm got the expected results in almost the same time as the results achieved by default PostgreSQL's optimization algorithms. The results confirm that Kruskal's algorithm is a feasible method for query optimization.

1. Introduction

The query optimization purpose is to retrieve the information as quick as possible. One of the most used methods to determine the join sequence in query optimization process is Dynamic Programming algorithm, proposed in System-R by [12]. In this algorithm, for a given query, all possible query execution trees are constructed and evaluated through an exhausting search over the points of search space. In each step, high cost trees are eliminated and in the end of the execution, only the lowest cost tree is kept as the optimal solution. The final tree is used to retrieve the information from database. This method explores all possible execution plans, consequently can indicate the optimal execution tree. However, the amount of possible execution plans increases exponentially with the number of relations in a query, and the execution time and space necessary to generate all possible plans become impracticable. The query optimization problem is NP-complete, as proven by [7].

As the time and space complexity in Dynamic Programming is exponential, some algorithms were developed to produce a good join order in polynomial time, like Heuristic, Randomized and Greedy algorithms. They are used to optimize queries with high number of relations, finding sub-optimal solutions in acceptable amount of time. These methods have lower execution cost, however there is no guarantee that a good solution will be found. Therefore, developing an algorithm which is able to find a sub-optimal solution in a reasonable time means to create an extremely efficient query optimizer.

This paper presents a Kruskal's Algorithm implementation in query optimization process, to determine the join sequence that has the lowest cost and to find the best query execution tree. Among the existing algorithms, the Greedy Algorithm of Kruskal was chosen because of its simple code and adequacy of its definition to the query optimization process. The availability and clarity of the PostgreSQL source code [1] were fundamental to the successful implementation of Kruskal's algorithm and observation of its behavior in a real database environment.

This paper is organized in sessions as follows: Section 2 describes the query optimization method studied in this research, presenting the reasons why the Kruskal's algorithm was the chosen method. Details of the Kruskal's implementation in the PostgreSQL DBMS are presented in Section 3. Section 4 presents the experiments with Kruskal's algorithm in the query optimizer and compares this method with other ones. Finally, Section 5 contains the conclusions and the future works.

2. Case Study: Kruskal's Algorithm

Greedy algorithms find the *minimum spanning tree* of a graph, which is a tree that connects all the vertices of a graph and the total cost of its edges is minimized. In query optimization, the optimal query execution plan can be described as a *minimum spanning tree* of the graph that represents the query.

296

Kruskal and Prim are Greedy algorithms and their implementation are simple due to their reduced code size. They are polynomial-time algorithms, presenting lower complexity than Dynamic Programming. On the other hand, greedy algorithms take the best immediate solution in each step, without regarding future consequences, and sometimes produces a solution that may not be the best one. Comparing Kruskal's and Prim's algorithms, Kruskal's algorithm presents the most adequate way to build the final solution in the query optimization process, because when the most profitable joins are performed first, the joins that will be formed after are going to have their cost reduced, mainly joins between tables with high number of tuples. Moreover, algorithms similar to Kruskal's algorithm were presented in others query optimization researches. The KBZ is a heuristic join ordering algorithm proposed by [10]. It finds the tree with the lowest product of edge weights, which is the *minimum spanning tree* of a cyclic join graph, and also presents good results for star queries. [8] has introduced an efficient rank-join order heuristic to help to choose a near-optimal join order. [5] has presented a polynomial-time greedy algorithm called GOO that generates good quality plans for object-oriented queries.

In our approach, the queries are represented as a graph where the edges *(i,j)* are weighted with the cost of the join between i and j. The cost is based on system statistics about tables and their attributes, like number and size in bytes of tuples, cardinality and selectivity.

The algorithm starts calculating the join cost between two relations and continues until all the possible pairs of relations have their costs calculated. After that, the join with lowest cost is chosen and the edge *(i,j)* that represents it is included in the query execution tree. If two or more joins have the same cost, one of them is chosen in a random manner. In the next step, the join with the second lowest cost is chosen and evaluated whether it can be included or not in the query execution tree. This evaluation guarantees that an edge will not be added in the query execution tree if it forms a cycle in the graph. The algorithm keeps searching to the next join with lowest cost that was not analyzed yet. Then the evaluation is made and the join can be included in the tree or not. This step is repeated until all the relations of the query have been included into the query execution tree, resulting in the final query plan.

3. Kruskal's Algorithm Implementation on PostgreSQL

For a practical study of Kruskal's algorithm in query optimizer, we choose the PostgreSQL open source DBMS. PostgreSQL was chosen because has several features, making possible the optimization evaluation for complex queries. Another reason for this choice is a problem de-

tected in PostgreSQL query rewrite by [4]. The optimizer did not simplify clauses *where* that had *OR* operations duplicated and the query was not executed, presenting response-timeout interval exceeded. After the manual query rewrite, the result was given in a feasible time. Although the error have been corrected by PostgreSQL developer community in [3], this fact indicated that PostgreSQL optimizer is not totally efficient yet, demonstrating a certain fragility in its query rewrite.

A detailed evaluation of PostgreSQL's algorithm and the developed Kruskal's algorithm was possible because of PostgreSQL code availability. The PostgreSQL query optimizer is composed by two distinct methods to generate the execution plan of the queries: Dynamic Programming and Genetic algorithm called GEQO.

The main method uses Dynamic Programming Algorithm, performing a near-exhaustive search over the possible strategies space, as described by [6]. This algorithm is based on the System-R and is very similar to the algorithm described by [11]. This method is mostly used by queries with less than 11 relations because it can take an enormous amount of time and memory space when the number of joins in the query grows large. First, for each individual relation, all the possible plans that perform a scan in the relation are generated. If the query has only one relation, the plans created are compared and the cheapest is chosen. For queries with more than one relation, the next step is generate plans to perform the joins between two relations. All the possible join operations between a pair of relations are created. If the query has more than two relations, the next step consists in making the join between one of the tables that are not yet in the plan and a join done previously. This step is repeated until all the relations of the query have been included in the execution plan. Different execution sequences are analyzed and the cheapest one is chosen. The final result can be represented by a binary tree that indicates the order in which the physical operations must be executed.

The *Genetic Query Optimization* module (GEQO) was implemented by [13] and allows the PostgreSQL query optimizer to support large join queries through a non-exhaustive search. The GEQO is used automatically in PostgreSQL for queries with 12 or more relations. It is a heuristic optimization method which operates through non-deterministic, randomized search. The set of possible solutions for the optimization problem is considered as a population of individuals. The adaptation degree of an individual to its environment is specified by its fitness. Through simulation of the evolutionary operations recombination, mutation and selection, new generations of search points that show a higher average fitness than their ancestors are found. However, according with [13] it is not clear that solving query optimization with a genetic algorithm designed for traveling salesman problem (TSP) is appropriate. In the

TSP case, the cost associated with any partial tour is independent of the rest of the tour, but this is certainly not true for query optimization. Thus is questionable if edge recombination crossover is the most effective mutation procedure.

The Kruskal's algorithm for query optimization was developed in C/C++, to keep the compatibility with PostgreSQL modules. The *function call* to Kruskal's algorithm was included in the PostgreSQL optimizer function that starts GEQO and regular optimizers. *RelOptInfo* is the PostgreSQL data structure that represents both base relations (single tables) and join relations. This structure was also used in Kruskal's function.

A *RelOptInfo* structure is created for all possible joins between pairs of tables, and the possible physical join methods are added in this structure as *paths*. If the pair does not contain join clause (*where*) between the relations, one *path* representing the Cartesian product is generated. The estimate cost for each *path* is calculated by the PostgreSQL's module, using the optimizer tables statistics. If the query has only two tables, the cheapest *path* is chosen and returned to the initial PostgreSQL's function. Otherwise, the Kruskal's algorithm in fact begins.

In Kruskal's function, an *array* with all the relations pairs is created and sorted by the estimate join costs. At each iteration, the lowest cost join is evaluated. If the addition of this join does not generate a cycle in the final execution tree, it must be added to the solution tree. Otherwise, this join is discarded and a new iteration starts, until all relations of the query have been into the final execution tree.

The Kruskal's algorithm can build *left-deep trees*, *right-deep trees* and *bushy trees*. As this algorithm generates *bushy trees*, the amount of possible solutions increases, since there are a larger set of possible trees shapes. The results achieved by [9] have led to the conclusion that query optimization in the space of both *deep and bushy trees* is easier than in the space of only *left-deep trees*, since the bushy shape provides more strategies as alternatives, what would produce outputs of better quality as well.

The final execution tree is generated in the *result_rels* list. In the beginning of the algorithm, *result_rels* is empty and the *RelOptInfo* that represents the first join chosen is added to this list. To determine how will occur the join between *n* relations, from the second join approved for addition into the tree, an evaluation needs to be done. Both relations of the pair which is candidate to be added are compared with the relations that have already been in the *result_rels* list, and three situations can occur:

- The relations *(i,j)* that are in the join which is candidate to be added have not been in any other join of *result_rels*. In this case, the *RelOptInfo* of the new join *(i,j)* is added to *result_rels*.

- The two relations *(i,j)* that are in the join which is can-

didate to be added have already been in other joins *(i,x)* and *(j,y)* of *result_rels*. In this case, the join between *RelOptInfo* structures of *(i,x)* and *(j,y)* that are in *result_rels* list is performed, resulting one new *RelOptInfo* representing *join(join(i,x),join(j,y))*. This new *RelOptInfo* is a *bushy tree* that is added to the *result_rels* list, while *RelOptInfo* that represents joins *(i,x)* and *(j,y)* are removed from the list.

- One of the relations *(i,j)* that is in the join which is candidate to be added have already been in another join *(i,x)* of *result_rels*. In this case, the join between the *RelOptInfo* of *(i,x)* that is in *result_rels* and the *RelOptInfo* of the base relation *(j)* is performed, resulting one *RelOptInfo* of *join(join(i,x),j)*, that is a *left-deep tree*. This new structure is added to the *result_rels* list while *RelOptInfo* that represents *join(i,x)* is removed from the list.

In the end of the algorithm, the *RelOptInfo* with the final execution tree, which is considered the optimal solution and contains all the relations of the query, will be in *result_rels*. This final plan is returned to the initial PostgreSQL's function to be executed.

4. Results

The implementation and the experiments have been done in a computer with processor Intel Pentium III - 800 MHz with 256KB integrated cache, 256MB of memory SDRAM 100MHz and operational system Debian Linux 3.1 (Sarge) with kernel Linux 2.4.27 i686. The PostgreSQL used was 8.2devel, which has a large code rewrite in query optimizer module comparing to PostgreSQL 8.1, providing more clarity in the implementation.

The PostgreSQL's code is organized in modules and only *allpath.c* was modified to add the *function call* to the Kruskal's algorithm in PostgreSQL query optimizer, in *make_rel_from_joinlist()* function. If the Kruskal's algorithm should be used, the boolean variable *enable_kruskal* is set to *true* at the beginning of the *allpath.c*.

The PostgreSQL tool *psql*, that is a terminal-based frontend to PostgreSQL, was used to type in queries interactively, issue them to PostgreSQL and check the query results. The *timing* parameter was set to *true* to show the amount of time necessary to retrieve the data.

4.1 Kruskal's Algorithm Validation

The purpose of the first test was to validate the Kruskal's algorithm feasibility in PostgreSQL query optimization. We expected as result an execution plan with the same format of the execution plans generated by standard PostgreSQL's algorithms.

```
SELECT mat_id
FROM  material, objeto, estado;

            QUERY PLAN KRUSKAL
--------------------------------------------------------------------
Nested Loop  (cost=41558.35..2686568549.17 rows=114719400000 width=4)
 -> Seq Scan on material  (cost=0.00..1088.82 rows=67482 width=4)
 -> Materialize  (cost=41558.35..64369.35 rows=1700000 width=0)
    -> Nested Loop  (cost=23.75..34047.35 rows=1700000 width=0)
       -> Seq Scan on objeto  (cost=0.00..23.60 rows=1360 width=0)
       -> Materialize  (cost=23.75..36.25 rows=1250 width=0)
          -> Seq Scan on estado  (cost=0.00..22.50 rows=1250 width=0)
```

Figure 1. The execution plan generated by the Kruskal's algorithm.

The first query executed by Kruskal's algorithm is shown in Figure 1, with three tables and no join clauses. The table *object* has 15 rows, the table *status* has 5 rows and the table *material* has 70259 rows, therefore the join between the two smaller tables should happen first and after occur the join between the third table and the first join result. The execution plan generated by the Kruskal's algorithm demonstrates that Kruskal's algorithm works as expected and is shown in Figure 1.

The output of Kruslkal's algorithm is shown in Figure 2. The following steps have been observed in the Kruskal's algorithm execution:

- First, the estimated costs for each possible joins are calculated. *join(material, object), join(material, status) and join(object, status)*

- After that, it is evaluated if the join will be reject or add to the execution tree, starting with the lowest cost *join(object, status)*. The first join is always included.

- Then, the next join from the list (*join(material, status)*) is evaluated and one of its tables (*status*) is in the join added previously. In this case, the *join(object, status)* is removed from the list and a new join between base relation *material* and *join(object, status)* is generated and added to the list.

- Finally, the last *join(material, object)* is discarded because if it had been included, it would form a cycle in the tree .

4.2 Comparison between Optimization Methods

The TPC-H methodology [2], developed by Transaction Processing Performance Council (TPC), is a bench-

```
Kruskal's algorithm begin

NumEdge = 0, edgeTail = 1, edgeHead = 3, edgeWeight = 2204572.500000
NumEdge = 1, edgeTail = 1, edgeHead = 2, edgeWeight = 2398574.000000
NumEdge = 2, edgeTail = 2, edgeHead = 3, edgeWeight = 46522.500000

tail: 2, head: 3, cost: 46522.500000 > included
The first edge is always included.

tail: 1, head: 3, cost: 2204572.500000 > included
Rel2: 3 is already been in the final tree.
The left-join between single rel 1 and join (2,3) is made.

tail: 1, head: 2, cost: 2398574.000000 > discarded

cheapest->total_cost = 2998234522.500000 num_relids = 3
Kruskal's algorithm end
```

Figure 2. The output of Kruslkal's algorithm.

mark that measures performance of decision support systems, like data warehouse, data mining and business intelligence. The TPC-H defines a synthetic database and a set of queries with high complexity degree to evaluate DBMS features in large data volumes. TPC-H was used to comparing the algorithms performance and *dbgen* tool was used to populate the database tables. The TPC-H contains data scales from 1GB up to 1TB. In this work, we used the 1GB data scale because the goal was to evaluate the difference between the algorithms and not the databases performance in a wide scale.

There are 22 decision support queries in TPC-H benchmark. These queries have high complexity degree and different access types. They examine a large percentage of the data available and include diverse databases operations. Their parameters are modified every each execution and the *qgen* tool was used to generate them. The *power test*, which measures the execution time of each query, was executed for a single user. The 22 queries had been executed 10 times sequentially, using Kruskal's and PostgreSQL default's algorithms.

The TPC-H queries do not have the minimum number of tables necessary to activate GEQO algorithm, therefore only the near-exhaustive search algorithm could be compared with Kruskal's algorithm by TPC-H. Other queries have been created to test the difference between GEQO and Kruskal's algorithm and will be presented later in this Section.

The query Q8 could not be executed by Kruskal's algorithm due to an error that locked up the database unexpectedly. The comparison could not be done and the error was not analyzed in this work.

The majority of the queries have gotten the same execution plan by Kruskal's algorithm and by PostgreSQL's default algorithm. There are 13 queries in this situation and results are shown in Table 1, as described below:

- eight queries (Q1, Q3, Q6, Q13, Q14, Q15, Q17, Q19)

Queries TPC-H	Average execution time (ms)	
	Kruskal's alg.	Default alg.
Q1	58.269	59.075
Q3	30.695	31.414
Q4	97.470	94.735
Q6	57.025	57.039
Q11	9.863	9.503
Q12	30.864	30.501
Q13	57.904	58.250
Q14	56.805	57.142
Q15	57.499	57.853
Q16	21.132	20.938
Q17	56.900	57.027
Q19	57.857	58.377
Q22	timeout	timeout

Table 1. Comparison between the average execution time by Kruskal's and PostgreSQL default's algorithms, for queries which presented the same execution plan in both algorithms.

Queries TPC-H	Average execution time (ms)	
	Kruskal's alg.	Default alg.
Q2	24.500	15.603
Q5	30.865	30.859
Q7	30.675	30.582
Q9	30.945	30.429
Q10	30.708	30.680
Q18	31.152	30.511
Q20	205	timeout
Q21	30.674	30.438

Table 2. Comparison between the average execution time by Kruskal's and PostgreSQL default's algorithms, for queries which presented different execution plans in each algorithm.

have gotten the average execution time a little lower when executed by the Kruskal's algorithm, because this algorithm does not generate as many solutions in the search space as Dynamic Programming Algorithm and a lower time is needed to indicate the solution.

- four queries (Q4, Q11, Q12, Q16) have gotten a lower average execution time by the PostgreSQL's default algorithm. The query Q4 was the one that has presented the highest average difference between Kruskal's and PostgreSQL default's algorithms, and the other queries have had almost the same execution time for both algorithms.

- one query (Q22) kept executing for 200 minutes without response, in both algorithms, and the excessive time was considered timeout.

There are 8 queries that have gotten different execution plans by Kruskal's and PostgreSQL default's algorithms, as described below. Table 2 shows the execution time and Table3 the costs of the plans generated.

- six queries (Q5, Q7, Q9, Q10, Q18, Q21) had a little better average execution time using PostgreSQL's default algorithm, where the time difference between the two algorithms were always lower than 0.5 second. Some execution plans generated by Kruskal's algorithm have presented lightly higher costs than the ones generated by PostgreSQL's default algorithm, others have presented equal costs although the join order were

Queries TPC-H	Plan execution cost	
	Kruskal's alg.	Default alg.
Q2	117617.38..117617.38	57847.19..57847.19
Q5	22.80..22.81	22.75..22.76
Q7	41.40..41.43	23.05..23.09
Q9	27.30..27.34	27.30..27.34
Q10	8838.01..8838.02	17.53..17.54
Q18	21.14..21.17	21.14..21.17
Q20	433.60..434.60	3372633.77..3372633.78
Q21	25.77..25.77	25.77..25.77

Table 3. Minimum and maximum costs of the execution plans generated by Kruskal's and PostgreSQL default's algorithms, for queries which presented different execution plans in each algorithm.

different. The query Q10 has presented an extremely higher cost by Kruskal's algorithm but its average execution time was almost the same for both evaluated algorithms.

- one query (Q2) has presented a much higher average execution time using Kruskal's algorithm, practically the double of the execution time obtained by PostgreSQL's default algorithm. This happened because the cost of execution plan generated by Kruskal's algorithm was higher than the cost of plan generated by PostgreSQL's default algorithm.

- one query (Q20) has presented an extremely lower average execution time using Kruskal's algorithm. The query kept executing for 233 minutes without response in PostgreSQL's default algorithm, and the excessive time was considered timeout. This occurred because of the extremely high execution plan cost generated by PostgreSQL's default algorithm, while a extremely low cost plan was generated by Kruskal's algorithm.

One difference between the implemented algorithm and PostgreSQL's Dynamic Programming Algorithm is that Kruskal's algorithm generates only one query execution tree, that will be the final tree, while the PostgreSQL's default algorithm generates a lot of trees and compares them to choose the final solution. Therefore, for queries with a large number of relations, building the final plan by Kruskal's algorithm will be faster than by exhausting search algorithm

The query execution times in both evaluated algorithms are almost the same, indicating that the results generated by Kruskal's algorithm in query optimization are at least so good as the ones obtained by the PostgreSQL's algorithm.

The PostgreSQL GEQO algorithm was not tested with the TPC-H queries because those queries does not have the minimum number of tables necessary to activate GEQO algorithm by default. Therefore, two queries with more than 11 relations were created for the experiments. The query Q23 has join clauses between all tables and the algorithm should define the better join order. The query Q24 does not have any *where* clause and a Cartesian product will occur between the relations.

In our experiment, each execution of the same query using the Genetic Algorithm have generated different execution plans. This occurred due to characteristic of this kind of algorithm, that uses random values as fitness. The Table 4 shows the results gotten in execution of queries Q23 and Q24 by Kruskal's and Genetic Algorithms.

Query Q23 has presented a lot of variation in its several execution times by GEQO algorithm, whereas the execution times by Kruskal's algorithm have kept the regularity. The average execution time obtained in this experiment was lower in Kruskal's algorithm, but the result could be differ-

Queries	Differents execution plans?	Execution time (ms)	
		Kruskal's alg.	Genetic alg.
Q23	yes	26.779	30.609
		26.043	8.352
		27.668	12.199
		26.590	124.516
		26.376	662
		26.362	20.392
		26.175	41.954
		26.177	9.288
average		26.484	31.006
Q24	yes	1.131	1.430
		1.108	1.187
		1.108	1.188
		1.160	1.368
		1.103	1.191
		1.103	1.188
		1.103	1.194
average		1.117	1.250

Table 4. Comparison between the average execution time by Kruskal's and PostgreSQL GEOQ algorithms.

Queries	Execution plan cost	
	Kruskal's alg.	Genetic alg.
Q23	175.30..179109.06	106.54..5122.23
		2292.94..37963.44
		9.97..31.69
		4005.88..9400.47
Q24	0.00..274.44	24.52..224.72

Table 5. Minimum and maximum costs of the execution plans generated by Kruskal's and PostgreSQL GEOQ algorithms.

ent in other experiments because the execution time in Genetic Algorithm depends on the random values generated as fitness.

Query Q24 has presented better execution times in all the tests by Kruskal's algorithm. All the execution plans generated by GEQO have gotten the same costs although the join order were different for each plan. The minimum cost of the plans generated were always lower by Kruskal's algorithm than by GEQO, what has provided a profit in Kruskal's algorithm execution, although the maximum cost of the plans generated by Kruskal's algorithm were lightly higher. The execution plans costs for queries Q23 e Q24 are presented on Table 5.

Comparing Kruskal's and PostgreSQL GEOQ algorithms, Kruskal's algorithm has presented better average results in all the experiments. It keeps higher cost and execution time regularity than GEOQ. In most of the tests between Kruskal's algorithm and PostgreSQL Dynamic Programming, Kruskal's algorithm has gotten the expected results in almost the same time as the results reached by PostgreSQL's Dynamic Programming algorithm. Therefore, Kruskal's algorithm can be considered a feasible method for query optimization, specially for large queries.

5. Conclusions

Throughout the years, the most diverse methods of query optimization and their combinations have been studied and implemented, not only in commercial DBMS available but also in projects developed by universities and research laboratories. However, none of these methods performs the optimization process in a totally satisfactory way for all of the query classes and there is not an optimum method. Therefore, new researches on this area are still interesting.

The researches on query optimization became easier with the free software movement and the availability of DBMS source codes, making possible the comparison of the methods proposed with methods already implemented, by implementing the studied theory in a real environment. In this research, a different query optimization methodology was proposed, using the Kruskal's algorithm to generate the optimal query execution tree. The algorithm was implemented and evaluated in PostgreSQL query optimizer.

In most of the experiments, Kruskal's algorithm presented good results, getting the expected results in better or in almost the same time as the results achieved by default PostgreSQL's optimization algorithms. Therefore it can be considered a feasible method for query optimization. The algorithm has given encouraging results and there are three advantages using Kruskal's algorithm: the easy implementation due to its reduced code size, the polynomial-time execution and the reduced memory space required to generate only one query execution tree, that will be the final tree, while the PostgreSQL Dynamic Programming generates several trees and then compares them to choose the final solution. Therefore, for queries with a large number of relations, building the final plan by Kruskal's algorithm will be faster than by exhausting search algorithm

The results presented by Kruskal's algorithm in optimization of queries involving large numbers of joins are good. When using it for this set of queries, it is guaranteed that the desired results will be gotten in a feasible time, what is not constant and certain when using Genetic Algorithm because of its random search.

One important future work is to perform a broad test to determine more precisely which set of queries would be benefited by this algorithm. Another future work is to improve the cost estimative considering the reweighting of

the edges in the graph after each part of the plan be constructed, since size and selectivity of the joins that would happen in sequence could be benefited by the joins realized previously.

References

[1] *PostgreSQL, object-relational database management system*, acessed in 03/05/2005. http://www.postgresql.org.

[2] *Benchmark H (Decision Support) Standard Specification*, acessed in 10/03/2006. http://www.tpc.org/tpch.

[3] *Documentation of code changes in PostgreSQL optimizer*, acessed in 2003. http://developer.postgresql.org/cvsweb.cgi/pgsql/src/backend/optimizer/README.

[4] E. C. de Almeida. Estudo de viabilidade de uma plataforma de baixo custo para data warehouse. Master's thesis, Universidade Federal do Paran, 2004.

[5] L. Fegaras. A new heuristic for optimizing large queries. In *Database and Expert Systems Applications, 9th International Conference, Vienna, Austria, August 24-28*, pages 726–735, 1998.

[6] Z. Fong. The design and implementation of the postgres query optimizer. Technical report, Univ. of California, Berkeley, CA, 1986.

[7] Ibaraki, Toshihide, Kameda, and Tiko. On the optimal nesting order for computing n-relational joins. *ACM Transactions on Database Systems*, September 1984.

[8] I. F. Ilyas, W. G. Aref, and A. K. Elmagarmid. Supporting top-k join queries in relational databases. *The VLDB Journal*, September 2004.

[9] Y. E. Ioannidis and Y. C. Kang. Left-deep vs. bushy trees: an analysis of strategy spaces and its implications for query optimization. In *ACM-SIGMOD*, 1991.

[10] R. Krishnamurthy, H. Boral, and C. Zaniolo. Optimization of non-recusrsive queries. In *Proc. of the Conference on Very Large Data Bases*, pages 128–137, 1986.

[11] P. Selinger and et. al. Access path selection in a relational data base system. In *ACM-SIGMOD Conference on Management of Data*, 1979.

[12] P. G. Selinger, M. M. Astrahan, D. D. Chamberlin, R. A. Lorie, and T. G. Price. *Database Systems - Access Path Selection in a Relational Database System*. Morgan Kaufman, 1979.

[13] M. Utesch. *Genetic query optimization in database systems*, 1997. http://www.postgresql.org/docs/8.0/interactive/geqo.html.

On Transversal Hypergraph Enumeration in Mining Sequential Patterns

Dong (Haoyuan) Li
École des Mines d'Alès
LGI2P, Parc Georges Besse
30035 Nîmes
France
Haoyuan.Li@ema.fr

Anne Laurent
LIRMM, CNRS
161 rue Ada
34392 Montpellier
France
laurent@lirmm.fr

Maguelonne Teisseire
LIRMM, CNRS
161 rue Ada
34392 Montpellier
France
teisseire@lirmm.fr

Abstract

The transversal hypergraph enumeration based algorithms can be efficient in mining frequent itemsets, however it is difficult to apply them to sequence mining problems. In this paper we first analyze the constraints of using transversal hypergraph enumeration in itemset mining, then propose the ordered pattern *model for representing and mining sequences with respect to these constraints. We show that the problem of mining sequential patterns can be transformed to the problem of mining frequent ordered patterns, and therefore we propose an application of the* Dualize and Advance *algorithm, which is transversal hypergraph enumeration based, in mining sequential patterns.*

1. Introduction

As one of the most concentrated topics in data mining research, mining frequent itemsets has received much attention. A lot of algorithms for this problem have been developed [1] since the first introduction of the *apriori* (also called *level-wise*) algorithm in mining association rules [1, 2, 9], where how to efficiently find all frequent itemsets is the major subtask.

The *apriori* (*level-wise*) algorithm considers the *specialization relation* (denoted by $\preceq$) between itemsets, so that the search of all frequent itemsets can be performed by walking up in the subset lattice of itemsets imposed by $\preceq$, one level at a time. [8] detailed this approach. However, when the most specific frequent itemsets appear at high levels in this search, the number of all frequent itemsets may be too large and the time of computing may not be acceptable.

[6] proposed the *Dualize and Advance* algorithm that only finds all most specific frequent itemsets using irre-

---

[1] See the FIMI (Frequent Itemset Mining Implementations Repository) Web site for a collection of implementations. (http://fimi.cs.helsinki.fi/)

dundant dualization done by transversal hypergraph enumeration, instead of finding all frequent itemsets. This approach is limited to itemset mining because the application of transversal hypergraph enumeration requires that the structure of patterns being discovered (e.g. itemset) satisfies the "representing as sets".

In this paper we are interested in porting transversal hypergraph enumeration based algorithms to sequential pattern mining. The rest of this paper is organized as follows. Section 2 introduces the transversal hypergraph enumeration on itemset mining. In Section 3 we analyze the constraints on applying transversal hypergraph enumeration. In the next Section 4 we formalize sequences with our proposition of the *ordered pattern* with respect to the above constraints. In Section 5 we show that with ordered patterns the *Dualize and Advance* algorithm can be used in mining sequential patterns. The final section is a short conclusion.

2. Transversal Hypergraph Enumeration on Itemset Mining

Given a data set **r** over relation R, we use the term *language*, denoted by $\mathcal{L}$, for expressing properties or defining subgroups of the data. $\mathcal{L}$ represents the structure of patterns being discovered in data mining and the computational task can therefore be considered as finding all sentences $\varphi \in \mathcal{L}$ that defines a sufficiently large subclass of **r**. With the *specialization relation* $\preceq$ between all sentences of $\mathcal{L}$ in **r**, considering a set $\mathcal{S} \subseteq \mathcal{L}$ such that $\mathcal{S}$ is closed downwards under the relation $\preceq$, the *positive border* $\mathcal{B}d^+(\mathcal{S})$ consists of the most specific sentences in $\mathcal{S}$ and the *negative border* $\mathcal{B}d^-(\mathcal{S})$ consists of the most general sentences that are not in $\mathcal{S}$ [8]. Figure 1 illustrates the notion of border.

In the problem of mining frequent itemsets addressed by a frequency threshold, the positive border consists of a set of the most specific frequent itemsets and the negative border consists the most general non-frequent itemsets. That is, all

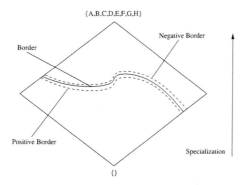

Figure 1. Border and specialization relation.

itemsets inside the border, from the vision of specialization, must be frequent but the ones outside the border cannot be frequent.

A collection $\mathcal{H}$ of subsets of R is a simple *hypergraph* [4], if no element of $\mathcal{H}$ is empty and if $X, Y \in \mathcal{H}$ and $X \subseteq Y$ imply $X = Y$. A hypergraph $\mathcal{H} = (V, E)$ consists of a finite collection E of sets over a finite set V. The elements of E are the *edges* of the hypergraph, and a *transversal* of $\mathcal{H}$ is a set $T \subseteq V$ that intersects all the edges of E. If no $T' \subset T$ is a transversal, we say that this transversal is *minimal*. The set $Tr(\mathcal{H})$ of all minimal transversals of a hypergraph $\mathcal{H}$ is called the *transversal hypergraph* of $\mathcal{H}$. [8] showed that if the language $\mathcal{L}$ satisfies the requirement of representing as sets, the negative border $\mathcal{B}d^-(\mathcal{S})$ can be computed by transversal hypergraph enumeration from the positive border, that is, $Tr(\mathcal{B}d^+(\mathcal{S})) = \mathcal{B}d^-(\mathcal{S})$.

Definition 1 (Representing as Sets [6]). *Let $\mathcal{L}$ be the language, $\preceq$ a specialization relation, and $\mathcal{R}$ a set; denote by $\mathcal{P}(\mathcal{R})$ the powerset of R. A function $f : \mathcal{L} \to \mathcal{P}(\mathcal{R})$ is a representation of $\mathcal{L}$ (and $\preceq$) as sets, if f is one-to-one and surjective, f and its inverse are computable, and for all θ and φ we have $\varphi \preceq \theta$ if and only if $f(\varphi) \subseteq f(\theta)$. This transformation is called representing as sets.*

Based on the conclusions of [8], the *Dualize and Advance* algorithm first finds a most specific sentence, $\theta \in \mathcal{L}$ from an initial sentence φ, such that $\varphi \preceq \theta$. Once a set of most specific sentences is found, the algorithm computes the negative border of the sentences found by using transversal hypergraph enumeration, and restarts its upward search from this negative border. If progress can be made, the positive border can be made from the negative border and thus the approach is guaranteed to succeed. The time complexity of the *Dualize and Advance* algorithm depends on the complexity of transversal hypergraph enumeration. [5] presented an incremental algorithm for the transversal hypergraph computation with time complexity $T(I, i) = (I + i)^{O(\log(I+i))}$, thus the time complexity of the *Dualize and Advance* algorithm could be concluded as

$t(|\mathcal{B}d^+| + |\mathcal{B}d^-|)$, where $t(n) = n^{\mathcal{O}(\log n)}$, while using at most $|\mathcal{B}d^-| + width(\mathcal{L}, \preceq)|\mathcal{B}d^+|$ queries.

For itemset mining, we have already the language $\mathcal{L}$ represented as sets if we consider the empty set $\{\} \in \mathcal{L}$. Therefore the *Dualize and Advance* algorithm can be applied to the problem of mining frequent itemsets. However, the language for mining sequential patterns could not satisfy the requirement of representing as sets.

3. Constraints on Representing as Sets

In this section we analyze the constraints on representing as sets. The problem of representing as sets is to find a invertible mapping function f, with which we have the structure imposed on the language $\mathcal{L}$ by $\preceq$ being isomorphic to a powerset $\mathcal{P}(\mathcal{R})$, where $\mathcal{R}$ is an finite set. This problem restricts the application of transversal hypergraph enumeration in data mining.

If an invertible mapping function $f : S \to \mathcal{P}(\mathcal{R})$ exists, the size of S must be a power of 2. For the problem of finding frequent itemsets, given relation R of items, let S be the set of all subsets of R defined by the language $\mathcal{L}$. If we consider $\{\}$ as a subset of R, then $S = \mathcal{P}(\mathcal{R})$ is a powerset and $|S| = 2^{|R|}$, thus an identity mapping $f(S) = S$ can be used in this case.

Given a data set on relation R of items, let $\mathcal{L}_{set}$ be the language of describing all itemsets generated from R and $\mathcal{L}_{seq}$ be a class of sentences that defines all sequences generated from R where the number of sentences depends on the maximal length of sentence. Obviously the number of sequences defined by the language $\mathcal{L}_{seq}$ is not a power of 2, thus $\mathcal{L}_{seq}$ cannot be mapped to a powerset by any invertible function.

Furthermore, if there exists an invertible function maps $\mathcal{L}_{seq}$ to $\mathcal{L}_{set}$, for example functions g and g^{-1}, then let $h = g \circ f$ we have that the language $\mathcal{L}_{seq}$ can be mapped to a powerset by h. In fact it does not exist such an invertible function h. So that we have the following two properties.

Property 1. *There does not exist any invertible mapping function that maps the language $\mathcal{L}_{seq}$ to a powerset.*

Property 2. *It does not exist any invertible function that maps the language $\mathcal{L}_{set}$ to language $\mathcal{L}_{seq}$ of defining sequences.*

The language $\mathcal{L}_{seq}$ of defining sequences does not satisfy the conditions on representing as sets, it does not exist any mapping function maps $\mathcal{L}_{seq}$ to a powerset.

The goal of representing as sets is to apply the transversal hypergraph enumeration to a powerset $\mathcal{P}(\mathcal{R})$ and then to retransfer the results from the powerset $\mathcal{P}(\mathcal{R})$ back to the description language $\mathcal{L}$ via the inverse function f^{-1}. This invertible transformation is based on the isomorphism on the specialization relation $\preceq$ over the mapping function f.

Property 3. *Mapping function f must be bijective.*

If a mapping function f has not the inverse function f^{-1}, after computing the transversal hypergraph, a set $X_\varphi \in \mathcal{P}(\mathcal{R})$ may not have an inverse mapping to be applied in the transformation from $X_\varphi \in \mathcal{P}(\mathcal{R})$ to the language $\varphi \in \mathcal{L}$.

In particular, for itemsets we have $\mathcal{L} \equiv \mathcal{P}(R)$, thus for all $f(\varphi) = X_\varphi$ we have $\varphi = X_\varphi$ and therefore we can simply write the identity mapping as $f(X) = X$.

Property 4. *Mapping function f must be isomorphic to the specialization relation $\preceq$.*

The mapping function for representing as sets transfers the language $\mathcal{L}$ to a powerset $\mathcal{P}(\mathcal{R})$ and then the transversal hypergraph enumeration on $\mathcal{P}(\mathcal{R})$ can be used to reduce the complexity of computing the negative border of the theory $\mathcal{T}h(\mathcal{L}, \mathbf{r}, q)$. The isomorphism requires f is monotone with respect to the specialization relation $\preceq$, that is,

$$\varphi \preceq \theta \iff f(\varphi) \preceq f(\theta).$$

4. Representing Sequences as Sets

Given a data set $\mathbf{r}$ over n rows of relation R of items, we say that a *pattern* is an itemset $X \subseteq R$. Let $\mathcal{L}_R$ denote the language defining all subsets of R, a pattern can be uniquely defined by a sentence in the language $\mathcal{L}_R$. Without losing generality, we denote the pattern as I_φ corresponding to the sentence $\varphi \in \mathcal{L}_R$. The language $\mathcal{L}_R$ describes the powerset of R if we consider the empty set $\{\}$ as a part of $\mathcal{L}_R$. The size of $\mathcal{L}_R$ is therefore $|\mathcal{L}_R| = 2^{|R|}$.

We define the *ordered pattern* as a pair (I_φ, o) where $I_\varphi \subseteq R$ is a pattern and $1 \leq o \leq n$ is an integer, the row number of the pattern. We call o the *order* of an ordered pattern. Therefore an ordered pattern is a pattern associated with an order, it can be rewritten as follows,

$$(I_\varphi, o) = \{(R_1, o), (R_2, o), \dots, (R_j, o)\},$$

where $R_1, R_2, \dots, R_j \in R$ and $|I_\varphi| = j$. The pair (R_i, o) is an *ordered item*, where $R_i \in R$. Let R_A denote the set of ordered items on R, we have $R_A = \{(R_i, o) \mid R_i \in R, 1 \leq o \leq n\}$, and $|R_A| = |R| \cdot n$.

Let $\mathcal{L}_A$ denote the language defining all subsets of R_O, it can be defined as following,

$$\mathcal{L}_A = \mathcal{P}(\{(X, o) \mid X \in R, 1 \leq o \leq n\}).$$

The size of $\mathcal{L}_A$ is $|\mathcal{L}_A| = 2^{n \cdot |R|}$.

We have the following characteristics of ordered patterns.

- **Union**: $I_\gamma = I_\varphi \cup I_\theta \iff (I_\gamma, o) = (I_\varphi, o) \cup (I_\theta, o)$.

- **Inclusion**: $I_\varphi \subseteq I_\theta \iff (I_\varphi, o) \subseteq (I_\theta, o)$.

- **Incomparability**: $i \neq j \Rightarrow (I_\varphi, i) \neq (I_\varphi, j)$.

- **Equivalence**: $\{(R_i, i), (R_j, j)\} = \{(R_j, j), (R_i, i)\}$.

When we consider the pair (R_i, o) as a single item, to find all frequent ordered patterns is the same task as finding frequent itemsets.

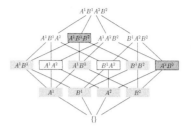

Figure 2. Finding frequent ordered patterns.

Example 1. Given data set r with items $R = \{A, B\}$, let language $\mathcal{L}^2$ define all ordered patterns with the order $o \leq 2$, we depict the language $\mathcal{L}^2$ as a lattice shown in Figure 2. Assume a set of sentences $\mathcal{S} \subseteq \mathcal{L}_a^2$ closed downwards to the relation $\preceq$, $\mathcal{S} = \{A^1, B^1, A^2, B^2, A^1B^1, A^1B^2, B^1B^2, A^2B^2, A^1B^1B^2\}$, and $\mathcal{S}$ includes the maximal ordered pattern sets $\{A^1B^1B^2, A^2B^2\}$.

The negative border $\mathcal{B}d^-(\mathcal{S}) = \{A^1A^2, B^1A^2\}$. For this problem, we already have $\mathcal{L}_a^2$ represented as sets and the mapping function f is an identity mapping. With the application of hypergraph transversals, we have therefore $\mathcal{B}d^+(\mathcal{S}) = \{A^1B^1B^2, A^2B^2\} \Rightarrow \mathcal{H}(\mathcal{S}) = \{A^2, A^1B^1\}$, thus we have the minimal transversals of $\mathcal{H}(\mathcal{S})$ that $\mathcal{T}r(\{A^2, A^1B^1\}) = \{A^1A^2, B^1A^2\}$, and thus the application of hypergraph transversals returns the correct answer. $\square$

We use the *sequential relation* between patterns in a sequence. The sequential relation is a total order $\mapsto^o$ that a pattern I_φ is precedent to another pattern I_θ if $I_\varphi \mapsto^o I_\theta$. Let o denote the order of the sequential relation, defined as follows: given a sequence s with length of k, if for no I_γ in s we have $I_\gamma \mapsto^o I_\varphi$, then $o = 1$; otherwise, $o = max(\{o' \mid I_\theta \mapsto^{o'} I_\varphi\}) + 1$. Note that $I_\theta \neq I_\varphi$ is not required for computing $I_\theta \mapsto^o I_\varphi$. In particular, for a sequence with length k, we define $o = k$ if for no I_γ in s we have $I_\varphi \mapsto^o I_\gamma$, and the order o is therefore an integer such that $1 \leq o \leq k$.

Given data set over relation R of items, let s^k denote a sequence consists of k patterns, then s^k can be formally described as follows.

$$s^k = \langle I_{\varphi_1} \mapsto^1 I_{\varphi_2} \mapsto^2 \dots \mapsto^{k-1} I_{\varphi_k} \mapsto^k \emptyset \rangle,$$

where $I_{\varphi_1}, I_{\varphi_2}, \dots, I_{\varphi_k} \subseteq R$ are k patterns. We use an empty set to bound a sequence. If we consider a pattern and its followed sequential relation as a pair, such as $(I_{\varphi_i}, \mapsto^o)$, then we can represent a sequence as a set of pairs, that is,

$$s^k = \{(I_{\varphi_1}, \mapsto^1), (I_{\varphi_2}, \mapsto^2), \ldots, (I_{\varphi_k}, \mapsto^k)\},$$

where the trailing empty set can be safely removed. It is easy to see that the above form of sequence can be represented by k ordered patterns, such as,

$$s^k = \{(I_{\varphi_1}, 1), (I_{\varphi_2}, 2), \ldots, (I_{\varphi_k}, k)\}.$$

Definition 2 (Sequence). *A sequence can be represented by a set of ordered patterns with consecutive orders starting from 1.*

Now let us consider a language $\mathcal{L}_O$ of generally defining all ordered patterns over relation R of items and given maximal order n, without distinguishing the form of representation. Let $\mathcal{L}_{seq}$ denote the language of defining all sequences over attributes R with given maximal length n, we have $\mathcal{L}_{seq} \subset \mathcal{L}_O$. Semantically, under the context of transaction database, we have following properties.

Property 5 (From Ordered Patterns to Sequence). *Each non-empty sentence in $\mathcal{L}_O$ stands for a list of transactions with their order in transaction time, corresponding to a sequence. Multiple sets of ordered patterns can be represented as one sequence in semantics.*

Property 6 (From Sequence to Ordered Patterns). *Each non-empty sentence in $\mathcal{L}_{seq}$ stands for a sequence of transaction, which can be only represented by a set of ordered patterns with consecutive orders starting from 1.*

Therefore, a *production function* p can be used in transforming a set of ordered patterns to a sequence. Given a sentence $\varphi \in \mathcal{L}_O$, such as,

$$\varphi = \{(I_{\varphi_1}, o_1), (I_{\varphi_2}, o_2), \ldots, (I_{\varphi_k}, o_k)\},$$

where $o_1 < o_2 < \ldots < o_k$ and $k \leq n$. The production $p(\varphi)$ returns a new sentence $\theta \in \mathcal{L}_O$ such that,

$$\theta = \{(I_{\varphi_1}, 1), (I_{\varphi_2}, 2), \ldots, (I_{\varphi_k}, k)\}.$$

We say that the sentence θ is the *alias* of the sentence φ, which represents a sequence.

It is remarkable that the production function p is not invertible, so that it does not imply that this representation satisfies the requirement of representing as sets.

5. Mining Sequential Patterns with Transversal Hypergraph Enumeration

We propose the *HSP* algorithm for mining sequential patterns with transversal hypergraph enumeration. Given

a transactional database over relation R, the task of mining sequential patterns is to find maximal frequent sequences with respect to given *minimal support* [3]. We use the language $\mathcal{L}_A$ for representing sequences and use the *Dualize and Advance* algorithm in finding the positive border of all interesting sentences of $\mathcal{L}_A$. The sequential pattern mining process is specified within the *Dualize and Advance* algorithm by a predicate q_hsp that determines whether the sequence corresponded to each sentence is frequent or not. This procedure returns all most specific sentences, i.e., all most specific frequent ordered patterns and their aliases. Finally the *HSP* algorithm returns all frequent sequential patterns with respect to these aliases.

Due to the limit of space, this paper only introduce the algorithm of q_hsp that is defined as follows (shown as Algorithm 1). Given a set $\mathcal{S}$ of customer sequences and a sentence $\varphi \in \mathcal{L}_A$, q_hsp evaluates φ against each $s \in \mathcal{S}$. If φ does not exist in any s, q_hsp returns $false$ without further evaluations. Otherwise, q_hsp computes the alias $\theta \in \mathcal{L}_A$ of φ and expands θ to obtain all sentences $\mathcal{E}$ ($\varphi \notin \mathcal{E}$) having the same alias θ. q_hsp then evaluates $\tau \in \mathcal{E}$ in each customer sequence, and updates the rank of θ for computing the support of θ. If the support of θ is $\geq minimal\_support$ q_hsp stores θ as a frequent sequence and returns $true$ otherwise q_hsp returns $false$. The approach of *Dualize and Advance* requires that q_hsp is monotone to the specialization relation $\preceq$ on the language $\mathcal{L}_A$.

Property 7. *The predicate q_hsp is monotone to the specialization relation $\preceq$ on the language $\mathcal{L}_A$.*

Proof. We already have that the sentences of $\mathcal{L}_A$ respect the specialization $\preceq$. If a sentence $\varphi \in \mathcal{L}_A$ is interesting, then we have the alias $\theta \in \mathcal{L}_A$ interesting, means that the sequence s_θ represented by θ is frequent, and φ exists in at least one customer sequence $s \in \mathcal{S}$. And according to the relation $\preceq$ on $\mathcal{L}_A$, any generalization of φ must be exist in at least one customer sequence $s \in \mathcal{S}$, and any sub-sequences of s_θ must be frequent. Thus we have that for $\gamma \in \mathcal{L}_A$ and $\gamma \preceq \varphi$, if $q\_hsp(\mathcal{S}, \varphi) = true$, then $q\_hsp(\mathcal{S}, \gamma) = true$.

Next we show that for $\gamma \in \mathcal{L}_A$ and $\gamma \preceq \varphi$, if $q\_hsp(\mathcal{S}, \gamma) = false$, then $q\_hsp(\mathcal{S}, \varphi) = false$.

$q\_hsp(\mathcal{S}, \gamma) = false$ means that γ does not exist in any customer sequence $s \in \mathcal{S}$ or the sentence represented by the alias $\psi \in \mathcal{L}_A$ of γ is not frequent. In the first case, no specialization of γ can exist in any customer sequence $s \in \mathcal{S}$. In the second case, the sequence represented by the alias of any specialization of γ cannot be frequent. Thus for any sentence $\varphi \in \mathcal{L}_A$ and $\gamma \preceq \varphi$, we have $q\_hsp(\mathcal{S}, \varphi) = false$. $\square$

The predicate q_hsp is monotone to the specialization relation $\preceq$ on $\mathcal{L}_A$ and it updates correctly the frequency of sequences with respect to the definition of *support* for sequential patterns. Therefore the model of ordered patterns and the q_hsp predicate can address the problem of mining sequential patterns within the *Dualize and Advance* algorithm where the transversal hypergraph enumeration is applicable.

Algorithm 1: Algorithm of the q_hsp predicate.

1   **if** *exits* $\gamma \preceq \varphi$ *not interesting* **then**
2 | **return false**;
3   **end**
4    $alias\_rank \leftarrow 0$;
5   **foreach** $s \in \mathcal{S}$ **do**
6 | $rank \leftarrow$ evaluate φ against s;
7 | **if** $rank > 0$ **then**
8 | | update $alias\_rank$ by $rank$;
9 | | remove s from $\mathcal{S}$;
10 | **end**
11   **end**
12   **if** $alias\_rank = 0$ **then**
13 | **return false**;
14   **end**
15   $\theta \leftarrow$ alias of φ;
16   $\mathcal{E} \leftarrow$ all sentences with alias θ but excluding φ;
17   **foreach** $s \in \mathcal{S}$ **do**
18 | **foreach** $\tau \in \mathcal{E}$ **do**
19 | | $rank \leftarrow$ evaluate τ against s;
20 | | **if** $rank > 0$ **then**
21 | | | update $alias\_rank$ by $rank$;
22 | | | remove s from $\mathcal{S}$;
23 | | **end**
24 | **end**
25   **end**
26   **if** $alias\_rank/number\_of\_slices \geq min\_supp$ **then**
27 | store_alias(θ);
28 | **return true**;
29   **end**
30   **return false**;

According to the *Dualize and Advance* algorithm, the complexity of the *HSP* is polynomial in $|\mathcal{B}d^+|$ and $T(|\mathcal{B}d^+|, |\mathcal{B}d^-|)$ where $T(n) = n^{\mathcal{O}(\log(n))}$ [5, 6, 7].

Given a set $\mathcal{S}$ of customer sequences, assume the final result contains N aliases, then in the worst case the number of all most specific sentences is $|\mathcal{B}d^+| = N|\mathcal{S}|$. In the worst case, each evaluation of a sentence $\varphi \in \mathcal{L}_A$ requires $|\mathcal{S}| + |\varphi|(|\mathcal{S}| - 1)$ queries without caching, where $|\varphi|$ is the number of all sentences with the same alias with φ, not including φ, and $|\mathcal{S}|$ is the number of customer sequences.

6. Conclusion

We analyzed the constraints of using transversal hypergraph enumeration on itemset mining and proposed the *HSP* approach for mining sequential patterns with the *Dualize and Advance* algorithm. We introduced the model of ordered patterns with respect to the constraints on applying transversal hypergraph enumeration in itemset mining. We showed that the problem of mining sequential patterns could be addressed by the language $\mathcal{L}_A$ for finding frequent ordered patterns and we presented a predicate for determining whether the sequence corresponded to each sentence is frequent. This predicate is monotone on $(\mathcal{L}_A, \preceq)$. The *HSP* approach is interesting when the lengths of frequent sequential patterns are large. We are currently investigating the comparison between different approaches to sequential patterns mining.

References

[1] R. Agrawal, T. Imielinski, and A. N. Swami. Mining association rules between sets of items in large databases. In *SIGMOD Conference*, pages 207–216, 1993.

[2] R. Agrawal and R. Srikant. Fast algorithms for mining association rules in large databases. In *VLDB*, pages 487–499, 1994.

[3] R. Agrawal and R. Srikant. Mining sequential patterns. In *ICDE*, pages 3–14, 1995.

[4] C. Berge. *Hypergraphs. Combinatorics of Finite Sets (third edition)*. Amsterdam: North-Holland, 1973.

[5] M. L. Fredman and L. Khachiyan. On the complexity of dualization of monotone disjunctive normal forms. *J. Algorithms*, 21(3):618–628, 1996.

[6] D. Gunopulos, R. Khardon, H. Mannila, S. Saluja, H. Toivonen, and R. S. Sharm. Discovering all most specific sentences. *ACM Trans. Database Syst.*, 28(2):140–174, 2003.

[7] D. J. Kavvadias and E. C. Stavropoulos. Evaluation of an algorithm for the transversal hypergraph problem. In *Algorithm Engineering*, pages 72–84, 1999.

[8] H. Mannila and H. Toivonen. Levelwise search and borders of theories in knowledge discovery. *Data Min. Knowl. Discov.*, 1(3):241–258, 1997.

[9] H. Mannila, H. Toivonen, and A. I. Verkamo. Efficient algorithms for discovering association rules. In *KDD Workshop*, pages 181–192, 1994.

The Requirements for Ontologies in Medical Data Integration: A Case Study

Ashiq Anjum, Peter Bloodsworth, Andrew Branson, Tamás Hauer, Richard McClatchey, Kamran Munir, Dmitry Rogulin, Jetendr Shamdasani

CCS Research Centre, CEMS Faculty, University of the West of England, ColdharbourLane, Frenchay, Bristol BS16 1QY, UK

Email: *{Ashiq.Anjum, Peter.Bloodsworth, Andrew.Branson, Tamas.Hauer, Richard.McClatchey, Kamran.Munir, Dmitry.Rogulin, Jetendr Shamdasani}@cern.ch*

Abstract

Evidence-based medicine is critically dependent on three sources of information: a medical knowledge base, the patient's medical record and knowledge of available resources, including where appropriate, clinical protocols. Patient data is often scattered in a variety of databases and may, in a distributed model, be held across several disparate repositories. Consequently addressing the needs of an evidence-based medicine community presents issues of biomedical data integration, clinical interpretation and knowledge management. This paper outlines how the Health-e-Child project has approached the challenge of requirements specification for (bio-) medical data integration, from the level of cellular data, through disease to that of patient and population. The approach is illuminated through the requirements elicitation and analysis of Juvenile Idiopathic Arthritis (JIA), one of three diseases being studied in the EC-funded Health-e-Child project.

1. Introduction

1.1 The problem in general

Information technology today is widely adopted in modern medical practice, especially supporting digitized equipment, administrative tasks, and data management but less has been achieved in the use of computational techniques to exploit the medical information in research or practice. There is an emerging demand for the integration and exploitation of heterogeneous biomedical information for improved clinical practice, medical research and personalized healthcare [1]. The application of computational and mathematical techniques in applying the laws of medicine to solve clinical problems is difficult because these laws are not mathematical in nature. Biology and especially medicine are "knowledge based disciplines" relying greatly on observed similarities rather than on the application of precise rules [2], [3].

The Health-e-Child (HeC) project [1] aims to develop an integrated platform for European paediatrics, enabling data integration between spatially separated clinicians and bringing together information produced in different departments or multiple hospitals. In this context vertical integration means establishing a coherent view of the child's health to which information from each vertical level contributes, from molecular through cellular to patient. The HeC project will study the data integration requirements of clinicians treating paediatric heart diseases, Juvenile Idiopathic Arthritis (JIA) and child brain tumours and will provide demonstrators for decision-support, knowledge management and disease modelling. Clinicians from the hospitals of the Gaslini Institute (Genoa, Italy), Great Ormond Street (London, UK) and the Necker Institute (Paris, France) are working with computer scientists, knowledge engineers and bioinformaticians to produce project deliverables in a 4-year Integrated Project initiated at the start of 2006, supported by the eHealth Unit of the EC's ICT Framework 6 programme. In this paper we consider the usage of ontologies within HeC. Paediatric rheumatology and in particular Juvenile Idiopathic Arthritis is used as a concrete example of the associated requirements.

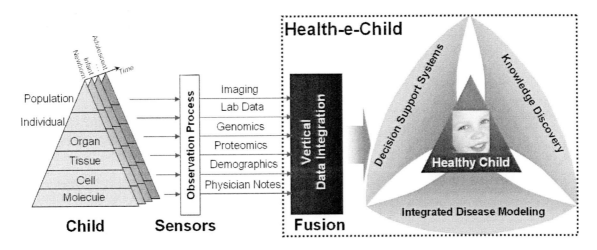

Figure 1: The conceptual approach of 'vertical data integration' in Health-e-Child

In order to understand the clinical processes and constraints inherent in the HeC study, a process of rigorous requirements elicitation was initiated at the project outset. Use-case and conceptual data models were incrementally and iteratively developed and validated as the main requirements models in consultation with key clinical staff in order to ensure that the HeC requirements engineering process addressed the needs of the specific user communities. The emphasis of the HeC requirements process is on providing "universality of information." Its corner stone is the integration of information across biomedical abstractions, whereby all layers of biomedical information are 'vertically integrated' (see fig 1) to provide a unified view of a child's biomedical and clinical condition. The next section introduces JIA – one of the integration areas studied in HeC which well illustrates the importance of 'vertical' integration.

2. Paediatric Rheumatology

2.1 Juvenile Idiopathic Arthritis

Juvenile Idiopathic Arthritis (JIA) [4] has a resemblance to Rheumatoid Arthritis, but with an onset in childhood (defined as before 16 years of age). The disease is characterized by a generalized inflammation affecting multiple joints, but there is a wide range of conditions that are collectively labelled JIA and the group of patients is not uniform. Although the disease is thought to have molecular or cellular origin, the accepted diagnosis of JIA is mostly clinical. JIA is a chronic disease with active periods that may involve a number of joints, though not necessarily the same ones every time, leaving permanent damage that may result in serious functional disability in the long term. The

evaluation of the disease activity is based on clinical and lifestyle assessment scores (pain, limited range of motion, swelling), while the damage progression is assessed by a doctor's evaluation of images (X-ray, ultrasound, MRI), the standardization is achieved by various scoring schemata.

2.2. Clinical requirements for modelling JIA data

It is apparent that the strategy for tackling JIA in clinical practice relies on data spanning a wide range of 'vertical' heterogeneity: molecular, organ-specific, and lifestyle information all contribute to various aspects of diagnosis, evaluation, and treatment. This is the case with many other diseases, but in JIA the lack of sufficient understanding of the linkage of information across the vertical axis and modalities is evident and interesting to study. Some of the outstanding questions that we identified as candidate issues to study are:

- The diagnosis is clinical, mostly negative, while the origin is probably molecular. Assessments are based on imaging, while the treatment is local (molecular, organ), as well as global (molecular). How do these interact?
- How can the clinical variables for disease activity and damage be standardised?
- Correlations can be made between patient assessment and disease progression. Which are the early predictors of damage?
- What are the short and long term effects of treatment procedures?
- Are there markers which distinguish between reversible and permanent organ damage?
- Can we identify more homogeneous groups of patients for better classification of JIA subtypes and better planning for treatment response?

- Are there any hereditary elements, do these correlate with other autoimmune diseases?

To answer these questions, clinicians need to test their theories on a statistically significant representation of the population. Of considerable importance are the so-called "fishing" experiments: individual centres generating ideas based on some individual case reports that can be tested against larger population or clinical trials.

3. Addressing JIA Requirements in Health-e-Child

3.1. HeC information technology solutions addressing JIA problems

The requirements mentioned in the previous sections drive the development of the HeC prototype system. Potential solutions are very heterogeneous and in effect pose new requirements on the system from an IT point of view; ultimately all these serve the same purpose in fulfilling the needs of the clinicians. From the applications' point of view the following techniques have been proposed in order to address the clinical requirements with respect to JIA:

- Knowledge Discovery (KD) algorithms using statistical learning and data mining techniques to find a better classification of the JIA (homogeneous groups of patients) based on the joint analyses of all available heterogeneous biomedical data (e.g. clinical, imaging, genomics, proteomics).
- Image-based techniques including semi-automatic segmentation of the synovitis to speed-up and improve the scoring (an inflamed synovia might be an early predictor of the severity of the disease); semi-automatic evaluation of joint damage; image registration across time to be able to compare the different studies of the same patient or between different (groups of) patients.
- Decision Support System (DSS) for individualized evaluation/treatment monitoring using disease progression and treatment outcomes.

These applications place additional requirements on the data management facilities provided by the platform. For example, the DSS system must be trained on large amounts of sample data, preferably from different populations; the knowledge acquired by the clinicians needs to be shared across different clinical communities; the information stored in the hospital databases should be made available for sophisticated query processing to assist applications as well as to enable end-users to analyse the data.

3.2 Modelling requirements

In the HeC project, requirements are specified in a joint effort with the participating clinicians. To support the HeC objectives, a set of models for representing biomedical information is necessary. At the first approximation, (borrowing the terminology from description logics), the information at hand may be split into terminology and assertions. In both cases, we need to observe constraints: existing knowledge should be reused, at the same time the knowledge base should be aligned to existing data models (patient record formats, examination templates, clinical protocols). To these ends, a three layer database model has been produced to stack clinical data, its defining meta-data, with semantic information attaching that to medical concepts and drawing relationships between.

The following features have been identified as part of the set of rheumatology use-cases in HeC:

1. Identify those MRI baseline measures (degree of synovitis, bone marrow oedema etc) that are most predictive of future severe radiological damage.
2. Identify more homogeneous groups of patients (suitable for aetiopathogenetic studies) taking account clinical assessment, immunologic, genetic, proteomic and radiological findings.
3. Identify a panel of candidate protein biomarkers in JIA that can predict which patients will develop erosive, disabling diseases.

All these examples stress the importance of the integrating the diverse medical data (clinical, epidemiological, imaging, genomic, proteomic etc.) that represent the patient's information at different levels of granularity (vertical levels). The semantic link between these levels is obvious: entities are in a part-of hierarchy, but the extreme complexity of the human body and its processes usually do not allow for drawing straightforward conclusions from parts to the whole. To establish a basis for the semantic coherence of the integrated data and facilitate accessibility of external information for querying and analysis by clinicians, the mappings from clinical data to the external medical knowledge (e.g. biomedical ontologies and databases) should be provided. For example, to answer the third question the clinical data needs to be aligned with external knowledge sources to identify genetic markers that can be present in JIA.

Another important requirement for our modelling is the temporal dimension. Time is a key issue in paediatric research and practice. Clinicians are usually interested in analysing patients' data over time (see the first example above). The paediatrics domain adds an additional complexity due to the fact that the child is growing and the observations in time should be aligned with the anatomical changes as well as the knowledge about how a particular disease may affect these changes. The clinical process usually follows a given time order (symptoms, study, diagnosis, treatment, follow-up, etc.). In addition, some symptom/diagnosis and treatment concepts are time-related (for example, a diagnostic criterion for JIA is persistence of some symptoms for a given time; medication is prescribed with a time profile, etc).

4. Ontologies in Health-e-Child

An ontology represents a shared, agreed and detailed model of a problem domain. One advantage for the use of ontologies is their ability to resolve any semantic heterogeneity that is present within the data. Ontologies define links between different types of semantic knowledge. They can particularly aid in the resolution of terms for queries and other general search strategies, thus improving the search results that are presented to clinicians. The fact that ontologies are machine processable and human understandable is especially useful in this regard [5]. There are many biomedical ontologies in existence although few, if any, support vertical integration. For example consider the Gene Ontology (GO) [6] which only defines structures regarding genes and GALEN [7] that is limited to anatomical concepts. In both cases there are no links to the other vertical levels that we have defined. We are currently investigating the scope for reusing these ontologies, or parts thereof, which have been identified by experts in both knowledge representation and clinical matters.

Many medical ontologies do not cover the paediatrics domain adequately, for example there is a difference between the physiology of a fully grown adult and that of a child; there are also some similarities, for example they both have one heart and two lungs. Hence, it would not be sensible to reuse these ontologies in their entirety; instead we propose the extraction of the relevant parts and then the integration of these into a coherent whole, thereby capturing most of the HeC domain. However it should be noted that integrating these ontologies into one single (upper level) ontology will not be sufficient to capture the entire HeC domain, and therefore we will have to model the missing attributes and extend these existing ontologies to suit our needs. Although there are other upper level ontologies present today, such as DOLCE [8] and SUMO [9], they are considered to be too broad to be included in the project.

The traditional ontology engineering process is an iterative process consisting of ontology modelling and ontology validation. We have chosen to evaluate the different methodologies that are available to us for the development of our vertical domain model. These include, for example CommonKADS [10] and Diligent [11]; this evaluation process is ongoing. A methodology that deserves special consideration is proposed by Seidenberg and Rector [12] in which a strategy for modular development of ontologies is proposed, to support the re-use, maintainability and evolution of the ontology to be developed. This methodology consists of untangling the ontology into disjoint independent trees which can be recombined into an ontology using definitions and axioms to represent the relationships in an explicit fashion.

4.1 Ontologies and data integration

Ontologies are extensively used in data integration systems because they provide an explicit and machine-understandable conceptualization of a domain. There are several approaches to data integration which we will now consider in further detail as described by Wache et al. in their article [13]. In the single ontology approach, all source schemas are directly related to a shared global ontology that provides a uniform interface to the user. However, this approach requires that all sources have nearly the same view on a domain, with the same level of granularity. One example of a system using this approach is SIMS [14]. In the multiple ontology approach, each data source is described by its own (local) ontology separately. Instead of using a common ontology, local ontologies are mapped to each other. For this purpose, additional representation formalisms are necessary for defining the inter-ontology mappings. The OBSERVER system [15] is an example of this approach.

In the hybrid ontology approach, a combination of the two preceding approaches is used. In the hybrid approach a local ontology is built for each source schema, which is not mapped to other local ontologies, but to a global shared ontology. New sources can be added with no need for modifying existing mappings. The single and hybrid approaches are appropriate for building central data integration systems, the former being more appropriate for so-called Global-as-View (GaV) systems and the latter for Local-as-View (LaV) systems. One drawback associated with the single global approach is the need for maintenance when new information sources are added to the representation. The hybrid architecture allows for greater flexibility in this regard with new sources being represented at the local level. The multiple ontology approach can be best used to construct pure peer-to-peer data integration systems, where there are no super-peers.

A mapping discovery process involves identifying similarities between ontologies in order to determine which concepts and properties represent similar notions across heterogeneous data samples in a (semi-) automatic manner. One of the major bottlenecks in generating viable integrated case data is that of mapping discovery. There exist two major approaches to mapping discovery. A top-down approach is applicable to ontologies with a well-defined goal. Ontologies usually contain a generally agreed upper-level ontology by developers of different applications; these developers can extend the upper-level ontology with application-specific terms. Examples of this approach are DOLCE [8] and SUMO [9].

A heuristics approach uses lexical structural components of definitions to find correspondences with heuristics. For example, [16] describes a set of heuristics used for the semi-automatic alignment of domain ontologies with a large central ontology. PROMPT [17] supports ontology merging, guides users through the process and suggests which classes and properties can be merged and FCA-Merge [18] supports a method for comparing ontologies that have a set of shared instances. IF-Map[19] identifies the mappings automatically by the information flow and generates a logic isomorphism [20].

Based on medical ontologies e.g. UMLS [21], GO [6] and GALEN [7] HeC is investigating the mapping heuristics for integrated case data. It is evaluating the relative quality of several of these mapping discovery methods for integrated case data. As a consequence it is in the process of providing an optimal combination of the best methods with respect to the accuracy and computation times.

4.2 Semantics support for DSS

Another interesting feature of ontologies is that they can aid in the creation of similarity metrics. This has already been attempted by many projects for example in [22] to gauge the similarity between genes using the GO ontology and by Resnik in [23] to gauge the similarity between different words with the WordNet Thesaurus. This technique can aid in the integration of the other sub-projects in HeC such as the DSS by creating a similarity metric based on the HeC ontology, hence creating a common base for the training and classification phases of the DSS. Furthermore the HeC ontology can be used within the project in the creation of ontology based training data, e.g. to classify different diseases; this can be achieved by using the rule base of the ontology within an expert system [24]. The HeC ontology can be used to annotate different data sets such as images for easy access later, creating a semantic image database.

4.3 Semantic query enhancement and optimization

Ontologies as mentioned previously can aid in the area of query enhancement. An example is when an image is annotated according to the HeC ontology with the concept of a 'Jaw'. The clinician inputs a simple query into the system, presented here in natural language, stating "Give me all X-Ray images of Jaws for children with a particular disease in a specific age group" then the system will return all of the X-Rays in the database that have been annotated with the concept Jaw. However, when the system uses the power of the HeC ontology it will determine that teeth have a 'part-of' relation to a 'Jaw'. Hence, the system will not only return a result set of images annotated with the concept of Jaw but it will also return images annotated with the concept of teeth as well. Therefore, the clinician will be able to take advantage of an enhanced search such as this to aid in their experiments.

Query enhancement as the previous example demonstrates is important because it allows the system to provide clinicians with more targeted information. During the requirements analysis phase of the project it became clear that clinicians often struggle to create the complex queries necessary to capture all the data that they require in a study. This may cause too many or too few results to be returned thus undermining the research being undertaken.

By using the conceptual model that the HeC ontology provides we can take basic queries from users and translate them into more complex context aware searches. This reduces the amount of time taken by clinicians to locate and group the dataset they require which, in turn minimises the load on the system as fewer searches are necessary. Query optimisation also assists in this regard by using the HeC ontology to aid the creation of efficient data access paths by semantically altering the initial query to find a more efficient execution path within the database. Both query enhancement and optimisation are crucial in delivery of intuitive data access for clinicians whilst at the same time ensuring the scalability and overall stability of the system.

5. Conclusions

In this paper we have used JIA as one disease to illustrate concretely the kind of medical problems we are trying to solve in the HeC project. Many of those are not JIA specific but appear in other areas of medicine possibly with different weights of relevance, importance etc. The HeC project aims to provide generic solutions without focusing on one particular study. We have selected three considerably different disease areas (paediatric heart diseases, Juvenile Idiopathic Arthritis (JIA) and child brain tumours) to investigate the problems related to differences and commonalities across the paediatric domain. Clinical requirements have been collected during the elicitation sessions with the medical experts and these requirements have been driving the development of the technological solutions to tackle these problems.

The integration of the diverse medical data (clinical, epidemiological, imaging, genomic, proteomic etc.) that represent the patient's information at different levels of granularity is very important as the clinical knowledge will span across different medical disciplines allowing clinicians to discover interesting findings and infer new medical knowledge. As indicated, future work in the project will enable appropriate knowledge representations including ontologies to be implemented to aid the process of vertical data integration and address the differences across these three disease domains.

References

[1] The Information Societies Technology Project: Health-e-Child EU Contract IST-2004-027749.

[2] Stevens R. et al., "Using OWL to model biological knowledge". *International Journal of Human Computer Studies*, Vol 65 no. 7 pp 583-594, 2007.

[3] Baker et al, "An ontology for bioinformatics applications", *Bioinformatics*, 15(6):510-520, 1999.

[4] Paediatric Rheumatology: http://www.printo.it/pediatric-rheumatology/, Accessed 4/4/2007.

[5] Gomez-Perez, A. Corcho, O. Fac. de Inf, "Ontology languages for the Semantic Web", IEEE Intelligent Systems, Jan/Feb 2002, volume: 17, Issue: 1 ,On page(s): 54- 60 ISSN: 1541-1672

[6] Ashburner M. et al, "Gene Ontology: tool for the unification of biology". *National Genetics,* Vol 25: pages 25-29, 2000.

[7] Rector, A. et al., "OpenGALEN: Open source medical terminology and tools". In *Proc. of the American Medical Informatics Association Symposium* 2003, pages 982-985.

[8] A Gangemi, N Guarino, C Masolo, A Oltramari,, "Sweetening ontologies with DOLCE" *Proceedings of EKAW*, 2002 .

[9] Niles, I. and Pease, A.. "Sumo: Towards a standard upper ontology". In *Proc. of the international Conference on Formal ontology in information Systems* - Volume 2001

[10] Schreiber, G. Et al., "CommonKADS: a comprehensive methodology for KBS development". *IEEE Expert*, Dec 1994 Volume: 9, Issue: 6 On page(s): 28-37 ISSN: 0885-9000

[11] Tempich, C et al., "An argumentation ontology for DIstributed, Loosely-controlled and evolvInG Engineering processes of oNTologies (DILIGENT)", *Lecture Notes in Computer Science* , Volume 3532/2005 , 241-256

[12] Seidenberg, J. & Rector, A. 2006. "Web ontology segmentation: analysis, classification and use". In *Proc. Of 15th international Conference on World Wide Web* (Edinburgh). WWW '06. ACM Press, New York, 13-22.

[13] Wache, H. et al,, "Ontology-Based Integration of Information - A Survey of Existing Approaches*", IJCAI Workshop on Ontologies and Information Sharing*, 2001

[14] Arens, Y. Knoblock, C. A. Shen, W. M. , "Query Reformulation for Dynamic Information Integration", *Journal of Intelligent Information Systems*, 1996, VOL 6; No. 2, pages 99-130, Kluwer Academic Publishers.

[15] Mena, E. et al., "OBSERVER: An Approach for Query Processing in Global Information Systems Based on Interoperation Across Pre-Existing Ontologies", *Distributed & Parallel Databases*, 2000, Vol 8; No. 2, pages 223-271, Kluwer Academic publishers.

[16] Philpot, A., Fleischman, M., & Hovy, E., "Semi-Automatic Construction of a General Purpose Ontology", *Proc. of the International Lisp Conference.* New York, 2003

[17] Noy & Musen , "The PROMPT suite: interactive tools for ontology merging and mapping", *International Journal of Human-Computer Studies*, 2003 - Elsevier, Vol 59, pages 983–1024.

[18] Stumme, G. & Madche, A., "FCA-Merge: Bottom-Up Merging of Ontologies*", Proc. 17th Intl. Conf. on Articial Intelligence (IJCAI '01)*, Seattle,USA, 2001, pp 225-230.

[19] Kalfoglou, Y. Schorlemmer, M. "IF-Map: An Ontology-Mapping Method Based on Information-Flow Theory", *Lecture Notes in Computer Science*, 2003, Vol 2800, pages 98-127 Springer-Verlag.

[20] Blackburn, P. Seligman, J. , "Hybrid Languages", *Journal of Logic Language and Information* , 1995, VOL 4; pages 251-272 , Kluwer Acaademic Publishers

[21] Bodenreider, O. ,"The Unified Medical Language System (UMLS): integrating biomedical terminology", *Nucleic Acids Research Journal*, 2004, VOL 32; NUMBER 1; SUPP, pages 267-270, Oxford University Press.

[22] Sevilla, J. L. et al., 2005. "Correlation between Gene Expression & GO Semantic Similarity". *IEEE/ACM Trans. Comput. Biol. Bioinformatics* 2, 4 (Oct. 2005), 330-338.

[23] Resnik, P., "Disambiguating noun groupings with respect to WordNet senses", In *Third Workshop on Very Large Corpora* pp54-68 MIT, USA. The Association for Computational Linguistics, 1995.

[24] JESS, the Rule Engine for the Java™ Platform, http://herzberg.ca.sandia.gov/jess/, Accessed 2/4/2007

IDEAS 2007

Author Index

Notes

 **IEEE Computer Society Conference Publications Operations Committee**

CPOC Chair

Phillip Laplante
Professor, Penn State University

Board Members

Thomas Baldwin, *Manager, Conference Publishing Services* (CPS)
Mike Hinchey, *Director, Software Engineering Lab, NASA Goddard*
Paolo Montuschi, *Professor, Politecnico di Torino*
Linda Shafer, *Professor Emeritus, University of Texas at Austin*
Jeffrey Voas, *Director, Systems Assurance Technologies, SAIC*
Wenping Wang, *Associate Professor, University of Hong Kong*

IEEE Computer Society Executive Staff

Angela Burgess, *Publisher*

IEEE Computer Society Publications

The world-renowned IEEE Computer Society publishes, promotes, and distributes a wide variety of authoritative computer science and engineering texts. These books are available from most retail outlets. Visit the CS Store at *http://www.computer.org/portal/site/store/index.jsp* for a list of products.

IEEE Computer Society *Conference Publishing Services* (CPS)

The IEEE Computer Society produces conference publications for more than 200 acclaimed international conferences each year in a variety of formats, including books, CD-ROMs, USB Drives, and on-line publications. For information about the IEEE Computer Society's *Conference Publishing Services* (CPS), please e-mail: cps@computer.org or telephone +1-714-821-8380. Fax +1-714-761-1784. Additional information about *Conference Publishing Services* (CPS) can be accessed from our web site at: *http://www.computer.org/cps*

IEEE Computer Society / Wiley Partnership

The IEEE Computer Society and Wiley partnership allows the CS Press *Authored Book* program to produce a number of exciting new titles in areas of computer science and engineering with a special focus on software engineering. IEEE Computer Society members continue to receive a 15% discount on these titles when purchased through Wiley or at: *http://wiley.com/ieeecs*. To submit questions about the program or send proposals, please e-mail dplummer@computer.org or telephone +1-714-821-8380. Additional information regarding the Computer Society's authored book program can also be accessed from our web site at:
http://www.computer.org/portal/pages/ieeecs/publications/books/about.html

Revised: 16 March 2007

CPS Online is a new IEEE online collaborative conference publishing environment designed to speed the delivery of price quotations and provide conferences with real-time access to all of a project's publication materials during production, including the final papers. The *CPS Online* workspace gives a conference the opportunity to upload files through any Web browser, check status and scheduling on their project, make changes to the Table of Contents and Front Matter, approve editorial changes and proofs, and communicate with their CPS editor through discussion forums, chat tools, commenting tools and e-mail.

The following is the URL link to the CPS Online Publishing Inquiry Form:
http://www.ieeeconfpublishing.org/cpir/inquiry/cps_inquiry.html